By Variorum Publications:

Neoplatonism and Early Christian Thought
Essays in Honour of A. H. Armstrong
Eds. H. J. Blumenthal & R. A. Markus

CHRISTOPHER WALTER
Art and Ritual of the Byzantine Church

Variorum Reprints Collected Studies Series:

SEBASTIAN BROCK
Syriac Perspectives on Late Antiquity

HENRY CHADWICK
History and Thought of the Early Church

ROBERT M. GRANT
Christian Beginnings: Apocalypse to History

FRANÇOIS HALKIN
Martyrs Grecs. IIe-VIIIe s.

R. A. MARKUS
From Augustine to Gregory the Great

AVERIL CAMERON
Continuity and Change in 6th Century Byzantium

GILBERT DAGRON
La Romanité chretienné en Orient:
héritages et mutations

J. M. FIEY
Communautés syriaques en Iran et Irak des origines à 1552

JEAN DAUVILLIER
Histoire et institutions des églises orientales au moyen âge

M. J. KISTER
Studies in Jāhiliyya and Early Islam

R. B. SERJEANT
Studies in Arabian History and Civilisation

SAMUEL M. STERN
Medieval Arabic and Hebrew Thought

East of Antioch

Professor Dr Han J. W. Drijvers

Han J. W. Drijvers

East of Antioch

Studies in Early Syriac Christianity

VARIORUM REPRINTS
London 1984

British Library CIP data

Drijvers, Han J. W.
East of Antioch
– (Collected studies series; CS198)
1. Church history – Primitive and early church, ca.30–600
2. Syria – Church history
I. Title II. Series
270.1 BR 160

ISBN 0–86078–146–1

Published in Great Britain by Variorum Reprints
20 Pembridge Mews London W11 3EQ

Printed in Great Britain by Paradigm Print
Gateshead

VARIORUM REPRINT CS198

CONTENTS

GNOSTICISM

This volume contains a total of 340 pages.

PREFACE

The studies brought together in this volume are the fruits of a long standing interest in the history and thought of early Syriac Christianity as it manifested itself in the area between Antioch and Edessa. In its various forms this Christian tradition reflects the remarkable hybrid culture of that thoroughly bilingual area, where Greek and Syriac, East and West, found a cultural synthesis that stood open to many influences and, therefore, does not lend itself to one-sided explanations or simple alternatives. These studies further mirror the attitude of a historian whose interest is mainly focused on the complicated relations between a specific cultural and social situation and the works of literature and art it produces. From this viewpoint they seek to elucidate various aspects of a complex cultural and religious pattern, of which too many sides are still unknown.

The first section deals with general aspects of the Syriac-speaking branch of the early Church and attempts to make some advance on W. Bauer's famous study of orthodoxy and heresy. It pays attention to the Abgar legend and the specific religious situation in which that legend originated. The Syrian saint and his severe asceticism also finds a place in this variegated pattern in which Tatian's encratism exerted a paramount influence.

The next four studies are devoted to the enigmatic Odes of Solomon and seek to locate them in the religious conflicts of the third century, when Marcion and Mani were the main opponents of a nascent orthodoxy, while sharing a common symbolism and imagery. They illustrate how subtle were the dividing-lines in the sophisticated religious milieux of that time.

The most outstanding exponent of early Syriac Christianity was Bardaiṣan, the Aramaic philosopher of Edessa. Since the publication of my *Bardaiṣan of Edessa* (Assen, 1966) a renaissance of Bardaiṣan studies has given rise to new discussions about the real nature and contents of his religious and philosophical doctrine, its background, sources and relations with Manichaeism. These three articles dedicated to Bardaiṣan elucidate my views and position in the continuing scholarly discussion.

The study of Bardaiṣan has made clear to me how artificial are the differences between gnosticism and Christianity, when seen against the background of the historical reality of the second and third century in the Syriac-speaking area. The last section of this volume is, therefore, dedicated to gnosticism and related matters, and these papers again illustrate my method and approach, directed principally to the understanding of complex historical developments more than to the shaping of well-defined conceptions that only have a tenuous connection with historical reality. Consequently I do not suggest a contrast, by concluding this volume with a paper on the persistence of paganism in what was supposedly the first Christian kingdom in the world. Paganism had a long life and history in Syria and Mesopotamia, and a minute study of *Cults and Beliefs at Edessa* (Leiden, 1980) revealed how much nascent and mature Christianity owed to and preserved of its pagan fellow-citizen at the time when both lived east of Antioch.

HAN J. W. DRIJVERS

Groningen University
February 1984

I

EAST OF ANTIOCH

Forces and Structures in the Development of Early Syriac Theology

East of Antioch ran the ancient silk route that linked the great cities of the west with Iran and India and China in the east. It crossed the Euphrates, passed Edessa and Nisibis and ran farther east through the Iranian highlands. At Edessa it met a north-south road which linked Amida, modern Diyarbekir, with Hierapolis, Aleppo and the other great Syrian centres. Edessa, therefore lay at the junction of these ancient routes which connected it with the west Syrian area [1]. Along these roads Roman armies marched to the east in order to fight the Parthians and Sassanians, caravans carried silk, spices and other precious products from the east to the luxurious Roman cities in the west, missionaries and pilgrims travelled with little luggage and great ideas and dreams. Along these roads Christianity became known through merchants and travellers in that east Syrian and northern Mesopotamian area, where Aramaic was the main spoken language, but Greek too was widely known and understood. [2]

In that border area, where east and west met, the new Christian belief developed forms and practices which at first sight seem very different from what we know from the west. So the region has fascinated the scholarly world, and various theories have arisen to explain its origin and particular traditions. Most of these theories are characterized by a certain romantic flavour probably due to the use of Aramaic or Syriac, the local Edessene dialect, which supposedly is very close to Jesus' own language. Ever since F.C. Burkitt's _Urchristentum im Orient_ - note the emphasis on _Ur_ - the use of that particular language has been considered a real cultural frontier and barrier, so that religious ideas and concepts expressed in Syriac or going back to traditions current in that language have usually been considered as largely untouched by Greek culture and idiom. If that is so, it is argued, they may have preserved authentic traditions about and _logoi_ of Jesus which have not been kept in the Greek speaking church of the west due to the predominance of the Greek language and the transformation it brought about in Jesus' original gospel, in the _kerygma_ of the _Urgemeinde!_ [3] And so we hear about the apostle Addai travelling through the desert and bringing Jesus' message to Edessa, if not to king Abgar V, then at least to king Abgar the Great in the last decades of the second century, so that that tiny kingdom became the first Christian kingdom in the world. [4] But before Addai's and Abgar's time, so we are told, the apostle Judas Thomas, Jesus' twin brother, brought the gospel to the Edessene area, or else an early Christian group in that city enhanced its status by appropriating the name of Thomas. That must have happened in a very early period, before the four gospels were written down, since that particular name Judas Thomas has only been preserved in Syriac traditions. Due to the cultural isolation of the Syriac-speaking area, which protected it against hellenizing influences from the west, precious authentic words of Jesus' himself and gospel traditions of the Jerusalem congregation have been kept in the cradle of Syriac-speaking Christianity and have been lost elsewhere. [5] One more example of the very special attraction that early Syriac writings exert on some minds. About five years ago the New York Times, announcing on its front page a well-known American Pseudepigrapha project, informed its readers, after quoting one of the Odes of Solomon, that 'it is possible that the author of that song met Jesus one day in Galilee or had a vision similar to that of Paul on the Damascus Road and later recalled the event'. In that case we would not only have original traditions, but even original experiences which found concrete shape in these songs. [6]

All this sounds very attractive: an out-of-the-way place in the Roman Empire, with a local dialect very close to the language Jesus spoke, preserved and transmitted original and authentic Christian traditions going back to the circle of the disciples and the Jerusalem community, which in other parts of the Empire remained unknown or were lost. And all this was due to the activities of the apostle Judas Thomas, Jesus twin brother, and the enigmatic apostle Addai, whom Eusebius identified with Thaddaeus, one of the seventy. [7]

Will this romantic and nostalgic picture stand firm, when it is confronted with the available sources and other historical data?

First of all a preliminary remark must be made. The east Syrian and northern Mesopotamian area, where Edessa was the centre of early Syriac-speaking Christianity, was not so isolated and untouched by Greco-Roman civilisation as is often assumed. Edessa was linked by intensely busy highroads with the other Syrian cities. It had all the characteristics of a Greco-Roman city in an area in which a Semitic culture was indigenous. It was thoroughly bilingual:

Greek philosophy was taught there in Syriac disguise, but local religious traditions were expressed in Greek artistic and literary forms. Like Palmyra, Edessa was an exponent of Near Eastern Hellenism, where cultural traditions of Semitic origin were transmitted in Greek disguise and vice versa.[8)] The border area fostered a continuous exchange of goods and ideas, and stood open to influences from all directions. That means that the question of language is not decisive: almost all writings that originate in that area and date back to the first three centuries A.D. are handed down in a Syriac and a Greek version, and it is often very difficult to establish which was the original.[9)] I would like to add: it is not that important either! Whoever was literate in that particular time and area usually knew both languages, and it may even be supposed that most texts were written down in two versions from the very outset. That does not mean that writings and ideas stemming from the east Syrian region belong without any differentiation to the mainstream of Greek Christian literature as we know it from more western areas, but their special features are not exclusively due to the fact that they were written by chance in Syriac and often also transmitted in Greek. Rather, the whole cultural and religious situation determined their particular contents and tendencies, which react on and reflect that situation. Who stood, then, by the cradle of Christianity, in that remarkable city that often looks like a melting-pot?

Marcion and Tatian were the most influential personalities in the shaping of that typical Syriac theology which gave rise to so many speculations and fantasies. Its whole development can be explained as due to their influence, to reactions to, polemics against and a further, sometimes poetical, elaboration of their ideas. It all ends up with Ephrem Syrus in the second half of the fourth century, who spent most of his intellectual energy in fighting Marcion's followers, and Bardaiṣan and Mani, who both stood in a certain relation to the heretic from Pontus. Within such a framework of historical development even the traditions about the apostle Judas Thomas find their organic place and date, like the enigmatic apostle Addai, who is supposed to have brought the gospel to king Abgar as a result of the king's correspondence with Jesus. In the further elaboration and substantiation of my main thesis it will turn out that these developments in the east Syrian area stood in continuous exchange with Antioch, and even exercised a fundamental influence on the basic ideas of later Antiochene theology, in particular diophysitism.

The Chronicon Edessenum mentions three names that were of importance for local religious developments: Marcion, who left the church in 137, Bardaiṣan, who was born on July 11th of the year 154, and Mani, who according to the same chronicle was born in 240 - the date of his spiritual birth, the time of his second revelation. In fact he was born in 216. [10] There is a whole range of arguments for a strong Marcionite influence in the east Syrian area, where these three figures dominated the scene for a long time.

According to Hippolytus and Eusebius Bardaiṣan of Edessa, the Aramaic philosopher, wrote dialogues against the followers of Marcion, among which was his excellent dialogue on Fate. Eusebius knew these dialogues in Greek, a translation due to Bardaiṣan's pupils, and gives long quotations from the Dialogue on Fate, which is identical with the well-known Syriac Book on the Laws of Countries, which originates in Bardaiṣan's circle. [11] It contains a dialogue between Bardaiṣan and the astrologer Awida, who started the discussion with the following question: 'If God is One, as you say He is, and He has created Mankind intending you to do what you are charged to, why did He not create Mankind in such wise that they could not sin, but always did what is right? Thereby His desire would have been fulfilled'. Bardaiṣan's reply contains a very concise formulation of the problem in question: 'Tell me, my son Awida, what do you think: The God of the Universe is not One, or He is One and does not desire man's conduct to be good and just?' [12] A better wording of Marcion's central problem can hardly be conceived. It is in any case clear, that Bardaiṣan disputed with the Marcionites in this area, roughly around 200 A.D. The controversy centred around Marcion's doctrine of two gods, the righteous and cruel god of the Old Testament, creator of the world, and God the Father of Jesus Christ, the Unknown God of Mercy. Bardaiṣan defended God's unity: the creator made the best possible world, using his noetic power in sending His Word of Thought or First Word towards the material elements in order to create harmony. This creative intellectual principle is at the same time God's instrument of salvation that teaches man how to live in accordance with the intention of the creator and to do what is good and right. This instrument was, therefore, identified by Bardaiṣan with Jesus Christ. [13] But in the theology of the Aramaic philosopher at the court of King Abgar the Great it is possible, besides a particular interpretation of the biblical message, to establish certain philosophical influences as well. Leaving aside the fact that Bardaiṣan, following in the tradition of Greek philosophy, taught an uncreated matter that was brought into order by the Word of Thought, his concept of Word of Thought shows great similarity to Tatian's Logos doctrine.[14)]

Bardaiṣan's dialogues against the Marcionites were widely known and used in the Syrian area. Parts of them, in particular of the Book of the Laws of Countries, were used in the Grundschrift of the Pseudo-Clementine writings that dates back to the first half of the third century and was written somewhere between Antioch and Edessa.[15)] That is in perfect accordance with the anti-Marcionite tendency of that Grundschrift, in which Simon Magus defends a Marcionite position which is attacked by Petrus. In this context it is of special interest that other doctrinal characteristics of the Pseudo-Clementine Grundschrift also betray Bardesanite influence. It is very remarkable that according to that Grundschrift evil found its origin in the mixture of the four basic elements after their coming forth from God. That reminds us of Bardaiṣan's cosmology, in which evil comes into being through the accidental mixture of the four elements which to begin with were in perfect harmony.[16)]

The learned author of that Grundschrift most likely made extensive use of Bardesanite writings and concepts, perhaps prompted to that use through the reputation of the Aramaic philosopher as an opponent of Marcion's views and influence.[17)]

Bardaiṣan's writings also found their way into the Vita of Aberkios, the famous fighter against the Marcionites in the Syrian area, who travelled through the whole of Syria, crossed the Euphrates and came to Nisibis preaching the Gospel of the one and only God. His Vita tells us about his meeting with Bardaiṣan somewhere in northern Mesopotamia between Edessa and Nisibis. There Aberkios sees a delegation of Christians arriving with at their head Bardaiṣan, distinguished from all others by his descent and wealth. We may suppose that Bardaiṣan came to see and honour Aberkios, with whom he shared a strong abhorrence of the Marcionites. Did these gentlemen speak Syriac with each other, or Greek? Aberkios like Bardaiṣan surely knew Syriac, otherwise his action against the Marcionites in the East Syrian and Northern Mesopotamian area would have been ineffective. But Aberkios knew perfect Greek too, as witness his famous tomb inscription which bears all the characteristics of his literary education and knowledge of Greek poetry. [18)]

All this must be dated to the years around A.D. 200 and into the first half of the third century. But Marcionite influence remained strong in later times too. For the Syriac-speaking area one of the main testimonies for Marcionism's powerful position is provided by the Odes of Solomon. These at first sight enigmatic poems of an ecstatic character, which usually are dated so early, reveal some of their secrets when their very precise wording is closely analysed. God the creator is described as knowing no envy. It is almost a standing epithet throughout the whole collection, and clearly conceals a reference to Marcion and his followers, who considered the creator god as a god of envy. One example from Ode 4: (God is being addressed):

> Sprinkle upon us Thy sprinklings
> And open Thy bountiful springs which abundantly supply
> us with milk and honey,
> For there is no regret with Thee
> That Thou shouldest regret anything which Thou has
> promised.
> Since the result was manifest to Thee
> For that which Thou gavest, Thou gavest freely
> So that Thou will not draw back and take it again.
> For all was known to Thee as God
> And set in order from the beginning before Thee;
> And Thou, O Lord, hast made all. [19)]

The well-known Marcionite motif of the repentance of the creator (die Reue des Schöpfers) is attacked here, and stress is placed on the unity of God's actions, that from the outset aimed at man's salvation. Again and again the odes emphasize that God the creator is also God the Saviour, and that the whole process of man's history from creation till the end is guided by divine providence. Only against the background of Marcion's doctrine can such specific phrases and theological accents become understandable and stand revealed in their full meaning.

The Marcionites had a long history in Syria. Ephrem Syrus severely combats them and is, therefore, a main source for the knowledge of their doctrines. But in the fifth century whole villages were still Marcionite according to Theodoret. [20] On their role in Syria I would like also to make one further suggestion. From the period before Chalcedon we have a whole collection of inscriptions from the Syrian area professing one god: heis theos. I am pretty sure that these inscriptions attack the Marcionites, since they are in particular found in regions where Marcionite presence is also documented in later times. Another example of the fact that the substantial influence of Marcion's church shaped the theology and formulas of his orthodox opponents. [21]

In all likelihood Tatian the Syrian and pupil of Justin belonged to Marcion's opponents too, at least when he remained loyal to that aspect of his teacher Justin. As a pagan he was converted to Christianity, the true philosophy, in Rome, and returned to the East about 170 A.D., where he was still active in the Syriac-speaking area for some time. The exact date of his death is unknown. [22] Only two of his works have been preserved. The Diatessaron probably composed after Tatian's return to the east, and most likely in a Greek and a Syriac version. I assume that the Greek was the first version, based on Greek versions of the four gospels, but that the Syriac one was produced at about the same time. [23] But what does 'original' mean in a thoroughly bilingual situation? The other work is the Oratio ad Graecos, in which an outline of Tatian's theology is to be found. [24]
Western sources credit Tatian with the founding of the sect of the Encratites, but Syriac sources silently pass by him and do not seem to know of his existence at all. [25] That seems very odd, but finds its explanation, in my view, in the fact that Tatian's religious ideas, leaving aside some of his more philosophical insights, were common coin in the East Syrian area, so that there was no explicit need to mention his name as the founder of a special sect as Irenaeus and others did. Tatian is at the same time an exponent of that Syriac spiritual climate and its powerful promotor. Later writings and developments in the Syriac-speaking region cannot be understood without regard to his view of Christian doctrine and practice. In particular, third century writings like the Syriac apocryphal Acts of Thomas and the Odes of Solomon reflect his ideas to such an extent that they can be considered a commentary on them. [26] They illustrate his doctrinal views, in the form of adventurous stories and poetic, very sophisticated, hymns. I will substantiate this thesis after an outline of Tatian's

theological position.[27)]

God's Logos, sprung forth from Him by His mere will, the firstborn work of the Father (5,1), also called Spirit (7,1), made Man an image of immortality, so that he might share God's lot and have immortality also. Man, like the angels created before him, has free will, whereas the power of the Word, having foreknowledge of the future, prevents wickedness by issuing prohibitions. Then came one who was cleverer than the rest because he was first-born, and men and angels followed along with him and proclaimed as god the traitor to God's law, and so the power of the Word banished the arch-rebel and his followers from life with him. Man, made in the image of God, became mortal, since the more powerful spirit departed from him. Man has two spirits, one called soul (psyche), and the other pneuma, the seat of God's image and likeness. First men were endowed with both, but they lost immortality, because free will destroyed them. God has done nothing bad, it was we who exhibited wickedness, but we who exhibited it are still capable of rejecting it (11.2). Originally the spirit was the soul's companion, but left it, when the soul was unwilling to follow it, although a spark remained behind. The junction of body, soul and spirit is of a particular nature expressed by Tatian in the following way: The bond of the flesh is soul, but it is the flesh which contains the soul. If such a structure is like a shrine, a temple (naos), God is willing to dwell in it through the spirit his representative. That dwelling of the spirit in the soul is called union (syzygia) by Tatian, and through this union man is enabled to mount to the realms above where the spirit leads him (13,2). To gain salvation, then, is to search for what we once had and have lost, to link the soul to the Holy Spirit and to busy ourselves with the union ordained by God. We must yearn for our ancient condition, and reject everything that impedes our regaining it, i.e. passions and sexuality, since we are convinced that the spirit in conjunction with the soul can obtain the heavenly garment of immortality. It is possible for everyone who is stripped of passion to obtain this adornment and hasten back to his ancient kinship (20,3). That union is accomplished through a permanent struggle against the demons, which are only visible to those who are guarded by the spirit of God. Demons cause illnesses which cannot be healed by medicines, but only through reliance on the power of God. Demons, the embodiment of evil, will be there as long as the world exists, because the Lord of the universe gave license to their frolics until the world comes to an end. When the soul is not united with spirit it is ignorant of the truth and will die. However, it will not die if it has obtained knowledge of God, because the soul is preserved by the spirit, just as was the darkness by the light that shone in it. That implies a process of rebirth. Tatian says about himself that he, in imitation (mimesis) of the Word, having been begotten again and obtained understanding of the truth, is bringing to order the confusion in kindred matter (5,3).

From these quotations from the Oratio ad Graecos the main lines of Tatian's doctrine will already have become clear.
Salvation is recuperation of Man's original immortal condition, in which soul and spirit were united and Man knew the truth and lived in kinship with God, wearing the heavenly garment of immortality, and free from the demons. That salvation is accomplished by the Holy Spirit's indwelling in the human's body as in a temple. One gets the impression that the Holy Spirit is identical with the Logos and His manifestation. Salvation was possible because a spark of the spirit was left in the soul, which was awakened by the servant of the suffering God (15,3). Salvation, therefore, is a timeless process. It has a beginning in the creation of the world by the Logos and is brought about every time that Man, using his free will in the right way, stirred and awakened by God's Spirit, His Logos, which is active during the whole of world history, wins the truth. Then he becomes immortal again, soul and spirit are united, bodily passions are overcome, he obtains the right insight, truth and wisdom, he lives again in the heavenly regions in kinship with God. From this system as represented by the Oratio ad Graecos it is fully understandable that Tatian began his Diatessaron with the Prologue of St John's Gospel, in which is described how God's Logos dwelt among us in order that we might become sons of God again.[28)] This Prologue contains the core of Tatian's theology and anthropology, including his encratism. Becoming sons of God again means being born, not of blood, nor of the will of the flesh, nor of the will of man, but of God.

The Syriac Acts of Thomas and the Odes of Solomon illustrate Tatian's concepts and their main tenets are in complete accordance with his views.

The Acts of Thomas were written in the first half of the third century in the Edessene area.[29] They describe the powerful acts of Judas Thomas, Jesus' twin, whose main activities aim at breaking off marriages and at persuading young couples to refrain from sexual intercourse. His successes were great and in particular many women said goodbye to their planned wedding and dedicated themselves to the heavenly wedding feast, the union with their heavenly spiritual bridegroom. This encratism is not inspired by pure and simple hate of the body, but is a means of salvation, of restoring Man's original state. The royal bride and bridegroom in the first book of the Acts, who both renounce marriage - they preserved themselves from the filth of intercourse, and became pure temples, according to the wording of these Acts -, return to their original state, the state of Man before he made the wrong use of his free will. In that state corruption is taken away from them and they are no longer ashamed. They found life and became immortal. The bride is betrothed to her true Husband, the power and wisdom and will of the Father, who invited her to the true wedding feast. The bridegroom praises God, who removed him from corruption and sowed life in him, who led him to a better state, who showed him how to find himself and to put away from him the things that are not his.[30]

The tenor of all stories about the heavenly wedding and the entering of the heavenly bridal chamber is the same, it is a poetical phrasing based on biblical parables of the Tatianic concept of the union of soul and spirit, which means a return to the state of immortality before Man made wrong use of his will.[31] All the terms that occured in the Oratio ad Graecos turn up again. Making the wrong use of free will means death according to Tatian, and that is illustrated in the Third Act, the story of the raising of a handsome young man. When Thomas sees his dead body he prays as follows:

'Lord of the souls which abide in the body, ...come, Lord, at this moment for the sake of the dust which Thy holy hands have fashioned'. And he said again: 'This deed has not taken place without the instigation of the enemy, who does these things. But the enemy, who does these things has not dared to attempt it through one who is alien to him, but through one who is subject to his will'.[31] This is an exact parallel with Tatian's explanation of the origin of evil and death in the world. Man has free will to choose; following the enemy implies becoming mortal, losing the spirit of immortality, dying. In Tatian's view the arch-rebel is a demon, who in in the story of the Acts of Thomas appears as a black snake. The snake introduces himself in the following way: 'I am the son of him, who makes himself like unto God to those who obey him that they may do his will. I am the son of him, who is ruler over everything that is created under heaven etc.' [33] Compare that with the following sentence from Tatian's Oratio, describing the origin of evil in the world: 'Then came one who was cleverer than the rest because he was first-born, and men and angels followed along with him and proclaimed as god the traitor to God's law' (7,2).

When the youth had come to life again by the hand of Judas Thomas, he addressed a long prayer to the Lord: ...'Thou art He who didst make Man, as Thy Godhead willed, with the fashioning of Thy hands, that he might be ruler above; and didst create for him another creation, that he might strive against it with the free will which Thou gave him. But the free nature of man went astray and he became subject to his fellow; and that fellow became an enemy of him, because he found that he had been unmindful of his free will'. [34]

Salvation from this miserable state is brought about by the sending of the Word. The young man phrases it as follows: 'but thou, O Merciful, through thy great mercy, didst spread over us Thy goodness, and didst send to our human race the Word, the Disposer of all created things, through Thy glorious Son. And He, through His Free-will, which Thou gavest Him - Thy goodness aiding Him - came and found us in those works which our human race did from the first day. And Thou didst enter into a reckoning with us for our sins, but didst bring me to life through Thy goodness, ...' [35]

Again we come across a clear Tatianic conception. Salvation consists of imitating the incarnate Word, as Tatian said: 'I too, in imitation of the Word, have been begotten again, namely to eternal life' (5,3). Unlike the first and all men, the man Jesus, aided by the indwelling of the eternal Word, made the right use of his free will, destroyed the enemy, and opened the path to a better earth. This process of mimesis is a life-long struggle, again a Tatianic concept, but in the end man will win the war and obtain the crown of victory. This war is conducted in particular against sexual passions, since sexuality entered the world through man's wrong use of his will, which distorted the original harmony and unity. The enemy, therefore, manifests himself in sexual seductions. When a woman in the Fifth Act of Thomas is afflicted by a demon, who at night wants to have intercourse with her, she prays to the Lord: '....drive away from me this affliction, that I may be free and may be united to my former nature ' (V, 43).[36)]

It is of particular interest that in all the adventures of Judas Thomas only he and some believing intimates are able to see the demons. When he delivered the woman from her erotic demon, the story goes on, the enemy came and stood before him, no one seeing him except the Apostle and the woman. That is a Tatianic idea again: 'None of the demons possesses a particle of flesh, but their constitution is spiritual like that of fire and air. Only those who are guarded by the spirit of God can easily perceive the bodies of demons, but the others cannot' - so Tatian puts it in his Oratio (15,3).

Again and again we come across Tatianic concepts in the Acts of Thomas often with a similar or almost similar terminology, in which the basic pattern is clear. Man, created with soul and spirit lost the latter, because he responded to the call of the first-born angel, who became the enemy par excellence. So Man lost his original immortality and became a mortal, sexual being. God's creative and saving activity, that started with the creation of the world by His Word, used that same Logos during the whole of world history to restore Man's original situation. At the end His Word came to dwell in a human body, which, therefore, could make the right use of his free will. That was God's only Son, who was in all aspects a single being. As God's only-begotten son he lived a single life, a-sexual, demonstrating Man's original unity.[37)] He left his family and urged his disciples to do the same, bringing back also in this way the state before the fall. You may recall: A man shall leave his father and his mother, and shall cleave unto his wife: and they shall be one flesh. And they were both naked the man and his wife and were not ashamed. In Tatian's view that verse meant that the sexual difference had been abolished: man and woman were one again. God's eternal Logos will dwell as the Holy Spirit in each man that hears the Gospel and believes it, so that he gets the right knowledge of just and wrong and can lead an encratitic life which brings him back to his original state and makes him immortal again. He has won the war against the enemy and found the pearl. When Tatian describes his conversion to Christianity he uses the following wording: 'God's word held power over our property like a kind of 'hidden treasure'; in digging it up we were covered with dust, but provide the occasion of guaranteeing its possession. For everyone who recovers his own property wins possession of the most precious wealth'. (Oratio 30,1). This whole process of salvation implies that man becomes identical with Christ. Just as God's Logos dwelt in the man Jesus and gave him the power, the wisdom and the will of the Father, so Jesus dwells in those who believe in him in the form of the Spirit that man lost in the beginning, and gives him wisdom, the right will, power, in short: immortal life. [38)]

This basic theological and anthropological pattern is expressed in the Acts of Thomas and in Tatian's Oratio in a way that shows great similarity to later Antiochene diophysitism as it was developed by Diodorus and Theodore of Mopsuestia. [39)]

A few examples from Tatian and the Acts of Thomas might illustrate this. When Tatian speaks about the composition of body, soul and spirit, he puts it this way: 'If such a structure, i.e. the body with the soul, is like a temple, God is willing to dwell in it through the spirit, his representative'. The body is like a temple, when it is guarded in chastity and purity. About that theme we read in the Acts of Thomas:'Purity is the athlete who is not overcome. Purity is worthy before God of being to him a familiar handmaiden. Purity is the temple of God, and everyone who guards it guards His temple and the Messiah dwells in him' (IX, 85). Therefore the Acts of Thomas never say that the Word became flesh, but that the first-born Son of the Father put on the body. I quote: 'Jesus who art in the Father and the Father in Thee, and ye are on in power and in will and in glory and in essence, and for our sake Thou wast named with names, and art the Son and didst put on the body' (V, 48). [40)] The Acts of Thomas consequently make a clear distinction between what Christ did as man and what He did as God. I quote from a prayer of Thomas to Jesus:'Jesus, born a man, slain, dead: Jesus, poor and catching fish for dinner and supper; Jesus, satisfying many thousands with a little bread. Jesus resting from the fatigue of a journey like a man, and walking upon the waves of the see like a God'(V, 47). It is like reading Theodore. [41)]

That is an indication of a continuous relation between Antioch and the East Syrian area, which made substantial contributions

to the early development of Antiochene theology. In this context Lucian of Antioch, the founder of the Antiochene School, is of special interest, since he got his philosophical and theological training in the School of Edessa, but moved shortly after 260 A.D. to Antioch.[42)] He surely must have known the Acts of Thomas and possibly related literature, to which the Odes of Solomon belong. These songs represent the same theological pattern as the Acts of Thomas, also due to Tatian's paramount influence.
The best illustration of this thesis is a quotation from the third Ode that is almost programmatic:

> I love the Beloved and my soul loves Him
> And where His rest is, there also am I.
> And I shall be no stranger,
> because there is no jealousy with the Lord Most High and Merciful.
> I have been united to Him, because the Lover has found the Beloved.
> Because I love Him that is the Son, I shall become a son.
> Indeed he who is joined to Him who is immortal,
> Truly shall be immortal.
> And he who delights in the Life
> Will become living.
> This is the Spirit of the Lord, which is not false,
> Which teaches the sons of men to know His ways.
> Be wise and understanding and vigilant.[43)]

Tatian's central concepts are present in these lines: Man becomes an immortal son of God when he is united to God's beloved Son, who is represented as the Spirit of the Lord. In this way Man also becomes wise and learns the truth, God's eternal ways. That is the reason why in these Odes all the passages that seem to be sung by Christ are actually spoken by the Odist himself, who as a son of God is identical with the Son of God, reborn from his Spirit, and guided by the Spirit to a heavenly place.[44)]
A comparison of a text from Tatian's Oratio with a quotation from Ode 36 will make that perfectly clear. First then Tatian: 'If the soul gains union with the divine Spirit it is not unaided, but mounts to the realms above where the spirit leads it; for the spirit's home is above, but the soul's birth is below' (13,2).
And now Ode 36:

> I rested on the Spirit of the Lord

And she raised me on high.
And made me to stand on my feet in the high place of the Lord,
Before His perfection and His glory,
While I was praising Him by the composition of His Odes.
The Spirit brought me forth before the Lord's face
And whereas I am a man,
I was named enlightened, son of God. [45)]

Further quotations might be adduced, but the main tenor is clear. The celestial Word, made spirit from the Spirit and Word from the power of the Word, to cite Tatian once more (7,1), is an active element that created the world and men, embodies Man's free will, and during the whole of world history aids him to return to his original state.
He put on a body and dwells like the divine Spirit in it, in order to give man his original spirit back.

This christological - anthropological pattern has a Platonic background and cannot be understood without taking into consideration the main philosophical trends that were current during the second and third century A.D. In the Odes of Solomon we find that pattern disguised in a very poetical, but at the same time sophisticated wording, which presents the same characteristics of early Antiochene theology that we have found earlier. Even the term prosopon occurs in its technical sense! [46)]

Until now the apostle Judas Thomas has not entered the scene on which Marcion and Tatian are the main actors. What about him and his Gospel that is assumed to represent a very old independent Gospel tradition? The apostle Judas Thomas, Judas the Twin, is the principal character of the Syriac Acts of Thomas, transmits Jesus' secret words in the Gospel of Thomas that is preserved in Coptic but goes back to a Syriac original, and receives other revelations from the Saviour in the Book of Thomas the Contender. [47)]
In the Syriac tradition Judas not Iskarioth is identified with Judas the brother of the Lord and considered in particular to be His twin brother, and therefore identified with the well-known apostle Thomas. [48)] In the Acts of Thomas Judas appears in the form of Jesus and the other way round. [49)] Both are identical and play puss in the corner. Whence stems this particular interest in an apostle Judas Thomas, who is unknown in traditions current outside Syria? I believe that Judas the twin brother of the Lord

is the most perfect representative of the state of salvation, which implies an identification with the Saviour, God's Word and Spirit dwelling in a human being. Who is more like the Lord than His own twin brother? They are two, but at the same time one; they represent each other and are interchangeable. The Tatianic concept of salvation aiming at a complete union with the Lord - but of an a-sexual nature! - gave rise to a special interest in an apostle who shows the greatest similarity to Jesus himself and, therefore, embodies the pure state of salvation with all the power of life-giving and healing that belongs to that state of regained immortality. Let me put it this way: the apostle Judas Thomas has not brought the Gospel to the east Syrian area, but the particular interpretation of the Gospel that prevailed in that area focussed on the twin brother of the Lord, who as a human person identical with the heavenly brother represents salvation *par excellence*.[50)]

That particular view of the relation between Man and his Saviour goes back to Tatian and we find it *in nuce* in his *Oratio* and in the preserved fragments of his *Diatessaron*, in which the figure of Judas Thomas occurs for the first time.[51)] Judas not Iskarioth was identified as Judas the brother of the Lord, more precisely the twin brother of the Lord, and he is, therefore, one and the same as the Apostle Thomas, whose name means 'twin'. The result was Judas Thomas, not a historical but a theological person, representing re-born man, born of God like the only begotten Son, his brother.

The much-discussed *Gospel of Thomas* does not contain, therefore, in my view an independent tradition of *logia* of Jesus, but its whole contents and message can and must be understood as an elaboration and illustration of the main elements of Tatian's christology and anthropology. That is the reason why so many *logia* represent *Diatessaron* readings, which always betray a typical encratitic Tatianic point of view.[52)] The *Gospel of Thomas* has the same doctrine on the divine *pneuma* that we met with in Tatian. It glorifies the solitary, the single one, in whom the difference between male and female has been removed and who, like a little child, does not know shame, again a Tatianic concept. The single ones, who overcame sexual passions and so abolished the difference between male and female, get back the spirit of God which dwells within them, their original image is restored, and they enter the kingdom of God from which they originate: Let me give one quotation that might illustrate this point:

> Jesus said: Blessed are the solitary and elect, for you shall find the kingdom; because you come from it, and you shall go there again. Jesus said: If they say to you: From where have you originated? say to them: We have come from the Light, where the Light has originated through itself. It stood and revealed itself in their image. If they say to you: Who are you? say: We are His Sons and we are the elect of the Living Father (49-50).[53)]

This background of the Gospel of Thomas also explains the many analogies between it and the Acts of Thomas and Odes of Solomon.

The main outlines of the traditio-historical development that we have tried to lay bare determine the main forces that were at work east of Antioch. Marcion and Tatian, two opponents from the beginning, fixed the structures of early Syriac theology. Marcion's influence was paramount and opposed by Bardaisan and Tatian. The latter shaped the Judas Thomas traditions and literature like the Odes of Solomon, which in their turn polemize against Marcion.

All this did not happen in splendid isolation, but in continuous exchange with what was going on in Antioch and the western area, where the same Marcion was a real danger. Tatian was deeply influenced by Platonism and Stoicism, and that philosophical flavour can be detected in all Syriac literature based on his ideas. It even can be considered the first phase of later Antiochene theology, for which the foundations were laid in the Syriac-speaking area. That was one direction in which this whole tradition developed. Another more radical direction is linked with Mani and Manichaeism.[54)]

Mani was the other heir of this remarkable mixture of clear cut philosophical concepts regarding Man's body, soul and spirit, their origin and destination, the reflective poetical dress in which these concepts were often disguised, and the harsh life style enforced by the pursuit of divine truth in the context of our rebellious and obstinate corporeal existence. The divine Spirit that was active during the whole of world history found at last a dwelling place in Mani, the Apostle of Jesus Christ and the promised Paraclete. He assimilated almost the whole tradition before him. The Diatessaron was his Bible, the Acts of Thomas and the Gospel of Thomas belonged to his library, he had a high esteem for Marcion and took over much from Bardaiṣan. He wrote hymns and Psalms like the Odes of Solomon, and based himself on the Christian tradition in the way it was understood and interpreted in the Syriac speaking area in which he was born.[55)] In that area the most outstanding Manichaean missionary was Addai, who travelled widely in Syria and northern Mesopotamia. Manichaeism, precisely because it associated itself so closely with the existing local traditions, was such a threat for the Christian community at the centre of that Syriac area, Edessa, that the Christians there seized the Manichaean missionary and transformed him into the Christian apostle Addai, who preached the Gospel to King Abgar, as Mani too preached to kings and queens. The Addai story has clear anti-Manichaean tendencies, and as a historical fiction functioned in a situation in which Manichaeism was a real threat.[56)]

It is a funny thing. Both supposed apostles of Edessa found their origin in theological and historical speculation. Judas Thomas' cradle is Tatian's theology. Addai owes his Christian existence to Mani's activities. They were not the personalities that shaped Syriac theology. Those were Marcion, Bardaiṣan and Tatian. That is the reason why Ephrem Syrus in the fourth century has much in common with Tatianic traditions, and spent most of his life fighting against Marcion, Bardaisan and Mani, whereas he passes by Judas Thomas and Addai in silence!

Until now we have dealt mainly with theological and philosophical ideas which, notwithstanding important differences, have one thing in common: a strong emphasis on asceticism, the command of the body and its passions in order to create room for the divine spirit, truth and wisdom. It deserves a special inquiry, why such ascetic trends found a fertile soil in the Syriac-speaking area, east of Antioch.[57)] But while revelations of the divine spirit may merit a life-long enkrateia, for the fruits of my mind one hour of war against sleep and other passions is more than enough.

Notes

1. L. Dillemann, Haute Mésopotamie orientale et pays adjacents. Contribution à la géographie historique de la région, du Ve s. avant l'ère chrétienne au VIe s.de cette ère, Paris 1962, 147 ff.; J.B. Segal, Edessa 'the blessed City', Oxford 1970, 3 f.; Drijvers, Hatra, Palmyra und Edessa. Die Städte der syrisch-mesopotamischen Wüste in politischer, kulturgeschichtlicher und religionsgeschichtlicher Beleuchtung, ANRW II, 8, 1977, 864; J. Ferguson, China and Rome, ANWR II, 9,2, 1978, 585 - 587.

2. On Greek and Aramaic in northern Mesopotamia vide Fergus Millar, Paul of Samosata, Zenobia and Aurelian: The Church, local Culture and political Allegiance in third-century Syria, JRS 61, 1971, 2 - 5; R. Schmitt, Die Ostgrenze von Armenien über Mesopotamien, Syrien bis Arabien, in: Die Sprachen im römischen Reich der Kaiserzeit, Beihefte der Bonner Jahrbücher 40, 1980, 187 - 214; S. Brock, From Antagonism to Assimilation: Syriac Attitudes to Greek Learning, East of Byzantium: Syria and Armenia in the formative Period, ed. N.G. Garsoïan - Th.F. Mathews - R.W. Thomson, Dumbarton Oaks 1982, 19.

3. F.C. Burkitt, Urchristentum in Orient, Tübingen 1907; H. Koester, 'Gnomai Diaphoroi', HThR 58, 1965, 279 - 318; R. Murray, Symbols of Church and Kingdom. A Study in Early Syriac Tradition, Cambridge 1975, 4 ff.; idem, The Characteristics of the Earliest Syriac Christianity, East of Byzantium, 3 - 16; G. Quispel, The Gospel of Thomas revisited, Colloque international sur les textes de Nag Hammadi, ed.: B. Barc, Quebec-Louvain 1981, 218 - 266, esp. 234 ff.; W. Cramer, Der Geist Gottes und des Menschen in frühsyrischer Theologie, MBT 46, Münster 1979, 7 - 13, cf. Drijvers, ZKG 1981, 354 - 358.

4. J.J. Gunther, The Meaning and Origin of the Name 'Judas Thomas', Le Muséon 93, 1980, 113 - 148, esp. 129 ff. is the most recent scholar to advocate this view; cf. E. Kirsten, art. Edessa, RAC VI, 1966, Sp. 570; I. Ortiz de Urbina, Le origini del cristianesimo in Edessa, Gregorianum 15, 1934, 82 - 91 and many others; on king Abgar the Great see Drijvers, A Tomb for the Life of a King. A recently discovered Edessene Mosaic with a Portrait of King Abgar the Great, Le Muséon 95, 1982, 167 - 189.

5. H. Koester, Gnomai Diaphoroi. The Origin and Nature of Diversification in the History of Early Christianity, HThR 58, 1965, 279 - 318 = J.M. Robinson - H. Koester, Trajectories through Early Christianity, Philadelphia 1971, 114 - 158; J.J. Gunther, The Meaning and Origin of the Name 'Judas Thomas'; G. Quispel, The Gospel of Thomas revisited; W.H.C. Frend, the Gospel of Thomas. Is Rehabilitation Possible?, JThS N.S. XVIII, 1967, 13 - 26; H.-Ch. Puech, En quête de la Gnose II. Sur l'évangile de Thomas, Paris 1978, 54 is, however, very doubtful about the authenticity of these logia.

6. Writings From the Time of Jesus Sought Around World by Scholars; Interview with Dr. James Charlesworth of Duke University; cf. J.H. Charlesworth - R.A. Culpepper, The Odes of Solomon and the Gospel of John, CBQ 35, 1973, 298 - 322; idem, Tatian's Dependence upon apocryphal Traditions, The Heythrop Journal 15, 1974, 5 - 17.

7. Eusebius, H.E. I, xiii, 4.

8. Drijvers, ANRW II, 8, 885 - 896; idem, Cults and Beliefs at Edessa, EPRO 82, Leiden 1980, 1 - 18.

9. Cf. the discussion about the original language of Tatian's Diatessaron, B.M. Metzger, The Early Versions of the New Testament. Their Origin, Transmission, and Limitations, Oxford 1977, 30 ff.; for the original language of the Odes of Solomon of which Ode 11 is preserved in a Greek version vide J.A. Emerton, Some Problems of Text and Language in the Odes of Solomon, JThS NS xviii, 1967, 372 - 406; idem, Notes on some Passages in the Odes of Solomon, JThS NS xxviii, 1977, 507 - 519; Bardaiṣan's writings were extant in a Syriac and a Greek version, cf. Eusebius, H.E., IV, 30, cf. Drijvers, Bardaiṣan of Edessa, Studia Semitica Neerlandica VI, Assen 1966, 63 ff.; if the Gospel of Thomas discloses features that connect it with a Syriac miliou, it must have been extant in a Syriac and a Greek version before it was translated into Coptic, cf. J.-E. Ménard, Le milieu syriaque de l'Évangile selon Thomas et de l'Évangile selon Philippe, RSR 42, 1968, 261 - 266; A.F.J. KLijn, Christianity in Edessa and the Gospel of Thomas, NovT 14, 1972, 70 - 77; A. Guillaumont, Les sémitismes dans l'Évangile selon Thomas. Essai de classement, Studies in Gnosticism and Hellenistic Religions, pres. to Gilles Quispel, EPRO 91, Leiden 1981, 190 - 204.

10. Chronica minora I, ed, I. Guidi, CSCO. Script. Syri 1,3 (textus); CSCO, Script Syri 2,4 (versio); cf. W. Bauer, Rechtgläubigkeit und Ketzerei im ältesten Christentum, BHTh 10, Tübingen 1934, 20 ff.

11. Eusebius, H.E. IV, 30; Hippolytus, Refutatio VII, 31; cf. Bardaiṣan of Edessa, 60 ff.; Eusebius, Praep. Evang. VI, 9, 32; VI, 10, 1 - 48; for recent literature vide Drijvers, art. Bardesanes, TRE V, 206 - 212.

12. Drijvers, The Book of the Laws of Countries. Dialogue on Fate of Bardaiṣan of Edessa, Assen 1965, 5; cf. M. Hoffmann, Der Dialog bei den christlichen Schriftstellern der ersten vier Jahrhunderte, TU 96, Berlin 1966; A. Dihle, Zur Schicksalslehre des Bardesanes, Kerygma und Logos, Festschrift C. Andresen, Göttingen 1979, 123 - 135.

13. Bardaiṣan of Edessa, 100 ff.; T. Jansma, La notice de Barḥadbešabba ᶜArbaïa sur l'hérésie des Daisanites, Mémorial Khoury-Sarkis, Louvain 1969, 91 - 106; cf. in general A. Dihle, Das Problem der Entscheidungsfreiheit in frühchristlicher Zeit. Die Überwindung des gnostischen Heilsdeterminismus mit den Mitteln der griechischen Philosophie, in: Gnadenwahl und Entscheidungsfreiheit in der Theologie der Alten Kirche, Oikonomia 9, Erlangen 1980, 9 - 31.

14. Tatian, Oratio 5 (ed. M. Whittaker, Oxford 1982); M. Elze, Tatian und seine Theologie, Göttingen 1960, 70 ff.

15. Ps. Clem. Recogn. IX, 19 - 29; cf. G. Strecker, Das Judenchristentum in den Pseudoklementinen, TU 70, Berlin 1958, 256 ff.; F. Stanley Jones, The Pseudo-Clementines: A History of Research, The Second Century 2, 1982, 1 - 33, 63 - 96, esp. 20 ff.

16. Ps. Clem. Hom. XIX; cf. H.J. Schoeps, Aus frühchristlicher Zeit, Religionsgeschichtliche Untersuchungen, Tübingen 1950, 39 ff.

17. On this particular point further research is needed, cf. C. Colpe, ThLZ 93, 1968, 436; F. Stanley Jones, The Second Century 2, 1982, 23.

18. Bardaiṣan of Edessa, 170 f.; H. Grégoire, Bardesane et S. Abercius, Byzantion 25 - 27, 1955 - 1957, 363 - 368; W. Wischmeyer, Die Aberkiosinschrift als Grabepigramm, JAC 23, 1980, 22 - 47.

19. Ode of Solomon 4, 10 - 15, ed. J.B. Charlesworth, The Odes of Solomon, sec. ed. Scholars Press 1977; Drijvers, Die Oden Salomos und die Polemik mit den Markioniten im syrischen Christentum, Symposium Syriacum 1976, Or. Chr. An. 205, Roma 1978, 39 - 55; M. Lattke, Die Oden Salomos in ihrer Bedeutung für Neues Testament und Gnosis, 2 Vols, Orbis Biblicus et Orientalis 25/1-2, Freiburg - Göttingen 1979 contains many mistakes in his translation of the Syriac text and adds nothing to a better understanding of the Odes of Solomon; cf. E. Muehlenberg, Marcion's Jealous God, Disciplina Nostra, Essays in Memory of Robert P. Evans, ed. D.F. Winslow, Patr. Mon. Series 6, Philadelpha 1979, 93 - 113.

20. For Ephrem's polemics with the Marcionites, vide B. Aland, Marcion. Versuch einer neuen Interpretation, ZThK 70, 1973, 420 - 447; Bauer, Rechtgläubigkeit und Ketzerei, 27 - 31; Theodoret, H.E.V. 31; Harnack, Marcion, 156 ff.; J.M. Fiey, Les Marcionites dans les textes historiques de l'église de Perse, Le Muséon 83, 1970, 183 - 188.

21. E. Peterson, ΕΙΣ ΘΕΟΣ, FRLANT 24, Göttingen 1926; W. Liebeschuetz, Problems arising from the conversion of Syria, in: The Church in Town and Countryside, ed. by D. Baker, Studies in Church Hist. 16, Oxford 1979, 22 f.

22. On Tatian vide M. Elze, Tatian und seine Theologie, Göttingen 1960; G.F. Hawthorne, Tatian and his Discourse to the Greeks, HThR 57, 1964, 161 - 188; L.W. Barnard, The Heresy of Tatian - Once Again, JEH 19, 1968, 1 - 10.

23. Metzger, Early Versions of the New Testament, 30 ff.; A. Vööbus, Early Versions of the New Testament. Manuscript Studies, Stockholm 1954, 9 - 31; T. Baarda, The Gospel Quotations of Aphrahat the Persian Sage, Diss. A'dam 1975, 322 ff.

24. J. Quasten, Patrology I, 221 - 224; Elze, Tatian und Seine Theologie; Hawthorne, Tatian and his Discourse to the Greeks; a recent and reliable edition is Tatian, Oratio ad Graecos and Fragments, ed. and transl. by M. Whittaker, Oxford 1982.

25. F. Bolgiani, La tradizione erescologica sull' encratismo, Atti della Acad. d. scienze de Torino xci, 1956 - 1957, 1 - 77; 343 - 419; XCVI, 1961 - 1962, 537 - 664; art. Enkrateia, RAC VI, Sp.

352 ff.; A. Guillaumont, Christianisme et gnoses dans l'Orient préislamique, Annuaire du Collège de France 1981 - 1982, 425 - 431; Murray, Symbols of Church and Kingdom, 280.

26. D. Plooij, Eine enkratitische Glosse im Diatessaron. Ein Beitrag zur Geschichte der Askese in der alten Kirche, ZNW 22, 1923, 1 - 16; A.F.J. Klijn, The Influence of Jewish Theology on the Odes of Solomon and the Acts of Thomas, Aspects du judéo-christianisme, Paris 1965, 167 - 179; Y. Tissot, Encratisme et actes apocryphes, Les actes apocryphes des apôtres. Christianisme et monde païen, Genève 1981, 109 - 119.

27. I follow Tatian's Oratio ad Graecos, ed. Whittaker; cf. Elze, Tatian und seine Theologie; A. Grillmeier, Christ in Christian Tradition, I, sec. ed. Atlanta 1975, 111 f.; H. Dörrie, Platonica Minora, München 1976, 52, Anm. 214.

28. Vööbus, Early Versions of the New Testament, 15; Metzger, The Early Versions of the New Testament, 27 f.; Baarda, The Gospel Quotations of Aphrahat, 55 ff.

29. A.F.J. Klijn, The Acts of Thomas. Introduction, Text, Commentary, Leiden 1962, 18 - 26; G. Bornkamm in Hennecke-Schneemelcher, Neutestamentliche Apokryphen II, 308; Y. Tissot, Les actes apocryphes de Thomas: exemple de recueil composite, Les actes apocryphes des apôtres. Christianisme et monde païen, 223 - 232.

30. W. Wright, Apocryphal Acts of the Apostles, repr. A'dam 1968, 155 - 159 (Engl. transl.); cf. G. Blond, L'encratisme dans les actes apocryphes de Thomas, Recherches et Travaux 1, 1946, 5 - 25; Y. Tissot, Encratisme et Actes apocryphes, Les actes apocryphes des apôcryphes des apôtres, 118 f.

31. cf. H.-G. Gaffron, Studien zum koptischen Philippusevangelium unter besonderer Berücksichtigung der Sakramente, Diss. Bonn 1969, 191 - 219; E. Peterson, Frühkirche, Judentum und Gnosis, Rom - Freiburg - Wien 1959, 200 - 208; H.-Ch. Puech, En quête de la Gnose II. Sur l'évangile selon Thomas, Paris 1978, 233 ff.

32. Wright, Apocryphal Acts of the Apostles, 170; cf. Tatian, Oratio ad Graecos, 11, 2.

33. Wright, Apocryphal Acts of the Apostles, 171

34. Wright, Apocryphal Acts of the Apostles, 174.

35. Wright, Apocryphal Acts of the Apostles, 174.

36. Wright, Apocryphal Acts of the Apostles, 184; cf. Guillaumont, Christianisme et gnoses dans l'Orient préislamique, 428 ff.; A. Rousselle, Porneia. De la maîtrise du corps à la privation sensorielle IIe - IVe siècles de l'ère chrétienne, Paris 1983, 167 ff.

37. St. John's Gospel 1, 18; the Syriac ihidaya has the meaning of monachos and monogenes, cf. Puech, En quête de la Gnose II. Sur l'évangile selon Thomas, 240, 283 f.; P. Nagel, Die Motivierung der Askese in der alten Kirche und der Ursprung des Mönchtums, TU 95, 1966, 15 f.; A. Adam, review of A. Vööbus, History of Asceticism in the Syrian Orient, in: Askese und Mönchtum in der alten Kirche, ed. K. Suso Frank, WdF 409, Darmstadt 1975, 244 ff.; Baarda, The Gospel Quotations of Aphrahat, 70 - 72.

38. This basic pattern is expressed in poetical disguise in the so-called Hymn of the Pearl in the Acts of Thomas, cf. H. Kruse, The Return of the Prodigal. Fortunes of a Parable on its Way to the Far East, Orientalia 47, 1978, 163 - 214, esp. 189 ff.; in general P.-H. Poirier, L'hymne de la perle des Actes de Thomas. Introduction, Texte-Traduction, Commentaire, Louvain-La Neuve 1981 (with bibliography).

39. Grillmeier, Christ in Christian Tradition, 352 - 360; 421 - 439; D.S. Wallace-Hadrill, Christian Antioch. A study of early Christian thought in the East, Cambridge 1982, 117 ff.; an excellent introduction is R.A. Norris, Manhood and Christ. A Study in the Christology of Theodore of Mopsuestia, Oxford 1963; see my forthcoming study Early Forms of Antiochene Christology, Mélanges van Roey, Louvain 1984.

40. Wright, Apocryphal Acts of the Apostles, 220 - 221; 187 - 188; cf. Norris, Manhood and Christ, 216 - 228; R. Devreesse, Essai sur Théodore de Mopsueste, Rome 1948, 113 - 114.

41. Wright, The Apocryphal Acts of the Apostles, 187; Norris, Manhood and Christ, 197 - 201.

42. E.R. Hayes, L'école d'Edesse, Paris 1930, 123; Quasten, Patrology II, 142 - 144; art. Lucian, RGG IV, Sp. 463 f.: G. Bardy, Recherches

sur Saint Lucien d'Antioche et son école, Paris 1936.

43. J.B. Charlesworth, The Odes of Solomon, Ode 3,5–11; cf. Die Oden Salomos und die Polemik mit den Markioniten im syrischen Christentum, 42.

44. Cf. R. Abramowski, Der Christus der Salomooden, ZNW 35, 1936, 67 f. and my Early Forms of Antiochene Christology.

45. Ode 36, 1–3 (ed. J.B. Charlesworth); cf. R. Tonneau, Les homélies catéchétiques de Théodore de Mopsueste, Rome 1949, Hom. 1, 4, p. 9 for an exact parallel; Norris, Manhood and Christ, 168 – 172.

46. Ode 17, 4; 22, 11; 25, 4; 31, 5; cf. Abramowski, Der Christus der Salomooden, 67; Norris, Manhood and Christ, 228 – 233.

47. The Gospel according to Thomas, Coptic Text established and transl. by A. Guillaumont, H.-Ch. Puech, G. Quispel, W. Till and Yassah ᶜabd al Masīḥ, Leiden – London 1959; The Nag Hammadi Library in English, ed. J.M. Robinson, San Francisco – London 1977, 117 – 130; the literature on the Gospel of Thomas is immense, the best commentary is H.-Ch. Puech, En quête de la Gnose II, Sur l'évangile selon Thomas, Paris 1978; J.D. Turner, The Book of Thomas the Contender, SBL Diss. Series 23, Scholars Press 1975; The Nag Hammadi Library in English, 188 – 194.

48. A.F.J. Klijn, John XIV 22 and the Name Judas Thomas, Studies in Johan pres. to J.N. Sevenster, Leiden 1970, 88 – 96; Puech, En quête de la Gnose II, 40 – 46; 213 – 216; 222 – 224.

49. Klijn, John XIV 22 and the Name Judas Thomas, 95, n. 4; J.A. Delaunay, Rite et symbolique en Acta Thomae vers. syr. I, 2 a et ss., Mémorial Jean de Menasce, éd. Ph. Gignoux, Acta Iranica, Teheran 1974, 11 – 34; Puech, En quête de la Gnose, 90, 216.

50. Cf. Puech, En quête de la Gnose II, 214: 'Thomas serait, en conséquence, conçu comme le 'frère mystique' du Christ, un 'frère' qui en est le reflet, l'image, la réplique parfaite'; Klijn, John XIV 22 and the Name Judas Thomas, 96.

51. Oratio 5, 2 – 3: 'Just as the Word begotten in the beginning in turn begot our creation by fabricating matter for himself, so

I too, in imitation of the Word, having been begotten again and obtained understanding of the truth and bringing to order the confusion in kindred matter'; Since the reading Judas Thomas occurs in the Old Syriac Gospels at John XIV, 22, it is most likely that it is a Diatessaron reading, cf. F.C. Burkitt, Evangelion da-mepharreshe, Vol. II, Cambridge 1904, 146 f.

52. Cf. G. Quispel, L'Évangile selon Thomas et le Diatessaron, VigChr 13, 1959, 87 - 117; idem, Tatian and the Gospel of Thomas, Leiden 1975, 174 ff.; Tj. Baarda, Luke 12, 13 - 14, Text and Transmission from Marcion to Augustine, Studies for Morton Smith at Sixty, ed. J. Neusner, Leiden 1975, 107 - 162, esp. 155 with decisive arguments against Quispel's thesis of a common Aramaic gospel source for Tatian's Diatessaron and the Gospel of Thomas.

53. Translation according to Guillaumont, Puech, Quispel; Puech, En quête de la Gnose II, 166 - 182 for a detailed commentary.

54. A. Böhlig, Christliche Wurzeln im Manichäismus, Mysterion und Wahrheit, Leiden 1968, 202 - 221; idem, The New Testament and the Concept of the Manichean Myth, The New Testament and Gnosis, Essays in honour of R.McL. Wilson, Edinburgh 1983, 90 - 103; E. Rose, Die manichäische Christologie, Wiesbaden 1979; a fresh inquiry into the precise relations between Mani and Syriac Christianity in its various forms is an urgent desideratum.

55. Cf. P. Nagel, Die apokryphen Apostelakten des 2. und 3 Jahrhunderts in der manichäischen Literatur. Ein Beitrag zur Frage nach den christlichen Elementen im Manichäismus, Gnosis und Neues Testament, Berlin 1975, 149 - 182; J.-D. Kaestli, L'utilisation des actes apocryphes des apôtres dans le manichéisme, Gnosis and Gnosticism, ed. M. Krause, Nag Hammadi Studies VIII, Leiden 1977, 107 - 116; A. Böhlig, Das Böse in der Lehre des Mani und des Markion, Makarios-Symposium über das Böse, ed. W. Strothmann, Wiesbaden 1983, 18 - 35.

56. See my forthcoming paper Addai und Mani. Christentum und Manichäismus im dritten Jahrhundert in Syrien, Symposium Syriacum 1980, Or. Chr. Anal., Rome 1984; A Tomb for the Life of a King. A recently discovered Edessene Mosaic with a Portrait of King Abgar the Great, Le Muséon 95, 1982, 188 f.

57. Notwithstanding the wealth of literature on early Syriac asceticism, the social roots of this particular phenomenon are still practically unknown; see now A. Rousselle, Porneia. De la maîtrise du corps à la privation sensorielle IIe - IVe siècles de l'ère chrétienne, Paris 1983.

LIST OF ABBREVIATIONS

ANRW	Aufstieg und Niedergang der römischen Welt
BHTh	Beiträge zur historischen Theologie
CBQ	Catholic Biblical Quarterly
CSCO	Corpus scriptorum Christianorum orientalium
EPRO	Etudes préliminaires aux religions orientales dans l'empire romain
HThR	Harvard Theological Review
JAC	Jahrbuch für Antike und Christentum
JEH	Journal of Ecclesiastical History
JRS	Journal of Roman Studies
JThS	Journal of Theological Studies
NovT	Novum Testamentum
OrChrAn	Orientalia Christiana Analecta
RAC	Reallexikon für Antike und Christentum
RGG	Religion in Geschichte und Gegenwart
RSR	Recherches de science religieuse
ThLZ	Theologische Literaturzeitung
TRE	Theologische Realenzyklopädie
TU	Texte und Untersuchungen zur Geschichte der altchristlichen Literatur
WdF	Wege der Forschung
ZKG	Zeitschrift für Kirchengeschichte
ZNW	Zeitschrift für die neutestamentliche Wissenschaft
ZThK	Zeitschrift für Theologie und Kirche

II

EDESSA UND DAS JÜDISCHE CHRISTENTUM*

Die Verbindung des Namens der Stadt Edessa mit einer bestimmten Strömung in der Geschichte des ältesten Christentums zu einem fast programmatisch klingenden Titel birgt eine grosse Anzahl von Problemen in sich, die vor allem hinter dem Terminus „jüdisches Christentum" stecken.[1] Edessa – Urhai im Syrischen – ist eine von den Seleukiden im Norden Mesopotamiens gegründete hellenistische Stadt, das „earliest center of Syriac-speaking Christianity",[2] wie es auf einer neuerdings erschienenen Karte der „lands of the Bible today" heisst. Edessa war aber mehr als nur das „earliest center of Syriac-speaking Christianity". Es war eine Stadt mit einer autochthonen semitischen Bevölkerung, die hauptsächlich arabischer Herkunft war; wo Juden und Griechen wohnten; wo die Parther einen grossen Einfluss ausübten; wo das Judentum, der Paganismus und das Christentum nebeneinander lebten; wo man sich der Astrologie und der Philosophie widmete, so dass die Stadt das Athen des Orients genannt wurde. Sie lag an der Grenze des Einflussbereiches der Römer und Parther und hat diese Lage mit grosser Diplomatie, Schlauheit und Perfidie ausgenutzt, um so lange wie möglich ihre Unabhängigkeit zu behaupten. In diesem Komplex von Einflüssen und Ausstrahlungen ist, vermutlich schon ziemlich früh, auch das Evangelium Jesu von Nazareth verkündigt worden. Die Annahme liegt nahe, dass die Formen dieser Verkündigung einerseits durch das Ursprungsland, Palästina, bedingt sind, anderseits durch die religiöse und kulturelle Lage in Edessa selbst, wo sie mit den religiösen Formen, die es dort

---

* Vortrag auf der Patristiker-Tagung in Driebergen, 2. Januar 1969.

1 M. Simon, Problèmes du judéo-christianisme, *Aspects du judéo-christianisme* (Paris 1965) pp. 1–17; M. Simon und A. Benoit, *Le Judaïsme et le Christianisme antique* (Paris 1968) pp. 258 svv.

2 *National Geographic*, december 1967, wall map supplement: Lands of the Bible today.

schon gab, eine Symbiose einging. Es ist im allgemeinen zu bedauern, dass die Autoren, die sich mit der Geschichte des ältesten Christentums in Edessa befasst haben, dieser komplexen synkretistischen Lage keine oder zu wenig Aufmerksamkeit gewidmet haben.[3] Man bekommt vielmehr den Eindruck, dass sie ohne weiteres das Christentum oder das jüdische Christentum extrapolieren und in „Reinkultur" behandeln. Es ist um so frappanter, dies festzustellen, als die Methode der Religionsgeschichtlichen Schule, die innerhalb der Religionswissenschaft nur noch wenige Anhänger hat, in dieser Weise – namentlich auf dem Gebiet der alten Kirchengeschichte – eine Nachblüte erlebt.

Mit dem Obenstehenden ist der Rahmen für diese Untersuchung über Edessa und das jüdische Christentum gegeben worden. Zunächst ist eine Übersicht der politischen, kulturellen und religiösen Geschichte Edessas, soweit sie für die Entstehung und die Geschichte des lokalen Christentums von Bedeutung ist, eine conditio sine qua non. Dann werden die Beziehungen zwischen den einzelnen Religionen die Aufmerksamkeit in Anspruch nehmen, wonach die Stellung des Christentums besser bestimmt werden kann, sowohl was seinen eigenen Charakter als auch sein Verhältnis zu den anderen Religionen betrifft. Dann erst tritt die Frage nach den Ursprüngen dieser ganz eigenen Form des Christentums und damit das Problem des jüdischen Christentums in den Gesichtskreis. Ich wähle also eine methodische Themenbehandlung, die von der bisher angewandten abweicht. W. Bauer charakterisierte in seinem Buch *Rechtgläubigkeit und Ketzerei im ältesten Christentum* das edessenische Christentum als häretisch, in diesem Fall als marcionitisch, welche Charakterisierung für das Problem des Ursprungs ihre Konsequenzen hat.[4] Dieser Ursprung ist denn auch marcionitisch, und die Marcioniten sind die ältesten Christen in Edessa. Diese Charakterisierung geht auf spätere kirchliche Qualifikationen römischen Ursprungs zurück und eignet sich also nicht dazu, eine religiöse Grösse in ihrem Milieu angemessen zu charakterisieren. Gibson, Barnard u.a. richteten ihr Augenmerk hauptsächlich auf die Ursprünge und gingen den Weg von Pälestina, unter Umständen Qumran, nach Edessa. Es ist wohl vernünftiger zu sehen,

[3] So bzw. J.C.L. Gibson, From Qumran to Edessa or the Aramaic Speaking Church before and after 70 A.D., *The Annual of Leeds Oriental Society* V (1963-65, Leiden 1966) pp. 24–39; G. Quispel, The Discussion of Judaic Christianity, *Vig. Chr.* 22 (1968) 81–93; L.W. Barnard, The Origins and Emergence of the Church in Edessa during the First Two Centuries A.D., *Vig Chr.* 22 (1968) 161-175.

[4] W. Bauer, *Rechtgläubigkeit und Ketzerei im ältesten Christentum*, BHTh 10 (Tübingen 1934) S. 27.

welche Wege in Edessa eigentlich zusammenkamen, auf denen das Christentum dort bekannt geworden sein mag. Deshalb ist die Frage, ob dieses Christentum orthodox oder häretisch ist, für eine historische Betrachtungsweise nicht von Bedeutung, eher eine Behinderung. Historisch ist es nur interessant, wie und unter welchen Einflüssen sich aus den komplexen christlichen Formen des zweiten Jahrhunderts n.Chr. später in Edessa die Polarisation von Orthodoxie und Häresie vollzogen hat. Diese Polarisation ist aber der Endpunkt einer Entwicklung, an deren Anfang sich eine seleukidische Stadt befindet, wo das Christentum noch nicht bekannt ist.

Einige Momente aus der Geschichte dieser Stadt sind für unser Thema wichtig. Die Bevölkerung der Stadt bestand grösstenteils aus freiheitsliebenden Arabern.[5] Nach der Niederlage Demetrius' II. machte sich König Osroes (137-125 v.Chr.) selbständig, aber er wurde schon bald ein Vasall der Parther. Das Eintreffen des Pompejus im Osten brachte auch für Edessa Veränderungen mit sich, da er König Abgar II. 64 v.Chr. zum Verbündeten machte, damit Edessa als ein Pufferstaat zwischen Rom und den Parthern dienen sollte. Crassus hat hier im Jahre 53 v.Chr. durch den Verrat der Edessener den Tod gefunden. Es gab viele Beziehungen zu Adiabene. Um 50 v.Chr. wurde dieses Reich Edessas Lehnsherr, und sein Einfluss blieb dort viele Jahre gross. König Abgar VII. (109-116 n.Chr.) war sogar ein Enkel der berühmten Königin Helena von Adiabene. Die Liebe zu den Römern war nicht gross. Abgar VII. unterwarf sich 114 n.Chr. dem Trajan, erhob sich aber 116 wieder, bis er 118 abermals von Rom abhängig wurde. Im Jahre 163 brach sogar in Edessa eine pro-parthische Revolution aus, wodurch König Ma'nu zu den Römern floh, die ihn 165 wieder in seine Rechte einsetzten. Sein Nachfolger war der berühmte König Abgar VIII. der Grosse (177-212), der von 210 an zusammen mit Abgar IX. regierte. Letzterer wurde 214 von Caracalla abgesetzt, worauf Edessa 216 seine Unabhängigkeit ganz und gar einbüsste.[6]

Diese wenigen Bemerkungen mögen deutlich machen: (a) eine grosse

---

[5] R. Duval, *Histoire politique, religieuse et littéraire d'Édesse jusqu'à la première croisade* (Paris 1892) pp. 24 svv.; J. B. Segal, *Edessa and Harran* (London 1963) p. 9; J. B. Segal, The Jews of North Mesopotamia before the Rise of the Islam, *Sepher Segal* (Jerusalem 1965) p. 40.

[6] Duval, *o.c.*; E. Kirsten, Art. Edessa, *RAC* IV (1959); D. Oates, *Studies in the Ancient History of Northern Iraq* (London 1968) pp. 67–80; A. Maricq, *Classica et Orientalia* (Paris 1965) pp. 27–32.

Abneigung in Edessa gegen die Römer; eigentlich eine grosse Abneigung gegen jede Zentralgewalt im Westen; (b) politische Verbindungen mit der Adiabene, dem jüdischen Fürstentum östlich des Tigris;[7] (c) Zusammenarbeit mit den Parthern gegen die Römer. G. Widengren hat nachgewiesen, dass die Juden und die Parther gegen die Römer gemeinsame Interessen hatten, die in parthischer und adiabenischer Hilfe während der jüdischen Aufstände gegen die Römer zum Ausdrück kamen. Überdies hatten die Juden wichtige Sektoren des Karawanenhandels in der Hand, u.a. den Seidenhandel, so dass sie den militärischen Schutz der Parther auf der grossen Seidenstrasse nach China nicht missen konnten.[8] Diese Seidenstrasse führte über Edessa und Zeugma nach Antiochia und im Osten über Arbela, die Hauptstadt der Adiabene.[9] Es kamen in Edessa noch mehr Karawanenstrassen zusammen, u.a. eine aus Palmyra. Wer von Jerusalem nach Edessa ging, wird in der Regel über Antiochien gereist sein.

Karawanenstrassen dienen sowohl dem wirtschaftlichen als auch dem religiösen Kontakt. „Plus nous pénétrons la compréhension des anciens cultes, plus leur homogénéité saute aux yeux. Le système de transhumance et celui du commerce par caravanes sur des pistes obligées et, somme toute, peu nombreuses, à l'écart des immensités sablonneuses, ont amené une remarquable, parce que continuelle diffusion des cultes“ sagt R. Dussaud mit Recht.[10] Die heidnische Religion in Edessa ist ein treffendes Beispiel für diese „diffusion des cultes“, zumal da dieser Paganismus auf die Bilder und Vorstellungen des Judentums und des Christentums in Edessa einwirkt und auch philosophisch interpretiert wird.

In der *Doctrina Addai* finden sich die Götter Bêl und Nebo, Bath-Nikal und Tarʿata, Sonne und Mond, und die Gestirne, die auch verehrt werden.[11] Es wird ausdrücklich festgestellt, dass die Bewohner Harrans gleichfalls Bath-Nikal verehren, während die Edessener den Kult des Adlers mit den Arabern teilen. Bath-Nikal ist vermutlich Ishtar, die Toch-

---

[7] Segal, The Jews of North Mesopotamia, pp. 40ff.

[8] G. Widengren, Quelques rapports entre juifs et iraniens à l'époque des Parthes, *Suppl. VT* IV (Leiden 1957) pp. 197–241; J. Neusner, *A History of the Jews in Babylonia* I (Leiden 1965) pp. 58ff.

[9] Segal, The Jews of North Mesopotamia, pp. 34f. (eine Karte auf S. 36).

[10] R. Dussaud, *La pénétration des Arabes en Syrie avant l'Islam* (Paris 1955) pp. 126 sv.

[11] *Doctrina Addai*, ed. Phillips, p. 24; cf. R. Duval, *Histoire d'Édesse*, pp. 74–80; C. Winckworth, On Heathen Deities in the Doctrine of Addai, *JThS* 25 (1924) 402ff.; Kirsten, Art. Edessa, *RAC* IV, Sp. 562f.

ter Nin-Gals, die Gemahlin Sins, des Mondgottes von Harran. Tar'ata ist Atargatis, die Dea Syria, die in Hierapolis, einer Stadt halbwegs zwischen Edessa und Antiochia, eine besondere Verehrung genoss. Die Götter Bêl und Nebo werden auch von Jakob von Sarug in seiner Homilie über den Fall der Götzenbilder als die wichtigsten Götter Edessas bezeichnet. Insbesondere Nebo, Nabu, der babylonische Gott der Schreiber, war in Edessa ein ausserordentlich wichtiger Gott. Theodor bar Khonai erzählt in seinem Scholienbuch, und zwar im Kommentar zu Jesaias 46:1, dass Nebo ein Mann aus Mabbug-Hierapolis war, der Schuljungen schreiben lehrte. Einer der Schüler machte, um sich seine Gunst zu erwerben, ein Bild des Schulmeisters und verehrte die. Nach einigen Generationen hatten die Menschen vergessen, dass Nebo ursprünglich ein Sterblicher war und nannten das Bild Gott.[12] Auch Ishodad von Merw (Mary) nennt in seinem Kommentar zur Genesis Nebo den Erfinder der Schrift, insbesondere der Pahlavischrift. Eine äusserst interessante Mitteilung treffen wir in der *Apologie des Pseudo-Melito* an, die am Ende des zweiten Jahrhunderts in Syrien geschrieben wurde. Diese Apologie berichtet, dass Nebo aus Mabbug die Gestalt des thrazischen Magiers Orpheus und zugleich des persischen Magiers Zarathustra ist. Pseudo-Lucianus teilt mit, dass Hermes, der Gott von Hierapolis, identisch ist mit Nebo.[13] Im synkretistischen Muster werden also Nebo, Hermes, Orpheus und Zarathustra identifiziert. Wenn wir dem noch hinzufügen, dass bei den Mandäern Nebo als die falsche Weisheit Christus (GR 124, 7ff.) gegenübergestellt wird, ist auch das Christentum im Ganzen vertreten. Vor nicht allzu langer Zeit ist in Edessa ein Mosaik aufgefunden worden, auf dem Orpheus abgebildet ist, während er vor den Tieren, u.a. vor einem Löwen und einem Raben, auf der Leier spielt.[14] Dieses Mosaik gleicht sehr dem Bildnis des David-Orpheus in der Synagoge von Doura-Europos, der ebenfalls vor den Tieren spielt.[15] Auch in Palmyra ist eine Tessera einer Gottheit gefunden worden, die

---

[12] Theodor Bar Khonai, *Liber Scholiorum*, ed. A.Scher, I, p. 369, 11–21; cf. B. Vandenhoff, Die Götterliste des Mar Jakob von Sarug in seiner Homilie über den Fall der Götzenbilder, *Or. Chr. N.S.* 5 (1915) 236f.

[13] *Apologie Pseudo-Melitos*, ed. W.Cureton, *Spicilegium Syriacum* (London 1855) c. 5, p. 44; Luc., *Syr.* 38, cf. G.Goossens, *Hiérapolis de Syrie* (Louvain 1943) pp. 86 sv.

[14] J.B.Segal, New Mosaics from Edessa, *Archaeology* 12 (1959) 150–159; J.Leroy, Nouvelles découvertes archéologiques relatives à Edesse, *Syria* 38 (1961) 159–169; J.B. Segal, in: *Vanished Civilizations*, ed. E. Bacon (London 1963) p. 209 (eine farbige Abbildung).

[15] Eine Abbildung bei G.Widengren, Quelques rapports, p. 207.

auf einer Leier spielt. Nach dem Anschrift ist der Gottheit Nebo.[16] Die Leier hat vermutlich eine kosmische Funktion. Es gibt Texte, in denen es heisst, dass die Schüler Zarathustras und Ostanes' die siebensaitige Leier gebaut haben, um die Sphärenharmonie zu imitieren.[17] Die Pseudo-Clementinen wiederum identifizieren Zarathustra mit dem weisen Schreiber Baruch.[18] In dem Paganismus Edessas nimmt der Gott der Weisheit, der Sohn Bêls und Nanais oder Bêls und Atargatis'/Ishtars, also eine zentrale Stelle ein. Diese Weisheit hat eine kosmische und eine soteriologische Funktion, worauf die verschiedenen Identifizierungen deuten. Letztere verbinden Nebo auch mit manchen anderen Religionen, etwa mit iranischen und griechisch-hellenistischen Kulten, mit dem Judentum und vielleicht auch mit gnostischen Vorstellungen. Der Hermetismus, der später in diesen Gebieten, namentlich in Harran, viele Anhänger gehabt hat, geht aller Wahrscheinlichkeit nach auf die Verehrung des Gottes Nebo zurück.[19] Es fällt weiterhin die Verbindung mit der Stadt Hierapolis auf. Es gibt übrigens mehr Verbindungslinien zwischen Hierapolis und Edessa. Atargatis, die Dea Syria, wurde auch in Edessa verehrt, wie sich ergab aus der *Doctrina Addai* und dem *Buch über die Gesetze der Länder* von Bardaiṣan, wo steht, dass König Abgar die Entmannung zu Ehren der Atargatis verbot.[20] Die Biographie Bardaiṣans erwähnt sogar, dass er aus Hierapolis stammte.[21] Noch ein anderer Aspekt des edessenischen Paganismus ist für unser Thema von Belang, und zwar die Astrologie. Es ist möglich, die Astrologie in sehr allgemeinen Zügen zu schildern, wobei sehr leicht Termini wie Fatalismus u.ä. fallen. Es ist meine Absicht, über einen bestimmten – erst in den letzten Jahren besser bekannt geworden – Kult in der Stadt Edessa und ihrer Umgegend, und zwar über den Planetenkult von Sumatar, einiges

---

16 H. Seyrig, *Syria* 18, p. 120 und *Syria* 20, p. 304, Anm. 1; cf. J. Pirenne, *Sacra Pagina* 1 (Paris 1959) p. 291.

17 Bidez und Cumont, *Les Mages héllénisés* II, p. 286, n. 5; F. Cumont, *Recherches sur le symbolisme funéraire des Romains* (Paris 1942) p. 18, n. 4; p. 499 (Additions).

18 *Recogn.* 4, 27–29; *Hom.* 9, 3–5; cf. Bidez und Cumont, *Les Mages hellénisés* II, pp. 50 svv.

19 Cf. D. Chwolson, *Die Ssabier und der Ssabismus* (St. Petersburg 1856); R. Reitzenstein, *Poimandres* (Leipzig 1904) SS. 165ff.; A. Jeremias, Nebo, *Roscher* III, 45–68; J.G. Février, *La religion des Palmyreniens* (Paris 1931) pp. 97–99.

20 *Liber Legum Regionum*, ed. F. Nau, *Patrologia Syriaca* I, 2 (Paris 1907) Sp. 607, 11–15; *The Book of the Laws of Countries*, text and transl. by H.J.W. Drijvers (Assen 1965) p. 58, 21–22; cf. Bauer, *Rechtgläubigkeit und Ketzerei*, SS. 11ff.

21 H.J.W. Drijvers, *Bardaiṣan of Edessa*, Studia Semitica Neerlandica 6 (Assen 1966) pp. 188ff.

zu sagen. Dieser Ort liegt zwischen Harran und Edessa, etwa 50 km südöstlich letzterer Stadt. Sumatar liegt auf einem Plateau in den Tektekbergen in einer unwirtlichen Gegend. Man findet dort einen hohen kahlen Hügel vor, der die ganze Umgebung beherrscht, und auf dem ein Heiligtum gestanden hat. Nördlich und südlich dieses zentralen Berges befinden sich die Ruinen von acht Bauten, von denen sieben eins miteinander gemeinsam haben: es ist eine Grotte darunter, die man durch eine Öffnung, welche nach dem zentralen Berg gerichtet ist, betreten kann. Auf dem zentralen Berg findet man Inschriften und Reliefs, aus denen hervorgeht, dass das Heiligtum im Jahre 476 der seleukidischen Zeitrechnung, also 164–165 n.Chr., gegründet wurde und dem Gott Marilaha (d.h. Gott dem Herrn) geweiht war.[22] Segal hat plausibel gemacht, dass es sich hier um ein zentrales Heiligtum eines höchsten Gottes und um Tempel handelt, die den Sieben geweiht sind, d.h. den fünf Planeten, der Sonne und dem Mond. Er sieht darin eine Vorstufe der späteren Religion der Sabier in Harran, in der ein höchster Gott durch die Vermittlung der Sieben die Welt regiert.[23] Diese Vorstellung ist in Syrien nichts Ungewöhnliches: Jupiter Heliopolitanus ist der Herr der Planeten und als solcher der Herr des Fatums, das von den Planeten bestimmt wird.[24] In einem jüdisch-christlichen Kontext kehren diese Vorstellungen in den Lehren Bardaiṣans wieder.

Die Verehrung Nebo-Orpheus' in Edessa führte uns schon zur Synagoge von Doura-Europos und damit zum Judentum. Edessa hatte eine wichtige jüdische Gemeinschaft, die eine Synagoge im Zentrum der Stadt hatte.[25] Die Juden hatten einen grossen Anteil am Seidenhandel und an der Seidenbearbeitung, die in Edessa durchgeführt wurde, und waren angesehene Männer, die Zutritt zum Hofe hatten. Die Beziehungen zwischen Edessa und der Adiabene im Anfang des zweiten Jahrhunderts n.Chr., haben wahrscheinlich die Position der Juden gefestigt.[26] Damals ergriffen die Juden auch Partei für die Parther und machten aufs heftigste

[22] J.B.Segal, Pagan Syriac Monuments in the Vilayet of Urfa, *Anatolian Studies* 3 (1953) 97–119.

[23] Segal, *art. cit.*; *idem*, The Planet Cult of Ancient Harran, *Vanished Civilizations*, ed. E.Bacon (London 1963) pp. 210–220.

[24] F.Cumont, Le Jupiter Héliopolitain et les Divinités des Planètes, *Syria* 2 (1921) pp. 40–46; cf. O.Eissfeldt, *Tempel und Kulte syrischer Städte in hellenistisch-römischer Zeit*, Der alte Orient 40 (Leipzig 1941) S. 50.

[25] J.B.Segal, The Jews of North Mesopotamia, p. 40; J.Neusner, *A History of the Jews in Babylonia* I (Leiden 1965) p. 14; 166–169.

[26] R.Duval, *Histoire*, p. 27; Neusner, *A History of the Jews* I, p. 46, 58ff. F.Haase, *Altchristliche Kirchengeschichte* (Leipzig 1925) SS. 70–111.

Front gegen Trajan, als er 115 in Syrien einen Feldzug unternahm.[27] Die wichtige Position der Juden erhellt auch aus einer merkwürdigen Mitteilung in der *Apologie Pseudo-Melitos* in bezug auf die Verehrung einer jüdischen Frau Kuthbi, die einem Patrizier Bakru das Leben gerettet hatte. Zum Gedächtnis dieser Tat wurde sie von den Heiden Edessas als eine Göttin verehrt.[28] Obwohl diese Mitteilung offenkundig falsch ist und die Überlieferung einen Fehler gemacht hat, indem sie „arabisch" in „hebräisch" änderte, was sich im Syrischen durch die Umstellung zweier Schriftzeichen ergibt, ist die Tatsache, dass dieser Fehler überhaupt auftritt, für die Position der Juden in Edessa aufschlussreich. Vermutlich handelt es sich hier um die Verehrung der nabatäischen Göttin Al-Kutba', die aus nabatäischen Inschriften bekannt ist.[29] In den Felsengräbern von Kirk Mağara, etwas mehr als ein Kilometer westlich von Edessa, gedenken drei Inschriften im Hebräischen und eine im Griechischen edessenischer Juden; Seleucus, Sohn des Izates, ist einer von ihnen.[30] Dass solch ein Judenname überhaupt vorkommt, wirft schon ein gewisses Licht auf den Charakter des edessenischen Judentums. J.Neusner hat mit Recht ausgeführt, dass dies nicht tannaitisch war, im Gegensatz zum Judentum der benachbarten Stadt Nisibis, wo eine jüdische Akademie war.[31] Von einem tannaitischem Judentum in Edessa ist uns nichts bekannt, und keiner von den Tannaim wird mit dieser Stadt in Verbindung gebracht. Wir müssen vielmehr an ein stark hellenisiertes synkretistisches Judentum denken, wie wir es auch in Doura-Europos antreffen. Auch dort gab es wenige Kontakte mit dem palästinensischen Judentum.[32] Die Juden in Doura waren angesehene Kaufleute, die Motive aller sie umgebenden Religionen verwendeten, um ihren Glauben zu gestalten. Hier hat man sich u.a. der Merkabah-Mystik gewidmet,

---

[27] Segal, The Jews of North Mesopotamia, p. 41; J.Neusner, The Conversion of Adiabene to Judaism, *JBL* 83 (1964) 60–66; Eusebius, *H.E.* IV, 2; J.Neusner, *A History of the Jews in Babylonia* I, pp. 70ff.

[28] W.Cureton, *Spicilegium Syriacum* (London 1855) p. 25.

[29] J.Strugnell, The Nabataean Goddess al-Kutba' and her Sanctuaries, *BASOR* 156 (1959) 29–36; J.T.Milik und J.Teixidor, New Evidence on the North Arabic Deity Aktab-Kutbâ, *BASOR* 163 (1961) 22–25.

[30] H.Pognon, *Inscriptions sémitiques de la Syrie, de la Mésopotamie et de la région de Mossoul* (Paris 1907/08) pp. 78 svv. J.B.Frey, *Corpus inscriptionum judaicarum* II (1952) pp. 340 ss.

[31] J.Neusner, *A History of the Jews in Babylonia* I, p. 169; *idem*, Studies on the Problem of Tannaim in Babylonia (Ca. 130–160), *Proceedings of the American Academy for Jewish Research* XXX (1962) pp. 87–91.

[32] J.Neusner, Judaism at Dura-Europos, *History of Religions* 4 (1964) 81–102.

wie aus den Freskos mit Abbildungen aus dem Buche Hesekiel in der Synagoge hervorgeht. Wir dürfen annehmen, dass ein derartiges Judentum auch in Edessa existierte, das mit der Kultur jener Zeit in jener Stadt in Fühlung stand. Es hat überdies Beziehungen zwischen Edessa und Doura gegeben, was man aus dem Fund des edessenischen Kaufkontrakts vom Jahre 243 n.Chr. in Doura ersehen kann.[33] Wenn die Verkündigung des Evangeliums sich auf bestehende jüdische Kreise gerichtet hat – und das ist sehr wahrscheinlich –, so ist diese Verkündigung in Edessa auch durch dieses hellenisierte Judentum geformt worden, das politisch und kulturell mit den Parthern auf gutem Fuss stand.[34]

Fast von selbst gehen wir vom Paganismus zum Judentum über, zwischen denen es übrigens niemals eine reinliche Scheidung gegeben hat. Nicht viel anders verhält es sich mit dem Christentum in Edessa, das einerseits etwas durchaus Eigenes hat, andrerseits durch viele Bande mit dem Paganismus und dem Judentum verbunden ist, mit denen es den kulturellen und religiösen Hintergrund gemeinsam hat. Es braucht in solch einer Lage nicht wunderzunehmen, dass auch die Formen, in denen das Christentum erscheint, nicht gleich sind, sondern mindestens ebenso verschiedenartig wie die der anderen Religionen. Seit Walter Bauer ist das Bild bedeutend komplizierter geworden. Bauer war der Ansicht, dass Marcion, Bardaiṣan und Mani das Gesicht des ältesten Christentums in Edessa bestimmt haben. Die Orthodoxie hingegen sei ein Spätling gewesen, der damit zufrieden sein musste, dass er nach Palût benannt wurde. Erst der rechtgläubige Bischof Kûnê erhöhte im Anfang des vierten Jahrhunderts das Ansehen der Orthodoxie, und auf ihn geht, nach Bauers Ansicht, die Fälschung zurück, die als Abgar-Legende bekannt ist.[35] Bauer stützt seine These grossenteils auf eine kritische Untersuchung der Gegebenheiten des *Chronicons Edessenum*. Es fällt auf, dass in Bauers Bild die Rolle Tatians äusserst unbedeutend ist; nur sein *Diatessaron* wurde in Edessa als Ersatz für das verstümmelte Evangelium Marcions benutzt. Andere Schriften, die dann und wann mit Edessa in Zusammenhang gebracht wurden, wie die *Oden Salomonis* und die apokryphen *Thomas-Acta*, fehlen ganz. Das hängt mit der Tat-

[33] A.R.Bellinger und C.B.Welles, A Third-Century Contract of Sale from Edessa in Oshroene, *YCS* V (1935) 93–154; J.A.Goldstein, The Syriac Bill of Sale from Dura-Europos, *JNES* 25 (1966) 1 ff.

[34] G.Widengren, Quelques rapports entre juifs et iraniens, *passim*; J.Neusner, Rabbi and Magus in third-century Sasanian Babylonia, *History of Religions* (1967) 169–178; *idem*, *A History of the Jews in Babylonia* I, 23 ff.

[35] Bauer, *Rechtgläubigkeit und Ketzerei*, S. 41.

sache zusammen, dass Bauer eigentlich nicht an den theologischen Konzeptionen der einzelnen Figuren und Schriften interessiert ist, sondern bloss an der Frage, ob sie von einem späteren kirchlichen Standpunkt aus orthodox oder häretisch sind. Sie sind häretisch, und der Ursprung dieser Qualifikation liegt, so meint Bauer, in Rom. Er hat also die traditionelle Reihenfolge von Orthodoxie und Häresie für eine Anzahl wichtiger Zentren des ältesten Christentums umgedreht, aber auch dieses Verfahren bleibt formell. G. Streckers Nachtrag hat daran im Grunde nichts geändert, da Strecker unter der Überschrift „Zum Problem des Judenchristentums" anhand der *Didaskalia* nachweist, dass in der durch die jüdische Geisteswelt stark beeinflussten syrischen Umwelt dieser Schrift Orthodoxie und Häresie, wie die Kirche beide Begriffe später interpretieren wird, ungetrennt waren. Etwas Ähnliches ist in den Pseudo-Clementinischen Schriften der Fall.[36] Strecker hat die anderen Schriften nicht zur Diskussion gestellt. Im Grunde hat er aber Bauers historisches Schema untergraben, indem er voraussetzt, dass Orthodoxie und Häresie in einer Anzahl von Schriften nicht zu trennen sind, m.a.W., dass diese Kategorien der historischen Wirklichkeit nicht gerecht werden. H. D. Altendorf schrieb mit Recht, dass eine Anwendung dieser theologischen Kategorien auf die historische Wirklichkeit „die urchristliche Geschichte in ein einigermassen wüstes Gemenge widerstreitender und sich ausschliessender theologischer Richtungen aufzulösen" droht.[37]

Historisch betrachtet ist jedoch wichtig, was diese „theologischen Richtungen" verbindet und trennt, sowohl unter sich als auch in bezug auf die anderen Religionen im lokalen Milieu, u.a. das Judentum. Das „Problem des Judenchristentums" tritt dann in einer anderen Weise erneut in dem Gesichtskreis. Zunächst muss festgelegt werden, wer und was als repräsentativ für das älteste Christentum in Edessa gelten dürfen. Folgende Schriften, Personen oder Gruppen bestimmen das Bild: das *Thomasevangelium*, die *Oden Salomos*, Bardaiṣan, die Quqiten, Tatian, die *Acta Thomae* und die darin enthaltenen Hymnen, während auch andere Schriften aus der Bibliothek Chenoboskions Beziehungen zu Syrien, in diesem Fall zu Edessa haben, z.B. das *Evangelium Philippi*.[38]

---

[36] G. Strecker, Zum Problem des Judenchristentums, Nachtrag zu der zweiten Auflage von *Rechtgläubigkeit und Ketzerei* (1964) SS. 258ff.

[37] H. D. Altendorf, *ThLZ* (1966) Sp. 192ff.; cf. E. Käsemann, *Jesu letzter Wille nach Johannes 17* (Tübingen 1966) S. 133.

[38] J.-E. Ménard, Le milieu syriaque de l'évangile selon Thomas et de l'évangile selon Philippe, *Revue des sciences religieuses* (1968) 261–266.

Zwar lässt sich nicht mit absoluter Sicherheit nachweisen, dass das *Thomasevangelium* in Edessa geschrieben wurde, aber ein aramäisches Original und der Name des Apostels Thomas, der mit Edessa verbunden ist, machen es doch wahrscheinlich.[39] Dasselbe gilt für die *Oden Salomos*, die ja vermutlich ursprünglich im Syrischen geschrieben wurden, wie eine genaue Vergleichung der griechischen und syrischen Fassung von Ode XI klarmacht.[40] Zwar ist damit nicht gesagt, dass die Oden in Edessa geschrieben wurden, aber sie sind doch in einem Gebiet beheimatet, dessen geistiges Zentrum Edessa war.[41] Höchst merkwürdig ist die Bilinguität mehrerer Schriften, u.a. der *Oden Salomos*, wovon auch eine griechische Fassung existiert hat, während fünf Oden in die koptische *Pistis Sophia* aufgenommen wurden. Auch vom *Thomasevangelium* existieren griechische Fragmente unter den Oxyrynchuspapyri, während die *Acta Thomae* in einer griechischen und einer syrischen Fassung überliefert worden sind. Man bekommt den Eindruck, dass die syrische Fassung der *Acta Thomae* sowie der *Oden Salomos* immer weniger „gnostisch" ist. Ist vielleicht die überlieferte syrische Version von späteren Generationen, die mehr an der Orthodoxie interessiert waren, zensiert worden?

Die *Oden Salomos* besingen das Heil des Individuums, das durch die Erscheinung Christi vom Tode ins Leben, vom Scheol ins Paradies, von der Unwissenheit zur Wahrheit, von der Vergänglichkeit zur Unvergänglichkeit hinübergewechselt hat. Der Mensch ist mit dem Geist wie mit einem neuen Gewand bekleidet. Christus, der Erlöser, wird in Termini beschrieben, die stark an die Bilder erinnern, mit denen die Weisheit, die Chokma, bezeichnet wird, obwohl die Inkarnation wohl genannt wird[42] (Ode XIX, 6ff.). A. F. J. Klijn, J. Daniélou und andere haben das jüdische oder jüdisch-christliche Element in den Oden stark betont.[43] Manche

---

[39] J.-E. Ménard, *art. cit.*; H.-Ch. Puech, *CRAI* (1957) 146–167; R. A. Guillaumont, Sémitismes dans les logia de Jésus retrouvés à Nag-Hamadi, *JA* 246 (1958) 113–132; cf. G. Quispel, *Makarius, das Thomasevangelium und das Lied von der Perle* (Leiden 1967) SS. 18ff.

[40] J. A. Emerton, Some Problems of Text and Language in the Odes of Solomon, *JThS* 18 (1967) 372–406.

[41] Cf. L. W. Barnard, *Vig. Chr.* 22 (1968) 166, n. 19.

[42] Contra A. F. J. Klijn: „... in the Odes of Solomon both the incarnation and the work of Christ, his death and resurrection, have been neglected", *Aspects du judéo-christianisme* (Paris 1965) p. 175.

[43] A. F. J. Klijn, The Influence of Jewish Theology on the Odes of Solomon and the Acts of Thomas, *Aspects du judéo-christianisme*, pp. 167–179; J. Daniélou, *Théologie du judéo-christianisme* (Tournai 1958) pp. 40–43.

gehen sogar soweit, Beziehungen zum *Hodayoth* aus Qumran und zu den mandäischen Hymnen festzustellen.[44] Auch gibt es Berührungspunkte mit dem *Evangelium Philippi* (Ode XIII, 1–2 im Vergleich zu Sent. 75 und 101 *Evang. Philipp.*).[45] Die Grundlinien der späteren syrischen Theologie werden in den *Oden Salomos* schon sichtbar: die Wiedererlangung des Status Adams vor dem Fall, die Situation im Paradies, wo die Gemeinschaft von Gott und Mensch noch nicht gelöst worden ist. Diese Wiedererlangung ist eine Art „realised eschatology", so dass es nicht zu verwundern ist, dass die Bilder der jüdischen und jüdisch-christlichen Apokalyptik in den Oden angetroffen werden. Der Mensch, der die Weisheit Gottes angenommen hat, ist vom Tode gerettet und hat das ewige Leben erworben. Diese Weisheit ist zugleich der Erlöser und das Gesetz, die den Menschen in den Stand setzt, gute Werke zu tun. Die optimistische Ethik der *Oden Salomos* erwächst m.E. aus der Gleichstellung von Weisheit und Gesetz, die kennzeichnend ist für die jüdischen apokalyptischen uns kosmologischen Vorstellungen und z.B. häufig in der syrischen *Baruchapokalypse* vorkommt.[46] Auch die asketischen Tendenzen ergeben sich aus dieser Paradies-Theologie, die zugleich eine Adam-Theologie ist: der Mensch soll z.B. nicht heiraten, was, wie man annahm, auch Adam nicht getan hatte.

Diese Züge verbinden die *Oden Salomos* einerseits mit dem Judentum, andererseits mit anderen christlichen Schriften und Gruppen in Edessa. Daniélou machte darauf aufmerksam, dass die Oden aus der Umgebung Bardaiṣans stammen müssen.[47] In Anbetracht des komplexen Charakters des Terminus „Erkenntnis" in diesen Hymnen können sie sogar ganz und gar in gnostischem Sinne interpretiert werden. Vieles hängt dabei von der genauen Unterscheidung der Ausdrücke „Gnosis" und „gnostisch" ab.[48] Inhaltlich gibt es allerlei Berühungspunkte zwischen den *Oden Salomos* und dem *Thomasevangelium*. Zwar bestehen auch Unterschiede; die Oden heben z.B. viel weniger stark eine asketische, enkratitische

---

44 J. Carmignac, Les affinités qumrâniennes de la onzième Ode de Salomon, *Revue de Qumran* 9 (1961) 71–102; K. Rudolph, War der Verfasser der Oden Salomos ein „Qumran-Christ"? Ein Beitrag zur Diskussion um die Anfänge der Gnosis, *Revue de Qumran* (1964) 523–555.

45 J.-E. Ménard, Le milieu syriaque de l'évangile selon Thomas et de l'évangile selon Philippe, *Revue des sciences religieuses* (1968) 261–266.

46 Cf. H.-F. Weiss, *Untersuchungen zur Kosmologie des hellenistischen und palästinischen Judentums*, TU 97 (Berlin 1966) 289ff.

47 Cf. Drijvers, *Bardaiṣan of Edessa*, p. 58; 210.

48 Cf. Drijvers, The Origins of Gnosticism as a religious and historical Problem, *Nederlands Theologisch Tijdschrift* 22 (1967/68) 321–351.

Lebenshaltung hervor. Die Vermutung liegt allerdings nahe, dass diese Unterschiede auch durch die einzelnen literarischen Gattungen bedingt werden. Die *Oden Salomos* besingen das erlangte Heil; das *Thomasevangelium* will vielmehr darüber belehren, wie man das Heil erwerben kann. Deshalb kann man dem *Thomasevangelium* eine deutliche Theologie abgewinnen, während man bei den *Oden Salomos* nur poëtische Bilder deuten kann.[49]

Es ist nicht der Ort, alle Probleme, die mit dem *Thomasevangelium* zusammenhängen, aufs neue zu besprechen.[50] Literarhistorisch sind die Probleme noch bei weitem nicht gelöst worden, obwohl feststeht, dass das Evangelium in der Form, wie wir es kennen, eine jüdisch-christliche Quelle, vermutlich auch das *Evangelium der Ägypter*, benutzt hat und sodann noch die Hand eines gnostischen Redaktors verrät. Puech hat darauf hingewiesen, dass der Text einer solchen Sammlung von Logia nicht feststeht, aus welchem Grunde sogar bezweifelt werden kann, ob das Evangelium überhaupt seine jetzige Form in Edessa bekommen hat.[51] Eine andere Möglichkeit wäre, dass die jüdisch-christliche Quelle von Edessa nach Ägypten gewandert und dort mit dem *Evangelium der Ägypter* zu dieser Sammlung von Logia zusammengefügt worden ist. Diese jüdisch-christliche Quelle ist möglicherweise das *Evangelium der Hebräer*, das im Osten bekannt war und auch als Quelle für Tatians *Diatessaron* gedient hat. Diese jüdisch-christlichen Logia zeigen allerlei Beziehungen zum Text der *Pseudo-Clementinischen Schriften* und zum abendländischen Text des Neuen Testaments.[52] Ob dies alles literarische Beziehungen sind, die auf Abhängigkeit schliessen lassen, ist eine Frage für sich. Es ist sehr wohl möglich, dass Logia Jesu, die in das uns bekannte *Thomasevangelium* aufgenommen worden sind, auch in anderen literarischen Traditionen verarbeitet wurden und bei anderen christlichen Gruppierungen eine Funktion gehabt haben. Sowohl die Naassener als auch die Manichäer haben ein *Thomasevangelium* gekannt, das mehr

---

[49] Cf. A.F.J. Klijn, Das Thomasevangelium und das altsyrische Christentum, *Vig. Chr.* 15 (1961) 153: „Eine deutlich umschriebene Heilslehre darf man hier also nicht erwarten."

[50] Cf. W.H.C. Frend, The Gospel of Thomas: Is Rehabilitation possible?, *JThS* 18 (1967) 13–26; G. Quispel, *Makarius, das Thomasevangelium und das Lied von der Perle*, SS. 18ff.; 65ff.

[51] H.-Ch. Puech, in: *Neutestamentliche Apokryphen*[3] I (Tübingen 1959) S. 221f.

[52] Cf. G. Quispel. The Gospel of Thomas and the Gospel of the Hebrews, *New Testament Studies* 12 (1966) 371–382; *idem*, L'Évangile selon Thomas et les Clémentines, *Vig. Chr.* 12 (1958) 181–196; *idem*, L'Évangile selon Thomas et le "Texte Occidental" du Nouveau Testament, *Vig. Chr.* 14 (1960) 204–215.

oder weniger mit dem uns bekannten identisch war, damit jedenfalls grosse Stücke gemeinsam hatte.[53]

Wenn das *Thomasevangelium* der Naassener und Manichäer mit der uns bekannten Schrift identisch war, deutet das immerhin darauf, dass die Logia in verschiedener Weise interpretiert werden konnten, was bei einer enkratitischen Schrift um so selbstverständlicher ist, als der Enkratismus auf verschiedenartige theologische Stämme gepfropft werden kann. Quispel hat darauf hingewiesen, dass das *Thomasevangelium* kein einziges Logion enthält, das gnostisch ausgelegt werden muss; alle Logia können hingegen aus einer jüdisch-christlichen und enkratitischen Tradition verstanden werden.[54] Parallelen zu bestimmten Logia aus gnostischen Schriften hält er deshalb für irreführend, da nur eine Exegese e mente auctoris wissenschaftlich akzeptabel ist und der Verfasser des *Thomasevangeliums* ein in der ersten Hälfte des zweiten Jahrhunderts n.Chr. in Syrien lebender jüdischer Christ war. Da die Traditionen des *Thomasevangeliums* unabhängig von denen der synoptischen Evangelien sind und ebenso alt wie sie, kann Quispel sagen, dass diese Traditionen orthodox sein müssen. Ich glaube, dass Bauers These hier in einer ähnlichen unhistorischen Weise verwendet wird – und zwar mit umgekehrten Vorzeichen – wie Bauer selbst vorgeworfen werden kann. Die Antithese Orthodoxie-Häresie wird nämlich nicht durch die Exegese e mente auctoris bedingt, angenommen, dass sie erschliessbar sei, sondern durch die verschiedenen Exegesen, die in späterer Zeit von einer Schrift gegeben werden und die sich gegenseitig ausschliessen können, während sie alle als Exegese e mente auctoris bezeichnet werden. In dergleichen Fällen erlangt eine Schrift, wie authentisch auch die darin enthaltene Tradition sein mag, sehr schwer das Prädikat kanonisch und damit orthodox. Eine Schrift wie das *Thomasevangelium*, von der es mehrere Fassungen gegeben hat, eine Schrift auch, die von grundverschiedenen Gruppen benutzt und dort zweifellos in verschiedener Weise interpretiert wurde, ist ein Schulbeispiel für diesen Hergang. Die Frage, ob das *Thomasevangelium* jüdisch-christlich und also orthodox, oder gnostisch und also häretisch ist, ist deshalb an und für sich von geringer Bedeutung. Die

---

[53] Cf. W.R.Schoedel, Naassene Themes in the Gospel of Thomas, *Vig. Chr.* 14 (1960) 225–234; E.M.J.M.Cornélis, Quelques éléments pour une comparaison entre l'évangile de Thomas et la notice d'Hippolyte sur les Naassenes, *Vig. Chr.* 15 (1961) 83–104; E.Hammerschmidt, Das Thomasevangelium und die Manichäer, *Or. Chr.* 46 (1962) 120–123; Puech, *Neutestamentliche Apokryphen*[3] I, SS. 203f.

[54] Quispel, *Makarius, das Thomasevangelium und das Lied von der Perle*, SS. 65–113.

Doktrin der betreffenden Schrift hat offenbar Anschluss gefunden bei dem, was in mehreren Gruppen lebte, und das Bildmaterial der Logia weist allerlei Übereinstimmungen mit anderen Texten auf.

Das *Thomasevangelium* lehrt den Weg vom Tode zum Leben, von der Welt der Vergänglichkeit zum Paradies des Lichtes. Da der Mensch selber nicht instande ist, diesen Weg zu finden, wird er von Jesus offenbart. Diese Offenbarung führt die wirkliche Lage des Menschen vor Augen und lehrt einen Heilsweg, der in einem enkratitischen Leben besteht, in dem sich der Mensch von Sexualität und Handel fernhalten soll. Er soll ein Einzelwesen werden und alle Bande, die ihn an das irdische Leben und die Familie binden, durchschneiden. Dann kann er allem Leid widerstehen und als Gleichbild Jesu in der Welt leben. Ebenso wie in den *Oden Salomos* wird im *Thomasevangelium* gelehrt, dass der Mensch zu seinem paradiesischen Status zurückkehren kann und soll. Die Ethik dieses Evangeliums, insbesondere die sexuelle, ist völlig darauf gerichtet.[55] Adam war ein asexuelles Wesen, in dem sich das Männliche und das Weibliche in gleichen Masse vorfanden; infolge seiner sexuellen Ethik wird der Mensch diesem Adam gleich werden. Das Logion 114 des *Thomasevangeliums* muss in diesem Kontext ausgelegt werden. Maria wird von Jesus zu einem Mann gemacht, damit auch sie ein lebendiger Geist (πνεῦμα) werde, denn nur so wird sie ins Himmelreich kommen können. Maria wird hier zu einem Mann, zu Adam, gemacht, dem Gott der Herr den lebendigen Odem in seine Nase eingeblasen hat (Gen. 2:7), ehe die Trennung zwischen Mann und Frau durchgeführt wurde.[56] Es gibt hier allerlei Beziehungen zu den Auffassungen Philons und zu jüdischen Adamspekulationen.[57] Das Heil wird auch im Bilde des Brautgemachs (Logia 75, 104) ausgedrückt, in das nur der „Einzelne“, d.h. das androgyne Wesen, eintreten kann. Es liegt hier offenbar eine Anspielung auf Gen. 2:24 vor, wo von „ein Fleisch werden“ die Rede ist, was als eine Rückgängigmachung der Trennung in Mann und Frau angesehen werden kann. Das Bild des Brautgemachs kommt in allerlei Schriften vor, u.a. bei den Naassenern, im *Philippusevangelium* (68, 104,

---

[55] Cf. A.F.J. Klijn, The "Single One" in the Gospel of Thomas, *JBL* 81 (1962) 271–278; G. Quispel, L'Évangile selon Thomas et les origines de l'ascèse chrétienne, *Aspects du judéo-christianisme*, pp. 35–52.

[56] Quispel, *Makarius, das Thomasevangelium*, SS. 104f.; Ursula Früchtel, *Die kosmologischen Vorstellungen bei Philo v. Alexandrien* (Leiden 1968) S. 35.

[57] Klijn, The "Single One" in the Gospel of Thomas, pp. 271–278. U. Früchtel, *o.c.*, SS. 27ff.

122ff.), bei Bardaiṣan, bei den valentinianischen Marcosianern, bei Ephrem Syrus, in den *Thomasacta* und in dem darin vorkommenden Brautlied Sophias.[57a] Das Bild, das sich auch im N.T. findet, ist also weit verbreitet; die Manichäer und Mandäer z.B. kennen es, was wieder eine Polyinterpretabilität erwarten lässt.[58] Im *Thomasevangelium* wird das Bild etwa in der gleichen Weise verwendet wie im N.T. Im *Philippusevangelium* wird von der geschlechtlichen Gemeinschaft des Vaters mit der Jungfrau gesprochen, der Jesus entspross (827).[59] Bei Bardaiṣan kennen wir die Vorstellung des Beischlafs des Vaters des Lebens mit der Mutter des Lebens, aus dem der Sohn hervorging.[60] Das Bild kann mithin als Bezeichnung des ursprünglichen paradiesischen Zustandes des Menschen, der für ihn wieder erreichbar geworden ist, verwendet werden. Auch kann es die Bezeichnung eines kosmischen Geschehens am Anfang der Zeiten sein, wie vermutlich bei Bardaiṣan und vielleicht bei den Quqiten.[61] Schliesslich kann es gebraucht werden, um die Vereinigung der Seele mit einem himmlischen Erlöser anzudeuten, welche Vereinigung im himmlischen Brautgemach vor sich geht. Allerlei Kombinationen dieser Interpretationen sind möglich, da in der Religion die Bilder einander nicht ausschliessen, sondern ergänzen. Dieses eine Bild führt uns so zu jüdischen Spekulationen über Adam, Eva und das Paradies und zu der Vorstellung eines Vaters und einer Mutter des Lebens, die einen Sohn erzeugen, in dem in Syrien sowohl Bêl, Atargatis und Nebo als auch Gott der Herr, Seine Weisheit und Sein Logos erkannt werden können. Das Bild kann durchaus spiritualisiert werden und eine Vereinigung der Seele mit ihrem himmlischen Erlöser andeuten, aber es lassen sich damit auch allerlei sexuelle Praktiken verbinden.

Eine systematische Untersuchung aller Texte, in denen dieses Bild vorkommt, und ihre Interpretation im Kontext wird ohne Zweifel die

---

[57a] Cf. Schoedel, Naassene Themes in the Gospel of Thomas, *Vig. Chr.* 14 (1960) 225–234; R.M.Grant, The Mysterie of Marriage in the Gospel of Philip. *Vig. Chr.* 15 (1961) 129–140; Ménard, Le milieu syriaque, pp. 261–266; Drijvers, *Bardaiṣan of Edessa*, p. 155ff. E.Preuschen, *Zwei gnostische Hymnen* (Giessen 1904) SS. 40ff. A.F.J.Klijn, *The Acts of Thomas* (Leiden 1962) pp. 172f.

[58] Thomas-psalm 11: *Psalmbook* 216, 14; 217, 17; K.Rudolph, *Die Mandäer* II (Göttingen 1961) S. 317, Anm. 9; G.Widengren, *Mesopotamian Elements in Manichaeism*, *UUÅ* 3 (1946) pp. 109ff.

[59] Cf. J.-E.Ménard, *L'Évangile selon Philippe* (Paris 1967) pp. 202 sv.

[60] Cf. Drijvers, *Bardaiṣan of Edessa*, pp. 144ff.

[61] Drijvers, Quq and the Quqites, An unknown sect in Edessa in the second century A.D., *Numen* 14 (1967) 122ff.

ganze Skala von Möglichkeiten vorführen, die mit verschiedenartigen religiösen Hintergründen verbunden sind.

Das *Thomasevangelium* und die *Oden Salomos* gehören zu den archaischen Schriften der syrischen Theologie. Bestimmte Tendenzen dieser Schriften sind in den apokryphen *Thomasacta*, weiter entwickelt worden. A. F. J. Klijn schrieb diese Systematisierung in der Anlage vorhandener Gedanken dem Wirken Tatians zu.[62] Ohne jeden Zweifel hat Tatian auf das edessenische Christentum, mit dem er viele Verbindungen hat, Einfluss ausgeübt, obzwar er von Rom aus vermutlich nach Adiabene und nicht nach Edessa zurückkehrte.[63] Sein Enkratismus verbindet ihn mit dem *Thomasevangelium* und den *Thomasacta*; mit dem *Thomasevangelium* hat er ein Stück jüdisch-christlicher Überlieferung gemeinsam. Auch das Denken über den androgynen Charakter Adams finden wir bei ihm, wie aus einer kleinen Glosse im Text des Lütticher Diatessarons (Matthäus 19:4–9) hervorgeht, wo Jesus über die Ehe spricht. Wie Tatian behauptet, fügte Gott Mann und Frau zusammen, während Adam für die fleischliche Gemeinschaft zwischen Mann und Frau verantwortlich gemacht wird.[64] In der Theologie Tatians wird der Inkarnation und Passion wenig Aufmerksamkeit gewidmet; bei ihn steht der göttliche Logos, der die menschliche Seele rettet, im Mittelpunkt. Der Leib gehört ja zu der vergänglichen Welt; im Einverständnis mit dem göttlichen Geist, der die Seele ihrem himmlischen Ursprung zurückführt, wird die Seele gerettet (*Oratio ad Graecos* 13). Diese Anthropologie, die z.B. den *Thomasacta* entspricht und an die sich die Vorstellungen des Brautgemaches sehr gut anschliessen können, weist zudem treffende Ähnlichkeiten mit der Gedankenwelt Bardaiṣans auf. Tatian lehrt, dass diese anthropologische Dreiteilung drei Niveaus im Menschen entspricht. Der Leib ist vergänglich; die Seele kann gerettet und zu ihrem himmlischen Ursprung zurückgeführt werden; der Geist – eine Gabe Gottes für diejenigen, die Gott gehorchen – repräsentiert das „Bild Gottes". Das involviert den freien Willen des Menschen, der sich sein eigenes Heil wählen kann, das ihm durch den göttlichen Logos angetragen wird. Der Mensch ist dazu bestimmt, sogar über die Engel zu herrschen (*Oratio* 17, 6–8), aber wegen des Sündenfalls ist er jetzt den Engeln untergeordnet.[65] Bei

---

[62] Klijn, Das Thomasevangelium und das altsyrische Christentum, S. 157.

[63] A. Vööbus, *A History of Asceticism in the Syrian Orient* I (Louvain 1958) p. 38.

[64] Cf. Vööbus, *A History of Asceticism* I, p. 43.

[65] Cf. G. F. Hawthorne, Tatian and his Discourse to the Greeks, *HThR* 57 (1964) 161–188.

Bardaiṣan finden wir die gleiche gestufte Dreiteilung im Menschen; der Geist ist das höchste göttliche Element, in dem der freie Wille enthalten ist und der die Seele zu ihrem himmlischen Ursprung zurückführen kann. Der Mensch untersteht, so nimmt Bardaiṣan an, der Macht der Planeten, die seine physische Existenz und sein Schicksal bestimmen. Man kann sich fragen, ob die Rolle der Engel im Judentum und im Christentum, wie sie in Edessa anzutreffen ist, nicht der der Planeten analog ist, die ja in manchen Systemen von wesentlicher Bedeutung sind. Die sieben Erzengel würden dann mit den Sieben in einem System mit astrologischem Anstrich (wie bei Bardaiṣan) übereinstimmen.[66] Auch hier ergibt sich also wieder, dass eine bestimmte Gegebenheit von verschiedenen Seiten angefasst und interpretiert werden kann: eine gleiche Grundtatsache, nämlich die des Verhältnisses von Freiheit und Gebundenheit im menschlichen Dasein kann mit Vorstellungen, die einem jüdisch-christlichen sowie einem heidnisch-astrologischen Milieu entstammen, ausgedrückt werden. Es ist weiterhin bemerkenswert, dass genau dasselbe anthropologische Schema im Enkratismus Tatians und in der Lehre Bardaiṣans, die bestimmt nicht enkratitisch ist, funktioniert. Ähnliche Vorstellungen finden sich z.B. in der *Apologie des Athenagoras* und in den *hermetischen Schriften.*[67]

Ehe wir uns weiter mit Bardaiṣan befassen, wollen wir zuerst einiges über die Marcioniten sagen, die nach der Ansicht Bauers die älteste Form des Christentums in Edessa vertraten. Wir wissen freilich sehr wenig in bezug auf die Marcioniten in Edessa, abgesehen von der Bemerkung im *Chronicon Edessenum*, dass Marcion im Jahre 449 (137/38 n.Chr.) aus der katholischen Kirche austrat,[68] und von den Mitteilungen über die Polemik Bardaiṣans gegen Marcion über die Schöpfung.[69] Reste dieser Polemik finden wir noch in der *Vita des Aberkios*, eines grossen Gegners der Marcioniten im Osten.[70] Die Kontroverse zwischen

---

[66] Cf. G.H.Dix, The Seven Archangels and the Seven Spirits, *JThS* 28 (1927) 233–250; G.Furlani, I Sette Angeli de Yezidi, *Rendiconti della relle academia dei Lincei* VIII, 2 (1947) 141–161.

[67] Cf. A.J.Festugière, Sur une traduction d'Athénagore, *REG* 41 (1943) 367–375; *CH* XII, cf. *Hermès Trismégiste* I, ed. Nock-Festugière, pp. 193 svv.

[68] Cf. Bauer, *Rechtgläubigkeit und Ketzerei*, S. 20.

[69] Hippolytus, *Refutatio* VI, 35 (ed. Wendland); Eusebius, *H.E.* IV, 30 (ed. Schwartz); cf. Drijvers, *Bardaiṣan of Edessa*, pp. 167ff.

[70] Th.Nissen, Die Petrusakten und ein bardesanitischer Dialog in der Aberkiosvita, *ZNW* 9 (1908) 315–328; H.Grégoire, Bardésane et S.Abercius *Byzantion* 25–27 (1955–57) 363–368; cf. Drijvers, *Bardaiṣan of Edessa*, p. 170.

Marcion mit den Seinen und Bardaiṣan bezog sich auf die Schöpfung. Der Dualismus in der Gotteslehre Marcions wird von Bardaiṣan abgelehnt, der auf Gott als Schöpfer oder vielmehr als Ordner der chaotischen Materie nicht verzichten will. Der Dualismus Bardaiṣans steckt in der Materie, die eine Mischung von Chaos und Ordnung, von Gut und Böse ist, wo das Böse aber niemals eine eigene Macht besitzt, sondern aus der *privatio boni* besteht.[71] Schon im zweiten Jahrhundert war also die Lehre über die Schöpfung eine Kernfrage in der syrischen Theologie. Wahrscheinlich gab es in Edessa wohl Anknüpfungspunkte für den Marcionismus. Tertullian – *Adv. Marcionem* IV, 11 – sagt, dass manche Marcioniten sich selber bei der Taufe entmannten, womit sie alle Bande mit dem Schöpfer in drastischer Weise durchschnitten. Auch andere Formen der Askese waren unter den Marcioniten bekannt.[72] Tertullian bezichtigt übrigens in *Adv. Valent.* 30 die Valentinianer derselben Praktiken. Entmannung war im Kultus der Atargatis nicht ungebräuchlich; im *Buch der Gesetze der Länder* von Bardaiṣan wird mitgeteilt, dass König Abgar der Grosse, wenn auch mit geringem Erfolg, die Entmannung verbot. Noch im vierten Jahrhundert muss Rabbula, der Tyrann von Edessa, in seinen Canones für Kleriker dieses Verbot wiederholen. Die Vermutung liegt nahe, dass solch eine Sitte einfach durch den Marcionismus und unter Umständen durch den Valentianismus übernommen wurde, eine andere theologische Motivierung erhielt, sich aber faktisch nicht wandelte. Ähnliches ist der Fall mit dem Schuldbekenntnis und der Busse im Kultus der Dea Syria; diese bezogen sich speziell auf die Übertretung von Nahrungstabus und Reinheitsvorschriften betreffs des Tempels; dadurch haben sie eine täuschende Ähnlichkeit mit den Vorschriften, die das Judentum auf diesem Gebiet kannte und die im jüdischen Christentum teilweise gültig geblieben und in einigen Sekten sogar noch verschärft worden sind.[73]

Trotz der Polemik zwischen Bardaiṣan und Marcion gelten beide im Manichäismus als die Erneuerer der Kirche nach Paulus. Mani hat das kosmologische und anthropologische Schema Bardaiṣans radikalisiert, wodurch der Raum geschaffen wurde, in dem Marcions Askese einen Platz fand.[74] A. Böhlig hat dazu bemerkt: „Wenn aber gerade Markion

---

[71] Drijvers, *Bardaiṣan of Edessa*, p. 139.

[72] Vööbus, *A History of Asceticism* I, pp. 51ff.

[73] Cf. R. Pettazzoni, La confession des péchés en Syrie aux époques préchrétiennes, *Mélanges R. Dussaud* I (1939) 197–202.

[74] Drijvers, *Bardaiṣan of Edessa*, pp. 123ff.; 139ff.; 225ff.

und Bardesanes so sehr als wahre Lehrer der Kirche gefeiert werden, gilt es zu untersuchen, ob sich ihre Ansichten auch sonst im Manichäismus wiederfinden."[75] Merkwürdigerweise weist der Manichäismus mehr Charakteristika auf, die in Edessa zum ersten Mal angetroffen werden oder dort ihren Ursprung finden: Bardaiṣan (und Marcion), die ganze Thomastradition des *Thomasevangeliums*, der *Thomaspsalmen* und *Thomasacta*, der Titel Arzt für Mani, der genau dem Titel Arzt Jesu entspricht usw.[76] Mani hat das Christentum augenscheinlich in seiner edessenischen Form kennen gelernt.

Bardaiṣan, der schon verschiedentlich genannt wurde, ist ein typischer Vertreter dieses edessenischen Christentums und dadurch so schwer zu charakterisieren. Die jüngste Charakterisierung ist aus der Feder L.W. Barnards geflossen, der die Doktrin Bardaiṣans folgendermassen umschreibt: „a Syrian Jewish-Christian Gnosis similar to that which appears in the Gospel of Thomas."[77] A. Böhlig nennt, indem er über „Probleme des manichäischen Lehrvortrages" handelt, in diesem Zusammenhang Bardaiṣan Manis Lehrmeister, in dessen Umgebung er das Christentum hat kennengelernt; Bardaiṣan aber „fühlte sich noch als häretischer Christ".[78] Diese ziemlich willkürlichen Charakterisierungen beschwören sofort das ganze Problem eines jüdischen Christentums im Syrien, eventuell einer jüdisch-christlichen Gnosis, herauf und im Zusammenhang damit die Frage von Orthodoxie und Häresie. Barnards Charakterisierung ist zum Teil grundfalsch: das *Thomasevangelium* ist enkratitisch, und Bardaiṣan war bestimmt kein Enkratit; im Gegenteil, seine weltliche Gesinnung wird ihm z.B. von Ephrem Syrus heftig vorgeworfen.[79] Wenn wir dem Terminus „Gnosis" einen sehr umfassenden Inhalt geben, so kann man bei Bardaiṣan davon sprechen, nicht aber von „Gnostizismus", da die Merkmale der gnostischen Systeme des zweiten Jahrhunderts bei ihm fehlen.[80] Ob diese „Gnosis" jedoch ausschliesslich

---

[75] A. Böhlig, Christliche Wurzeln im Manichäismus, *Mysterion und Wahrheit*, (Leiden 1968) S. 208.

[76] Jesus wird in der *Doctrina Addai* „guter Arzt" genennt; cf. Jos. Ott, Die Bezeichnung Christi als ἰατρός in der urchristlichen Literatur, *Der Katholik* 90 (Mainz) 454–458; Böhlig, *Mysterion und Wahrheit*, S. 262; *idem*, Christliche Wurzeln im Manichäismus, *Mysterion und Wahrheit*, SS. 202–221.

[77] L.W. Barnard, The Origins and Emergence of the Church in Edessa during the First Two Centuries A.D., *Vig. Chr.* 22 (1968) 171.

[78] Böhlig, Probleme des manichäischen Lehrvortrages, *Mysterion und Wahrheit*, S. 243.

[79] Drijvers, *Bardaiṣan of Edessa*, p. 161.

[80] Drijvers, *Bardaiṣan of Edessa*, p. 224; *idem*, Bardaiṣan, die Bardaiṣaniten und

eine „Jewish-Christian Gnosis“ ist, könnte bezweifelt werden. Ich möchte das an einigen Beispielen erläutern. Das anthropologische Schema Bardaiṣans, das er z.B. mit Tatian gemeinsam hat, nämlich Leib, Seele und Geist, entspricht einer kosmologischen/theologischen Trias von Materie – planetarischen Mächten – Gott oder physischer Determination – Schicksal – Freiheit.[81] Jede Trias stellt auch eine ethische Gradation dar, indem der letzte Terminus absolut gut, frei und harmonisch ist, der erste aber ein geordnetes Chaos, d.h. unfrei ist und dadurch die Möglichkeit des Bösen in sich trägt. Fundamental in diesem Bild der Schöpfung und des Menschen ist die Vorstellung von der Vermischung der vier Urelemente, die durch einen Zufall entstanden ist. Diese Vermischung stört die ursprüngliche Harmonie und ist sowohl die Ursache des Bösen als auch die Möglichkeit dazu, da die Finsternis einerseits als ein fünftes Element gesehen wird und andrerseits die Bezeichnung der abstrusen Situation der vier reinen Elementen ist. Dieses Bild hat Parallelen in der iranischen Welt, wo der Begriff gumečisn für die Kosmologie von fundamentaler Bedeutung ist.[82] Andrerseits finden wir in den Pseudo-Clementinen auch die Vorstellung, dass der Teufel, das Böse und die Dämonen aus der κρᾶσις der Elemente entstanden sind. In den *Ps.-Clementinischen Recogn.* 9,17–29 hat sich ein Teil des Dialogs über das Fatum von Bardaiṣan, das sogenannte *Buch der Gesetze der Länder* erhalten. Dieser Teil gehörte schon zu der Grundschrift, die im Anfang des dritten Jahrhunderts verfasst wurde. Dadurch finden sich in den Ps.-Clementinen genau dieselben Vorstellungen über Freiheit und Gebundenheit wie bei Bardaiṣan. Auch die Grundschrift sagt aus, dass die Konstellation Gewalt über Charakter und Lebenslauf hat, wenn auch der Freiheit Raum gelassen wird.[83] Die einfachste Erklärung für diese gegenseitige Verwandtschaft ist die Annahme, dass der Autor der Grundschrift die Doktrinen Bardaiṣans und vielleicht seine Schriften gekannt hat.[84] G. Quispel ist

---

die Ursprünge des Gnostizismus, *Le Origini dello Gnosticismo* (Leiden 1967) SS. 307–314.

[81] Cf. Drijvers, *Bardaiṣan of Edessa*, pp. 76–95; 152–161; 218ff.; Hawthorne, Tatian and his Discourse to the Greeks, pp. 167ff.; Klijn, Das Thomas-evangelium und das altsyrische Christentum, SS. 157ff.

[82] Cf. Widengren, *Mesopotamian Elements*, p. 44, n. 1; H.S. Nyberg, Questions de cosmogonie et de cosmologie mazdéennes, *JA* 119 (1931) 29 svv.; cf. G. Widengren, *Die Religionen Irans* (Stuttgart 1965) S. 304; *idem*, Quelques rapports entre Juifs et Iraniens, p. 235.

[83] Cf. B. Rehm, Bardesanes in den Pseudoclementinen, *Philologus* 93 (1938) 218–247; Drijvers, *Bardaiṣan of Edessa*, p. 62.

[84] Cf. Drijvers, *Bardaiṣan of Edessa*, pp. 60–76.

auch der Ansicht, dass der Autor der Grundschrift einen Teil einer Schrift aus der Schule Bardaiṣans in sein Werk integriert hat, er glaubt aber, dass die Lehre der Vermischung, die sowohl in der Grundschrift als auch bei Bardaiṣan vorkommt, ein Beispiel von „Jewish-Christian influence upon Bardesanes" ist.[85] Es liegt viel näher anzunehmen, dass der Autor der Grundschrift auch diese Lehre von Bardaiṣan entlehnt hat, wie sich auch weiterhin in den Ps.-Clementinischen Schriften Einfluss Bardaiṣans nachweisen lässt.[86] Dieser Autor, der ein typischer Literat war, hat vielerlei disparate Gegebenheiten in seinem Œuvre verarbeitet; auch persische Vorstellungen finden sich bei ihm.[87] H. J. Schoeps ist der Meinung, dass nicht das Werk Bardaiṣans, der ja ein Gnostiker war, vom Verfasser der Grundschrift benutzt wurde, sondern eine jüdische Apologie gegen die Astrologie.[88] Obschon dies nicht sehr wahrscheinlich ist, berührt es sich doch mit einer früher von P. Wendland gemachten Feststellung, dass der Dialog über das Fatum von Bardaiṣan auffallende Übereinstimmungen mit Philons Abhandlung *De Providentia* aufweist.[89] Es ist möglich, dass Bardaiṣan und Philon in gleicher Weise aus den philosophischen Abhandlungen gegen das Fatum, die vielleicht alle auf Carneades zurückgehen, geschöpft haben. Es ist auch möglich, dass Philons Werk in Edessa ziemlich früh bekannt war. Dem Œuvre Philons entstammen auch Gedanken aus dem *Thomasevangelium*, die enkratischen Tendenzen in Edessa und selbst die Schöpfungsvorstellungen Bardaiṣans.[90] Eine systematische Untersuchung über diese Beziehungen wäre sicherlich empfehlenswert. Wenn also Bardaiṣan und das Judentum in diesem Punkte übereinstimmen, so ist dieses ein stark hellenisiertes, philosophisch eingestelltes Judentum, wie es dem Charakter des edessenischen Judentums entspricht. In diesem Zusammenhang muss konstatiert werden, dass auch auffallende Ähnlichkeiten zwischen Anschauungen Bardaiṣans und der *Hermetica*, namentlich dem *Poimandres*, bestehen. Im Traktat XII, 5–9 finden wir auch eine Fatumlehre, die eine frappante

---

85 G. Quispel, The Discussion of Judaic Christianity, *Vig. Chr.* 22 (1968) 89.

86 *Recogn.* 3,15; 5,13 (= *Hom.* 10,5); 5,25 (= *Hom.* 11,8); 5,27 (= *Hom* 11,10); 8,44; 8,56; cf. Rehm, Bardesanes in den Pseudoclementinen.

87 Cf. H. J. Schoeps, Iranisches in den Pseudoklementinen, *ZNW* 51 (1960) 1–10.

88 H. J. Schoeps, Astrologisches im pseudoklementinischen Roman, *Vig. Chr.* 5 (1951) 88–100.

89 P. Wendland, *Philos Schrift über die Vorsehung. Ein Beitrag zur Geschichte der nacharistotelischen Philosophie* (Berlin 1892) SS. 27ff.

90 Cf. U. Früchtel, *Die kosmologischen Vorstellungen bei Philo von Alexandrien* (Leiden 1968) SS. 14ff.

Ähnlichkeit mit der Bardaiṣans hat: die Körper sind dem Fatum unterworfen, aber das Gute und das Böse dem νοῦς, der die Freiheit impliziert.[91] Die gnostischen Schriften aus Chenoboskion kennen auch derartige Vorstellungen, u.a. die *Schrift ohne Titel.*[92] Der Kult der Planeten von Sumatar mag aber auch als Modell für die Entwicklung dieser Gedanken gedient haben, die also auch ein heidnisches Gegenstück hatten.

Wir dürfen als Schlussfolgerung ziehen, dass Bardaiṣans Lehre über die Schöpfung und die Menschen zwar Parallelen zu jüdischen Denkern oder Gruppen, aber ebenfalls zu heidnisch-philosophischen oder astrologischen aufweist. Ein aut-aut ist hier nicht angebracht, vielmehr ein et-et.

Ähnliches kommt in Bardaiṣans Gotteslehre vor. Einesteils findet man die Vorstellung von einem Gott, der sein Wort vom Denken zur Materie sendet, um die Unordnung, die in ihr herrscht, zu beheben. Dies erinnert an jüdische Spekulationen über die Weisheit als göttliche Emanation, die die Welt schafft.[93] Dieses Wort vom Denken kann auf Christus deuten. Andernteils findet man auch die Vorstellung von einem Vater und einer Mutter des Lebens, die einen Sohn erzeugen; Vater und Mutter werden gleichzeitig mit dem Bild der Sonne und des Mondes bezeichnet. Wir können dabei an die geläufige syrische Vorstellung von der Trinität denken, aber auch an Atargatis und Bêl, deren Sohn Nebo ist. Die heftigen Ausfälle Ephrems gegen derartige Vorstellungen Bardaiṣans lassen vermuten, dass sie doch anders waren als die gewöhnlichen trinitarischen Vorstellungen und bestimmt weniger keusch. Die Vorstellung von der Mutter des Lebens ist ganz gewiss nicht vom Judentum abzuleiten, wo Sophia die einzige weibliche Gestalt ist. Sophias Funktion wird aber bei Bardaiṣan vom Sohn übernommen. So entstehen Verbindungen mit heidnischen religiösen Vorstellungen. Der Sohn kann Jesus sein, aber auch Hermes-Nebo. Das Gleiche finden wir bei den Naassenern, wo Hermes der Logos ist, der die Aufgabe des Psychopompos erfüllt.[94] Die *Oracula Chaldaica* verschaffen uns auch Vergleichsmaterial: sie kennen die Trias Sonne, Mond und Weisheit, d.h. Merkur.[95] Diese Beispiele sind verhältnismässig willkürlich gewählt worden, machen

---

[92] Cf. *Hermès Trismégiste* I, ed. Nock und Festugière, pp. 193–195: A.J. Festugière, *Hermétisme et mystique païenne* (Paris 1967) pp. 60 svv.

[92] *Schrift ohne Titel*, ed. Böhlig/Labib, 173,28–30; cf. Böhlig, *Mysterion und Wahrheit*, S. 125.

[93] Cf. H.-F. Weiss, *Untersuchungen zur Kosmologie*, SS. 189ff.

[94] Hippol. *Ref.* 8.27 seqq.; cf. W. Foerster, Die Naassener, *Studi di storia religiosa della tarda antichità* (Messina 1968) pp. 27ff.

[95] Cf. H. Lewy, *Chaldaean Oracles and Theurgy* (Cairo 1956) p. 221.

aber deutlich, dass streng genommen bei Bardaiṣan nicht von einem jüdischen Christentum geredet werden kann. Er ist vielmehr ein Produkt des edessenischen Synkretismus seiner Zeit. Vor allem Einflüsse der hellenistischen Philosophie sind nachweisbar.[96] Wenn überhaupt bei Bardaiṣan von einer Art Gnosis die Rede ist, ist sie nicht nur jüdisch-christlich, sondern ein Komplex von allerlei Elementen verschiedenen Ursprungs, die auch in ganz andere Systeme hineinpassen. Wenn Bardaiṣan sich als Christ fühlte, dann auf jeden Fall nicht nur als Christ, sondern auch als Philosoph, Dichter und Astrologe, der sich auf Gedankengänge einliess, die sich später nicht mehr mit dem Christentum vertrugen. Er fühlte sich also nicht als „häretischer Christ"; man kann ihn höchstens als einen Christen bezeichnen, der später zu den Häretikern gerechnet wurde.

Es ist merkwürdig, wie die Wissenschaft manchmal von einem Extrem ins andere fällt. Nach der Zeit, in der alles Christliche in Edessa als gnostisch oder doch als abhängig vom Gnostizismus galt, überwiegt heute die Tendenz, jeden Gnostizismus von Edessa fernzuhalten und dort nur dem Enkratismus und dem jüdischen Christentum Heimatrecht zu verleihen. Obwohl die Meinungen über die anderen Gruppierungen und Schriften des essenischen Christentums noch differieren, steht doch unumstösslich fest, dass die Quqiten jedenfalls eine primitive Form des Gnostizismus repräsentieren. Überdies leben sie nicht isoliert, sondern haben Verbindungen mit den anderen Gruppen und Strömungen in Edessa. Es braucht hier nicht wiederholt zu werden, was an anderer Stelle ausführlich auseinandergesetzt wurde.[97] Die Quqiten sind ohne Zweifel Gnostiker, denn ihnen ist die Vorstellung vom Fall der Mutter des Lebens, der himmlischen Sophia, in die Materie, geläufig. Sie wird daraus befreit, dadurch, dass sie Sieben Jungfrauen opfert, die in der Materie zurückbleiben. Ihrerseits werden diese Jungfrauen von ihren himmlischen Bräutigamen, von denen Jesus von Nazareth einer ist, befreit. Diese Jungfrauen sind aller Wahrscheinlichkeit nach Isis, die Dea Syria, Athena in Hatra u.a. Diese gnostische Vorstellung ist jedoch primitiv: es gibt einen Fall und eine allmähliche Rehabilitation, nicht aber einen Bruch im göttlichen Pleroma zwischen einem guten allerhöchsten Gott und einem schlechten Demiurgen. Die Schöpfung der Welt vollzieht sich durch zweiundvierzig Kämpfe der himmlischen

[96] Drijvers, *Bardaiṣan of Edessa*, pp. 163ff.; 218–223.

[97] Drijvers, Quq and the Quqites. An unknown sect in Edessa in the second century A.D., *Numen* 14 (1967) 104–129.

Äonen, Kinder des Vaters und der Mutter des Lebens, mit der lebendig gemachten Materie, die als ein Bild dargestellt wird. Diese Zahl 42 hat wahrscheinlich etwas zu tun mit Spekulationen des jüdischen babylonischen Lehrers Rabh (gest. 247) über einen geheimen Namen Gottes, der aus 42 Buchstaben besteht. Mit diesem Namen hätte Gott die Welt geschaffen.[98] Es haben also jedenfalls in dieser Sekte Spekulationen existiert, die mit esoterischen jüdischen Doktrinen verwandt sind, wie auch aus der Kosmologie der Quqiten hervorgeht. Daneben kennen sie aber strenge Reinheitsvorschriften, die durch die Überlieferung mit analogen Gewohnheiten Samariter in Zusammenhang gebracht werden. Diese Reinheitsvorschriften und ihre Sexualethik passen wieder organisch in ihre Anschauung über die Schöpfung und den Fall der Mutter des Lebens. Wenn wir gleichzeitig in der Kosmologie noch einen astrologischen Einfluss nachweisen können, dadurch, dass die Planeten und Zodiakalgestirne als Kinder des Vaters und der Mutter des Lebens angesehen werden, haben wir so ziemlich alles, was sich in Edessa findet, Revue passieren lassen: Judentum, Paganismus, Christentum, Astrologie, Gnostizismus und Enkratismus. Es scheint, das quqitische Vorstellungen auch in späteren Hymnen vorkommen. In den manichäischen *Thomaspsalmen* wird von einer Tochter berichtet, die einem Löwen oder Drachen entrissen und ins Brautgemach geführt wird. Die Manichäer haben auch dieses überlieferte Material selbständig verarbeitet.

Das gleiche ist der Fall mit den *Acta Thomae* und den darin aufgenommenen Hymnen, dem sogenannten *Lied von der Perle* und dem *Hochzeitslied der Sophia*. G.Quispel hat, in den Spuren A.F.J.Klijns tretend, den jüdisch-christlichen Charakter des Liedes von der Perle betont und das *Thomasevangelium* und die *Homilien des Makarius* aufgeführt, um dieses Lied aus der jüdisch-christlichen, enkratitischen Tradition zu erklären.[99] Dem steht gegenüber, dass dieses Lied in den mandäischen und manichäischen Hymnen zahlreiche Parallelen hat und in der *Kephalaia Manis* ausführlich expliziert wurde.[100] Die Auffassung der Iranisten steht so in geradem Widerspruch mit der Quispels u.a., was im verschiedenartigen Ausgangspunkt begründet liegt. Quispel wählt

---

[98] *Talmud Babli*, *Qiddushin* 71a (briefliche Mitteilung G.Scholems 28.9.'67).

[99] A.F.J.Klijn, The so-called Hymn of the Pearl, *Vig. Chr.* 14 (1960) 154–164; G.Quispel, Das Lied von der Perle, *Eranos-Jahrbuch* 1965 (Zürich 1966) SS. 1–24; *idem*, *Makarius, das Thomasevangelium und das Lied von der Perle*, SS. 39–64.

[100] Cf. G.Bornkamm, *Neutestamentliche Apokryphen*³ II (Tübingen 1964) SS. 304f.; dort alle Belegstelle.

den seinigen in der neutestamentlichen Parabel und in der Form, in der sie im *Thomasevangelium* vorkommt. Die Iranisten, u.a. Widengren, gehen von der manichäischen Interpretation aus an das Lied heran.[101] Mit J.E. Ménard bin ich der Ansicht, dass dazwischen eine Entwicklung liegt, die zugleich eine Verschiebung in der Interpretation des Bildes vom Königssohn und der Perle bewirkt. Ménard führt aus, dass das Lied christlich sei und aus einer jüdisch-christlichen Quelle stamme. Es sei später gnostisch bearbeitet worden und sei letzten Endes manichäisch. Die gnostische Bearbeitung sei persischen Vorstellungen über das Daēna zu verdanken.[102] Es ist fraglich, ob sich die verschiedenen Bearbeitungen in dem Lied, wie wir es jetzt kennen, unterscheiden lassen, aber es bleibt jedenfalls wahr, dass mehr Interpretationen möglich sind als nur eine enkratitische. In diesem Zusammenhang ist die Tatsache bemerkenswert, dass auch von diesem Lied mehrere Fassungen vorliegen, eine „gnostische" und eine weniger „gnostische", eine syrische und eine griechische. Wir haben es hier wiederum mit einer Erscheinung zu tun, die auch beim *Thomasevangelium* und bei den *Oden Salomos* festgestellt wurde. Die *Thomasacta* wurden auch von den Manichäern benutzt. Damit soll nicht betritten werden, dass Makarius in legitimer Weise von jüdisch-christlichen Theologoumena, die das *Lied von der Perle* enthält, Gebrauch gemacht hat. Die manichäische Exegese ist jedoch nicht weniger legitim. Beide Auslegungen sind nicht eine Exegese e mente auctoris, sondern Beispiele aus der Geschichte der Exegese dieses Liedes.

Eine bunte Reihe von Personen, Schriften und Auffassungen ist damit durchaus nicht erschöpfend behandelt worden. Daraus mag klar geworden sein, dass sie alle einen eigenen Charakter haben und doch auch genügend Übereinstimmungen aufweisen, um sie zusammen zu behandeln. Sie sind durchweg Exponenten einer sehr komplexen kulturellen und religiösen Situation im Edessa des zweiten Jahrhunderts. Diese Situation ist nicht statisch, sondern hat eine Entwicklung durchgemacht. In einem bestimmten Augenblick ist dort die christliche Verkündigung in irgendeiner Form gehört und ins Ganze aufgenommen worden. Wenn dieser Moment als Anfangspunkt einer Entwicklung gewählt wird, so ist der

---

[101] G. Widengren, Der iranische Hintergrund der Gnosis, *ZRGG* 4 (1952) 97–114. A. Adam hat einen Zwischenweg versucht und deutet den Text als Endprodukt der Entwicklung einer jüdisch-mesopotamischen Gnosis aus vorchristlicher Zeit, A. Adam, *Die Psalmen des Thomas und das Perlenlied als Zeugnisse vorchristlicher Gnosis*, Beiheft ZNW 24 (Berlin 1959).

[102] J.E. Ménard, Le Chant de la Perle, *Revue des sciences religieuses* (1968) 289–325.

Endpunkt eine Situation, in der Häresie und Orthodoxie einander gegenüberstanden. Das Problem lässt sich auch anders formulieren: welches ist der Grund, dass eine jüdisch-christliche Evangeliumstradition schliesslich in eine gnostische Bücherei gerät und dass Bardaiṣan und Tatian allmählich verketzert wurden? Die Endphase ist nicht vom allerersten Anfang zu trennen, wie die erste Zeile eines Romans in gewissem Sinne für das ganze Buch entscheidend ist. Die Meinungen über diesen allerersten Anfang sind geteilt, so dass auch weiterhin keine Einstimmigkeit erzielt wird.

J. Daniélou,[103] O. Cullmann,[104] J. C. L. Gibson,[105] G. Quispel,[106] A. Vööbus[107] u.a. nehmen einen palästinensischen Ursprung des ältesten edessenischen Christentums an, worauf sektiererische jüdische Gruppen aus Qumran noch eingewirkt hätten. Nach 70 n.Chr. hätten sich Juden und jüdische Christen in Transjordanien vermischt und von dort Syrien erreicht. Für die älteste Herkunft der Mandäer gälte dasselbe. W. Bauer nahm an, dass das Christentum in marcionitischer Vermummung Edessa zuerst von Westen aus um 150 n.Chr. erreicht hätte.[108] Mit „Westen" meint Bauer vermutlich Antiochia. Auch J. Leroy vertritt eine antiochenische Herkunft.[109] Die Bekehrung Edessas ist auch mit der Adiabenes in Zusammenhang gebracht, und zwar auf Grund der alten Beziehungen zwischen den beiden Städten und vor allem auf Grund der Gegebenheiten aus der *Chronik von Arbela*. Jetzt, da J. M. Fiey nach J. Assfalg überzeugend nachgewiesen hat, dass die *Chronik von Arbela* eine Fälschung von der Hand A. Minganas ist, werden alle Argumente der Autoren,

---

103 J. Daniélou, *Théologie du Judéo-Christianisme* I (Tournai 1958) pp. 68 svv.; *idem*, *Das Judenchristentum und die Anfänge der Kirche* (Köln 1964) SS. 11f.

104 O. Cullmann, Das Thomasevangelium und die Frage nach dem Alter der in ihm enthaltenen Tradition, *Vorträge und Aufsätze* 1925–1962 (Tübingen 1966) SS. 566–588; *idem*, Die neuentdeckten Qumrantexte und das Judenchristentum der Pseudoklementinen, *Vorträge und Aufsätze*, SS. 241–259.

105 J. C. L. Gibson, From Qumran to Edessa or the Aramaic Speaking Church before and after 70 A.D., *The Annual of Leeds Oriental Society* V (1963–65, Leiden 1966) pp. 24–39.

106 Quispel, *Makarius, das Thomasevangelium und das Lied von der Perle*, SS. 5ff.; *idem*, The Discussion of Judaic Christianity, *Vig. Chr.* 22 (1968) 81–93 und zahlreiche andere Aufsätze.

107 A. Vööbus, *A History of Asceticism* I, pp. 4ff.

108 Bauer, *Rechtgläubigkeit und Ketzerei*, SS. 27ff.

109 J. Leroy, *Les manuscrits syriaques à peintures. Contribution à l'étude de l'iconographie des églises de langue syriaque*, 2 Vols (Paris 1964) p. 22; cf. *BiOr* 25 (1968) 169–173.

die diese Chronik als eine echte Quelle benutzen, gegenstandslos.[110] Der Kronzeuge für einen direkt palästinensischen und jüdisch-christlichen Ursprung des edessenischen Christentums ist Tobias bar Tobias, ein Jude aus Palästina, bei dem Addai, als er aus Jerusalem nach Edessa gekommen war, Wohnung nahm und der ihn am Hof des Königs Abgar einführte. Die *Doctrina Addai*, die dies erwähnt, ist aber zu sehr eine Apologie der Orthodoxie aus späterer Zeit, wie W. Bauer überzeugend erwiesen hat, um als eine zuverlässige historische Quelle benutzt werden zu können. Ein palästinensischer Ursprung im Kreise der Jünger, die naturgemäss Juden waren, passt in die Apologie, die die *Doctrina Addai* eben ist, da sie den „prestige de l'origine" vertritt. Natürlich ist das edessenische Christentum letzten Endes palästinensischen Ursprungs und ist es als solches jüdisches Christentum; es ist allerdings sehr zweifelhaft, ob es eine direkte Verbindung von Jerusalem nach Edessa gab, so dass sich dort ein Teil der ältesten Traditionen unverändert und unversehrt hätte erhalten können. Die christliche Verkündigung ist dort vielmehr allmählich, auf verschiedenen Wegen bekannt geworden, sowohl von Transjordanien als auch von Antiochia aus. Die Achse Jerusalem-Edessa ist eine moderne Fassung der *Doctrina Addai*. Die Vielgestaltigkeit dieses ältesten Christentums in Edessa und seine Verbindungen mit jüdischen und heidnischen Vorstellungen spricht auch gegen einen direkten palästinensischen Ursprung und für ein Bekanntwerden auf verschiedenen Wegen. Natürlich haben die Juden sowohl aktiv als auch passiv in diesem Entwicklungsprozess eine Rolle gespielt, aber sie waren sicherlich nicht die einzigen und zudem stark hellenisiert. Es ist auch fraglich, ob man in dieser Zeit jüdisch und griechisch, jüdische und heidnische Christen deutlich trennen kann.[111] Sogar in späterer Zeit ist dies schwer. Die Inschrift von Kartir (Ende des dritten Jahrhunderts), die Nazoräer neben Christen nennt, meint mit der ersten Gruppe höchstwahrscheinlich die Mandäer oder ihre Vorläufer und nicht jüdische Christen, die sich

---

[110] J.-M. Fiey, Auteur et date de la Chronique d'Arbèles, *L'Orient Syrien* 12 (1967) 265–302; J. Assfalg, Zur Textüberlieferung der Chronik von Arbela. Beobachtungen zu Ms. or. fol. 3126, *OC* 50 (1966) 19–36. Vööbus, *A History of Asceticism* I, pp. 4ff., Gibson, *art. cit.*, p. 32, Simon und Benoit, *Le Judaïsme et le Christianisme antique*, p. 111, Barnard, The Origins and Emergence of the Church in Edessa, pp. 173f., J. Neusner, The Conversion of Adiabene to Christianity, *Numen* 13 (1966) 144–150 benutzen die Chronik als eine echte Quelle.

[111] Cf. J. Leroy, Art. Hellénistique, juif, chrétien, *Cahiers Sioniens* (1956) 157–162; H. Dörrie, *Erasmus* 15 (1963) Sp. 715; W. Grundmann, Geschichte und Botschaft des Urchristentums in ihrer religiösen Umwelt, *Umwelt des Urchristentums*, ed. J. Leipoldt und W. Grundmann, I (Berlin 1965) SS. 416ff.

dann neben den heidnischen Christen aus Antiochia fänden.[112] Die Beziehungen zwischen Antiochia und Edessa, die wohl in Frage gestellt worden sind, hat es entschieden gegeben. Man braucht noch nicht an den orthodoxen Palut zu denken, der von dort aus seine Weihe erhalten hätte. Die Mosaiken in Edessa sind höchstwahrscheinlich von Handwerkern aus Antiochia angefertigt worden; sie weisen auch deutliche stilistische Übereinstimmungen mit den antiochenischen Mosaiken aus dem zweiten Jahrhundert auf. Das deutet auf manchen Kontakt.

Wir dürfen feststellen, dass Termini wie jüdisch-christlich oder gnostisch u.ä. keine adäquate Bezeichnungen des ältesten Christentums in Edessa sind. Es ist „a typical example of hellenistic syncretism – wide open to further influences and developments".[113] Alte Traditionen mögen sich erhalten haben, aber die waren direkt „further influences and developments" unterworfen. Ein Aspekt dieser „developments" ist die auftretende Trennung zwischen Orthodoxie und Häresie, die eigentlich erst im vierten Jahrhundert greifbare Gestalt annimmt. Zwischen dem vierten Jahrhundert und dem chaotischen zweiten Jahrhundert liegt die aufsteigende Entwicklung des Manichäismus, der insbesondere die christliche Tradition in seine edessenische Gestalt aufgenommen und christliche Schriften edessenischen Ursprungs benutzt hat. Anthropologie und Kosmologie des Manichäismus sind eine konsequente Entwicklung dessen, was im edessenischen Christentum des zweiten Jahrhunderts enthalten war. Mani ging durch die Tür, die von Bardaiṣan angelehnt worden war, sagt Ephrem Syrus.[114] Die Entstehung des Manichäismus fällt in dieselbe Zeit, in der die Stadt Edessa ihre Selbständigkeit einbüsste und eine römische Kolonie wurde. Ist das der Grund, dass die Häresie in Syrien oft politische Aspekte zeigt?

Es will mir scheinen, dass der Manichäismus die Polarisation von Orthodoxie und Häresie herbeigeführt hat. Mani ist in Edessa der Ketzer κατ' ἐξοχήν, mit dem allerlei Personen und Schriften in Verbindung stehen oder gebracht werden. Die Verketzerung Bardaiṣans z.B. setzte

---

[112] Gegen Quispel, The Discussion of Judaic Christianity; cf. K. Rudolph, *Die Mandäer* I: *das Mandäerproblem* (Göttingen 1960) S. 57, Anm. 3; S. 115.

[113] H. Koester, ΓΝΩΜΑΙ ΔΙΑΦΟΡΟΙ: The Origin and Nature of Diversification in the History of Early Christianity, *HThR* 58 (1965) 304; cf. H. Koester, Häretiker im Urchristentum als theologisches Problem, *Zeit und Geschichte*, Dankesgabe an R. Bultmann (Tübingen 1964) SS. 61–76.

[114] *S. Ephraim's Prose Refutations of Mani, Marcion, and Bardaisan*, ed. C.W. Mitchell, Vol. I (London 1912) p. 122 (syrischer Text), p. xc (Übersetzung); cf. Drijvers, *Bardaiṣan of Edessa*, pp. 225f.

sich erst durch, nachdem er von Ephrem Syrus mit Mani, der ja die letzten Konsequenzen aus seinen Lehren zog, in Zusammenhang gebracht worden war. Anschauungen, die in Schriften des zweiten Jahrhunderts, wie dem *Thomasevangelium* und in späteren wie z.B. den *Thomasacta*, latent vorhanden sind, werden vom Manichäismus expliziert und in ein konsequent dualistisches asketisches System aufgenommen. Mir scheint, dass zu erwägen wäre, ob die verschiedenen Rezensionen von „edessenischen" Schriften, welche Rezensionen sich in eine „gnostische" und eine „orthodoxe" unterschieden lassen, nicht irgendwie mit dem Gebrauch, den die Manichäer davon machten, zusammenhängen. Was anfangs in religiösen und kulturellen Hinsicht vieldeutig war, fiel in zwei Pole auseinander. So lässt sich erklären, dass in späteren Jahrhunderten eine „orthodoxe" Version der *Thomasacta* und des *Thomasevangeliums* in der syrischen Kirche nach wie vor verwendet wurde. Gruppen aber, die in späteren Jahrhunderten auf das kulturelle und religiöse Erbe des zweiten Jahrhunderts zurückgingen, wie Audianer und Messalianer, wurden in dieser Weise häretisch. Dieses Erbe war zu belastet. Einen analogen Hergang zeigt uns die Überlieferungsgeschichte der *Ps.-Clementinischen Schriften.*

Extreme rufen Extreme hervor; das geschieht in religiosis und in der Wissenschaft. Häresie und Orthodoxie sind in Edessa zu Extremen geworden, wodurch sich keine von beiden hat behaupten können. Der Manichäismus hat dort einige Spuren hinterlassen, und der Orthodoxie abendländischer Prägung war hier nur ein kurzes Leben beschieden. Die Antithese Orthodoxie-Häresie hat dort beim Schisma im fünften Jahrhundert andere Formen angenommen. Die Synthese finden wir nicht am Ende, sondern am Anfang, im zweiten Jahrhundert, als im Spiel der religiösen Kräfte in einer Stadt an der Grenze von Ost und West alles noch möglich war.

Groningen, Acacialaan 54

III

RECHTGLÄUBIGKEIT UND KETZEREI IM ÄLTESTEN SYRISCHEN CHRISTENTUM

Wenn man als Thema für eine Vorlesung im Rahmen des Symposium Syriacum „ Rechtgläubigkeit und Ketzerei im ältesten syrischen Christentum " wählt und nachher die Tagesordnung zu Gesicht bekommt, die diesen Vortrag auf den 31. Oktober ansetzt, wird man sich einer Spannung zwischen dem Theologen und dem Historiker in einer Person inne. Sind doch Rechtgläubigkeit und Ketzerei theologische, dogmatische Begriffe und das älteste syrische Christentum ist ein historisches Phänomen, das geographisch und zeitlich näher bestimmt werden kann. Eine Klärung dieses Spannungsverhältnisses ist umsomehr notwendig, als das Thema eine Variante und Erweiterung des Titels des berühmten Buches von Walter Bauer ist, das auch eine Diskussion über die Anwendung theologischer Begriffe auf historische Erscheinungen entfesselt hat [1]. Das Christentum fängt auf irgendeine Weise mit Jesus von Nazareth an und ist gleichzeitig ein dauernder Versuch, deutlich zu machen, wie und auf welche Weise der Glaube in jeder historischen Situation mit Jesus von Nazareth anfängt. Das Christentum ist eine stetige Neuinterpretation des Jesus von Nazareth, seiner Person und seines Wirkens, eine Neuinterpretation, die im Neuen Testament anfängt und bis heute andauert. In diesem Sinne verstanden, ist das älteste syrische Christentum

---

[1] W. BAUER, *Rechtgläubigkeit und Ketzerei im ältesten Christentum.* 2te Auflage, hrsg. mit einem Nachtrag v. G. STRECKER, *BHTh* 10, Tübingen 1964 ; eine Zusammenfassung in W. BAUER, *Aufsätze und kleine Schriften,* hrsg. v. G. STRECKER, Tübingen 1967, S. 229-233 ; cf. H. D. ALTENDORF, *ThLZ* 91, 1966, Sp. 192-195 für eine kritische Besprechung und *idem, Zum Stichwort : Rechtgläubigkeit und Ketzerei im ältesten Christentum, ZKG* 80, 1969, S. 61-74 ; *vide* weiter H. KÖSTER, *Häretiker im Urchristentum als theologisches Problem, Zeit und Geschichte,* Dankesgabe an R. Bultmann, Tübingen 1964, S. 61-76 ; H. KÖSTER u. J. M. ROBINSON, *Entwicklungslinien durch die Welt des frühen Christentums,* Tübingen 1971, ein Band mit früher erschienenen Aufsätzen ; H. D. BETZ, *Orthodoxy and Heresy in Primitive Christianity, Interpretation* 19, 1965, p. 299-311 ; M. SIMON-A. BENOIT, *Le Judaïsme et le Christianisme antique,* Paris 1968, p. 289 ss. : orthodoxie et hérésie dans le christianisme des premiers siècles.

die Gesamtheit aller Interpretationen Jesu von Nazareth durch Personen und Gruppen im kulturellen und geographischen Bereich, den wir als „ Syrien " bezeichnen. In diesem Beziehung stehen sie mit ihren Erwartungen und Ideologien Jesu gegenüber und versuchen, in der jeweiligen kulturellen Situation den Sinn des Lebens zum Ausdruck zu bringen. Selbstverständlich kann das auf mehrfache Weise geschehen und das Bild des ältesten Christentums ist deshalb weit entfernt von Einförmigkeit. Wenn man das älteste Christentum in diesem Gebiet auf die ersten drei Jahrhunderte A. D. einschränkt, ist „ ältestes " fast synonym mit „ unbekannt " oder , dunkel ". Unsere Kenntnisse vom Anfang und von der weiteren Geschichte des Christentums in dieser Gegend sind fragmentarisch und hypothetisch. Welche Schriften gehören zu diesem Bereich und welche Gruppen haben dort Einfluss ausgeübt ? Das sind alles Fragen, die nicht eindeutig beantwortet werden können. Erst mit Ephraem am Ende des vierten Jahrhunderts haben wir festeren Boden unter den Füssen. Bei Ephraem kommen Rechtgläubigkeit und Ketzerei zusammen, weil er in der Auseinandersetzung mit den Häretikern seine Rechtgläubigkeit entwickelt und bewahrt und darin seine Interpretation Jesu gibt. Bei Ephraem sind Rechtgläubigkeit und Ketzerei fast dialektisch miteinander verbunden : die Häresien liefern Themen, die rechtgläubig interpretiert werden, und das Bild Ephraems von Person und Wirken Jesu gibt ihm Waffen zur Bestreitung der Häretiker, mit denen er teilweise in gleichen kulturellen Tradition steht. Erst bei Ephraem werden die Häretiker zu Ketzern, ist die Polarisierung vorläufig definitiv geworden als Endpunkt einer langen Entwicklung.

Mit diesen summarischen Gedanken ist der Rahmen dieses Vortrages abgesteckt worden, dessen Thesen nun mit Belegen unterbaut werden sollen. Zunächst beschäftigen wir uns mit methodischen Fragen, weiter arbeitend in der Spur Walter Bauers und seiner Kritiker. Zweitens betrachten wir das Phänomen des altsyrischen Christentums und versuchen, es näher zu umschreiben und zu charakterisieren, und drittens betrachten wir das Oeuvre und die Theologie Ephraems als die Resultante einer rechtgläubigen und häretischen Entwicklung.

Wie bekannt hat W. Bauer das traditionelle kirchliche Schema — Unglaube, Rechtgläubigkeit, Irrglaube — umgekehrt und für eine Anzahl Gebiete glaubwürdig gemacht, dass die Reihenfolge : Unglaube, Irrglaube, Rechtgläubigkeit den wirklichen geschichtlichen Ereignissen eher angemessen ist. Er verwendet diese Termini, wie der spätere kirchliche Sprachgebrauch als normative Bezeichnungen. Mit anderen Worten : Das Christentum z.B. im Edessa des zweiten Jahrhunderts A. D. hat Merkmale, die die spätere orthodoxe Kirche als ketzerisch betrachtet. Der Ursprung dieser Rechtgläubigkeit ist in Rom zu suchen und dem Einfluss Roms ist es zu verdanken, dass die Orthodoxie sich in fast allen Ländern der damaligen Welt endgültig durchgesetzt hat.

Die zweite These Bauers kann man charakterisieren als Produkt der konstruktiven Phantasie des Verfassers, die lebhaft mit dem Argumentum e Silentio spielt, und damit eine elegante und gelehrte Fiktion entwickelt [2]. Die erste These bedeutet einen wertvollen Beitrag zur Geschichte des frühen Christentums und eröffnet der Forschung neue Gebiete. Bauer hat klar und deutlich dargestellt, dass die Entwicklung des christlichen Glaubens und seiner Institutionen nicht überall in der damaligen Oikoumene gleichartig verlaufen ist, und hat damit neue Anregungen zu historischen Forschungen von örtlich und zeitlich beschränkter Art gegeben. Das Problem „ Rechtgläubigkeit und Ketzerei " ist damit nicht gelöst, solange die Forschung daran festhält, diese Begriffe deduktiv zu verwenden und als Wesens- oder Strukturbezeichnungen aufzufassen. Die Schwierigkeit mit dem Bauerschen Buche ist, dass er einerseits rein historisch arbeitet, indem er deutlich darstellt, dass die Geschichte des Christentums an verschiedenen Orten eine andere gewesen ist, mitbestimmt von örtlichen kulturellen und sozialen Verhältnissen, anderseits aber Begriffe aus dem theologisch-dogmatischen Bereich anwendet auf diese unterschiedenen historischen Situationen, um sie zu charakterisieren. Daraus entsteht ein Kurzschluss unvergleichbarer Grössen, resultierend in einer Mischung von statischer und dynamischer Geschichtsauffassung.

In der theologischen Wissenschaft hat die gelehrte Welt eine starke Neigung zu einer statischen Geschichtsauffassung, worin das Christentum die zentrale Rolle spielt und alle anderen kulturellen und religiösen Phänomene den Hintergrund bilden und höchstens gewisse Einflüsse ausgeübt und erlitten haben. Man studiert gewisse Schriften und Gestalten, versucht festzustellen, ob diese Schriften orthodox oder nicht mehr orthodox oder häretisch sind, welche Einflüsse dazu beigetragen haben können, und welche Folgen das für spätere Erscheinungen gehabt hat.

Als Norm handhabt man gewöhnlich bei solchem Verfahren das biblische Kerygma oder den biblischen Christus oder die Wahr-

---

[2] ALTENDORF, *ZKG* 80, 1969, S. 64.

heit des Neuen Testaments, woran alle späteren Erscheinungen dann gemessen werden. Es ist aber unmöglich, dass das Neue Testament eine Norm für spätere Phänomene abgibt, da das Neue Testament nicht eindeutig ist. Wir kennen den biblischen Christus nicht, nur eine Vielfalt an Interpretationen innerhalb der Schriften, die spätere Generationen als das kanonische Neue Testament bezeichnet haben. Der irdische inkarnierte Christus versteckt sich hinter diesen Interpretationen, die untereinander verschieden sind. Überdies sind die späteren Entwicklungen, die je von einem Apostel ausgehen, oft in entgegengesetzter Richtung gegangen. Von Paulus gehen Wege zu Lukas und weiter zu den apostolischen Briefen und der späteren Orthodoxie. Aber auch Markion und die Gnostiker berufen sich auf den Heidenapostel. Und mit Johannes hat es eine gleiche Bewandtnis. Am Anfang gab es noch keine feste Norm für Wahrheit und Unwahrheit innerhalb des christlichen Glaubens. Wir können höchstens sagen, dass verschiedene Leute in verschiedenen Situationen sich mit Erscheinung und Verkündigung des irdischen Christus auseinandergesetzt haben auf eine Weise, die ihnen und ihrer kulturellen und religiösen Situation angemessen war. Auf welche Weise wir die Geschichte des frühen Christentums auch betrachten, wir haben es immer mit dem hermeneutischen Problem einer Spannung zu tun [3]. Es ist die Spannung zwischen dem vereinzelten historischen Ereignis Jesus in all seiner Zufälligkeit und der Abfolge verschiedener Sprachwelten — sagen wir Kulturen —, in denen dieses Ereignis jeweils neu zum Ausdruck kommen musste. Es gab paradoxe Lösungen, wie diejenige des Paulus, radikale Lösungen, wie die der christlichen Asketen und vernünftige Lösungen, wie die Forderung der Apologeten, ein Bündnis zwischen der christlichen Botschaft und der Kultur ihrer Umwelt herzustellen. In der Entwicklung der ersten drei Jahrhunderte hat sich aus allen diesen Lösungen in der Tradition eine rechtgläubige Theologie entwickelt, die aber nicht von den vorangehenden Entwicklungen losgelöst werden kann und auch selber nur ein Stadium in einer kontinuierlichen Entwicklung ist.

Diese hier kurz skizzierte Betrachtungsweise der Geschichte der ersten christlichen Jahrhunderte (und der Geschichte der christlichen Religion überhaupt!) impliziert, dass Begriffe wie ‚jüdisch', ‚griechisch', ‚hellenistisch' und dgl., womit die Umwelt und der Hintergrund des Christentums in seinen ersten Jahr-

---

[3] KÖSTER in KÖSTER-ROBINSON, *Entwicklungslinien*, S. 261.

hunderten meistens gekennzeichnet werden, ein wenig problematisch sind. Man hat sich daran gewöhnt, nur die Entwicklung des Christentums ins Auge zu fassen und die andere Phänomene und ihr Verhältnis zum christlichen Glauben als Hintergrund zu betrachten. Daraus resultiert ein Gesamtbild dieser Jahrhunderte, in dem nur das Christentum sich entwickelt und die anderen Religionen und Kulturen starr und unveränderlich zu sein scheinen. Es ist aber fraglich, ob man in diesen Jahrhunderten z.B. das Judentum und den Hellenismus als gesonderte Grössen scharf unterscheiden kann. Die historische Wirklichkeit ist vielmehr, dass Anhänger der jüdischen Religion in vielen Gebieten auch Träger der hellenistischen Kultur gewesen sind, und dass hellenistische Einflüsse auf das entstehende Christentum und seine Lehrbegriffe — διδαχή — über das Judentum gewirkt haben [4]. Als religionswissenschaftliche Kategorien sind ‚jüdisch', ‚hellenistisch' und dgl. noch beizubehalten, aber als deduktive Wesensbezeichnungen sind sie unbrauchbar, um historischen Verhältnissen und Abläufen gerecht zu werden. Alle diese Begriffe verhalten sich zu der historischen Wirklichkeit wie Platons Ideen zur sozialen Wirklichkeit seiner Zeit. Es sind idealistische Abstraktionen, die ungeeignet sind für ein induktives historisches Verfahren. Damit ist das Problem des Synkretismus in seiner vollen Komplexität gestellt worden, ein Synkretismus, der nicht als die Summe verschiedener kultureller Einflüsse oder Begriffe oder Vorstellungen betrachtet werden kann, sondern vielmehr in der kulturellen Mehrdeutigkeit von allerlei Vorstellungen besteht [5]. Überdies hat sich herausgestellt, dass zu gleicher Zeit z.B. Judentum, Christentum und hellenistische Religionen Schriften hervorgebracht haben, die sich mit demselben Problemen befassen, z.B. apokalyptische Schriften [6]. Das bedeutet, dass wir zuerst das Milieu kennenlernen sollen, in dem die Vorstellungen ihren Platz ind ihre Funktion haben und

---

[4] Köster in Köster-Robinson, *Entwicklungslinien*, S. 256.

[5] Cf. Drijvers, *Edessa und das jüdische Christentum*, *VigChr* 24, 1970, p. 4-33 ; *idem*, The Origins of Gnosticism as a religious and historical Problem, *NedTheolTijdschr.*, 22, 1966/67, pp. 321-351 ; *idem*, Bardaiṣan von Edessa als Vertreter des syrischen Synkretismus im zweiten Jahrhundert A. D., erscheint zunächst in den *Göttinger Orientforschungen* ; diese Vieldeutigkeit findet sich insbesondere im Bereich der Kunst, vide G. Kretschmar in J. Gutmann (ed.), *No Graven Images*. Studies in Art and the Hebrew Bible, N. Y. 1972, p. 159 ; Th. Klauser, *Studien zur Entstehungsgeschichte der christlichen Kunst*, *JbAC* 1, 1958, 20-51 ; 2, 1959, 115-145 ; 3, 1960, 112-133.

[6] Köster in Köster-Robinson, *Entwicklungslinien*, S. 253.

auf kulturell mehrdeutige Weise zum Ausdruck gebracht werden können, der kulturellen Situation gemäss. A-priori-Anwendung deduktiver Begriffe ist im diesem Rahmen ein hemmender Faktor beim Versuch, die geschichtliche Wirklichkeit zu verstehen und zu erklären.

Für das Problem „ Rechtgläubigkeit und Ketzerei im ältesten Christentum " überhaupt und im ältesten syrischen Christentum insbesondere folgt daraus, dass Rechtgläubigkeit und Ketzerei nur als historische Begriffe aufzufassen sind, und dass man die geistigen Auseinandersetzungen des zweiten Jahrhunderts „ nicht als species in einem vorhandenen Genus der Ketzerbekämpfung versteht, sondern als historisches Phänomen sui generis " [7].

Wenn man zweitens mehr Klarheit gewinnen will über den begrenzten Bereich, der mit dem geographischen Namen „ Syrien " angedeutet zu werden pflegt, dann ist es auffallend, dass der Euphrat oft als wichtige Grenze betrachtet wird zwischen einerseits Coele-Syrien- sagen wir das Gebiet um Antiochien- und anderseits Osrhoene, das Gebiet rundum Edessa. W. Bauer hat diese Gebiete in seinem Buch gesondert behandelt und das ist durchwegs so geblieben. Nur ist sich die gelehrte Welt darüber nicht einig, welche Schriften im zweiten Jahrhundert in Coele-Syrien entstanden sind und welche in Osrhoene. Entstehungsort und -Zeit der *Oden Salomos* sind z.B. unbekannt. Es gibt Gelehrte, die behaupten, dass die Oden in einem syrisch-sprachigen Gebiet entstanden sind [8] und deshalb als Zeugnisse für eine spezifisch syrische Theologie in Anspruch genommen werden müssen [9]. Andere halten das Griechische als Originalsprache der *Oden Salomos* für wahrscheinlicher und denken dann an Antiochien als Entstehungsort [10]. Derzeit hat H. Schlier viele Parallelen aus den *Oden Salomos* zu den theologischen Vorstellungen der Ignatiusbriefe angeführt, die

---

[7] ALTENDORF, *ZKG* 80, 1969, S. 74.

[8] A. ADAM, *Die ursprüngliche Sprache der Salomon-Oden*, *ZNW* 52, 1961, S. 141-156 ; A. VÖÖBUS, *Neues Licht zur Frage der Originalsprache der Oden Salomos*, *Le Muséon* 75, 1962, S. 275-290 ; J. A. EMERTON, *Some Problems of Text and Language in the Odes of Solomon*, *JThS* 18, 1967, p. 372-406.

[9] A. F. J. KLIJN, *Das Thomasevangelium und das altsyrische Christentum*, *VigChr* 15, 1961, p. 153f. ; idem, *The Influence of jewish Theology on the Odes of Solomon and the Acts of Thomas*, *Aspects du Judéo-Christianisme*, Paris 1965, pp. 167-179 ; W. CRAMER, *Die Engelvorstellungen bei Ephräm dem Syrer*, *OrChrAn* 173, Roma 1965, S. 25-28.

[10] I. ORTIZ DE URBINA, *Patrologia Syriaca*, altera editio, Roma 1965, p. 228.

zweifelsohne in Antiochien beheimatet sind [11]. Als zweites Beispiel dürfen die pseudoklementinischen Schriften genannt werden, deren sogenannte Grundschrift, die *Kerygmata Petrou*, aller Wahrscheinlichkeit nach irgendwo in Coele-Syrien im Anfang des dritten Jahrhunderts in griechischer Sprache geschrieben ist. Die *Kerygmata Petrou* haben Beziehungen zum Edessenischen Christentum und zu Vorstellungen, die in Antiochien zu Hause sind, so dass G. Strecker schreibt : „ Das Judenchristentum der KP befindet sich auf der Grenzscheide zwischen dem griechischen und edessenischen Syrien " [12]. G. Strecker führt als Belege für diese These an, dass die paulinischen Briefe und die Apostelgeschichte in der KP-Schrift nicht positiv zitiert sind, und dass nur das Alte Testament und die vier Evangelien als heilige Schriften herangezogen werden, was eine auffallende Parallele im Kanon der edessenischen Christen hat. Die Grundschrift enthält aber auch theologische Konzeptionen, die edessenischen Schriften parallel sind. Die Gesetze der Länder, die in Bardaiṣans berühmtem Dialog *De Fato* als Belege dafür angeführt werden, dass die menschliche Freiheit stärker ist als die Macht des Fatums, haben auch ihren Platz in der pseudoklementinischen Grundschrift, wo sie eine gleiche Funktion haben [13]. Die Schöpfungslehre des Bardaiṣan kennt die Vorstellung der Vermischung der reinen Elemente, die zur Folge hat, dass das Böse aktiv wird, i.c. die Finsternis eine Chance hat, sich mit den reinen Elementen zu vermischen. Im pseudoklementinischen Roman entsteht das Böse desgleichen aus einer Art „ krasis ". Wenn H. J. Schoeps behauptet, dass „ diese Lehre von der Mischung alleiniges Eigentum des Homilisten ist ", hat er mit dieser Behauptung zweifelsohne Unrecht [14]. Es scheint daher angebracht, eine Untersuchung darüber durchzuführen, ob die Anschauungen des Bardaiṣan sich auch weiter im pseudoklementinischen Roman noch finden, welche Untersuchung hier nicht verfolgt werden kann [15]. Es gibt also gewisse Indizien, das Osrhoene und Coele-Syrien nicht

---

[11] H. SCHLIER, *Religionsgeschichtliche Untersuchungen zu den Ignatiusbriefen*, *BZNW* 8, Giessen 1929, *passim*.

[12] G. STRECKER, Nachtrag zu W. BAUER, *Rechtgläubigkeit und Ketzerei*, S. 262.

[13] Cf. B. REHM, *Bardesanes in den Pseudoclementinen*, *Philologus* 93, 1938, S. 218-247 ; DRIJVERS, *Bardaiṣan of Edessa*, Assen 1966, p. 60-76 ; cf. C. COLPE, *ThLZ* 93, 1968, Sp. 436.

[14] H. J. SCHOEPS, *Der Ursprung des Bösen und das Problem der Theodizee im pseudoklementinischen Roman*, *RechScRel.* 60, 1972, S. 136.

[15] Eine derartige Untersuchung wird demnächst vom hiesigen Autor veröffentlicht.

ganz verschiedene Welten gewesen sind, und dass ein Austausch von Ideen und Schriften stattgefunden hat. Dasselbe gilt auch für den weiteren Bereich der Kultur : es ist am wahrscheinlichsten, dass die Mosaiken, die in Edessa /Urfa in ziemlich grosser Anzahl gefunden wurden, von Mosaiklegern aus Antiochien gelegt worden sind, oder ihr Muster in Antiochien haben. Im ganzen Süden der Türkei findet sich eine Reihe von Mosaiken, von Antiochien bis Edessa reichend, an einer wichtigen Verkehrstrasse entlang. Es ist daher nicht allzu kühn anzunehmen, dass das Christentum, der christliche Glaube, in Edessa bekannt geworden ist von Antiochien aus. Wenn man von Jerusalem nach Edessa reiste, führte der Weg über Antiochien.

Syrien im weitesten Sinne ist also ein ausgedehntes Gebiet mit einer Vielfalt an kulturellen Formen und mit mindestens zwei Sprachen : Griechisch und Aramäisch, c.q. Syrisch. In Antiochien war gewiss das Griechische vorherrschend, in Edessa das Syrische, obwohl man in der letztgenannten Stadt bestimmt Griechisch gekannt hat. Es gibt griechische Inschriften aus Edessa und die berühmte Grabschrift des Amaššemeš ist zweisprachig: griechisch und aramäisch [16]. Ich selber fand in Sumatar Harabesi im Tektek-Gebirge Reste einer zweisprachigen Inschrift, griechisch und aramäisch, wahrscheinlich aus dem Anfang des dritten Jahrhunderts vor Christi Geburt. Der Einfluss der parthischen Kultur hat sich in Osrhoene Geltung verschafft, wie sich in Kleidung und Schmuck der auf den Mosaiken abgebildeten Leute und aus der Glyptik zeigt [17]. Einfluss der Parther ist in Coele-Syrien nicht anzunehmen, und so gibt es allerhand Unterschiede im geographischen Raum Syrien. Auch der christliche Glaube bildet hier keine Ausnahme und hat eine Vielfalt an Formen entwickelt. Syrien ist die Heimat des Bischofs Ignatius von Antiochien, aber dort ist auch der Gnostiker Saturnilus zu Hause. Der Ursprung des Gnostizismus überhaupt wird in Syrien gesucht, auf jeden Fall ist Syrien ein Musterbeispiel für ein Gebiet, wo synkretistische religiöse Formen leicht entstehen können.

Es scheint darum angebracht und methodisch am richtigsten, in diesem kulturell und religiös uneinheitlichen Gebiet einen Teil

---

[16] Cf. J. Pirenne, *Aux origines de la Graphie syriaque*, *Syria* 40, 1963, pp. 109-115 ; J. B. Segal, *Edessa, 'the blessed City'*, Oxford 1970, p. 29 und Pl. 30b ; Drijvers, *Old-Syriac (Edessean) Inscriptions*, Leiden 1972, p.x.

[17] Cf. D. Schlumberger, *l'Orient hellénisé, l'Art grec et ses héritiers dans l'Asie non méditerranéenne*, Paris 1970, p. 102, 205 ; Segal, *Edessa*, p. 39ff. ; B. Ehlers, *Kann das Thomasevangelium aus Edessa stammen ?*, *NovTest* 12, 1970, S. 294ff.

zu isolieren und gesondert zu betrachten. In kleinem Umfange zeigen sich dort die gleichen Phänomene, wie im ganzen Gebiet; sie sind aber bequemer zu analysieren und miteinander in Verbindung zu setzen. Es liegt nahe, hier Edessa zu wählen, nicht nur weil W. Bauers These von Rechtgläubigkeit und Ketzerei sich am glänzendsten an der Geschichte des Christentums in dieser Stadt demonstrieren lässt und in gewissem Sinne mustergültig ist für seine weiteren Ausführungen — wobei ich bequemlichkeitshalber die methodischen Bedenken übergehe —, aber auch weil ziemlich viel bekannt ist vom kulturellen, sozialen und religiösen Milieu in dieser Stadt im zweiten und dritten Jahrhundert A. D., als das Christentum hier bekannt wurde und sich weiter entwickelte.

Die Verkündigung des christlichen Glaubens in Edessa hat einen nichtapostolischen Ursprung; vielmehr soll man annehmen, dass die christliche ‚didache' dort bruchstücksweise bekannt geworden ist, im Laufe des zweiten Jahrhunderts, vielleicht schon früher [18]. Die in der *Doctrina Addai* geschilderten Ereignisse dienen ja nur apologetischen Zwecken, um die spätere Rechtgläubigkeit unmittelbar mit dem Herrn und einem Briefwechsel mit Ihm in Verbindung zu bringen. Auch kann man dieser Schrift nicht ein ursprüngliches sogenanntes Judenchristentum entnehmen, das in Edessa im zweiten Jahrhundert zu Hause gewesen wäre [19]. Überdies ist dieses Judenchristentum eine theologische Abstraktion, die sich historisch nicht definieren lässt. Das einzige, was feststellbar ist, ist die Anwesenheit von Markioniten im zweiten Jahrhundert, gegen die Bardaiṣan bekanntlich in Dialogen polemisiert hat. Reste dieser Dialoge finden sich in der *Vita des Aberkios*, eines heftigen Anti-Markioniten im Orient [20]. Damit sind die wichtigsten Persönlichkeiten des edessenischen Christentums in seinen Anfängen gleich genannt worden: Markion und Bardaiṣan. Daneben gab es noch andere Gruppen, z.B. die des Palût, des Vorläufers der späteren Orthodoxie in Edessa. Wie mehrfach betont, klagt Ephraem, dass die Rechtgläubigen Palutianer genannt werden [21]. Daraus kann man ableiten, dass Palut Haupt einer Gruppe ge-

---

[18] BAUER, *Rechtgläubigkeit und Ketzerei*, S. 6ff.; SEGAL, *Edessa*, p. 62ff.

[19] Cf. DRIJVERS, *Edessa und das jüdische Christentum*, p. 30ff.; EHLERS, *Thomasevangelium*, S. 293ff.

[20] Cf. Th. NISSEN, *Die Petrusakten und ein bardesanitischer Dialog in der Aberkiosvita*, *ZNW* 9, 1908, S. 315-328; H. GRÉGOIRE, *Bardesane et S. Abercius*, *Byzantion* 25-27, 1955-57, p. 363-368; DRIJVERS, *Bardaiṣan*, p. 170f.

[21] EPHRAEM, *Hymni contra Haereses* 22, 5,6, ed. E. BECK, *CSCO, Script. Syri* 76, Louvain 1957; BAUER, *Rechtgläubigkeit*, S. 22-26.

wesen ist, die als die geistigen Vorfahren Ephraems betrachtet werden kann. Ob daneben noch andere Gruppen oder Strömungen in Edessa beheimatet gewesen sind, ist eine umstrittene Sache. Die *Oden Salomos*, das *Thomasevangelium* und die *Thomas-Akten*, die Quqiten und Tatian werden bald für das edessenische Christentum in Anspruch genommen, bald mit ebenso starker Überzeugung abgelehnt. Es ist unmöglich, im Rahmen dieses Vortrages alle Argumente pro und contra zu analysieren, um ein sicheres Resultat zu gewinnen. Ich möchte nur behaupten, dass es wahrscheinlich ist, dass das *Thomasevangelium* sowie die *Thomas-Akten* und die *Oden Salomos* schon früh in Edessa bekannt geworden sind, obwohl nicht zu beweisen ist, dass diese Schriften dort geschrieben wurden [22]. Sie haben Einfluss auf die Textgeschichte der neutestamentlichen Schriften in Edessa ausgeübt und sind zusammen mit anderen Teilen und Traditionen des edessenischen Christentums des zweiten Jahrhunderts vom Manichäismus übernommen worden. Es ist sehr auffallend, dass der Manichäismus viele Schriften und Traditionen in sein Religionssystem hineingepasst hat, die alle auf irgendeine Weise zu Edessa in Beziehung gesetzt werden. Marcion und Bardaiṣan gelten als die zwei Gerechten, die die Kirche nach Paulus gekannt hat und die die richtige christliche Tradition weitergegeben haben bis an Mani [23]. Der Manichäismus hat das *Thomasevangelium* benützt und die *Thomasakten*; das Lied von der Perle ist in Manis *Kephalaia* ausführlich expliziert [24]. Das bedeutet nicht, dass das *Thomasevangelium*, das die Manichäer gekannt haben, identisch gewesen ist mit der Schrift, wie sie in Nag Hammadi gefunden wurde. Solche Schriften sind im Laufe der Zeit in mehreren Rezensionen bekannt gewesen, die

---

[22] Cf. B. Ehlers, *Kann das Thomasevangelium aus Edessa stammen?* Ein Beitrag zur Frühgeschichte des Christentums in Edessa, *NovTest* 12, 1970, S. 284-317; A. F. J. Klijn, *Christianity in Edessa and the Gospel of Thomas*. On Barbara Ehlers, *Kann das Thomasevangelium aus Edessa stammen? NovTest* 14, 1972, pp. 70-77. cf. Drijvers, *Edessa und das jüdische Christentum*, S. 16ff. und W. Cramer, *Engelvorstellungen*, S. 28: ' Das Thomasevangelium....., so steht doch seine Bedeutung für die syrische Theologie fest. '

[23] *Kephalaia*, 13, 30ff.; cf. A. Böhlig, *Christliche Wurzeln im Manichäismus*, *Mysterion und Wahrheit*, Leiden 1968, S. 208 ff.; H.-Ch. Puech, *Le Manichéisme, son fondateur, sa doctrine*, Paris 1949, p. 70 u. Anm. 268; O. Klima, *Manis Zeit und Leben*, Prag 1962, S. 135 ff. und mein Aufsatz, *Mani und Bardaiṣan*. Ein Beitrag zur Vorgeschichte des Manichäismus, der demnächst erscheinen wird in den *Mélanges H.-Ch. Puech*, Paris 1973.

[24] Cf. G. Bornkamm, *Neutestamentliche Apokryphen*³ II, Tübingen 1964, S. 304 f, wo alle Belege.

ihre Funktion hatten im Prozess, der aus der Vielfalt der christlichen Formen die Polarisation von Rechtgläubigkeit und Ketzerei entwickelte. Das gleiche gilt für die *Oden Salomos*, von denen die griechische Version der elften Ode ‚ gnostischer ' ist als die syrische [25]. Auch die griechische Text der *Thomas-Akten* ist, gnostischer ' als der syrische, wie sich besonders bei einer Vergleichung der beiden Versionen des Perlenliedes herausstellt. Es ist sehr wahrscheinlich, dass diese syrischen Versionen eine orthodoxe Zensur bilden und deshalb bewahrt geblieben sind.

Wie oben behauptet wurde, ist Edessa nicht so isoliert gewesen, dass Schriften aus anderen Gegenden — z.B. Coele-Syrien — ihren Weg dorthin nicht fanden.

Es scheint mir also durchaus möglich zu sein, bestimmte religiöse Themen, die eine zentrale Rolle im Christentum Edessas im zweiten Jahrhundert spielten, herauszuarbeiten und mit diesem Verfahren das religiöse Mosaik der Stadt in Hauptlinien zu rekonstruieren. Am meisten charakteristisch ist das Thema der Wiedergewinnung des verlorenen Paradieses, das wir sowohl in den *Oden Salomos* wie auch in anderen Schriften aus diesem Milieu finden. Den Weg zurück zum Paradies findet der Mensch, wenn er die Weisheit geschenkt bekommt oder wenn diese ihm offenbart wird und wenn er die richtige Lebensweise innehält. Das kann in eine Kombination von Gnosis und Askese oder Enkratismus resultieren, wodurch die Seele gerettet wird und nach ihrem Ursprung zurückkehren kann. Durchwegs wird das Heil beschrieben mit Bildern, die das Paradies schildern, u.a. das Bild des göttlichen Brautgemachs [26]. Es ist im voraus klar, dass eine solche Thematik in ganz verschiedenen Richtungen entwickelt werden kann. Im Markionismus finden wir eine stark entwickelte Askese auf der Grundlage einer anti-kosmischen Theologie und eines dualistischen Gottesbegriffes. Im bardaiṣanitischen System wird eine Art Monotheismus beibehalten, so dass überliefert wird, dass Bardaiṣan den Dualismus der Markioniten stark bestritten hat. Der unter Bardaiṣans Namen überlieferte Dialog *De Fato*, das *Buch der Gesetze der Länder* hat eine anti-markionitische Tendenz [27]. Die Weisheits-

[25] Cf. J. A. Emerton, *Some Problems* und Drijvers, *Edessa und das jüdische Christentum*, S. 14.

[26] Cf. R. M. Grant, *The Mysterie of Marriage in the Gospel of Philip*, *VigChr* 15, 1961, p. 129-140 (*Philippusevangelium* 68, 104, 122ff) ; G. Widengren, *Mesopotamian Elements in Manichaeism*, Uppsala 1946, p. 109 ff.

[27] Cf. den Anfang des *Buches der Gesetze der Länder* : ' Si unus est Deus... qui et ipse homines creavit volens id quod iussi estis facere quare homines non ita creavit ut peccare non possent, sed in omni tempore quod

Theologie hat Verbindungen mit jüdischen Auffassungen, die Weisheit betreffend, zeigt aber auch Verwandtschaft mit hermetischen Lehren, die sich auch in Syrien, speziell Harran, entwickelt haben [28]. Kurz, eine Thematik, die das Heil schildert als die Wiedergewinnung des Paradieses durch die richtige Erkenntnis und die dazu gehörige Lebensführung, hat Anklänge an das Judentum und seine Hokma-Traditionen (das Gesetz = die offenbarte Weisheit), knüpft an bei paganen philosophischen Vorstellungen, findet Anschluss bei einheimischen mesopotamischen Überlieferungen, wie G. Widengren gezeigt hat [29], kann auf voll-entwickelte gnostische Systeme hinauslaufen, aber auch in christliche Bilder gekleidet werden, die dem Corpus Paulinum und den johanneïschen Schriften entlehnt sind. Das bedeutet nicht, dass alle diese kulturellen Traditionen in Edessa des zweiten Jahrhunderts scharf unterschieden werden können, oder dass nur eine Tradition vorherrschend gewesen sei. Vielmehr sind die überlieferten Vorstellungen in kultureller oder religiöser Hinsicht mehrdeutig und gestatten mehrere Interpretationen. So ist es durchaus möglich, die *Oden Salomos* ganz gnostisch zu interpretieren, wenn Parallelen aus dem Mandäismus zur Interpretation herangezogen werden, aber auch eine mehr ‚orthodoxe' Auslegung gehört durchaus zu den „legitimen" Möglichkeiten [30]. Dasselbe gilt für das *Thomasevangelium*, das in die Tradition der richtigen christlichen innerweltlichen Askese gestellt werden kann, aber auch eine gnostische Auslegung erlaubt. Das bedeutet nur, dass die Formen, die das Christentum in Edessa und Syrien überhaupt zeigt, nicht vom kulturellen Kontext losgelöst werden können und nur in diesem Kontext ihre Funktion haben. Die vorherrschende Stellung, die die einheimische Kultur dem christlichen Glauben gegenüber einnimmt, hat zur Folge, dass Jesus von Nazareth in erster Linie

---

bonum est facerent ' mit dem folgenden anti-markionitischen Zitat aus den Pseudoklementinen : ' Quomodo potest unum atque idem et bonum esse et iustum,' *Recognitiones*, col. 1299, cf. A. Vööbus, *A History of Asceticism in the Syrian Orient* I, Louvain 1958, p. 45.

[28] Drijvers, *Bardaiṣan of Edessa and the Hermetica. The aramaic Philosopher and the Philosophy of his Time*, *JEOL* 21, 1969-70, Leiden 1970, p. 190-210. R. Reitzenstein, *Poimandres*, Leipzig 1904, S. 166ff.

[29] Widengren, *Mesopotamian Elements*, *passim* und *idem*, *Heavenly Enthronement and Baptism. Studies in Mandaean Baptism*, *Religions in Antiquity*, ed. J. Neusner, *Essays in Memory of E. R. Goodenough*, Leiden 1968, pp. 551-582, spez. 571ff.

[30] Cf. K. Rudolph, *War der Verfasser der Oden Salomos ein « Qumran-Christ »? Ein Beitrag zur Diskussion um die Anfänge der Gnosis*, *Revue de Qumran* 4, 1964, S. 523-555.

Überbringer und Offenbarer einer himmlischen erlösenden Weisheit ist und damit den Weg zum Paradies wieder öffnet. Sein irdisches Leben ist von viel geringerer oder von keinerlei Bedeutung. In einigen Fällen bedeutet das, dass die Stellung Jesu sekundär ist und dass nachher für Ihn eine Stelle im System eingeräumt wird, z.B. im kosmogonischen und Erlösungsmythos der Quqiten und in Bardaiṣans Denken [31]. Die Formen des christlichen Glaubens sind noch nicht exklusiv und antithetisch, sondern rezeptiv und assimilationsfähig. Es ist durchaus möglich, dass sich daneben in Edessa auch Formen oder Gruppen entwickelt haben, die eine mehr ausgesprochene ‚christliche' Haltung hatten, — man kann in diesem Zusammenhang denken an Palut und seine Anhänger —, aber eine Art Symbiose aller dieser Gruppen darf man voraussetzen, ohne Ansprüche auf den alleinigen Besitz der Wahrheit.

Am besten lässt sich diese Auffassung der Geschichte des Christentums in Edessa darlegen an der Linie, die von Bardaiṣan über Mani nach Ephraem läuft. Aus allen vorhandenen Zeugnissen kann man Bardaiṣans Denken in Hauptlinien rekonstruieren und zu gleicher Zeit stellt sich dann heraus, dass dieses Denken Elemente von ganz verschiedener Herkunft in sich aufgenommen hat. Das soll man sich nicht als einen künstlichen Prozess vorstellen, sondern vielmehr als einen unbewussten Eklektizismus, wobei das Milieu die Bilder und Motive liefert. Die Kosmologie des aramäischen Philosophen wird gekennzeichnet durch die Vorstellung der Vermischung der reinen Elemente/Wesenheiten miteinander und dadurch mit der Finsternis. Diese Störung der ursprünglichen Harmonie durch einen blinden Zufall ist Ursache des Bösen in der Welt. Der Herr der Elemente sendet dann das Wort des Denkens, um aus dem Gemisch die Welt zu schaffen, nachdem dieses die Finsternis teilweise vertrieben hat. Die Schöpfung umfasst die Erde und die Planeten und Sterne; letztere enthalten ein geringeres Quantum Finsternis und spielen eine Rolle bei der Schöpfung des Menschen, dessen Körper von den Planetmächten aus dem Gemisch der reinen Elemente mit der Finsternis geschaffen wird. Nach der Harmonie, die vor dem Anfang aller Zeiten war, gibt der Zufall also Anlass zu der Schöpfung der Welt, wo drei Ebenen unterschieden werden können: Gott, die Sterne und Planeten und die Erde. Ganz parallel dazu gibt es drei Ebenen, die für das mensch-

[31] DRIJVERS, *Quq and the Quqites. An unknown sect in Edessa in the second century A.D.*, *Numen* 14, 1967, pp. 104-129; namentlich Theodor bar Konais Bericht über die Quqiten ist in diesem Zusammenhang von Interesse; DRIJVERS, *Bardaiṣan of Edessa and the Hermetica*, p. 206.

liche Dasein bestimmend sind : den Geist, die Seele und den Körper. Der Körper gehört zur Natur, Physis, wo Unfreiheit herrscht, mit anderen Worten, wo die Vermischung, die Störung der Harmonie, vollkommen ist. Die Seele gehört zu den Planetmächten, die die Schicksale des Menschen während seines irdischen Lebens bestimmen. Diese Schicksale sind nicht für alle Menschen gleich, wie die Gesetze der Natur, also gibt es auf dieser Ebene eine grössere Freiheit. Der Geist ist Gabe Gottes, vollkommen frei und deshalb der Sitz der Moral. Das Befolgen der Gebote, summarisch der goldenen Regel, trägt bei zum Vertreiben der Finsternis. Die zentrale Stelle im Schöpfungs- und Erlösungsprozess wird also vom Geist gespielt ; einerseits vom Wort des Denkens, anderseits vom menschlichen Geist, dem Göttlichen im Menschen. Nur dieser Geist ist imstande, am Anfang und während der Menschheitsgeschichte das Böse zu bekämpfen. Wenn die Finsternis ganz und gar vertrieben worden ist, tritt die ursprüngliche Harmonie wieder ein und ist das Intermezzo der Welt- und Menschheitsgeschichte wieder zu Ende gekommen [32]. In der Überlieferung wird das Wort des Denkens, das die Welt schuf, dem Logos, dem präexistenten Christus, gleichgestellt. Dieser Christus ist auch derjenige, der den menschlichen Geist aufweckt, diesen seines Ursprungs bewusst macht und der Seele den Weg zurück zu ihrem Ursprung, dem Brautgemach des Lichtes, zeigt. Diese Kenntnis ist moralisch und intellektuell und deshalb erlösend. Bardaiṣan hat seine Lehre auch in Hymnen verbreitet, von denen Ephraem Auszüge bewahrt hat. Dort finden wir den Vater und die Mutter des Lebens und andere symbolische Gestalten, die Anklänge an gnostische Systeme in Syrien aufweisen [33].

Wenn man das Ganze, das hier sehr summarisch zusammengefasst ist, überschaut, gibt es eine Reihe von Möglichkeiten, dieses System geistesgeschichtlich einzuordnen. Es hat enge Verwandtschaft mit der Hermetik, wo im ersten und dreizehnten Traktat des *Corpus Hermeticum* der Nous eine parallele Funktion wie das

---

[32] *Vide* : *Bardaiṣan of Edessa, passim* ; Bardaiṣan von Edessa als Repräsentant des syrischen Synkretismus, und Das Bild des Bardaiṣan in der syrischen literarischen Überlieferung ; beide letztgenannte Aufsätze werden veröffentlicht werden in den *Göttinger Orientforschungen* und enthalten eine Diskussion mit resp. B. Ehlers, Bardesanes von Edessa-ein syrischer Gnostiker, *ZKG* 1970, 334-351, und W. Strothmann, *Bardaiṣan in der syrischen Literatur*, das auch in den *Göttinger Orientforschungen* veröffentlicht wird ; dort alle Literatur und Belege.

[33] Cf. W. Bousset, *Hauptprobleme der Gnosis*, Göttingen 1907, S. 16, 96ff. ; Widengren, *Mesopotamian Elements*, p. 16ff.

Wort des Denkens hat [34]. Die Rolle der Planeten im Schöpfungsprozess ist vergleichbar mit der der sogenannten neuen Götter in Platons *Timaeus*, so dass Bardaiṣan bestimmte Traditionen des Platonismus weiterführt und auch sonst spätantike philosophische Auffassungen vertritt, namentlich auf dem Gebiet der Elementenlehre. Es ist aber auch möglich, Bardaiṣans System in erster Linie zu betrachten als philosophisch-gnostische Auslegung der ersten Kapitel des Buches Genesis, wie das in jüdischen Kreisen und von Gnostikern geschah. Als Astrologe ist es der Erbe einheimischer mesopotamischer Lehren und überdies ist ein gewisser Einfluss des Mazdaïsmus unverkennbar, speziell wo Bardaiṣan die Auffassung vertritt, dass Gott und die reinen Elemente sich innerhalb eines begrenzten Raumes befinden [35]. Bardaiṣans Anthropologie ist fast derjenigen des Tatians gleich, wie aus einer Vergleichung des dreizehnten Kapitels der *Oratio ad Graecos* mit Bardaiṣanitischen Vorstellungen hervorgeht [36]. Wir können noch einige Zeit auf diese Weise fortfahren, aber es ist klar, dass Bardaiṣans Christentum aufgeklärt und weltoffen ist, und ganz in der kulturellen Tradition seiner Stadt und Welt steht. Doch wird er z.B. von Euseb nicht als ein echter Häretiker betrachtet. Der Kirchenhistoriker spricht mit Respekt über ihn, obwohl er nicht ganz frei ist von häretischen Überresten (*H. E.*, IV, 30).

Erst Ephraem am Ende des vierten Jahrhunderts bekämpft die Bardaiṣaniten aufs heftigste, weil er die Manichäer und ihre Lehren als die konsequente Fortsetzung der Bardaiṣanitischen Auffassungen sieht. Eine Vergleichung der Bardaiṣanitischen Kosmologie mit der Manichäischen ergibt, dass Mani das ‚Scenario' der Schöpfung dualistisch radikalisiert hat und damit die Erlösung der menschlichen Seele inhaltlich anders bestimmt. Das Böse hat bei Mani eine eigene Aktionsfähigkeit und deshalb ist Reinigung im menschlichen Körper unmöglich : man soll die Finsternis nicht bestreiten oder vertreiben, sondern ihr entfliehen und das geschieht in der Askese. Bei Bardaiṣan ist die Gnosis dagegen Verwirklichung der menschlichen Freiheit und Realisierung des

---

[34] *Bardaiṣan of Edessa and the Hermetica*, passim.

[35] Cf. P. Boyancé in U. Bianchi, *Le Origini dello Gnosticismo*, Leiden 1967, pp. 344-352 ; U. Bianchi, *Bardesane Gnostico. Le Fonti del Dualismo di Bardesane, Umanità e Storia*. Scritti in Onore di Adelchi Attisani, p. 1-15 ; R. C. Zaehner, *Zurvan, A Zoroastrian Dilemma*, Oxford 1955, p. 197f.

[36] Cf. G. F. Hawthorne, *Tatian and his Discourse to the Greeks*, *HThR* 57, 1964, p. 161-188 ; cf. Drijvers, *Edessa und das jüdische Christentum*, S. 20f.

Ethos im irdischen Dasein. Die Probleme und Themen sind gleich, die Lösung grundverschieden [37].

Wenn wir uns nun Ephraem zuwenden, fällt es auf, dass er sosehr von seinen Gegnern in Anspruch genommen wird, dass er wiederholt in seinen theologischen und exegetischen Ausführungen sich von ihren Fragen leiten lässt und bis in die gewählte Terminologie von ihnen abhängig ist. Einige Beispiele genügen und sind dafür exemplarisch. Wie bekannt, ist der Begriff *itjâ* ein zentraler Begriff in Bardaiṣans Kosmologie, womit er ungeschaffene Wesenheiten andeutet, die sich miteinander vermischen und aus denen die Welt geschaffen wird. Ephraems Exegese von Gen. 1,1-5 wird von dieser Bardaiṣanitischen Lehre vollkommen beherrscht bis in alle Einzelheiten der Auslegung, wie Jansma dargestellt hat [38]. Ausdrücklich sagt Ephraem, dass Wasser, Wind, Feuer, Licht und Finsternis keine *ityê* sind, sondern erschaffene Dinge, und in dieser Reihenfolge ist Bardaiṣans Auffassung das Modell gewesen. Ephraem nennt in seiner Interpretation diese Elemente auch Naturen, *keyânê*, und stimmt damit mit dem Buch der Gesetze der Länder überein, das auch an einigen Stellen *ityê* und *keyânê* als Synomyme verwendet [39]. Dasselbe findet man in Ephraems Prose Refutations, wo er Licht und Finsternis auch *keyânê* = Naturen nennt [40]. Ich bin der Meinung, dass Ephraem nicht den Terminus *keyânê* verwendet, um ‚das Kreatürliche besser auskommen zu lassen', wie Jansma behauptet, sondern um die Aufmerksamkeit mehr auf die Qualitäten der Wesenheiten zu lenken, als auf ihren ontischen Status. Ephraem reserviert den Terminus *ityâ* für Gott und verwendet ihn gleichwertig mit *itutâ*, nicht nur in seinen antihäretischen Schriften, sondern auch z.B. in seinen Reden über den Glauben [41]. Auffallend ist auch, dass in der Theologie Ephraems das Wort *keyânê* eine eigenartige Doppelbedeutung hat; einerseits „konkretes Individuum" anderseits „umfassende Natur". Dom Beck schreibt diese Doppelbedeutung der Eigenart des orien-

---

[37] Cf. *Mani und Bardaiṣan. Ein Beitrag zur Vorgeschichte des Manichäismus*, Mélanges H.-Ch. Puech, Paris 1973.

[38] T. JANSMA, *Ephraems Beschreibung des ersten Tages der Schöpfung. Bemerkungen über den Charakter seines Kommentars zur Genesis*, *OrChrPer* 37, 1971, 295-316.

[39] *Buch der Gesetze der Länder*, ed. F. NAU, *PS* I, 2, col. 548; 551; 579, 17; 611, 12.

[40] *S. Ephraim's Prose Refutations of Mani, Marcion, and Bardaisan*, ed. C. W. MITCHELL (completed by A. A. Bevan and F. C. Burkitt), Vol. II, London 1921, p. 196, 24-26.

[41] E. BECK, *Ephraems Reden über den Glauben*, *Studia Anselmiana* 33, Roma 1953, S. 1-4, wo die Belege und Kommentar dazu.

talischen Denkens zu, das Mangel an Abstraktionsfähigkeit besitzt [42]. Man kann aber fragen, ob Ephraem auch hier nicht von Bardaiṣan abhängig ist, weil diese Doppelbedeutung auch im *Buch der Gesetze der Länder* zu finden ist [42].

In Ephraems Anthropologie ist eine ausgesprochene voluntaristische Einstellung vorherrschend. Die Willensfreiheit ist die Gottesebenbildlichkeit der Menschen ; diese Freiheit ist an den menschlichen Geist gebunden [43] und überdies verbunden mit der menschlichen Fähigkeit zum Sprechen, mit der Gabe des Wortes. Derselbe Beck sagt, dass diese letzte Verbindung ungriechisch ist und für Ephraem kennzeichnend [44]. Wiederum fällt auf, dass auch Bardaiṣan die menschliche Freiheit mit dem Geist verbunden hat und dort die Möglichkeit zum moralischen Handeln lokalisierte. Auch Ephraem kennt den Gegensatz von Natur und Freiheit wie Bardaiṣan ; das folgende Zitat könnte ohne weiteres dem *Buche der Gesetze der Länder* entnommen sein, stammt aber in Wirklichkeit aus Ephraems *Hymnus De Conf. et Mart.* 3,5 :

> Kraft seiner Natur hungert der Mensch, kraft seines Willens fastet er.
> Kraft seiner Natur begehrt der Mensch, kraft seines Willens hält er sich rein. [45]

Wir übergehen ganz banale Übereinstimmungen, wie eine trichotomische Anthropologie, in der auch Ephraem philosophische Konzeptionen vertritt oder das Bild des Brautgemachs, womit Ephraem das himmlische Heil beschreibt.

Es ist ganz in der Tradition der syrischen Theologie, wenn Ephraem das Heil, das Christus brachte, als eine Wiedergewinnung des Paradieses sieht:

> Er (Christus) kleidete sich in Adam und öffnete damit
> das Tor des Paradieses durch seine Rückkehr [46].

Darum wird seine göttliche Natur von Ephraem auch stärker betont als die menschliche Natur. Speziell Termini wie *ityâ* und *keyânâ* und ihre christologische und theologische Anwendung

---

[42] E. Beck, *Reden über den Glauben*, p. 8 ; cf. Cramer, *Engelvorstellungen*, S. 113-117, 169f ; z.B. col. 559, 10, 15 ; 560, 12 und 564,9 *keyânâ* = umfassende Natur, col. 563, 2 und 611, 7, 12, 22 *keyânâ* = konkretes Individuum.

[43] Ephraem, *Hymni de Fide*, III, 31, cf. E. Beck, *Reden über den Glauben*, S. 65 ; *Hymni de Paradiso* VI, 10, 15 ; cf. Beck, *Ephraems Hymnen über das Paradies*, *Studia Anselmiana* 26, Roma 1951, pp. 53-55.

[44] *Reden über den Glauben*, S. 46, Anm. 2.

[45] Zitiert von Beck, *Reden über den Glauben*, S. 88.

[46] *Contra Haereses* XXVI, 6, 10.

geben einen ‚ Einblick in die völlig ungeklärte Terminologie der syrischen Kirche zur Zeit Ephraems ‘, wie Dom Beck nach eingehenden Untersuchungen feststellte [47]. Findet diese ungeklärte Terminologie ihre Ursache in den vorangehenden Jahrhunderten, in denen von Rechtgläubigkeit und Ketzerei noch nicht die Rede war, nur von Verschiedenheit der christlichen Formen ? Als erster hat Ephraem den Nachdruck gelegt auf Jesu irdisches Leben, sein Kreuz und Leiden, aber doch ist der Christus für ihn eher der vom Himmel gekommene Gott, als der Mensch aus Nazareth. Auch darin gleicht er seinen Gegnern. Was wir brauchen, um in diesen Dingen mehr Klarheit zu gewinnen, ist eine Geschichte der syrischen Theologie, anfangend mit den Zeugnissen des zweiten Jahrhunderts und auslaufend auf Ephraem, ständig vergleichend, wobei Übereinstimmungen und Unterschiede herausgearbeitet werden sollen, wobei Entwicklungen von Begriffen verfolgt werden und bestimmte Motive in ihrer Verbreitung und Funktion untersucht werden. Intuitiv gewinnt man den Eindruck, dass Rechtgläubigkeit und Ketzerei mehr miteinander gemeinsam haben, als man zu glauben geneigt ist, und dass die Unterschiede oft nichttheologischer Natur sind. Die Entwicklung von Rechtgläubigkeit und Ketzerei war ‚ ein Scheidungsprozess von grundsätzlicher Wichtigkeit, darüber war man sich in der Forschung immer klar ; aber nicht darüber, was dieser Prozess für beide Seiten eigentlich bedeutete ‘ [48]. Ephraems Theologie ist das Ergebnis aller vorangehenden christlichen Traditionen in Edessa, die er zugleich zum grössten Teil als häretisch betrachtet und bekämpft. Darin steht er einzigartig da. Im Grunde wird das Problem von Rechtgläubigkeit und Ketzerei nur von einer Frage beherrscht : inwieweit ein Mensch ganz neu anfangen kann im Leben und im Glauben. Bardaiṣan hat das nicht gewollt, Ephraem hat es nicht gekonnt. Damit sind Übereinstimmung und Unterschied zwischen Rechtgläubigkeit und Ketzerei theologisch und historisch angegeben und damit sind wir zurück gekommen zum Anfang dieses Referates. Vielleicht ist die Spannung zwischen dem Theologen und dem Historiker in einer Person identisch mit derjenigen zwischen Rechtgläubigkeit und Ketzerei in derselben Person. Aber kann man anderes erwarten von jemandem, der auf der Suche ist nach dem wahren, dem „ rechtgläubigen “ Bardaiṣan von Edessa ?

---

[47] *Reden über den Glauben*, S. 86.

[48] K. Rudolph, *Einige grundsätzliche Bemerkungen zum Thema « Schisma und Häresie » unter religionsvergleichendem Gesichtspunkt*, *Ex Orbe Religionum. Studia Geo Widengren oblata* II, Leiden 1972, S. 338.

IV

Hellenistic and Oriental Origins

'THE holy men who minted the ideal of the saint in society came from Syria', so we are told by Peter Brown in his well-known article on 'The Rise and Function of the Holy Man in Late Antiquity'.[1] Brown traces the rise of the holy man back into the villages of the Syrian countryside which, especially during the fourth and fifth century, were passing through a crisis of leadership and were in need of a good patron. The holy man living on the edge of the desert and the *oikoumene* took on the role of mediator in village life and as a stranger exercised his power in the complicated network of Syrian rural society. Although his role is applicable to urban conditions, the specific characteristics of the Syrian villages surrounded by desert provide a sufficient explanation for the rise and function of the holy man who, in complete social disengagement, coming as a stranger from the desert, was able to solve the problems of life and thought of simple folk. Brown's emphasis on the Syrian countryside as the primary stage of the holy man relieved him from a closer examination of the cultural background of the saints: a sociological approach replaces a wider cultural one which also inquires after the cultural sources for the lifestyle of the holy men and asks what is specifically Syrian in it.

Does Syria have a specific cultural identity which distinguishes it from other regions in the Roman Empire? Syria as well as Mesopotamia is a thoroughly bilingual country; large groups of the population could speak and understand Greek besides their native tongue and many Lives of saints and other works were translated from Syriac into Greek or vice versa. That is why we speak of the *tréfonds oriental* of Byzantine hagiography.[2]

But is a linguistic frontier equal to a cultural frontier in the hellenized Orient? To consider the Syriac-speaking villages as untouched by Hellenistic civilization seems too simple, however attractive the idea of a barbarian saint might be. Furthermore it is misleading to consider Northern Mesopotamia as an area that was

1. P.R.L. Brown, 'The Rise and Function of the Holy Man in Late Antiquity', *JRS* 61 (1971), 80-101, esp. 82. Cf. id., *The World of Late Antiquity from Marcus Aurelius to Muhammad* (London 1971), 101: 'In villages dedicated for millennia to holding their own against nature, the holy man had deliberately chosen "anti-culture" – the neighbouring desert, the nearest mountain crags. In a civilisation identified exclusively with town life, the monks had committed the absurd – they had "made a city in the desert".'
2. See P. Peeters, *Le tréfonds oriental de l'hagiographie byzantine* (SubsHag 26 [1950]), 165.

free from contacts with the West and therefore characterized by a strong and unbroken Semitic tradition which made itself manifest in Edessene Christianity as distinct from its Antiochene hellenized counterpart in Coele-Syria. There is something like Greek in Syriac disguise and a local cultural tradition in Greek dress, so that the division of languages in Syria and Mesopotamia is not identical with different cultural tradition.[3] The hellenistic and the oriental do not exclude each other and, therefore, remain to be defined. Yet it seems to be true that Syria developed a special type of saint with a lifestyle of his own, who made his appearance in towns and villages in Syria and Mesopotamia and there represented divine power.[4] In a sense his rise and function is independent of local geography which only provides a scene, but does not dictate the role. That is explicitly stated by Theodoret in a touching remark at the end of the Life of Maisymas (14): Those who practise ascesis are not hindered by a stay in towns or villages, because they prove that it is also possible to attain the summit of virtue surrounded by crowds.[5]

It is, therefore, appropriate to analyse some Lives of Eastern saints more closely, not only to analyse these images as products of the society around the holy man, but also to have a closer look at the inherent ideology of the Lives. The holy man represents the needs of the society and a religious ideology in a characteristic lifestyle. His life is symbolical, his actions, cures and deeds of power refer to a religious myth and make plain how religious behaviour has sociological and ideological components.[6]

The holy man of Edessa

A typical example of a Syriac life of a saint is the legend of the Man of God from Rome, who lived his holy life at Edessa.[7] It dates from the second half of the fifth century and tells the story of an anonymous nobleman from Rome, the only child of rich parents, who was born through prayers and the special grace of God, a prerogative that he shares with Isaac, Samuel, John the Baptist and other biblical prototypes of holy men. In humility he devoted himself to gain 'great science'

3. See Fergus Millar, 'Paul of Samosata, Zenobia and Aurelian: The Church, local culture and political allegiance in third-century Syria', *JRS* 61 (1971), 1-17, esp. 2ff; id., *JJS* 29 (1978), 3ff; H. Drijvers, *Aufstieg und Niedergang der römischen Welt* viii (1977), 885ff. A Vööbus, *History of Asceticism in the Syrian Orient,* (CSCO Sub 14 and 17 [1958], i.140 is of a different opinion: in his view, Mesopotamia 'had remained almost untouched by Hellenism and contacts with the West'. Cf. R. Schmidt, 'Die Sprachen im römischen Reich der Kaiserzeit', *BJb* 40 (1980), 196ff.

4. A. Vööbus, op.cit.; S.P. Brock, 'Early Syrian Asceticism', *Numen* 20 (1973), 1-19; P. Canivet, 'Le monachisme syrien selon Théodoret de Cyr', *ThH* 42 (1977), 255; A.J. Festugière, *Les moines d'Orient* (Paris 1961-5), i (= *Culture ou sainteté).*

5. Theodoret, *H.Ph.* xiv; cf. Canivet, op.cit., 248 and 263 on Maisymas.

6. See J.A. Delaunay, 'Rite et symbolique en ACTA THOMAE vers. syr. I.2a et ss', *Mémorial Jean de Menasce,* ed. P. Gignoux (Tehran 1974), 11-24.

7. A. Amiaud, 'La légende syriaque de Saint Alexis l'homme de Dieu', BEHEt 79 (1889); cf. A. Baumstark, *Geschichte der syrischen Literatur* (Bonn 1922), 96; and C.E. Stebbins, 'Les origines de la légende de Saint Alexis', *Revue Belge de Philologie et d'Histoire* 51 (1973), 497-507.

(*yd't' sgy't'*) and despised all earthly things. His parents arranged a bride for him and a wedding-feast to which the whole city was invited. But on the first day of this feast the holy man escaped his bride and his city, found a ship and sailed to Seleucia in Syria, whence he arrived at Edessa. There he used to stay in the church, fasting in the daytime and living off alms, since he gave away his riches (as well as all he got and did not need) to the poor. The night, when all were asleep, he spent praying with extended arms, that is in the form of the cross – exactly the same gesture as Symeon the Stylite took up on his column. One night the *paramonarius* saw him like that and asked him where he was from. At last after long persuasion he told him the truth. When the holy man fell ill the *paramonarius* brought him to hospital. But he was absent when he died and was buried at the special cemetery for strangers. When the *paramonarius* heard what had happened he ran to the bishop Rabbula and told him how holy a man had stayed in his city and died there. Thereupon the bishop and the *paramonarius* went to the cemetery and ordered the grave to be opened. But the holy body had disappeared and only his rags were left. Since that day Rabbula devoted himself to take care of strangers, poor people, widows and orphans and even stopped his building activities to give all his attention to these pious deeds.

The holy man as alter Christus

This tale dealing with an anonymous stranger formed the starting point for the well-known legend of St Alexis via a more elaborated version that became known in Byzantium. Leaving aside all complicated questions that are connected with the further development of this legend it can be stated that the primitive form represents some typical traits of a Syrian life of a saint. Although there are some minor deviations, the lifestyle of the Man of God is an *imago Christi.* His youth is like Jesus' youth during which he 'increased in wisdom and stature and in favour with God and man' (Luke 2:52). Like Jesus he left his glory behind at the same time as he left his bride and became a *monogenēs* or *monachos,* in Syriac an *yhydy',* living in humility (cf. Phil. 2).[8] In Edessa he lived among the poor as a completely anonymous stranger from abroad, representing Christ on earth. His nightly prayer amidst the sleeping people in the church court is a symbolic imitation of Jesus' prayer in Gethsemane, when all his disciples fell asleep, and actually an *imitatio passionis Christi.* The *paramonarius* is a kind of counterpart of Peter; this becomes completely clear after the saint's death when the *paramonarius* and bishop Rabbula went to the tomb as once Peter and John did according to the Gospel of

8. On the *yhydy'* see A. Adam, 'Grundbegriffe des Mönchtums in sprachlicher Sicht', *Zeitschrift für Kirchengeschichte* 4te Folge iii.65 (1953-4), 209ff; and E. Beck, 'Zur Terminologie des ältesten syrischen Mönchtums', *Studia Anselmiana* 38 (1956), 254-67. A. Adam criticises the views of Beck and Vööbus in *Gottingische geiehrte Anzeiger* 213 (1960), 127-45 and in *Askese und Mönchtum in der Alten Kirche,* ed. K. Suso Frank (Darmstadt 1975), 230-54, esp. 244ff. See also G. Nedungatt, 'The Convenanters of the Early Syriac-Speaking Church', *OCP* 39 (1973), 205ff.

John 20:3ff. It is not without reason that Rabbula's care of poor people and strangers is explicitly emphasized as a consequence of the saint's life and death.

In this legend the Syrian holy man has nothing in common with the good patronus, but is rather an *alter Christus* with a strong integrating function in the urban society he inhabits. Cities in Syria and Mesopotamia, especially during the fourth and fifth century, were crowded with poor and starving people and the suffering of homeless strangers was terrible in the severity of winter.[9] The holy man broke through all social boundaries and classes and represented help and justice in the merciless social structure of an ancient city, in which a stranger especially was a social outcast. In fact he did not have a position *vis-à-vis* the community, mediating between that community and the outside world, but rather worked within the population and fully belonged to it. The great emphasis laid on Rabbula's work of relief for the poor and sick is a natural consequence of the saint's actions. Rabbula indeed established permanent hospices for men and women and infirmaries for diseased and in particular for lepers.[10] The pious Euphemia did the same at Amida in the sixth century.[11] The life of the holy man of God at Edessa, therefore, does not only afford a description of his life and death, but also makes an appeal on the hearer and reader, and functions as a source of social change. It seems to me a necessary task of historical research to analyse the *Wirkungsgeschichte* of the Lives of the holy men and their influence on the society. These Lives represent not only products of the society around the holy man, but in turn exercise a certain influence on that society. They offer an ideal life that asks for imitation in exactly the same way as Christ's life is symbolically represented by the holy man in his stylized and ritualised behaviour. The empty grave of the holy man at Edessa, therefore, is not a miraculous addition to the legend meant to link it to the story of his second life after his return in his father's house in Byzantium, the New Rome, but an essential part of the original legend that highlights the role of the holy man as an *alter Christus.*[12]

Jacob of Nisibis

The second life I would draw to your attention is the *vita* of Jacob of Nisibis, with which Theodoret opens the *Historia Religiosa.*[13] This *vita* is also preserved in a

9. See J.B. Segal 'Mesopotamian Communities from Julian to the Rise of Islam', *Proceedings of the British Academy* 41 (1955), 116ff and id., *Edessa 'the blessed City'* (Oxford 1970), 147ff.
10. G.G. Blum, 'Rabbula von Edessa. Der Christ, der Bischof, der Theologe', CSCO Sub 34 (1969), 70ff.
11. John of Ephesus, 'Lives of the Eastern Saints' 12 (PO 17.1.166ff).
12. Amiaud, op.cit. (n.7 above), xlvii suggests that the empty grave was 'indispensible pour faire une histoire populaire de la vie de l'humble ascète inconnu qui fut plus tard Saint Alexis'. Cf. Stebbins, op.cit. (n.7 above), 499ff.
13. Theodoret de Cyr, *Histoire des moines de Syrie,* ed. P. Canivet and A. Leroy-Molinghen (SC 234 [1977]), i.160. Cf. P. Peeters, 'La légende de S. Jacques de Nisibe', *AnalBoll* 38 (1920), 285-373; P. Bedjan, *Acta Martyrum et Sanctorum* (Paris 1890ff), 4.262-3 (Jacob

Syriac version like that of Julian Saba, the second life that Theodoret describes. Jacob was born in Nisibis in the latter part of the third century and as a young man he chose the ascetic life in the desert. He lived in the open air on fruits and herbs, did not use fire and maltreated his body. His soul, however, received spiritual food and the holy man acquired the image of God's glory. Hence he had foreknowledge of the future and could work miracles. Theodoret tells us some of these, such as the punishment of some bold girls at a spring and of an unjust judge. Theodoret explicitly refers to Moses and to Jesus' gentleness in telling these miracles which actually are a kind of *sēmeia.* The holy man Jacob became so well-known and famous that he was called to the bishop's see of Nisibis. Reluctantly he went there, but did not change his food or his clothes: only the place, but not his way of life, as Theodoret puts it. At Nisibis he took care of the poor and diseased, the widows and orphans; he punished the wicked and practised justice. He even raised a dead beggar, imitating in everything the Lord's grace. He seems to have attended the Council of Nicaea, but his work at Nisibis culminated in his brave behaviour during a siege by Sapor. The story in the *Historia Religiosa* gives the strong impression that Jacob organised the population during that siege not only through prayer but also through hard work in the rebuilding of walls that were broken by the force of the artificially dammed waters of the local river. Like Moses, Jacob prayed to God, who sent darkness and fleas to disconcert the enemy. He even appeared on the walls of Nisibis dressed in purple and with the royal diadem to confuse Sapor, who had attacked Nisibis because he believed the king was not there. The enemy withdrew; and as long as Jacob lived Nisibis was not taken by the barbarians. It is not surprising that the tomb of this *promachos* became the real centre of the city, or that the people of Nisibis took his body with them when they left their city on its being ceded by Jovian to the Persians (363).[14]

Although this Life and its striking details are for the greater part legendary – Jacob of Nisibis died in 337-8 and the *vita* refers to a siege of Nisibis by Sapor in 350 – it gives quite an exact picture of what was expected of the saint.[15] His *vita* actually depicts his ideal role, which is partly the same that is played by Ephrem in Nisibis according to his legendary Syriac *vita.* The best explanation of these elements in the Syriac *vita* of Ephrem as well as in Theodoret's story of Jacob of Nisibis is that the third siege of Nisibis by Sapor (as described by a letter of bishop Vologeses of Nisibis preserved in the *Chronicon Paschale,* by the *Orationes* of Julian and possibly other texts) gave rise to these legendary *vitae* in which the dominant role

of Nisibis); ibid., 6.380-4 (Julian Saba); Ephrem Syrus, *Carmina Nisibena* ed. E. Beck (CSCO, S 92-3 [1961]), Hymns xiii-xvi; also Canivet, op.cit (n.4 above), 104.

14. See G.W. Bowersock, *Julian the Apostate* (Cambridge Mass. 1978), 118; R. Turcan, 'L'abandon de Nisibe et l'opinion publique', *Mélanges d'archéologie et d'histoire offerts à André Piganiol,* ed. R. Chevallier (Paris 1966), 875-90.

15. See Canivet, op.cit. (n.4 above), 107-8, and P. Peeters, op.cit. (n.13 above), 289, 296-312.

of the holy men was strongly emphasised.[16] That role is pre-eminently an urban one: the holy man organizes the resistance against the enemy with all means available and therefore functions as the social centre of the city even after his death. This function is even corroborated by his other social activities on behalf of the poor and diseased. That holds true for Jacob of Nisibis, for Ephrem Syrus, for the Man of God at Edessa and for many other saints whose lives are described by Theodoret or are to be found in the various Syriac sources, such as Aphraates at Edessa and Antioch (*Historia Religiosa* 8), Theodosios at Antioch, Abraham at Harran *et al.*[17]

The role of ascesis

If we have found strong indications that the role of the holy man is independent of the place where he manifests his power, so that, next to his appearance in the Syrian villages, his protecting and integrating function in the urban centres should be stressed, the question arises what forces contributed to his rise and characteristic lifestyle. Two elements are of special importance: the social disengagement of the holy man, which expresses itself in his favoured stay in the desert and other barren places, and his ascesis (often called the mortification of his body) through a remarkable diet and demanding bodily exercises. Both elements are interwoven: the desert is the place of solitude par excellence, where human existence reaches its lowest level, or in the view of the ascetic himself the summit of virtue and wisdom. 'Where did all this madness come from?', exclaims E.R. Dodds, and for lack of a satisfying answer to this desperate and intriguing question he states that contempt for the human condition and hatred of the body was a disease endemic in the entire culture of the period, of which some Christian and Gnostic manifestations are the most extreme, but which also show themselves in pagans of purely Hellenic education.[18] A. Vööbus, therefore, attributes the ascetic practice of the Syrian holy men to the strong influence of the Manichees and their anti-cosmic and anti-bodily dualism.[19] Vööbus is partly followed by P. Canivet, when he states: 'le mal réside dans la matière' and considers this to be an all-explaining ground for the ascetic practice of

16. See B. Outtier, 'Saint Ephrem d'après ses biographies et ses oeuvres' *Parole de l'orient* iv (1973), 22; Julian, *Or.* i and ii, ed. F.C. Hertlein, 22-4, 33-9, 79-80; *Chronicon Paschale, PG* 92. 724B.14-728A.8; also Canivet, op.cit. (n.4 above), 104-8.
17. Julian Saba played an important role at Antioch (Theodoret, *H.Ph.* 2). For Theodosius (*H.Ph.* 10) see Canivet, op.cit. (n.4 above), 182-5. Abraham, bishop of Harran (*H.Ph.* 17) took care of widows and strangers and played a stabilising role in social tensions. See also J.H.W.G. Liebeschuetz, *Antioch. City and Imperial Administration in the Later Roman Empire* (Oxford 1972), 234ff on the urban function of the Syrian saints and hermits.
18. E.R. Dodds, *Pagan and Christian in an Age of Anxiety. Some Aspects of religious experience from Marcus Aurelius to Constantine* (Cambridge 1965), 34.
19. Vööbus, *History of Asceticism* i.158ff. For a severe criticism of Vööbus see the works cited in n.8 above. See also A. Guillaumont. 'Perspectives actuelles sur les origines du monachisme' in *The Frontiers of Human Knowledge. Lectures held at the Quincentenary Celebrations of Uppsala University 1977*, ed. T.T. Segerstedt (Uppsala 1978), 111-23.

the Syrian saints and their mortification of the body.[20] But is the Christian ascetic practice an expression of contempt for the human condition and hatred of the body as such?

It should be emphasised that the social role of the holy men is in flagrant contradiction of such an explanation. The Manichaean *electi* are a religious elite which never interferes with the troubles of the body social, but always lives at a safe distance from the cares and worries of daily life. We never hear about their social activities or care of the poor.[21] Contrary to Christianity, Manichaeism never became a social movement: its doctrinal idèology leads away from the trivial and material aspects of human life. The Christian holy men are always ready to participate in the daily life of common people and the social elite in order to protect and integrate that life. They may cherish the ideal of virginity, but when necessary they repair a marriage and they pray for barren women. That does not agree with a general atmosphere of hatred of the body and contempt for the human condition.

It is noteworthy that often when the ascetic practice of the holy man is discussed (as by Theodoret), such discussion involves mention of his special wisdom and eventually his *apatheia.* The *vita* of Julian Saba as told by Theodoret is a good example of such a pattern.[22] These elements find their unity in the *imago Christi* which is represented by the saint in his lifestyle.[23] Actually that lifestyle is an exact replica of the essential elements in early Syrian Christology. To phrase it in a theological way: anthropology is part of christology. It might be useful therefore to sketch the main lines of early Syrian thinking on Christ before returning to our problem.

Early Syrian christology

The literary heritage of the early Syriac-speaking Church (which is essentially part of Antiochene theological traditions) comprises some apocryphal Acts of the Apostles, of which the Syriac Acts of Thomas are the most important, the Syriac Odes of Solomon (dating from the second part of the third century) and the remnants

20. Theodoret de Cyr, op.cit. (n.13 above), i.45.

21. See G. Widengren, *Mani und der Manichäismus* (Stuttgart 1961), 97ff; O. Klima, *Manis Zeit und Leben* (Prague 1962), 84 ff; K. Rudolph, *Die Gnosis. Wesen und Geschichte einer spätantiken Religion* (Leipzig 1977), 362ff.

22. Theodoret, *H.R.* ii.3. Cf. ibid., Prologue 2-3; on Theodoret's use of *apatheia,* ibid. 148 n.6. See also Canivet, op.cit. (n.4 above), 273; P. Harb, 'Les origines de la doctrine de 'la-hašūšūtā (Apatheia) chez Philoxène de Mabbug', *Parole de l'orient* 5 (1974), 227-41. The article 'Apatheia' by G. Bardy in *Dictionnaire de spiritualité* i.727-46 remains fundamental. Since asceticism in Syria was not merely a rural movement but also had strong roots in the towns and cities, philosophical influences on its very beginnings cannot be denied *a priori.*

23. Canivet, op.cit. (n.4 above), 275-9. In the Syriac *Acts of Thomas,* the apostle is depicted as Christ's earthly 'double', and each is repeatedly identified completely with the other. Cf. H. Drijvers, 'Spätantike Parallelen zur altchristlichen Heiligenverehrung unter besonderer Berücksichtigung des syrischen Stylitenkultus, *Erkentnisse und Meinungen* ii, ed. G. Weissner [*Göttinger* Orientforschungen/Reihe: Syriaca 17], 77-113. The stylites in particular represent Christ and his passion in their ritualised lifestyle.

of Tatian's *Diatessaron.*[24] In all that literature Christ is considered God's eternal thought and will, incarnate in a human body in order that man might return to the original state in which he was created according to God's thought and will. Christ manifests the divine will by his obedience unto death, which means by dominating human passions and strivings, revealing in this way God's eternal thought concerning the salvation of mankind.[25] The lifestyle of the holy man is an imitation of Christ's passion, a training of his will in dominating his passions and human strivings; so he shows a certain Christ-conformity. Virginity is not the ideal of the holy man because he is filled with a deep hatred of the human body, but because Christ was an *ihidaya,* in fact the *iḥidaya* or *monogenēs.*[26] The doctrine of the free will of man which can control all his passions and guide his body is therefore an essential part of all forms of theology in the Syrian area, however different these may be. The best illustration of this are the Acts of Thomas, with which the *vita* of the Man of God at Edessa has some striking literary and ideological parallels. In the hard exercise of his will the holy man gains insight into God's saving thought – asceticism and the acquirement of wisdom are two sides of the same *imitatio Christi* – and he displays this insight in his acts of power, which always aim at the salvation of men. The desert is the place of trial and hence preeminently the place for exercising the will; at the same time the desert is between servitude and slavery and the promised land. That is why the holy man is also depicted as a *Moyses redivivus,* just as Christ was an *alter Moyses.*[27]

From philosophia to apatheia

The combination of self-discipline by exercising the human will and the acquisition of wisdom is part of the hellenistic philosophical tradition. Hence Theodoret can describe the ascetic life as a *philosophia aiming at apatheia.* That does not mean that Christian asceticism in its Syrian manifestation is due to the influence of Greek philosophical tradition, as Reitzenstein and Leipoldt believed.[28] There is a

24. In general see R. Murray, *Symbols of Church and Kingdom. A Study in Early Syriac Tradition* (Cambridge 1975), 24ff. On the date of the Odes of Solomon see H. Drijvers, 'Kerygma und Logos in den Oden Salomons dargestellt am Beispiel der 23. Ode', *Kergyma und Logos. Festschrift Carl Andresen,* ed. A.M. Ritter (Göttingen 1979), 153-72, esp. 171; and id., 'The 19th Ode of Solomon: its Interpretation and Place in Syrian Christianity', *JThS* (1980), 337-55. On Tatian see M. Elze, *Tatian und seine Theologie* (Göttingen 1960). A fresh enquiry into Tatian's encratism and its influence on early Syrian asceticism seems to be required.
25. See Drijvers, 'Kerygma und Logos', 159ff. This theological concept is also found in Addai's sermons in the Syriac *Doctrina Addai,* ed. G. Phillips (London 1876), and is an essential element in the doctrinal parts of the Syriac apocryphal *Acts of Thomas.*
26. See A. Guillaumont, op.cit. (n.19 above), 114ff. As to the development of the word *monachos,* the term occurs in the Coptic *Gospel of Thomas:* cf. H.-Ch. Puech, *En quête de la gnose* ii (=*Sur l'Evangile selon Thomas*) (Paris 1978), 178, 216, 222, 236, 240.
27. See J. Daniélou, *Sacramentum Futuri* (Paris 1950), 131-200. A good example is provided by the miracle of the well in the *vita* of Julian Saba (*H.R.* 2, 7-8).
28. R. Reitzenstein, 'Historia monachorum und Historia Lausica', *Forschungen zur Religion und Literatur des Alten und Neuen Testaments* 24 (1916); J. Leipoldt, 'Griechische Philo-

common pattern, of which the Syrian holy man is a characteristic variant, formed and guided by the life of Christ as understood in Syria. Perhaps this may be related to certain philosophical trends, since Christ as thought and will of God has some relation with Middle Platonism, and this life can itself be considered a kind of philosophical life. But its main characteristic is the holy man as *imago Christi* and continuation of the incarnation, so that the divine manifests itself in human shape by transforming that shape into an instrument of God's thought and will. And that might be the ground for the combination of spiritual and ascetic life with philosophical learning which is quite common in the early and later Syrian Church.[29]

Sociology and ideology

If the rise and function of the holy man in Syrian towns and villages are determined by that ideal of *imitatio Christi* which strives for the transcendence of human existence by controlling the most fragile part of it, the body, the final question is: what is the influence of a written and preached religious tradition on human behaviour in a given historical and social situation? In other words, what is the interaction between sociological and ideological elements in a society? It seems that Christianity's most distinct ideological type, the saint, exercised the strongest influence on the society of Late Antiquity, in the Syrian villages as well as in the towns. The special character of the Syrian holy men is rooted in earlier phases of theological thinking, but it fully unfolds during the fourth and fifth centuries. His special way of functioning in the Syrian society of that period, therefore, should be explained by a fresh examination of the structure of that society and its specific needs.

sophie und frühchristliche Askese', *Berichte über die Verhandungen der sächsischen Akademie der Wissenschaften zu Leipzig P.H.* 106.4 (1961).

29. See A. Guillaumont, 'Un philosophe au désert: Euagre le Pontique', *RHR* 181 (1972), 29-56; and P. Harb, op.cit. (n.22 above), 227. It can be assumed that at Edessa, for example, there was a strong unbroken philosophical tradition from pagan times, of which the so-called 'Letter of Mara bar Serapion to his Son' is an expression (ed. W. Cureton, *Spicilegium Syriacum* (London 1855), 43-8.

V

DIE LEGENDE DES HEILIGEN ALEXIUS UND DER TYPUS DES GOTTESMANNES IM SYRISCHEN CHRISTENTUM

Die Legende des heiligen Alexius, die Ende des zehnten Jahrhunderts in Rom bekannt wurde und sich von dort in viele Versionen verbreitete, da sie sich im europäischen Mittelalter einer großen Beliebtheit erfreute, geht zum Teil auf die syrische Vita des anonymen Gottesmannes in Edessa zurück[1]. Diese älteste Schicht der Legende des heiligen Alexius ist in Edessa Anfang des fünften Jahrhunderts entstanden und wurde vielleicht im sechsten Jahrhundert ein wenig erweitert. Jedenfalls stammen die ältesten syrischen Handschriften aus dem sechsten und ein Manuskript möglicherweise noch aus dem fünften Jahrhundert[2]. Diese älteste Version der Legende endet mit dem Tode und der Bestattung des Heiligen in Edessa. Eine spätere Version, die in Handschriften aus dem neunten bis dreizehnten Jahrhundert bezeugt ist, kennt die Heimkehr des Heiligen aus Edessa in seine Vaterstadt nach seinem Tode und seiner Auferstehung oder beschreibt sie als Flucht vor der Verehrung der edessenischen Bevölkerung, nachdem seine wahre Identität bekannt wurde[3]. Diese Version ist den abendländischen Fassungen ähnlicher und ist in Konstantinopel aus einer Verschmelzung der ältesten edessenischen Fassung mit der bekannten griechischen Legende des Juan Calibita wahrscheinlich im siebten Jahrhundert entstanden[4]. Die mittelalterlichen europäischen Versionen gehen also über ein byzantinisches Original auf die syrische edessenische Legende des Gottesmannes zurück. Diese Legende ist ein charakteristisches Beispiel einer syrischen Heiligenvita, deren Hauptmerkmale in der weitverbreiteten Alexiuslegende noch erhalten sind, die demnach in den Fassungen des Mittelalters Spuren vom Typus des syrischen Heiligen repräsentiert[5].

Der heilige Mann als kennzeichnende Figur in der Religionsgeschichte der Spätantike erschien zuerst in Syrien. Im Gegensatz zur Kirche des lateinischen Westens, wo die Märtyrergräber Fixpunkte der Religiosität und Organisation wurden, blieb der heilige Mann, der in seinem Leben und Auf-

treten die Glaubensideale verkörperte und Gottes Macht und Weisheit tatsächlich zeigte, eine Dauererscheinung im östlichen Christentum[6]. Die vielen Heiligenviten der syrischen Helden der Askese gewähren einerseits Erkenntnisse der Gesellschaft und ihrer Erwartungen, denen der heilige Mann der Legende gemäß entsprach, sie bieten anderseits ein festes Muster von Qualitäten, die jeder Heilige zum Teil besaß und die für die Kenntnis der Theologie der syrischen Kirchen aufschlußreich sind[7]. Anstatt einer Erörterung dieser Heiligenleben als Produkte religiöser Psychopathologie oder Neurose der spätantiken Gesellschaft[8], sind sie viel mehr als wichtige Quellen der Theologiegeschichte zu verwenden, die als Äußerungen von Glaubensreflektion und Glaubensideale auch Einsichten bieten, in den sozialen Kontext, in dem sie entstanden sind.
Der heilige Mann verdeutlicht eine bestimmte Typologie, die für das Glaubensverständnis des syrischen Christentums, dessen Schwerpunkt in Nordmesopotamien lag, kennzeichnend ist, und sie wirft Licht auf die Gesellschaft, in der er funktioniert. Nach der Darstellung der Typologie des heiligen Mannes soll deshalb nach den geistigen Kräften und kulturellen Einflüssen, die auf diese Typologie eingewirkt und sie überhaupt hervorgebracht haben, gefragt werden, damit das sozial-kulturelle Milieu des syrischen Christentums, in dem der heilige Mann auf ganz charakteristische Weise funktioniert hat, mindestens in Umrissen herausgestellt wird. Das ist umso notwendiger, da das syrische Christentum von vielen Gelehrten als eine eigenständige Größe angesehen wird, die in ihren Anfängen von hellenistischen Einflüssen frei gewesen sei und ein authentisches semitisches Christentum bewahrt hätte, das der Jerusalemer Urgemeinde ganz nahe gestanden habe[9]. Dann erst wird sich auch herausstellen, inwieweit die Alexiuslegende eine Sondererscheinung der mittelalterlichen Religiosität ist und auf welche Weise sie sich in andere theologische Strömungen einordnen läßt.
Der Verfasser der syrischen Vita des edessenischen Gottesmannes nennt in der Einleitung den Heiligen einen Engel, weil er alle Genüsse des Lebens verschmähte[10]. Sein Leben war so außerordentlich, daß die menschliche Sprache es kaum beschreiben kann, eine Behauptung, die an den Schluß des Johannesevangeliums erinnert[11]. Seine Eltern wohnten in Rom, gemeint ist das neue Rom - Konstantinopel, sie waren reich und von adliger Familie.

Leider waren sie kinderlos, aber nach vielen Tränen und Gebeten wurde ihnen ein Sohn geboren, der bei Gott und den Menschen beliebt war. Als er im Schulalter war, zeigte er kein Interesse für Bildung und Gelehrsamkeit dieser Welt, sondern gab sich in Demut einer großen nichtweltlichen Kenntnis hin. Sklaven konnten ihn nicht amüsieren, und die schönsten Sklavinnen, die seine Mutter ihm sandte, würdigte er keines Blickes, sondern starrte auf den Boden. Im heiratsfähigen Alter suchten ihm seine Eltern eine Frau und bereiteten alles für die Hochzeit vor. Die ganze Stadt wurde zum Fest eingeladen. Am Hochzeitstage, als die Braut erscheinen sollte, entschloß sich der Bräutigam, sie und das Fest zu verlassen und begab sich mit einem der Brautführer zum Hafen. Dort übergab er dem Brautführer sein Pferd und entfernte sich von ihm. Er bat inbrünstig zu Gott, ihm eine Tür zu öffnen und ihm die Sehnsucht seines Herzens zu befriedigen. Sofort kam ein Schiff, das ihn schnell unter göttlicher Vorsehung nach Seleucia in Syrien brachte. Von dort zog er als Bettler durch das Land und erreichte schließlich Edessa, die Stadt der Parther, wo er bis zu seinem Tode blieb. Tagsüber verbrachte er die Zeit fastend in der Kirche und weigerte sich, etwas anzunehmen. Abends stellte er sich mit ausgestreckter Hand an die Tür der Kirche und erhielt Almosen der Kirchenbesucher. Hatte er genug bekommen, schloß er die Hand, und verschenkte, was er seiner Meinung nach zuviel bekommen hatte. Die Nacht verbrachte er im Freien mit den Armen der Stadt, aber wenn jene schliefen, stand er auf und begann mit ausgestreckten Armen, in Kreuzform, zu beten. Morgens betrat er wieder als einer der ersten die Kirche. Auf diese Weise lebte er in Edessa und erzählte niemandem ein Wort über sein früheres Leben in Reichtum und Ehren, nicht einmal seinen Namen gab er bekannt. Er war ein anonymer Fremdling, der von einem heimischen Sklaven, der ausgesandt war, seinen Herrn zu suchen, nicht wiedererkannt wurde, weil er allen früheren Glanz und alle Herrlichkeit abgelegt hatte.

Eines nachts, als er in Kreuzform betend stand, wurde er von einem eifrigen Kirchendiener, einem Paramonarius, beobachtet, der ihn auch weiterhin auf diese Weise beten sah. Dieser bat ihn eindringlich ihm zu sagen, wer er wirklich sei, was der heilige Mann endlich tat. Sein Beispiel brachte den Paramonarius dazu, noch eifriger zu fasten und zu beten, als er dies zuvor schon tat, denn er sagte sich: "wenn jemand, der in größten Ehren erzogen wurde, derartiges ertragen kann, was müssen dann wir elende Menschen nicht tun, um unser Heil zu bewirken"[12].

Nach langer Zeit wurde der heilige Mann krank, weigerte sich aber, beim Paramonarius Wohnung zu nehmen oder ins Hospital zu gehen. Endlich gab er nach und wurde unter der Bedingung ins Hospital gebracht, daß der Paramonarius für ihn nicht mehr tun dürfe, als für andere Fremde in der Stadt. Jener besuchte ihn täglich, war aber durch Gottes Vorsehung nicht dabei, als der heilige Mann starb, so daß die Krankenpfleger ihn sogleich hinausschaften zum Fremdenfriedhof[13]. Als der Paramonarius von seinem Tode hörte, eilte er zum Bischof Rabbula, berichtete ihm vom heiligen Fremden, der gestorben und begraben war, und bat inbrünstig, daß diesem reinen Körper Ehre erwiesen würde. Gemeinsam eilten sie zum Grabe, wo der Bischof den Auftrag erteilte, dies zu öffnen. Gemeinsam betraten sie das Grab, fanden es aber leer, allein die Lumpen des Fremden fanden sich darin. Fassungslos standen sie eine Weile da, und dann begann Bischof Rabbula zu geloben, künftighin nur noch für Arme und Fremde zu sorgen. Speziell Fremde und Ausländer waren von nun an das Ziel seines frommen Eifers, um bei Gott Gnade zu finden[14].

Das Nachwort der Vita erwähnt, daß der Paramonarius, dem der Heilige sein Leben erzählt hatte, seine Herrlichkeit wie seine Niedrigkeit, dieses bekanntgemacht hat, damit es in Erinnerung behalten werde[15].

Diese syrische Vita steht nicht vereinzelt da, sondern weist allerhand Parallelen mit anderen syrischen Heiligengeschichten und apokryphen Apostelakten auf. An erster Stelle springen die Übereinstimmungen mit der biblischen Überlieferung des Lebens Jesu in die Augen. Der Lebenslauf des Gottesmannes ist geradezu eine genaue Illustration des Lebens Jesu, wie es Paulus im Philipperbrief 2,5ff. summarisch beschreibt: "Ein jeglicher sei gesinnt wie Jesus Christus es auch war, welcher, wenngleich er in göttlicher Gestalt war, hielt er's auch nicht für einen Raub,Gott gleich zu sein, sondern entäußerte sich selbst und nahm Knechtsgestalt an, ward gleich wie ein andrer Mensch ..... erniedrigte sich selbst, und ward gehorsam bis zum Tode ...."[16]. Sein Leben endet darum mit dem leeren Grab, ein Erzählmotiv, das zur ursprünglichen Gestalt der Legende gehört und nicht später eingefügt wurde, um des Heiligen Rückkehr zum väterlichen Hause nach seinem Tode in Edessa zu ermöglichen, wie die Alexiuslegende es erzählt[17].

Das Über- und Nicht-mehr-Menschliche wird gleich am Anfang der Legende betont, wenn gesagt wird, daß man den Heiligen einen Engel nennen sollte. Der Zug der *Vita Angelica* ist im syrischen Christentum sehr früh bezeugt und geht auf Tatian zurück, dessen Interpretation der Sadduzäerperikope, die in der *Vetus Syra* nachhallt, das engelgleiche Leben nicht auf die Zeit nach der Auferstehung bezieht, sondern in die Gegenwart verlegt[18].

Die *Vetus Syra* zur Stelle Lk 20,34ff liest:

34. Jesus sagte zu ihnen: die Söhne dieser Welt zeugen und werden gezeugt, sie nehmen Frauen, und Frauen gehören den Männern an.

35. Diejenigen aber, welche würdig sind, jene Welt und die Auferstehung von den Toten zu erlangen, nehmen keine Frauen, und die Frauen gehören nicht den Männern an.
36. Sie können auch nicht mehr sterben, denn sie sind den Engeln gleich geworden, als Söhne Gottes Söhne der Auferstehung[19].

Der Text der *vetus syra* mit der Betonung des Gegensatzes zwischen "Zeugen" und "gezeugt werden" einerseits, und den Söhnen Gottes, die den Engeln gleich nicht mehr zeugen, ist bestimmt vom Wortlaut des Johannesprologs beeinflußt worden. Joh 1,12 - 13: "Wie viele ihn aber aufnahmen, denen gab er Macht, Gottes Söhne zu werden, die an seinen Namen glauben; welche nicht von dem Geblüt, noch von dem Willen des Fleisches, noch von dem Willen des Mannes, sondern von Gott geboren sind". Die Kinder oder Söhne Gottes sind gleichsam von Gott wiedergeboren, den Engeln gleich geworden, und enthalten sich von jedem sexuellen Verkehr. Sexuelle Abstinenz ist in gewissem Sinne eine Voraussetzung, um die Auferstehung zu erlangen, d.h. um Söhne Gottes zu werden.
Die Geburt des Gottesmannes war Gottes Gnade zu verdanken, der das Gebet der Eltern erhörte, so daß er eigentlich von Gott geboren war. Darin gleicht er Isaak, Samuel und insbesondere Johannes dem Täufer, der für die syrischen Asketen ein glänzendes Beispiel war, so daß sie sogar sein Fasten in der Wüste nachahmten[20]. Schon als Kind zeigte der heilige Mann eine spezielle Vorliebe für das große Wissen, d.h. das Wissen Gottes, gleich wie der zwölfjährige Jesus im Tempel (Lk 2,47-52). Wie alle Heilige verläßt der Gottesmann seine Familie und befolgt damit das evangelische Gebot Mt 10,37: "Wer Vater oder Mutter mehr liebt als mich, der ist meiner nicht wert ..." Lk 14,26ff.: "Wenn jemand zu mir kommt, und hasset nicht seinen Vater, Mutter, Weib, Kinder, Brüder, Schwestern, auch dazu sein eigenes Leben, der kann nicht mein Jünger sein". Auch Jesus verließ seine Familie, obwohl er eine spezielle Beziehung zu seiner Mutter Maria unterhielt. In diesem Zusammenhang ist es bemerkenswert, daß syrische Heilige ebenfalls oft durch spezielle Bande mit ihren Müttern verbunden sind, wie z.B. Symeon der Jüngere und Theodor von Sykeon. Das kann dem Oedipuskomplex oder der Unsicherheit der Vaterrolle zugeschrieben werden[21]. Es ist aber durchaus möglich, hierin eine klare Nachahmung von Jesu Verhältnis zu Maria zu sehen. Auch das neutestamentliche Fastengebot wird in der Vita des Gottesmannes konkretisiert, Mk 2,20: "Es wird aber die Zeit kommen, daß der Bräutigam von ihnen genommen wird; dann werden sie fasten"[22].

Der Heilige ist ein Fremdling, der wie Jesus keine Stelle hatte, wohin er sein Haupt legen konnte[23]. Sein nächtliches Beten ist eine Nachahmung von Jesu Gebet in Gethsemane, als alle Jünger schliefen, wie die Leute um den Gottesmann. Es ist tatsächlich eine *Imitatio Passionis Christi*, und deshalb nimmt der Heilige die Kreuzform beim Beten an[24]. Symeon der Stylit pflegte stehend auf seiner Säule zu schlafen und betete in der Haltung des Kreuzes mit ausgestreckten Armen. Säule und Heiliger zusammen bilden auf diese Weise eine Art Kreuz. Als Symeon während seiner irdischen Existenz die Säule allmählich erhöhte, symbolisiert diese Handlung nicht nur die räumliche Entfernung von den Menschen, sondern auch die Erhöhung am Kreuze, die ursprünglich der Himmelfahrt gleich kam, so daß der Heilige allmählich ein Himmelswesen wurde[25].
Der Paramonarius in der edessenischen Legende gleicht ein wenig dem Simon Petrus, namentlich als er den Heiligen vor dem Leiden schützen wollte. Das zeigt sich besonders, wenn er zusammen mit dem Bischof zum Grabe eilt, wie einst Petrus und Johannes (Joh 20,3ff.) und es leer fanden. Der anonyme Fremdling war seinem Herrn völlig gleich geworden und unter Hinterlassung seiner Lumpen auferstanden.
Die Legende des Gottesmannes in Edessa beschreibt ihn also wie einen *alter Jesus*, der durch Leiden und Askese seinem Herrn identisch wird. Es ist äußerst auffallend, daß der Heilige gar keine soziale Rolle spielt. Er ist nur da, schenkt weg, was er zuviel bekommt, heilt aber keine Kranke, weckt keine Toten auf, verrichtet keine Wunder, erteilt keine Ratschläge, und prophezeit nicht die Zukunft, obwohl alle diese Züge in vielen syrischen Heiligenleben zum normalen Bild des Heiligen gehören[26]. Der Mann kommt als Fremder, niemand kennt seinen Namen, und er verschwindet als Fremder nur mit Hinterlassung seiner Lumpen im leeren Grab. Seine Existenz in Edessa hat nur Wirkung auf den Paramonarius, der sein Fasten intensiviert und auf Bischof Rabbula, der sich den Fremden und Armen widmet. Sein Leben war exemplarisch, eine Darstellung innerhalb der menschlichen Gesellschaft des göttlichen Lebens der Auferstehung. Seine Macht war nicht auf das Heil oder die Erlösung seiner Mitmenschen gerichtet, sondern auf die eigene Gottgleichheit, die durch Nachahmung der Inkarnation, durch Wiedergeburt, wiederhergestellt wird. Selbstverständlich hatte der spätantike Heilige eine soziale Rolle, die von PETER BROWN großartig beschrieben worden ist. Es scheint aber fragwürdig, ob die Aufgabe des Historikers erfüllt wäre, wenn er die Figur des Heiligen als Produkt der ihn umgebenden Gesellschaft analysiert hat, wie P. BROWN behauptet: "It is for the historian, therefore, to analyse this image as a product of the society around the holy man"[27].

BROWN's historischer Analyse nach hat die gesellschaftliche Situation im vierten und fünften Jahrhundert auf dem syrischen Lande, wo die Dörfer einen Patron brauchten, das Emporkommen der Heiligen gleichermaßen provoziert. Dort fanden sie ihre Aufgabe und demonstrierten ihre Macht in einem sozialen Machtvakuum.
Der Typus des heiligen Mannes, wie die Legende des edessenischen Gottesmannes ihn fast in Reinkultur schildert, hat aber ältere Wurzeln in der Theologie der syrischsprachigen Kirche während des zweiten und dritten Jahrhunderts, wo das Thema der Christusgleichheit der Gläubigen das Zentrum der theologischen Reflexion bildete.
Hauptquellen für die Kenntnis jener Periode sind die Schriften Tatians, des Verfassers des 'Diatessarons', die syrischen apokryphen 'Thomasakten' und die 'Oden Salomons'[28]. Andere Thomasschriften kommen auch in Anbetracht sowie Teile manichäischer Texte[29]. Obwohl eine vollständige Analyse dieser und anderer Schriften einer zukünftigen Arbeit vorbehalten bleiben muß, können die Hauptmerkmale dieser Theologie in ihren Hauptlinien skizziert werden.
Judas Thomas Didymus, die Hauptfigur der apokryphen 'Thomasakten', ist nach der Bedeutung seines Namens Jesu Zwilling[30]. Er ist nicht nur der Zwilling Jesu, sondern wird in den Akten auch auf eine künstlich raffinierte Weise als *alter Jesus* dargestellt. Die Motive der Erzählung und Thomas' Benehmen haben oft symbolische Bedeutung, die der Geschichte erst ihren wahren Sinn geben.
Gleich am Anfang der Akten wird erzählt, wie Jesus seinen Sklaven Judas Thomas für zwanzig Silberlinge dem Kaufmann Habban verkauft. Habban fragte Thomas: "Ist jener Ihr Herr?" Thomas antwortet bejahend und darauf teilt Habban ihm mit, daß sein Herr ihn verkauft hat. Judas aber schwieg! Das erinnert sehr stark an die eigentliche Passionsgeschichte, die mit dem Verrat Judas und Jesu Verhalten vor Pilatus beginnt. Das Motiv der zwanzig Silberlinge entstammt wohl der Geschichte von Joseph, der für zwanzig Silberlinge von seinen Brüdern nach Ägypten verkauft wird (Gen 37,28), und deutet deshalb schon daraufhin, daß Jesus und Judas Brüder sein sollen. Am nächsten Morgen steht Judas auf, betet: "Herr, Dein Wille geschehe!", und geht dann mit den zwanzig Silberlingen zu Habban. Beide gingen darauf an Bord eines Schiffes, wo Judas Habban seinen Beruf mitteilt; er sei Zimmermann und könne vieles in Holz und Stein anfertigen, auffallenderweise speziell die Dinge, die im Evangelium eine symbolische Bedeutung haben: Pflug, Joch, Tempel, und Paläste. In einen Hafen angekommen, gingen sie ans Land und hörten in der Stadt, daß der König für die Heirat seiner Tochter ein großes

Fest vorbereitete. Jedermann war eingeladen und gebeten zu kommen, weshalb auch Habban und Thomas hingingen, um nicht den Zorn des Königs zu erregen, weil sie Fremde waren. Judas Thomas war bei Tisch, aber er aß und trank nichts. Gefragt, warum er nichts esse, antwortete er: 'Ich bin hier hergekommen um etwas, das besser ist als essen und trinken, nämlich um der Ruhe des Königs Willen und um seinen Willen zu erfüllen. Am Ende der Mahlzeit pries Judas Thomas Gott, machte das Kreuzzeichen auf seinem Haupt, salbte seine Nasenlöcher und Ohren mit Öl, machte das Kreuzzeichen über das Herz, setzte einen Myrtenkranz auf sein Haupt und nahm einen Stab aus Rohr in die Hand. Wenn jemand ihn auf die Wange schlug, sagte Thomas: "Gott wird dir in der kommenden Welt vergeben, aber in dieser Welt wird Er seine Macht zeigen ..." und darauf begann er das Lied von der Kirche zu singen: "Meine Braut ist eine Tochter des Lichts, sie hat die Herrlichkeit der Könige"[31].

Diese Geschichte ist in kunstvoller Weise auf dem Stramin der Passionsgeschichte geschrieben und endet tatsächlich mit der Kreuzigung: die Worte, die Thomas zu dem, der ihn schlägt, spricht, sind eine freie Nachahmung der Worte, die Jesus am Kreuz zu einem der Übeltäter spricht (Lk 23, 42-43). Die vorherige Verkleidung am Ende der Mahlzeit hat nichts mit einem Taufritual zu tun, wie man oft behauptet hat, sondern Thomas verkleidet sich als leidender Jesus[32].

Die Mahlzeit hat auch symbolische Bedeutung; einerseits ist sie das königliche Hochzeitsfest des Gleichnisses (Mt 22, 1-14), anderseits erinnert sie an das letzte Abendmahl, wo Jesus selbst nichts aß, und an die himmlische Mahlzeit im Königreich Gottes, wo die ewige Ruhe herrscht[33]. Es nimmt deshalb nicht Wunder, daß dieser Abschnitt mit dem Hymnus auf die Kirche endet. Als Thomas ihn beendet hatte, war sein Anblick völlig verändert, und er strahlte überirdische Schönheit aus. Er betete dann zu Jesus ein langes Gebet, in dem die ganze Heilsgeschichte gleichermaßen zusammengefaßt wurde. Jesus wird angerufen als der Führer seiner Gläubigen, als Bringer des Lebens, der sich mit dem ersten Menschen bekleidete, als Kraft, Weisheit, Wissen und Wille des Vaters, der die Glorie der Göttlichkeit in menschlicher Gestalt offenbarte und den Weg nach oben für die Menschen öffnete. Judas Thomas, der sich dann in der Gestalt Jesu zeigte, überredete darauf die königliche Braut und ihren Bräutigam, sich von jeder geschlechtlichen Berührung fernzuhalten und sich nur auf die himmlische Hochzeit zu verlassen[34]. Die Braut sagt ausdrücklich, daß durch die Virginität menschliches Verderben von ihr genommen worden ist, und der Bräutigam sagt aus, daß der Fremde ihm gezeigt hat, wie er das, was nicht eigentlich zu seinem Wesen ge-

hörte, ablegen könnte[35].
Der Mensch kehrt gleichsam zum Paradies zurück. Durch die Virginität braucht er sich nicht mehr zu schämen, weil die Tat der Schande von ihm genommen worden ist. Das verweist auf den Sündenfall, für den der Mensch mit der Sexualität gestraft wird; Gen 3,16: "du sollst mit Schmerzen Kinder gebären; und dein Verlangen soll nach deinem Manne sein; und er soll dein Herr sein". Das steht im Gegensatz zur Situation vor dem Sündenfall; Gen 2,24f: "Darum wird ein Mann Vater und Mutter verlassen, und seinem Weibe anhangen, und die werden sein wie ein Fleisch. Und sie waren beide nackt, der Mann und sein Weib, und schämten sich nicht". Durch die Virginität kehrt der Mensch zur Situation vor dem Sündenfall zurück, wo der Unterschied zwischen Mann und Frau gleichermaßen aufgehoben ist: sie werden sein ein Fleisch! Deshalb ist das Verlassen der Familie auch so wichtig; es führt zurück zum Paradies[36].
Aus diesem kurzen Überblick eines Teiles der 'Thomasakten' zeigt sich Einiges, was für die einschlägige Thematik wichtig ist. Judas Thomas ist Christus ähnlich, er erscheint in der Gestalt Christi, und zeigt ein Verhalten, das auf symbolische Weise Christi Leben und insbesondere die Passion nachahmt. Thomas ist mit Stab und Krone ein *alter Christus,* wie der Gottesmann in Edessa, wenn er mit ausgestreckten Armen betet. Dieses christusähnliche Leben weist einige Hauptmerkmale auf, die es als solches charakterisieren und dafür grundlegend sind.

1. Ein Mensch soll Vater und Mutter verlassen und in die Fremde gehen. Thomas war ein Fremder, als Sklave verkauft, wie der Mann Gottes ein Fremder war. Oft wird noch hinzugefügt, daß er einer angesehenen Familie entstammt. Ebenso wie der Mann Gottes kam auch Thomas aus einer vornehmen Familie, wie ein Eselfüllen, worauf er in eine Stadt hineinreitet (!) , zu ihm sagt: "Zwilling des Messias, der teilhat am verborgenen Wort des Lebensschenkers, Freigeborener, der Sklave wurde, Sohn einer großen Familie, der seiner Glorie beraubt wurde"[37]. Das Leben des Heiligen verläuft mit dem Leben Jesu parallel.

2. Der wahre Gläubige fastet und pflegt eine absolute Virginität. Thomas schaut keine Frau an. Der Mann Gottes verläßt seine Braut, ohne sie berührt zu haben (*intactam sponsam relinquens)*[38]. Thomas' wichtigste Aktivität während seines öffentlichen Auftreten ist, Männer und insbesondere verheiratete Frauen zu einem Leben in strikter Enthaltsamkeit zu bekehren, weil ein solches Leben eine *conditio sine qua non* ist für das himmlische,

paradiesische Leben und die himmlische Hochzeit, die den Menschen mit Christus vereint. Der Geschlechtstrieb, die Scham, war die Folge einer falschen Verwendung des menschlichen Willen,so daß der Mensch dem Teufel unterworfen und sterblich wurde. Dadurch verlor er auch die richtige Einsicht in Gottes Willen, der Welt und Menschen nur wollte und schuf für sein Heil, das der Mensch durch die Sünde verlor.

Sexualität, falsche Verwendung des Willens, Sterblichkeit, Herrschaft des Teufels und der Dämonen, Unkenntnis der Pläne Gottes, das sind die Hauptmerkmale des irdischen Lebens. Jesu Kommen und Auftreten war eine von Gott in Gang gesetzte Gegenbewegung, durch die seine ewige Heilsintention, die schon in der Schöpfung wirksam war, sich sichtbar manifestierte. In Gegensatz zum sterblichen Menschen verkörpert er das Leben und kann den Menschen zum ewigen von Gott gewollten Leben zurückführen.
Die beschreibenden, epischen Passagen in den 'Thomasakten' werden deshalb durch lange Gebete unterbrochen, die die Erzählung gleichsam kommentieren und für die Kenntnis der frühsyrischen Christologie von größter Wichtigkeit sind[39]. Sie bestehen zum größten Teil aus christologischen Titeln und Epiklesen, die einen sehr reflektierten Eindruck machen. Einige Beispiele mögen das verdeutlichen. Thomas betet zu Jesus: "Du bist die Kraft und die Weisheit, das Wissen und der Wille deines Vaters .... Du vertriebst den Bösen aus seiner Macht .... Du riefst mit deiner Stimme zu den Toten und sie wurden lebendig .... Du wurdest aus der Höhe abgesandt, weil Du den lebendigen und vollkommenen Willen deines Senders vollziehen konntet"[40]. In einem anderen Gebet wendet Thomas sich zu Gott: "Dein Wille bahnte den Weg von deinem Geheimnis zur Offenbarung. Du breitest deine Gnaden über uns aus in dem, der durch deinen Willen kam und einen Körper annahm .... ihm hast du den Namen des Sohnes gegeben, er, der dein Wille und die Kraft deines Denkens war"[41]. Es ist bemerkenswert, daß nirgends von der Vergebung der Sünden gesprochen wird. Jesus verkörpert Gottes Willen und Denken; er erschlägt den Teufel und treibt Dämonen aus, er verläßt seine Familie und ist als eingeborener Sohn Gottes selbstverständlich ein *monachos,* einzig und allein, was im Syrischen mit dem Begriff *īḥīdāyā* ausgedrückt wird[42]. Er war ein Königssohn, der in die Fremde ging und dort Unwissenheit und Verderben ein Ende bereitete, weil er Gottes Denken und Willen war. Verderben hat in diesem Zusammenhang immer eine sexuelle Konnotation.
Der Mensch ist durch seinen Willen imstande, diese Erlösung nachzuahmen und so selbst zu vollziehen. Er kann durch die christusähnliche Virgini-

tät und das Leben eines *īhīdāyā* die verlorengegangene Gottähnlichkeit, das Bild Gottes, zurückgewinnen, gleichsam von Gott wiedergeboren werden, nicht "aus dem Willen des Fleisches, noch aus dem Willen eines Mannes" (Joh 1,12) so wie Jesus selbst von Gott geboren wurde, ohne den Willen des Fleisches oder aus dem Willen eines Mannes. Göttliche und menschliche Aktivität laufen hier genau parallel; Gott wird Mensch, damit der Mensch wieder Bild Gottes, ja fast Gott wird. Gottes Willen und Denken wird menschenähnlich, damit des Menschen Willen und Denken auf diese Weise wieder gottähnlich und wie von Gott gewollt werden. Es scheint unzweifelhaft, daß einer derart asketisch orientierten Soteriologie wesenhaft die Vorstellung von der Selbsterlösungsfähigkeit des Menschen eignet. Im Rahmen der 'Thomasakten' hat das nichts mit Gnostizismus im Sinne einer dualistischen antikosmischen Erlösungslehre zu tun, wie jene in vielen Systemen ausgebildet wurde und im Manichäismus einen vorläufigen End- und Höhepunkt fand[43]. Der inkarnierte göttliche Wille und das göttliche Denken zeigten und lehrten den Menschen, wie er seinen Willen richtig verwenden soll und kann, damit er, was er einst im Paradies durch eine falsche Verwendung seines Willens verloren hatte, zurückgewinnt[44]. Auf diese Weise kann Judas Thomas, jeder Heilige und im Grunde jeder Mensch die Gestalt und das Verhalten Jesu zeigen[45].

Die syrischen 'Thomasakten' sind deshalb nicht als volkstümliche Literatur zu betrachten, die Einblick in die Volksfrömmigkeit geben und zur Gattung der Erbauungs- und Unterhaltungsliteratur gehören[46]. Sie sind auf sehr kunstvolle Weise strukturiert und stammen vielmehr aus gelehrten, jedenfalls gebildeten Kreisen, wie die Mehrheit der frühsyrischen Literatur, die überwiegend von Tatian's und Bardaiṣan's philosophischer Bildung geprägt und von Marcion's Fragestellungen beherrscht wurde[47].

In solchen Kreisen sind auch die zweiundvierzig syrischen 'Oden Salomos' in der zweiten Hälfte des dritten Jahrhunderts entstanden[48]. Sie weisen eine reflektierte, stark symbolische Theologie und Christologie auf, deren Zentrum die Identität des Gläubigen und seines Herrn bildet, die zugleich der Schlüssel für das richtige Verständnis der Oden ist. Ode 3 ist in diesem Zusammenhang aufschlußreich:

4. Wer ist's, der die Liebe zu begreifen vermag, außer dem, der geliebt wird?
5. Ich glühe für den Geliebten, und es liebt ihn meine Seele, und wo sein Ruhelager ist, bin auch ich.
6. Und ich werde kein Fremdling sein, weil es keine Mißgunst gibt bei dem

Herrn, dem höchsten und liebevollen.
7. Ich bin vermählt, weil der Liebende den Geliebten fand, weil ich ihn, den Sohn lieben sollte, daß ich selbst Sohn sein möchte.
8. Denn, wer mit dem verbunden ist, der unsterblich ist, wird auch unsterblich sein.
9. Und wer am Leben (= Christus, Verf.) Wohlgefallen hat, wird lebendig sein.
10. Das ist der Geist des Herrn, der ohne Trug, der die Menschen lehrt, daß sie seine Wege kennen.
11. Seid weise, und habt Erkenntnis und seid wachsam[49].

Alle vorherigen Elemente treten hier wieder auf. Der Gläubige ist mit Christus vereint, was in Vs.7 mit dem Bild der Hochzeit ausgedrückt wird, er ist selber Sohn Gottes geworden und daher unsterblich, kennt Gottes Heilswege und wird daher aufgerufen wachsam zu sein[50]. Er schläft nicht mehr, so wie Judas Thomas und der Mann Gottes in Edessa immer wachen. Der Sänger der Oden ist ein Erlöster, der seinem Herrn identisch geworden ist. Diese Identität wird auch auf symbolische Weise in der Haltung des Sängers dargestellt; Ode 42:

1. Ich streckte meine Hände aus und nahte mich meinem Herrn; denn das Ausbreiten meiner Hände ist sein Zeichen.
2. Und mein Ausstrecken ist das ausgestreckte Holz, das angebracht wurde auf dem Wege des Aufrichtigen[51].

Genauso wie der Mann Gottes nachts in der Haltung des Kreuzes betet, so streckt der Sänger seine Hände aus und bildet eine Kreuzform.
Die Christologie der 'Oden Salomos' kennt eine konsistente Terminologie. Christus ist der Wille und das Denken Gottes, wie sich in Ode 9 herausstellt:

3. Das Wort des Herrn und seine Willensregungen sind ein heiliger Gedanke, den er gedacht hat über seinen Christus.
4. Denn im Willen des Herrn beruht euer Leben, und sein Gedanke ist ewiges Leben, und unvergänglich ist eure Vollendung.
5.Werdet reich in Gott dem Vater, und nehmet an den Gedanken des Höchsten. Seid stark und lasset euch erlösen durch seine Gnade.
6. Denn ich verkündige Frieden euch, seinen Heiligen, daß alle, die darauf hören, nicht im Kampfe fallen werden,

7. und weiter die, die ihn erkannt haben, nicht zugrunde gehen werden, und daß, die ihn annehmen, sich nicht (mehr) schämen werden[52].

Der Gläubige hat Gottes Gedanke und Willen angenommen, damit er im Kampfe gegen den Satan siegen wird und die Scham der Sünde von ihm weggenommen wird. Dadurch wird die Situation vor dem Sündenfall wiederhergestellt, wie sie in Gen 2,24f. beschrieben worden ist. Der Mensch wird so eine neue Person, christusähnlich, ein Fremder, wie Ode 17 ihn schildert:

1. Ich bin bekränzt worden durch meinen Gott, und mein Kranz ist lebendig.
2. Und ich bin gerechtfertigt worden durch meinen Herrn, meine Erlösung ist nun unvergänglich.
3. Ich bin befreit worden von den Eitelkeiten und bin nicht verurteilt.
4. Meine Fesseln sind durch ihn zerrissen worden, Antlitz und Gestalt einer neuen Person habe ich empfangen und wandelte in ihr und bin erlöst worden[53].
5. Und das Denken der Wahrheit (= Christus) leitete mich und ich ging ihm nach und ging nicht irre.
6. Und alle, die mich sahen, erstaunten,und wie ein Fremder kam ich ihnen vor[54].

Die Beispiele dieser Theologie und Christologie der 'Oden Salomos' lassen sich beliebig vermehren; das Wesentliche hat sich aber schon herausgestellt. Erlöst-Werden ist ein intellektueller und ein Willensprozeß, in dem der Mensch Gottes Denken und Willen, wie jene in Jesu Gestalt angenommen hatten, nachahmt. Gottes Denken und Willen waren auch in der Schöpfung wirksam, die wie die Inkarnation ein Exponent der göttlichen Providentia *(mdbrnwt')* ist. Immer wieder wird in den 'Oden' die Macht Gottes betont, wie sie in der Schöpfung und in Christus ans Licht tritt,so daß auch jener Aspekt der 'Oden' mit ihrer anti-markionitischen Tendenz in Übereinstimmung ist[55].

Diese komplementären christologischen und anthropologischen Konzeptionen bilden den Hintergrund und den Boden, auf dem der charakteristische Typus des syrischen Heiligen sich entwickeln konnte. Diese Theologie war schon am Anfang des dritten Jahrhunderts, als die Thomasakten entstanden, vollentwickelt, also in einer Zeit, in der der heilige Mann als solcher noch nicht auf der Bildfläche des syrischen Christentums erschienen war. Vorstufen finden sich bei Tatian, dessen Lehre von der Wiederherstellung der Gottebenbildlichkeit zugleich seine kämpferische Ethik begründet[56]. Der

heilige Mann ist also eine prägnante Entwicklung eines allgemein gültigen Typus des Christgläubigen, der sich nun einmal bei Vermeidung des Aussterbens nicht in vollem Rigorismus durchführen läßt. Die syrischsprachige Kirche kennt jenen Typus als die "Söhne und Töchter des Bundes" (*bny wbnt qym')*[57]. Für die Kenntnis der Geschichte des syrischen Christentums ist es jedenfalls bemerkenswert, daß das Emporkommen des Heiligen als eine Art Idealtypus und Paradigma des Glaubens parallel läuft mit dem Verschwinden der "Söhne und Töchter des Bundes" als eine spezielle Kategorie in der Kirche[58].
Woher stammt nun diese christologisch - anthropologische Grundkonzeption? Ist der christliche Heilige so grundverschieden vom paganen *theios aner,* wie P. BROWN wahrhaben will, wenn er behauptet, daß der *theios aner* seine Macht aus der überlieferten oft okkulten philosophisch - religiösen Weisheit bezog, der christliche Heilige aber aus dem Über- und Nicht-mehr-Menschlichen; daß der *theios aner* sich selbst erlöst, der Heilige immer von Christus erlöst wird[59]? Im frühsyrischen Christentum wird aber das Erlösungswerk Christi gar nicht betont! Vielmehr sind es Gottes Weisheit, Denken und Wille, die den Menschen aufwecken, und derer Nachahmung zur Erlösung führt. Heiligkeit in diesem Sinne ist nicht nur asketische Praxis und moralische Perfektion durch eine richtige Anwendung des Willens, sondern hat auch ein intellektuelles Element, insoweit als der Mensch seinen Willen nur dann richtig anwenden kann, wenn er weiß, was vorher schief gegangen war und warum. Daher betonen die 'Thomasakten' und die 'Oden Salomos', daß der Gläubige Einsicht hat in die Pläne Gottes und die Erkenntnis seiner Wege ihn von Anfang bis Ende trägt[60]. Dieses Element bringt den syrischen Heiligen wieder in die Nähe des paganen Philosophen der Spätantike. Der pagane *theios aner* war ein asketischer Philosoph, der über spezielle spirituelle Gaben verfügte[61]. In diesem Sinne war der syrische Heilige auch ein Philosoph, und einige Quellen betiteln die asketische Lebensführung der heiligen Männer deshalb als Philosophie[62]. Die Übereinstimmung mit dem paganen Bereich wird noch stärker, wenn man die gängige Definition der Weisheit als Inbegriff aller Philosophie in Anbetracht zieht: *scientia rerum divinarum et humanarum,* die grundlegend war für die platonische Lehrtradition[63]. Der Kenntnis der *res divinae* kommt nicht ohne Grund der erste Rang zu, und sie ist genau die Kenntnis, die in den 'Oden Salomos' immer wieder als charakteristisch für den Gläubigen betont wird. Dazu muß auf die zentrale Bedeutung des platonischen Telosgedankens der *homoiosis theọ* als Endziel menschliches Philosophierens hingewiesen werden, wodurch der Philosoph in den Bereich der Göttlichkeit aufsteigt[64].

Die Philosophie führt über die ethische und über die rationale Vollkommenheit zur *homoiosis theǭ* . Weil die Gottheit reiner *nous* ist, ist dieser Lebensprozeß nur rationaler Art, was die Abwendung von *to pathetikon,* i.e. von der Askese, einschließt. Der Gegensatz zwischen *fides* und *intellectus* ist in der platonisierenden Philosophie deshalb undenkbar[65].
Die frühsyrische Christologie, die Christus als Denken und Willen Gottes betrachtet, hat auch Parallelen im zeitgenössischen Mittel- und Neuplatonismus, wo Betrachtungen über Gottes Denken und Wollen Gang und Gäbe waren, die ihren Einfluß auf Justin, Tatian und Irenaeus nicht verfehlten[66]. Justin, I Apol. 60,1ff. führt aus, daß Gott am Anfang vor der Schöpfung eine geistige Potenz hervorbrachte, die seine Herrlichkeit, seine Weisheit und sein Wort verkörpert, in menschlicher Gestalt in der Geschichte erschien und Gottes Willen darstellt[67]. Justin's Reflexionen gehen auf im Mittelplatonismus gängige Timaeusauslegungen zurück[68]. Athenagoras, Suppl. 10, nennt den Sohn Gedanken und Wort Gottes, von dem und für den alles geschaffen ist und der den Willen Gottes zum Ausdruck bringt[69]. Tatian und Theophilus von Antiochien äußern verwandte Ideen, die ebenso von platonischen Schultraditionen beeinflußt worden sind[70].
Irenaeus' Ausführungen über Gottes Denken und Willen in der Schöpfung, in der Er seine Güte zeigte, sind ebenso von Platon's Darlegungen im 'Timaeus' aus zu verstehen[71].
Der edessenische Philosoph Bardaişan zeigt in der Kosmologie und Anthropologie starken Einfluß vom Mittelplatonismus. Er betitelt das noetische Prinzip in der Schöpfung als das Wort des Denkens Gottes, das sich in Christus in der Welt manifestierte. In seiner rationalen Willensethik zeigt er nahe Verwandtschaft mit Alexander von Aphrodisias auf[72].
Dies und anderes mehr weist darauf hin, daß die zeitgenössische Philosophie genauso wie im hauptsächlich griechischsprachigen West- und Coelesyrien auch ihren Einfluß auf die Ausbildung der syrischsprachigen Theologie in Ostsyrien geübt hat. Die Sprachgrenze in Syrien war fließend; in Antiochien, Apamea und Chalcis - Zentren der Philosophie und Gelehrsamkeit - wurde auch Syrisch gesprochen und verstanden, wie in Edessa das Griechische üblich war. Die angenommene Sprachgrenze war jedenfalls keine kulturelle Barriere[73]. Die Ausbildung des speziellen Typus des heiligen Mannen im syrischen Christentum auf der Grundlage der frühsyrischen Christologie und Anthropologie zeigt deutlich, daß und in welchem Umfang in allen Entwicklungstufen die griechische Bildung und Philosophie aktiv an diesem Prozeß beteiligt waren.

Das bedeutet nicht, daß der syrische Heilige und der pagane philosophische *theios aner* in allen Hinsichten vergleichbar sind. Für die Philosophen der Spätantike gehörte religiöses Erleben als gesteigertes Erleben des Logos ausschließlich zum Bereich der Philosophie, in der für Gefühl und Affekt kein Platz ist[74]. Für die syrischen Heiligen war die Christusgestalt das Paradigma ihres Lebensstils und zugleich Ursprung und Ziel ihrer Erkenntnis, dem sie sich allmählich anglichen. Das Prozeß der Angleichung ist deshalb nicht nur rational, sondern auch emotional bestimmt. Für den paganen *theios aner* war jeder Erkenntnisvorgang zugleich auch ein Prozeß des Angleichens, an dessen Ende er den Göttern gleichartig geworden ist, so daß ihm allmählich göttliche Kräfte zuwachsen. Das Epitheton *theios* bezieht sich aber nur auf die Teilhabe am göttlichen Nous und zeigt sich nie in einem symbolhaften Verhalten, das dem syrischen Gottesmanne eignet.

Das sozial - kulturelle Milieu des frühen syrischsprachigen Christentums, in dem der Typus des Gottesmannes seinen Ursprung hat, weist einen stark intellektuellen Charakter auf, das in allen überlieferten Schriften - orthodoxen wie ketzerischen - zu Tage tritt. Sie sind Produkte einer intellektuell-symbolischen Glaubensreflexion mit den Kategorien des zeitgenössischen Denkens. Es gibt deshalb keine Gründe, das syrischsprachige Christentum als eine eigenständige vom Griechischsprachigen grundverschiedene Größe zu betrachten, die vom Hellenismus frei geblieben wäre. Der syrische Gottesmann hat in seinem symbolhaften Verhalten und in seiner sozialen Funktion die Einheit von Denken und Willen bewahrt, die zum Erbe der griechischen Bildung gehört und das Charakteristikum par excellence der frühsyrischen Theologie war. Sie war und blieb Ausgangspunkt für jedes religiöse Handeln und Denken und bildete die bleibende Anziehungskraft dieser heiligen Männer.

Es wundert daher nicht, daß die hervorragendsten Figuren des syrischen Christentums, wie der Mann Gottes in Edessa und Symeon der Stylit, die den Typus des Gottesmannes am prägnantesten zeigen, im europäischen Mittelalter große Verehrung fanden[75]. Als *alter Christus* treten sie neben Franziskus von Assisi und andere Heilige, die die intellektuellen und spirituellen Kräfte des christlichen Glaubens verkörpern und deshalb eine bleibende paradigmatische Funktion behalten werden[76].

ANMERKUNGEN

[1]Das Bekanntwerden der Legende des heiligen Alexius in Rom steht zweifelsohne im Zusammenhang mit der Ankunft des Sergius, Erzbischof von Damaskus, in Rom, der 977 verbannt und von Papst Benedikt VII. mit der Sorge für die Kirche des heiligen Bonifatius betraut wurde. In dieser römischen Bonifatius-Kirche findet sich das älteste Denkmal des Alexius im Westen. Vgl. L.DUCHESNE, Les lêgendes chrétiennes de l'Aventin, MAH 10 (1890) 234ff.; A.AMIAUD, La lêgende syriaque de Saint Alexis l'homme de Dieu, Paris 1889, XXXVII - XXXVIII; C.E.STEBBINS, Les origines de la lêgende de Saint Alexis, RBPH 51 (1973) 497ff.; Die Literatur über die mittelalterlichen Fassungen ist sehr umfangreich. Ich führe in Auswahl die Wichtigste an: H.F.MASSMANN, Sanct Alexiusleben in acht gereimten mittelhochdeutschen Behandlungen, Quedlinburg-Leipzig 1843. M.RÖSSLER, Die Fassungen der Alexiuslegende mit besonderer Berücksichtigung der mittelenglischen Versionen, Wien-Leipzig 1905; DIES. Sankt Alexius, Altfranzösische Legendendichtung des 11. Jh., hrg. von ..., Halle/Saale 1941[2]; Versiones espangnolas de la leyenda de San Alejo, Nueva Revista de Filologia Hispanica 3 (1949) 329ff. V.L.DEDECK-HÉRY, The Life of Saint Alexius, New York 1932. G.EIS, Beiträge zur mittelhochdeutschen Legende und Mystik, Untersuchungen und Texte, Berlin 1935, Nachdruck Nendeln 1967. G.ROHLFS, Sankt Alexius. Altfranzösische Legendendichtung des 11. Jh., hrg. von ..., Tübingen 1963[4], 11-13 Bibliographie. L.GNÄDINGER, Eremitica. Studien zur altfranzösischen Heiligenvita des 12. und 13. Jahrhunderts, Tübingen 1972. F.WAGNER, Die Alexiuslegende des Brüsseler Codex Nr. 8883-94 (Fs. I.Schröbler, PBB 95, Sonderband) Tübingen 1973, 144-169. H.F.ROSENFELD, 'Alexius', in: VL Bd.1 (1978[2]) 226-235, hier Bibliographie.

[2]Vgl. A.AMIAUD, La lêgende syriaque..., XIII ff.; A.BAUMSTARK, Geschichte der syrischen Literatur, Bonn 1922, 96; das älteste Manuskript ist: Britisches Museum, London, Add.15.644, vgl. A.AMIAUD, aaO., I ff.; BHO, 10-11.

[3]A.AMIAUD, aaO., XIII ff.; C.E.STEBBINS, Les origines de la lêgende de Saint Alexis ... aaO.; 499ff.

[4]A.AMIAUD, aaO., XI; P.PEETERS, Le tréfonds oriental de l'hagiographie byzantine, Bruxelles 1950, 178 nimmt auch an, daß die abendländischen Fassungen auf ein byzantinisches Original zurückgehen; darauf weisen die

griechischen Eigennamen hin. F.HALKIN, Une lêgende grecque de Saint Alexis. BHG 56d, AnBoll 98 (1980) 5 - 16, macht darauf aufmerksam, daß die Art, in der in par. 3 über die weltberühmte Ikone von Edessa gesprochen wird, auf eine Entstehung vor 730 hinweist.

[5]Es ist noch eine offene Forschungsfrage, inwieweit die abendländischen Versionen charakteristische Züge der syrischen Legende erhalten oder umgewandelt haben. Von großer Wichtigkeit hierfür sind die historischen Beziehungen zwischen Syrien und dem Westen, die erneut erforscht werden sollten; vgl. P.SCHEFFER - BOICHORST, Kleine Forschungen zur Geschichte des Mittelalters IV. Zur Geschichte der Syrer im Abendlande, MIÖG 6 (1885) 521 - 551; L.BREHIER, ByzZ 12 (1903) 1-39; P.LAMBRECHTS, L'antiqué classique 6 (1937) 35-61.

[6]P.BROWN, The Rise and Function of the Holy Man in Late Antiquity, JRS 51 (1971) 80 - 101; DERS., The Making of Late Antiquity, Harvard 1978, 12ff.; The Cult of the Saints. Its Rise and Function in Latin Christianity, Chicago - London 1981, 1ff.: The Holy and the Grave; für eine Kritik an Brown's Ansichten siehe J.SUMPTION, TLS 1 (May 1981) vgl. H.J.W.DRIJVERS, Hellenistic and Oriental Origins, in: The Byzantine Saint,University of Birmingham Fourteenth Spring Symposium of Byzantine Studies, ed. by S.HACKEL, Studies Supplementary to Sobornost 5 (1981) 25 - 33.

[7]Vgl. S.P.BROCK, Early Syrian Asceticism, Numen 20 (1973) 1 - 19; A.GUILLAUMONT, Aux origines du monachisme chrétien. Pour une phénoménologie du monachisme, Spiritualité orientale 30 (1979); P.CANIVET, Le monachisme syrien selon Théodoret de Cyr,ThH 42 (1977); P.NAGEL, Die Motivierung der Askese in der Alten Kirche und der Ursprung des Mönchtums (TU 95) 1966; G.KRETSCHMAR, Die Theologie des Heiligen in der frühen Kirche, in: Aspekte frühchristlicher Heiligenverehrung, Oikonomia 6 (1977) 77 - 125.

[8]Das ist die Ansicht von E.R.DODDS, Pagan and Christian in an Age of Anxiety. Some Aspects of religious Experience from Marcus Aurelius to Constantine, Cambridge 1965, 34 - 36.

[9]Diese Ansicht vertreten z.B. A.VÖÖBUS, History of Asceticism in the Syrian Orient I (CSCO Syr14) 1958,140; W.CRAMER, Der Geist Gottes und

des Menschen in frühsyrischer Theologie, MBTh 46 (1979) 6ff.; R.MURRAY, Symbols of Church and Kingdom. A Study in Early Syriac Tradition, Cambridge 1975,2ff.

[10]A.AMIAUD, La lêgende syriaque..,aaO., 1.; für die Vita Angelica siehe P.NAGEL, Die Motivierung der Askese...., 34ff. mit berechtigter Kritik über die Ansichten von S.FRANK, AGGELIKOS BIOS. Begriffsanalytische und begriffsgeschichtliche Untersuchung zum "engelgleichen Leben" im frühen Mönchtum, Münster 1964.

[11]Joh 21,25; derartige Schlußwendungen sind traditionell, vgl. R.BULTMANN, Das Evangelium des Johannes, Göttingen 1957,540, Anm. 3, wo mehrere Beispiele angeführt werden, sowohl aus dem jüdischen als auch aus dem griechischen Bereich.

[12]A.AMIAUD, La lêgende syriaque...,aaO.

[13]A.AMIAUD, aaO., 8.; für den Fremdenfriedhof siehe G.DAGRON, Le christianisme dans la ville byzantine, DOP 31 (1977) 18 und Anm. 81.

[14]A.AMIAUD, aaO., 9; diese Angabe stimmt inhaltlich mit der Rabbulavita überein, vgl. G.G.BLUM, Rabbula von Edessa. Der Christ, der Bischof, der Theologe (CSCO, Syr 34) 1969,70ff.

[15]A.AMIAUD, aaO., 9; der Paramonarius spielt die Rolle des Augen- und Ohrenzeugen, um die Authentizität der Legende zu verbürgen, obwohl er höchstwahrscheinlich nicht der Verfasser der Legende ist, vgl., A.AMIAUD, aaO., XIVII.

[16]Dieser Hymnus im Philipperbrief beschreibt die drei Stadien der Offenbarungsgeschichte Christi, vgl., E.KÄSEMANN, Kritische Analyse von Phil.2. 5-11, ZThK 47 (1950) 313 - 360; G.BORNKAMM, On Understanding the Christhymn (Phil.2.6-11), Early Christian Experience, London 1969, 112 - 122; A.GRILLMEIER, Christ in Christian Tradition, London 1975^{2}, 20ff.

[17]Für die Behauptung von C.E.STEBBINS, Les origines de la lêgende de saint Alexius..., aaO., 499: "Cette première lêgende syriaque est dêpourvue de tout élément miraculeux. La résurrection du saint n'en fait pas encore partie" gibt es keinen Grund in den überlieferten Fassungen. Sie geht

zurück auf eine mündliche Mitteilung von ASSEMANI an JEAN PIEN, den ersten kritischen Herausgeber der Alexius Legende, vgl., A.AMIAUD, La Légende syriaque ..., XXXVII-XXXVIII; H.J.W.DRIJVERS, Hellenistic and Oriental Origins..., 28.

[18]CLEM.ALEX., Strom.III,87; vgl., M.ELZE, Tatian und seine Theologie, Göttingen 1960, 116ff.; P.NAGEL, Die Motivierung der Askese..., aaO., 37f.

[19]F.C.BURKITT, Evangelion da-Mepharreshe, Cambridge 1904,I,386 und sein Kommentar zur Stelle: II,299.

[20]S.P.BROCK, The Baptist's diet in Syriac sources, OrChr 54 (1970) 113 - 124; DERS., Early Syrian Asceticism, Numen 20 (1973) 4ff.

[21]P.BROWN, The Rise and Function of the Holy Man in Late Antiquity, 99; E.R.DODDS, Pagan and Christian in an Age of Anxiety..., aaO., 77ff.

[22]Vgl., P.NAGEL, Die Motivierung der Askese ..., aaO., 5, der darauf hinwies, daß dieses Logion zur Gemeindetheologie gehört.

[23]Vgl., A.GUILLAUMONT, Le dépaysement comme forme d'ascèse dans le monachisme ancien, AEPHE.R. (1968-69) 31 - 58 = Aux origines du monachisme chrétien, 89 - 116.

[24]Vgl., E. STOMMEL, Zemeion ekpetaseos (Didache 16,6) RömQ 48 (1953) 21 - 42; A.GRILLMEIER, Der Logos am Kreuz, München 1956, 67 - 80; DERS., Christ in Christian Tradition ..., aaO., 61ff.

[25]Vgl., H.J.W.DRIJVERS, Spätantike Parallelen zur altchristlichen Heiligenverehrung unter besonderer Berücksichtigung des syrischen Stylitenkultes. Aspekte frühchristlicher Heiligenverehrung, Oikonomia 6 (1977) 68f.; THEODORETUS, Hist.Rel. XXVI,12.

[26]Vgl., P.CANIVET, Le monachisme syrien, 117 - 145; P.BROWN, The Rise and Function of the Holy Man ..., 87ff.; A.ADNES - P.CANIVET, Guérisons miraculeuses et exorcismes dans l'Histoire Philothée de Théodoret de Cyr,RHR (1967) 54 - 82; 150 - 179.

[27]P.BROWN, The Rise and Function of the Holy Man ..., aaO., 81.

[28]Für Tatian siehe M.ELZE, Tatian und seine Theologie, Göttingen 1960; für das Diatessaron siehe L.LELOIR, Le Diatessaron de Tatien, L'Orient syrien 1 (1956) 208 - 231; 313 - 334; T.BAARDA, The Gospel Quotations of Aphrahat the Persian Sage, Diss. Amsterdam 1975 mit fast vollständiger Bibliographie; die Thomasakten werden zitiert nach der Edition von W.WRIGHT, Apocryphal Acts of the Apostles, 2 Tle London 1871 (reprint Amsterdam 1968); vgl., G.BORNKAMM, in: HENNECKE - SCHNEEMELCHER, Neutestamentliche Apokryphen II, Tübingen 1964, 297ff.; die Oden Salomons werden zitiert nach die Edition von W.BAUER, Die Oden Salomons (Kleine Texte 64) Berlin 1933; vgl., W.BAUER, in: HENNECKE - SCHNEEMELCHER II, 576ff.; die letzte Edition von M.LATTKE, Die Oden Salomons in ihrer Bedeutung für Neues Testament und Gnosis, 2 Bde,Freiburg - Göttingen 1979, enthält in der Übersetzung viele Fehler; die Frühdatierung der 'Oden' ist nicht zu halten, vgl., H.J.W.DRIJVERS, The 19th Ode of Solomon. Its Interpretation and Place in Syrian Christianity, JThS 31 (1980) 337 - 355; DERS. Odes of Solomon and Psalms of Mani. Christians and Manichaeans in Third-Century Syria, Studies in Gnosticism and Hellenistic Religions presented to Gilles Quispel, ed. R.VAN DEN BROEK - M.J.VERMASEREN, EPRO 91, (1981) 117 - 130; R.MURRAY's Darlegungen in: Symbols of Church and Kingdom ..., aaO., 24ff.: The Literature and the Writers, sind deshalb an vielen Stellen zu korrigieren.

[29]An erster Stelle das Thomasevangelium, dessen Semitismen auf ein syrisches Original hinweisen, vgl., zuletzt A.GUILLAUMONT, Les sémitismes dans l'Évangile selon Thomas, Studies presented to GILLES QUISPEL, Leiden 1981, 190 - 204; H.-CH.PUECH, En quête de la Gnose II. Sur l'évangile selon Thomas, Paris 1978; es scheint mir wahrscheinlich, daß das Thomasevangelium im selben Kreise wie die Thomasakten entstanden ist und das die Evangelientraditionen teils vom Diatessaron beeinflußt oder abhängig sind,so daß hier keine alten authentischen Logia vorliegen, sondern spätere Bearbeitungen evangelischer Traditionen, die durch eine Kombination messerscharfer Theologie mit poetischer Sprache charakterisiert werden; wichtig ist auch das Buch von Thomas dem Athleten, vgl., J.D.TURNER, The BOOK of Thomas the Contender, Missoula 1975, 233ff.; für das manichäische Schrifttum kommen in Betracht die koptischen manichäischen Psalmen, Homilien und Kephalaia, die alle auf syrische Originale zurückgehen, und der Kölner Mani Codex, der ebenfalls vom Syrischen ins Griechische übersetzt

worden ist, vgl., A.HENRICHS - L.KOENEN, Ein griechischer Mani - Codex P.Köln, inv.nr.4780, ZPE 5 (1970) 104ff.; A.HENRICHS, The Cologne Mani Codex reconsidered, HSCP 83 (1979) 352ff.; siehe meine in Kürze erscheinende Arbeit: Christ and Man in Early Syrian Theology.

[30]Vgl., A.F.J.KLIJN, John XIV 22 and the Name Judas Thomas, Studies in John presented to J.N.Sevenster, NTS 24 (1970) 88 - 96; J.J.GUNTHER, The Meaning and Origin Of the Name "Judas Thomas", Le Muséon 93 (1980) 113 - 148,hat ganz revolutionäre Ansichten des Ursprungs und der frühen Geschichte des syrischsprachigen Christentums, die jedoch nicht unbestritten bleiben sollen, vgl., H.J.W.DRIJVERS, Addai und Mani, Christentum und Manichäismus im dritten Jahrhundert in Syrien, Akten des III. Symposium Syriacum (im Druck).

[31]W.WRIGHT, Apocryphal Acts of the Apostles ..., aaO., 146 - 150; für das Brautlied siehe: G.HOFFMANN, Zwei Hymnen der Thomasakten, ZNW 4 (1903) 273ff.; E.PREUSCHEN, Zwei gnostische Hymnen, Gießen 1904; G.BORNKAMM, in:HENNECKE - SCHNEEMELCHER II, 302f.; eine neue Bearbeitung und Analyse scheint notwendig trotz A.F.J.KLIJN, The Acts of Thomas Leiden 1962, 168 - 179 und R.MURRAY, Symbols of Church and Kingdom ..., aaO., 133ff.

[32]Vgl., J.A.DELAUNAY, Rite et symbolique en ACTA THOMAE vers.syr.I,2a et ss., Mêmorial Jean de Menasce, éd. Ph.GIGNOUX, Acta Iranica, Teheran 1974, 11 - 34.

[33]Das Mahlzeitmotiv innerhalb den Thomasakten läßt sich in aller Verwikkeltheit und Vieldeutigkeit genauso analysieren wie das Motiv der Verkleidung, wie ich in einer künftigen Arbeit darzulegen hoffe; vgl., V.ARNOLD-DÖBEN, Die Bildersprache des Manichäismus, Arbeitsmaterialien zur Religionsgeschichte 3, Köln 1978, 78ff.; R.MURRAY, Symbols of Church and Kingdom ..., aaO., 131ff.

[34]Das Motiv der himmlischen Hochzeit ist weitverbreitet im syrisch-mesopotamischen Raum und begegnet in gnostischen wie in 'rechtgläubigen' Kreisen; vgl., G.WIDENGREN, Mesopotamian Elements in Manichaeism (King and Savior II), UUA 1946:3, 109ff.; H.-G.GAFFRON, Studien zum koptischen Philippusevangelium unter besonderer Berücksichtigung der Sakramente, Inaugural-Dissertation Bonn 1969, 191 - 219; R.MURRAY, Symbols of Church

and Kingdom ..., aaO., 131ff.; 254ff.

[35]W.WRIGHT, Apocryphal Acts of the Apostles ..., aaO., 157: '... that I am not veiled, (is) because the veil of corruption is taken away from me; and that I am not ashamed, (is) because the deed of shame has been removed far from me ....that I have not had intercourse with a husband, the end whereof is bitter repentance, (is) because I am betrothed to the true Husband.' 158: '... who did not withhold Thy mercy from me who was lost, but didst show me (how) to seek for myself and to put away from me the things that are not mine.'

[36]Diesselbe Vorstellung begegnet in Logion 114 des Thomasevangeliums: Simon Peter said to them: let Mary go out from among us, because women are not worthy of the Life. Jesus said: See, I shall lead her, so that I will make her male, that she too may become a living spirit, resembling you males. For every woman who makes herself male will enter the Kingdom; vgl., G.QUISPEL, Makarius, das Thomasevangelium und das Lied von der Perle, Leiden 1967, 104f., der aber die Vorstellung als alexandrinisch betrachtet; H.-CH.PUECH, En quête de la Gnose II.Sur l'évangile selon Thomas, Paris 1978, 239s.; A.F.J.KLIJN, Das Thomasevangelium und das altsyrische Christentum, VigChr 15 (1961) 146 - 159; DERS., Christianity in Edessa and the Gospel of Thomas, NT(1972) 70 - 77.

[37]W.WRIGHT, Apocryphal Acts of the Apostles ..., aaO., 180.

[38]Vgl., BAUDOUIN DE GAIFFIER, Source d'un texte relatif au mariage dans la Vie de S.Alexis BHL 289, AnBoll 63 (1945) 48 - 55; DERS., Intactam sponsam relinquens. A propos de la Vie de S.Alexis, AnBoll 65 (1947) 157 - 195.

[39]A.F.J.KLIJN, The Acts of Thomas. Introduction, Text, Commentary, Leiden 1962 hat diese Gebete fast unbeachtet gelassen; vgl., R.MURRAY, Symbols of Church and Kingdom ..., aaO., 27.

[40]W.WRIGHT, Apocryphal Acts of the Apostles ..., aaO., 153f.

[41]W.WRIGHT, Ebda, 207f.

[42]Vgl., A.ADAM, Grundbegriffe des Mönchtums in sprachlicher Sicht, ZKG 65

(1953-54) 209 - 239; E.BECK, Ein Beitrag zur Terminologie des ältesten syrischen Mönchtums, Antonius Magnus Eremita, Stud.Anselm.38 (1956) 254 - 267; A.VÖÖBUS, History of Asceticism in the Syrian Orient I, 97 - 108; A.GUILLAUMONT, Monachisme et êthique judêo-chrêtienne, Aux origines du monachisme chrêtien, 47 - 66; R.MURRAY, The Exhortation to Candidates for Ascetical Vows at Baptism in the Ancient Syrian Church, NTS 21 (1974 - 75) 58 - 79; DERS., Symbols of Church and Kingdom ..., 12 - 16; G.NEDUNGATT, The Covenanters of the Early Syriac-Speaking Church, OrChrPer 39 (1973) 205ff.

43 Daß die 'Thomasakten' gnostisch seien, ist eine weitverbreitete Ansicht, die z.B. von G.BORNKAMM, HENNECKE-SCHNEEMELCHER II, 300ff., von G.WIDENGREN, Mesopotamian Elements in Manichaeism. passim, K.RUDOLPH, Die Gnosis.Wesen und Geschichte einer spätantiken Religion, Leipzig 1977, 245ff. u.a. vertreten wird. Die Alternative gnostisch - nicht gnostisch wird aber der Eigenart dieser Schriften nicht gerecht, vgl., H.DÖRRIE, Gnostische Spuren bei Plutarch, Studies presented to Gilles Quispel, Leiden 1981, 114 - 116: "... die Äußerungen religiösen Denkens und Empfindens sind in den Jahrhunderten von Poseidonios bis Plotin, ja bis zu Proklos von einem ganz bestimmten Stil geprägt; ... Und es ist eine Zeitlang verführerisch gewesen, alle Äußerungen, die diese Gepräge tragen, "gnostisch" zu nennen. Damit ist nichts gewonnen, solange nicht die notwendige Unterscheidung gewonnen ist, um innerhalb des weiten Komplexes, der von spätantiker Frömmigkeit geprägt ist, die einzelnen Phänomene vom einander zu sondern".

44 Vgl., A.DIHLE, Das Problem der Entscheidungsfreiheit in frühchristlicher Zeit. Die Überwindung des gnostischen Heilsdeterminismus mit den Mitteln der griechischen Philosophie, in: Gnadenwahl und Entscheidungsfreiheit in der Theologie der Alten Kirche, OIKONOMIA 9 (1980) 9-31.

45 Das stellt sich z.B. heraus bei einer genauen Analyse des Perlenliedes in den Thomasakten, das sowohl über Adam's Vertreibung aus dem Paradiese und seiner Rückkehr handelt, als über die Entsendung und Rückkehr Christi, und daher das Wesentliche der Theologie der Thomasakten enthält.

46 So z.B. W.CRAMER, Der Geist Gottes und des Menschen in frühsyrischer Theologie, Münster 1979,23ff.

[47]Vgl., M. ELZE, Tatian und seine Theologie, Göttingen 1960; H.J.W. DRIJVERS, Bardaiṣan of Edessa, SSN 6, Assen 1966, passim; A.DIHLE, Zur Schicksalslehre des Bardesanes, Kerygma und Logos. (Festschrift für Carl Andresen) hrg. v. A.M.RITTER, Göttingen 1979, 123 - 135, wies auf Verbindungen zur platonischen Tradition hin; für den Einfluß der Markioniten im syrischen Bereich siehe H.J.W.DRIJVERS, Die Oden Salomos und die Polemik mit den Markioniten im syrischen Christentum, Symposium Syriacum 1976, OrChrA 205 (1978) 39 - 55; W.BAUER, Rechtgläubigkeit und Ketzerei im ältesten Christentum, BHT 10 (1934) 27ff.; zur Gattung der halb-philosophischen gelehrten Literatur gehören auch die 'Pseudoklementinen'. Es ist nicht ohne Grund, daß das älteste syrische Manuskript aus dem Jahre 411 v. Chr., Britisches Museum London, Add. 12150,eine syrische Fassung der 'Pseudoklementinen' enthält, die ebenfalls antimarkionitische Tendenzen aufweisen vgl., H.SCHOEPS, Theologie und Geschichte des Judenchristentums, Tübingen 1949, 305ff.; für Marcion's philosophische Fragestellungen siehe J.G.GAGER, Marcion and Philosophy, VigChr 26 (1972) 53 - 59.

[48]Vgl., H.J.W.DRIJVERS, Oden of Solomon and Psalms of Mani. Christians and Manichaeans in Third-Century-Syria, Studies presentes to GILLES QUISPEL, Leiden 1981, 117 - 130. Diese Spätdatierung wird bestätigt durch Diatessaronlesarten, wie sie z.B. in Ode 17,9 gefunden werden, wo Mt 16,18 nach dem Diatessaron zitiert wird und Einfluß von Ps 107,16 vorliegt, vgl., BURKITT, Evangelion Da-Mepharreshe II, 119, 156; vgl., R.MURRAY, Symbols of Church and Kingdom ..., aaO., 228 - 236; 324 - 329.

[49]Übersetzung nach W.BAUER, Die Oden Salomos, Kleine Texte 64 (1933) mit geringen Änderungen vom Verfasser.

[50]Wachsam (syr. *ᶜyr'*) gehört zur asketischen Terminologie; vgl., P.NAGEL Die Motivierung der Askese ..., aaO., 43.

[51]Vgl., Ode Sal 27 und 37, wo dasselbe Motiv begegnet; vgl, A.Grillmeier, Christ in Christian Tradition ..., aaO., 61.

[52]Übersetzung nach W.BAUER, Die Oden Salomos, mit einer Änderung in v. 7: Bauer: "und daß, die (ihn) annehmen, nicht zuschanden werden sollen"; das hier verwendete Verb *bht* = sich schämen wird auch in Gen 2,25 verwendet, worauf Ode Sal 9,7 anspielt. LATTKE'S Übersetzung: "nicht verwirrt werden

mögen" ist grundfalsch.

[53]Das Syrische verwendet hier für Person das Griechische *prosopon!* Schimmert hier die dogmatische Verwendung dieses Begriffes schon durch? vgl., R.ABRAMOWSKI, Der Christus der Salomooden, ZNW 35 (1936) 67, der darauf hinwies,daß wir hier bei der Verwendung dieses Ausdrucks den Übergang zu einem Terminus sich vollziehen sehen, der in der späteren antiochenischen Schule charakteristisch ist.

[54]Vgl., APHRAATES, Demonstrationes (PS I,1) 248,25: Wer das Bild der Engel erlangt, der sei fremd vor den Menschen; vgl., H.J.W.DRIJVERS, Kerygma und Logos in den Oden Salomos dargestellt am Beispiel der 23. Ode, Kerygma und Logos (Festschrift für CARL ANDRESEN Göttingen 1979) 153 - 172, wo die Theologie der 'Oden' ausführlich dargelegt worden ist.

[55]Siehe z.B. Ode 7,6 - 9; 9,14 - 20; 11,4; 16,8 - 20; 23,12; 36,8.

[56]M.ELZE, Tatian und seine Theologie ..., aaO., 97; Oratio ad Graecos, c.11.

[57]G.NEDUNGATT, The Covenanters of the Early Syriac-Speaking Church, OCP 39 (1973) 191-315; 419-444.

[58]Vgl., A.VÖÖBUS, Celibacy, a Requirement for Admission to Baptism in the Early Syrian Church, PETSE 1 (1951) 35ff.: The Question of Duration; R.MURRAY, The Exhortation to Candidates for ascetical Vows,NTS 21 (1974-5) 59 - 80.

[59]P.BROWN, The Rise and Function of the Holy Man, 92; DERS., The World of Late Antiquity from Marcus Aurelius to Muhammad, London 1971,97ff.

[60]Z.B. Ode Sal 6,4-6; 7,13; 11,4; 18,13 - 15; Thomasakten, ed. W.WRIGHT, Apocryphal Acts of the Apostles ..., aaO., 154,205f.207 etc.

[61]Vgl., L.BIELER, Theios Aner. Das Bild des "göttlichen Menschen" in Spätantike und Frühchristentum,2Tle, Wien 1935 - 36, 60 - 96; H.DÖRRIE, Die Religiosität des Platonismus im 4. und 5. Jahrhundert nach Christus, in: De Jamblique à Proclus, Entretiens surl'antiquité classique XXI, Genève 1975, 257 - 281; J.LEIPOLDT, Griechische Philosophie und frühchristliche Askese,BVSAW.PH 106,4 (1961) 16ff.

[62]THEODORETUS,Hist.Rel., Prol.2,SC 234,127s.149, Anm.8; Thomasevangelium, Log.13; THEODORETUS, Therap.I,38; XII,28; vgl., P.CANIVET, Le monachisme syrien ..., aaO., 68ss.; A.GUILLAUMONT,Aux origines du monachisme syrien..., aaO.; vgl., A.M.MALINGREY, 'Philosophia'. Etude d'une groupe de mots dans la littérature grecque,Paris 1961.

[63]SEXTUS EMPIRICUS,Adv.math.IX,13; IX,123; CICERO, Off.I,43,153; II,2,5; ALBINUS, Didaskalikos,Prol.; SENECA,Epist.89,5; QUINTILIAN, Inst.I 10,5; ORIGENES,Cels. III 72; CLEM.ALEX.Paed.II 2,25; Strom. I,5,30; vgl., H.DÖRRIE, Die Religiosität des Platonismus ..., aaO.; 257,Anm.1.

[64]PLATON, Theaitet 176 AB; Staat 10,613 A; Phaidon 82A; Gesetze 4, 715 E - 716 B; Phaidros 248 A; ALBINUS, Didaskalikos,c.28; siehe auch PLATON, Timaeus 90 D; vgl., H.DÖRRIE, Der Platonismus in der Kultur- und Geistesgeschichte der frühen Kaiserzeit, in: Platonica Minora, München 1976, 178,198f.,223; E.R.DODDS, Pagan and Christian in an Age of Anxiety ..., aaO., 74ff.; H.MERKI, Homoiōsis Theō, Freiburg i.Schweiz 1952.

[65]Vgl., H.DÖRRIE, Die Religiosität des Platonismus im 4. und 5. Jahrhundert nach Christus ..., aaO., 259ff.; PORPHYRIUS, De Abst.00.49; Ad Marc.11.

[66]Vgl., C.ANDRESEN, Justin und der Mittlere Platonismus,ZNW 44 (1952-53) 157 - 195; N.HYLDAHL, Philosophie und Christentum. Eine Interpretation der Einleitung zum Dialog Justins, Kopenhagen 1966; J.C.M.VAN WINDEN, Le Christianisme et la philosophie, Kyriakon (Festschrift für J. QUASTEN, Münster 1970) 205 - 213; E.F.OSBORN, Justinus Martyr.BHTh 47 (1973) M.ELZE, Tatian und seine Theologie, Göttingen 1960; E.P.MEIJERING, Irenaeus' Relation to Philosophy in the Light of his Concept of Free Will, Romanitas et Christianitas (Studia J.H.WASZINK oblata, Amsterdam 1973) 221 - 232.

[67]Vgl., JUSTIN, Dial.76,1; 128,3-4; C.ANDRESEN, Justin und der Mittlere Platonismus..., aaO., 190; J.DANIÉLOU, Message évangélique et culture hellénistique, Tournai 1961,317ss.; A.GRILLMEIER, Christ in Christian Tradition ..., aaO., 92f.

[68] Timaios 34 A-B; 36 B; vgl., C.ANDRESEN, Justin und der Mittlere Platonismus..., aaO., 188ff.; ALBINUS, Didaskalikos 10, (ed. HERMANN, 164,16ff.)

[69]Vgl., J.DANIÉLOU, Message évangélique et culture hellénistique..., aaO., 319f.; W.BARNARD,God, the Logos, the Spirit and the Trinity, Studia Theologica 24 (1970) 70 - 92.

[70]TATIAN, Oratio ad Graec.5; M.ELZE, Tatian und seine Theologie ...,aaO., 70ff.; THEOPHILUS, Ad Autol.I,3; J.DANIÉLOU, Message évangélique...,aaO., 324ff.; vgl., Ad Autol.II,10.

[71]Adv.haer.3,25,5; 5,4,2; 3,23,1; vgl., Timaeus 29 D - 30 A; vgl., Meijering, Irenaeus' Relation to Philosophy ..., aaO., 222ff.

[72]H.J.W.DRIJVERS, Bardaiṣan of Edessa ...,aaO., 96ff.; A.DIHLE, Zur Schicksalslehre des Bardesanes, Kerygma und Logos (Festschrift f.C. ANDRESEN) 123 - 135.

[73]Vgl., FERGUS MILLAR, Paul of Samosata, Zenobia and Aurelian: The Church, local Culture and political Allegiance in Third-Century Syria, JRS 61 (1971) 2ff.; DERS., JJS 29 (1978) 3ff.; H.J.W.DRIJVERS,ANRW VIII (1977) 885ff.; R.SCHMIDT, Die Sprachen im römischen Reich der Kaiserzeit,BoJ.B 40 (1980)196ff.

[74]Vgl., H.DÖRRIE, Die Religiosität des Platonismus, 261ff.; DERS., Überlegungen zum Wesen antiker Frömmigkeit, Pietas (Festschrift für B.Kötting, 1980) 3 - 14; vgl., E.R.DODDS, Pagan and Christian..., aaO., 30ff.;

[75]Vgl., J.NASRALLAH, Survie de Saint Siméon l'Alepin dans les Gaules, Syria 61 (1974) 171 - 197.

[76]H.W.van OS, St.Francis of Assisi as a second Christ in early Italian painting, Simiolus 7 (1975) 3 - 20.

LITERATUR

Auswahl zum Thema: 'Mann Gottes im syrischen Christentum'

Les Actes apocryphes des apôtres. Christianisme et monde paien, Genève 1981.

ADAM A., Grundbegriffe des Mönchtums in sprachlicher Sicht, ZKG 65 (1953/54) 209-239.

AMIAUD A., La légende syriaque de Saint Alexis l'homme de Dieu, Paris 1889.

BECK E., Ein Beitrag zur Terminologie des ältesten syrischen Mönchtums, Antonius Magnus Eremita, Stud. Anselm. 38, Roma 1956, 254-267.

BIELER L., Theios Aner. Das Bild des "göttlichen Menschen" in Spätantike und Frühchristentum, 2 Tle, Wien 1935/36 (reprint Darmstadt 1976).

BLOND G., L'encratisme dans les Actes Apocryphes de Thomas, Recherches et Travaux 1/2 (1946) 5-25.

BROCK S.P., The Baptist's diet in Syriac sources, OrChr 54 (1970) 113-124.

DERS., Early Syrian Asceticism, Numen 20 (1973) 1-19.

BROWN P., The Rise and Function of the Holy Man in Late Antiquity, JRS 51 (1971) 80-101.

DERS., The Making of Late Antiquity, Harvard 1978.

DERS., The Cult of the Saints. Its Rise and Function in Latin Christianity, London/Chicago 1981.

CANIVET P., Le monachisme syrien selon Théodoret de Cyr, ThH 42, Paris 1977.

DELEHAYE H., Les Saints Stylites, SHG 14 Bruxelles 1923.

DODDS E.R., Pagan and Christian in an Age of Anxiety. Some Aspects of religious Experience from Marcus Aurelius to Constantine, Cambridge 1965.

DÖRRIE H., Platonica Minora, Studia et Testimonia Antiqua VIII, München 1976. (Mit Bibliographie zum Mittleren und Neuen Platonismus).

DRIJVERS H.J.W., Spätantike Parallelen zur altchristlichen Heiligenverehrung unter besonderer Berücksichtigung des syrischen Stylitenkultes, Aspekte frühchristlicher Heiligenverehrung, OIKONOMIA 6 (1977) 54-76.

DERS., Hellenistic and Oriental Origins, The Byzantine Saint, University of Birmingham Fourteenth Spring Symposium of Byzantine Studies, ed. by S.HACKEL, Studies Suppl. to Sobornost 5 (1981) 25-33.

FRANK K. Suso., (Hrg.), Askese und Mönchtum in der Alten Kirche (WdF CCCCIX) Darmstadt 1975.

DE GAIFFIER B., Source d'un texte relatif au marriage dans la Vie de S.Alexis, BHL 289, AnBoll 63 (1945) 48-55.

DERS., Intactam sponsam relinquens. A propos de la Vie de S. Alexis, AnBoll 65 (1947) 157-195.

GUILLAUMONT A., Aux origines du monachisme chrêtien. Pour une phênomênologie du monachisme. Spiritualitê Orientale 30 (1979).

LEIPOLDT J.,Griechische Philosophie und frühchristliche Askese, BVSAW.PH 106, 4 (1961).

KRETSCHMAR G., Ein Beitrag zur Frage nach dem Ursprung frühchristlicher Askese, ZThK 61 (1964) 27-67.

MURRAY R., The Exhortation to Candidates for Ascetical Vows at Baptism in the Ancient Syrian Church, NTS 21 (1974/75) 58-79.

DERS., Symbols of Church and Kingdom. A Study in Early Syriac Tradition, Cambridge 1975.

NAGEL P., Die Motivierung der Askese in der Alten Kirche und der Ursprung des Mönchtums, TU 95, Berlin 1966.

NEDUNGATT G., The Covenanters of the Early Syriac-Speaking Church, OCP 39 (1973) 191-215; 419-444.

PEETERS P., Le tréfonds oriental de l'hagiographie byzantine, Bruxelles 1950.

STEBBINS C.E., Les origines de la lêgende de Saint Alexis, RBPH 51 (1973) 497-507.

VÖÖBUS A., Celibacy, a Requirement for Admission to Baptism in the Early Syrian Church, PETSE 1, Stockholm 1951.

DERS., History of Asceticism in the Syrian Orient I/II (CSCO Subs. 14, 17) Louvain 1958/60.

Texte und Literatur zur Alexiuslegende im Mittelalter siehe oben Anm. 1.

Facts and Problems in Early Syriac-Speaking Christianity

The publication of a reprint of the well-known *Doctrina Addai* offers a good opportunity for a critical reconsideration of all real and supposed facts and problems in the study of early Syriac-speaking Christianity, for which this legendary tale of its origins is of crucial importance.[1] Since Walter Bauer's *Rechtgläubigkeit und Ketzerei* first appeared in 1934, most scholars considered the *Teaching of Addai* and the famous Abgar legend about his correspondence with Jesus and subsequent conversion as sheer fantasy, only meant to support the claims of an "orthodox" minority at Edessa to an apostolic origin.[2] The few who like to maintain a historical kernel for the legend always transferred the historical background from the time of Abgar V Ukkama (4 B.C. - A.D. 7 and A.D. 13 - 50) to the reign of Abgar VIII the Great (A.D. 177-212) and his supposed conversion to Christianity.[3] Some others saw the story about the conversion of the royal dynasty of Adiabene to Judaism, as told by Flavius Josephus, as model for an analogous story of the royal house of Osrhoëne and pointed to Jewish or Jewish-Christian origins of local

[1] *The Teaching of Addai,* trans. George Howard (Chico: Scholars Press, 1981). See review in *The Second Century* 2 (1982) 125f.

[2] W. Bauer, *Rechtgläubigkeit und Ketzerei im ältesten Christentum (BHTh* 10; Tübingen, 1934; 2nd ed. 1963); Engl. trans., *Orthodoxy and Heresy in Earliest Christianity,* ed. by R.A. Kraft and G. Krodel (Philadelphia, 1971); for a detailed survey H.J.W. Drijvers, "Rechtgläubigkeit und Ketzerei im ältesten syrischen Christentum," *Symposium Syriacum 1972 (OrChrA* 197; Rome, 1974) 291-310.

[3] *Int. al.* E. Kirsten, "Edessa," *RAC* III, 569 - 570; J.J. Gunther, "The Meaning and Origin of the Name 'Judas Thomas'," *Le Muséon* 93 (1980) 129ff.

Christianity brought about by its close ties with Jerusalem and Jewish sects like the Essenes.[4] This view seemed to find some support in the *Doctrina Addai*: "When Addai came to the city of Edessa he dwelt in the house of Tobias, the son of Tobias the Jew, who was from Palestine."[5] The same scholars consequently considered most literary products of Syriac-speaking Christianity, like the *Odes of Solomon* and the *Acts of Thomas,* as typical representatives of Jewish-Christian theology. They considered the collection of 42 hymns, known as *Odes of Solomon,* to be of a very early date (end of the first or beginning of the second century A.D.) and constituting the spiritual link to Syriac Christianity's Jewish origins.[6]

When the *Gospel of Thomas* was discovered and first published in 1959, its striking parallels with concepts in the *Acts of Thomas* and in other texts from the Syriac-speaking area were immediately noticed; therefore, its origin in such a milieu has been generally accepted.[7] In particular the name Judas Thomas or Didymus Judas Thomas, which is a combination of Judas not Iscariot (John 14:22) and Thomas called Didymus (John 20:24), is a phenomenon characteristic of and restricted to early Syriac literature, occurring in the Vetus Syra, in the *Acts of*

[4] J.B. Segal, *Edessa, 'the Blessed City'* (Oxford, 1970) 68-70; *idem,* "When Did Christianity Come to Edessa?" *Middle East Studies and Libraries.* A Felicitation Volume for Prof. J.D. Pearson, ed. by B.C. Bloomfield (London, 1980) 179 - 191; L.W. Barnard, "The Origins and Emergence of the Church in Edessa during the first two Centuries A.D.," *VigChr* 22 (1968) 161 - 175; G. Quispel, "The Discussion of Judaic Christianity," *VigChr* 22 (1968) 86; R. Murray, *Symbols of Church and Kingdom.* A Study in Early Syriac Tradition (Cambridge, 1975) 4ff.

[5] *The Teaching of Addai,* ed. Howard, 11.

[6] A.F.J. Klijn, "The Influence of Jewish Theology on the Odes of Solomon and the Acts of Thomas,' *Aspects du Judéo-Christianisme* (Paris, 1965) 167 - 179; Murray, *Symbols of Church and Kingdom,* pp. 24ff.; J.H. Charlesworth, *The Odes of Solomon* (Oxford, 1973) vii; *idem,* "Tatian's Dependence upon Apocryphal Traditions," *The Heythrop Journal* 15 (1974) 5-17; J.H. Charlesworth and R.A. Culpepper, "The Odes of Solomon and the Gospel of John," *CBQ* 35 (1973) 298 - 322.

[7] H.-Ch. Puech, *En quête de la Gnose* II. Sur **l'évangile selon Thomas** (Paris, 1978) *passim;* G. Quispel (among numerous articles on this subject), "The *Gospel of Thomas* Revisited," *Colloque international sur les textes de Nag Hammadi,* ed. B. Barc (Québec -Louvain, 1981) 218 - 266; A.F.J. Klijn, "Das Thomasevangelium und das altsyrische Christentum," *VigChr* 15 (1961) 146 - 159; *idem,* "Christianity in Edessa and the Gospel of Thomas," *Novum Testamentum* 14(1972) 70-77; A Guillaumont, "Les sémitismes dans l'évangile selon Thomas. Essai de classement," *Studies in Gnosticism and Hellenistic Religions Presented to Gilles Quispel,* ed. R. van den Broek and M.J. Vermaseren (EPRO 91; Leiden, 1981) 190 - 204.

Thomas, in Ephrem Syrus, in the *Doctrina Addai* and in Eusebius, *Church History* I. 13, where the bishop of Caesarea gives a Greek translation of essential parts of the Abgar correspondence and Abgar legend.[8] The name Judas Thomas = Judas the Twin most likely goes back to Tatian's *Diatessaron,* unless it represents an original tradition which was suppressed in the canonical gospels and only preserved in the East Syrian area, together with a whole collection of extra-canonical but authentic sayings of Jesus such as those found in the *Gospel of Thomas.*[9]

If that would be the real course of events, Judas Thomas, the apostle of Parthia, must be considered the first preacher of the gospel in the East Syrian area with Edessa as center, where a partly independent gospel tradition was preserved. The shadowy figure of Addai was then a product of the creative fantasy and propaganda of "orthodox" circles about A.D. 300 which managed to get Eusebius to believe in the historical value of their faked Edessene acts.[10] Quite recently J.J. Gunther advocated another view of the Christianization of Edessa, in which he tried to preserve the historical character of the *Doctrina Addai* as well as that of the Thomas tradition.[11] In his view Judas Thaddaeus was the original apostle of Syria. In the second quarter of the second century the Edessenes with Encratite tendencies conflated Judas Thaddaeus with Thomas, the apostle of the East, into Judas Thomas. In the same period the Abgar and Addai story was invented at the Christian court of King Abgar the Great under instigation of his court philosopher Bardaiṣan, who deposited the alleged acts of Abgar and Addai in the local archives. The original reverence for Thaddaeus fell into oblivion, but his name was still remembered among non-Encratite members of the church, who eventually referred to him as Addai, just as Eusebius did.

From the foregoing data, several problems arise which are interconnected. What is the historical value and *Sitz im Leben* of the *Doctrina Addai,* and who was the alleged Christian apostle Addai? What is the age of the local Edessene traditions about Judas Thomas, the Twin of Jesus,

[8] U. Monneret de Villard, *Le leggende orientali sui magi evangelici (Studi e Testi* 163; Rome, 1952)46 n.1; A.F.J. Klijn, "John XIV 22 and the Name Judas Thomas," *Studies in John presented to J.N. Sevenster (NovTest Suppl.* 24; Leiden, 1970) 88-96.

[9] This view is held a.o. by G. Quispel, see *art.cit.* and H. Koester, "Gnomai Diaphoroi, *HThR* 58 (1965) 279-318 = H. Koester and J.M. Robinson, *Entwicklunslinien durch die Welt des frühen Christentums* (Tübingen, 1971) 118 - 134.

[10] So H. Koester following W. Bauer, *Entwicklungslinien,* pp. 133f.

[11] J.J. Gunther, "The Meaning and Origin of the Name 'Judas Thomas'," *Le Muséon* 93 (1980) 113 - 148.

and how do they relate to Christian origins at Edessa? In this context it should be noticed that Walter Bauer considered the Abgar and Addai legend as pure fantasy and did not give any attention to the *Acts of Judas Thomas* or their place and function in the history of early Syriac-speaking Christianity.

Even if the *Doctrina Addai* is a piece of historical fiction that was completely unknown before the time of Eusebius of Caesarea, who for the first time reports on the correspondence between Jesus and Abgar V and the conversion of the Edessene king and quotes the letters, the question still remains unanswered how it was that the legend arose and in which historical situation it functioned. The legend surely came into existence before Eusebius' time. A comparison of the Syriac version, the text of Eusebius, and the Greek papyrus fragments that have been preserved leads to the conclusion that there must have been a Syriac original of which at the same time a Greek version was known, as was quite normal in this bilingual area where a Syriac and a Greek version of most writings existed side by side. It is most likely that our version of the *Doctrina Addai,* the text of Eusebius, and the Greek papyri all go back to that Syriac original, which must date back to the second half of the third century.[12] The structure and characteristic elements of the Abgar legend become clear and find their explanation in a historical situation in that particular period in which Manichaeism threatened and competed with Christian belief and behavior in Edessa. The name of the apostle Addai, the correspondence of Jesus and Abgar, the special relationship between the king and the apostle, and the occurrence of a portrait of Jesus painted by Ḥanan and brought to the king find all their special meaning in a milieu dominated by the followers of Mani and the Manichaean mission.

An apostle called Addai is completely unknown in the first centuries of Christianity and occurs only in later Edessene traditions that go back to the *Doctrina Addai.* Eusebius, who could not think of it as the name of an apostle, changed it into Thaddaeus one of the seventy, although Thaddaeus is not the Greek translation of the Semitic name Adda(i).[13] In

[12]R. Peppermüller, "Griechische Papyrusfragmente der Doctrina Addai," *VigChr* 25 (1971) 289 - 301.

[13]Matthew 10:3 and Mark 3:18 reckon Thaddaeus to the twelve apostles; Eusebius, *Hist. eccl.* I.xiii.4: "Thaddaeus, who was himself reckoned among the number of the seventy disciples . . . ." In Palmyrene onomastics the name occurs as *'d'*; cf. J.K. Stark, *Personal Names in Palymyrene Inscriptions* (Oxford, 1971) 65; in Hatra *'d'* and *'dy* are to be found (inscriptions 58[1], 46, 56, 57[1] etc.); Greek transcriptions are *Adda(s), Addaios,* and *Addai.* Cf. H. Wuthnow, *Die semitischen Menschennamen in griechischen Inschriften und Papyri des Vorderen Orients* (Leipzig, 1930) 12.

Manichaean traditions, however, Addai/Adda is one of the best known missionaries who belonged to the inner circle around the apostle of light and who was active in the Syrian-Mesopotamian area in the years 261-62 and earlier. In these times Addai, together with Abzakaya, preached the Manichaean gospel in Karka d^{e} Beth Selog according to the reliable martyr acts of that town.[14] He was one of the first disciples of Mani, who sent him about A.D. 240 from Vēh-Ardašir to the Roman Empire, where he healed and converted the Palmyrene queen Zenobia and even came to Alexandria.[15] Adda's important place among Mani's disciples also becomes clear in his being mentioned in the Cologne Mani Codex.[16] His name is familiar to the *Acta Archelai,* to Epiphanius, to Theodoret, to the Nestorian Chronicle, and to Michael Syrus; and he was known as author of many treatises on Manichaean doctrine which were combatted by Titus of Bostra and Diodore of Tarsus.[17]

According to Christian and Manichaean tradition there were two apostles called Addai. The Manichaean preached and healed in Roman Syria, the Christian preached and healed at the court and in the city of king Abgar. The one was sent by Mani, the other by Jesus through Judas Thomas. The legend of the Christian apostle Addai arose in the same time as the Manichaean Addai was active in the same region. Traditions on both apostles show a certain resemblance and analogy, and both even might be identical, in which case the Christian Addai is a borrowing from Manichaeism.

The relation between king Abgar and Jesus is due to a correspondence. Eusebius quotes a letter from Abgar to Jesus and the latter's reply, although the *Doctrina Addai* only mentions the king's letter and has

[14]G. Hoffmann, *Auszüge aus syrischen Akten persischen Märtyrer (AKM* VII, 3; Leipzig, 1880) 46; cf. H. - Ch. Puech, *Le manichéisme, son fondateur, sa doctrine* (Paris, 1949) 49 and n. 196; J. - M. Fiey, "Vers la réhabilitation de l *'histoire de Karka d' Bēt Slōh," An Boll* 82 (1964) 197; Theodor bar Koni, *Liber Scholiorum,* ed. A. Scher, *CSCO.S* 26, 345 calls him Ado; Michael Syrus, *Chronicon* I, 199, however, Addai.

[15]W.B. Henning, "Mitteliranische Manichaica aus Chinesisch-Turkestan I," *SPAW.PH* (1933) 301 - 306; W. Sundermann, "Iranische Lebensbeschreibungen Manis," *AcOr* 36 (1974) 126ff.; *idem,* "Zur frühen missionarischen Wirksamkeit Manis, "*Acta Orient. Hung.* 24 (1971) 93ff.; C. Schmidt and H.J. Polotsky, "Ein Mani-Fund in Ägypten. Originalschriften des Mani und seiner Schüler," *SPAW.PH* (1933)28; cf. H.H. Schaeder in *Gnomon* 9 (1933) 344.

[16]A. Henrichs and L. Koenen, "Ein griechischer Mani-Codex (P. Colon. inv. nr. 4780)," *ZPE* 5 (1970) 111 and n. 132.

[17]Cf. F. Forrester Church and G. G. Stroumsa, "Mani's Disciple Thomas and the Psalms of Thomas, *VigChr* 34 (1980) 49; J. Quasten, *Patrology* III (Utrecht, 1960) 359ff.; O. Klima, *Manis Zeit und Leben* (Prague, 1962) 499, n. 159.

Ḥanan write down Jesus' oral reply, which he brings to the king together with Jesus' portrait. Was the original version of the legend that Ḥanan brought the letter as well as the portrait to Edessa, or did the motif of the portrait replace the answer written by Jesus himself? Why does Eusebius mention two letters and no portrait? The alternative of letter or oral reply is no fundamental question. A dictation given by Jesus and written down by Ḥanan differs only slightly from a written answer. Doctrinal reasons might have caused this, because Jesus had not written a letter, according to later traditions.[18] It seems, therefore, plausible that the original version of the legend knew two letters, as Eusebius did. That he did not mention the portrait could likewise be caused by dogmatic reasons; the pious bishop was an opponent of images in Christian cult.[19] We might, therefore, assume that two letters and the portrait were part of the original version of the Abgar legend. External reasons can corroborate this assumption.

Mani, "the apostle of Jesus Christ," wrote numerous letters to Manichaean communities and individual persons, the whole collection of which was part of the Manichaean canon.[20] The Cologne Mani Codex has preserved some fragments of Mani's letter to his followers at Edessa, in which he describes himself as mediator of divine truth. Mani and his followers took himself for the Paraclete promised by Jesus, according to John 16:7, 8.[21] Two different concepts merged into this idea. On the one

[18] Augustine, *Contra Faust.* 28.4; Jerome, *In Ez.* 44.29; *Decretum Gelasianum* 5. 8. 1, 2; cf. W. Bauer in Hennecke and Schneemelcher, *Neutestamentliche Apokryphen* I, 325.

[19] Eusebius, *Hist. eccl.* VII. 18; *Epistola ad Constantiam Augustam* (Migne, PG 20. 1545); cf. S. Runciman, "Some Remarks on the Image of Edessa," *CHJ* 3 (1929-30) 242; K. Schäferdiek, "Zu Verfasserschaft und Situation der Epistula ad Constantiam de imagine Christi," *ZKG* 91 (1980) 177-186; Averil Cameron, *The Sceptic and the Shroud.* An Inauguaral Lecture, King's College (London, 1980) 7f. and n.29.

[20] Klima, *Manis Zeit und Leben,* pp. 420ff.; G. Widengren, *Mani und der Manichäismus* (Stuttgart, 1961) 82f.; Schmidt and Polotsky, "Ein Mani-Fund in Ägypten," pp. 24ff.; the codex P. 15998 which contained Mani's collected letters in Coptic was destroyed during the Second World War, cf. A. Böhlig, "Die Arbeit an den koptischen Manichaica," *Mysterion und Wahrheit* (Leiden, 1968) 184.

[21] *CMC* 64,8 - 65,18 contains parts of Mani's letter to Edessa; A. Henrichs and L. Koenen, *ZPE* 5 (1970) 108f. and n. 24; *ZPE* 19 (1975) 64ff.; *The Cologne Mani Codex "Concerning the Origin of his Body,"* ed. and transl. R. Cameron and A.J. Dewey (Chico, 1979) 50-5.; on Mani as the Paraclete see P. Nagel, "Der Parakletenspruch des Mani (Keph 14, 7-11) und die altsyrische Evangelienübersetzung," *Festschrift z. 150. jähr. Bestehen des Berliner Ägyptischen Museums, Mitt. aus der Ägypt. Sammlung* 8 (Berlin, 1973) 303 - 313; H.- Ch. Puech, *Sur le manichéisme* (Paris, 1979) 18 - 20; L. Koenen in *Illinois Classical Studies* 3 (1978) 154ff.; 167 - 176.

hand there was the biblical doctrine of the Paraclete, the Spirit of Truth, manifested in Mani's revelation; on the other hand, the idea of a heavenly twin or double, on which the Thomas literature had a clear influence. Just as Thomas was the earthly representative of Jesus in heaven, his twin or alter ego, so Mani had a heavenly twin, who inspired his revelations.[22]

A comparison with these Manichaean data can foster the right understanding of Abgar's correspondence with Jesus. Abgar's letter to Jesus begins as follows: Abgar Ukkama to Jesus the good Physician who has appeared in the land of Jerusalem.[23] This last expression has an exact parallel in Mani's self-designation: "I am a physician [doctor] from Babylon," as he announced himself in the presence of king Shapur.[24] The central role of healing in Addai's relation to king Abgar finds an analogue in Mani's healing of king Shapur and other royal personnages.[25] The miraculous healing power of both apostles brought the kings to the confession of their supernatural origin and mission.[26]

Jesus' answer to Abgar is still more revealing:

> Blessed are you who though not having seen me have believed in me. For it is written concerning me that those who see me will not believe in me, but those who do not see me will believe in me. With regard to the fact that you have written to me that I should come to you, that for which I was sent here is now finished and I ascend to my Father who sent me. But when I have ascended to Him I will send you one of my disciples who will heal and make your particular illness well and will turn all who are with you to eternal life. As for your city may it be blessed and may no enemy ever [or: the enemy never] again rule over it.[27]

[22]Cf. K. Rudolph, "Die Bedeutung des Kölner Mani-Codex für die Manichäismusforschung, *Mélanges H.-Ch. Puech* (Paris, 1974) 478f. and n. 3; P. Nagel, "Die apokryphen Apostelakten des 2. und 3. Jahrhunderts in der manichäischen Literatur, Ein Beitrag zur Frage nach den christlichen Elementen im Manichäismus, *Gnosis und Neues Testament* (Berlin, 1973) 178 and n. 143.

[23]*Doctrina Addai,* ed. and transl. G. Howard, 7; Eusebius *Hist. eccl.* I.13.6; cf. Jes P. Asmussen, *X^{u}ĀSTVĀNĪFT.* Studies in Manichaeism (Copenhagen, 1965) 231f.

[24]*M 566* I, ed. F.W.K. Müller, *APAW* (1904) 87; cf. L.J.R.Ort, *Mani.* A Religio-historical Description of his Personality (Leiden, 1967) 50ff.; 95ff.; *M 1306* I, ed. W.B. Henning, *Journal of the Greater India Society* 11 (1944) 85ff.; W. Sundermann, "Iranische Lebensbeschreibungen Manis," 130ff.

[25]Sundermann, "Iranische Lebensbeschreibungen Manis, 131f.

[26]*Doctrina Addai,* ed. G. Howard, p. 13: "At his entrance before him a marvelous vision appeared to Abgar in the face of Addai. As soon as Abgar saw the vision he fell down and did obeisance to Addai"; cf. Paul at Damascus! P. 15: "Abgar marveled and was astonished for just as he had heard about Jesus that he worked and performed healings so also Addai himself without drugs of any kind performed healings in the name of Jesus."

[27]*Doctrina Addai,* ed. G. Howard, p. 9.

The beginning of the letter is a variant unknown elsewhere of Jesus' logion to Thomas in John 20:29. His promise to Abgar to send him one of the disciples is a variant of the Paraclete text in John 16:7-8: "If I go not away, the Paraclete will not come to you, but if I depart I will send him to you. And when he is come, he will reprove the world of sin, and of righteousness, and of judgment!" That is the very text that played such an enormous role in Mani's revelation and formed the link par excellence with the Christian tradition.[28] Instead of sending the Paraclete, Jesus is promising a disciple, just as Mani, the apostle of Jesus Christ, considered himself the revelation of the Paraclete and was identified with it by his followers. The whole structure of the answer gives the impression that the apostle Addai enters into competition with Mani, who believed himself the promised Paraclete, so that it turns out that Jesus' answer in the Abgar legend is directed against Manichaean claims and the Manichaean mission. If such an assumption is true, the beginning of the letter also could stem from Manichaean tradition, which maintains that the eye-witnesses falsified Jesus' words and doctrine and that only some *electi* in later generations, among whom is Mani in the first place, had the right understanding of Jesus' preaching.[29]

After Christ's ascension Judas Thomas sent Addai to Edessa. In a sense this forms an anomaly in the story. Had not Jesus himself promised to send a disciple? One possible solution is that Judas Thomas was the first apostle of Edessa, who was replaced in the Abgar legend by Addai. When the legend, however, displays a clear anti-Manichaean tendency, so that the Christian apostle Addai is a borrowing from Manichaeism, who played exactly the same role with king Abgar as Mani did with Shapur, another solution presents itself. Addai functioned like an alter Mani and was the fulfillment of the Paraclete text just as Mani was. If that be true, the relation between Judas Thomas and Addai can be compared to that of Mani's heavenly twin = Syriac *tauma* and the Apostle of Light. Addai's mission is at the same time his vocation to preach the truth and heal illnesses. That is the very task ordered to Mani by his heavenly twin during his second revelation.[30]

[28]Cf. n. 22; A. Böhlig, *Die Gnosis* III. Der Manichäismus (Zürich, 1980) 24 and 308, n. 84.

[29]A. Böhlig, "Christliche Wurzeln im Manichäismus," *Mysterion und Wahrheit,* 207ff.; the view of the falsification of Jesus' words was held by the Marcionites and is a well-known element in the Pseudo-Clementine writings.

[30]Ort, *Mani,* 77ff.; Nagel, "Die apokryphen Apostelakten des 2. und 3. Jahrhunderts," 178; Rudolph, *Mélanges H.-Ch. Puech,* 478.

After Addai's arrival at Edessa he performed many miracles and healings and was called to the king's court. He cured the toparch, who became promotor of the gospel and the church and Addai's special patron. Again a certain analogy with Shapur, in his role of Mani's patron and promotor of Manichaean doctrine, comes to the fore. Mani belonged to Shapur's retinue for a couple of years.[31]

The last motif worth some closer examination is the famous portrait of Jesus that was painted by Ḥanan and taken with him for king Abgar, who gave it a place of honor in his palace. The portrait does not have any relation with the Edessa icon, which was mentioned for the first time at the end of the sixth century by Evagrius.[32] In the foregoing centuries the only mention of a portrait of Jesus was found in the *Doctrina Addai*, but that was a purely literary tradition, whereas a real portrait or icon did not exist. When the nun Egeria visited Edessa in 384, she saw Abgar's palace and heard about the correspondence, but she silently bypassed the portrait in her travel story.[33] The motif of a portrait of Jesus also has its place in the anti-Manichaean character of the *Doctrina Addai*.

A portrait or image of Mani played an essential role in Manichaean cult and mission. At the Bema Feast, the feast of Mani the Paraclete, in which the remission of sins by the Paraclete was the kernel of the whole celebration, an image of Mani the Paraclete stood upon the Bema or tribunal.[34] It was invoked and celebrated in the Bema psalms, of which the Coptic Manichaean Psalm Book contains a whole collection.[35] Eusebius of Caesarea saw an image of Mani that was venerated by

[31]*Kephalaia* I, 15.31 -34; Alexander of Lykopolis, *Contra Manich.* 4.20; cf. Widengren, *Mani und der Manichäismus,* 37f.; Sundermann, "Zur frühen missionarischen Wirksamkeit Manis, 100ff.

[32]Evagrius, *Hist. eccl.* IV. 27, ed. Bidez and Parmentier, pp. 174 - 176; cf. Averil Cameron, *The Sceptic and the Shroud,* 4ff.

[33]*Peregrinatio Aetheriae* 19, *SC* 21 (1948) 162 - 171; cf. P. Devos, "Egérie à Edesse. S. Thomas l'Apôtre. Le roi Abgar," *AnBoll* 85 (1967) 382-400.

[34]C.R.C. Allberry, "Das Manichäische Bema-Fest," in G. Widengren, ed., *Der Manichäismus* (WdF 168; Darmstadt, 1977) 321; J. Ries, "La Fête de Bêma dans l'Eglise de Mani, *REAug* 22 (1976) 218 - 233; P. Nagel, "ZOOGRAPHEIN und das 'Bild' des Mani in den koptisch-manichäischen Texten, *Eikon und Logos,* ed. H. Goltz (Halle [Saale] 1981) 199 - 238.

[35]C.R.C. Allberry, *A Manichaean Psalm - Book,* Part II (Stuttgart, 1938) 26, 1-5 mentions Mani's image.

Manichaeans, and he reports on that in his letter to the empress Constantia.[36] A bust of Mani, such as stood on the Bema, is pictured on a gem in a collection at Paris; the identity of the person in question is confirmed by a Syriac inscription: m'ny šlyḥ' dyšwʿ mšyḥ' = Mani, the Apostle of Jesus Christ.[37] The formula is almost indentical with the opening of Mani's Living Gospel, "I, Mani, Apostle of Jesus Christ, through the will of God, the Father of Truth. . . ."[38]

The portrait of Jesus in the *Doctrina Addai,* therefore, can be considered a Christian counterpart of Mani's image. Ḥanan brought it to Abgar together with Jesus's Gospel, as Mani's image and the preaching of the Paraclete went together.

The whole structure and the various motifs of the *Doctrina Addai* should be explained against the background of a historical situation in Edessa in which the Manichaean version and interpretation of Christian belief was the most powerful rival of a nascent "orthodox" version of the same tradition. It is noteworthy that Manichaeism, as such, is never mentioned in the *Doctrina Addai,* but all motifs and elements of the Abgar legend constantly allude to Manichaean concepts and practices. That might refer to a situation in which the "orthodox" (Palutians, as Ephrem Syrus will call them later) formed a minority that played a subordinate role in the local religious pattern.

Hereby the *Doctrina Addai* is given its organic place in the religious development at Edessa, where it arose in the second half of the third century as an anti-Manichaean treatise. It is not pure fantasy, has nothing to do with the conversion of the royal family of Adiabene, nor with a Golden Age of church and state at Edessa during the reign of Abgar VIII, nor with the activities of Thaddaeus, one of the Seventy and the supposed first apostle of Edessa. Rather it should be understood in the light of the Manichaean mission, concepts, and practices as known in Edessa.

The *Odes of Solomon,* often considered ecstatic Jewish-Christian hymns of salvation dating back to the very beginnings of the church, turn

[36]Eusebius, *Epistula ad Constantiam Augustam,* ed. I.B. Pitra, *Spicilegium Solesmense* I (Paris, 1852) 383f.; cf. A. Adam, *Texte zum Manichäismus* (Berlin, 1954) 106; cf. H. -Ch. Puech, *Sur le manichéisme* (Paris, 1979) 257ff., where all relevant texts are quoted.

[37]P.de Menasee - A. Guillou, "Un cachet manichéen de la Bibliothèque Nationale," *RHR* 131 (1946) 81 - 84; cf. Adam, *Texte zum Manichäismus,* 105.

[38]*Cologne Mani Codex* 66,4 ff.; Mani imitates Paul, e.g. 2 Cor. 1:1; *cf.* H.H. Schaeder, "Urform und Fortbildungen des manichäischen Systems, "*Vorträge der Bibliothek Warburg* IV (Leipzig, 1927) 129f.; Henrichs and Koenen, *ZPE* 5 (1970) 198ff.

out to be highly symbolic hymns with a very reflective wording which are based on second-century Antiochene theology and which betray the influence of Tatian's *Diatessaron* and Encratite ideas, contain outspoken anti-Marcionite polemics, and combat the congregation of Mani, who is entitled the Corruptor in Odes 33 and 38.[39] In particular, this last ode is a typical example of a concealed manner of polemic which constantly presupposes a substantial knowledge of Christian and Manichaean doctrine and symbolism.

1. I ascend to the Light of Truth as into a chariot,
   And the Truth led me and caused me to go.
2. And caused me to pass over chasms and rifts
   And saved me from cliffs and waves.
3. And became to me a Haven of Salvation,
   And set me on the level of immortal life.
4. And He went with me and made me rest and did not allow me to err,
   Because He was and is the Truth.
5. And there was no danger for me, because I walked with Him,
   And I did not err in anything because I obeyed Him.
6. For Error fled away from Him,
   And did not resist Him.
7. But the Truth was proceeding on the right way,
   And whatever I did not know He declared to me.
8. All the drugs for Error,
   And those pitfalls which are considered the sweetness of death,
9. And the author of the Corruption.
   I looked on when the corrupted Bride was adorned
   And the Bridegroom who corrupts and is corrupted.
10. And I asked the Truth: Who are these?
    And He said to me: This is the Deceiver and the Error.
11. And they imitate the Beloved and His Bride
    And they cause the world to err and corrupt it.
12. And they invite many to the wedding feast,
    And give them to drink the wine of their drunkenness,
13. So that they vomit up their wisdom and knowledge
    And they make them mindless.

[39] H.J.W. Drijvers, "Die Oden Salomos und die Polemik mit den Markioniten im syrischen Christentum," *Symposium Syriacum 1976* (*OrChrA* 205; Rome, 1978) 39 -55; *idem,* "Kerygma und Logos in den Oden Salomos dargestellt am Beispiel der 23. Ode," *Kerygma und Logos. Festschrift f. C. Andresen,* ed. A.M. Ritter (Göttingen, 1979) 153-172; *idem,* "The 19th Ode of Solomon. Its Interpretation and Place in Syrian Christianity," *JTS* 31 (1980) 337-355; *idem,* "Odes of Solomon and Psalms of Mani. Christians and Manichaeans in Third-Century Syria," *Studies in Gnosticism and Hellenistic Religions Presented to Gilles Quispel,* ed. R. van den Broek and M.J. Vermaseren (*EPRO* 91; Leiden, 1981) 117 -130.

14. Then they abandon them
And so they go about like mad and corrupted men.[40]

As in all other *Odes of Solomon,* the "I" is the redeemed believer who has gained immortal life and true Wisdom, so that he cannot err, and who has become in a sense identical with Christ, the Light of Truth.[41] Guided by the Truth, the believer is shown an anti-church, a false imitation of the Beloved and his Bride. The whole wording and imagery of Ode 38 contain some hints that this corrupted couple disguises Mani and the Manichaean church. All the symbols and images in Ode 38 have exact parallels and counterparts in the Manichaean Psalm-Book, and they give the impression that they are used on purpose in order to attack related concepts in Manichaean doctrine. The Light of Truth has a counterpart in the Spirit of Truth, which denotes Mani in the Bema Psalms.[42] The way of Truth to salvation is symbolized as a voyage by boat on a dangerous sea to a safe haven, the Haven of Salvation. This symbolism is rather rare in the Syriac area, but very frequent in the Manichaean Psalms and in Manichaean literature in general.[43] The imagery of Bride, Bridegroom, and the Wedding-Feast is very common in Manichaean literature to denote the Manichaean church, and the Manichaeans are the only Gnostics who used that symbolism to denote the church, often in combination with the parable in Matthew 25.[44] When the Odist emphasizes that the false Bride and Bridegroom cause the world to err and make men drunken, his wording gives the impression that he is perverting Manichaean statements about their church.[45] In stressing the

[40]Cf. Drijvers, "Odes of Solomon and Psalms of Mani," pp. 119ff.; my translation differs in various points from that given by J.H. Charlesworth, *The Odes of Solomon* (Oxford, 1973, 2nd ed. Chico: Scholars Press, 1977).

[41]Cf. Ode 10. 1ff.; 28; 36; 41.7.

[42]Cf. e.g. Allberry, *A Manichaean Psalm - Book,* 9,3-10; 22,6-10; cf. "Odes of Solomon and Psalms of Mani," 123ff.

[43]V. Arnold-Döben, *Die Bildersprache des Manichäismus,* Arbeitsmaterialien zur Religionsgeschichte 3 (Köln,1978) 63-70; cf. *Keph.* 8 and A. Böhlig, "Der Synkretismus des Mani," *AAWG* 96 (1975) 148f. on *ochema; idem, Mysterion und Wahrheit,* pp. 230f.; *Psalm-Book,* 52, 16-18; 58, 14; 63, 13-14; 77, 14-16; 95, 8; 151, 31-152, 5; 166,11 etc.

[44]Arnold-Döben, *Die Bildersprache des Manichäismus,* pp. 78-85; G. Widengren, *Mesopotamian Elements in Manichaeism,* UUA (1946) 3. 109-122; *Psalm-Book, 37, 25 -32; 154, 5-6; 159, 1-3.* For the rite of the wedding chamber in the Gospel of Philip, but with a different meaning, see R.M. Grant, "The Mystery of Marriage in the Gospel of Philip," *Vig Chr* 15(1961) 129-140; J-E Ménard, L'Évangile selon Philippe (Paris, 1967) 202f.

[45]Cf. *Psalm-Book,* 8, 22-26;9,3-9;26, 11ff;56,15-25; 193, 25; Ephrem Syrus, *Hymni contra Haereses,* ed. E. Beck, *CSCO.S* 76-77 (Louvain, 1957) 24, 4-7; 47, 3-4; *Odes of Solomon* 33 refers to the same opponent called the Corruptor and is a second instance of polemics against the Manichaean church.

madness and corruption of the Manichaeans he uses the traditional word-play in Mani's name that often is connected with Greek *mania* and *manikos.*[46]

These are only a few examples of the sophisticated use of well-known Manichaean imagery in this ode in order to attack the Manichaean church. *Odes of Solomon* 38 is, therefore, the oldest anti-Manichaean document known so far, having been written during or shortly after Mani's lifetime in one of the central regions of his mission, the bilingual Syrian area. The whole collection of forty-two odes was in all likelihood composed in the city of Edessa, which had an important Manichaean congregation and likewise a substantial number of Marcionites, the other target of the Odist. A date about A.D. 275, therefore, seems to be likely, taking into account the doctrinal elements in other odes that seem to refer to Christological controversies in the second half of the second century and the fact that Lactantius is the first *pater ecclesiae* who quoted the *Odes of Solomon.*[47]

It is noteworthy that the *Odes of Solomon* displays the same concealed manner of polemics as we detected in the *Doctrina Addai,* another indication of a weak position of the group to which the *Odes of Solomon* belonged, probably the same that produced the *Doctrina Addai.*

The third century in Edessa, which H. Koester considered very unclear and practically unknown, has become much clearer and actually has begun to show a kind of historical pattern, in particular when the figure of the apostle Thomas is closely looked at.[48] Judas Thomas Didymus, Judas the Twin, is the hero of the well-known *Acts of Thomas,* which were originally written in Syriac, most likely in the first half of the third century and in Edessa.[49] The same Judas Thomas is the receiver of Jesus'

[46]Eusebius, *Theophania* IV, 30; Cyril of Jerusalem, *Catecheses* VI. 19; Titus of Bostra, *Contra Manichaeos Libri quattuor,* ed. P.A. de Lagarde (Hannover, 1924^2) 70, 33; 72, 2; Serapion of Thmuis, ed. R.P. Casey, III, 9-23.

[47]Drijvers, "Odes of Solomon and Psalms of Mani," pp. 127ff.; cf. G.G. Stroumsa, "Aspects de l'eschatologie manichéenne," *RHR* 198 (1981) 166 n. 14: "Une étude systématique des Odes et de certains textes manichéens, en particulier le Psautier copte, promet une riche récolte." For this systematic study, which the present author is working on, the *Cologne Mani Codex* is of paramount importance; cf. Henrichs and Koenen, *ZPE* 44 (1981) 201-318 *passim.*

[48]On Thomas A.F.J. Klijn, *The Acts of Thomas* (Leiden, 1962) 27ff.; H. Koester, "Gnomai Diaphoroi," *HThR* 58 (1965) 279-318 = Koester and Robinson, *Entwicklunslinien,* 118-134, esp. 124ff.

[49]A. Baumstark, *Geschichte der syrischen Literatur,* p. 15; Klijn, *The Acts of Thomas,* pp. 1ff.; 13ff.; see also Y. Tissot, "*Les actes de Thomas, exemple de recueil composite,*" *Les Actes apocryphes des Apôtres.* Christianisme et monde païen (Genève, 1981) 223ff.

secret words according to the *Gospel of Thomas* and the *Book of Thomas the Contender*.[50] Both writings were preserved in the Coptic library of Nag Hammadi, but most likely written in Syriac in Edessa.[51] Given the bilingual character of the Syrian area, most Syriac writings were known in a Greek version too, which in its turn was translated into Coptic. The Syriac *Odes of Solomon* were also in a Greek version, of which some Odes found their way into the Coptic *Pistis Sophia*. The Coptic Manichaean texts, the *Psalm-Book,* the *Homilies,* and the *Kephalaia,* all go back to a Syriac original through a Greek translation. Even the famous *Cologne Mani Codex* was originally written in Syriac.[52]

Edessa, therefore, turns out to be the center of traditions linked with the apostle Thomas, who was considered Jesus' twin. All writings connected with his name have essential doctrinal elements in common, of which a particular anthropology and Christology are paramount. Anthropological views found their expression in a severe Encratism. For an even partial reconstruction of the milieu in which these Thomas writings originated, a sketch and rough analysis of the underlying religious pattern is a first task, leaving aside the question of the age and authenticity of singular traditions and *logia* in the *Gospel of Thomas* and related literature. Even when separate *logia* and *agrapha* are authentic sayings of Jesus, that does not mean that the whole context of a writing as such represents original traditions of, *e.g.,* the Aramaic-speaking Christian community in Jerusalem and Palestine, as often is assumed.[53]

The central theme of the theology of the Thomas literature is man's regaining of paradise lost through the right use of his mind and will as taught and revealed by Jesus the Savior. Sin and atonement are not emphasized and are actually absent. Like Jesus the only Son of God

[50] *L'Evangile selon Thomas,* ed. and transl. by A. Guillaumont, H. -Ch. Puech, G. Quispel (Leiden, 1959); cf. H.-Ch. Puech, *En quête de la gnose* II. Sur l'évangile selon Thomas (Paris, 1978); J.D. Turner, *The Book of Thomas the Contender* (Chico: Scholars Press, 1975); cf. J.M. Robinson, ed. *The Nag Hammadi Library* (New York, 1977) 117ff.; 188ff.

[51] Cf. Turner, *The Book of Thomas the Contender,* 114ff.; 233; Quispel, "The *Gospel of Thomas* Revisited," 254ff.

[52] Henrichs and Koenen, *ZPE* 5 (1970) 104ff.; A. Henrichs, "The Cologne Mani Codex Reconsidered," *HSCP* 83 (1979) 352ff.

[53] See in particular the well-based and severe criticism of Quispel's and Koester's views by Tj. Baarda, "Luke 12, 13 - 14. Text and Transmission from Marcion to Augustine," *Studies for Morton Smith,* ed. J. Neusner, I (Leiden, 1975) 107-162, esp. 155, who proves in the case of logion 72 that the text of the *Gospel of Thomas* is due to dogmatic views and *not* to an independent Gospel tradition of *logoi.*

(*monogenēs),* man should become a "single one," an *iḥidaya,* which implies the actual abolition of the difference between male and female, a reinstatement of man's situation before the "fall" according to Gen. 2:24-25: "Therefore shall a man leave his father and his mother, and shall cleave unto his wife; and they shall be *one* flesh. And they were both naked, the man and his wife, and were not ashamed!" Abstinence from sexual intercourse, a main characteristic of Syrian Encratism, was not born from hatred of the body as such, but served a higher aim, the return to man's original state. It is, therefore, quite comprehensible, that Encratite practice and right knowledge of God's saving plans always went together. Both were revealed by Jesus, the incarnation of God's wisdom and will, a paradigm of man as he should be according to God's plans. The true believer, therefore, is in a sense identical with Christ, because he has regained his original estate which Christ represents and reveals.[54] The identity of Christ and the believer, one of the central elements in the *Gospel of Thomas,* finds a symbolic expression in the whole structure and the various tales of the *Acts of Thomas,* in which Thomas appears as an *alter Christus.*[55] Another element in the same complex is the symbolism of the bridal chamber or heavenly wedding feast, where man is united with his heavenly *alter ego* and the original state of harmony is restored.[56] In fact, the wedding symbolism based on a special version and exegesis of the parable of Matthew 25:1-13 is another expression of the return to paradise, where man finds eternal rest (*anapausis*) after a wakeful life.[57]

Although this is a summary in outline of a very complicated anthropological pattern, the main elements may be clear. The cardinal question is whether this theological concept was part of the early tradition and interpretation of Jesus' *logia* linked with the apostle Judas Thomas, brother of Jesus, whose real name was suppressed in the

[54] A typical example of this identity is *Odes of Solomon* 3,7: "Because I love Him that is the Son, I shall become a son"; cf. Drijvers, "Odes of Solomon and Psalms of Mani," p. 121; *idem,* "Die Legende des heiligen Alexius und der Typus des Gottesmannes im syrischen Christentum," *Eichstätter Beiträge* 4 (1982) 187-217; H.-Ch. Puech, *En quête de la gnose* II, 177, who refers to *Gospel of Thomas,* logion 61, 108 and the *Acts of Thomas;* see also pp. 211-219.

[55] Cf. J.A. Delaunay, "Rite et symbolique en ACTA THOMAE vers. syr. I, 2a et ss.," *Mémorial Jean de Menasce,* ed. Ph. Gignoux, *Acta Iranica* (Teheran, 1974) 11-34.

[56] H.-G. Gaffron, *Studien zum koptischen Philippusevangelium unter besonderer Berücksichtigung der Sakramente* (Diss. Bonn, 1969) 191-219; R. Murray, *Symbols of Church and Kingdom,* pp. 131ff; 254ff.

[57] Cf. P. Nagel, *Die Motivierung der Askese in der Alten Kirche und der Ursprung des Mönchtums* (Berlin, 1966) 85, 97; Puech, *En quête de la gnose* II, 167 - 178; 263-269.

canonical gospels but preserved in the Syriac-speaking area east of the Euphrates, or that this concept of man's identity with Christ was due to other influences and secondarily linked with Thomas, the Twin, whose very name made him an apt person for such speculations. In that case, the name of the apostle Thomas Didymus has secondarily been extended to Judas Thomas Didymus in order to make him a real twin of Jesus, of whom Judas was a brother. The relationship between Jesus and Thomas consequently functioned as an ideal paradigm of the relation between every believer and his Lord, in particular when we take into account that those believers are blessed that have not seen and yet have believed (John 20:29), which is the precise position of the circles that produced this literature.

In trying to solve at least some of the complicated problems posed by the *Gospel of Thomas* and its relations to other Thomas literature and older traditions, it seems methodologically sound to look for a period and a person or group in which this whole complex of Christological and anthropological concepts had an organic place. It seems to me that the often neglected person of Tatian as a typical representative of Syrian Encratism in the second half of the second century is a good starting point.[58] With him all characteristics of this Thomas theology are found in philosophical disguise in the *Oratio ad Graecos* and in tendentious variants in his *Diatessaron,* so far it can be reconstructed.[59] According to Tatian the human soul and divine *pneuma* form a *suzugia,* which implies the return to man's original estate.[60] These are the underlying philosophical ideas of the theology of man's identity with Christ.[61] Even the symbolism of the bridal chamber may go back to such ideas of the *suzugia* of soul and *pneuma.* A first and very attractive and rewarding task in the study of early Syriac-speaking Christianity is, therefore, a systematic research of the influence and *Wirkungsgeschichte* of Tatian's

[58]M. Elze, *Tatian und seine Theologie* (Göttingen, 1960); cf. R. Murray, *Symbols of Church and Kingdom,* p. 280: "Tatianic peculiarities have already been noted several times in this work, but our authors were evidently unaware that they were peculiarities, and no early Syriac writer ever names Tatian."

[59]Cf. L. Leloir, "Le diatessaron de Tatien," *L'Orient Syrien* 1 (1956) 208 - 231; 313-334; R. Murray, "Reconstructing the Diatessaron," *The Heythrop Journal* 10 (1969) 43-49 (a critical review of I. Ortiz de Urbina, *Vetus Evangelium Syrorum et exinde excerptum Diatessaron Tatiani* [Madrid, 1967]); for a full bibliography concerning the Diatessaron see Tj. Baarda, *The Gospel Quotations of Aphrahat the Persian Sage* (Diss. Amsterdam, 1975); Y. Tissot, "Encratisme et Actes apocryphes," *Les Actes apocryphes des Apôtres,* pp. 109 - 119.

[60]Tatian, *Or.* 15.1; cf. Elze, *Tatian und seine Theologie,* 90ff.

[61]Elze, *Tatian und seine Theologie,* 94ff.; Puech, *En quête de la gnose* II, 119, 149.

theology in the Thomas literature, other apocryphal acts of apostles of Syrian origin and Encratite character, and other writings, like those of the Pseudo-Clementines.[62] It should be noted that the much discussed problem of the common variants of the *Gospel of Thomas* and the *Diatessaron* can be solved within the same context. Instead of assuming an independent Jewish-Christian gospel that was used as well by the author of the *Gospel of Thomas* as by Tatian, it seems a much simpler and more satisfying explanation to assume that the author of the *Gospel of Thomas* used Tatian's *Diatessaron*; at least this would apply to the author of an original Syriac version that might have been different from the preserved Coptic version.[63] It is of course quite possible that Tatian and, consequently, the author of the *Gospel of Thomas* knew and made use of extracanonical gospel traditions that can be old and authentic, but that does not mean that the *Gospel of Thomas* as such is a representative of an independent gospel tradition.[64] This assumption means a considerable change in the usual dating of the *Gospel of Thomas.* A date about A.D. 200 seems plausible and offers, moreover, a good explanation of the close relations between *Gospel* and *Acts of Thomas,* which often are emphasized.[65]

This whole complex of theological literature originally written in Syriac or extant in a Syriac and a Greek version is characteristic of Christian belief as understood and practiced in the Syriac-speaking area, of which Edessa was the center, about A.D. 200. The variegated pattern of Encratite theology had a counterpart in Bardaiṣan's certainly not Encratite views.[66] Furthermore, the strong influence of the Marcionites

[62]E. Peterson, "Bemerkungen zum Hamburger Papyrus - Fragment der Acta Pauli," *Frühkirche, Judentum und Gnosis* (Rome - Vienna, 1959) 204 - 208; see 206, n. 86.

[63]Puech, *En quête de la gnose,* p. 53 emphasized that at least two versions of the *Gospel of Thomas* were known, an "orthodox" one and a "heterodox" one; the same holds true for the *Acts of Thomas* and perhaps other writings from the same area and period; for *Gospel of Thomas* and *Diatessaron* see G. Quispel, "L'Évangile selon Thomas et le Diatessaron," *VigChr* 13 (1959) 87 -117 and Tj. Baarda, "Luk. 12, 13 -14. Text and Transmission."

[64]It seems to me extremely unlikely that Tatian made use of extracanonical material or even of an apocryphal gospel in composing his Diatessaron; when J.H. Charlesworth, "Tatian's Dependence upon Apocryphal Traditions, "*The Heythrop Journal* 15 (1974) 5-17 tries to prove that peculiar gospel traditions reflected in *Odes of Solomon* 24 influenced Tatian, since Ode 24 and the baptism story in the *Diatessaron* have some variants in common, the most plausible solution of this phenomenon is that the author of the *Odes of Solomon* knew the *Diastessaron,* as I hope to demonstrate in a forthcoming article. S. Gero, "The Spirit as a Dove at the Baptism of Jesus," *NovTest* 18(1976) 17-35 also wrongly assumes that Ode 24 contains an old and independent baptism tradition.

[65]Cf. Puech, *En quête de la gnose* II, 43ff.; 177.

[66]Drijvers, *Bardaisan of Edessa* (Assen, 1966) 192.

should be stressed, who were heavily opposed by Bardaiṣan and his followers and by the Syrian Encratites.[67] Polemic with Marcion is, therefore, a distinguishing mark of all Syrian theology in its different forms from the very beginning of Syriac literature forward.

Through Tatian, Bardaiṣan, and possibly other channels Greek philosophy, mainly Middle Platonism, contributed to the theological framework of Syriac-speaking Christianity and linked it with the Greek-speaking West, in particular with Antioch. Systematic research on philosophical elements in this theology is an urgent need for two reasons: first, to liberate Syriac-speaking Christianity from its romantic isolation and to give it its right place as a branch of early Christian theology that was developed in Antioch; second, to get a better insight into Greek culture in Syriac disguise, of which Edessa was a main center.[68]

When Mani made his appearance on the religious stage of Syria and started his mission in A.D. 240, he took over the whole Christian tradition and literature and developed it into a radically dualistic doctrine.[69] Tatian's *Diatessaron* was the Gospel text in use with the Manichaeans; they took over the apocryphal acts of Peter, Andrew, John, Thomas, and Paul and formed these into a coherent corpus.[70] The *Gospel of Thomas* was read by the Manichaeans, and they knew Bardaiṣan's writings, which were the base and starting point of Manichaean cosmology.[71] Although it is generally assumed that Christian doctrine

[67]Drijvers, *Bardaisan*, pp. 169 - 171; Baarda, "Luke 12, 13-14 Text and Transmission," pp. 120ff.; Drijvers, "Die Oden Salomos und die Polemik mit den Markioniten"; Bauer, *Rechtgläubigkeit und Ketzerei*, pp. 21ff.; 27ff.

[68]Cf. Drijvers, "Hatra, Palmyra und Edessa. Die Städte der syrisch-mesopotamischen Wüste in politischer, kulturgeschichtlicher und religionsgeschichtlicher Beleuchtung," *ANRW* II, 8 (Berlin, 1977) 887ff.; F. Millar, "Paul of Samosata, Zenobia, and Aurelian. The Church, Local Culture and Political Allegiance in Third-Century Syria," *JRS* 61 (1971) 2ff.: Syriac and Greek in the East Syrian Regions and Mesopotamia.

[69]That becomes clear from the *Cologne Mani Codex* and holds true for nearly all aspects of Manichaean doctrine; cf. E. Rose, *Die manichäische Christologie* (Wiesbaden, 1979) 177-182; G.G. Stroumsa, "Aspects de l'eschatologie manichéenne," *RHR* 198 (1981) 163-181.

[70]P. Nagel, "Die apokryphen Apostelakten des 2. und 3. Jahrhunderts in der manichäischen Literatur. Ein Beitrag zur Frage nach den christlichen Elementen im Manichäismus," *Gnosis und Neues Testament* (Berlin, 1973) 149 - 182.

[71]E. Hammerschmidt, "Das Thomasevangelium und die Manichäer," *OrChr* 46 (1962) 120-123; Puech, in Hennecke and Schneemelcher, I. 203f.; *idem, En quête de la gnose* II, 39; Drijvers, "Mani und Bardaiṣan. Ein Beitrag zur Vorgeschichte des Manichäismus," *Mélanges Puech* (Paris, 1974) 459 - 469.

and tradition reached Mani through a Gnostic filter, in particular Marcionites and Bardaiṣanites, it seems more in accordance with historical reality to suppose that the whole Christian tradition and literature of the Syriac-speaking East contributed to Mani's doctrinal system and mythology.[72] Traditio-historical research on these connections seems promising and is a third task for further study. It is often noticed that most writings of early Syriac-speaking Christianity existed in two versions, a more "orthodox" one and a "heretical" one.[73] A plausible explanation of this remarkable fact is that Manichaean adoption of existing writings transformed and adapted them to Manichaean doctrine. That process of taking over called forth a counter action and caused a dividing of the ways. The *Odes of Solomon* as well as the *Doctrina Addai* are milestones on this road to the radical opposition between orthodoxy and heresy, of which Ephrem Syrus is our first and most outstanding witness. Facts and problems of Syriac-speaking Christianity are determined by a complicated historical process that started with the many-colored pattern that can be detected about A.D. 200, on which Manichaeism and later orthodoxy heavily drew, and ended with a sharp opposition of both. Notwithstanding their sharp contests, both shared a common heritage of Christian tradition and practice.

[72]A. Böhlig, "Christliche Wurzeln im Manichäismus, *Mysterion und Wahrheit*, pp. 208ff.; Nagel, "Die apokryphen Apostelakten," 149ff.; Drijvers, "Odes of Solomon and Psalms of Mani," p. 130.

[73]See n. 63.

VII

DIE ODEN SALOMOS UND DIE POLEMIK MIT DEN MARKIONITEN IM SYRISCHEN CHRISTENTUM.

Seit der im Jahre 1909 von J. Rendel Harris gemachten Entdeckung eines aus dem sechzehnten Jahrhundert stammenden syrischen Manuskriptes, das fast alle Salomo zugeschriebenen Oden und Psalmen enthält, haben diese Hymnen Patristiker, Religionshistoriker, Syrologen und Neutestamentler beschäftigt. Der zufällige Fund einer zweiten Handschrift im Britischen Museum, die einige Oden und alle Psalmen enthält, und die Tatsache, dass die koptische Pistis Sophia fünf Oden (1,5,6,22 und 25) bewahrt hat, machten es Rendel Harris und Mingana möglich, Oden und Psalmen mit ausführlichen Einleitungen und Erläuterungen zwischen 1916-20 zu edieren [1]. Als im Jahre 1959 der griechische Papyrus Bodmer XI veröffentlicht wurde, der die elfte Ode in einer griechischen Version enthält, die ausführlicher ist als die syrische, entbrannte die Diskussion über die Originalsprache der Oden aufs neue, eine Debatte, die bis heute noch nicht endgültig entschieden ist.[2] Überdies gaben die Veröffentlichungen neuer gnostischer,

---

[1] Rendel Harris - A. Mingana, *The Odes and Psalms of Solomon*, 2 Vols, Manchester 1916-1920 ; eine andere viel benutzte Ausgabe ist die von Walter Bauer, *Die Oden Salomos*, Kleine Texte 64, Berlin 1933 ; Bauer gab eine verbesserte Übersetzung der Oden in : E. Hennecke - W. Schneemelcher, *Neutestamentliche Apokryphen*, 3te Aufl., Bd II, Tübingen 1964, 576-625 ; die letzte Edition ist herausgebracht worden von J. H. Charlesworth, *The Odes of Solomon*, ed. with transl. and notes, Oxford 1973 ; siehe für eine kritische Besprechung dieser Ausgabe, G. Reinink, *Journal for the Study of Judaism* 5, 1974, 64-68 ; und S. P. Brock, *JBL* 93, 1974, 623-625 ; gerne danke ich Herrn Reinink für seine kritische Hilfe und wertvollen Anregungen. In diesem Aufsatz wird ständig auf die Übersetzungen von Rendel-Harris, Bauer und Charlesworth Bezug genommen.

[2] M. Testuz, *Papyrus Bodmer X-XII*, *Bibl. Bodmeriana*, Cologny-Genève 1959 ; siehe A. Adam, Die ursprüngliche Sprache der Salomon-Oden, *ZNW* 52, 1961, 141-156 (ursprünglich Aramäisch geschrieben) ; A. Vööbus, Neues Licht zur Frage der Originalsprache der Oden Salomos, *Le Muséon* 75, 1962, 275-290 (Syrisch ist die Originalsprache) ; A. F. J. Klijn, *Ned. Theol. Tijdschr.* 14, 1959-60, 447f. ; *idem*, *Aspects du judéo-christianisme*, Paris 1965, 169 (Griechisch ist die Originalsprache) ; M. Philonenko, Conjecture sur un verset de la onzième Ode de Salomon, *ZNW* 53, 1962, 264 (Griechisch); siehe J. A. Emerton, *Some Problems of Text and Language in*

namentlich mandäischer Texte und hebräischer Hymnen und Psalmen aus Qumrân neue Antriebe zur wissenschaftlichen Diskussion der vielen in den Oden liegenden Fragen.[3]

Heutzutage sind die Ansichten über Art und Wesen dieser zweiundvierzig Oden noch ebenso verschieden, wie zur Zeit Rendel Harris. Man ist sich nicht einig über die ursprüngliche Sprache der Oden, Griechisch oder Syrisch. Im ersten Falle sind sie vielleicht in Antiochien entstanden, im letzteren Falle in Edessa. Es gibt Autoren, die für eine frühe Entstehungszeit plädieren, im ersten Jahrhundert oder in der ersten Hälfte des zweiten Jahrhunderts, und enge Beziehungen zu den Hodayôt aus Qumran betonen, wodurch der judenchristliche Charakter der Hymnen ins Licht gerückt wird. Andere Forscher betrachten die Oden als gnostisch und sehen starke Übereinstimmungen mit der poetischen Literatur der Mandäer. Die Oden sind als ein Handbuch für den Taufunterricht beschrieben worden und mit dem valentinianischen oder nicht-valentinianischen Evangelium Veritatis in Beziehung gebracht worden.[4] Ein Übersichtsartikel in der *RGG* endet mit dem inspirierenden Satz : ,, Das in den Oden vorliegende Bildmaterial enthält allerdings noch viele ungelöste Fragen.“ [5] Der letzte Herausgeber und Übersetzer der Oden, J. H. Charlesworth, ist der Meinung, dass ,, One of the main hindrances to understanding the Odes has been the lack of a critical text.“ Er hofft, dass ,, such a text, together with translation, notes and bibliography ... will help clarify the interpretation of the Odes and assist further study.“ [6] In einer kritischen Rezension von Charlesworth's Buch spricht S. Brock aber von ,, one of the most puzzling products of early Christianity“, sodass auch in dieser Ausgabe Text und Übersetzung noch nicht alle ungelösten Fragen gelöst haben [7].

---

the Odes of Solomon, *JThS* 18, 1967, 372-406 (Syrisch ist die Originalsprache); die These J. Carmignac's, *Revue de Qumran* III, 1961, 71-102 und IV, 1963, 429-432 dass Hebräisch die Originalsprache sei, hat sich auch nicht bewährt.

[3] Siehe z. B. J. Carmignac, *Un qumranien converti au christianisme : L'auteur des Odes de Salomon*, *Qumran-Probleme*, hg. v. H. Bardtke, Berlin 1963, 75-108 ; K. Rudolph, *War der Verfasser der Oden Salomos ein ,, Qumran-Christ“ ?* Ein Beitrag zur Diskussion um die Anfänge der Gnosis, *Revue de Qumran* IV, 1964, 523-555.

[4] E. Segelberg, *Evangelium Veritatis. A Confirmation Homily and its Relation to the Odes of Solomon*, *Orientalia Suecana* 8, 1959, 3-42 ; siehe die ausführliche Bibliographie in Charlesworth's Edition.

[5] S. Schulz, *RGG*³, Bd. V. 1339-1342.

[6] Charlesworth, *The Odes of Solomon*, vii.

[7] Brock, *JBL* 93, 1974, 623.

Zu einer eingehenden Analyse dieses Bildmaterials stehen zwei grundsätzlich verschiedene Wege offen. Der eine besteht in einer Analyse der literarischen Bilder und der darin enthaltenen religiösen Gedanken, ferner aus dem Sammeln verschiedener Parallelen aus der kulturellen Umwelt, wodurch dann den Oden ihre Stellung in der Geistesgeschichte des syrischen Christentums zugewiesen werden kann. Dieser Weg ist bis heute fast ausschliesslich begangen worden und eine imponierende Reihe von Veröffentlichungen zeigt, dass man auf diese Weise überallhin gelangen kann, von Qumran über Jerusalem und Antiochien bis nach Edessa, ohne genau zu wissen, wo und in welcher Zeit man sich befindet.

Der zweite Weg wird fast niemals begangen, liegt aber ebenso nahe wie der erste : nicht das Sammeln von Parallellen, sondern das Aufsuchen von Ansichten, gegen die die Oden Front machen. Fast alle überlieferten Schriften des Urchristentums aus dem zweiten und dritten Jahrhundert haben einen apologetischen und polemischen Charakter, und die Oden sind von dieser Regel keine Ausnahme, wie sich herausstellen wird.

Die Oden Salomos besingen in oft sehr extravaganten Bildern das Heil, das der gläubige Sänger mit einem Kranze auf dem Haupt, mit dem Trinken aus der Quelle des Lebens, mit dem Erlangen der richtigen Kenntnis, mit der Heimkehr ins Paradies und dem Erreichen der Unsterblichkeit vergleicht [8]. Jenes Heil wird dem Gläubigen reichlich gespendet und er hört nicht auf, dies in den Oden auf viele Weisen zu besingen. Gott schenkt das Heil ohne Missgunst, sagt der Sänger, und das führt W. Bauer, einen der Übersetzer der Oden, zu der folgenden erklärenden Anmerkung bei Ode 3, 6 : ,, Dass der Herr ohne Missgunst ist, wird immer wieder betont : 7,3 ; 11,6 ; 15,6 ; 17,12 ; 20,7 ; 23,4 ; dazu Johannesakten 55 : ,, Wir hören, dass der Gott, den du verkündest, ein neidloser Gott ist." Ein solcher Gott spendet ,, reichlich", entsprechend dem griechischen ἄφθονος, ἀφθονία." [9] Die sieben Stellen in den Oden, die diese Eigenschaft Gottes betonen, verdienen eine eingehende Untersuchung hinsichtlich der Terminologie und des Kontextes.

---

[8] Die Übereinstimmungen mit der Gedankenwelt des Johannes-Evangeliums sind handgreiflich, wie F. M. Braun, *L'énigme des Odes de Salomon*, *Revue thomiste* 57, 1957, 597-625 = *Jean le théologien et son évangile dans l'église ancienne*, Paris 1959, I, 224-251, dargetan hat.

[9] W. Bauer, in : *Hennecke-Schneemelcher* Bd. II, 579, Anm. 7 ; siehe auch W. C. van Unnik, ΑΦΘΟΝΩΣ ΜΕΤΑΔΙΔΩΜΙ, *Med. Kon. Vlaamse Acad.*, Kl. d. Lett. XXXIII, 1971, Nr. 4, Brussel 1971, 58, Anm. 3 und *idem*, *De* ἀφθονία *van God in de oudchristelijke literatuur*, *MNAW. L*, N. R. 36, Amsterdam 1973, 11 und Anm. 181.

Ode 3,6 : Diese Ode besingt die Einheit zwischen dem liebenden Gott und dem gläubigen Menschen, sie gehört zu den sogenannten Individualoden, wo der einzelne seine Glaubenserfahrungen besingt :

6 :	ܘܠܐ ܐܗܘܐ ܢܘܟܪܝܐ	Und ich werde kein Fremdling sein,
	ܡܛܠ ܕܠܝܬ ܚܣܡܐ ܠܘܬ	Weil es keine Missgunst gibt bei dem
	ܡܪܝܐ ܡܪܝܡܐ ܘܡܪܚܡܢܐ	Herrn, dem höchsten und barmherzigen.

In den folgenden Versen wird das Ergebnis dieser Gnade besungen : der Gläubige wird unsterblich (Vs. 8) und erwirbt Erkenntnis Gottes. Das syrische Wort für Missgunst, das in diesem Kontext benutzt wird, ist ܚܣܡܐ = *invidia*, φθόνος. Die üblichen Übersetzungen geben es folgendermassen wieder : ,, For with the Lord Most High and Merciful, there is no *grudging*" (Rendel Harris) ; ,, Weil es keine Missgunst gibt bei dem Herrn ..." (W. Bauer) ; ,, Because there is no jealousy with the Lord Most High and Merciful." (Charlesworth).

Ode 7,3 : Diese Ode hat die Menschwerdung Gottes zum Thema ; Gott wird Mensch, damit wir Ihn erfassen können.

3 :	ܡܥܕܪܢܐ ܓܝܪ ܐܝܬ ܠܝ ܠܡܪܝܐ	Denn einen Helfer habe ich zum Herrn.[10]
	ܐܘܕܥܢܝ ܢܦܫܗ ܕܠܐ ܚܣܡܐ ܒܦܫܝܛܘܬܗ	Er machte sich in seinem Edelmut mir bekannt als (jemand) ohne Missgunst,
	ܪܒܘܬܗ ܓܝܪ ܒܒܣܝܡܘܬܗ ܐܙܥܪܬ	Denn seine Freundlichkeit machte seine Grösse klein.

Die syrischen Ausdrücke *'wd'ny npšh dl' ḥsm'* haben die Bedeutung, dass Gott sich dem Ich dieser Ode bekannt macht als ein Wesen, das keine Missgunst kennt. Die Wörter *dl' ḥsm'* bilden an sich einen negativen Nominalsatz, der durch die Partikel *d* mit *npšh* verbunden ist und diese Form genauer bestimmt. Die Übersetzungen

---

[10] Die Bauersche Übersetzung : ,, denn ein Helfer ist er mir zum Herrn " verfehlt die Pointe ; durch die Wortstellung wird ein Helfer besonders betont ; er, der mein Herr ist, ist nicht Herrscher über mich, sondern mein Helfer. Auch Charlesworth's Übersetzung : ,, For there is a Helper for me, the Lord " hat dieses Paradoxon nicht zum Ausdruck gebracht.

interpretieren diese Konstruktion ohne Grund adverbial : „ He hath shown Himself to me without grudging" (Rendel Harris) ; „ Er liess sich selbst mich erkennen ohne Missgunst" (Bauer) ; „ He has generously shown Himself to me." (Charlesworth). Die Erlösung wird dann in dieser Ode weiter geschildert als die Kenntnis Gottes, die die Trennung zwischen Gott und Mensch aufhebt. Die hier vorgeschlagene Deutung der Formel *dl' ḥsm'* findet eine Stütze in Ode 11,6.

Ode 11,6 : Der Gegenstand dieser Ode ist die Beschneidung des frommen Herzens durch Gott mit Hilfe des Heiligen Geistes.

6 : ܘܡܝܐ ܡܡܠܠܐ ܩܪܒܘ ܠܣܦܘܬܝ܂	Und redendes Wasser berührte meine
ܡܢ ܡܒܘܥܗ ܕܡܪܝܐ ܕܠܐ ܚܣܡ	Lippen aus der Quelle des Herrn, der keine Missgunst kennt.

Die nächsten Verse 7 und 8 erzählen, wie der Sänger von diesem lebenden Wasser trank, sodass er berauscht wurde ; dieser Rausch verlieh ihm aber richtige Erkenntnis, sodass er die Eitelkeiten der Welt fahren liess. Das Syrische verwendet hier *dl' ḥsm* = ohne Missgunst wie eine Determination des Herrn, zwar im Status absolutus und nicht im Status determinatus, wie in 3,6 und 7,3, aber es gibt in dergleichen Ausdrücken keinen wesentlichen Unterschied zwischen den beiden Status[11]. Auch hier wird eine adverbiale Übersetzung geboten : „ From the fountain of the Lord plenteously." (Rendel Harris) ; „ From the fountain of the Lord generously." (Charlesworth) ; Bauers Übersetzung „ Aus der Quelle des Herrn ohne Missgunst" suggeriert ebenso eine adverbiale Funktion.

Ode 15,6 : Die belebenden Strahlen der himmlischen Sonne haben Augen und Ohren des Erwählten geöffnet und ihm das Betrachten seiner Erkenntnis geschenkt.

6 : ܐܘܪܚܐ ܕܛܥܝܘܬܐ ܫܒܩܬ ܘܐܙܠܬ ܠܘܬܗ ܘܩܒܠܬ ܦܘܪܩܢܐ ܕܠܐ ܚܣܡܐ	Den Weg des Irrtums habe ich verlassen und ich bin hingegangen zu ihm und habe Erlösung empfangen von Ihm, der keine Missgunst kennt.

[11] Siehe TH. NÖLDEKE, *Kurzgefasste syrische Grammatik*, reprint Darmstadt 1966, Par. 202, F. 4, wo Beispiele gegeben werden, wie der Status absolutus und der Status determinatus in solchen Ausdrücken ohne Unterschied verwendet werden.

Die darauf folgenden Verse beschreiben, wie der Sänger Unvergänglichkeit angezogen hat und wie das unsterbliche Leben erschienen ist im Lande des Herrn. Die Übersetzungen geben *dl' ḥsm'*, das gleich auf *mnh* = von Ihm folgt und das determiniert, unveränderlich als einen adverbialen Ausdruck wieder : ,, And I have received Salvation from Him abundantly.“ (Rendel Harris and Charlesworth) ; ,, ... und habe empfangen Erlösung von ihm ohne Missgunst “ (Bauer) was auch eine adverbiale Deutung suggeriert.

Ode 17,12 : Durch Gottes Erlösung ist der Sänger, der in dieser Ode zugleich auch der Christus ist, eine vollkommen neue Person geworden. Er ist zu der höchsten Wahrheit und Erkenntnis geführt, wodurch er die Tore der Unterwelt sprengen und die Seinen erlösen kann. Auf diese Beschreibung des Descensus ad Inferos folgt

12 : ܘܝܗܒܬ ܝܕܥܬܝ ܕܠܐ ܚܣܡ Und ich gab meine Erkenntnis ohne Missgunst
ܘܒܥܘܬܝ ܒܚܘܒܐ ܕܝܠܝ und meine Fürbitte durch meine Liebe [12].

Die Formel *dl' ḥsm* mag in diesem Falle nach *yd'ty* = meiner Erkenntnis eine adverbiale Nuance haben. Der Erlöser schenkt den Seinigen die Erkenntnis, die er zuvor von Gott empfangen hat, ohne Missgunst. Darin ist impliziert, dass ohne Missgunst nicht rein adverbial verwendet wird in der Bedeutung von , reichlich ‘, sondern eine Qualität der Ich-Figur bezeichnet, die keine Missgunst kennt. Diese Interpretation findet eine Stütze in der zweiten Hälfte dieses Verses, wo Liebe gleichfalls ein Characteristicum des Erlösers ist, das der Formel ,, ohne Missgunst “ ganz parallel läuft. Es ist bemerkenswert, dass im diesem Kontext wiederum das Schenken von Leben und Kenntnis und das Sein ohne Missgunst zusammen begegnen als ein religiöser Gedanke. Die Übersetzungen geben es folgenderweise wieder : ,, And I imparted my knowledge without grudging “ (Rendel Harris) ; ,, And I gave my knowledge generously.“ (Charlesworth) ; ,, Und ich gab meine Erkenntnis ohne Missgunst “. (Bauer).

---

[12] Bauer’s Übersetzung : ,, ... und meine Fürbitte voller Liebe “. bringt den instrumentalen Charakter der Präposition *b* ungenügend zum Ausdruck ; der Erlöser schenkt Erkenntnis, weil er ohne Missgunst ist und, seine Fürbitte, weil er Liebe hat. Charlesworth’s Deutung von *b'wt'* als ,, resurrection “ (... And my resurrection through my love) muss ebenso als falsch betrachtet werden.

Ode 20,7 : In dieser Ode redet das Ich zu der Gemeinde und fordert sie auf, dem Herrn Gerechtigkeit und Reinheit von Herzen zu opfern und den Nächsten nicht zu betrügen. Der Prediger fährt dann folgendermassen fort :

ܠܒܫ ܕܝܢ ܠܒܣܝܡܘܬܗ ܕܡܪܝܐ ܕܠܐ ܚܣܡܐ	Ziehe vielmehr an die Güte des Herrn, der keine Missgunst kennt,
ܘܬܐ ܠܦܪܕܝܣܗ	Und komme in sein Paradies und mache
ܘܥܒܕ݂ ܠܟ ܟܠܝܠܐ ܡܢ ܐܝܠܢܗ	dir einen Kranz von seinem Baum.

Der Baum des Herrn ist der Baum des Lebens, der dem Menschen Unsterblichkeit schenkt. Eine genaue Parallele, die bisher noch keine Beachtung fand, zu den Gedanken in Ode 20,7 findet sich bei Ephrem Syrus, Hymnen de Paradiso 12,15 und 17 :

12,15 : Zwei Bäume stellte er in das Paradies, — den Baum des Lebens und den der Erkenntnis, — zwei Quellen, gesegnete, aller Güter. Durch diese beiden Dinge, die preiswürdigen, kann der Mensch das Ebenbild Gottes werden, mit Leben ohne Tod und Erkenntnis ohne Irrtum.

12,17 : Er wollte nämlich nicht geben den Kranz ohne Mühe.- Zwei Kränze hatte er Adam im Wettkampf ausgesetzt,- die zwei Bäume sollten sein die Kränze für seinen Sieg. Hätte Adam gesiegt, sofort hätte er gegessen und das Leben gewonnen, hätte er gegessen und das Wissen gewonnen, unverletzliches Leben, unverwirrbares Wissen.[13]

Diese beiden Strophen können überdies Ode 11,6, deren Text oben schon angeführt wurde, noch genauer erklären. Auf bildlich-symbolische Weise identifiziert Ephrem Baum der Erkenntnis und Quelle der Erkenntnis. Daraus ergibt sich, dass das Trinken aus der Quelle des Herrn, die Erkenntnis schenkt, dem Essen vom Baume der Erkenntnis gleich ist.

---

[13] E. Beck, *Des heiligen Ephraem des Syrers Hymnen de Paradiso und contra Julianum*, hg. und übers., *CSCO.S*, 78-79, Louvain 1957, 53 sq. (Textus), 49 (Versio) ; nur in der letzten Zeile der Strophe 15 weiche ich von Beck's Übersetzung ab, wo er *bḥy' dl' mwt' wḥkmt' dl' tw'yy* wiedergibt mit ,, durch Leben ohne Tod und Erkenntnis ohne Irrtum." m. E. hat die Präposition *b* in diesem Kontext die Bedeutung von ‚ mit, bestehend aus '.

Die Übersetzungen geben alle *dl' ḥsm'* in Ode 20,7, — obwohl es hier am klarsten ist, dass *dl' ḥsm'* eine Eigenschaft Gottes ist — eine adverbiale Deutung. „ But put on the grace of the Lord without stint“ (Rendel Harris); „ But put on the grace of the Lord generously“, (Charlesworth); „ Ziehe vielmehr an die Güte des Herrn ohne Missgunst“ (Bauer). Bauer behauptet in einer erklärenden Anmerkung, dass „ Ohne Missgunst = reichlich gespendet“, ist, womit er die Formel zu Gottes Güte in Beziehung setzt. Der Zusammenhang, in dem Ode 20,7 fungiert, ist eine Schilderung des Zurückkehrens zum Paradies, des Erwerbens des Lebens und der Erkenntnis.

Die letzte Stelle, die in diesem Zusammenhang wichtig ist, ist Ode 23,4.

Ode 23,4: Ode 23 handelt über einen Himmelsbrief der zur Erde herabkommt, und in dem Gottes Wille beschrieben steht.[14] Bevor der Sänger im Vers 5 über diesen Brief zu reden anfängt, fordert er die Gläubigen mit den folgenden Worten auf:

4: ܗܠܟܘ ܒܝܕܥܬܗ ܕܡܪܝܡܐ	Wandelt in der Erkenntnis des Höchsten
ܘܬܕܥܘܢ ܛܝܒܘܬܗ ܕܡܪܝܐ ܕܠܐ ܚܣܡܐ	Und dann werdet ihr erkennen die Güte des Herrn, der keine Missgunst kennt
ܘܠܕܝܠܗ ܘܠܫܘܡܠܝܐ ܕܝܕܥܬܗ	So dass ihr über Ihn jubelt und seine Erkenntnis vollkommen wird.

Rendel Harris und Charlesworth übersetzen *dl' ḥsm'* adverbial:

„ And ye shall know the grace of the Lord without grudging“;
„ And you will know the grace of the Lord generously.“

Bauers Übersetzung verrät, dass er sich dessen bewusst war, dass *dl' ḥsm'* in diesem Zusammenhang eine Apposition zu Herrn ist, die eine göttliche Qualität andeutet. Er übersetzt aber: „ und ihr werdet erkennen die Güte des Herrn (‚die) ohne Missgunst (spendet)“, sodass er *dl' ḥsm'* sich auf die Güte beziehen lässt. Dadurch kann er seine Interpretation *dl' ḥsm'* = reichlich gespendet behaupten.

---

[14] Siehe meinen Aufsatz: *ALUOS* VIII, 1977, wo eine Interpretation dieser Ode, „ the most difficult of all the hymns in the collection“ (Rendel Harris) geboten wird.

In Ode 3,6 ; 11,6 ; 20,7 und 23,4 ist die feste Formel *dl' ḥsm'* unmittelbar mit *mry'* = Herrn verbunden. In Ode 7,3 folgt es gleich auf *npšh* = sich (nämlich den Herrn) selbst, und in Ode 15,6 auf *mnh* = von Ihm (nämlich dem Herrn). Die einzige übrige Stelle, Ode 17,12, spricht von der Erkenntnis des Erlösers, des Christus, die er schenkt, da er keine Missgunst kennt. Die Formel „ohne Missgunst" ist also in fast allen Fällen mit dem Herrn verbunden und fungiert überdies in einem festen theologischen Kontext, der durch Leben und Erkenntnis als paradiesische Gaben bestimmt wird. Dort wo es sich in den Oden um diese Gaben handelt, die im Paradies für den Menschen bereit liegen und ihm die Rückkehr dorthin ermöglichen, wird betont, dass die Missgunst keine Rolle spielt. Daraus ergibt sich, dass die feste Formel *mry' dl' ḥsm'* und ihre Derivate interpretiert werden müssen als ‚der Herr, der keine Missgunst kennt' oder ‚der Herr der ohne Missgunst ist', in welchem Kontext *dl' ḥsm'* mit Nachdruck als eine Qualität Gottes vorgeführt wird. Die Formel *mry' dl' ḥsm'* ist so vielen anderen idiomatischen Ausdrücken in der syrischen Sprache analog, in denen ein mit *dl'* = ohne anfangender Ausdruck in Postposition nach einem Substantiv eine Eigenschaft des Substantivs beschreibt, z. B. *ḥy' dl' mwt'* = Leben ohne Tod oder unsterbliches Leben ; *ḥkmt' dl' dwwd'* = Kenntnis ohne Verwirrung oder deutliche Kenntnis ; *'nš dl' hymnwt'* = ein Mensch ohne Glauben oder ein ungläubiger Mensch, usw.

Das syrische Wort *ḥsm'* ist das Äquivalent des griechischen φθόνος, sodass *dl' ḥsm'* dem griechischen ἀφθονία oder οὐ φθονεῖν entspricht. In der Geschichte des Christentums innerhalb und ausserhalb der Alten Kirche war es nur ein Denker, der wiederholt betonte, dass der Schöpfer dem Menschen im Paradies Leben und Erkenntnis aus Missgunst vorenthalten hatte, nämlich Markion.[15] Die ganze Überlieferung hinsichtlich Markions Lehre stimmt darin überein : die Boshaftigkeit des markionitischen Schöpfergottes dem fremden und gnädigen Gott gegenüber zeigt sich vor allem in seinem missgünstigen Vorgehen im Paradies : so schreibt Irenäus : *A ligno vitae longe transtulit hominem invidens ei lignum vitae* (Iren. III, 23,6), wo der Bischof von Lyon aller Wahrscheinlichkeit nach

[15] Siehe A. von Harnack, *Marcion. Das Evangelium vom fremden Gott*, 2te Aufl., TU 45, Leipzig 1924 = Reprint, Darmstadt 1960, 100, 105 ; cf. Barbara Aland, *Marcion. Versuch einer neuen Interpretation*, *ZThK* 70, 1973, 420-447 ; W. C. van Unnik, *Der Neid in der Paradiesgeschichte*, *Essays in Honour of Alexander Böhlig*, Leiden 1972, 120-132 erörtert die verschiedenen Weisen, auf welche das Motiv des Neides in der Paradiesgeschichte verwendet wird.

aus Markions Antithesen zitiert.[16] Auch die Pseudo-Klementinischen Schriften, die bekanntlich stark anti-markionitisch sind — erwähnen alle bösen Eigenschaten des alttestamentlichen Schöpfergottes z. B. sagt Simon in Hom. III, 38 sqq., einem Streitgespräch zwischen Petrus und Simon Magus, der markionitische Auffassungen vertritt : (39,3) „Wenn es von Adam heisst : ‚Wir wollen ihn hinaustreiben, damit er nicht etwa seine Hand ausstrecke, den Baum des Lebens berühre, davon esse und ewig am Leben bleibe' so beweist das *etwa* (μήπως) seine Unwissenheit und der Satz *davon esse und ewig am Leben bleibe* seinen Neid noch dazu (καὶ φθονεῖ).[17] Gottes Missgunst enthält dem ersten Menschen also den Baum des Lebens vor. Dieselbe böse Eigenschaft ist der Grund dafür, dass er Adam das Essen vom Baum der Erkenntnis verbot. Dagegen polemisiert Theophilus von Antiochien in der rund 190 A. D. geschriebenen Apologie Ad Autolycum II, 25 : „... Darum war Gott nicht missgünstig, auf ihn, wie einige annehmen, wenn er verbot, nicht von der Erkenntnis zu essen." Mit ‚einige' sind hier die Markioniten gemeint und namentlich Apelles, der in den Syllogismen die Missgunst Gottes ausführlich erörterte.[18]

Hat unsere Untersuchung bisher schon klar gemacht, dass es nicht abwegig ist anzunehmen, dass die erörterten Stellen in den Oden Salomos Front machen gegen Markion und seine Anhänger, so gibt es noch mehr Indizien in dieser Hymnensammlung für eine antimarkionitische Tendenz.

---

[16] Zitiert von HARNACK, *Marcion*, 271* ; cf. TERTULLIANUS, *Adversus Marcionem* (ed. E. Evans, Oxford 1972), II, 4, 6 und IV, 38, 2.

[17] Zitiert von HARNACK, *Marcion* 278*f. ; die Deutsche Übersetzung ist von J. IRMSCHER, *Hennecke-Schneemelcher*, Bd II, 385 ; für den Antimarcionitismus der Pseudoklementinen siehe H. SCHOEPS, *Theologie und Geschichte des Judenchristentums*, Tübingen 1949, 305ff. : der Kampf gegen den Marcionitismus ; G. STRECKER, *Das Judenchristentum in den Pseudoklementinen*, *TU* 70, 1958 ; A. SALLES, *Simon le magicien ou Marcion ?*, *VigChr.* 12, 1958, 197-224 versuchte darzulegen, dass sich keine marcionitischen Auffassungen hinter Simon Magus verbergen, welcher Versuch nicht überzeugend ist.

[18] THEOPHILUS OF ANTIOCH, *Ad Autolycum*, hg. v. R. M. Grant, Oxford 1970, 66ff. ; Grant's Hinweis auf Ambrosius, *De Paradiso* VI, 30 und Harnack, *Marcion*, 414-415 ist aber falsch, worauf schon W. C. van Unnik, Der Neid in der Paradiesgeschichte, 125 hingewiesen hat ; es ist aber klar, dass Theophilus gegen die Marcioniten polemisiert ; seine Polemik gehört zu den Quellen von Tertullian's *Adversus Marcionem*, *cf.* G. QUISPEL, *De bronnen van Tertullianus' Adversus Marcionem*, Leiden, 1943, 41.

Ode 3,6 : Und ich werde kein Fremdling sein,

Weil es keine Missgunst gibt bei dem Herrn, dem Höchsten und Barmherzigen.

Bekanntlich lehrte Markion zwei Götter, den unwissenden und missgünstigen Gott des Alten Testaments, den Schöpfer dieser Erde, und den höchsten Gott, den Vater Jesu Christi, der dem Menschen gegenüber ein Fremder ist. Der Schöpfer ist den Menschen bekannt, weil er diese Welt geschaffen hat, der höchste Gott ist Welt und Menschen unbekannt, bis der Christus erscheint, der ihn offenbart. Daher sind die Menschen jenem fremden und gnädigen Gott gegenüber ‚*extranei*' (Tertullianus, Adv. Marc. 1,11,1)[19]. Das Syrische Wort *nwkry'* = fremd, das in Ode 3,6 begegnet, wird von Ephrem in seinen polemischen Schriften dazu verwendet um den fremden Gott der Markioniten zu bezeichnen[20]. Ode 3,6 betont also, dass die Beziehung zwischen Gott und Mensch nicht durch Fremdheit gekennzeichnet ist, dass dieser Gott keine Missgunst kennt, und zugleich wird Er mit Nachdruck der Höchste und Barmherzige genannt, sodass der Vers Front macht gegen mehrere Elemente in Markions Lehre. Dieselbe Ode 3,10 betont, dass Gott *ohne Trug* ist, speziell wenn sein Geist die Menschen lehrt, seine Wege zu kennen.[21] Der Trug des Schöpfergottes ist fester Bestand-

[19] Harnack's Hinweis, *Marcion*, 267* auf Tert. I, 3 ist falsch ; Tertul. I, 11, 1 : *Quale est enim ut aliquid extraneum deo sit, cui nihil extraneum esset, si quis esset ? quia dei hoc est, omnia illius esse et omnia ad illum pertinere, vel ne statim audiret a nobis. Quid ergo illi cum extraneis ?* siehe auch Tertul. I, 23,3 : *Scio dicturos atquin hanc esse principalem et perfectam bonitatem, cum sine ullo debito familiaritatis in extraneos voluntaria et libera effunditur, secundum quam inimicos quoque nostros et hoc nomine iam extraneos diligere iubeamur,* woraus klar hervorgeht, dass die Menschen dem höchsten Gott gegenüber Fremde sind.

[20] E. Beck, *Des Heiligen Ephraem des Syrers Hymnen contra Haereses,* hg. u. übers., *CSCO.S.* 76-77, Louvain 1957, z. B. XXX, 9 ; XXXIII, 2 ; XXXIV, 3 ; XXXV, 1, XXXVII, 1 ; C. W. Mitchell (ed.), *S. Ephraim's Prose Refutations of Mani, Marcion, and Bardaisan,* 2 Vols, London 1912-1921 (Reprint 1969), z. B. Against Marcion I, II, Vol. II, 59, Z. 41 ; 71, Z. 32 ; 80, Z. 4 ; 125, Z. 1 usw. ; die Vorstellung begegnet ebenso in Vol. I, the Discourses addressed to Hypatius ; auch E. Beck, *Des heiligen Ephraem des Syrers Hymnen de Nativitate (Epiphania), CSCO. S.* 82-83, Louvain 1959, Nat. 17,17 : Es bleibt kein Raum für die Fremdheit (Christi). Nicht ist fremd der Sohn des Herrn des Alls dem Herrn des Alls, wo Ephrem sich gegen die Markioniten richtet.

[21] Ode 3,10 : *hd' hy rwḥh dmry' dl' dglwt'*
dmlp' lbnynš' dnd'wn 'wrḥth

Bauer's Übersetzung : „Das ist der Geist des Herrn, der ohne Trug, der

teil seines Sündenregisters im markionitischen Schrifttum. Das Register in den Homilien des Pseudoklemens (II,43) erwähnt den Trug des Schöpfers wiederholt an erster Stelle ; ψεύδεται ... ; es stammt wohl aus den Antithesen Markions.[22]

Auch Ode 4, 11-15 ist in diesem Rahmen aufschlussreich. In dieser Ode wird besungen, wie Gott seinen Gläubigen Gemeinschaft mit Ihm geschenkt hat, und wie diese Gaben nicht zurückgenommen werden können.

Vs. 11-15 : Bei dir ist ja keine Reue,
dass du Reue empfändest über etwas, was du verheissen hast.
Und der Ausgang ist dir offenbar,
Denn was du gabst, ohne Entgelt gabst du (es),
so dass du dich also nicht anders entschliessen und es wieder nehmen wirst.
Denn alles war dir als Gott offenbar
und stand von Anfang an bereit vor dir.

Das syrische Wort *twt'* = Reue begegnet wieder in Ephrems polemischen Schriften, wo er die Markionitische Lehre der ‚Reue des Schöpfers' bestreitet ; diese Reue ist mit einer Änderung der Meinung verbunden. Es gereut Gott, dass er die Menschen geschaffen hat in Unwissenheit dessen, wass sie tun würden, und er will die Schöpfung ungeschehen machen.[23] So sagt Tertullian adv. Marc. II, 28, 1-2 : *Mutavit sententias suas deus noster, proinde qua et vester. Qui enim genus humanum tam sero respexit, eam sententiam mutavit qua tanto aevo non respexit. Paenituit mali in aliquo deum nostrum, sed et vestrum. Eo enim, quod tandem animadvertit ad hominis salutem, paenitentiam dissimulationis pristinae fecit debitam malo facto.*[24] Auch der markionitische Simon Magus sagt in den

die Menschen lehrt, dass sie seine Wege kennen" macht nicht klar, ob *dl' dglwt'* zum Geist oder zum Herrn gehört. M. E. spricht nichts dagegen auch in diesem Falle *dl' dglwt'* mit Herrn zu verbinden.

[22] Zitiert von Harnack, *Marcion*, 278* ; cf. Tertul. II, 28,2 : *Si et mentitum alicubi dicis creatorem ...* ; Origenes, Hom. IX, 3 in Gen. 22,17 spricht von der ‚*iniquitas*' des Schöpfers ; Iren. I, 27,2 : *Is qui a lege et prophetis annuntiatus est deus malorum factor et bellorum concupiscens et inconstans quoque sententia et contrarius sibi ipse.*

[23] Ephrem Syrus, *Hymnen contra Haereses* XX, 1-3 ; XXXI, 2 ; XXX, 1 ; *Prose Refutations* II, 122, Z. 27.

[24] Cf. Harnack, *Marcion* 268*f. wo Harnack aber Tertullian II, 28 unrichtig und tendenziös zitiert ; *cf.* auch Adamantius, *Dial.* II, 6 ; Tertull. II, 7,3 : ... *nonne exclamaret Marcion, O dominum futilem, instabilem, infi-*

pseudo-klementinischen Homilien (III, 39) : „ Und wenn geschrieben steht : , Gott reute es, dass er den Menschen geschaffen hatte', so weist das auf Sinnesänderung und Unwissen. Denn er bereute bezeichnet das Nachdenken, durch das einer, der nicht weiss, was er will, seine Absichten festzulegen sucht ..." [25]. Reue, Sinnesänderung und Unwissenheit sind die Eigenschaften des markionitischen Schöpfergottes. Dagegen betonen die Verse 11-15 von Ode 4, dass Gott keine Reue hatte, dass er sich nicht anders entschliessen wird und dass alles Ihm von Anfang bis zum Ende bekannt war, d. h. im Gegensatz zu Markions Auffassungen wird die Providentia Dei betont. Diese polemische Diskussion mit Markions Auffassungen hat genaue Parallelen in den philosophischen Widerlegungen der epikureischen Lehre, wie sie in der spätantiken Schulphilosophie begegnen.[26]

Ganz im Einklang mit den bisher besprochenen anti-markionitischen Tendenzen in den Oden ist der Anti-Doketismus, wie er z. B. klar aus den Versen 6-11 der 19ten Ode hervorkommt : ausdrücklich wird betont, dass die Geburt Christi nicht *spyq'yt* geschah, womit m. E. angedeutet wird, dass die Geburt nicht leer oder eitel, d. h. ein fassbares Ereignis war, wie auch aus Vs. 10 hervorgeht : ... und sie gebar in Sichtbarkeit (*bthwyt'*) ... Charlesworth's Übersetzung ... And she bore according to the manifestation ... ist ganz verfehlt und übersieht die Pointe.[27]

---

delem, rescindentem quae instituit. Siehe auch Tertull. IV, 41,1 : ... *noli iam de creatore circa Adam retractare quae in tuum quoque deum retorquentur ; aut ignorasse illum, qui non ex providentia obstitit peccaturo, aut obsistere non potuisse si ignorabat, aut noluisse si et sciebat et poterat.* Wichtig sind in diesem Zusammenhang Tertullian's Erörterungen in II, 5 über die Praescientia Dei.

[25] Übersetzung von J. Irmscher in : *Hennecke-Schneemelcher*, II, 385.

[26] Cf. J. G. Gager, *Marcion and Philosophy, VigChr.* 26, 1972, 53-59, wo die Beziehungen zwischen Marcion's Auffassungen in Tertul. *Adv. Marcion* II, 5,1 2, Epicurus, *De ira dei* 13,20-21 und Sextus Empiricus, *Pyrr.* 3,9-11 aufgedeckt worden sind.

[27] Der Terminus *spiq'yt* spielte eine Rolle in dem späteren christologischen Streit und in den Diskussionen zwischen Nestorianern und Monophysiten ; Bauer's Übersetzung , zwecklos ' wird der Meinung auch nicht gerecht : R. Abramowski, *Der Christus der Salomooden, ZNW* 35, 1936, 54 gibt die Übersetzung : „ denn es geschah nicht *von ungefähr* ". R. M. Grant, *The Odes of Solomon and the Church of Antioch, JBL* 63, 1944, 364ff. behauptete den Doketismus der Oden : „ we can probably conclude that the Christ of the Odes of Solomon was not really born, ...", was nicht im Einklang ist mit Ode 19,6-10.

Nicht ohne Grund wird im letzten Vers dieser Ode :

ܘܐܚܒܬ ܒܦܘܪܩܢܐ
ܘܢܛܪܬ ܒܒܣܝܡܘܬܐ
ܘܚܘܝܬ ܒܪܒܘܬܐ

eine Analogie hergestellt zwischen den Aktivitäten der Maria, d. h. Lieben, Bewahren, und Zeigen, ans Tagelicht Bringen, und den göttlichen Qualitäten der Erlösung, Freundlichkeit und Grösse. Die üblichen Übersetzungen machen diese Analogie nicht klar.[28]

Wenn diese Ausführungen überzeugend sind und die Oden Salomos klare antimarkionitische Tendenzen zeigen, müssen sie viel später datiert worden, als es gewöhnlich geschieht. Sie sind dann in eine Reihe zu stellen mit z. B. Theophilus von Antiochien, Ad Autolycum, Bardaiṣans anti-markionitischen Dialogen und der antimarkionitischen Grundschrift der Pseudo-Klementinen.[29] Die Zeit um 200 A. D. kommt dann frühenstens in Betracht. Die antimarkionitische Tendenz der überlieferten alt-syrischen Literatur kann bis in Ephrems Oeuvre verfolgt werden. Schon vor vielen Jahren sind die starken Übereinstimmungen zwischen Ephrems Hymnen de Nativitate und den Oden Salomos ans Licht gerückt worden.[30] Auch die Genesisauslegung, am ersten der Paradiesgeschichte, zeigt die gleiche anti-markionitische Tendenz, wie sie z. B. aus der Schatzhöhle klar hervorgeht und die sich bis in spätere exegetische Arbeiten der syrisch-sprechenden Kirche verfolgen lässt.[31] Mittelbar sind die Oden dadurch ein Zeugnis geworden für die vorherrschende Stellung, die die Markioniten in der Geschichte des alt-syrischen Christentums einnahmen.[32] Es ist nicht ohne

---

[28] In dem in Anm. 14 angezeigten Aufsatz werde ich auch diese Fragen erörtern.

[29] Für Theophilus siehe die noch immer wichtige Arbeit von F. Loofs, *Theophilus von Antiochien adversus Marcionem und die anderen theologischen Quellen bei Irenaeus*, *TU* 46, 2, 1930 ; über Bardaisan's anti-markionitische Dialoge siehe Eusebius, *H. E.* IV, 30 ; Hippolytus, *Refutatio*, VI, 35 ; VII, 31 ; Bardaisan's *Buch der Gesetze der Länder* zeigt eine klar anti-markionitische Tendenz.

[30] A. J. Wensinck, *Ephrem's Hymns on Epiphany and the Odes of Solomon*, *Expositor*, Ser. 8, Vol. 3, 1912, 108-112 ; Rendel Harris, *Ephrem's Use of the Odes of Solomon*, *ibidem*, 113-119.

[31] Siehe z. B. I. M. Vosté - C. van den Eynde, *Commentaire d'Išo'dad de Merv sur l'Ancien Testament*. I. Genèse, *CSCO. S.* 126 (Textus), 156 (Versio), Louvain 1950-1955, S. 81 ad Gen. 3,5 : C. Bezold, *Die Schatzhöhle*, hg. u. übers., Leipzig 1883, 6 : „Und als der *Satan* Adam und Heva sah, welche im Paradiese glänzten, wurde der Empörer verzehrt und geröstet vor *Neid*."

[32] Siehe W. Bauer, *Rechtgläubigkeit und Ketzerei im ältesten Christentum*, *BHT* 10, Tübingen 1934, 27ff.

Bedeutung, dass die anti-markionitischen Schriften bewahrt geblieben und alle anderen fast völlig verschwunden sind ! In diesem Prozess sind auch die Oden Salomos bewahrt geblieben, nicht weil sie gnostisch wären, oder judenchristlich oder so etwas, sondern weil sie authentischen Gedanken der syrischen Theologie am Anfang des dritten Jahrhunderts Ausdruck verleihen, die in der Gedankenwelt der Antiochener und Ephrems wieder auftauchen und auch in den späteren theologischen Werken ihre Rolle spielten. Ein Beispiel sei in diesem Rahmen ein wenig weiter ausgeführt, um darzulegen, dass die Oden nicht am Anfang einer theologischen Entwicklung stehen, sondern Gedanken verkündigen, die nur aus einer theologischen Reife zu verstehen sind. Die Inkarnation Christi findet ihren Grund nach den Oden in dem Willen und dem Gedanken Gottes.

Ode 9,3 :

ܡܠܬܗ ܕܡܪܝܐ ܘܨܒܝܢܘܗܝ	Das Wort des Herrn und seine Willensregungen
ܡܚܫܒܬܐ ܩܕܝܫܬܐ ܕܐܬܚܫܒ	(sind) ein heiliger Gedanke, den er gedacht hat über seinen Ge-
ܥܠ ܡܫܝܚܗ	salbten.

Vergleiche dazu Ode 23,5, wo der Christus mit dem Bilde eines Briefes symbolisiert wird :

ܘܡܚܫܒܬܗ ܗܘܬ ܐܝܟ ܐܓܪܬܐ	Und sein Gedanke war wie ein Brief,
ܘܨܒܝܢܗ ܢܚܬ ܡܢ ܪܘܡܐ	Und sein Wille kam herab aus der Höhe

Wille und Gedanke Gottes sind Ausdruck seiner gnädigen Fürsorge, die schon am Anfang (*mn bršyt*) den Christus vorbereitete (Ode 41, 9,10). Es gibt daher nicht zwei Messiasse, ein ewiges Wort und einen Sohn des Höchsten, der auf der Erde erschien, sondern beide sind einer. Diese Gedanken der 41-sten Ode machen nicht Front gegen jüdische Vorstellungen der Qumrân-Gemeinde, wie Carmignac and Charlesworth meinen,[33] sondern sind eine Vorstufe der christologischen Streitigkeiten des vierten Jahrhunderts und nur von daher zu verstehen. In diesem Lichte ist Ode 41,15 zu verstehen :

[33] Cf. J. Carmignac, *Qumran-Probleme*, hg. v. H. Bardtke, Berlin 1963, 80f. ; J. H. Charlesworth, *Les Odes de Salomon et les manuscripts de la mer morte*, *RB* 77, 1970, 522-549, spez. 524ff. und sein Kommentar auf Ode 41,15, *The Odes of Solomon*, 143.

ܡܫܝܚܐ ܒܫܪܪܐ ܚܕ ܗܘ
ܘܐܬܝܕܥ ܡܢ ܩܕܡ ܬܪܡܝܬܗ
ܕܥܠܡܐ

ܕܢܚܐ ܢܦܫܬܐ ܠܥܠܡ ܒܫܪܪܐ
ܕܫܡܗ

Der Gesalbte ist in Wahrheit einer, und es war von ihm bekannt (i. e. bei Gott) vor der Gründung der Welt,
dass er die Seelen in Ewigkeit durch die Wahrheit seines Namens lebendig machen würde.

In der festen Formel „der Wille und Gedanken" Gottes klingen schon die theologischen Ausdrücke der antiochenischen Theologie an. Eine genaue Parallele dazu findet sich wiederum in Theophilus, Ad Autolycum II, 22; wo die Identität des Logos und des Sohnes betont wird; der Logos wohnt im Herzen Gottes (vgl. Ode 41,10) und als Gott machen wollte (ἠθέλησεν), was er geplant hatte (ἐβουλεύσατο; cf. *mhšbt'*), erzeugte er diesen Logos als den Erstgeborenen der ganzen Schöpfung, womit wir wieder bei der Christologie sind.[34]

Es würde den Rahmen dieses Aufsatzes sprengen, ausführlich alle literarischen und theologischen Parallelen aus dem Phänomenbestand aufzuführen, der gewöhnlich „altsyrische Theologie" genannt wird. Die Rolle des göttlichen Willens bei der Menschwerdung Christi in Ephrems Theologie ist nur allzu bekannt.[35] Bei den Nestorianern ist es ein bekanntes Theologumenon und wird z. B. in Theodor bar Konais Scholienbuch ausführlich erörtert.[36]

Zusammenfassend: Es hat sich herausgestellt, dass die Oden Salomos klare antimarkionitische Tendenzen aufzeigen, sowohl in der theologischen Terminologie als in den dort vertretenen Auffassungen. Diese Gedankenwelt verbindet die Oden mit Schriften, die im syrischen Raum um 200 A. D. und später entstanden sind, und die eine Vorstufe für die theologischen Weiterentwicklungen bilden, wie sie in der antiochenischen Theologie einerseits und in Ephrems theologischer Gedankenwelt anderseits vor sich gegangen sind. Folgerichtig sind die Oden von diesen Gedanken und Bildern aus zu erläutern. Theologisch und sprachlich sind die Oden zwischen Antiochien und Edessa beheimatet; das geht aus den Sprachen her-

---

[34] Theophilus, *Ad Autolycum*, II, 22: τὸν λόγον τὸν ὄντα διὰ παντὸς ἐνδιάθετον ἐν καρδίᾳ θεοῦ. πρὸ γάρ τι γίνεσθαι τοῦτον εἶχεν σύμβουλον, ἑαυτοῦ νοῦν καὶ φρόνησιν ὄντα. ὁπότε δὲ ἠθέλησεν ὁ θεὸς ποιῆσαι ὅσα ἐβουλεύσατο, τοῦτον τὸν λόγον ἐγέννησεν προφορικόν, πρωτότοκον πάσης κτίσεως, ...

[35] Cf. E. Beck, *Ephraems Reden über den Glauben*, *Studia Anselmiana* 33, Rom 1953, 23ff.

[36] Theodorus bar Koni, *Liber Scholiorum* I, ed. A. Scher, *CSCO*. S. 19, 1910, S. 10, Frage 12,13; S. 16, Fr. 34; S. 17, Fr 35; S. 20, Fr. 47.

vor, in denen sie überliefert sind, und aus den Gedanken, die in ihnen zum Ausdruck kommen. Dass sie in syrischer Sprache fast vollständig erhalten geblieben sind, steht ohne Frage in Zusammenhang mit ihren „rechtgläubigen" anti-markionitischen und antidoketischen Vorstellungen und ist ein mittelbarer Beweis für den starken Einfluss der Markioniten in der Gegend um Edessa. „The Odes of Solomon still deserve a full introduction and commentary" schrieb S. B. Brock 1974. Ein solcher Kommentar wird dem Charakter dieser Hymnen am besten gerecht, wenn sie betrachtet werden als ein hymnischer Ausdruck theologischer Reflexionen, die ihre historische Stelle finden zwischen Theophilus von Antiochien und dem Verfasser der pseudo-klementinischen Grundschrift einerseits und den Antiochenern und Ephrem anderseits.

VIII

Kerygma und Logos in den Oden Salomos dargestellt am Beispiel der 23. Ode

Die Anwendung der Kategorien Kerygma und Logos auf die Oden Salomos mit der Absicht, die damit bezeichnete geistesgeschichtliche Thematik auch in diesen 42 Hymnen aufzudecken, muß jedem, der sich je mit ihnen beschäftigt hat, erkünstelt vorkommen. Fast immer werden die syrischen Oden Salomos als typische Erzeugnisse einer orientalischen Frömmigkeit betrachtet, reich an kühnen Bildern ohne eine Spur logischer Rationalität[1]. Nicht nur die Eigenart der Oden würde sich der Thematik von Kerygma und Logos widersetzen, sondern auch ihre Entstehungszeit nach Meinung vieler noch im ersten Jahrhundert, in welcher Periode des Christentums "it was easier to be unorthodox than to be logically exact"[2]. Aber auch wenn man die Entstehung der Oden in einer späteren Periode ansetzt, bleibt das Problem der abstrusen Bildersprache, die sich oft einer logischen Interpretation zu entziehen scheint.

Das gilt um so mehr für die 23. Ode, die von J. Rendel Harris "the most difficult of all the hymns in the collection" genannt worden ist[3]. Sie ist eine Bildrede über einen Himmelsbrief, der durch ein Rad erfaßt durch die Welt rollt. Bis heute hat sie sich jeder kohärenten Interpretation widerspenstig gezeigt, obwohl allerhand Versuche gemacht worden sind, sie zu deuten. W. R. Newbold erklärte das Rad als den Zodiakus und deutete die ganze Ode in einem gnostisch-astrologischen Rahmen,

---

[1] Diese Ansicht vertreten z. B. R. M. Grant, The Odes of Solomon and the Church of Antioch, JBL 63, 1944, 363; H. Chadwick, Some Reflections on the Character and Theology of the Odes of Solomon, KYRIAKON. Festschrift J. Quasten, Vol. I, Münster 1970, 267; A. Adam, Lehrbuch der Dogmengeschichte, I. Die Zeit der Alten Kirche, Gütersloh 1965, 142ff.

[2] So J. Rendel Harris in: J. Rendel Harris – A. Mingana, The Odes and Psalms of Solomon, Vol. II, Manchester 1920, 78; auch A. Adam. o.c., 142ff., J. H. Charlesworth, Les Odes de Salomon et les manuscrits de la mer morte, RB 67, 1970, 522ff.; J. H. Charlesworth/R. A. Culpepper, The Odes of Solomon and the Gospel of John, CBQ 35, 1973, 298–322; J. H. Charlesworth, The Pseudepigrapha and Modern Research, Missoula 1976, 189ff. et al. behaupten eine Entstehungszeit am Ende des ersten oder Anfang des zweiten Jahrhunderts, wie im allgemeinen üblich ist.

[3] J. Rendel Harris/A. Mingana, The Odes and Psalms of Solomon II, 336.

in welchem der descensus des Christus beschrieben wird[4]. Viele Einzelheiten der Ode bleiben aber bei diesem Deutungsversuch, der keine Anerkennung gefunden hat, ungeklärt. J. Rendel Harris glaubt, daß die Ode im Grunde die Inkarnation besingt, sieht Anklänge an den 40. Psalm und Jesaja 8 und 9 und ist der Meinung, daß das NT gar nicht erwähnt wird, sondern nur alttestamentliche Testimonien angeführt werden. Das Rätsel des Rades kann er aber auch nicht lösen[5]. H. Greßmann, ganz in der Tradition der religionsgeschichtlichen Schule, sucht den Ursprung des Himmelsbriefes und des Rades in chinesischen und indischen Vorstellungen, die sich in Ostsyrien mit jüdisch-christlichen Gedanken verschmolzen hätten – eine Meinung, die auch keine Zustimmung gefunden hat[6]. R. Abramowski behauptete resigniert, daß Ode 23 „aus der Arkandisziplin stammt und für uns nicht mehr deutbar ist"[7]. In letzter Zeit hat nur J. Daniélou dieser Ode einige Aufmerksamkeit gewidmet im Rahmen seiner Rekonstruktion der theologischen Strukturen des sogenannten Judenchristentums. Er betrachtet den Brief als den Logos und das Rad als das Kreuz. Das Rad sollte daher einen descensus absconditus symbolisieren, gefolgt durch einen ascensus gloriosus. Die Verborgenheit des descensus würde noch angedeutet durch das Siegel des Briefes, das ihn gegen den bösen Archonten schützt. Daniélous Meinung nach wäre also in Ode 23 die Rede von der kosmischen Symbolik des Kreuzes mit besonderer Betonung der Vertikalbewegung[8].

Angesichts dieser verschiedenen und einander widerstreitenden Deutungsversuche scheint es angebracht, Ode 23 aufs neue unter stetigem Vergleich mit den anderen Oden zu analysieren und so ihren kerygmatischen Gehalt und die dahinter liegenden Traditionen aufzudecken und möglicherweise darzustellen, wie jene mit der Gesamtthematik Kerygma und Logos verbunden sind. Obwohl viele Übersetzungen der Oden vorhanden sind, soll eine neue der Analyse vorangehen, zumal die neueste Edition und Übersetzung manche Fehler aufweisen[9].

---

4 W. R. Newbold, The Descent of Christ in the Odes of Solomon, JBL 31, 1912, 168–209.

5 J. Rendel Harris/A. Mingana, The Odes and Psalms of Solomon II, 336–340.

6 H. Gressmann, Ode Salomos 23, SPAW 1921, 616–624.

7 R. Abramowski, Der Christus der Salomooden, ZNW 35, 1936, 51; cf. W. Bauer in: E. Hennecke/W. Schneemelcher, Neutestamentliche Apokryphen II, Tübingen 1964, 603: „Über Vermutungen gelangt man nicht hinaus."

8 J. Daniélou, Théologie du Judéo-Christianisme, Tournai 1958, 306f.; Daniélou wird gefolgt von R. Murray, Symbols of Church and Kingdom. A Study in Early Syriac Tradition, Cambridge 1975, 240.

9 J. H. Charlesworth, The Odes of Solomon, edited with translation and notes, Oxford 1973; cf. G. J. Reinink, Journal for the Study of Judaism 5, 1974, 64–68 und S. P. Brock, JBL 93, 1974, 623–625; die meist benutzte deutsche Übersetzung ist W. Bauer, Die Oden Salomos, in: Hennecke/Schneemelcher, Neutestamentliche Apokryphen II, 576–625; cf.

1. Die Freude ist der Heiligen,
Und wer sollte sie anziehen, außer ihnen allein?
2. Die Gnade ist der Auserwählten,
Und wer sollte sie empfangen außer jenen, die auf sie trauen von Anfang an?
3. Die Liebe ist der Auserwählten,
Und wer sollte sie anziehen außer jenen, die sie besessen haben von Anfang an?
4. Wandelt in der Erkenntnis des Höchsten,
Und dann werdet ihr erkennen die Gnade des Herrn, der keine Mißgunst kennt,
So daß ihr über Ihn jubelt und seine Erkenntnis vollkommen wird[10].
5. Und sein Gedanke war wie ein Brief,
Und sein Wille kam herab aus der Höhe.
6. Und er wurde gesandt wie ein Pfeil vom Bogen,
Der entsandt wird mit Gewalt.
7. Und es eilten zu dem Briefe viele Hände,
Um ihn zu packen und zu nehmen und zu lesen.
8. Er aber entfloh ihren Fingern,
Und sie bekamen Angst vor ihm und vor dem Siegel auf ihm,
9. Weil es ihnen nicht erlaubt wurde, sein Siegel zu lösen.
Denn die Kraft, die auf dem Siegel war, war stärker als sie.
10. Es folgten aber dem Briefe jene, die ihn gesehen hatten,
Um zu erfahren, wo er sich niederließe.
Und wer ihn lese,
Und wer ihn höre.
11. Ein Rad nun nahm ihn in Empfang,
Und er kam auf es.
12. Und ein Zeichen war mit ihm verbunden
des Königtums und der Providentia.
13. Und alles, was das Rad störte,
Mähte es nieder und schnitt es ab.
14. Und eine Menge, die bestand aus Gegnern, drängte es zurück,
Und schüttete die Flüsse zu
15. Und ging hinüber, rodete viele Wälder aus[11],
Und legte einen breiten Weg an.
16. Das Haupt kam herab zu den Füßen,
Weil bis zu den Füßen das Rad gelaufen war
Und das, was auf ihm gekommen war.

---

idem, Die Oden Salomos, Kleine Texte 64, Berlin 1933. Meine Übersetzungen sind oft von den Bauerschen verschieden, wenn dafür inhaltliche oder philologische Gründe vorliegen.

[10] Im ersten Glied folge ich die Lesart des Ms. H. dmrym' = des Höchsten; Ms.N. liest dmry' = des Herrn; cf. Drijvers, Die Oden Salomos und die Polemik mit den Markioniten im syrischen Christentum, Symposium Syriacum 1976, OrChrAnal 205, Roma 1978, 46.

[11] Ms.N. liest ʿmm' = Völker statt ʿb' = Wälder.

17. Der Brief enthielt ein Gebot,
    Daß sich alle Länder versammelten.
18. Und an seinem Kopfe zeigte sich das Haupt, das sich offenbarte,
    der wahre Sohn vom höchsten Vater.
19. Und er erbte alles und nahm es in Besitz.
    Und die Absicht der vielen nun scheiterte.
20. Alle Verführer nun flohen kopfüber
    Und die Verfolger wurden schlaff und erloschen.
21. Der Brief nun wurde eine große Tafel,
    Die beschrieben war vom Finger Gottes ganz und gar.
22. Und der Name des Vaters (war) darauf
    Und der des Sohnes und der des Heiligen Geistes,
    Zu herrschen in Ewigkeit der Ewigkeiten.
    Hallelujah!

Analyse und Kommentar

1–3: Diese Verse bilden einen Prolog zu der Ode, der in ganz gleich konstruierten Sätzen – ein Nominalsatz, der eine Behauptung enthält, gefolgt durch einen rhetorischen Fragesatz – eine heilsgeschichtliche Beziehung darstellt zwischen Gottes gnädigen Eigenschaften und den Seinigen, die von Anfang der Welt an bestanden hat. Freude (ḥdwt') begegnet oft in den Oden Salomos (7,1,2,17; 15,1; 31,3,6; 32,1), ist immer der Erfolg der Inkarnation des Herrn und daher der Alleinbesitz seiner Gläubigen, Heilige genannt. Deshalb werden in 2 und 3 jene Qualitäten Gottes erwähnt, die in der Menschwerdung zum Ausdruck kommen, Gnade und Liebe. Gnade (ṭybwt') wird in den Oden nur für Gott verwendet und kann eben so ein Äquivalent des Christus sein; z.B.

9,5: Werdet reich in Gott dem Vater,
Und nehmet an den Gedanken des Höchsten!
Seid stark und lasset euch erlösen durch seine Gnade.

33,1: Es eilte aber wiederum herbei die Gnade und vertrieb das Verderben,
Und sie stieg auf es herab, um es zunichte zu machen.
(cf. 33,10; 34,6; 41,3)

Auch Liebe (ḥwb') wird fast ausschließlich von Gott ausgesagt (6,2; 7,19; 11,2; 16,2,3; 40,4; 41,2,6) und manifestiert sich in Christus (17,12; 42,7,9). Es ist nicht ohne Interesse, daß diese spezifische Verwendung von Gnade und Liebe zu Sprachgebrauch und Theologie des Johannes gehört (cf. Joh 1,16,17; 3,14,35). Dasselbe gilt für die Betonung des „von Anfang an“ (mn bryšyt), das wiederum auf den Johannesprolog verweist, wo der Logos Gottes des Anfangs sich in seiner inkarnierten Gnade offenbart (cf. 4,14; 6,4; 7,14; 41,9). Gnade und Liebe sind nur für Gottes Auserwählte – eine Kategorie, die von Anfang an dagewesen ist. Sie sind vorzeitlich erwählt und für das Heil vorherbestimmt (cf. 8,14–21) und werden deshalb aufgerufen, in Gottes Wegen zu wandeln (cf. 33,13). In gewissem Sinne sind sie identisch mit den in Joh 1,12 erwähnten Kindern Gottes, die sich von der im vorangehenden Verse genannten Kategorie, die das Licht der Welt nicht angenommen hat, unterscheiden (cf. Joh 1,5). Wenn die Auserwählten das ihnen bereitete Heil angenommen haben, kennen sie die Freude und gehören zu den Heiligen Gottes, in denen der höchste Gott erkannt wird (7,16) und die das Königreich Christi (= die Kirche) als Wohnung haben (22,12)[12].

Der Prolog der 23. Ode beschreibt also die Einheit der Heilsgeschichte von Anfang an, während derer Gottes Gnade sich entfaltet und von seinen Auserwählten erkannt wird.

4: Dieser Vers bildet nach dem thetischen Prolog den Übergang zu dem erzählenden Teil der Ode und ruft die Gläubigen auf, in der Erkenntnis des Höchsten zu wandeln. Erkenntnis hat in den Oden Salomos die Bedeutung von Erkenntnis des Heils, das im Laufe der Weltgeschichte, die zugleich von Anfang bis Ende Heilsgeschichte ist, von Gott seinen Auserwählten bereitet worden ist. Die Heilsgeschichte ist also ein Weg, worauf die Kenntnis sich mehrt und Unkenntnis vertrieben wird; z.B. 6,6:

Es mehrte seine Erkenntnis der Herr,
Und er bemühte sich, daß erkannt würde, was durch seine Gnade uns geschenkt war (cf. 7,21; 12,3).

Das Hören des Wortes der Wahrheit ist daher mit dem Erhalten der Erkenntnis identisch (8,8), ja, das Wort der Erkenntnis (= der inkarnierte Logos) ist dem Vater der Erkenntnis gleich (7,7). Mit dieser Phraseologie sind wir wieder beim johanneischen Gedankenkreis zurück, wo Erkenntnis des Sohnes Erkenntnis Gottes meint[13].

Das zweite Glied von Vers 4 enthält eine antimarkionitische Tendenz in der Betonung, daß der Herr keine Mißgunst kennt; das führt zurück zum Paradies und zum Anfang der Heilsgeschichte[14]. Das dritte Glied spielt dagegen in der Erwähnung der Vollkommenheit der Erkenntnis Gottes (d.h. daß Gott auf vollkommene Weise erkannt wird) auf die Inkarnation an. Das wird klar aus Ode 7, die die Menschwerdung des Herrn zum Thema hat; 7,12–13:

---

[12] Ephräm Syrus, Carmina Nisibina 15,9 und 19,6, ed. E. Beck, CSCO, Script. Syri 92–93, Louvain 1961, kennt die Heiligen als eine Spezialkategorie in der Kirche, die aber nicht genauer bestimmt werden.

[13] Cf. J. H. Charlesworth/R. A. Culpepper, The Odes of Solomon and the Gospel of John, CBQ 35, 1973, 298–322 für die vielen Anklänge am vierten Evangelium, die die Oden aufweisen.

[14] Cf. Drijvers, Die Oden Salomos und die Polemik mit den Markioniten, 46ff.

Er hat Ihn gegeben, so daß Er (Gott) sich denen zeigen würde, die sein sind,
Damit sie den erkannten, der sie gemacht hat,
Und nicht meinten, von sich selbst her zu sein.
Denn zur Erkenntnis hin hat Er seinen Weg angelegt,
Hat ihn breit und lang gemacht und zur völligen Vollkommenheit geführt[15].

Auch hier ist das johanneische Gedankengut handgreiflich, wie in der verwandten Stelle 41,13–14:

Der Sohn des Höchsten ist erschienen
Mit der Vollkommenheit seines Vaters.
Und das Licht ging auf von dem Wort,
Das von Anfang in Ihm (Gott) war.

Die ganze Thematik der ersten vier Verse der 23. Ode wird also beherrscht vom Gedanken der Einheit der Heilsgeschichte, während derer Gott von Anfang an seine Gnade zeigt, d. h. seine Erkenntnis mehrt – ein Prozeß, der in der Menschwerdung zur Vollkommenheit geführt wird. In Anbetracht der johanneischen Eigenart dieser Thematik, die auch in der Wortwahl zum Ausdruck kommt, wundert es nicht, daß der erzählende Teil der Ode, der – um die Erkenntnis Gottes tatsächlich zur Vollkommenheit zu führen – die Inkarnation und die darauf folgenden Ereignisse im heilshistorischen Prozeß beschreibt, auch, wie sich herausstellen wird, Anklänge an das vierte Evangelium aufweist.

5–6: Christus, der inkarnierte Logos verkörpert den Gedanken (mḥšbt') und Willen (ṣbyn') Gottes nach der Theologie der Oden Salomos, wie besonders klar wird aus 9,3–5:

Das Wort des Herrn und seine Willensregungen
(Sind) ein heiliger Gedanke, den er über seinen Gesalbten gedacht hat.
Denn im Willen des Herrn beruht euer Leben,
Und sein Gedanke ist ewiges Leben,
Und unvergänglich ist eure Vollkommenheit.
Werdet reich in Gott dem Vater,
Und nehmet den Gedanken des Höchsten an.
Seid stark und lasset euch erlösen durch seine Gnade.

Wort und Gedanke Gottes sind wirksam in der Schöpfung, so 16,8,9:

Denn das Wort des Herrn ergründet, was unsichtbar ist,
Und ermittelt seinen Gedanken.
Denn es schaut das Auge seine Werke
Und das Ohr vernimmt seinen Gedanken.

Und ebenso 6,19:

Und die Welten sind durch sein Wort geworden
Und durch den Gedanken seines Herzens.

---

[15] Cf. Joh 1,10,11 und Charlesworth/Culpepper, art. cit., 303.

Sie verkörpern aber auch seine Erlösung in Christus, 17,5:

Und der Gedanke der Wahrheit leitete mich,
Und ich folgte ihm und ging nicht irre (cf. 12,7; 21,5; 41,10)[16].

Es ist in diesem Zusammenhang wichtig, daß die Oden für „folgen“ genau dasselbe Wort verwenden, wie die Evangelien für das Folgen Jesu, nämlich 'zl btr, das auch im 10. Vers der 23. Ode begegnet (cf. Mt 4,22; Joh 1,37 usw.).

Daß Christus den Gedanken und Willen Gottes darstellt, findet sich nicht nur in den Oden Salomos, sondern auch bei den Apologeten, in den Thomas-Akten und bei Ephräm Syrus. Justinus, Apol 61,1 sagt, daß Gott am Anfang vor der Schöpfung eine geistige Potenz hervorbringt, die seine Herrlichkeit, seine Weisheit und sein Wort verkörpern, in menschlicher Gestalt in der Geschichte erscheint und Gottes Willen darstellt und ihm dient[17]. Athenagoras, Suppl. 10 nennt den Sohn Gedanken und Wort Gottes, von dem und für den alles geschaffen ist und der den Willen Gottes zum Ausdruck bringt[18]. Tatianus, Oratio ad Graec. 5 äußert verwandte Ideen, wenn er behauptet, daß das Wort am Anfang durch den Willen Gottes hervorkam[19]. Zum Schluß sei Theophilus von Antiochien erwähnt, der Ad Autol. II,22 reflektiert über den Logos Gottes, der sein Sohn ist, sein Geist und Gedanken, der Gottes Willen durchführt und sich in der Welt manifestiert[20]. In den Ausführungen der Apologeten sind Beziehungen zum mittleren Platonismus, besonders zu Albinus und dessen Timaeusauslegung nachweisbar, wie C. Andresen et al. dargelegt haben[21]. Die göttlichen Qualitäten werden auf den Sohn übertragen, der Gottes Logos, Weisheit, Dynamis, Geist, Gedanken und Willen verkörpert und deshalb Gottes Aktivität in der Welt repräsentiert[22].

---

16 Bauers Übersetzung des zweiten Gliedes von 12,7: „denn Licht und Helligkeit für das Denken ist es (sc. das Wort)“, soll geändert werden in: „denn Licht und der Aufgang des Gedankens ist es“; dnh' = Aufgang wird oft für die Inkarnation des Logos verwendet; so auch 21,5, wo Bauer übersetzt: „Und überaus hilfreich war mir der Ratschluß des Herrn“; es soll lauten: „Und überaus hilfreich war mir der Gedanke des Herrn (sc. der inkarnierte Logos).“

17 Cf. Justinus, Dial. 76,1; 128,3–4; J. Daniélou, Message évangélique et Culture hellénistique, Tournai 1961, 317 ff.; C. Andresen, Justin und der mittlere Platonismus, ZNW 44, 1952–53, 157–195, spez. 190.

18 Cf. Daniélou, Message évangélique, 319 f.

19 Cf. M. Elze, Tatian und seine Theologie, Göttingen 1960, 70 ff., für eine genaue Analyse von Tatians Logoslehre.

20 Cf. Theophilus, Ad Autol. I,3; Daniélou, Message évangélique, 324 ff.

21 C. Andresen, Justin und der mittlere Platonismus, ZNW 44, 1952–53; 157–195; M. Elze, Tatian und seine Theologie, Göttingen 1960; Daniélou, Message évangélique et culture hellénistique, Tournai 1961.

22 So Theophilus, Ad Autol., II,10.

Es ist anzunehmen, daß gleiche philosophische Einflüsse, die bei den Apologeten die Interpretation des Johannesprologs in Zusammenhang mit der Lehre Gottes und der Schöpfung mitgestaltet haben, auch mittelbar oder unmittelbar auf die Theologie der Oden Salomos eingewirkt haben. Sie bleiben nicht auf die Oden beschränkt, sondern sind auch in den apokryphen Thomas-Akten nachweisbar. In einer der vielen Lobreden des Apostels, die oft einen Lehrcharakter aufweisen, sagt er:

And Thou, because Thou art Lord of all, hast a care for the creatures, so that Thou spreadest over us Thy mercy in *Him who came by Thy will* (ṣbynk) and put on the body, Thy creature, which *Thou didst will* and form according to Thy glorious *wisdom*. He whom Thou didst appoint in Thy *secresy* and establish in Thy *manifestation*, to Him Thou hast given the name of *Son*, He who was *Thy Will*, the *Power of Thy Thought* (ṣbynk ḥyl' dmḥšbtk); so that Ye are by various names, the Father and the Son and the Spirit for the sake of the government of Thy creatures, for the nourishing of alle natures, and Ye are *one in glory and power and will;* and Ye are divided without being separated, and are one though divided[23]. '

Die klarsten Parallelen zu den Oden finden sich bei Ephräm Syrus. Im ersten Kapitel seines Diatessaronkommentars im Rahmen der Auslegung von Joh 1,1 betont Ephräm die Wesensgleichheit Gottes mit dem Wort und nennt den Sohn den Gedanken des Vaters. Weiter beschreibt er häufig die Person Christi als die Manifestation von Gottes Willen und Macht, z.B. Hymnus de Nat. 4,165–166:

So hat auch, während er ganz im Mutterleib wohnte,
sein unsichtbarer Wille das All betreut.
Denn siehe, daß er ganz am Kreuze hing,
Seine Macht aber alle Geschöpfe erschütterte[24].

Der inkarnierte Gedanke und Wille Gottes, sein Logos, wird einem Brief verglichen, der sehr rasch aus der Höhe in die Welt geschickt wird. Die Vorstellung eines himmlischen Buches oder Briefes ist ziemlich weitverbreitet (cf. Ez 1; Apk 5,1–3). Das Buch enthält Gottes Plan mit der Welt und ihrer Geschichte, der in Gestalt einer Apokalypse offenbart werden kann[25]. Es wundert daher nicht, daß der inkarnierte Logos,

---

[23] W. Wright, Apocryphal Acts of the Apostles, London 1871 (reprint Amsterdam 1968), 207f.; A. F. J. Klijn, The Acts of Thomas, Leiden 1962, hat diesen Passus nicht kommentiert; cf. Justinus, Apol 61,1; Tatianus, Oratio 5.

[24] L. Leloir, Saint Éphrem, commentaire de l'évangile concordant, Dublin 1963, I,3; idem, Éphrem de Nisibe. Commentaire de l'évangile concordant ou diatessaron, SC 121,43f.; Hymnus de Nat. 4,165–166, ed. E. Beck, CSCO, Script. Syri 82–83, Louvain 1959; cf. Hymnus de Nat. 3,5–6; 23,2–4; Hymnus contra Haereses 32,15; 36,6; Hymnus De Azymis 20,1ff., und E. Beck, Ephraems Reden über den Glauben, Studia Anselmiana 33, Rom 1953, 88ff.

[25] Cf. J. Daniélou, Théologie du Judéo-Christianisme, 151ff.; H. Bietenhard, Die

der von Anfang bis Ende Gottes Plan durchführt, jenem himmlischen Brief verglichen wird, ja gewissermaßen dieser selbst ist. Im Bereich der syrischen Literatur begegnet dieser Brief im sogenannten Perlenlied der Thomas-Akten, wo er auch die Offenbarung Christi symbolisiert[26], und in den Pseudo-Ephrämschen Maria-Hymnen, wo der Brief die Nachricht Gabriels an Maria enthält[27]. Das Bild ist noch weiter entwickelt bei Jakob von Sarug, der den Schoß Mariens „einem versiegelten Briefe voller Geheimnisse" vergleicht[28].

Die Schnelligkeit, mit der der Logos herabkam, ist ein geläufiges Motiv in den Oden; so 12,5:

Denn die Schnelligkeit des Wortes läßt sich nicht erzählen,
Und wie seine Erzählung, so ist auch seine Schnelligkeit und seine Schärfe[29].

und 33,1:

Es eilte wiederum herbei die Gnade und vertrieb das Verderben
Und sie stieg auf es herab, um es zunichte zu machen (cf. 39,4).

7–10: In diesen Versen werden zwei Kategorien von Menschen einander gegenübergestellt: die vielen Hände, die den Brief packen wollten, aber ohne Erfolg, weil es ihnen nicht erlaubt wurde, und jene, die ihm folgten, weil sie ihn gesehen hatten. In Anbetracht der vorhergehenden Verse, die das Herabkommen des Logos beschreiben und auf Joh 1,1 ff. anspielen, scheint es nicht zu weit hergeholt, die zwei Kategorien auch im Johannesevangelium zu suchen. Tatsächlich werden sie im Prolog gleich nacheinander erwähnt: Joh 1,11,12: Er kam in das Seine, und die Seinen nahmen ihn nicht auf. So viele ihn aber aufnahmen, denen gab er Anrecht darauf, Kinder Gottes zu werden, denen, die an seinen Namen glauben . . . Ode 23,7–9 macht den Eindruck, eine Ausle-

---

himmlische Welt im Urchristentum und Spätjudentum, Tübingen 1951, 251; eine Parallele in Evangelium Veritatis 19,35–20,15.

[26] Cf. Wright, The Apocryphal Acts, 241; E. Preuschen, Zwei gnostische Hymnen, Gießen 1904, 21, LL.40–68; A. F. J. Klijn, The so-called Hymn of the Pearl, VigChr 14, 1960, 154–164 und idem, The Acts of Thomas, widmet diesem Brief und seiner Bedeutung keine besondere Aufmerksamkeit. Ich plane dieses Thema in einem gesonderten Aufsatz zu erörtern.

[27] Cf. Th. J. Lamy, Sancti Ephraem Syri Hymni et Sermones II, Mechelen 1896, 593, 641; III, 969; Rendel Harris in Rendel Harris-Mingana, The Odes and Psalms of Solomon II, 337 f. betrachtete diese Hymnen als authentisch Ephrämisch; cf. aber I. Ortiz de Urbina, Patrologia Syriaca, ed. alt., Roma 1965, 73.

[28] Cf. R. C. Chesnut, Three Monophysite Christologies, Oxford 1976, 115, Anm. 11: Hom. 39; 94; Brief 36.

[29] Bauer, in: Hennecke-Schneemelcher II,593, Anm. 1 betrachtet den Text als sichtlich in Unordnung, und Charlesworth, The Odes of Solomon, 61, übersetzte qlylwt' = Schnelligkeit mit ‚subtlety' and ‚swiftness'. Ich glaube, daß die Schnelligkeit des Wortes hier auf paradoxe Weise zum Ausdruck gebracht wird. Das Motiv entstammt Ps 21,13.

gung von Joh 1,11 zu sein, die darlegt, weshalb die Seinen = die Juden ihn nicht aufgenommen haben: weil es ihnen nämlich nicht erlaubt wurde. Im Wortlaut dieser Verse hat daneben noch Joh 1,5 mitgespielt und im allgemeinen der Gedanke des vierten Evangelisten, daß Jesus sich beharrlich den Juden entzogen hat, die ihn ja nicht verstanden (cf. Joh 2,24; 3,10; 5,18; 6,15,52; 7,10–13,31 ff.; 8,59 etc.). Das stellt sich klar heraus im Vers 8, der Joh 10,39 zitiert: Da suchten sie wiederum, sich seiner zu bemächtigen. Und er entkam aus ihrer Hand (cf. Joh 11,52; 13,33)[30].

Die Angst der Juden und ihrer Führer vor dem Christus ist ein geläufiges Thema in den Evangelien (cf. Mk 11,18; Joh 11,47 ff.) und wird in den Oden ihrer Unkenntnis zugeschrieben, für die sie prädestiniert waren – eine Tradition, die auch im vierten Evangelium begegnet: Joh 12,37–43; 15,25. Das wird durch die Behauptung angedeutet, daß es ihnen nicht erlaubt wurde, das Siegel des Briefes zu lösen. Siegel (ḥtm') hat die einfache Bedeutung von Eigentumszeichen, wie in Ode 4,7:

Ist doch dein Siegel bekannt
Und erkannt werden daran deine Geschöpfe[31].

Dadurch sind sie vom Heil Christi ausgeschlossen. Die anti-jüdische Tendenz großer Teile der altsyrischen Literatur kommt auch hier ans Tageslicht. Die Juden werden in Vers 7 bezeichnet als „viele Hände“, wo „viele“ eine negative Nebenbedeutung hat; cf. Vers 19: die Absicht der vielen scheiterte; und 25,5:

Ich wurde aber verachtet und verworfen in den Augen der Vielen.

Dieser letzte Vers ist ein freies Zitat von Jes 53,3 mit Hinzufügung von „in den Augen der Vielen“. Das ist ein weiterer Beweis dafür, daß die Oden christlichen Kreisen entstammen, die sich selber als eine (intellektuelle) Elite gegenüber den Juden betrachteten, welche den Christus nicht besiegt haben, weil er stärker war als sie.

---

[30] Dieses Zitat fehlt bei Charlesworth-Culpepper, art. cit.

[31] Siegel bedeutet hier nicht Taufsiegel, wie z. B. E. Dinkler, Signum Crucis. Aufsätze zum Neuen Testament und zur christlichen Archäologie, Tübingen 1967, 93 und Anm. 64 behauptet; cf. auch W. Heitmüller, Sphragis. Neutest. Studien Georg Heinrich zu seinem 70. Geburtstag, 1914, 48 f.; Art. Sphragis, PRE 2.R,II/2,1361 ff.: Siegelschutz ist ein rechtliches Legitimationsmittel, cf. Ez 9,4 ff., Gen 4,15, Ex 13,9, Jes 44,5, I Kön 20,41, Ps. 15,6–9 und Dinkler, Signum Crucis, 16 f.; Daniélou, Théologie du Judéo-Christianisme, 235 betrachtet das Siegel als Schutzzeichen gegen die bösen Archonten, was nicht richtig ist. Das l' šlyṭ hw' lhwn in Vs. 9 kontrastiert mit šwlṭn' in Joh 1,12: Es wurde ihnen (sc. den Juden) nicht erlaubt das Siegel zu lösen, den Gläubigen dagegen wird die Macht geschenkt Kinder Gottes zu werden.

Vers 10 beschreibt die andere Kategorie mit Worten, die auf Joh 1,37–39 anspielen (die Berufung der ersten Jünger):

Und die beiden Jünger hörten ihn reden und folgten Jesus nach. Als aber Jesus sich umwandte und sie nachfolgen sah, sagte er zu ihnen: Was begehrt ihr? Da sagten sie zu ihm: Rabbi (das heißt übersetzt: Lehrer), wo hältst du dich auf? Er sagt zu ihnen: Kommet, so werdet ihr es sehen! Sie kamen nun und sahen, wo er sich aufhielt, und blieben jenen Tag bei ihm.

Auch die Betonung des Sehens gehört zum johanneischen Sprachgebrauch (cf. Joh 1,14,47,52 usw.). Lesen und Hören des Briefes setzt die Lösung des Siegels voraus, und deshalb ist vielleicht die Annahme nicht zu weit hergeholt, daß in der Verwendung des Verbums šr' = sich niederlassen (intrans.) auch die transitive Bedeutung ‚lösen' (z.B. eines Siegels) oder ‚öffnen' (z.B. eines Briefes) mitklingt. Die Betonung des Hörens im Vers 10 gehört zur johanneischen Theologie, die eine unmittelbare Beziehung zwischen Hören, Folgen und Wissen kennt (cf. Joh 1,37; 3,32ff.; 4,42; 9,27; 10,3 etc.).

11: Dieser Vers erwähnt das rätselhafte Rad, mit dem ein Zeichen verbunden war, das im Vers 12 als ein Zeichen des Königtums und der (göttlichen) Providentia beschrieben wird. Dies Zeichen ('t') meint in den Oden Salomos immer das Kreuz. So 27:

Ich streckte meine Hände aus
Und hielt heilig meinen Herrn.
Denn das Ausbreiten meiner Hände ist sein Zeichen ('t'),
Und mein Ausstrecken ist das aufgerichtete Holz.
Hallelujah! (cf. 42,1)

Und 29,7–8:

Und er (Christus) zeigte mir sein Zeichen
Und leitete mich mit seinem Licht,
Und er gab mir den (Herrscher-)Stab seiner Macht,
Damit ich die Pläne der Völker unterwerfen solle.

Diese Verse machen in ihrem Parallelismus klar, daß das Kreuz als Machtzeichen verstanden wird, als Herrscherstab, was fast identisch ist mit dem Kreuz als Zeichen des Königtums. Ode 39,7 betrachtet das Kreuz sogar als ein Mittel, gewaltige Wasserströme zu überqueren, mit einer Symbolik, die Ex 14,15–31, dem Durchziehen des Schilfmeeres, entlehnt ist, wie Ode 29,7–8 auf den Exodus aus Ägypten anspielt[32].

---

[32] Cf. Justinus, Dial. 86; 138,2 und Daniélou, Théologie du Judéo-Christianisme, 300ff.; dieselbe Symbolik im Perlenlied, 64–65:
Meinen Brief, der mich erweckte,
fand ich vor mir auf dem Wege;

Diese Interpretation des Kreuzes als ein Machtzeichen des Logos findet sich auch bei Justinus und Irenäus. Justinus, Apol., 55 nennt das σχῆμα τοῦ σταυροῦ das Symbol der Macht und Herrschaft des Logos[33]. Derselbe Gedanke begegnet Apol., 60: das Kreuz ist die δύναμις θεοῦ, und Justinus referiert dann Plato, Timaeus 34 a.b und 36 b.c, wo der Philosoph behauptet, daß der höchste Gott seinen Sohn als ein Chi im Weltall bildete[34]. Daher kann Justinus, Dial. 73,1–2 sagen, daß der Herr seine Königsherrschaft vom Kreuz aus ausübte[35]. Irenäus repräsentiert dieselbe Gedankenlinie; Demonstr. 56 sagt er, unter Verweisung auf Jes 9,6: die Herrschaft kommt auf seine Schulter, daß das Kreuz das Zeichen von Christi Königsherrschaft ist[36]. Es wundert daher nicht, daß Irenäus, Demonstr. 79 das Kreuz beschreibt als das Wort Gottes, das die Wirklichkeit durchdringt und das Symbol der göttlichen Führung ist[37]. Adv. Haeres. V,17,4 redet dementsprechend von der οἰκονομία des Holzes (= des Kreuzes)[38]. Das griechische οἰκονομία ist mit dem syrischen mdbrnwt' identisch und bedeutet die göttliche Providentia. Der Gedanke ist klar: das Kreuz ist das Zeichen, mit welchem Gott seinen Logos in der Welt darstellt, und ist daher das Zeichen par excellence seiner Herrschaft und Führung. Justinus und Irenäus beschreiben darum ausführlich alle Typen des Kreuzes im AT (Apol. 55; Dial. 86; Demonstr. 46). Diese Gedanken bilden den Hintergrund und Ursprung von Ode Salomos 23,12: das Zeichen des Königtums und der Providentia, und überdies der sehr komplexen Kreuzsymbolik des Ephräm Syrus[39].

Ephräm kennt auch die Verbindung von Kreuz mit Königsherrschaft; Hymnus de Nativ. 18,3:

---

ihn, der mit seiner Stimme mich geweckt hatte,
mich wieder mit seinem Lichte leitend. (übersetzt v. E. Preuschen)
Rendel Harris in seinem Kommentar zu den Oden hat diese Exodussymbolik nicht beachtet.

[33] Cf. Daniélou, Théologie du Judéo-Christianisme, 294 ff.; Dinkler, Signum Crucis, 36 f.; 65,155.

[34] Cf. Dinkler, Signum Crucis, 36 f.; Daniélou, Théologie, 310 f.; idem, Message évangélique, 319; Andresen, ZNW 44, 1952, 188 f.; W. Bousset, Platons Weltseele und das Kreuz Christi, ZNW 14, 1913, 273–285.

[35] Cf. Justinus, Dial. 86, wo er die ganze Kreuzsymbolik, wie sie sich in den alttestamentlichen Typen findet, darstellt.

[36] Cf. Justinus, Dial. 73,1–2; G. Q. Reijners, The Terminology of the Holy Cross in Early Christian Literature, Nijmegen 1965, 62.

[37] Cf. W. Bousset, Platons Weltseele und das Kreuz Christi, 273 f.; E. Stommel, RQ 48, 1953, 35 ff.; Daniélou, Théologie, 296; cf. Tert., Adv. Marc. 3,22; Evang. Philipp. 95, ed. W. C. Till, Berlin 1963, 122, 18–22.

[38] Cf. G. Q. Reijners, The Terminology of the Holy Cross, 60 f.; Daniélou, Message évangélique, 327 ff.; Tatianus, Oratio 5; Irenäus, Adv. Haeres. IV,6,7; IV,20,6–7; Ephräm Syrus, Comment. Diatessaron 7.

[39] Cf. P. Yousif, Le symbolisme de la croix dans la nature chez saint Éphrem de Nisibe, Symposium Syriacum 1976, OrChrA 205, Roma 1978, 207–228.

Seine Geburt in den Tagen des Königs
Mit dem Namen „Strahl" (= Augustus) – Symbol und Wirklichkeit
trafen einander: König und König,
Strahl und Aufgang. Sein Kreuz trug
jene Königsherrschaft. Gepriesen sei, der sie erhob[40].

Das Kreuzzeichen ist mit einem Rad verbunden, das den Brief = den Logos in Empfang nahm. Der Text der Verse 11 und 12 widerspricht also der Gleichsetzung von Kreuz und Rad, die Daniélou als gegeben annahm[41]. Die Bedeutung des Rades muß daher anderswo gesucht werden.

Im Rahmen der biblischen Symbole verweist das Rad auf den Wagen Gottes, die Merkabah, wie sie in Ez 1 ausführlich als Sitz der göttlichen Herrlichkeit beschrieben wird. Die vier Räder der Merkabah sind aufs engste verbunden mit den vier Tieren, können nach allen vier Seiten gehen und gingen, wo der Geist sie hintrieb (Ez 1,15–21).

Die Kombination der Merkabah und des Kreuzes findet sich mehrfach bei Ephräm Syrus, z.B. Hymnus de Virg. 21,10:

Das Kreuz ist eingezeichnet jenem Wagen,
An dem die (lebendigen) Cherubim gespannt sind[42].

Ephräm deutet die Tiere von Ez 1 also als Cherubim und stellt so eine Verbindung zur Bundeslade (Ex 37,6–9) her. Ephräms Hymnus de Azymis 13 beschreibt die Antinomien des gottmenschlichen Leidens und Sterbens Christi und bringt das Paradoxon auf folgende Weise zum Ausdruck: Hymnus de Azymis 13,8:

Er fuhr auf dem (Wagen des) Kreuzes,
Während er unsichtbarerweise auf dem (Gottes)wagen der Cherubim fuhr[43].

Christus thronte auf der Merkabah und verließ sie, so Hymnus de Fide 17,8:

Den Wagen der vier Lebewesen verließ er und stieg hinab
Und schuf sich das Kreuz zum Gefährt nach den vier Richtungen.
Er verließ die Seraphim und Cherubim
Und stieg hinab und ertrug den Spott der Kreuziger[44].

---

[40] E. Beck, Des Heiligen Ephraem des Syrers Hymnen de Nativitate, CSCO, Script. Syri, 82–83, Louvain 1959, 83f.; cf. Yousif, art. cit., 223, Anm. 32.

[41] Daniélou, Théologie, 306f.; Daniélous Übersetzung von Ode 23,10–17 ist ziemlich ungenau.

[42] E. Beck, Des Heiligen Ephraem des Syrers Hymnen de Virginitate, CSCO. S 94–95, Louvain 1962, 67.

[43] E. Beck, Des Heiligen Ephraem des Syrers Paschahymnen, CSCO. S 108–109, Louvain 1964, 16.

[44] E. Beck, Des Heiligen Ephraem des Syrers Hymnen de Fide, CSCO. S 73–74, Louvain 1955, 52; cf. Hymnus de Fide 4,18; 55,4; Hymnus de Ecclesia 29,14; Yousif, art. cit., 212, 224.

166

Im Lichte dieser Ephräm-Stellen können die Verse 11 und 12 gedeutet werden. Das Rad steht als pars pro toto für den Wagen Gottes, seinen Thron, dem das Kreuz wie vier Speichen eingezeichnet ist. Wenn das Rad den Brief in Empfang nimmt, ist das eine Art Inthronisation[45]. Diese Deutung wird bestätigt durch die Wortwahl in Vers 12: der inkarnierte Logos nimmt Platz auf dem Thron der Herrlichkeit Gottes und das Kreuz ist das Zeichen seiner Königsherrschaft! Mit diesem Paradoxon wird der Anfang des öffentlichen Lebens Christi beschrieben. In Anbetracht der vorhergehenden Verse, die eine Art Paraphrase des Johannesprologs bilden, darf man annehmen, daß die Verse 11 und 12 auf Joh 1,14 anspielen: „Und das Wort ward Fleisch und wohnte unter uns, und wir schauten seine Herrlichkeit, eine Herrlichkeit, wie sie der einzige (Sohn) von seinem Vater hat, voll Gnade und Wahrheit." Im Inthronisationsgedanken spielt die christologische Auslegung des 110. Psalms eine Rolle, Ps 110,1: „Es spricht der Herr zu meinem Herrn: ‚Setze dich zu meiner Rechten, bis daß ich hinlege deine Feinde als Schemel für deine Füße.'"

Die Ephräm-Stellen machten klar, daß Merkabah und Bundeslade in gewissem Sinne identifiziert werden. Bei einem Vergleich von Num 10,33ff., Deut 1,33, 1.Sam 4 und 5 stellt sich heraus, daß die Bundeslade Gott als Führer seines Volkes ersetzen kann und daneben als Sitz seiner Herrlichkeit fungiert. Die Ikonographie der jüdischen Religion bestätigt diese Identifikation: in der Synagoge in Dura-Europos z.B. wird die Bundeslade auf einem Wagen dargestellt[46].

13–15: Auf ganz konsequente Weise wird daher in diesen Versen das öffentliche Leben Jesu, der Zug der Herrlichkeit Gottes durch die Welt oder der Werdegang seines Logos, beschrieben mit Bildern, die alttestamentlichen Stellen, die christologisch gedeutet werden, entlehnt worden sind. Ps 68, Ps 110 und Ex 14, die Erzählung vom Durchziehen des Schilfmeers, kommen hier in Betracht. Ps 68 beschreibt Gottes Triumphzug, spielt auf den Exodus an (Vs. 8,9), das Vertreiben der Feinde (Vs. 22) und erwähnt Gottes Wagen (Vs. 18). Die christologische Deutung von Ps 68 ist ganz traditionell, begegnet schon in Eph 4,7–9 und überdies bei Justinus, Dial. 39,4; 87,6, Irenäus, Demonstr. 83 und Ode Sal 10,3[47]. Dasselbe gilt für Ps 110, der auch den Sieg über die

---

[45] Cf. Daniélou, Théologie, 281; idem, Études d'exégèse judéo-chrétienne, Paris 1966, 42ff.

[46] Cf. E. Goodenough, Jewish Symbols in the Greco-Roman Period, VII,176, und II,182, Anm. 100; J. Gutmann, The Dura-Europos Synagogue: A Re-evaluation (1932–1972), Missoula 1973, 142ff.; J. Maier, Vom Kultus zur Gnosis. Bundeslade, Gottesthron und Märkābāh, Salzburg 1964, 55ff.

[47] J. Rendel Harris, The Odes and Psalms of Solomon, II,265; Daniélou, Théologie, 283ff.

Feinde beschreibt und, worauf in den Oden mehrfach Bezug genommen wird, speziell für die häufige Verwendung des christologischen Titels ‚die Rechte' (sc. Hand)[48].

Wenn der Odist Wörter wie Abschneiden und Ausroden verwendet, verbirgt sich dahinter die Symbolik des Kreuzes als ein Beil oder eine Pflugschar. Das Kreuz als Beil geht zurück auf die christologische Interpretation von 2.Kön 6,1–7, die sich bei Justinus, Dial. 86,6 und Irenäus, Adv. Haeres. V,17,4 findet. Irenäus bezieht überdies Mt 3,10 in seine Auslegung ein und stellt das Wort Gottes, den Logos, dem Beil gleich[49]. Die Identifikation des Kreuzes mit einer Pflugschar wurzelt in der christologischen Exegese von Jes 2,3–4: „und viele Nationen werden sich aufmachen und sprechen: ‚Kommt, lasset uns hinaufziehen zum Berge des Herrn, zu dem Hause des Gottes Jakobs, daß er uns seine Wege lehre und wir wandeln auf seinen Pfaden; denn von Zion wird die Weisung ausgehen, und das Wort des Herrn von Jerusalem.' Und er wird Recht sprechen zwischen den Völkern und Weisung geben vielen Nationen; und sie werden ihre Schwerter zu Pflugscharen schmieden und ihre Spieße zu Rebmessern." Diese Exegese findet sich bei Justinus, Apologie 39,1; Dial., 110,3, und bei Irenäus, Adv. Haeres. IV,34,4[50].

Wenn er dagegen spricht vom Zuschütten der Flüsse und, wie eine Variante im Ms.N (B.M. Add. 14538) liest, vom Ausroden der Völker, spielt die auf den Logos bezogene Interpretation von Ex 14 eine Rolle, die bei Justinus, Dial., 86; 138,2, im Perlenlied, Verse 62–68 und in Ode Sal 39,8–11 begegnet (cf. Ode 29,7–8)[51].

Ode 39 macht diese hier vorgeschlagene Deutung noch wahrscheinlicher, wenn sie im Vers 7 in einer symbolischen Auslegung des Durchzuges durch das Schilfmeer sagt:

Denn das Zeichen (= Kreuz) an ihnen (sc. den Gläubigen) ist der Herr
Und das Zeichen ist der Weg derer, die hinübergehen im Namen des Herrn.

Kreuz und Herrlichkeit Gottes legen einen breiten Weg an, wie Ode 23 sagt, und dieser Weg ist dem Durchzug durch das Schilfmeer gleich (cf. auch Jes 2,3–4)[52].

---

[48] Cf. Ode 8,6,20; 14,4; 18,7; 19,5; 22,7; 25,2,9; 28,15; 38,20 und Daniélou, Études d'exégèse judéo-chrétienne, 42ff.: La session à la droite du Père.

[49] Cf. Daniélou, Théologie, 299f.; J. Carcopino, Le mystère d'un symbole chrétien, Paris 1955, 69–76.

[50] Cf. J. Daniélou, La charrue symbole de la croix (Irénée, Adv. Haer., IV,34,4), RSR 42, 1954, 193–204; J. Doignon, RSR 43, 1955, 535–544; A. Grillmeier, Der Logos am Kreuz. Zur christologischen Symbolik der älteren Kreuzigungsdarstellung, München 1956, 64f.; cf. Irenäus, Adv. Haeres. IV,56,3; Demonstr. 86.

[51] A. F. J. Klijn, The Acts of Thomas, Leiden 1962, 281, widmet dieser Symbolik des Exodus keine Aufmerksamkeit in seinem Kommentar zur Stelle.

[52] Ephraem Syrus, Sermo de Domino Nostro, ed. E. Beck, CSCO, S 116–117, Louvain

16: Wenn die vorhergehenden Verse sich auf das Auftreten des inkarnierten Logos beziehen, ist anzunehmen, daß Vers 16 das Ende seines öffentlichen Lebens, die Kreuzigung, beschreibt. Das Herabkommen zu den Füßen darf man auffassen als eine symbolische Andeutung der Erniedrigung, weil Füße als bildliche Umschreibung für Niedrigkeit oder Unterseite verwendet werden können (so Ephräm, Hymnus de Paradiso 1,4). Haupt (ryš') bedeutet in den Oden Salomos immer den Messias; so 17,15–16:

Denn sie sind mir Glieder geworden
Und ich ihr Haupt.
Preis dir, unserem Haupte, Herr, Christus!

und 24,1:

Die Taube flog auf das Haupt unseres Herrn Christus,
Weil er ihr Haupt war[53].

Das Herabkommen des Hauptes zu den Füßen ist also eine Umschreibung für die Erniedrigung, d.h. die Kreuzigung, die stattfindet, weil das Rad zu den Füßen gelaufen war, d.h. die Herrlichkeit Gottes sich erniedrigt hat und mit ihr, was auf dem Rad gekommen war, d.h. der dort inthronisierte Logos, der Sohn Gottes (cf. Phil 2,8). Die hier vorgenommene Umschreibung der Kreuzigung wird bildlich dargestellt in den apokryphen Petrus-Akten 38, wo die Kreuzigung Petri kopfunter beschrieben wird[54].

17–22: Die Verse 5–16 beschreiben auf eine symbolische Weise die Inkarnation des Logos, sein Leben und seine Kreuzigung, und es ist daher wahrscheinlich, daß die übrigen Verse dieser Ode die nächsten Ereignisse der Heilsgeschichte enthalten. Vers 17 sagt, daß der Brief ein Gebot enthielt, daß alle Länder sich versammelten, und spielt auf Stellen wie Joh 11,52; 12,32; Act 1,8; 2,39; Ephes 2,14–16, Phil 2,10 an, die alle auf verschiedene Weise von der einigenden Kraft des Wortes Gottes in der Verkündigung reden. Im Lichte der vorhergehenden Verse kommen auch alttestamentliche Stellen, wie Jes 2,2–4 und Ps 67 in Betracht.

1966, c. IV, vergleicht das Kreuz mit einer „Brücke über den Tod, damit darauf die Seelen vom Reich der Toten ins Reich der Lebenden hinübergehen (können)"; für eine gnostische Interpretation des Weges vide Newbold, art. cit., 186f.

[53] St. Gero, The Spirit as a Dove at the Baptism of Jesus, NT 18,17–35, interpretiert Ode 24,1 als die Quelle – obwohl in verstümmelter Form – von Mk 1,10, der Geschichte der Taufe Jesu. M. E. hat Ode 24,1 ff. nichts mit der Taufe Jesu zu tun, sondern bezieht sich auf „apokalyptische" Ereignisse, die anknüpfen bei einer christologischen Exegese der Sintflutgeschichte. Ich hoffe das demnächst detailliert darzulegen.

[54] Lipsius-Bonnet, Acta Apostolorum Apocrypha I,94–97; Hennecke-Schneemelcher II,220f.; cf. Ephräm Syrus, Carmina Nisibena 59,2; Yousif, Le symbolisme de la croix, 222.

Speziell Jes 2,2–4 spielt eine wichtige Rolle bei Justinus und Irenäus, die darstellen, daß es nach der Inkarnation ein neues Gesetz gibt, das alle Völker durch die Verkündigung des Evangeliums vereinigt[55].

18: Dieser Vers enthält ein Wortspiel mit ryš', das Kopf eines Briefes bedeuten kann, aber auch Haupt = Messias und Anfang und damit zurückverweist auf die Spekulationen über den Anfang der Welt und die Rolle des Sohnes Gottes im Schöpfungsprozeß[56]. Es ist nicht ungereimt anzunehmen, daß Vers 18 dadurch eine apologetische und anti-häretische Tendenz bekommt in der Betonung der Identität des wahren Sohnes des höchsten Vaters, der von Anfang der Welt an da war, mit dem Gekreuzigten[57].

Im ganzen Passus sind weiter zwei Sachen sehr auffallend. An erster Stelle die alttestamentlichen Ausdrücke: das Wort Gottes wird ein Gebot (pwqdn', ein hapax in den Oden), das alle Länder vereinigt; dadurch erbt der Sohn Gottes alles und nimmt es in Besitz, ein Ausdruck, der immer im AT verwendet wird für die Inbesitznahme des verheißenen Landes (Deut 1,8; 4,1 etc.); und das Wort Gottes wird eine große Tafel, beschrieben vom Finger Gottes, ein Bild, das immer für die Tafeln des mosaischen Gesetzes verwendet wird. Das Evangelium wird so eine Nova Lex, die bis in Ewigkeit bleibt, und die Trinität bekannt macht[58]. Auf diese Weise umfaßt die 23. Ode die ganze Geschichte von Anfang bis in Ewigkeit.

An zweiter Stelle ist diese alttestamentliche Terminologie mit einer anti-jüdischen Tendenz verbunden. Das Gebot ist für die Länder, der Sohn Gottes erbt alles und nimmt es in Besitz, die Absicht der vielen (= der Juden) scheitert, und die Verfolger werden schlaff. Mit den Verfolgern sind auch die Juden gemeint, wie sich aus Ode 42,5 ergibt, wo der Christus spricht:

Es starben alle meine Verfolger,
Und es suchten mich die, die auf mich hofften, weil ich lebendig bin.

---

[55] Justinus, Dial. 11,1; 24,1, wo eine anti-jüdische Tendenz ans Licht kommt; Irenäus, Adv. Haeres. IV,34,4; V,17,4 enthält einen Anklang an Eph 2,14–16; Irenäus, Demonstr. 86,87; cf. Daniélou, Théologie, 218f.; 303ff.; F. Loofs, Leitfaden zur Dogmengeschichte, 303.

[56] Cf. Daniélou, Théologie, 221 über die Bedeutung und Funktion von κεφαλή und ἀρχή.

[57] Für anti-häretische Tendenzen in den Oden Salomos cf. Drijvers, Die Oden Salomos und die Polemik gegen die Markioniten im syrischen Christentum, Symposium Syriacum 1976, OrChrA 205, Roma 1978, 39–55; idem, The 19th Ode of Solomon. Its Interpretation and Place in Syrian Christianity, wird demnächst in ALUOS erscheinen.

[58] Cf. Daniélou, Théologie, 216ff.; Ephräm Syrus, Hymnus de Ecclesia 44,13–21, ed. E. Beck, CSCO, S. 84–85, Louvain 1960, redet sehr ausführlich vom Evangelium als neuen Tafeln.

Es ist ein weitverbreiteter Gedanke in der syrischen Theologie, daß durch die Kreuzigung die Juden verworfen wurden und die Völker die Gnade und Auserwählung bekamen. Ephräm, Comm. Diatessaron XXI,14,19 sind dafür gute Beispiele[59].

Wie das Rad als Symbol der göttlichen Herrlichkeit auf Joh 1,14 verweist, so ist der letzte Teil der Ode in gewissem Sinne eine Ausführung von Joh 1,15–17. Der Täufer betont, daß der Christus vor ihm gewesen ist: „Denn er war als erster vor mir (cf. der Messias als Anfang und Haupt) . . . Denn das Gesetz ist durch Mose gegeben worden, die Gnade und die Wahrheit ist durch Jesus Christus gekommen." Die Antithese von Moses und Jesus Christus wird im letzten Teil von Ode 23 vollständig ausgeführt!

Der letzte Vers der Ode knüpft ganz folgerichtig an Joh 1,18 an: „Niemand hat Gott jemals gesehen; der einzige Sohn, der im Schoße des Vaters ist, der hat Kunde (von ihm) gebracht." Es wundert nicht, daß diese Kunde Gottes, die nur durch das Evangelium als Nova Lex zustande kommt, im letzten Vers der Ode trinitarisch ausgeführt wird. Der Brief, der inkarnierte Logos, macht Gott bekannt durch das geschriebene Wort Gottes (die große vom Finger Gottes beschriebene Tafel), dessen Verständnis Sache des Heiligen Geistes ist. Wiederum gibt es eine genaue Parallele bei Irenäus, Demonstr. 26: „„. . . dans le désert, Moïse reçoit de Dieu la loi, le Décalogue, sur les tables de pierre écrites par le doigt de Dieu (Ex 31,18) – et doigt de Dieu est ce qui sort du Père – dans le Saint-Esprit."[60] Es gibt darum keinen Grund, die Erwähnung des Sohnes und des Heiligen Geistes als eine spätere doxologische Zufügung zu betrachten, wie Daniélou es tut im Nachfolge von P. Battifol[61]. Vielmehr kommen wir mit dieser trinitarischen Formel in die Nähe der früh-antiochenischen Trinitätstheologie, wie sie z.B. Theophilus, Ad Autol. II,10 repräsentiert, der auch beim Johannesprolog anschließt[62].

Schlußfolgerungen

Die Analyse der 23. Ode Salomos hat gezeigt, daß sie eine sehr kohärente Struktur aufweist, in welcher die Heilsgeschichte vom Anfang bis

---

[59] Ed. L. Leloir, Saint Éphrem. Commentaire de l'évangile concordant, XXI,14: Expansae erant manus Moysis, et extendit ea Deus pandendo, donec collaberentur inimici eorum (sc. Israelitarum) (Ex 17,8–14). Extenderunt isti (sc. Iudaei) manus Filii eius (sc. Dei) super crucem, et quia egerant contrarium illi (beneficae extensioni manuum), fecit eis etiam contrarium illi (beneficae) extensioni manuum suarum; collapsi sunt, et erectio iterum non fuit eis.

[60] Irénée de Lyon, Démonstration de la prédication apostolique, ed. L. M. Froidevaux, SC 62, 1959, 73 und Anm. 2.

[61] Daniélou, Théologie, 161, Anm. 1.

[62] Cf. Daniélou, Théologie, 220; G. Kretschmar, Studien zur frühchristlichen Trinitätstheologie, Tübingen 1956, 27–33.

Ende dargestellt wird und die auf einer höchst reflektierten ‚sophisticated' Auslegung des Johannesprologs unter Heranziehung anderer biblischer Perikopen und Gedanken beruht. Das Ganze zeigt einerseits eine starke Übereinstimmung mit den theologischen Gedanken des Justinus, Irenäus und Theophilus, also mit Kreisen, die Verbindungen zu Antiochien haben, andererseits finden sich manche der verwendeten Bilder nur in den Schriften Ephräms des Syrers wieder und sind dort in ausgeführter Form anzutreffen. Das trifft besonders für das Bild des Rades, abcr auch für dic christologischen Gedanken zu. Die Ode weist antijüdische Elemente auf, was sie mit großen Teilen der alt-syrischen Literatur verbindet, und zeigt Bekanntschaften mit philosophischen Systemen, die Einfluß auf die Apologeten und namentlich Justinus und Irenäus gehabt haben. Vor allem aber findet sich in dieser Ode, wie in den anderen, eine symbolisch-typologische Schriftauslegung, die sich auf den Gedanken der Einheit der Heilsgeschichte stützt und die sich genau so bei Ephräm findet[63].

Die 23. Ode Salomos – und die ganze Sammlung! – läßt sich deshalb am besten in die erste Hälfte des dritten Jahrhunderts datieren, also zwischen den Schriftstellern des zweiten Jahrhunderts im Umkreis Antiochiens und Ephräm Syrus im vierten Jahrhundert. Eine spätere Entstehungszeit kommt auch noch in Betracht, da die ersten Zeugnisse der Oden Lactantius und die Pistis Sophia sind – rund 300 A.D. – und Cyrillus von Jerusalem und Ephräm Syrus im vierten Jahrhundert die meisten Parallelen zu den Oden aufweisen[64]. Die 23. Ode macht überdies klar, daß die ganze Sammlung der 42 Oden das wichtigste Bindeglied zwischen Ephräms Theologie und exegetischen Methoden und der antiochenischen Theologie des zweiten und dritten Jahrhunderts ist und daß sie deshalb fast die einzige bekannte Vorstufe und Quelle der Ephrämschen Theologie bildet.

Die Kreise, denen die Oden entstammen, sind schwieriger zu bestimmen. Dem Charakter der 23. Ode entspricht es am besten, ihren Ursprung in gelehrten Kreisen zu suchen, wo ihr Verfasser unter Aufwand all seiner philosophischen, theologischen und exegetischen Kenntnisse

---

[63] Ephräms Exegese ist in dieser Hinsicht niemals genau untersucht worden; als Ersatz dient gewissermaßen R. Murray, Der Dichter als Exeget: der Hl. Ephräm und die heutige Exegese, ZKTh 100, 1978, 484–494; auch L. Leloir, Doctrines et méthodes de S. Éphrem d'après son commentaire de l'évangile concordant, CSCO, Sub 18, Louvain 1861, schenkt diesen geistesgeschichtlichen Beziehungen keine Aufmerksamkeit; sie bleiben auch unbeachtet von T. Kronholm, Motifs from Genesis 1–11 in the genuine Hymns of Ephrem the Syrian, Lund 1978.

[64] J. Rendel Harris/A. Mingana, The Odes and Psalms of Solomon, II,40 ff.; 61 ff.; cf. A. J. Wensinck, Ephrem's Hymns of Epiphany and the Odes of Solomon, Expositor Ser. 8,3, 1912, 108–112; Rendel Harris, Ephrem's Use of the Odes of Solomon, Expositor 1912, 113–119.

172

das Kerygma auf eine symbolische Weise gestaltete, die nur dem Anschein nach poëtisch und unlogisch ist, in Wirklichkeit aber alle Feinheit besitzt, die auch das Thema Kerygma und Logos kennzeichnet. Sie sind deshalb nur für eine Elite bestimmt, sowohl in unserer Zeit als zweifelsohne auch in der Zeit ihrer Entstehung.

IX

THE 19TH ODE OF SOLOMON: ITS INTERPRETATION AND PLACE IN SYRIAN CHRISTIANITY

THE Odes of Solomon are characterized by S. P. Brock in a review of a recent edition of these hymns as 'one of the most beautiful, and at the same time, most puzzling products of early Christianity'.[1] Since the appearance of the first edition of these Odes in 1909, followed by Rendel Harris and Mingana's extensive edition of 1916–20, no *communis opinio* has been reached on the time and place of their origin, on the nature of their religious ideas, or on the language in which these Odes were originally written.[2] In the words of J. Quasten: 'Though they were published as long ago as 1909 they have since baffled all attempts to determine their exact character.[3] In the context of this article it is quite superfluous to quote all the different views relating to the Odes of Solomon, which usually reflect prevailing fashions and methods in the field of ancient Christianity and patristics. They are considered by some as products of an early Jewish-Christian Gnosticism and by others as non-Gnostic hymns related to the Hodayôt from the Qumrân-community; the Christology of the Odes is described by some as docetic, by others as perfectly orthodox. Thus H. Chadwick argues that the Odes are indeed orthodox Christian, but represent a 'Christianity of an unusual kind', a view supported by the complaint that a 'vague and cloudy language' prevails in these ancient Christian hymns.[4] Similar thoughts had earlier been expressed by R. M. Grant: 'The Christianity of the ancient Near East was by no means as accurately and dogmatically defined as that of the regions more influenced by Rome.'[5] Apart from the question as to whether such a characterization

[1] S. P. Brock (review of *The Odes of Solomon*, edited with translation and notes by J. H. Charlesworth, Oxford, 1973), *J.B.L.* xciii (1974), pp. 623–5.

[2] Rendel Harris–A. Mingana, *The Odes and Psalms of Solomon*, 2 vols. (Manchester, 1916–20); for a discussion of problems connected with the Ode, cf. W. Bauer, in E. Hennecke–W. Schneemelcher, *Neutestamentliche Apokryphen*, 3te Aufl., Bd. II (Tübingen, 1964), pp. 576 ff.; M. Erbetta, *Gli Apocrifi del N.T.* i. 1, *Vangeli* (1975), appendix; A. Adam, *Lehrbuch der Dogmengeschichte*, Bd. I (Gütersloh, 1965), pp. 142 ff.; J. A. Emerton, 'Some Problems of Text and Language in the Odes of Solomon', *J.T.S.* N.S. xviii (1967), pp. 372–406.

[3] J. Quasten, *Patrology*, i (Utrecht–Antwerp, 1975), p. 160.

[4] H. Chadwick, 'Some Reflections on the Character and Theology of the Odes of Solomon', *KYRIAKON: Festschrift J. Quasten*, i (Münster, 1970), pp. 266–70, esp. 267.

[5] R. M. Grant, 'The Odes of Solomon and the Church of Antioch', *J.B.L.* lxiii (1944), pp. 363–77, esp. 363.

should be regarded as a praise or a blame it should be stated that on the whole it is not valid and not even an adequate labelling of the Odes of Solomon.

Since Rendel Harris's standard work appeared the 42 Odes 'still deserve a full introduction and commentary' (Brock): in most cases they are only used as a source for extracting quotations that in turn are used as parallels to other texts or as arguments in support of a certain theory about ancient Syriac Christianity. The works of J. Daniélou, A. F. J. Klijn, R. Murray, and others may be mentioned in this context.[1]

The present author prefers another method for many reasons: to reach firmer conclusions it seems more expedient first to analyse the different Odes and to compare the religious conceptions in them. In this way something like a theology of the Odes of Solomon can be sketched in outline. This theology or these theological concepts can be compared to other theological systems known from ancient Syrian Christianity to determine differences and similarities and, where possible, to assign to the Odes their place in a process of historical development. This working method can be compared to a system of concentric circles going from the centre to the outside, instead of comparing loose phrases outside their context to each other. In a sense it is of no importance which Ode or Odes is or are chosen for analysing and comparing with the others. The choice of the 19th Ode is based on remarks which Harris and others made about this hymn; in his words: 'This Ode is, in modern eyes, altogether grotesque, and out of harmony with the generally lofty strain of the rest of the collection.' On the first discovery of the Odes Harris supposed that it was a later addition, but it is one of the best attested, quoted by Lactantius in his *Divinae Institutiones* iv. 12. 3 and having much in common with other Odes, e.g. the 8th and the 35th, so that there is no reason to eject the 19th Ode from the whole collection. Harris tried to explain this 19th Ode, but did not succeed; especially the difference he discerned between the first and the second part of the Ode was a hindrance for its understanding: 'The second part of the Ode is really more perplexing than the first: the first is grotesque, without an evolution of ideas; it might easily have been produced at a single sitting; but the second part appears to present the doctrine of the Virgin Birth in a highly evolved form. . . . Can we really refer this kind of speculation to the borders of the first century?'[2]

[1] Cf. J. Daniélou, *Théologie du Judéo-Christianisme* (Tournai, 1958); A. F. J. Klijn, 'The Influence of Jewish Theology on the Odes of Solomon and the Acts of Thomas', *Aspects du Judéo-Christianisme* (Paris, 1965), pp. 167–79; R. Murray, *Symbols of Church and Kingdom: a Study in early Syriac Tradition* (Cambridge, 1975).

[2] Harris–Mingana, *The Odes*, ii, pp. 304 f.

One of the very few scholars who has ever tried to do any systematic research on the Odes, R. Abramowski, in an article on the Christology of the Odes of Solomon, also met with great difficulties in interpreting the 19th Ode. After having given a partial translation starting with verse 7, he states: 'So schwierig, fast unmöglich die Einzelauslegung erscheint, so klar ist die Tatsache der Geburt des Gottessohnes. . . .'[1] The previously cited H. Chadwick also has great difficulties with the 19th Ode: 'Another grotesque image occurs in Ode 19. . . .'[2] In sharp contrast to Rendel Harris's opinion, especially on the second part of Ode 19, is a statement by J. Quasten: 'The content of these hymns breathes throughout the spirit of an exalted mysticism, which seems to be influenced by the Gospel of St. John. Most of them contain general praises of God with no traces of theological or speculative thought.'[3] Difficulty and grotesquerie going hand in hand are so attractive that this combination, which seems to make a coherent interpretation impossible may be a sufficient justification for the choice made here. In view of the many translations available, which often vary considerably, a new translation is offered here; arguments for certain translations, that are at the same time interpretations will be adduced in the commentary.[4]

1. A cup of milk was offered to me
   And I drank it with the sweetness of the Lord's kindness.
2. The Son is the cup,
   And He who was milked is the Father;
   And She who milked Him is the Holy Spirit;
3. Because His breasts were full,
   And it was undesirable that His milk should be spilt without purpose,

[1] R. Abramowski, 'Der Christus der Salomooden', *Z.N.W.* xxxv (1936), pp. 44–69, esp. 54; Abramowski's translation of Ode 19: 7–11 is wrong in essential points.

[2] H. Chadwick, 'Some Reflections', p. 269.

[3] J. Quasten, *Patrology*, i, p. 162.

[4] In the numbering of the verses I follow Harris–Mingana; Ode 19 has been completely translated by Rendel Harris, W. Bauer, J. H. Charlesworth, J. H. Bernard, H. Grimme, G. Diettrich, J. Labourt–P. Batiffol, to mention only the best known translations (full bibliography in J. H. Charlesworth, *The Odes of Solomon*, pp. 149–67). Ode 19 has been partly translated by R. Murray, *Symbols Of Church and Kingdom*, p. 315; J. Daniélou, *Théologie du Judéo-Christianisme*, p. 238 (a rather tendentious translation of vv. 6–8); R. Abramowski, 'Der Christus der Salomooden', p. 54; A. F. J. Klijn, *Edessa: De stad van de apostel Paulus* (Baarn, 1962), pp. 60 f. The present author has refrained from discussing all variants and faults in the translations available; he differs on many points from the translation given by J. H. Charlesworth, who gives many wrong translations and misunderstandings of the Syriac text: cf. G. J. Reinink, *Journal for the Study of Judaism*, v (1974), pp. 64–68 for a critical review; see now the most recent edition by Michael Lattke, *Die Oden Salomos in ihrer Bedeutung für Neues Testament und Gnosis*, 2 vols. (Fribourg–Göttingen, 1979).

4. The Holy Spirit opened Her womb
And mixed the milk of the two breasts of the Father,
5. And gave the mixture to the world without their knowing.
And those who take (it) are in the perfection of the right Hand.
6. The womb of the Virgin caught (it)
And she received conception and gave birth.
7. And the Virgin became a mother through great mercy.
8. And she laboured and bore a Son without suffering pain,
Because it did not happen without purpose.
9. And she did not require a midwife
Because He delivered Her.
10. As a man she bore by will,
And she bore with display,
And acquired (her Son) with great power.
11. And she loved (Him) with redemption,
And guarded (Him) with kindness,
And showed (Him) with greatness.
Hallelujah

Commentary

V. 1. The odist celebrates the salvation which was granted to him, the Lord's kindness, as a cup of milk; by drinking this cup he appropriates this kindness. The word ܚܠܝܘܬܐ 'sweetness' occurs also in Ode 28: 15, where it is a designation for the gracious quality of Christ, who endures the bitterness of his enemies by His sweetness; a second instance of ܚܠܝܘܬܐ is Ode 38: 8, where it is used in contrast to pains.[1] The term ܒܣܝܡܘܬܐ 'kindness' is consistently used in the Odes as a designation for God's grace (7: 3; 11: 21; 17: 7; 42: 16); in Ode 14: 3 it is used as a synonym for mercy:

> Turn not away Thy mercy from me, O Lord,
> And take not Thy kindness from me.

In Ode 20: 9 kindness and grace are synonyms:

> And His glory will go before thee;
> And thou shalt receive of His kindness and His grace;

Man can be justified by God's kindness, hence Ode 25: 12: 'And I was

[1] Charlesworth translates verse 8b.: ܘܚܒ̈ܠܐ ܗܢܘܢ ܕܡܬܚܫܒܝܢ ܕܚܠܝܘܬܐ ܗܝ ܕܡܘܬܐ 'And pains of death which are considered sweetness', which misses the ironical wordplay; the translation should be: 'And those pains which are considered to be the sweetness of death!'

justified by His kindness....' Considering the fact that sweetness is a quality of Christ, and kindness always means God's grace and mercy, the meaning of verse 1 should be that God's grace is offered to the singer in the shape of a cup of milk filled with the gracious qualities, the sweetness, of His Son. By drinking this cup man appropriates God's kindness that is offered to him in the earthly manifestation of sweet milk, i.e. Christ's gracious work: sweetness (of Christ) is a manifestation of kindness (of God)! Therefore the translation of ܒܚܠܝܘܬܐ ܕܒܣܝܡܘܬܗ ܕܡܪܝܐ should be 'with the sweetness of the Lord's kindness' rather than 'in the sweetness of the Lord's kindness', as all current translations have. All the remaining verses of Ode 19 are an elaboration of verse 1: how man can appropriate God's kindness.

V. 2. This verse puts the essence of verse 1 into a Trinitarian context: God's kindness, His milk, is given to the world by His Son, the cup. The Holy Spirit takes this kindness out of God the Father; She puts into effect the kindness that is hidden in God, She milks Him.

Vv. 3, 4, 5. These three verses contain the grotesque images which were such a hindrance for an intelligible interpretation. Verse 3 states that God is full of grace, kindness, symbolized by His breasts full of milk; this kindness is given through the activity of the Holy Spirit, who fulfils God's economy or providence; the giving of the milk is according to God's purpose—that is the only correct interpretation of ܠܐ ܣܦܝܩܐܝܬ—literally 'not empty'.

V. 4. Harris in the *editio princeps* and Harris–Mingana in the 1920 edition considered the reading 'her bosom' problematic and as originating under the influence of the preceding and following feminine verbs. They altered the text to read 'his bosom' and were followed by Grimme, Gressmann, and Bauer. Both manuscripts, however, have ܥܘܒܗ̇ 'her bosom' or 'womb'. The idea expressed in this verse is that the Holy Spirit functions as the womb of the Father in which His grace in the shape of the milk from His two breasts is received—she 'opened her womb'—and thereupon brought forth and given to the world. The milk from the two breasts of the Father is, so to speak, his 'sperma', 'used for self-fertilization', to let His grace be born! In other and perhaps more dogmatically defined terms: the Logos being with and in God is brought forth by the Holy Spirit and as λόγος προφορικός given to the world. Related ideas are expressed in Ode 8: 16, but now God Himself is the acting person through the intermediary of Christ:

> I fashioned their members,
> And my own breasts I prepared for them,
> That they might drink my holy milk and live by it.

In Ode 19: 4, 5 the milk is a mixture coming from two breasts: God's grace is composed of two different constituents. This mixture of two components is given to the world, without their knowing, i.e. while the inhabitants of the world, mankind, did not know or notice it. Those who take it, however, are in the perfection of the right hand. The right hand of God is in the context of the Odes of Solomon an image of His helping care and salvation:

Ode 8: 6. For the right hand of the Lord is with you,
And He will be your helper.

Ode 8: 20. I wanted to fashion mind and heart,
And they are mine,
And upon my right hand I have set my elect ones.[1]

Ode 25: 2. Because Thou wast the right hand of salvation
and my Helper.

Two fundamental ideas in verse 5, namely that God's grace was given to the world without their knowing, and that those who take it become God's children, and are in the perfection of His right hand, are a clear allusion to, or variant on, St. John's Gospel i. 10–12:

ܒܥܠܡܐ ܗܘܐ. ܘܥܠܡܐ ܒܐܝܕܗ ܗܘܐ. ܘܥܠܡܐ ܠܐ ܝܕܥܗ ܀
ܠܕܝܠܗ ܐܬܐ ܘܕܝܠܗ ܠܐ ܩܒܠܘܗܝ. ܐܝܠܝܢ ܕܝܢ ܕܩܒܠܘܗܝ. ܝܗܒ
ܠܗܘܢ ܫܘܠܛܢܐ ܕܒܢܝܐ ܕܐܠܗܐ ܢܗܘܘܢ. ܠܐܝܠܝܢ ܕܡܗܝܡܢܝܢ
ܒܫܡܗ.

He was in the world, and the world was made by Him, and *the world knew Him not.* He came unto His own, and His own received Him not. But *as many as received Him*, to them *gave He power to become children of God,* to them that believe on His name.

This clear reference to the proem of St. John's Gospel, where the Evangelist described the incarnation of the Logos, also gives the clue to a correct understanding of the other grotesque images of Ode 19. John i. 14–18 reads in the Peshiṭta version:

ܘܡܠܬܐ ܦܓܪܐ ܗܘܐ ܘܐܓܢ ܒܢ ܘܚܙܝܢ ܫܘܒܚܗ ܫܘܒܚܐ
ܐܝܟ ܕܝܚܝܕܝܐ ܕܡܢ ܐܒܐ ܕܡܠܐ ܛܝܒܘܬܐ ܘܩܘܫܬܐ ܀
ܝܘܚܢܢ ܐܣܗܕ ܥܠܘܗܝ ܘܩܥܐ ܘܐܡܪ ܗܢܘ ܗܘ ܕܐܡܪܬ ܕܒܬܪܝ،

[1] The subject of this verse is God who expresses His will to fashion mind and heart of men that they know Him. Charlesworth's translation 'I willed and fashioned mind and heart' does not take into account that two verbs are linked by *w*- and may express one action or idea in Syriac. The verse contains a clear allusion to John i. 10–12.

ܐܬܐ ܘܗܘܐ ܠܗ ܩܕܡܝ. ܡܛܠ ܕܩܕܡܝ ܗܘܐ ܡܢܝ ܘܡܢ ܡܠܝܘܬܗ
ܚܢܢ ܟܠܢ ܢܣܒܢ ܘܛܝܒܘܬܐ ܚܠܦ ܛܝܒܘܬܐ. ܡܛܠ ܕܢܡܘܣܐ
ܒܝܕ ܡܘܫܐ ܐܬܝܗܒ. ܩܘܫܬܐ ܕܝܢ ܘܛܝܒܘܬܐ ܒܝܕ ܝܫܘܥ
ܡܫܝܚܐ ܗܘܬ. ܐܠܗܐ ܠܐ ܐܢܫ ܚܙܝܗܝ ܡܡܬܘܡ. ܝܚܝܕܝܐ
ܐܠܗܐ ܗܘ ܕܐܝܬܘܗܝ ܒܥܘܒܐ ܕܐܒܘܗܝ ܗܘ ܐܫܬܥܝ.

And the Word became flesh, and dwelt among us, and we beheld His glory, the glory of the only begotten of the Father, full of grace and truth. John bare witness of Him, and cried, saying: This was He of whom I spoke: He that cometh after me was before me, for He was earlier than me. And of His fulness have all we received, and grace for grace. For the law was given by Moses, but truth and grace came by Jesus Christ. No man has ever seen God; the only begotten Son, God, which is in the womb of His Father, He told (about Him).

The Vetus Syra extant for these verses in the Curetonian version shows some very significant variants:

v. 14: ܘܡܠܬܐ ܦܓܪܐ ܗܘܬ ܘܐܓܢܬ ܒܢ.

And the Word became a body. . . .

ܕܝܚܝܕܝܐ ܕܡܢ ܐܒܐ ܟܕ ܡܠܐ ܛܝܒܘܬܐ ܘܩܘܫܬܐ

. . . the only begotten of the Father, as He was full of grace and truth

v. 17: ܘܛܝܒܘܬܐ ܘܩܘܫܬܐ ܒܝܕ ܝܫܘܥ ܡܫܝܚܐ ܗܘܐ

. . . and grace and truth came by Jesus Christ. . . .

v. 18: ܝܚܝܕܝܐ ܒܪܐ ܕܡܢ ܥܘܒܗ ܕܐܒܘܗܝ ܗܘ ܐܫܬܥܝ.

the only begotten Son, which is from the womb of His Father, He told (about Him).[1]

In distinction to the other versions the Vetus Syra states that the Father is full of grace and truth (note the consistent wording of verses 14 and 17), which came to the world by Jesus Christ, His Son, who originates *from* the womb of His Father. Here lies the origin of the images of Ode 19: 3–5! The wording that the Son comes 'from the womb of His Father' introduces a female element into the Father's personality. That female element of the Father which gives birth to the Son is represented by the (female) Holy Spirit who functions as the womb of the Father, from where His grace and truth, the milk of His two breasts, His only begotten Son, are born. Father, Holy Spirit, and

[1] Vetus Syra quoted after A. Smith Lewis, *The Old Syriac Gospels or Evangelion da-Mepharreshê* (London, 1910).

Son are three divine hypostases, who function in a sexually coloured interacting process to express the idea that God's grace and truth are given to the world as His only begotten Son, who is from the womb of His Father.

Similar allusions to, or variants of, the proem of St. John's Gospel occur in Ode 8: 14–20, which should be compared to John i. 10–12.[1] Another instance of a very condensed wording of this prologue is Ode 36: 3:

ܝܠܕܬܢܝ ܡܢ ܩܕܡ ܐܦܘܗܝ ܕܡܪܝܐ

ܘܟܕ ܒܪܢܫܐ ܐܝܬܝ

ܐܬܟܢܝܬ ܢܘܗܪܐ ܒܪܗ ܕܐܠܗܐ

(The Spirit) brought me forth before the Lord's face,
And whereas I am a man,
I was named enlightened, Son of God.

It should be noted that the Syriac phrase ܡܢ ܩܕܡ ܐܦܘܗܝ ܕܡܪܝܐ also bears the notion that the Son was born of the Lord. The role of the Holy Spirit is exactly the same in the conception expressed in Ode 36: 3 as in Ode 19.

The same symbolism of divine milk, breasts, and bosom occurs in Clement of Alexandria, *Paedagogus* I. vi. 35. 3: The Logos is Christ's milk; I. vi. 42. 1–2: Being virginal, the mother church does not produce milk, she is feeding her children with the Logos, that is holy milk; I. vi. 43. 3–4: The Logos is the Father's milk and bosom; I. vi. 45. 1: The Lord is nourishing milk; I. vi. 46. 1: Christ, the Logos, is milk provided by the breasts of the Father's goodness (cf. I. vi. 49. 3). Irenaeus, *Adv. Haeres.* iv. 38. 1 is also acquainted with this imagery: The Lord is breastfeeding the faithful 'quasi a mammilla carnis eius nutriti'. Besides some New Testament milk-feeding texts like I Cor. iii. 1–2, Hebrews v. 12–13, and 1 Peter ii. 2, Genesis xlix. 25 in particular forms the background for this exegesis of the prologue of St. John's Gospel and links it to the Annunciation story which is retold in verse 6 of Ode 19. The text of Genesis xlix. 25, 26 is worth quoting, especially since it is a blessing of Joseph: '. . . Even by the God of thy father, who shall help thee; and by the Almighty, who shall bless thee with blessings of *heaven* above, blessings of the *deep* that lieth under, blessings

[1] Other allusions to or paraphrases of John are to be found in Ode 7: 4–9, 12–16; Ode 12: 3–4; Ode 41, etc. An exact parallel to Ode 7: 3 '. . . Because His kindness has diminished His majesty' is found in Ephrem Syrus, *Hymn. de Nativitate* 23. 3 (ed. Beck, *C.S.C.O.*, *SS.* 82/83): 'Deine Güte hat dich zu einem Kinde, deine Güte hat dich zu einem Menschen gemacht,—hat deine Größe verengt, erweitert'; cf. Eusebius, *Dem. Evang.* vi. 9, who uses the same words in his comment on Psalm cxliv.

of the *breasts*, and of the *womb*: (26) The blessings of thy father have prevailed above the blessings of my progenitors unto the utmost bound of the everlasting hills: they shall be on the head of Joseph, and on the crown of the head of him that was separate from his brethren. . . .' The correlation between heaven and deep, and breasts and womb, brings the breasts into a heavenly sphere and the womb into an earthly one. This text, which Hippolytus, *Ben. Iac.* 27. 3, uses to explain the twofold birth of the Logos, from God and from the Virgin, causes the special interpretation of John's Prologue as birth in heaven and links it to the birth from the Virgin on earth.[1]

From verse 6, therefore, the scene of action shifts. After the introductory verse 1, verses 2–5 describe a *Prolog im Himmel* with God the Father and the Holy Spirit as dramatis personae; from verse 6 the world functions as a scene of action to which the mixture of grace and truth is given. The odist sticks closely to the prologue of St. John's Gospel, when in verse 6:

> The womb of the Virgin caught (it)
> And she received conception and gave birth,

he gives his version of John i. 14: 'And the Word became flesh and dwelt among us.' In this wording of the odist the influence of the text of Luke i. 26 ff., the Annunciation to Mary, is also perceptible, especially of Luke i. 31: 'For, behold, thou shalt conceive in thy womb, and bring forth a son. . . .' The relation between the proem of St. John's Gospel and the opening chapter of the Gospel of St. Luke is apparent in the Syriac version of the New Testament from a great similarity in wording, that in distinction to the Greek versions. Compare Luke i. 28: ܘܥܠ ܠܘܬܗ ܡܠܐܟܐ ܘܐܡܪ ܠܗ ܫܠܡ ܠܟܝ ܡܠܝܬ ܛܝܒܘܬܐ (And the angel entered unto her and said to her: Hail *thou that art full of grace*) with John i. 14: ܫܘܒܚܐ ܐܝܟ ܕܝܚܝܕܝܐ ܕܡܢ ܐܒܐ ܕܡܠܐ ܛܝܒܘܬܐ ܘܩܘܫܬܐ (. . . the glory of the only begotten of *the Father, full of grace* and truth). The words of the angel to Mary in Luke i. 30: ܐܫܟܚܬܝ ܓܝܪ ܛܝܒܘܬܐ ܠܘܬ ܐܠܗܐ (. . . for thou hast found *grace* with God . . .) form an explanation for the relation between Luke i. 28 and John i. 14: the grace of God entered into Mary through the intermediary of the Holy Spirit. Mary will conceive and bear a son, that shall be called the Son of the Highest. To her

[1] The references to Clement of Alexandria I owe to my colleague Averil Cameron of London University, to whom I express my warm thanks; for Hippolytus, *Ben. Iac.* 27. 3, see A. Grillmeier, *Christ in Christian Tradition*, i (Atlanta², 1975), pp. 114 f.

question to the angel how this is possible the answer is—Luke i. 35: ܪܘܚܐ ܕܩܘܕܫܐ ܬܐܬܐ ܘܚܝܠܗ ܕܥܠܝܐ ܢܓܢ ܥܠܝܟܝ (The *Holy Spirit* shall come and *the power of the Highest shall dwell in you*); compare with this verse John i. 14: ܘܡܠܬܐ ܒܣܪܐ ܗܘܐ ܘܐܓܢ ܒܢ. (And *the Word* became flesh and *dwelt among us*). The Syriac uses in both texts the same verb ܐܓܢ (aphel) with the meaning 'to lie down, to rest in, to dwell within', whereas the Greek has ἐπισκιάσει (Luke i. 35) and ἐσκήνωσεν (John i. 14). In these verses the explanation of the role of the Holy Spirit in the process of incarnation has to be sought, as expressed in Ode 19 and its well-considered combination of the proem of St. John's Gospel and the Annunciation to Mary. A final link between both Gospel texts lies in Mary's saying that she did not have intercourse with a man (ܕܓܒܪܐ ܠܐ ܚܟܝܡ ܠܝ). The Vetus Syra (Curetonian version) reads in John i. 13:

ܐܝܠܝܢ ܕܠܐ ܒܕܡܐ ܘܠܐ ܡܢ ܨܒܝܢܐ ܕܦܓܪܐ ܘܠܐ ܡܢ ܨܒܝܢܐ
ܕܓܒܪܐ ܐܠܐ ܡܢ ܐܠܗܐ ܐܬܝܠܕ.

'The reading of the Curetonian in this verse appears to hover between *qui nati sunt* and *qui natus est*, *qui* being translated as plural and *natus est* as singular.'[1] The reading *qui natus est* can be considered as a testimony to the Virgin birth and is also found in Irenaeus, *Adv. Haer*. iii. 19. 2; iii. 16. 2; Augustine, *Confess*. vii. 9; Ambrose, in *Ps*. xxxvii; Tert., *De Carne Christi*, xix. vv. 7–9. The bringing forth of the Son by Mary full of grace, in whom the Holy Spirit dwelt, is completely parallel to the milking of the breasts of God the Father full of grace and truth by the Holy Spirit, who took this mixture in her opened womb and bore it to the world: in the Son are grace and truth like milk in a cup. Both are instruments for God's *oeconomia*. This parallelism on two levels is expressed by the repeating of the words ܠܐ ܡܣܪܩܐܝܬ—'not without purpose', in verses 3 and 8. In this perspective verses 8 and 9 are parallel expressions for the same idea: Mary bore a son without suffering pain, *because* it did not happen without purpose, but was a constituent phase of God's *oeconomia* or providence, and she did not require a midwife, *because* God delivered her, which help is also a carrying out of His plans. God's role as midwife goes back to the Christological interpretation of Psalm xxii, especially the verses 10 and 11:

ܡܛܠ ܕܐܢܬ ܐܦܩܬܢܝ ܡܢ ܡܪܒܥܐ
ܘܣܒܪܝ ܡܢ ܬܕܝܗ ܕܐܡܝ

[1] A. Smith Lewis, *The Old Syriac Gospels*, xxviii.

ܥܠܝܟ ܐܫܬܕܝܬ ܡܢ ܡܪܒܥܐ

ܘܡܢ ܟܪܣܗ ܕܐܡܝ ܐܠܗܝ ܐܢܬ.

For thou hast taken me from the womb
And art my trust from the breasts of my mother,
On thee I was cast from the womb
And from the belly of my mother thou art my God.

The same psalm is referred to in Ode 28.[1] It is clear that these verses are interpreted as testimonies to the miraculous birth of the saviour, where God played the role of midwife.[2] The wording of Ode 19: 9, especially the aphel of ܚܝܐ with the meaning 'to deliver', refers not only to Psalm xxii. 10–11 but also to Luke i. 47: ܘܪܘܙܬ ܪܘܚܝ ܒܐܠܗܐ ܡܚܝܢܝ (And my spirit hath rejoiced in God my Saviour). The meaning of ܡܚܝܢܐ is life-giver and it is a derivate from the aphel of ܚܝܐ, which verb in Ode 19: 9 is used to express God's delivering action in the birth of His Son. The exegesis of Luke 1. 47 confirms this interpretation, as ܡܚܝܢܐ, life-giver, Sôter, has the sense that through Mary God gives His life to the world.[3] Once again there is a link between this verse in the opening chapter of Luke's Gospel and the prologue of St. John's Gospel, verse 4, where the Vetus Syra reads: ܗܘ ܕܝܢ ܡܕܡ ܕܗܘܐ ܒܗ ܚܝܐ ܐܝܬܘܗܝ (That which was in Him [i.e. the Logos, Christ] was Life).[4] God's delivering of Mary functions as His life-giving to the world, for this life is in His and Mary's Son.

With regard to the Son's birth without human assistance Harris

[1] Cf. Ode 28: 16:

And I did not perish, for I was not their brother,
Nor was my birth like theirs.

Compare Ode 28: 13:

And they surrounded me like mad dogs
Who ignorantly attack their masters

to Psalm xxii. 17; see for further parallels Harris–Mingana, *The Odes*, pp. 360 ff.

[2] So Eusebius, *Dem. Evang.* x. 8; *Eclog. Proph.* ii. 13; Tertull. *De Carne Christi*, 20.

[3] Cf. *Th.W.N.T.*, Bd. vii. 1015: the use of sôter in Luke i. 47 is based on its occurrence and meaning in the O.T., where it is not a *terminus technicus* but denotes in general God's saving and lifegiving action towards Israel and mankind.

[4] *Codex Ephraemi rescriptus* reads: ὃ γέγονεν ἐν αὐτῷ ζωὴ ἦν. I. Ortiz de Urbina, *Vetus Evangelium Syrorum*, Biblia Polyglotta VI, Matriti 1967, p. 4, John i. 4: ܘܗܘܐ ܡܕܡ ܕܗܘܐ ܒܗ ܘܗܘܐ ܚܝܐ ܗܘ. The same reading occurs in the Diatessaron.

draws attention to the interpretation of Daniel ii. 34. 45, the stone cut without hands, as bearing witness to the miraculous birth. It appears to have been interpreted in two different ways, firstly that the Virgin had no consort, and secondly that she had no midwife's help. This interpretation occurs int. al. in Just. *Dial.* 76; Irenaeus, *Adv. Haer.* iii. 21. 7.[1]

Vv. 10–11. These concluding verses have always been a *crux interpretum*, as appears from the different translations and explanatory notes. The translation of Harris and Mingana reads:

> And she brought forth, as a man, by (God's) will:
> And she brought (Him) forth with demonstration
> And acquired (Him) with great dignity;
> And loved (Him) in redemption;
> And guarded (Him) kindly
> And showed (Him) in majesty.

In his commentary Harris writes: 'The concluding sentences of the Ode are almost unintelligible and without adequate motive.'[2] In the first edition of 1909 he made a conjecture in verse 11 and read, instead of ܘܐܚܒܬ ܒܦܘܪܩܢܐ 'and loved (Him) in redemption', ܘܐܚܒܬ ܒܦܘܪܡܢܐ—'and loved (Him) in his swaddling clothes'. In his second edition he remarks that this conjecture is too violent a change to find acceptance, but that there is something to be said for it. He therefore paraphased the last sentences of the Ode:

> It is a great honour (not a dishonour) to have borne him:
> She loved him in his swaddling clothes,
> And watched over him with fondling,
> And exhibited him proudly.

From his translation and paraphase it is clear that Harris refers all nouns in these last verses that are constructed with the preposition *b* to qualities of Mary or her child, except ܒܨܒܝܢܐ in verse 10 which he hesitatingly refers to God. From W. Bauer's translation one gets the impression that he refers all nouns to Mary's qualities and actions. J. H. Charlesworth does the same, whereas he refers ܒܨܒܝܢܐ in verse 10 to ܠܓܒܪܐ and translates: 'She brought forth like a strong man with desire'; the following sentence he translates: 'And she bore according to the manifestation', in which context 'manifestation' should also refer

[1] Harris–Mingana, *The Odes*, pp. 307–9.
[2] Ibid. 306.

to the manifestation by Gabriel in Luke i. 26 ff. It is obvious that Charlesworth considers all these nouns as qualities of Mary or as descriptions of her relation to the child.[1] From the preceding analysis of Ode 19 it appeared that this ode should be regarded as a very sophisticated elaboration of the proem of St. John's Gospel and the Annunciation to Mary, which both show great similarities of wording, especially in the Old Syriac versions. These two pericopes form the scriptural basis for a deliberately elaborated theological conception in which the mutual relations between God the Father, the Holy Spirit, and Mary with regard to the birth of the Son are precisely fixed. The Holy Spirit mediates between God the Father and Mary, as Christ is both a Son of God and of Mary through her intermediary. Especially the relation between God and Mary is the kernel of verse 9, and this relation is worked out in verses 10 and 11. The first part of verse 10: 'As a man she bore by will', is an allusion to John i. 13: 'only they can become children of God, which are born, not of blood, nor of the will of the flesh, nor of the will of man, but of God', to which verse the Curetonian version gives a Christological explanation. When the odist states that Mary bore as a man by will, he accentuates that she had no male consort in this birth process, just as the Father had no consort in bringing forth his Son, and that this birth does not occur without her will, but on the contrary that she bore her child by action of the will in which God's will is expressed: in the bearing and in the will there is a close cooperation between God and Mary: both will the child. From other odes, e.g. Ode 23: 5, it is clear that Christ is the incarnation of God's thought and will:

> And His (i.e. God's) *thought* was like a letter
> And his *will* descended from on high.[2]

Analogous to the first part of verse 10 the second part says that the birth is a visible event, in which Mary shows her child, and God's grace

[1] J. H. Charlesworth, *The Odes of Solomon*, p. 84.

[2] The same combination of the thought and will of God embodied in Christ is found in Ode 9: 3, 4; on the other hand, Christ is called God's thought, so Ode 16: 8, 9, 19; Ode 17: 5; Ode 21: 5; Ode 41: 10. Cf. R. Abramowski, 'Der Christus der Salomooden', p. 67, who draws attention to the role of this conception in the theology of Theodore of Mopsuestia; Ephrem Syrus calls Christ ܚܘܫܒܗ ܕܐܒܐ, 'the thought of the Father', Saint Éphrem, *Commentaire de l'Évangile concordant*, éd. et trad. L. Leloir (Dublin, 1963), i. 3, pp. 3 f. The same conception occurs in the Book of Scholia by Theodor bar Konai, i, p. 10, questions 12 and 13. The whole subject deserves a thorough diachronical investigation, starting with the earliest testimonies on Antiochene theology and its forerunners. Cf. Drijvers, 'Kerygma und Logos in den Oden Salomos dargestellt am Beispiel der 23. Ode', *Festschrift Carl Andresen* (Göttingen, 1979), 153–172.

and glory are displayed. In the Odes the verb ܚܘܝ 'to show, to display' is used only with God's grace or truth as object.[1] The same stress on the visibility of God's glory is found in the prologue of St. John's Gospel: e.g. verse 14: '. . . we *beheld* His glory, the glory as of the only begotten of the Father, full of grace and truth.' The accentuation on the visibility may have an anti-docetic tenor.[2] So the second part of verse 10 also has a twofold meaning: Mary bears her child, shows it, and thereby isplays God's grace. The third part is analogous to the other two: Mary acquired her child with effort of all her force and power, in which God's power becomes manifest. Will, display, and power refer on one hand to Mary, on the other to God, by whose will the child is born, in whom His glory and power are displayed.

The three parts of verse 11 have the same double tendency. On the one hand, Mary loves her son ܒܦܘܪܩܢܐ, i.e. in the situation in which he has been delivered from her, she guards or cherishes him ܒܚܝܣܢܘܬܐ, i.e. showing her kindness towards him, and she shows her child ܒܪܘܪܒܘܬܐ, i.e. with grandeur. On the other hand, in her loving, guarding, and showing she manifests God's redemption, kindness, and greatness. This aspect of verse 11 also appears from the fact that ܪܘܪܒܘܬܐ, ܚܝܣܢܘܬܐ, ܦܘܪܩܢܐ are used only for expressing divine qualities or actions in the context of the Odes.[3] Finally, it is noteworthy that the sequence of actions by Mary and the Father represents, on the one hand, the chronological order of events in a birth process, on the other hand, the divine order in the process of salvation: Mary is willing to beget her child, the process of bearing is beginning, and then she has begotten her son (v. 10). When the child has been born, she loves and cherishes it and at last she shows it to the others (v. 11). The process of salvation starts with God willing it, and then showing His power to realize it (v. 11). This means redemption and kindness towards mankind and manifests at last God's greatness (v. 11).

Some conclusions

The foregoing expositions may contain a closely reasoned interpretation of the 19th Ode of Solomon in which a well-defined Trinitarian theology regarding the incarnation is expounded in a hymnical but very reflected wording. Such an analysis of other Odes too will lead to the

[1] Ode 7: 25; Ode 8: 9; Ode 12: 2; Ode 24: 13; Ode 29: 7; Ode 38: 7.

[2] Cf. H. J. W. Drijvers, 'Die Oden Salomos und die Polemik mit den Markioniten im syrischen Christentum', Symposium Syriacum 1976, *OrChrA*, 205 (Roma, 1978), 39–55.

[3] Cf. the concordance in Harris–Mingana, *The Odes*, pp. 435–54, where all relevant texts are recorded.

outcome that the Odes were not written in a 'vague and cloudy language' and that their Christianity is 'as accurately and dogmatically defined' as in the regions more influenced by Rome. Moreover, the paraphrases of and allusions to certain pericopes of the Bible, as detected in Ode 19, also occur in other Odes: Odes 7, 12, and 41 are a kind of paraphrase of the prologue of St. John's Gospel and Psalm 22 is used in Odes 23 and 25, so that Ode 19 is not an exception within the whole collection.

The combination of the Prologue of St. John's Gospel and of the Annunciation to Mary is to be found in exactly the same order as in Ode 19 in Tatian's Diatessaron which begins with the Prologue followed by the Annunciation to Zacharias and Mary.[1] The great similarity in wording as shown by the Syriac versions in contradistinction to the Greek ones may be ascribed to the harmonizing tendencies of Tatian's Diatessaron which have worked in the Vetus Syra and in the Peshiṭta. Ode 19 is therefore based on exegetical and theological traditions that are found in the Diatessaron and the structure and wording of Ode 19 are comprehensible only through the underlying Diatessaron. The conclusion seems therefore justified that the earliest possible date for Ode 19—and most likely for all the Odes—is about A.D. 200, considering the fact that Tatian wrote his Diatessaron after his return to the Orient, i.e. after A.D. 175.[2] At the same time strong arguments are indirectly adduced for Syriac as the original language of the Odes, if the theological conceptions of Ode 19 are exclusively based on a Syriac text tradition of the New Testament.

This approximate date is in accordance with the fact that the theological ideas of Ode 19 are also found in writers of the end of the second century A.D. having relations with Antioch. Harris drew attention to some resemblance of ideas between Ignatius of Antioch and the Odes. In his opinion Ignatius was dependent on the Odes, which led him to a dating of the Odes at the end of the first century A.D.[3] On the other hand, he saw acutely that the Christology of the Odes is nearly

[1] Harris, *The Odes*, p. 311, in trying to find a scriptural basis for the text of Ode 19, sighed away, 'There seems to be a missing link to connect all these passages together.... We have not yet found it.' The remains of the Diatessaron in Syriac tradition have been collected by I. Ortiz de Urbina, *Biblia Polyglotta Matritensia*, vi (Madrid, 1967).

[2] I. Ortiz de Urbina, *Patrologia Syriaca*, altera editio (Rome, 1965), pp. 35 ff.; C. Peters, *Das Diatessaron Tatians* (Rome, 1939), 195 ff.

[3] Harris–Mingana, *The Odes*, p. 67; cf. J. de Zwaan, 'Ignatius and the Odist', *American Journal of Theology* (1911), pp. 617–25; in a sense Ign., *Ephes*. 7. 2 is the kernel of Ode 19; cf. Ign. *Smyrn*. i. 1, where F.-M. Braun, *Qui ex Deo natus est, Aux sources de la tradition chrétienne* (Neuchâtel, 1950), p. 22 sees a combination of John i. 13 and Luke i. 35 in the wording: *υἱὸν θεοῦ κατὰ θέλημα καὶ δύναμιν θεοῦ*; do we find here already theological ideas that are worked out by Tatian's Diatessaron?

identical to the Nicaenum: 'Nicene in a nascent form.'[1] The contradiction between these two statements he did not notice.

An exact parallel to Ode 19 is to be found in Irenaeus, *Adv. Haer.* iv. 38 (ed. Harvey, 293): 'Et propter hoc Dominus noster in novissimis temporibus, recapitulans in seipso omnia, venit ad nos, non quomodo ipse poterat, sed quomodo illum nos videre poteramus. Ipse enim in sua inenarrabili gloria ad nos venire poterat: sed nos magnitudinem gloriae ipsius portare non poteramus. Et propter hoc, quasi infantibus, ille qui erat panis perfectus Patris, lac nobis semetipsum praestavit, quod erat secundum hominem eius adventus, ut quasi a mammilla carnis eius nutriti et per talem lactationem assueti manducare et bibere Verbum Dei, et eum qui est immortalitatis panis, qui est Spiritus Patris, in nobis ipsis continere possimus.'[2] The allusions to the Prologue of St. John's Gospel are clear, whereas the so-called recapitulation theology of Irenaeus is explicitly mentioned. The theology of the Odes of Solomon may also be characterized as a form of recapitulation. The role of the Holy Spirit in Irenaeus' theology is identical to her role in Ode 19: the Holy Spirit '*semper cum patre erat*; olim et ab initio . . . revelat patrem; . . . per ipsam conditionem *revelat* verbum conditorem deum, et per mundum fabricatorem mundi dominum, et per plasma eum qui plasmaverit artificem, et *per filium eum patrem qui generavit filium*'.[3] As in Ode 19, there is mention in Irenaeus of a double birth of the Son, the birth of the λόγος ἄσαρκος and of the λόγος ἐν σαρκί, which preludes the later developments of the doctrine of the two natures.[4]

Another exact parallel to Ode 19 can be found in Eusebius, *Dem. Evang.* x. 8 (p. 499), where Eusebius digresses on the 22nd Psalm. Referring to verse 10 he writes: 'Just as thou wast my help when I assumed a human body, when from the womb of her that bare me, thou thyself, my God and Father, as if playing the midwife's part, didst draw forth from the womb that flesh which had been prepared for me of the Holy Ghost . . .'[5] While this parallel from Eusebius makes a date in the first

[1] Harris–Mingana, *The Odes*, p. 83.

[2] Irenaeus quoted after Irénée de Lyon, *Contre les hérésies*, livre iv, éd. A. Rousseau, *S.C.* 100 (Paris, 1965), iv. 38. 1, p. 946; cf. R. Murray, *Symbols*, p. 316; related ideas with Clemens Alex., *Paed.* i. 35. 3; i. 36. 1; i. 43. 3; i. 46. 1; see F. Loofs, *Leitfaden zum Studium der Dogmengeschichte*, hrsg. v. K. Aland (Tübingen, 1959), pp. 109 f.

[3] See Loofs, *Leitfaden*, pp. 109 f.; cf. Th. Rüsch, *Die Entstehung der Lehre vom Heiligen Geist bei Ignatius von Antiochia, Theophilus von Antiochia und Irenäus von Lyon* (Zürich, 1952), pp. 99 ff.

[4] Loofs, *Leitfaden*, pp. 113 ff; Rüsch, *Die Entstehung*, p. 102; Iren., *Epid.* 30.

[5] Harris–Mingana, *The Odes*, pp. 33 ff.; J. Daniélou, 'Le Psaume 21 et le mystère de la passion', *Études d'exégèse judéo-chrétienne* (Paris, 1966), p. 36. A systematic inquiry into the use of Psalm xxii in the Odes of Solomon would

half of the third century even more likely, parallels from the works of Ephrem Syrus also argue for a later date than A.D. 200. Already A. J. Wensinck and Harris had established the closest resemblance between Ephrem's Hymns on the Epiphany and the Odes of Solomon.[1] Harris made the important remark that this necessitates an inquiry among the literary antecedents of St. Ephrem, but such an inquiry has never been made. In view of the structure of Ode 19 based on the Diatessaron it seems preferable first to look at Ephrem's commentary on this Gospel harmony, preserved partially in Syriac and completely in Armenian translation.[2] The interpretation of the Prologue of St. John's Gospel as describing the birth of the Son from the womb of the Father based on the reading of Diatessaron and Curetonian versions of John i. 18: ܡܢ ܥܘܒܗ ܕܐܒܐ, and as such worked out in Ode 19, is confirmed by Ephrem in his commentary on the Diatessaron, where he says, citing John i. 18: '. . . and it [i.e. Scripture] says further: He is born from His (God's) womb' ܕܐܬܝܠܕ ܡܢ ܥܘܒܗ.[3] Ephrem explicitly states in his commentary on the first verse of St. John's Gospel that it deals with the 'divinity, the hypostasis, and the procreation of the Logos', ܐܠܗܘܬܐ ܘܩܢܘܡܐ ܘܝܠܕܐ;[4] this precisely embodies the theme of Ode 19. Describing the Son's birth Ephrem cites Daniel ii. 34, 45, like Irenaeus iii. 21. 7: '"Sans l'aide des mains." De même que, pour Ève, Adam remplit le rôle du père et de la mère, ainsi Marie pour Notre-

be clarifying and would contribute to determining its place in the historical development of Christian theology; cf. J. Daniélou, 'Le psaume 21 dans la catéchèse patristique', *Maison-Dieu*, xlix (1957), pp. 17–34.

[1] A. J. Wensinck, 'Ephrem's Hymns on Epiphany and the Odes of Solomon', *Expositor*, ser. 8, vol. iii (1912), pp. 108–12; Harris, 'Ephrem's use of the Odes of Solomon', *Expositor*, ser. 8, vol. iii (1912), pp. 113–19.

[2] Cited after L. Leloir, *Saint Éphrem, Commentaire de l'Évangile concordant*. Texte Syriaque (manuscript Chester Beatty 709) (Dublin, 1963); id. *Éphrem de Nisibe, Commentaire de l'Évangile concordant ou Diatessaron*, *SC* 121 (Paris, 1966).

[3] ܕܐܠܗܐ ܕܡܬܘܡ ܐܢܫ ܠܐ ܚܙܝܗܝ، ܝܚܝܕܝܐ ܕܡܢ ܥܘܒܗ ܕܐܒܘܗܝ، ܒܕܩ ܥܠܘܗܝ، ܘܐܢܐ ܡܢ ܐܒܐ ܢܦܩܬ ܐܬܝܬ. ܐܢ ܕܝܢ ܡܕܡ ܕܐܝܬܘܗܝ، ܠܐ ܡܬܝܠܕ ܐܡܪܬ. ܐܢܬ ܕܓܠܝܬܗ، ܠܟܬܒܐ ܕܐܡܪ ܕܐܝܬܘܗܝ، ܗܘܐ ܘܐܡܪ ܬܘܒ ܕܐܬܝܠܕ ܡܢ ܥܘܒܗ.

'*Deum quem numquam aliquis vidit, unigenitus, qui e sinu Patris sui, patefecit de eo. Et ego ex Patre exivi, veni* [John xvi. 28]. Si autem id quod est gigni dicis, mendacem vocasti Scripturam, nam dicit: *Erat*; et dicit iterum: *Genitus est e sinu eius*' (*Commentaire*, i. 2).

[4] *Commentaire*, ii. 5.

Seigneur.'[1] It is to be considered, whether Ode 19: 10: 'As a man she bore by will', besides being an allusion to John i. 13, also expresses this analogy between Mary and Adam, the man.

Like Ode 19: 8 Ephrem says: 'Le Seigneur . . . sortit d'un sein virginal, parce que cette vierge enfanta vraiment et réellement sans douleur.'[2]

Other parallels to Ode 19 are to be found in the hymns of Ephrem. The role of God's will in the incarnation is stressed in *Hymn. de Nativitate* 3. 5: 'Sich selber hat er durch seinen Willen verkörperlicht, für seine Häscher' and 3. 6: 'Gepriesen sei, den sein Wille geführt hat zu (Mutter)schoß und Geburt.'[3] The Son thus embodies His Father's will. Like Ode 19 Ephrem knows of a heavenly and an earthly birth of the Son: *Hymn. de Nat.* 27. 20:

> Von den (beiden) Geburten des Eingebornen
> ist die eine himmlisch, die andere irdisch.[4]

Sweetness as a designation of Christ's gracious qualities finds an exact analogy in *Hymn. de Nat.* 1. 52: 'Die Seele der Gerechten fühlte den Sohn, der die Lebensarznei ist, und sie trug Verlangen, daß er in ihren Tagen kommen möge und sie seine Süßigkeit verkosten könne' (cf. *Hymm. de Nat.* 18. 26). The stress on the visibility of the birth in which God's glory is displayed finds its analogies in *Hymn. de Nat.* 2. 9; 3. 2, 3, 4.

This enumeration of parallels is far from complete, but all theological

[1] *Éphrem de Nisibe, Commentaire*, ii. 3, p. 67; Leloir's remark, *Doctrines et méthodes de S. Éphrem d'après son commentaire de l'Évangile concordant, C.S.C.O.*, Subs. 18 (Louvain, 1961), p. 29: 'Sans doute Éphrem ajoute-t-il la citation de Daniel de son propre cru' is not right.

[2] *Éphrem de Nisibe, Commentaire*, ii. 6; cf. E. Beck, 'Ephraems Reden über den Glauben', *Studia Anselmiana*, xxxiii (Rome, 1953), pp. 95–107, where *Hymn. de Fide* 4. 2 is discussed.

[3] Cf. *Hymn. de Nativitate* 23. 2–4; *Contra Haereses* 32. 15; 36. 6; cf. Beck, 'Ephraems Reden über den Glauben', pp. 88 ff.

[4] An interesting text is *Hymn. de Virginitate*, 31. 1 (Beck, *C.S.C.O.*, *SS*, 94–5): 'Du, Christus, hast das Leben geschenkt der Schöpfung durch deine Geburt, durch jene (Geburt), die sichtbar geschah aus dem Schoß des Fleisches. Du, Christus, hast verwirrt das (menschliche) Wissen durch deine Geburt, durch jene (Geburt), die von Ewigkeit her aufging aus dem unsichtbaren Schoß (des Vaters).' It is noteworthy that Theodore of Mopsuestia in his commentary on the Gospel of St. John (ed. J.-M. Vosté, *C.S.C.O. SS*, 62–3) stresses the unity of the Logos and God the Father and does not speak about the birth of the Logos from the Father: 'Dicit autem: *qui est in sinu Patris*, quia inseparabiliter coniunctus est ei' (p. 27. 14–15 Versio; p. 39. 5–7 Textus). This may be an indication that Antiochene theology of the second century developed into different directions, one of which is represented through the line from Odes of Solomon to Ephrem.

conceptions of Ode 19 (and all other Odes!) are to be found in Ephrem's works, even in exactly the same combinations.

In the development of Syrian theology Ode 19 and the other Odes of Solomon should be placed between the Antiochene theologians of the end of the second century—Irenaeus, Justinus, Theophilus—and Ephrem at the end of the fourth century. Its theological ideas contain a working out of second-century conceptions directed through text and structure of the Diatessaron, and therefore a date in the first half of the third century or later is most likely. Like the theology of the second century in this region it is a doctrine of recapitulation, how to regain paradise lost, which is also characteristic of Ephrem. They form a link between Ephrem's works and theology and his theological and literary antecedents. Thus it becomes possible to bring theological writings and ideas from the Syrian area into a chronological order to sketch a historical development starting in the second half of the second century somewhere in or around Antioch and provisionally ending with Ephrem, with whom a new historical phase in Syrian theology begins.[1]

[1] The very loose relations between Antioch and Edessa as sketched out by W. Bauer, *Rechtgläubigkeit und Ketzerei im ältesten Christentum*, *B.H.Th.* 10, (Tübingen, 1934), pp. 22–5, need some revision in the light of the conclusions reached here.

X

ODES OF SOLOMON AND PSALMS OF MANI

Christians and Manichaeans in Third-Century Syria

The 42 Syriac Odes of Solomon have, ever since their discovery and first publication, been one of the most puzzling products of early Christianity. Their poetic language and imagery seems to baffle all attempts to determine their exact character, whereas the apparent lack of a coherent theological doctrine was the main reason for dating these ecstatic hymns of salvation at the end of the first or the beginning of the second century A.D., when the nascent christian faith was not yet exposed to the influence of Greek philosophical thought.[1]

Language and religious symbolism were considered true products of a real oriental christianity that preserved the authentic character of Jesus' preaching and salvation, and the Odes, therefore, have kept all the romantic flavour linked with such "prestige de l'origine". Recent research, however, has made clear that the Odes contain outspoken anti-Marcionite polemics, that they express christological conceptions in a highly symbolic and reflective wording that are based on second-century Antiochene theology with all its philosophical terminology, that they betray the influence of Tatian's Diatessaron and encratitic interpretation of christian tradition, and, therefore, originate in a bilingual culture and most likely are to date to the third century.[2]

---

[1] That is the opinion held by the first editor of the Odes, Rendel Harris in: Rendel Harris – Alphonse Mingana, *The Odes and Psalms of Solomon*, 2 Vols, Manchester 1916-1920, II, 61 ff.; the last editor J.H. Charlesworth, *The Odes of Solomon*. The Syriac Texts, sec. ed., Missoula 1977, holds the same view, *cf.* J.H. Charlesworth, *The Odes of Solomon — Not Gnostic*, in *CBQ* 31, 1969, 357-369; *idem*, *Les Odes de Salomon et les manuscrits de la Mer Morte*, in *RB* 77, 1970, 522-529; J.H. Charlesworth - R.-A. Culpepper, *The Odes of Solomon and the Gospel of John*, in *CBQ* 35, 1973, 298 ff.; M. Lattke, *Die Oden Salomos in ihrer Bedeutung für Neues Testament und Gnosis*, 2 Vols (Orbis Biblicus et Orientalis 25/1.2), 1979, apparently suggests an early date too.

[2] H.J.W. Drijvers, *Die Oden Salomos und die Polemik mit den Markioniten im*

Considering the anti-Marcionite tendency, the encratitic elements and the philosophical terminology, Edessa with its sophisticated culture could very well be their place of origin.

The Coptic Manichaean Psalm-Book has only partly been subjected to systematic research since its publication in 1938.[3] A. Baumstark emphasized its relationship with Syriac christian hymns, the influence of Tatian's Diatessaron, and its strongly christian character: "Man vermag sich des Eindrucks kaum zu erwehren, als seien in das manichäische Psalmbuch geradezu einzelne Texte christlich grosskirchlicher Herkunft in einer mehr oder weniger leichten Überarbeitung oder sogar ohne eine solche übernommen worden".[4] Later research confirmed that view.[5] The Manichaean psalms, therefore, play a paramount rôle in the discussion about christian roots and elements in Manichaeism.[6] Like nearly all original Manichaean writings these psalms were also written in Syriac and later on translated into Coptic, most likely through a Greek intermediary version. Since the Psalm-Book as we have it now dates from the first half of the fourth century, the original Syriac version came into existence in the second half of the third century.

The formal parallelism of the Manichaean Psalms with the Odes of Solomon is striking. Both were originally composed in Syriac and were also known in a Greek version, as is quite understandable in a bilingual cultural area. Part of the Greek version of Ode of Solomon 11

---

syrischen Christentum, in *Symposium Syriacum 1976 (OrChrA* 205), 1978, 39-55; *idem*, *Kerygma und Logos in den Oden Salomos dargestellt am Beispiel der 23. Ode*, in *Kerygma und Logos*. Beiträge zu den geistesgeschichtlichen Beziehungen zwischen Antike und Christentum, Festschrift Carl Andresen, hrsg. v. A. M. Ritter, Göttingen 1979, 153-172; *idem*, *The 19th Ode of Solomon: Its Interpretation and Place in Syrian Christianity*, in *JTS* 31, 1980, 337-355.

[3] C. R. C. Allberry, *A Manichaean Psalm-Book*, Part II, Stuttgart 1938.

[4] A. Baumstark, review of C. R. C. Allberry, *A Manichaean Psalm-Book*, in *OrChr* 36, 1941, 117-126, esp. 122.

[5] P. Nagel, *Die Psalmoi Sarakoton des manichäischen Psalmbuches*, in *OLZ* 62, 1967, 123-130; E. Segelberg, *Syncretism at Work: On the Origin of some Coptic Manichaean Psalms*, in *Religious Syncretism in Antiquity*. Essays in Conversation with Geo Widengren, ed. by B. A. Pearson, Missoula 1975, 191-203.

[6] *Cf.* A. Böhlig, *Christliche Wurzeln im Manichäismus*, in *Mysterion und Wahrheit*. Gesammelte Beiträge zur spätantiken Religionsgeschichte, Leiden 1968, 202-221; *idem*, *Der Synkretismus des Mani*, in *Synkretismus im syrisch-persischen Kulturgebiet*, *AAWG* 96, 1975, 144-169.

even has been preserved in a papyrus from Egypt dating from the end of the third century.[7] That the Manichaean Psalms must have been known in a Greek version too becomes clear from the many Greek words that the Coptic has preserved. The Manichaean Psalms as well as the Odes of Solomon were translated from Greek into Coptic, so that five Odes of Solomon found their way into the *Pistis Sophia*, in which they, like the canonical psalms, were interpreted in a gnostic way.[8] The Odes of Solomon and the Manichaean Psalms are thus, each in its own way, exponents of a Syriac hymnology that may go back to Bardaiṣan (154-222 A.D.), but which, very likely, is of much earlier date and which was eventually to find its most mature form with Ephrem Syrus (d. 373 A.D.).[9] It would, therefore, be highly interesting if the Odes and the Psalms were to have some material points of contact, beside their formal ones, in order to get new light on religious developments in third-century Syria, of which so little is known.

In this connection Ode of Solomon 38 is of special interest as regards its contents and imagery.

1. I ascended to the Light of Truth as into a chariot,
   And the Truth led me and caused me to go.
2. And caused me to pass over chasms and rifts
   And saved me from cliffs and waves.
3. And became to me a Haven of Salvation,
   And set me on the level of immortal life.
4. And He went with me and made me rest and did not allow me to err,
   Because He was and is the Truth.
5. And there was no danger for me, because I walked with Him,
   And I did not err in anything because I obeyed Him.

---

[7] M. Testuz, *Papyrus Bodmer X-XII*, Cologny-Genève 1959; *cf.* M. Lattke, *Die Oden Salomos*, Vol. I, 1-23; see also J.A. Emerton, *Some Problems of Text and Language in the Odes of Solomon*, in *JTS* 18, 1967, 372-406.

[8] *Odes of Solomon* 1 (complete?); 5, 1-11; 6, 8-18; 22 and 25; *cf.* A. Kragerud, *Die Hymnen der Pistis Sophia*, Oslo 1967; M. Lattke, *Die Oden Salomos*, I, 187-225.

[9] A. Baumstark, *OrChr* 36, 1941, 125f. already drew attention to Sumerian and Akkadian hymns; *cf.* G. Widengren, *Mesopotamian Elements in Manichaeism (King and Saviour II)*. Studies in Manichaean, Mandaean and Syrian-Gnostic Religion, *UUA* 1946 : 3, *passim*.

6. For Error fled away from Him,
   And did not resist Him,
7. But the Truth was proceeding on the right way,
   And whatever I did not know He declared to me.
8. All the drugs of Error,
   And those pitfalls which are considered the sweetness of death,
9. And the author of the Corruption.
   I looked on when the corrupted Bride was adorned
   And the Bridegroom who corrupts and is corrupted.
10. And I asked the Truth, Who are these?
    And He said to me: This is the Deceiver and the Error.
11. And they imitate the Beloved and His Bride
    And they cause the world to err and corrupt it.
12. And they invite many to the wedding feast,
    And give them to drink the wine of their drunkenness,
13. So that they vomit up their wisdom and knowledge
    and they make them mindless.
14. Then they abandon them
    And so they go about like mad and corrupted men.
15. Since there is not heart in them
    Neither do they look for it.
16. But I have been made wise so as not to fall into the hands of the Deceivers,
    And I rejoiced in myself because the Truth had gone with me.
17. And I was established and lived and was redeemed,
    And my foundations were laid on the hand of the Lord,
    For He planted me.
18. For He set the root,
    And watered it and fixed it and blessed it,
    And its fruits will be forever.
19. It penetrated deeply and sprang up and spread wide,
    And became full and large.
20. And the Lord alone was glorified
    In His planting and His cultivation
21. In His care and in the blessing of His lips,
    In the beautiful planting of His right hand

22. And in the existence of His planting,
And in the understanding of His Mind.[10]
Hallelujah.

"This Ode from its first verse is full of difficulties and obscurities" sighed R. Harris, the first editor of the Odes, and R. Murray completely agrees with him in declaring Ode 38 "very obscure".[11] Within the context of this paper it is not necessary to give a full commentary on this hymn, but for its understanding two points are crucial: who is the Light of Truth and who are the corrupted Bride and Bridegroom? R. Harris in his commentary on the Odes suggested that the Odist was attacking the Manichaean church, but rejected that idea because in his view the Odes date from the beginning of the second century A.D. "If it were not for the fact that antiquity has been established for the Odes, both as regards individual compositions, and as a collection, we should have been tempted to regard this attack on the heretical teachers who make men mad, as a conventional Patristic attack on Mani and his followers the Manichaeans". Since it is, however, clear from Ignatius' Letters that heretics had been classed with mad dogs from a very early time, Mani is "only a belated illustration" of that traditional polemical pattern.[12] R. Harris' suggestion is worth reconsidering in the light of the imagery in the Coptic Manichaean Psalm-Book.

As in all other Odes of Solomon, the "I" is the redeemed believer who has gained immortal life, insight into God's saving plans for mankind, true Wisdom so that he cannot err, and who has become in a sense identical with Christ. The believer becomes a son of God, born of God (cf. John 1, 12f.) like the only begotten Son.[13] The central

[10] My translation differs in various points from that given by J.H. Charlesworth, *The Odes of Solomon*, who often misunderstood the meaning of the text; *cf.* G.J. Reinink, *JSJ* 5, 1974, 64-68.

[11] R. Harris, *The Odes and Psalms of Solomon*, II, 394; R. Murray, *Symbols of Church and Kingdom. A Study in Early Syriac Tradition*, Cambridge 1975, 133.

[12] R. Harris, *The Odes and Psalms of Solomon*, II, 395.

[13] That becomes clear from *Ode* 41,7; *Ode* 36; *Ode* 10, 1 ff.; *Ode* 28; the usual division of these Odes between Christ and the Odist respectively as singers of the different parts of these Odes is, therefore, not in accordance with the theology of the Odes in general; see my forthcoming monograph on the Christology of the Odes of Solomon (*Subs. CSCO*).

terms in the first eight verses of this Ode: Light, Truth, immortal Life, the right way, rest, suggest the theological climate of St John's Gospel, so that the Light of Truth undoubtedly denotes Christ.[14] The Light of Truth is actually a combination of St John 1, 5: And the Light shineth in the darkness, and St John 1, 14: ... the only-begotten of the Father, full of grace and truth (cf. St John 1, 17; 14, 6; 16, 13). This Light of Truth guides the believers to eternal life to which He himself went (cf. St John 13, 31 ff.) and guides them in truth by His Spirit of Truth (cf. St John 16, 13: Howbeit when he, the Spirit of Truth, is come, he will guide you into all truth, for he shall not speak of himself, but whatsoever he shall hear, that shall he speak; and he will show you things to come). The gaining of immortal life is symbolized as a dangerous journey in a chariot that stands for the Light of Truth, and at the same time as an ascension to the Light. The symbol of the chariot is not uncommon in the Odes of Solomon; it occurs in Ode 23, 11 to denote Christ's earthly journey during which he made manifest God's glory, and goes back to the symbolism of God's chariot or merkabah that is mentioned in Ez. 1 and Ps. 68, 18.[15] The symbolism of waves and haven of salvation might go back to the story of the crossing of the Red Sea, which is a very common symbol for the journey from death to life, from danger to salvation. Remarkable is the occurence of the Greek word κίνδυνος to denote the danger that threatens man on his journey to Light and Life. It also occurs in Ode 39, 8 in a context that reminds of the crossing of the Red Sea which symbolically stands for the Way to the eternal life:

> put on the name of the Most High and know Him,
> And you shall cross without danger (κίνδυνος)
> Because rivers shall be obedient to you.

In the New Testament κίνδυνος only occurs in Rom. 8, 35 and II Cor. 1, 10 ff., where it indicates a danger that separates man from Christ.

---

[14] *Cf.* J. H. Charlesworth - R. A. Culpepper, *The Odes of Solomon and the Gospel of John*, in *ÇBQ* 35, 1973, 307, quoting *Ode* 18, 6 (*cf.* 11, 11, 19; 15, 1 f.) and comparing it with St John's Gospel 1, 5.

[15] *Cf.* Drijvers, *Kerygma und Logos in de Oden Salomos*, 165 ff.

Guided by the Truth the believer is shown an anti-church, a false imitation of the Beloved and His Bride. The Beloved is the Beloved Son, i.e. Christ as He is called at His baptism in the river Jordan (Matth. 3, 17 par.). The term is also to be found in Ode 8, 22 with exactly the same meaning. His Bride symbolizes the Church according to Rev. 21, 9-10. True insight into the erroneous character of this corrupted Couple of Bride and Bridegroom (cf. Matth. 25, 1-13) brings the believer great joy and he therefore praises God's planting. God's planting is a very common symbol in Syriac literature that goes back to the Gospel and Revelation of John (cf. John 15 and Rev. 22) and Old Testament texts like Is. 5 and Ps. 80.[16] When this planting, which at the same time is the tree of life, is called the planting of the Right Hand, the Church of Christ is meant, since Christ in the Odes of Solomon is commonly denoted as the Right Hand (Ode 8, 6, 20; 14, 4; 18, 7; 19, 5; 22, 7; 25, 2, 9); the term goes back to the christological interpretation of Ps. 110, 1.[17] In this planting, i.e. in Christ's Church the knowledge of God's plans ("the understanding of His Mind") is extant and can be attained, and in this way the last verse of the Ode is linked with the first, because the Light of Truth reveals and embodies God's Will and Thought.[18]

It is noteworthy that the believer is identified, as it were, with Christ and the earthly continuation of His incarnation, the Church. The assembly of believers, the sons of God (cf. John 1, 12-13) continue the earthly existence of the Son of God, who guides them in truth.

In this way the relation between and the identity of the Odist and the Light of Truth is clarified in broad outlines. But who are the corrupted Bride and Bridegroom? The wording and imagery of Ode 38 contain some hints that this corrupted Couple disguises Mani and the Manichaean church. All the symbols and images in Ode 38 have exact parallels and counterparts in the Manichaean Psalm-Book, and they often give the impression that they are used on purpose in order to attack related concepts in Manichaean doctrine.

---

[16] *Cf.* R. Murray, *Symbols of Church and Kingdom*, 95 ff.

[17] J. Daniélou, *Théologie du Judéo-Christianisme*, Tournai 1958, 282 ss.; *idem*, *Études d'exégèse judéo-chrétienne* (*Les Testimonia*), Paris 1966, 42-49: La session à la droite du Père.

[18] *Cf. Ode* 9, 3-5; 16, 8, 9; 6, 19; 17, 5 and 23, 5-6; Drijvers, *Kerygma und Logos in den Oden Salomos*, 158 ff. for more parallels.

The Light of Truth, undoubtly a title of Jesus in the Syriac Ode of Solomon which teaches his believer the truth and protects him from error, has a counterpart in the Spirit of Truth, which denotes Mani in the Coptic Bema Psalms, the first section of the Psalm-Book.

Ps. CCXXIII (9, 3-10):

> Let us worship the Spirit of the Paraclete.
> Let us bless our Lord Jesus who has sent to us
> the Spirit of Truth. He came and separated us from the Error
> of the world, he brought us a mirror, we looked, we saw the Universe in it.
> When the Holy Spirit came he revealed to us
> the way of Truth and taught us that there are two
> Natures, that of Light and that of Darkness, ...[19]

Just as the Light of truth, Jesus, leads his believer on the way of Truth to immortal life, so does the Paraclete-Spirit:

Ps. CCXXVII (22, 6-10):

> This is the way of Truth, this is the stairway
> that leads to the height, that will lead us up to the Light.
> From the beginning the First Man is this way and Jesus the Dawn and
> the Paraclete-Spirit they have summoned thee,
> o Soul, that thou mayest ascend to the height by it.[20]

Ode 38 describes the way of Truth to salvation as a journey in a chariot, which is the divine Truth itself, to the haven of salvation. The opening verses of this Ode seemingly contain a contamination of two different sets of symbolism; on the one hand the image of a journey in a chariot through a waste land, on the other hand a voyage by boat on a dangerous sea to a safe haven. The symbolism of ship and haven, which is very frequent in patristic literature, is rather rare in the Syriac area. It occurs, but incompletely, with Aphraates and several times in the Acts of Thomas, next to this single instance in the Odes of Solomon. It is, however, very frequent in the Manichaean Psalms and in Mani-

---

[19] On Mani as the Paraclete see O. Klíma, *Manis Zeit und Leben*, Prag 1962, 234 ff.; 365 ff.; on the Manichaean Bema-Feast *cf.* C.R.C. Allberry, *Das manichäische Bema-Fest*, in *ZNW* 37, 1938, 2-10 = *Der Manichäismus*, hrsg. v. G. Widengren, Darmstadt 1977, 317-327; J. Ries, *La fête de Bêma dans l'Église de Mani*, *REAug* 22, 1976, 218-233. *Cf.* Allberry, *Psalm-Book*, 20, 21-24.

[20] *Cf. Psalm-Book* 25, 3; 31, 23-24.

chaean literature in general.[21] The journey of the soul to the world of Light is often compared to a voyage by ship to a haven in Manichaean texts. Some quotations from the Manichaean psalms may illustrate the use of that symbolic complex, especially in the Psalms to Jesus.

Ps. CCXLV (52, 16-18):

> Come to me my Saviour (σωτήρ), the haven of
> my trust. Bestir thyself, o soul that watchest in the chains
> that have long endured, and remember the ascent into the
> air (ἀήρ) of joy.

Ps. CCXLIX (58, 14):

> I traversed (?) all places in haste, I found no haven save Christ.[22]

Ps. CCLIII (63, 13-14), where the soul speaks:

> Lo, the fight (ἀγών) I have finished; lo my ship I have brought to the shore, no storm has overwhelmed it, no wave has seized it.[23]

In the rather badly preserved Ps. CCLXII even the same Greek word for haven is used as in Ode 38 i.e. λιμήν, 77, 14-16:

> ... his ship into the harbour (λιμήν) ...
> the helmsman on high, his ....
> ... fashion it, that thou mayest make the voyage of the holy ones.[24]

In Ps. CCLXXV (95, 8) Jesus is called "haven of Light" and another text from the ψαλμοὶ Σαρακωτῶν calls Him "a ship, blessed are we if we sail upon it" (166, 11). The symbolism is fully elaborated in another of the ψαλμοὶ Σαρακωτῶν (151, 31 - 152, 5):

> The ship of Jesus has come to port, laden with garlands and gay palms.

---

[21] *Cf.* H. Rahner, *Symbole der Kirche*, Salzburg 1964, 239-564 and R. Murray, *Symbols of Church and Kingdom*, 250; *Acts of Thomas* (ed. W. Wright), 206, 19 (transl. 178); 322, 12-13 (transl. 288); Aphraates, *Dem.* XIV, 684, 4-5; for the Manichaean use of this symbolism see: V. Arnold-Döben, *Die Bildersprache des Manichäismus*, Arbeitsmaterialien zur Religionsgeschichte 3, Köln 1978, 63-70. *Cf. Keph.* 8 and Böhlig, *Der Synkretismus des Mani*, 148 f. on ὄχημα; *idem*, *Probleme des manichäischen Lehrvortrages*, in *Mysterion und Wahrheit*, 230 f.

[22] *Cf. Psalm-Book* 60, 24 f.; 66, 9; 83, 25 ff.; Arnold-Döben, *Die Bildersprache des Manichäismus*, 68-70.

[23] *Cf. Psalm-Book* 70, 3 ff.; 73, 7; 147, 34 ff.

[24] *Cf. Psalm-Book* 77, 21; 78, 23 f.; 139, 24.

> It is Jesus who steers it, he will put in for us until we embark. The holy ones are they whom he takes, the maidens are they whom he ... Let us also make ourselves pure that we may make our voyage ... The ship of Jesus will make its way up to the height. It will bring its cargo to the shore and return for them that are left behind.

The Odist explicitly states that he does not risk any danger (κίνδυνος) since he is companied by the Light of Truth. It is noteworthy and may not be mere coincidence that the same Greek word is used to describe the situation of man in the beginning at the creation of the world, during his earthly lifetime and after his death when he crosses over to the land of immortal life;
Ps. CCXXXVIII (39, 6-9):

> Let us bear up, my brethren, in fortitude, and let us ...
> and let us make away with the second danger (κίνδυνος) ...
> from the beginning we were rescued from the first, so ...
> ... we shall pass over and cross the last also.[25]

The imagery of Bride, Bridegroom and the Wedding-Feast is very common in Manichaean literature to denote the Manichaean Church.[26] Actually the Manichaeans are the only gnostics who used that symbolism often in combination with the parable in Matth. 25. Mani himself is called the Bridegroom of his Church; so Ps. CCXXXVII (37, 25-32):

> Let us all sing together unto Mani, the man of God
> on the holy perfect day, and let us be glad and
> learn the mysteries of the life of the Saviour (σωτήρ) Jesus
> and make festival and render glory to the Sage, the Paraclete.
> Light your lamps (λαμπάς) and ....
> And keep watch on the day of the Bema for the Bridegroom
> of joy and receive the holy rays (ἀκτίς) of Light.[27]
> cf. 154, 5-6:

[25] *Cf.* Allberry's note p. 39: The three dangers seem to be (I) the cosmic danger in the beginning, when the Dark threatened to defeat the Light, from which we were redeemed; (II) the danger in this present life, our corruption by the body and its lusts; (III) the danger that at the last assize we may be condemned and be bound for ever in the Bolos.

[26] Arnold-Döben, *Die Bildersprache des Manichäismus*, 78-85; Widengren, *Mesopotamian Elements in Manichaeism*, 109-122.

[27] See J. Ries, *La fête de Bêma dans l'Église de Mani*, in *REAug* 22, 1976, 218 ff.

The Bride is the Church, the Bridegroom is the Mind (νοῦς) of Light.
The Bride is the soul, the Bridegroom is Jesus.[28]

When Ode 38 emphasizes that the false Bride and Bridegroom cause the world to err and make men drunken, then this wording gives the impression that the Odist is perverting Manichaean statements about their own church; e.g.

Ps. CCXLVIII (56, 15-25):

Come, my Lord Jesus, the Saviour (σωτήρ) of souls, who hast saved me from the drunkenness and Error (πλάνη) of the world (κόσμος). Thou art the Paraclete whom I have loved since my youth: Thy Light shines forth in me like the lamp (λαμπάς) of light: thou hast driven away from me the oblivion of Error (πλάνη)

....

Christ and the church I have distinguished from the deceit (ἀπάτη) of the world (κόσμος).[29]

The whole passage in Ode of Solomon 38 that describes the false Church seems to contain more hidden clues pointing to Mani, especially in stressing the madness he causes so that people become mindless and even do not have a heart. That fits very well with the traditional word-play on Mani's name that often is connected with Greek μανία and μανικός: Eusebius, Theophania IV, 30: ... that madman of yesterday and of our own times, whose name became the titular badge of the Manichaean heresy; Cyril of Jerusalem, Cat. VI, 19: Thou must hate all heretics, but especially him who even in name is a *maniac*, who arose lately under the emperor Probus.[30]

The explicit mention of the *smmn' dṭywt'* = drugs of error in

---

[28] *Cf. Psalm-Book* 159, 1-3.

[29] On error and drunkenness in Manichaeism *cf. Psalm-Book* 8, 22-25; 9, 3-9; 26, 11 ff.; 193, 25; Ephrem Syrus, *Hymni contra Haereses* (ed. Beck, *CSCO*, S 76-77, Louvain 1957) 24, 4-7: Die falschen Lehrer aber ... glichen sich der Schönheit des Bräutigams an, um die Braut mit seiner Schönheit zu fangen; *cf. Hymn* 47, 3-4; *Ode of Solomon* 33 refers to the same opponent, also called the Corruptor, and should, therefore, be considered a second instance of polemics with the Manichaean church.

[30] Quoted by R. Harris, *The Odes and Psalms of Solomon*, Vol. II, 395; the word-play occurs with Titus of Bostra, *Contra Manichaeos Libri quattuor*, ed. P. A. de Lagarde, Hannover 1924², 70, 33; 72, 2; and Serapion of Thmuis, ed. R. P. Casey, III, 9-23 *et al.*; *cf.* E. Beck, *Ephräms Polemik gegen Mani und die Manichäer im Rahmen der zeitgenossischen griechischen Polemik und der des Augustinus*, (*CSCO Subs.* 55), Louvain 1978, 1 ff.

vs. 8 may also contain a hidden allusion to Mani's profession of physician and his miraculous healings. Moreover *smmn`* = drugs is a hapax in the Odes only occuring here.[31] In contradistinction to Mani's healings the Odist states that these drugs which seems to be sweet only lead to death and not to eternal Life.

The description of God's planting i.e. His Church in the last part of Ode 38 also deserves some attention. This Ode is the only one of the whole collection that uses this derivate of the root *nṣb* = to plant, namely *nṣbt`* = planting to denote the church. This use has exact parallels in the Manichaean Psalm-Book:

Ps. CCLXI (75, 28-30):

> I have known the way of the holy ones, these
> ministers of God who are in the church, the place wherein the
> Paraclete planted the tree of knowledge.[32]

Psalm of Thomas (218, 15-19):

> I went forth to plant a garden beyond
> the confines of this world, choosing and planting in it the plants
> that grew in the Living ones. I will give orders to the gardener:
> Attend to my trees, my new plants.[33]

Ode of Solomon 38, therefore, attacks the Manichaean church by using well-known Manichaean imagery like 'haven', 'danger', 'drugs', 'Bride and Bridegroom', 'drunkenness', 'planting' etc., which for the greater part occur only in this Ode and not in the other hymns of the collection. It also refers to traditional elements in polemics with the Manichaeans, such as the word-play with 'mad' and offers a very sophisticated example of christian anti-heretical literature which twists and perverts the central ideas of its opponents. The area and time in which the Odes of Solomon originate know only two heretical

---

[31] *Cf.* the text *M 566 I*: ... 'I am a doctor from Babylon'; *Psalm-Book* 46, 1-47: Lo, the great physician has come ... A skilful one is he in his work; his mouth also is sweet in its words. He knows how to cut a wound, to put a cool medicament upon it ... see L. J. R. Ort, *Mani.* A religio-historical description of his personality, Leiden 1967, 95ff.; *Psalm-Book* 152, 22-23 and Arnold-Döben, *Die Bildersprache des Manichäismus*, 97-107.

[32] *Cf. Ode of Solomon* 11, 18-21 and Arnold-Döben, *Die Bildersprache*, 25-30.

[33] *Cf.* G. Widengren, *Mesopotamian Elements in Manichaeism*, 18-30.

organisations of importance, Marcionites and Manichaeans. Although both built a solid ecclesiastical structure, only the Manichaeans come into consideration as the target of Ode 38 considering the whole phrasing and the use of images also known with Mani's followers. Since Mani got his second revelation on April 19 A.D. 240, this offers a terminus post quem for the dating of the Odes of Solomon.[34] A date around 275 A.D., therefore, seems to be likely and possible taking into account the doctrinal elements in other Odes of the collection that seem to refer to christological controversies in the second half of the third century.[35]

Ode of Solomon 38 is, therefore, the oldest anti-manichaean document known so far, having been written during or shortly after Mani's lifetime in one of the central regions of his mission, the bilingual Syrian area. Taking into account language and substance of this Ode it was in all likelihood composed in the city of Edessa, which had an important Manichaean congregation to which Mani addressed one of his letters. Fragments of this epistle have been preserved in the Cologne Mani Codex which itself goes back to a Syriac original.[36]

The concealed manner of polemic in Ode 38, which is only understandable for insiders with a substantial knowledge of christian and manichaean doctrine and symbolism that seem to have so much in common, throws a new light on the relations between Christians and Manichaeans in third-century Syria. On the one hand it might be an indication of a weak position of the 'orthodox' group which did not make possible any open controversy with the Manichaeans in which chapter and verse were given. On the other hand the differences

---

[34] L. Koenen, *Das Datum der Offenbarung und Geburt Manis*, in *ZPE* 8, 1971, 247-250; A. Henrichs-L. Koenen, *Ein griechischer Mani-Codex*, in *ZPE* 5, 1970, 119 ff.

[35] See *e.g. Ode* 41, 13-15:

The Son of the Most High appeared
in the perfection of His Father.
And Light dawned from the Word
that was before time in Him.
The Messiah is truly one
And He was known before the foundations of the world,
That He might give life to souls for ever by the truth of His name.

[36] A. Henrichs-L. Koenen, *Ein griechischer Mani-Codex*, in *ZPE* 5, 1970, 108 ff.; A. Henrichs-L. Koenen, *Der Kölner Mani-Kodex (P. Colon. inv. nr. 4780)*. Edition der Seiten 1-72, in *ZPE* 19, 1975, 64, 8 - 65, 18.

between Manichaean and 'orthodox' Christian seem to be so small that they are only intelligible for the learned circles in which the Odes of Solomon seem to originate. For the rest these differences are hardly conceivable especially for the general public. Christians and Manichaeans had a common fund of religious symbolism and language to express views on the world and salvation that in the long run became radically opposite, but that had a lot in common in the missionary situation of Manichaeism in an area with a variety of Christian groups and doctrines such as Edessa in the third century.

It has usually been assumed that the christian elements in Manichaeism reached Mani through a gnostic filter. Marcion and Bardaiṣan were made responsible for Mani's knowledge of christian tradition.[37] Such a restricted view on the relations between both groups seems hardly tenable in the light of the foregoing. It is rather more in agreement with the historical situation and development during the third century in the Edessean area to assume that Mani and Manichaeism heavily drew upon the whole of christian tradition and literature extant in that time without any restriction to a supposedly gnostic strain.[38] The Coptic Manichaean Psalm-Book and the Syriac Odes of Solomon both originate in the same area and the same time and demonstrate the common background that both share. The Manichaean Psalms are truly Manichaean products and do not give the impression of being revised Christian hymns as Baumstark thought. The Odes of Solomon refer to Christian concepts that may be labelled orthodox, and oppose heretical views of Marcionites and Manichaeans. Their common symbolism and imagery make clear how vague and narrow the dividing-lines between the various groups really were.

---

[37] A. Böhlig, *Christliche Wurzeln im Manichäismus*, in *Mysterion und Wahrheit*, 208ff.; *idem*, *Der Synkretismus des Mani*, 158ff.; K. Rudolph, *Gnosis und Manichäismus nach den koptischen Quellen*, in *Koptologische Studien in der DDR*, *WZ Halle* 1965 (Sonderheft), 158; *cf.* P. Nagel, *Die apokryphen Apostelakten des 2. und 3. Jahrhunderts in der manichäischen Literatur. Ein Beitrag zur Frage nach den christlichen Elementen im Manichäismus*, in *Gnosis und Neues Testament*, Berlin 1975, 149ff.

[38] A more comprehensive study of these relations is planned by the present author.

XI

BARDAIṢAN OF EDESSA AND THE HERMETICA

THE ARAMAIC PHILOSOPHER AND THE PHILOSOPHY OF HIS TIME

Introduction

Although nearly all currents of religious and spiritual thought of the second century have been drawn upon to help elucidate the teachings of Bardaiṣan of Edessa, the Hermetica have not until now been seriously considered for inclusion among the number. Astrology, gnosticism, the Christian apologists, Zurvanite theology, the cult of the Dea Syria, Jewish Christianity and other constituent parts of second century syncretism have been presented in turn, or all together, as background, explanation or ingredient of the doctrines of the Aramaic philosopher. Moreover, all these phenomena were to be found in Edessa, where Bardaiṣan (154-222) spent the greater part of his life at the court of Abgar VIII the Great [1]). O. G. von Wesendonk was the only one to relate Bardaiṣan and the Hermetica because of a passage in the Bardesanite Dialogue on Fate, the so-called *Book of the Laws of Countries* [2]). In this passage Bardaiṣan tries to prove to his interlocutor Awida that the power of Fate is limited, and man's lot is not completely determined [3]). In this connection Bardaiṣan speaks of the "Books of the Babylonian Chaldaeans" and the "Books of the Egyptians", whose teaching is the same [4]). With reference to this passage Von Wesendonk says: "Unter den ägyptischen Schriften wird man sich die hermetische Literatur vorstellen dürfen." If this suggestion is correct, we must suppose Bardaiṣan to have been acquainted with the astrological literature purporting to stem from Hermes Trismegistus [5]). In all the extensive "Geschichte der Leben-Bardaiṣan-Forschung" this is the only place where the Egyptian sage makes an appearance, while it is not even clear if it is really he.

Conversely, Bardaiṣan is not often mentioned either in the extensive literature on the Hermetic writings. In *Die Lehren des Hermes Trismegistus* J. Kroll

---

[1]) For a historical survey of all interpretations see H. J. W. Drijvers, *Bardaiṣan of Edessa, Studia Semitica Neerlandica* VI, Assen 1966, pp. 1-59.

[2]) O. G. von Wesendonk, *'Bardesanes und Mānī'*, AcOr(L) X, 1932, SS. 336-363; *The Book of the Laws of Countries. Dialogue on Fate of Bardaiṣan of Edessa, text and transl.* by H. J. W. Drijvers, Assen 1965, p. 38, 1. 25-40, 1. 7.

[3]) *Cf.* Drijvers, *Bardaiṣan of Edessa*, pp. 76 ff.

[4]) Von Wesendonk, *art. cit.*, S. 346; the Egyptian without more is often Hermes Trismegistus, *cf.* A.-J. Festugière, *'Une source hermétique de Porphyre'*, REG XLIX, 1936, pp. 586-595.

[5]) See A.-J. Festugiere, *La Révélation d'Hermès Trismégiste* I, 2ème éd., Paris 1950, pp. 89-186; *Corpus Hermeticum* III, *ed.* Nock-Festugière, Paris 1954, pp. XXXIX-LXII.

relegates the sage of Edessa to a footnote, where he refers to the relation of Fate and nature [6]). In W. SCOTT's big edition of the Hermetica one searches in vain for the name of Bardaiṣan, and equally so in the opus magnum of A.-J. FESTUGIÈRE *La Révélation d'Hermès Trismégiste* [7]). Both scholars discuss numerous related phenomea and philosophers, including Albinus, Numenius, Oracula Chaldaica etc., but they clearly do not regard Bardaiṣan as a philosopher having affinity with the Hermetica. Thus his name only appears sporadically in the edition of the Hermetic writings prepared by A. D. NOCK and A.-J. FESTUGIÈRE [8]). In the commentary on Poimandres 9, where the Stoic expression διοίκησις τοῦ κόσμου — administration of the world — is discussed, a note by F. CUMONT remarks that this Stoic conception of the seven planets governing the world is very close to the view expressed in the Poimandres, and is also found in Bardaiṣan's Book of the Laws of Countries [9]). The footnote in the work of J. KROLL reappears in a similar context in the introduction to the Excerpta XII-XIV of Stobaeus. Excerptum XII deals with the mutual relation of Nature and Fate. In the introduction to it, Bardaiṣan is mentioned and the way his ideas were rendered by D. AMAND [10]). Very occasionally, one comes across the name of Bardaiṣan in the secondary literature on the Hermetica and related matters. G. VAN MOORSEL classes him with "semi-gnosticism", where he also places the Hermetica, with no explicit adstruction [11]). A term like "semi-gnosticism" can only serve rather to cover uncertainty than to give a clear characterisation. K. E. MÜLLER mentions that Harmonios the son of Bardaiṣan introduced the doctrine of reincarnation into the system of his father, in which MÜLLER sees a clear parallel with the Hermetica, where the doctrine of reincarnation plays a great part [12]). Perhaps a few more instances might be cited, but the relation between Bardaiṣan and the Hermetica would appear to require more justification than the vague parallels and incidental mention of Bardaiṣan's name which is the meagre result of searching through the literature.

---

[6]) J. KROLL, *Die Lehren des Hermes Trismegistos*, Münster 1914, S. 227, Anm. 1.

[7]) W. SCOTT, *Hermetica*, 4 Vols, Oxford 1924-1936; A.-J. FESTUGIÈRE, *La Révélation d'Hermès Trismégiste*, 4 Vols, Paris 1949-1954.

[8]) A. D. NOCK/A.-J. FESTUGIÈRE, *Corpus Hermeticum*, 4 Tomes (Collection Budé), Paris 1945-1954.

[9]) *Corpus Hermeticum* I, p. 20, n. 27: 'Les planètes sont ,,les gouverneurs". *Cf.* par exemple Bardesane, *Livres des lois* (Patrol. Syriaca, II, 567 s.) où *gubernatores* rend exactement l'original. F.C.'

[10]) *Corpus Hermeticum* III, p. LXXIX, n. 2; D. AMAND, *Fatalisme et Liberté dans l'antiquité grecque*, Louvain 1945, pp. 228-257, esp. p. 246 svv.

[11]) G. VAN MOORSEL, *The Mysteries of Hermes Trismegistus, A phenomenologic study in the process of spiritualisation in the Corpus Hermeticum and latin Asclepius*, Utrecht 1955, p. 21.

[12]) K. E. MÜLLER, *Kulturhistorische Studien zur Genese pseudo-islamischer Sektengebilde in Vorderasien, Studien zur Kulturkunde* 22, Wiesbaden 1967, S. 346.

The philosophers and tendencies discussed at length by A.-J. FESTUGIÈRE as related to the Hermetica offer little to our purpose. In an article on Numenius and Ammonius, E. R. DODDS speaks about the psychology of the former. According to Numenius, man has two souls, a good one and an evil one, the latter deriving ἀπό τῶν ἔξωθεν προσφυομένων. The soul descends through the spheres of the planets, and on the way receives "certain increments of starry body". This conception is also found with the Hermetists, Basilidians and Manichaeans and "we are reminded also of the Gnostic Bardesanes, for whom man has 'a body from the Evil Ones and a soul from the Seven' "[13]. H. LEWY, in his great work on the Oracula Chaldaica, regards these oracles on the one hand and the Gnostics, including Bardaiṣan, on the other as parallel developments, originating from the "intermingling of Platonic ingredients" with Chaldaean and Iranian teachings[14]. Numenius — who was a contemporary of Bardaiṣan — and the Oracula Chaldaica are obviously at home in a syncretistic climate of "théologies orientales au second siècle" where all kind of ideas remind one of Bardaiṣan, because he belonged to the same mental climate[15]. In itself, this common syncretistic climate of the second century of our era is not enough to justify connecting Bardaiṣan with the Hermetica and the philosophical theology or theological philosophy of his time. Undoubtedly he will have shared certain thoughts with these, but that is hardly surprising in a period when the popular Platonic or Stoic philosophy was the common property of every intellectual or semi-intellectual who felt the urge to pronounce upon the problems of man and the cosmos.

The polemic writings of Ephrem Syrus (306-373) against Bardaiṣan make it plain that the Aramaic philosopher took part in the philosophical discussion of his day both in speech and in writing. He wrote a treatise against the Platonists, entitled "Of Domnus", in which he specifically attacked the Platonic distinction between σώματα and ἀσώματα. Ephrem says that this distinction is treated in a writing by Albinus "Of the incorporeal". Mistakenly, I formerly stated that nothing was known of this work by Albinus[16]. E. ORTH had already written in 1947 that this work of Albinus "Concerning the incorporeal" was to be found in the works of Galenus under the title ὅτι αἱ ποιότητες

[13]) E. R. DODDS, '*Numenius and Ammonius*' in: *Entretiens sur l'antiquité classique* V, *Les Sources de Plotin*, Genève 1960, p. 7 f.

[14]) H. LEWY, *Chaldaean Oracles and Theurgy, Mysticism, Magic and Platonism in the Later Roman Empire*, Le Caire 1956, p. 392.

[15]) *Cf.* H.-C. PUECH, '*Numénius d'Apamée et les théologies orientales au second siècle*' in: Annuaire de l'Institut de Philologie et d'Histoire orientales II, Bruxelles 1934, pp. 745-778; A.-J. FESTUGIÈRE, *La Révélation* IV, pp. 135 svv.; *cf. Les Sources de Plotin*, pp. 35-39 with corrections by PUECH on his article of 1934.

[16]) *S. Ephraim's Prose Refutations of Mani, Marcion, and Bardaisan* II, transcribed by C. W. MITCHELL and completed by A. A. BEVAN/F. C. BURKITT, London 1921, p. i-xxii (translation), 1-49 (syriac text); *cf.* DRIJVERS, *Bardaiṣan of Edessa*, p. 163.

ἀσώματοι (Tom. 19, pp. 463-484, ed. Kühn). Galenus studied philosophy with Albinus in Smyrna 149-151, so that Bardaiṣan may well have polemised against the views of Albinus [17]. Upon this point, the Aramaic philosopher agreed with the opinion of certain Stoics who held that the qualities of bodies are themselves material and not incorporeal. We are explicitly informed of this by Sergius of Resh 'Aina in the sixth *memra* of his writing on the categories of Aristotle. G. FURLANI was thus induced to regard Bardaiṣan as altogether a Stoic, both in his cosmology and doctrine of the elements of the world and in his doctrine of fate [18]. When Bardaiṣan, then, was considered as a philosopher, the first thing thought of was the Stoa. This not only applies to G. FURLANI, but before him already to H. H. SCHAEDER [19]. A title like "Bardaiṣan of Edessa and the Stoa" would therefore have been more appropriate for these lines.

Yet there are a number of arguments for the probability of the relationship set forth in the title, apart from a common spiritual climate. Muslim authors of later centuries write at length about the so-called Sabians in Harran, a town no more than thirty miles away from Edessa. These Sabians were accounted heathen, and probably only became Muslims in name. Their religion was an autochthonous Syrian paganism, with a strong astrological bias and clad in the aspect of philosophy. They were regarded as Hermetists and were intensely interested in philosophy and astrology [20]. According to tradition, they had temples dedicated to the Seven, five planets and sun and moon. In the fifties of the present century J. B. SEGAL made a new investigation of the ruins in Sumatar Harabesi, in the Tektek mountains, situated 50 km southeast of Edessa and 30 km northeast of Harran. These ruins consist of the remains of seven differently shaped buildings lying round a central mountain. Underneath each building there is a cave with its opening directed towards the central mountain. Very probably, the buildings represent temples dedicated to the Seven, who are subject to the deity of the central sanctuary named *marilaha*. The shape of the planetary sanctuaries accurately corresponds with the shape of the temples for the planets of the Sabians in Harran as described to us

---

17) E. ORTH, '*Les œuvres d'Albinos le Platonicien*' in: l'Antiquité Classique XVI, 1947, pp. 113 sv.; *cf.* A. H. ARMSTRONG, *The Cambridge History of Later Greek and Early Medieval Philosophy*, Cambridge 1967, p. 70, n. 3: P. LOUIS, *Albinos. Epitomé*, Thèse, Paris 1945, pp. 64 svv. = XI, 1 sqq.

18) G. FURLANI, '*Sur le stoïcisme de Bardesane d'Edesse*' in: ArOr IX, 1937, pp. 347-352; *idem*, *Encicl. Ital.* VI, 1938, pp. 167-168.

19) H. H. SCHAEDER, '*Bardesanes von Edessa in der Überlieferung der griechischen und syrischen Kirche*', ZKG 51, 1932, SS. 21-74; *cf.* DRIJVERS, *Bardaiṣan of Edessa*, pp. 46 ff.

20) *Cf.* D. CHWOLSOHN, *Die Ssabier und der Ssabismus*, 2 Tle, St. Petersburg 1856; R. REITZENSTEIN, *Poimandres*, Leipzig 1904, SS. 166 ff.

by Mas'udi and al-Dimesqi [21]). If this reconstruction is right, then in Sumatar Harabesi we have a sanctuary of the planets that was used until far into the Muslim period by the Sabians of Harran, thus taking back their religion to the second century A.D., when this planetary sanctuary was probably built, since the inscriptions several times give the date 476 of the Seleucidean era, corresponding to 164/165 A.D. [22]). The sanctuary was dedicated during the new moon of Šebat, a time that also had a religious significance for the Sabians.

If it is therefore not too bold a guess to connect the Hermetic Sabians, for whom Hermes was the founder of their cult, their prophet and their fount of wisdom, with the planetary sanctuary in Sumatar, it is clear that Bardaiṣan was also not unacquainted with the conceptions pertaining to this sanctuary. The Aramaic philosopher teaches that at the creation of the world the Seven were also assigned their fixed courses and charged with part of the government of the world. It is true they are not free in that, but are supposed to perform a task, and their transgressions will even be judged [23]). This cosmological conception, which forms part of a comprehensive view of life, is as it were a philosophical-astrological interpretation of the cult in Sumatar. However, Bardaiṣan was not only a philosopher. His adherents assembled with him in caves, where hymns were sung and various kinds of writings were read and expounded [24]). May we here also think of the caves under the temples of the planets in Sumatar? In any case the sanctuary there is a link between Bardaiṣan and the Hermetists of Harran. The latter were also philosophers and astrologers with a great interest in all kinds of esoteric teachings. In this, they are a late offshoot of the Hellenistic culture, which had perished nearly everywhere in these forms. The Hermetic literature in Arabic is thus a continuation of that in Greek of Hellenistic times, which in all probability was translated into Arabic via Syriac [25]). That is not to say that the Harranian Hermetists knew or had known the Hermetic writings that have been gathered in the so-called Corpus Hermeticum, nor that they knew just those astrological or alchemistic Hermetic treatises which have been preserved to us in Greek. Under the name of Hermes Tris-

---

[21]) J. B. SEGAL, *'Pagan Syriac Monuments in the Vilayet of Urfa'*, AnSt III, 1953, pp. 97-119; *idem, 'The Sabian Mysteries. The planet cult of ancient Harran* in: *Vanished Civilizations* (ed. E. Bacon), London 1963, pp. 201-220.

[22]) J. B. SEGAL, *'Some Syriac Inscriptions of the 2nd-3rd century A.D.'*, BSOAS XVI, 1954, pp. 97-120.

[23]) *Book of the Laws of Countries*, p. 14, l. 12-18; p. 28, l. 18-30, l. 3; *cf.* DRIJVERS, *Bardaiṣan of Edessa*, pp. 78-85.

[24]) E. BECK, *Des Heiligen Ephraem des Syrers Hymnen contra Haereses*, hrsg. u. übers. v. E. BECK, CSCO, *Script. Syri*, 76-77, Louvain 1957, I, 17, 18; *cf.* DRIJVERS, *Bardaiṣan of Edessa*, p. 162 f.

[25]) REITZENSTEIN, *Poimandres*, S. 173; *cf.* L. MASSIGNON, *'Inventaire de la littérature hermétique arabe'*, in: FESTUGIÈRE, *La Révélation* I, pp. 384 svv.

megistos a considerable body of literature was written, that was delivered to us partly in Greek (or Latin) and partly in Arabic. Hermetism is not a separate religion with its own canon of sacred writings, but an attitude of mind characterised by intensive preoccupation with esoteric philosophy and astrology and by a hankering after the mysterious; to people of this turn of mind Hermes Trismegistos was the bearer of revelation and the teacher of wisdom. This is the spiritual home of the Sabians, and perhaps also of Bardaiṣan [26]).

The name of Hermes, however, does not appear anywhere in the tradition regarding Bardaiṣan, let alone the name of Hermes Trismegistos. Only by ascribing the astrological "books of the Egyptians" to Hermes Trismegistos can one suppose Bardaiṣan to have been acquainted with the Egyptian god of wisdom. In Edessa and other Syrian towns, however, the god Nebo was worshipped, and he was identified with Hermes. This Nebo, the third person of the Babylonian triad Bêl-Nanai-Nabû, is named as one of the principal gods of Edessa in the Doctrina Addai, the Apology of Pseudo-Melito, the homily of Jacob of Sarug on the fall of the idols, and in other Syriac sources [27]). Nebo, then, is equalled with Hermes and thus Pseudo-Lucianus can call Hermes the god of Hierapolis-Mabbug [28]). This Nebo-Hermes is also identified with Orpheus, the divine singer, and so represented with the lyre. Later traditions relate that this lyre had seven strings and gave forth the harmony of the spheres [29]). The connection with Orpheus can be understood from the function of Hermes as Ψυχοπομπός: he conducted the souls to the realm of the dead, and in later times to the supreme god [30]). His function is the same with, for instance, the gnostic Naassenes, where he is the Logos with power over life and death, who leads those aroused from sleep to the realm of eternity [31]). In the great magical papyrus of Leiden = PGM, XIII, Hermes even has a function in the creation of the world. Here he is called "Mind" (Νοῦς) or "Reason" (Φρενές) and "lord

---

[26]) *Cf.* A.-J. FESTUGIÈRE, L'Hermétisme, *Hermétisme et Mystique païenne,* Paris 1967, pp. 28-87.

[27]) *Doctrina Addai, ed.* PHILLIPS, p. 24; *Apology of Pseudo-Melito, c.* 5; THEODORE BAR KHONAI, *Liber Scholiorum* (*ed.* A. SCHER) I, 369, 11-21; *cf.* DUVAL, *Histoire d'Édesse,* p. 75; P.-S. LANDERSDORFER, '*Die Götterliste des Mar Jacob von Sarug in seiner Homilie über den Fall der Götzenbilder* in: *Programm des Kgl. Gymnasiums Ettal,* München 1914, S. 23 ff. B. VANDENHOFF, '*Die Götterliste des Mar Jakob von Sarug in seiner Homilie über den Fall der Götzenbilder*', OrChr. N.S. 5, 1915, SS. 236 ff.

[28]) J. PIRENNE, *Sacra Pagina* I, Paris 1959, p. 291.

[29]) *Apology of Pseudo-Melito, c.* 5; F. CUMONT, *Syria* II, 1921, p. 44, n. 1; F. CUMONT, *Recherches sur le symbolisme funéraire des Romains,* réimpression 1966, p. 18, n. 4, p. 499 (additions).

[30]) *Cf.* K. KERÉNYI, *Hermes der Seelenführer, Albae Vigiliae* N.F. 1, Zürich 1944, *passim*; *Mém. Pyth.* ap. D. L. VIII, 31.

[31]) Hippol. *Refutatio* 8, 27 sqq.; *cf.* W. FOERSTER, '*Die Naassener*' in: *Studi di storia religiosa della tarda antchità,* Messina 1968, p. 27 f.

of the elements" [32]). So Hermes had a function for the salvation of the individual soul, guiding it through the spheres of the planets, and he could also manifest himself as the Nous which creates and maintains the world and is related with the nous of each individual. When a splendid mosaic of Orpheus is found in a tomb in Edessa, we may also recognise Nebo-Hermes there, who accompanies the soul on the road to the divine world [33]).

Although the sources are fairly meagre, we can yet conclude with some certainty that Nebo-Hermes had a very complex function in Edessa and other Syrian towns. He is the god of wisdom, who affords insight into the secrets of the cosmos; he is the god of writers, having invented writing, and he conducts the soul journeying through the spheres of the planets [34]). If Hermetism gained a place in this region, as it did in Harran, this undoubtedly goes back to the local cult of Nebo-Hermes. Bardaiṣan knew this cult, as Nebo was one of the chief gods of Edessa, with Bêl and Atargatis. Further investigation will have to show whether Bardaiṣan was acquainted with all the semi-philosophical conceptions that became attached to the worship of this god.

While the cult of the planets in Sumatar and the worship of Nebo-Hermes in Edessa are historical indications that it is by no means unreasonable to compare the teachings of the Aramaic philosopher and the Hermetic writings, there are also formal analogies to justify such a proceeding.

The Hermetists were not a community united in a cult, but people who sought individual salvation through a doctrine given by a teacher to his pupils by word of mouth or in writing. This form of transmission was taken from the philosophical schools of the time. The oral teaching or the written treatise is the medium for the transmission of truth, not a philosophical truth, but the theological truth ensuring the salvation of the soul. From a philosophical point of view the Hermetic writings are very mediocre productions, and eclectic as they are, they are swarming with contradictions and philosophical banalities. Their distinction is a religious inspiration, annexing all profane learning to make it further the cause of individual salvation: salvation through knowledge, but this knowledge must be believed. The whole of traditional Greek and Oriental learning and religion was forced towards this end with an almost monomaniac fanaticism that reminds one of the pietistic mysticism of eighteenth

---

[32]) *PGM*, XIII, 138-213(A) = 443-563(B); *cf.* FESTUGIÈRE, *Révélation* I, pp. 300 svv. *PGM*, XIII, b = V, 400-423; *cf.* FESTUGIÈRE, *Révélation* I, p. 295 sv. *cf.* E. KREBS, *Der Logos als Heiland im ersten Jahrhundert. Ein religions- und dogmengeschichtlicher Beitrag zur Erlösungslehre*, Freiburg i.B. 1910, SS. 34-36, 38 ff., 120 ff.; H. RAHNER, *Griechische Mythen in christlicher Deutung*, Zürich 1957, SS. 242 ff.

[33]) J. B. SEGAL, in *Vanished Civilizations* (ed. E. Bacon), London 1966, pp. 208 f.; *cf.* J. LEROY, *Les manuscrits syriaques à peintures* I, Paris 1964, pp. 88-92.

[34]) *Cf.* THEODORE BAR KHONAI, *Liber Scholiorum* (ed. A. SCHER) I, p. 369, l. 11-21 (commentary on Jes. 46:1); F. CUMONT, *Lux Perpetua*, Paris 1949, p. 301.

century preaching. No wonder that here and there the content bursts out of the framework, so that the Hermetica cannot offer a consistent system [35]).

We find the same characteristic in the teachings of Bardaiṣan and his followers. The Aramaic philosopher is really an Aramaic theologian, reflecting on the creation of the world and the essence of man, because that creation must be undone and man only reaches his true destination when after the journey to heaven the soul enters into the bridal-chamber of light. His cosmology and doctrine of fate, his anthropology and psychology are all directed towards the realisation of this individual salvation. Bardaiṣan presents his views like a philosopher in a circle of pupils, who are called upon to believe [36]). In this circle his works are read, including the "book of mysteries" and astrological treatises, for example the "Book about the signs of the Zodiac" [37]). Traditional religion is also given its due place in the Bardesanite circle. Hymns are sung, as the hymns to Isis have gained a place in the Hermetica [38]). Bardaiṣan wrote a book about India with its Brahmins and gymnosophists, and he shares this interest in the esoteric with the Hermetica and with a philosopher such as Numenius of Apamea, who stands very close to the Hermetic teachings [39]).

Because of the intention of Bardaiṣan's thought, logical contradictions do not form an insuperable barrier to understanding and believing, any more than they do in the Hermetica. The philosophical or physical conceptions are not intended as a model of reality, but as a theological interpretation of it. The different disposition of the four elements of the world before the creation, all on a level and also one above the other in order of weight, clearly demonstrates this intention. These four elements, taken from Stoic physics, function as intermediary between the theological concepts of light and darkness, which are constitutive of human existence [40]).

---

[35]) *Cf.* FESTUGIÈRE, *Hermétisme et mystique païenne*, pp. 28-50.

[36]) *Book of the Laws of Countries*, pp. 4-8 = *PS*, II, 536-543. Transmitting the knowledge of salvation in the form of an artificial dialogue is another point Bardaiṣan has in common with the Hermetists: cf. A. HERMANN/G. BARDY, Art. *"Dialog" RAC* 3, Sp. 928-955 and M. HOFFMANN, *Der Dialog bei den christlichen Schriftstellern der ersten vier Jahrhunderten, TU* 96, Berlin 1966, SS. 105-109; *cf.* K. RUDOLPH, *'Der gnostische "Dialog" als literarisches Genus* in: *Wissenschaftliche Beiträge Martin-Luther-Universität Halle-Wittenberg* 1968/1 (K 2), *Probleme der koptischen Literatur*, SS. 105 ff.

[37]) EPHREM SYRUS, *Contra Haereses* I, 14, 18 (*ed.* E. Beck); *cf.* DRIJVERS, *Bardaiṣan of Edessa*, pp. 157-163.

[38]) EPHREM SYRUS, *Contra Haereses* LV; *cf.* DRIJVERS, *Bardaiṣan of Edessa*, pp. 143 ff.; *Kore Kosmou*, 65-69, *cf. Hermès Trismégiste* IV, pp. cxlvii svv.

[39]) *Cf.* PUECH, *Numénius d'Apamée et les théologies orientales au second siècle*, pp. 770 svv.; DRIJVERS, *Bardaiṣan of Edessa*, p. 173 ff. = *FGH*, III, C, Fr. 719 = STOBAEI, *Anthologium* I (*ed.* Wachsmuth/Hense), 56 sqq.; W. BOUSSET, *Gött. Gel. Anz.* 1914, S. 716; E.-A. LEEMANS, *Studie over de wijsgeer Numenius van Apamea met uitgave der fragmenten*, Bruxelles 1937, pp. 35 vv.; A.-J. FESTUGIÈRE, *'Trois rencontres entre la Grèce et l'Inde'*, RHR CXXV, 1942-43, pp. 32-57.

[40]) DRIJVERS, *Bardaiṣan of Edessa*, pp. 136 ff.

The main themes in the philosophy of Bardaiṣan are the same in which the authors of the Hermetic treatises were interested. The creation of the world, the destiny of the soul, fate and free will, the essence of evil and the quest for the right course of action are discussed both in the Hermetica and in the doctrine of the Aramaic philosopher. Resemblance and difference will now be explicitly considered, in order to contribute to that "vertiefte religionsgeschichtliche Interpretation" of this Aramaic philosophy demanded by a reviewer [41]). Before proceeding with this, it is necessary to specify what we shall understand by Hermetica, since very different entities may be included under this name.

A.-J. Festugière distinguishes the popular Hermetica from the learned. The former include astrological and alchemistic writings and in general, works on the subject of occult sciences. The learned Hermetica comprise the Corpus Hermeticum and a number of fragments preserved int. al. in the work of Stobaeus. It is not possible to derive a coherent doctrine from the writings of the learned Hermetica. The tractates I, IV, VII, XIII and the beginning of XII contain a coherent doctrine of salvation, which one might call the Hermetic gnosis. All writings of the learned Hermetica are marked by a certain "tour d'esprit" directed towards the knowledge of God, which one might also call Hermetic.[42]). Since in the latter meaning the concept is not sufficiently specific — doing no more than suggest a certain spiritual climate — it cannot be used in that sense for the explicit comparison of Bardaiṣan and the Hermetica. Moreover, nearly all the parallels between Bardaiṣan and the Hermetica are found in the tractates mentioned above, and a few in the popular Hermetica. Apart from these latter, we shall in the following therefore understand by Hermetica the Hermetic gnosis of the Poimandres (tractate I) and the tractates IV, VII, XII and XIII and of those fragments agreeing therewith.

Bardaiṣan and the popular Hermetica

The Aramaic philosopher developed a cosmology in which the four pure elements: water, fire, wind and light, have a central place. Their structure is atomic, and each has a different colour, smell, taste, form and sound, corresponding to the five senses. The world originated because these elements by chance became confused, and were then ordered by the Word of Thought. Their atomic structure enables them to enter into an infinite number of combinations, and this was the origin of everything to be found in the world. Ephrem Syrus explicitly states that Bardaiṣan took his notions of the elements, with their structure and properties, from the Greeks [43]). The classical atomic

[41]) C. Colpe, *ThLZ* 93, 1968, Sp. 437; *idem*, in H. H. Schaeder, *Studien zur orientalischen Religionsgeschichte*, Darmstadt 1968, SS. 265-273.

[42]) Festugière, *Hermétisme et mystique païenne*, pp. 38 svv.

[43]) Drijvers, *Bardaiṣan of Edessa*, p. 137; *Ephrem Syrus, Prose Refutations* II, p. cvi (transl.) pp. 223:23-224:7 (syriac text).

theory comes from Democritus, who in Hellenistic times, however was not only regarded as the inventor of this theory, but also as the author of all kinds of apocryphal works on the magical qualities of plants and stones, as the writer of the *Physica et Mystica*, as an astrologer and philosopher, a magician bringing an esoteric doctrine [44]). Democritus had gained his wisdom from Egyptian priests and astrologers, Babylonian magicians and Indian gymnosophists [45]). The interests of Bardaiṣan, who discoursed with Indian gymnosophists and even wrote a book about India, are therefore entirely parallel with those ascribed to the Ionian natural philosopher in Hellenistic times [46]). The *Physica et Mystica* were the first fundamental work on Greek alchemy, and were followed by many other works under the name of Hermes, Ostanes and others. In the fourth century Zosimos is the principal alchemist, and he is also closely connected with the learned Hermetica. The basis of alchemy is that materials and qualities can be mixed and altered in such a way, that if only one knows the correct procedure any desired substance may be manufactured. After all, there were only a few primary elements to begin with, and everything was formed from these. It seems very probable that Bardaiṣan's conception of the atomic structure of the elements with their individual qualities, from whose different combinations everything originated, belongs to this philosophical-alchemistic tradition. That would also explain how it is that Bardaiṣan, in agreement with some Stoics, regarded the qualities of substances as corporeal and attacked the Platonist Albinus. The qualities can be mixed like atomic substances and give rise to other substances with other qualities. Among the Bardesanites there are even some who, consistently following this line, regard spirit and thought as composed of atoms [47]). These spiritual atoms may be mixed to a greater or lesser extent with the other ones, making the bodies more subtle. There are degrees, therefore, of materiality and spirituality, but everything remains material, even the soul of man[48]).

The doctrine of universal sympathy is the foundation of astrological literature, both the Hermetic and the Bardesanite branch. Astrology is not, however, the exclusive possession of the Hermetists or of Bardaiṣan and his followers, but is an element of general education in the Hellenistic period. A special development are the medical and botanical works on an astrological basis under the name of Hermes Trismegistos. The general principle is the existence of a relation between the human body and the cosmos, in particular the planets or

---

44) FESTUGIÈRE, *Révélation* I, pp. 23 svv.; F. CUMONT, *L'Égypte des astrologues*, pp. 122 sv.
45) FESTUGIÈRE, *Révélation*, I, p. 25.
46) DRIJVERS, *Bardaiṣan of Edessa*, pp. 173-175.
47) EPHREM SYRUS, *Prose Refutations* II, p. civ (transl.); p. 220:10-33 (syriac text).
48) DRIJVERS, *Bardaiṣan of Edessa*, pp. 118 ff.

the decanal stars. Man the microcosm is influenced by the macrocosm around him, because there is a special relation between some part of the body or human organ on the one hand and a planet or decanal star on the other [49]. As a similar relation exists between certain plants and planets or decanal stars, this theoretical insight led to the therapeutical use of these plants when a "corresponding" part of the body or organ was affected. Later Bardesanites were acquainted with this doctrine and its literature. Agapius of Mabbuğ and Michael Syrus tell us that according to Bardaiṣan there was a relationship between the parts of the human body and the planets: the brains come from the sun, the hair from Venus, the skin from the moon etc.[50]. Thus Ephrem Syrus and Michael Syrus can say that according to Bardaiṣan the Seven have created man. Analogous conceptions are found with the sect of the Audians in Edessa [51]. In view of the above, it is more than likely that Bardaiṣan was aquainted with ideas and writings, ascribed to Hermes Trismegistos and others, that dealt with alchemy and astrology.

Bardaiṣan and the Hermetic Gnosis

Although Bardaiṣan cannot be looked upon as belonging to the historical phenomenon of gnosticism as it manifested itself in the second century A.D., there is yet reason to speak of the gnosis of Bardaiṣan. In this connection, gnosis is defined as "knowledge of the divine mysteries reserved for an élite" [52]. This description also indicates exactly what is to be understood by the Hermetic gnosis: in that case it is revealed by Hermes Trismegistos. It is misjudging the true character of this gnosis to regard it as an intellectual process alone. Gnosis is both knowledge of the origin, essence and destiny of the world and of man, and also a means for man to live in the world or perhaps to escape from it. Gnosis reveals divine mysteries and also a way of life, and is the only manner of following this way of and to life. Gnosis is the unity of philosophy and ethics that shows man's true essence and how to act in accordance with it. Therefore gnosis is an expression of human selfrespect, and hence can induce the sense of belonging to an elite. God, the world, man and his destination are the central themes of the Hermetic and the Bardesanite gnosis, so that a theological, a cos-

---

49) FESTUGIÈRE, *Révélation* I, pp. 127 svv.

50) AGAPIUS OF MABBUG, *Kitâb al-ʾUnwân*, PO VII, pp. 518-521; MICHAEL SYRUS, *Chronicon* (*ed.* Chabot) I, pp. 109-111; BAR HEBRAEUS, *Sur les Hérésies*, *ed.* F. NAU, PO XIII, pp. 255-56.

51) DRIJVERS, *Bardaiṣan of Edessa*, p. 192; *S. Ephraem Syri Commentarii in Epistolas D. Pauli, a Patribus Mekitharistis translati*, Venetiis 1893, p. 118: . . . "neque hominem omnino dicunt a deo creatum, sed a septem rectoribus . . .".

52) *Cf.* U. BIANCHI (ed.), *Le Origini dello Gnosticismo*, Studies in the History of Religions XII, Leiden 1967, p. xxvi; *cf.* Drijvers, '*The Origins of Gnosticism as a religious and historical problem*', Ned. Theol. Tijdschrift 22, 1967/68, pp. 321-351.

mological, an anthropological and an eschatological aspect may be distinguished in them.

A. *Theology*

Bardaiṣan knows one God, enthroned in the light far above the elements, whose lord he is. This god is called good; he possesses the supreme power, which he can delegate in part to planetary beings. He did not himself create the world, but when the four pure elements happened to be brought into confusion and darkness seized the opportunity of mingling with them, he replied to their call for help by sending the "Word of Thought" who restored order but was unable to drive out darkness completely. Later traditions call this "Word of Thought" Christ, but the earliest traditions do not do so. The ordering principle is therefore the "Word", the Logos, and specifically the "Word of Thought". We may conclude from this that the supreme god is at the same time pure thought, the Nous. Ephrem Syrus in his hymns refers to a Father of Life and a Mother of Life, who together bring forth a son. This seems to contradict the conception of a single god. It is conceivable, however, that this supreme god was imagined as androgynous, while the hymns use the imagery of a Father and a Mother, who are even compared with Sun and Moon [53]).

The most detailed Hermetic theology we find in the first tractate of the Corpus Hermeticum, the Poimandres, a speech of revelation by Poimandres ὁ τῆς αὐθεντίας νοῦς to an ego. This tractate describes the creation of the world and of man and contains an eschatology. There is one supreme god, wholly light, the first Nous, androgynous and father of the Word. This Word keeps the mingled elements of earth and water in continual motion. Later the first Nous brings forth a second Nous, who as demiurge creates the Seven governors, whose administration is the Heimarmene. The Word then unites with the second Nous, his brother, and together they set the spheres of the planets revolving, which causes animal life to originate [54]). The conception of a creative Nous is general in the Hermetica [55]). Possibly the Word, as described in the Poimandres, betrays the influence of the LXX, as C. H. Dodd opines [56]). One gains the impression that originally the scheme only contained a supreme god and a Nous-demiurge ordering chaos. The author returns to this scheme when he has the Word unite with the second Nous, son of the androgynous first Nous.

---

[53]) Ephrem Syrus, *Contra Haereses* LV, 10; LV, 1.

[54]) *Poimandres* 9-11 = *Hermès Trismégiste* I, pp. 9 sv.; *cf.* Festugière, *Hermétisme et mystique païenne*, pp. 51 svv.

[55]) *E.g.* CH VIII; *cf.* Festugière, *Révélation* IV, pp. 59 svv.; pp. 123 svv.

[56]) C. H. Dodd, *The Bible and the Greeks*, London 1954, pp. 99 ff.

The theological scheme of the Poimandres and of the Hermetic gnosis in general is quite the same as that of Bardaiṣan, as even appears from the terminology employed. The Bardesanite Word of Thought functions in the same way as the Hermetic logos and Nous in their work of creation. The conception of the supreme god is to a great extent identical. In contrast to the gnostic systems of the second century, the Hermetica and Bardaiṣan do not regard the creation in itself as an evil: the demiurge is no presumptuous evil god owing to a fall, but a son of the supreme god, bearer of the Nous. Hence the cosmology is a harmonious sequel to the theology and not the story of a divine rebellion.

B. *Cosmology*

The cosmology of the Aramaic philosopher is based on a most simple scheme. Matter, originally consisting of four elements, at a certain moment came into confusion through an unknown cause. The ordering Word of Thought ended the confusion, although a certain quantity of darkness remained in the mixture. Matter as such is the cause of confusion in the world, so that purification is necessary. This view of matter goes back to Plato's *Timaeus* 52D 4 - 53 B 5 [57]). Matter alone without mind means confusion. It was at the creation, then, that mind entered into the world. Exactly how everything was created does not appear from the tradition, only that combinations of atoms in many different variations form the things of this world. The creation of man, not explicitly named in the tradition, is undoubtedly based on the same scheme: the body belongs to matter, soul and spirit are the gift of god [58]).

The same simple scheme also determines the cosmological conceptions of the Hermetic gnosis, at least in so far as the sensible world is concerned. In the intelligible world, the world of the archetypes, there is at first a unity of god and matter, the latter originating from the deity as an image of the archetypal world. Pythagorean speculations regarding the monad and the dyad are the foundation here [59]). From the elements came inanimate nature and animal life through the working of the creative Nous and the planets. Also the body of man is formed of the four elements [60]). This cosmology is taken from the Poimandres, but other tractates offer an analogous picture. In general, matter is here also accounted the cause of confusion, which requires to be checked by a creative spirit [61]).

In the Poimandres the creative Nous is god of fire and pneuma. In the cosmology of Bardaiṣan as transmitted by Theodore bar Khonai we find a con-

57) *Cf.* FESTUGIÈRE, *Révélation* II, pp. 117 svv.; III, p. xii.

58) EPHREM SYRUS, *Prose Refutations* II, p. lxxiii (transl.), p. 158 : 1-11 (syriac text); *cf. Bardaiṣan of Edessa*, pp. 218 ff.

59) FESTUGIÈRE, *Révélation IV*, pp. 32 svv.

60) *Poimandres* 17; *cf.* FESTUGIÈRE, *Hermétisme et mystique païenne*, pp. 55 svv.

61) *E.g.* CH VIII, IX.

ception of the same kind, when the creative Word of Thought is also called "wind of the heights", that is pneuma. It may be that Gen. 1 is of influence here [62]).

Obvious parallels between Bardaiṣan and the Hermetica are also seen in the conception and function of the planets in the cosmological process. In the Hermetic gnosis of the Poimandres the planets, set revolving by the creative Nous and the Word, create animal life. In the creation of man, the chief part is assigned to the archetypal Man who, desirous of creating, enters into the sphere of the planets. When archetypal Man creates the first human beings, their character is given them by the planets, thereby determining their animal existence. In this respect man is therefore subject to the planets [63]). The Bardesanite doctrine teaches that the "animal" existence of man is determined by the power of the Seven [64]). At the same time, Ephrem Syrus says that according to Bardaiṣan the human body was created by the Seven [65]). Also in this field we therefore see a clear agreement between Bardaiṣan and the Hermetica. From theology, cosmology has led us to man. His true being and his destiny are the real interest of the Hermetic authors and of Bardaiṣan, so that the anthropology determines the theology and cosmology and cannot be separated from them, as we see from the above.

C. *Anthropology*

From the *Book of the Laws of Countries* and from the polemic works of Ephrem Syrus Bardaiṣan's anthropology may be reconstructed. Man consists of body, soul and spirit. The body is subject to the laws of nature; the soul, which takes up residence in the body at the moment of birth, comes from the divine world of light, and descends through the spheres of the planets. Each of these imparts something of its qualities to the soul, and that is why the constellation of the stars at the moment of birth decides a man's weal and woe in the world. The spirit is a divine gift to man, tied to the soul, and is that which links man and god. The spirit conveys man's liberty to choose between good and evil. To act rightly is therefore in agreement with the true nature of man, who through his spirit (= liberty) is also master of Fate, although he is subject to it in body. To do what is right of one's own spiritual free-will encompasses the return of the spirit to its origin, the "Bridal-Chamber of Light". The opposition between matter and spirit, which determines the cosmology, returns in the anthropological setting as that between bondage and liberty, or human fate and human

---

[62]) DRIJVERS, *Bardaiṣan of Edessa*, p. 116; DODD, *The Bible and the Greeks*, pp. 103 f.

[63]) *Poimandres* 15; cf. FESTUGIÈRE, *Hermétisme et mystique païenne*, pp. 56 sv.

[64]) *Book of the Laws of Countries*, p. 32, l. 11-19; *cf.* DRIJVERS, *Bardaiṣan of Edessa*, pp. 86 ff.

[65]) See p. 200, n. 52.

essence. The human soul is the vehicle of animal life, and thus has an intermediate position between the body and the spirit [66]).

The anthropology of the Poimandres is altogether identical with the above. Man has a body, a soul and a spirit. The body is composed of the elements and is mortal, according to the course of nature. Soul and spirit determine the essential man, since they represent life and the light of god. Because the planets contributed to the creation of man he is subject to their power, although in essence he is also master of Fate. The nous is not only an intellectual, but also an ethical principle, as man is to live in accordance with his true being = the divine nous. Therefore salvation is reserved for those who do so live in accordance with this nous, that is to say the virtuous. Thus the author of the Poimandres can say that the nous is only given to the virtuous. We found the same correlation between nous and doing what is right with Bardaiṣan [67]). Nous, then, is both man's true being and his destiny, and the means of attaining it, if a man has the moral courage to act after his true nature [68]). This explains that both the Hermetists and the Aramaic philosopher turned their thoughts to the problem of bondage and liberty, or the power of Fate and free will, since the latter is a necessary condition for moral conduct and the ultimate attainment of salvation to be possible. As a result, their solution to the problem is very similar. Bardaiṣan restricted the power of Fate to the strictly corporeal, and showed in an empirical argumentation, by making use of the νόμιμα βαρβαρικά that human liberty is stronger than the power of Fate [69]). This view we also find in the Poimandres and in tractate XII [70]). Fate only works upon the body through the soul, the nous is above it, since that is an emanation of the divine Nous, as a sun-ray is of the sun. The idea as it is explained in tractate XII recalls the Stoa; the nous makes it possible for man to subdue the passions of the body. These passions are aroused by that which Fate has ordained for our corporeal existence. What Fate has appointed cannot be undone, but need not lead to evil if man only follows his nous. In this connection, as in the Book of the Laws of Countries, the question is discussed whether punishment is justified: man is only judged and punished for that which he does in freedom [71]). Here we meet with the ideal of the true sage, who appears in all kinds of variations in the religious history and philosophy of Hellenistic times. The true sage foi-

---

[66]) *Cf.* Drijvers, *Bardaiṣan of Edessa*, pp. 76-95; 152-157.

[67]) *Poimandres* 21-23; cf. *Hermétisme et mystique païenne*, pp. 58 svv.; *Book of the Laws of Countries* p. 16, l. 6-8; 18, l. 19-24.

[68]) *Cf.* Festugière, *Hermétisme et mystique païenne*, pp. 80 svv.; *Révélation* III, pp. 18 svv.

[69]) *Book of the Laws of Countries*, p. 41-63; cf. Drijvers, *Bardaiṣan of Edessa*, pp. 90 ff.

[70]) *Poimandres* 15, 24-26; *CH* XII, 5-9; *cf. Révélation* II, pp. 64 svv.; *Hermès Trismégiste* III, p. lxxix ss.; *Hermès Trismégiste* I, pp. 193 svv.; *Hermétisme et mystique païenne*, pp. 60 svv.

[71]) *Book of the Laws of Countries*, p. 14, l. 12-18.

lows his nous, and this makes him superior to Fate. Bardaiṣan and his followers share this view with the Hermetists. Zosimos in his treatise on the letter Omega quotes a Hermetic writing on the non-material to the effect that according to Hermes and Zarathustra the sages are above Destiny [72]).

Both in the Hermetic gnosis, then, and in the doctrine of Bardaiṣan the nous is something metaphysical in man, and so it is the road to salvation, attained when the spirit returns to its origin. All of life is a preparation for the attainment of full salvation, so that the soteriology is completely covered by the eschatology. This applies both to the individual and to the world, where good and evil are mixed together, yet this state of mixture will not endure forever.

D. *Eschatology and Soteriology*

The ties between body, soul and spirit which are formed at the birth of a human being, are broken again in dying, after which each part goes to its own destination. The whole tradition about Bardaiṣan is unanimous in saying he denied the resurrection of the body because the body was only material. To matter it returns, and the composing elements, being of an atomic structure, enter into new combinations [73]). The soul, to which the spirit is bound, is on the one hand material because it consists of subtle elements (light and fire?), on the other hand it consists of seven parts, having received something from each of the planets while descending to the body. Considering the material aspect of the soul, we may suppose it perishes at man's death. Considering the planetary aspect, the soul will, rising up through the spheres of heaven, render to each planetary sphere that which it had received until, pure nous, it enters in to the "Bridal-Chamber of Light" [74]). This return has become possible because Christ taught the truth, whereby the impediments caused by Adam's sin were removed [75]). The sin of Adam did not, therefore, bring about death, but it made the return of the soul impossible. Thus the truth brought by Christ has an ethical and an intellectual aspect. Christ teaches man the Good in accordance with his true being, and an understanding of that true being. He introduces man to freedom i.e. the nous, and shows him how to use that freedom in order to return to his origin. Faith and knowledge, according to the school of Bar-

---

[72]) *Hermès Trismégiste* IV, p. 117 sv., fragment 20 = *Zosimus* III xlix 3-4 = BERTHELOT/RUELLE, p. 229 = *Mages Hellénisés* II, p. 243; *cf.* FESTUGIÈRE, *Révélation* I, p. 44, 266 (translation).

[73]) EPHREM SYRUS, *Prose Refutations* II, p. cii (transl.), p. 215:13-44 (syriac text); DRIJVERS, *Bardaiṣan of Edessa*, pp. 139 ff.; *Prose Refutations*, II, p. lxvi (transl.), p. 143: 1-24 (syriac text); *cf. Bardaiṣan of Edessa*, p. 153 ff.

[74]) *Prose Refutations* II, p. lxxvii (transl.), p. 164:32-40 (syriac text).

[75]) *Prose Refutations* II, p. lxxvii (transl.), p. 164:41-165:12 (syriac text); *cf. Bardaiṣan of Edessa*, p. 155.

daiṣan, purify creation by liberating the nous from it, thus bringing creation to its completion [76]).

In the cosmology of Bardaiṣan as transmitted by Moses bar Kepha and Îwannîs of Dàrâ, the creative Word of Thought, the Nous, is said to be Christ. This makes the impression of being a later addition, as neither Ephrem Syrus nor Theodore bar Khonai have any such reference, nor does the conception appear in the Book of the Laws of Countries [77]). It is a plausible inference that the spiritual principle in creation, the Nous, is the most original. The human nous is identical with it, both in form and function, and constitutes the possibility of return to the world of light, if man shall have used the power of nous to order the chaos of existence and to push back evil. The fundamental conception would then be, that the creative nous is also the rescuing nous: this is a form of gnosis, not of gnosticism. If this is right, belief in the power of the human spirit, which is a divine spirit, would be the driving force in this doctrine of salvation that already begins at creation.

C. Colpe wrote in a review of *Bardaiṣan of Edessa*: "Es wäre für die Geschichte der Gnosis und die Vorgeschichte des Manichäismus, zu der Drijvers S. 225 f. selbst einiges sagt, entscheidend wichtig, zu wissen, ob eine Erlöserlehre wie diese ohne Einfluss oder Konkurrenz von Christologie konzipiert werden konnte oder nicht" [78]). The answer, in so far as possible, has been given above: the Christological elements are secondary and fitted into an existing schema, which we also find in the Hermetic gnosis and elsewhere. This schema, however, offers every possibility of connecting and assimilating it with a logos-Christology, so that it obtained a place in the Praeparatio Evangelica. The Hermetic fragments of Cyrillus make that very plain [79]).

The eschatology of the Hermetic gnosis is again most clearly set forth in the Poimandres. The body is yielded up to the ἀλλοίωσις, so that its component parts in other combinations can continue to work in the material universe, just as Bardaiṣan teaches. The soul consists of a material part, the ἄλογον and a non-material part, the λογικόν or νοητικόν. While it is said that the ἄλογον returns to matter, it is also stated that its component parts, the πάθη, return to the planets. The nous, the perfect spiritual man, stripped of everything that impeded him, enters into the Ogdoad and is absorbed in the divine beings, the

---

[76]) *Prose Refutations* II, p. xcvii (transl.), p. 206:31-39 (syriac text) cf. *Bardaiṣan of Edessa*, p. 141.

[77]) *Bardaiṣan of Edessa*, pp. 101 f ; 110.

[78]) C. Colpe, ThLZ 93, 1968, Sp. 437; *idem* in: Nachwort to H. H. Schaeder, *Studien zur orientalischen Religionsgeschichte*, S. 271: "War der absteigende Logos nur als Christus oder auch in Konkurrenz zu diesem oder auch rein innerhellenistisch mythologisierbar ?"

[79]) *Hermès Trismégiste* IV, pp. 126-146.

consummation of the gnosis (θεωθῆναι) [80]). The close agreement between Bardaiṣan and the Hermetic gnosis need be argued no further.

In the stricter sense, then, the Hermetic gnosis has no saviour,: the νοῦς is the way to salvation when it has received the gnosis, viz. that it comes from God and will return to Him, and if it has the courage to act accordingly in full liberty [81]). This gnosis is revealed by Hermes Trismegistos, as Jesus revealed this truth for Bardaiṣan. The central role, however, in the drama of man is played by the divine nous that delivers itself. There is no question of a fall, so that no saviour is required, only a teacher of wisdom, who makes man conscious of his nous, and points out the road of life to him.

Bardaiṣan and the philosophy of his time

In the second century philosophers were more particularly teachers to direct men wisely in their earthly existence. From the philosophical point of view they were eclectics, offering a doctrine of salvation rather than thinking out philosophical problems for themselves. All attention was directed upon those aspects of reality that are constitutive for human existence, i.e. upon cosmology and psychological anthropology. This is the intellectual climate of Bardaiṣan and the Hermetists, so it is obvious that many of his ideas will be similar to those of other thinkers of his day.

To illustrate this thesis, we have some parallel thoughts developed by Bardaiṣan and Numenius of Apamea, whom we already mentioned in the introduction. Numenius and Bardaiṣan have in common their interest in exotic phenomena and esoteric wisdom. They also have very much the same conception of the origin of the world. Numenius has a supreme god, pure spirit and perfect goodness (αὐτοαγαθόν). Next there is a second god, a creative νοῦς, who orders chaotic matter. This second god shares both in the purely spiritual world and in the matter which he orders into a cosmos. Thus the cosmos may be regarded as a third god, in a sense one with the second. In this way the entire schema shows a gradual decrease in spirituality [82]). The distinction between the second and the third god is really quite artificial, and only meant to express both aspects of the second νοῦς, belonging both to the intelligible and to the sensible world. To a great extent, then, the cosmology of Numenius is exactly like that of Bardaiṣan.

Their psychology is in the same case. Numenius distinguishes two souls in

[80]) *Poimandres* 24-26; *cf. Révélation* III, pp. 124 svv.; *Hermès Trismégiste* I, p. 25, n. 63; Addenda p. 303; F. CUMONT, *Lux Perpetua*, pp. 185 svv.

[81]) FESTUGIÈRE, *Hermétisme et mystique païenne*, pp. 80 sv.

[82]) *Cf.* PUECH, *Numénius d'Apamée*, pp. 755 svv.; E. R. DODDS, '*Numenius and Ammonius*' in: *Entretiens sur l'antiquité classique* V, *Les Sources de Plotin*, Genève 1960, pp. 3-32; *Révélation* III, pp. 42 svv.; IV, 123 svv.; LEEMANS, *Studie over den wijsgeer Numenius van Apamea*, Bruxelles 1937, pp. 35-75.

man that are interlinked, a material and a purely spiritual one. The purely spiritual soul is a part of the divine νοῦς, to which it returns after death if a man has led a virtuous life. The non-rational soul consists of very subtle matter forming the pneuma, which has accrued to the soul during the descent through the spheres of the planets. After death, the reverse route is followed [83]. The similarity to Bardaiṣan's teaching is evident.

The doctrine of the two souls or of the two constituent parts of the soul, is neo-Pythagorean. We also find neo-Pythagorean influence in the Oracula Chaldaica, which in their turn probably influenced Numenius [84]. The cosmology taught by the Oracula is more or less the same as that of Numenius and Bardaiṣan [85], but there are other resemblances also to the doctrine of the Aramaic philosopher. Bardaiṣan compares the Sun and Moon to the Father and Mother of Life, who plant a paradise together and people it with their descendants. This paradise is also called "isles of the blest" and is situated in heaven[86]. The Oracula regard paradise as the abode of Truth = the Sun, Virtue = the Moon and Wisdom = Mercury [87]. Bardaiṣan speaks of a Son, the child of a Father and a Mother [88]. This may be understood in a christological sense, or one may think of Nebo as son of Bêl and Atargatis, but in view of the parallel with the Oracula, one may also think of Hermes as embodiment of wisdom, the child of truth and virtue.

In the neo-Pythagorean catechism the question, what the isles of the blest were, was answered: "sun and moon" [89]. We find the same in the Oracula Chaldaica and with Bardaiṣan, whose ideas regarding paradise and the way to reach it are much the same. If such kinship between the Oracula and the Aramaic philosopher may be justly claimed, it would also suggest why Porphyrius was so interested in the work of the Edessene thinker. The neo-Platonist, indeed, in his *Peri stygos* and *De abstinentia ab esu animalium*, preserved fragments of Bardaiṣan's works [90]. Porphyrius was also the first neo-Platonist to attempt to harmonise the doctrine of the Oracula with neo-Platonism, quoting extensively from them in his writings [91]. The Oracula and the works of the

---

[83]) DODDS, '*Numenius and Ammonius*', pp. 7 ff.; LEEMANS, *Numenius van Apamea*, p. 63.

[84]) E. R. DODDS, *New Light on the "Chaldean Oracles"*, HThR LIV, 1961, pp. 263-273.; *idem*, *Numenius and Ammonius*, p. 10.

[85]) *Oracula Chaldaïca* (*ed.* KROLL), p. 14; H. LEWY, *Chaldean Oracles and Theurgy*, Le Caire 1956, pp. 137 ff.

[86]) *Bardaiṣan of Edessa*, p. 195; EPHREM SYRUS, *Contra Haereses* LV, 8, 10.

[87]) LEWY, *Chaldaean Oracles and Theurgy*, p. 221.

[88]) EPHREM SYRUS, *Contra Haereses* LV, 1; *cf. Bardaiṣan of Edessa*, pp. 144 ff.

[89]) A. DELATTE, *Études sur la littérature pythagoricienne*, 1915, pp. 249-268; *cf.* FESTUGIÈRE, *Révélation*, I, p. 16.

[90]) DRIJVERS, *Bardaiṣan of Edessa*, p.p 173-176.

[91]) LEWY, *Chaldaean Oracles*, pp. 3 ff.

Aramaic philosopher belong to the same spiritual climate, where the *regressus animae*, to vary the title of a work of Porphyrius, formed a centre of interest.

Conclusion

Living in a cultural centre of the first order in the north of Mesopotamia in the second century as he did, Bardaiṣan was in many ways linked with the philosophy of his time. He was influenced by it, and the way in which he worked out the traditional material for himself had much in common with the thought of the Hermetists and similar philosophers. Undoubtedly further research will show these ties to be even closer. The general trend, however, has become quite clear: the Aramaic philosopher has a place in a Hellenistic philosophical tradition where soul and matter, freedom and fate are the focal centres of interest, and thinking is directed upon the subject-matter of the Timaeus.

Yet Bardaiṣan's role is far greater than that of a brilliant representative of mediocre philosophical thought. He is always traditionally represented as the teacher of Mani, who "went through the door that Bardaiṣan had set ajar", as Ephrem Syrus put it, referring to the consistent dualistic development of the potentialities of Bardaiṣan's system [92]). H. H. SCHAEDER once set Mani in "vulgär-philosophische Tradition griechischen Ursprungs", on which he depends "durch christlich-gnostische Vermittlung" [93]). This is a good description of the part played by Bardaiṣan and of its importance, which the above makes more apparent. Besides Greek philosophy, SCHAEDER looked upon the "Heilsverkündigung Jesu" as the second root of Manichaeism, which he held to be a higher unity of the Christian doctrine of grace and the Greek concept of the world. The latter conclusion does not seem to be justified. The concept of the divine and the human nous in the tradition of Hellenistic philosophy does not need the impulse of Christianity to become a doctrine of salvation. The nous is embodied in many teachers of wisdom, of whom Jesus of Nazareth is one, beside Hermes Trismegistos, Orpheus, and Zarathustra. It may be that the Bardesanites helped to pass on this "Hermetic" tradition to Mani. In Manichaeism, Hermes Trismegistos is one of the "Heralds of the Good One to the World", together with Plato, Buddha, Zarathustra and Jesus, as Ephrem Syrus tells us [94]). The whole philosophical tradition of Hellenism thus exercised its influence

---

[92]) *Prose Refutations* I, p. xc (transl.), p. 122 (syriac text); *cf. Bardaiṣan of Edessa*, pp. 225 ff.

[93]) H. H. SCHAEDER, *'Der Manichäismus nach neuen Funden und Forschungen'*, in F. TAESCHNER, *Orientalische Stimmen zum Erlösungsgedanken*, Morgenland 28, Leipzig 1936, S. 99; *idem*, *'Urform und Fortbildungen des manichäischen Systems* in: *Vorträge der Bibliothek Warburg* IV, Leipzig 1927, SS. 65-157.

[94]) *Prose Refutations* II, p. xcviii; cf. F. C. BURKITT, *The Religion of the Manichees*, Cambridge 1925, p. 96; AUGUSTINUS, *Contra Faustum* XIII, 1; *cf. Hermès Trismégiste*, IV, p. 146.

upon Mani via Bardaiṣan, as this tradition must also be invoked for the explanation of Manichaean conceptions. To mention only one instance, it seems to me that the Manichaean view of the role of Sun and Moon in the process of salvation cannot be properly considered without having regard to the Oracula Chaldaica, Bardaiṣan and neo-Pythagorism.

The Aramaic philosopher also has a place at the head of a Hermetic tradition in Mesopotamia, which in a later period can be identified through notices referring to the Harranian Sabians and other Muslim sects. A new investigation of these Sabians will have to take account of Bardesanite traditions, since particularly in these circles an unbroken tradition of Hermetic philosophy existed from the second to the ninth century.

As Toth was worshipped in Egypt, so Mesopotamia worshipped Nabu or Nebo. In Hellenistic times both gods were equated with Hermes, god of wisdom. This is a symptom "eines babylonischen Hellenismus, der sich von der zeitgenössischen hellenistischen Kultur Syriens and Ägyptens nicht grundsätzlich unterschied" [95]). Bardaiṣan's philosophy clearly illustrates the truth of these words of Hans Heinrich SCHAEDER, who more than any other scholar of his generation has developed the theme "Der Orient und das griechische Erbe". "Bardaiṣan of Edessa and the Hermetica" is no more than a variation on this theme.

Groningen

---

[95]) SCHAEDER, '*Der Manichäismus nach neuen Funden und Forschungen*', S. 99.

XII

Bardaiṣan von Edessa als Repräsentant des syrischen Synkretismus im 2. Jahrhundert n. Chr.

Vor fünfeinhalb Jahren erschien mein Buch „Bardaiṣan of Edessa", eine Darstellung seines Lebens und Denkens und ein Versuch, aus den Nachrichten von ihm sein Erlebnismuster zu ermitteln: wie es im Edessa des 2. Jahrhunderts n.Chr.[0] in Wirklichkeit war. Das Wirkliche ist aber die Spannung zwischen Entwurf und Fertigem, so daß genügend Raum bleibt, die Geschichte Bardaiṣans, auf Grund der überlieferten Nachrichten aufs neue zu prüfen. Kein einziger Entwurf bleibt ohne Widerspruch, einmal deswegen, weil eine erneute Begegnung mit den Überlieferungen von und über Bardaiṣan stattfindet, zum anderen, weil der Autor und andere neue Erfahrungen gemacht haben. Dieses Symposium ist also der Anlaß, in einer Konfrontation mit mir selbst und anderen den alten Entwurf erneut zu prüfen und aufs neue zu versuchen, der Wirklichkeit Bardaiṣans näherzukommen.

Der ursprüngliche Entwurf wurde von Kritikern und Rezensenten auf Fehler untersucht, die Materialien sind ergänzt worden, und man hat den Wunsch geäußert, den Gegenstand neu zu untersuchen. Einige haben sich aufs neue in die Quellen vertieft und sind zu anderen Entwürfen gelangt oder haben sogar behauptet, es sei grundsätzlich unmöglich, auf Grund des überlieferten Materials Leben und Denken Bardaiṣans auch nur annäherungsweise darzustellen. Es ist kurzum die Rede von einem erneuten Interesse für Bardaiṣan innerhalb des ganzen Fragenbereichs, der mit der Geschichte des ältesten Christentums in Syrien als einer Komponente des Synkretismus im syrisch-persischen Kulturgebiet verbunden ist.

Den Rezensenten, die Mühe darauf verwenden, Fehler eines Autors bei der Deutung bestimmter Texte zu verbessern oder Druckfehler anzuzeigen, ist jeder zu Dank verpflichtet. Mein Dank gilt namentlich A. de Halleux, der die Interpretation einiger Texte des Philoxenos von Mabbug verbesserte, S. P. Brock, der dasselbe mit einem Text aus dem LV. Hymnus contra Haereses von Ephrem tat, sowie A. J. M. Davids und B. Aland, die, wie auch andere, die Aufmerksamkeit auf eine Reihe

---

[0] H. J. W. Drijvers, Bardaiṣan of Edessa, Studia Semitica Neerlandica 6, Assen 1966.

110

von Druckfehlern und Ungenauigkeiten lenkten[1]. Die Zahl der Dokumente über Bardaiṣan hat sich vergrößert, da Ph. Gignoux die Forschung auf einen Text von Narsai aus den Homilien über die Schöpfung aufmerksam machte, wo dieser mit Bardaiṣan und Mani polemisiert[2]. G. Vajda veröffentlichte einen Auszug aus dem *Kitāb at- Tauḥīd* von al-Māturīdī (gest. 944), der die Lehren der Manichäer, der Daiṣaniten und der Markioniten enthält. In diesem Rahmen zitiert er noch andere muslimische Autoren, die Bardaiṣan und seinen Jüngern einige Zeilen gewidmet haben, ohne jedoch der bekannten Überlieferung etwas Neues hinzuzufügen[3].

Diese revidierte und ergänzte Materialsammlung bietet aber noch zahllose Schwierigkeiten für den Versuch, von den disparaten Quellen her Aufschlüsse über Person und Denken Bardaiṣans zu gewinnen. T. Jansma, dessen Rezension meines „Bardaiṣan of Edessa" sich zu einer richtigen Monographie entwickelte, ist so sehr von der Verschiedenheit der Quellen beeindruckt, daß er es für unmöglich hält, die wirklichen Ansichten Bardaiṣans zu rekonstruieren[4]. Das „Buch der Gesetze der Län-

---

1 Folgende Rezensionen sind bis heute erschienen: Syria 43 (1966), S. 322–325 (J. Leroy); Ned. Theol. Tijdschr. 21 (1966/67), S. 45–47 (G. Quispel); L'Orient Syrien 12 (1967), S. 123–125 (Ph. Gignoux); Speculator 16,2 (1967) (P. Vermeülen); Recherches de Science Religieuse 1967, S. 143–147 (J. Daniélou); JA. 1967, S. 154–155 (G. Vajda); RSPhTh 51 (1967), S. 682 (P.-Th. Camelot); Le Muséon 1968, S. 273–274 (A. de Halleux); ThRv 64 (1968), S. 94f. (A.-Th. Khoury); ThLZ 93 (1968), Sp. 435–437 (C. Colpe); OLZ 63 (1968), Sp. 366–367 (W. Hage); RHR 1969, S. 211–213 (A. Guillaumont); BSOAS 32 (1969), S. 603–604 (J. B. Segal); Irénikon 3 (1969), S. 399–400 (E. D.); Etudes Grégoriennes 10 (1969), S. 182–183 (L.R.); JSS 1970, S. 114–115 (S. P. Brock); Kairos 1970, S. 147–151 (A. J. M. Davids); Edizione dell'ateneo, Roma 1970, S. 282–283 (M. Simonetti); ZRGG 22 (1970), S. 279 (E. Bammel); ZKG 1970, S. 334–351: Barbara Ehlers, Bardesanes von Edessa – ein syrischer Gnostiker. Bemerkungen aus Anlaß des Buches von H. J. W. Drijvers, Bardaiṣan of Edessa; Bulletin de Littérature ecclésiastique 2 (1971) (M. Delcor).

2 A. Mingana, Narsai Doctoris Syri Homiliae et Carmina II, S. 218, 5–15; vgl. Ph. Gignoux, L'Orient Syrien 12 (1967), S. 124–125. Inzwischen erschien S. Brock, Didymus the Blind on Bardaiṣan, JThS, NS 22 (1971), S. 530–531, der auf einen Text in Didymus' Psalmenkommentar (ed. A. Gesché/M. Gronewald, Bonn 1969, S. 182–184) über Bardaiṣans Leben aufmerksam machte: „Bardaiṣan lived in former times, in the days of Antoni(n)us the Roman emperor. At first he belonged to the school of Valentinus, but (later) he went over to the church and became a priest" (Übersetzung von S. Brock).

3 G. Vajda, Le témoignage d'al-Māturīdī sur la doctrine des Manichéens, des Daiṣanites et des Marcionites, Arabica 13 (1966), S. 1–38; 113–128, spez. 23–31.

4 T. Jansma, Natuur, lot en vrijheid. Bardesanes, de Filosoof der Arameeërs en zijn images, Cahiers bij het Ned. Theol. Tijdschr. 6, Wageningen 1969; siehe die Rezension von A. J. M. Davids, OrChr 55 (1971) S. 233–235.

der" zeigt uns einen Philosophen, dessen einziges Ziel darin besteht, die Möglichkeit der Freiheit, und damit ethischen Verhaltens, gegen den astralen Determinismus zu verteidigen. Der Bardaiṣan des Dialogs ist der rationale Philosoph, ein Monotheist, der in die Reihe der Apologeten, Philosophen und diskutierenden Rabbis hineingehört. Der Bardaiṣan des LV. Hymnus contra Haereses von Ephrem Syrus, in dem eine Anzahl Hymnenzitate von ihm vorkommen, ist ein überschwenglicher Dichter, welcher der Natur entnommene Bilder verwendet, um einen unverblümten Polytheismus zu lehren. Bardaiṣan, wie Ephrem ihn in den anderen Hymni contra Haereses und in seinen Prose Refutations of Mani, Marcion und Bardaiṣan zeichnet, ist ein äußerst widersprüchlicher Mensch. Obwohl Monotheist, lehrt er doch die Existenz einer Anzahl ungeschaffener *ityē* neben dem einen Gott. Er lehrt die Willensfreiheit, tut aber der Allmacht Gottes Abbruch, indem er diese Freiheit einschränkt. Er ist Astrologe, lehrt aber nicht einen konsequenten Determinismus, – kurz er ist, äußerlich gesehen, untadelig, lästert aber insgeheim den Namen Gottes. Ephrem sieht hinter Bardaiṣan, dem weltmännischen Hofmann, immer das bleiche asketische Antlitz Manis auftauchen, der „durch die Tür schritt, die von Bardaiṣan geöffnet worden war", wie Ephrem sagt. Schließlich gibt es noch den Dichter des kosmogonischen Mythos, der in vier Fassungen überliefert wurde. Jansma sieht zwar ein Grundmotiv, das der kosmogonische Mythos und der Dialog gemeinsam haben, glaubt aber, daß die gesamte Überlieferung so schlecht zu diesem Grundmotiv paßt, daß jede Rekonstruktion der Anschauungen Bardaiṣans von vornherein zum Mißlingen verdammt sei. Offenbar konnte der historische Bardaiṣan einen Ausgleich zwischen den großen Gegensätzen in seinem Geiste schaffen. Seine Lehre ermöglichte eine katholische Deutung, indem sie den Logos einführte, sowie eine manichäische, indem sie die Gestalt der passiven Finsternis zum aktiven Feind machte. In einer ausführlichen Auseinandersetzung mit Jansma, die an anderer Stelle erfolgte, habe ich die Meinung vertreten, daß es möglich ist, die Grundzüge des Dialogs, des kosmogonischen Mythos und der Daten aus den Hymni contra Haereses sowie der Prose Refutations von Ephrem zu einer getreuen Wiedergabe von Bardaiṣans Lehre zusammenzufügen – wenigstens zu einer Wiedergabe der Hauptzüge dieser Lehre. Im Dialog wird eine Anthropologie entwickelt, in der die Dialektik von Freiheit und Gebundenheit im Menschenleben eine zentrale Stelle einnimmt. Diese Anthropologie, die drei Ebenen im Menschenleben unterscheidet – Geist, Seele und Körper –, von denen erstere die Freiheit verkörpert und letztere die vollkommene Gebundenheit, ist eine Parallele zu Bardaiṣans Kosmologie. Diese wird im Dialog am Rande angedeutet und kennt eine Dialektik von Harmonie und Vermischung, die mit derjenigen von Freiheit und Gebundenheit übereinstimmt. Ephrem kennt sowohl Bardaiṣans Lehre von der eingeschränkten menschlichen Freiheit als auch seine Kosmologie, so daß diese drei Quellen die Stützen bilden, die die Rekonstruktion des Gerüstes der Lehren Bardaiṣans tragen müssen. Ephrem hat daneben noch Sondergut, das man aber nicht ohne weiteres unberücksichtigt lassen kann. Weil er eine gewissenhafte Wiedergabe der Gedanken Bardaiṣans bietet und ihre Ambiguität deutlich zeigt, scheint es mir methodisch falsch zu sein, das Ephremsche Sondergut, weil es zu dem Sonstigen im Widerspruch steht, von vornherein zu streichen oder es dem Harmonius, Bardaiṣans Sohn, zuzuschreiben, wie Jansma es mit den Hymnenfragmenten aus Hymnus LV tut. Bardaiṣans Lehre ist dualistisch in einem monistischen Rahmen und eignet sich deshalb für eine Weiterentwicklung in entgegengesetzten Richtungen[5].

Eine zentrale Stelle in der ganzen Überlieferung nimmt der kosmogonische Mythos ein, weil ein Vergleich der vier Rezensionen vielleicht zum ursprünglichen Bardaiṣanischen Mythos führen könnte. Jansma und Davids haben sich je mit einem Aspekt dieser Tradition beschäftigt. Jansma untersuchte die Fassung, die von Barḥadbešabbā ʿArbaya überliefert worden ist. Am Schluß dieser Fassung stehen die rätselhaften Worte:

> „Und was dasjenige betrifft, das noch nicht gereinigt ist, er wird am Ende kommen, es reinigen und folgendes sprechen: ‚Das Wesen, welches das, was neben ihm war, angriff, geriet in heftige Bewegung und hat dieses in die Tiefe verscheucht; die schwarze Finsternis erhob sich und hat die glänzenden Wesen geschwärzt.' "

In einer minuziösen und scharfsinnigen Analyse hat Jansma gezeigt, daß hier eigentlich eine Textkorruption vorliegt, die auf eine Variante in der ursprünglichen Fassung der Überlieferung zurückzuführen ist. Die reinen Elemente sind nämlich in einer horizontalen Ebene geordnet, aber Barḥadbešabbā läßt auch die Kenntnis einer vertikalen Ordnung nach Schwere erkennen. Ephrem kennt diese Ordnung neben der horizontalen ebenfalls. Das Ende der Zeiten und die Vollendung des Reinigungsprozesses ist dann das Werk des Logos, während die Worte „und folgendes sprechen" die Einleitung bilden zu einem Zitat von Bardaiṣan selbst. Diese Hypothese wird gestützt durch den metrischen Charakter des betreffenden Zitates, eines Verses von sechs Silben. Es hat also eine Überlieferung des kosmogonischen Mythos gegeben, die beide Fassungen

---

[5] H. J. W. Drijvers, De Schilder en de Kunstcriticus. Discussies rond een portret van Bardesanes, de filosoof der Arameeërs, NedThT 24 (1969), S. 89–104; T. Jansma, Bardesanes van Edessa en Hermogenes van Carthago, NedThT 24 (1969), S. 256–259; H. J. W. Drijvers, Het image van Bardesanes van Edessa, 24 (1969), S. 260–262.

erwähnte, welche Ephrem kannte[6]. Diese Hypothese ist in jeder Hinsicht akzeptabel; sie vermag außerdem einen Passus in dem kosmogonischen Mythos nach der Fassung des Theodor bar Konai zu erklären. Nachdem das reine Element ‚Wind' dasjenige, das neben ihm lag, erreicht hatte, sagt Theodors Text: „Das Feuer begann im Wald zu brennen, und ein dunkler Rauch ballte sich zusammen, der kein Produkt des Feuers war, und die reine Luft wurde in Verwirrung gebracht (...)". Wie H. H. Schaeder zum ersten Mal bemerkt hat, ist ʿ*b*ʾ, (Wald) hier eine Wiedergabe des griechischen ὕλη, „Materie". Das Feuer steigt also ab in die Materie, d.h. die Finsternis, die einen dunklen Rauch verbreitet, wodurch alle Elemente ihre glänzende Reinheit verlieren. Hyle (ὕλη) ist bei Theodor bar Konai also eine Bezeichnung für die Finsternis, wie B. Aland mit Recht bemerkt[7]. Dann ist aber festzustellen, daß die Fassung von Theodor bar Konai auf jeden Fall gekürzt ist. Ferner verdient die Tatsache Aufmerksamkeit, daß der kosmogonische Mythos nach Barḥadbešabbā als einziger der vier Fassungen sagt, daß der Logos, das Wort des Denkens, am Ende der Welt zurückkehren wird (also nach 6000 Jahren), um den Reinigungsprozeß zu vollenden. Dies ist nur noch im Buch der Gesetze der Länder zu lesen, wo der Logos eine didaktische Funktion am Ende der Zeiten hat. Man fragt sich, ob sich dies möglicherweise auf das Erscheinen Jesu von Nazareth bezieht, dessen Lehre eine neue Welt – in einer neuen Vermischung, sagt das Buch der Gesetze der Länder – einleitet. Wie dem auch sei, der kosmogonische Mythos nach Barḥadbešabbā hat einerseits Beziehungen zu den polemischen Schriften Ephrems: Barḥadbešabbā kennt, ebenso wie Ephrem, die beiden Ordnungsmodelle der reinen Elemente; andererseits, hinsichtlich der eschatologischen Funktion des Logos, berührt es sich mit dem Buch der Gesetze der Länder. Der äußerst kritische Jansma behauptet sogar, daß „Bardesanes eine Anspielung auf eine übereinstimmende Darstellung macht in einem Dialog, der von seinem Schüler Philippus zu Papier gebracht wurde (...)"; dort heißt es, daß die Ordnung und die Regel, die gegeben sind, und die Vermischung des einen mit dem anderen die Gewalt der Naturen eingeschränkt hat, damit sie weder ganz und gar schädlich seien, noch ganz und gar geschädigt würden, so wie sie schädlich waren und Schaden erlitten vor der Schöpfung der Welt[8].

Davids hat eine Reihe von Ausdrücken in der kosmogonischen Überlieferung untersucht. Er stellte fest, daß Moses bar Kephas Ausdruck,

---

[6] T. Jansma, La notice de Barḥadbešabba ʿArbaïa sur l'hérésie des Daiṣanites, in: Mémorial Mgn. Gabriel Khouri-Sarkis. Leuven, 1969, S. 91–106.

[7] Bardesanes von Edessa – ein syrischer Gnostiker, ZKG 1970 S. 347.

[8] Jansma, La notice de Barḥadbešabba, S. 97; Liber Legum Regionum, ed. F. Nau, PS II, col. 608; vgl: Drijvers, Bardaiṣan of Edessa, S. 93f.

daß die Elemente in Verwirrung gerieten, *'n mn gušm' w'n mn gdš'*, eine Korruption des Ausdrucks *'n mn šgm'* ist, die wir in den anderen überlieferten Texten finden. An zweiter Stelle macht er wahrscheinlich, daß dort, wo Barḥadbešabbā von der *rešanuthon gauwaita* der reinen Elemente, und wo Theodor bar Konai von der *rešithon gbita* spricht, der Text des letzteren korrupt ist, um so mehr, weil dort *rešanuthon gauwaita* mit *'uzza d-ḥattituthon* = ‚die sie in ihrer Eigenart bestimmende Kraft' übereinstimmt. Dies lesen wir im Buch der Gesetze der Länder, wo es über die Vermischung der *ityē* spricht, wobei diese *ityē* einen Teil ihrer *'uzza d-ḥattituthon* preisgeben müssen[9]. Schließlich weist Davids auf die Verwechslung von *paizin* und *pairin* in den Fassungen von Barḥadbešabba und Moses bar Kepha hin, wobei der ursprüngliche Wortlaut schwer festzustellen ist. Wiederum muß festgestellt werden, daß Davids inhaltliche Beziehungen zwischen der kosmogonischen Überlieferung und dem Buch der Gesetze der Länder erblickt, wo es sich um die Eigenschaften der *ityē* handelt.

Den kräftigsten Widerspruch erfuhr mein Entwurf von Bardaiṣans Lehre vonseiten B. Alands, die in zwei Aufsätzen eine Ansicht darlegte, die der meinigen radikal entgegengesetzt ist[10]. Der Titel des zweiten Aufsatzes: „Bardesanes von Edessa – ein syrischer Gnostiker" hat programmatische Bedeutung. B. Aland betrachtet Bardaiṣans Lehre als „durch und durch gnostisch". Indem sie sich auf die kosmogonischen Dokumente und einige Stellen bei Ephrem stützt, konstruiert sie einen kosmogonischen Mythos, der deutliche Übereinstimmung z. B. mit den Lehren des Apocryphon Johannis und des Satornil aus Antiochien aufweist. Die Vermischung der reinen Elemente sieht sie als einen „Fall", auf den die Schöpfung der Welt zurückgefürht wird. Die Welt ist von demiurgischen Astralmächten, namentlich von den sieben Planeten, geschaffen worden. Diese Archonten schaffen auf Veranlassung der Sophia auch den Menschen. Zwar erwähnen alle Fassungen des kosmogonischen Mythos, daß das Wort des Denkens, der Logos (Christus?) diese Welt aus den vermischten Elementen schuf, aber B. Aland sieht darin bloß „die Erstellung einer Art Plan für die Welt oder eines κόσμος νοητός". Entscheidend für eine gnostische Interpretation Bardaiṣans sind für sie zwei Stellen am Schluß der vierten Rede an Hypatius sowie der Kommentar

---

[9] A. J. M. Davids, Zur Kosmogonie Bardaiṣans. Textkritische Bemerkungen, ZDMG 120 (1970), S. 32–42; vgl. Liber Legum Regionum, ed. Nau, col. 548 und Drijvers, Bardaiṣan of Edessa, S. 78.

[10] B. Ehlers, Bardesanes von Edessa – ein syrischer Gnostiker, ZKG 1970, S. 334–351; B. Ehlers, Kann das Thomasevangelium aus Edessa stammen? Ein Beitrag zur Frühgeschichte des Christentums in Edessa, NovTest 12 (1970), S. 284–317.

Ephrems zum apokryphen Briefwechsel zwischen Paulus und den Korinthern. Ehe wir diese Deutung der Kosmogonie und die betreffenden Stellen aus der vierten Rede an Hypatius sowie den Kommentar zu der apokryphen Paulus-Korrespondenz näher betrachten, sei zunächst eine allgemeine Bemerkung gestattet[11].

Mit Recht weist meine Opponentin darauf hin, daß weitgehende, oft wörtliche Übereinstimmung zwischen Ephrem Syrus und der kosmogonischen Überlieferung besteht. Es ist ihr Verdienst, daß sie einige Beispiele dafür gegeben hat. Das Buch der Gesetze der Länder betrachtet sie als eine Quelle geringeren Wertes, die die Gedanken Bardaiṣans nicht adäquat wiedergibt. Der Wert dieser Quelle kann nur festgestellt werden aufgrund „eines gründlichen Vergleichs aller Quellen, um zu entscheiden, welche von ihnen den ursprünglichen Bardesanes am treuesten bewahrt hat". Weshalb vergleicht B. Aland dann aber nicht alle Quellen, um erst danach, wenn möglich, festzustellen, daß die Kosmogonie und die polemischen Stellen, die sich darauf beziehen, bei Ephrem „den ursprünglichen Bardesanes am treuesten bewahrt haben"? Damit soll nicht geleugnet werden, daß diese Übereinstimmung in der Tat vorliegt, wohl aber, daß dies die ganze Überlieferung bezüglich Bardaiṣans sei, und daß nur dieses Dokument seine ursprünglichen Auffassungen treu bewahrt hat. Ein Vergleich des Buches der Gesetze der Länder mit der kosmolgischen Überlieferung ist gleichfalls notwendig, ebenso wie ein Vergleich mit dem ganzen polemischen Werk Ephrems[12].

Das Buch der Gesetze der Länder kennt die Vorstellung der Vermischung der *ityē*, die dabei einen Teil ihrer eigenen Kraft, ihrer Freiheit verloren und ihrem Schöpfer unterworfen wurden. Offenbar sind die Planeten, die *στοιχεῖα* auch aus diesen *ityē* gebildet und teilweise frei, teilweise gebunden, wie alle anderen Astralmächte. Es gibt in der Welt eine Art Delegation der Macht in einer absteigenden Linie: Gott, die Engel, die Herrscher (*šaliṭanē*), die Lenker (*medabbranē*), die *στοιχεῖα* die Menschen und die Tiere. Die vorhergehenden haben eine begrenzte Macht über die folgenden. Die Herrscher und Lenker verkörpern das Fatum, wie es von Gott geschaffen wurde. Das Grundmotiv der Kosmologie finden wir also gleichfalls im Buch der Gesetze der Länder, ebenso wie alle *termini technici*, die eine Rolle in der Polemik Ephrems mit

---

11 Bardesanes von Edessa, S. 348ff., wo die diesbezüglichen Stellen angegeben sind.

12 Diesen Zeilen wurden geschrieben, bevor ich das Referat von B. Aland, „Das Fortwirken der Theologie des Bardesanes im manichäischen System" gehört und gelesen hatte. Frau Aland hat mir den Text ihres Referates nachher zur Verfügung gestellt, wofür ich ihr an dieser Stelle herzlich Dank sage. In anderem Zusammenhang hoffe ich ausführlich auf ihre Thesen eingehen zu können.

Bardaiṣan spielen. Der griechische Terminus ‚Archonten' ist eine genaue Wiedergabe des syrischen *šaliṭanē*. Ephrem hat aber auch Kenntnis von der Lehre der Freiheit und Gebundenheit, wie sie im Buch der Gesetze der Länder erörtert wird. Dort heißt es, daß der Mensch einen freien Willen hat, der von Gott gegeben und an den Nous gebunden ist. Daher kann der Mensch zwischen Gut und Böse wählen. Der Nous ist das Reich der Freiheit und des ethischen Verhaltens. Dies Reich ist aber begrenzt. Das Fatum, das sich im Lauf der Gestirne und der Planeten darstellt und vom Schöpfer bestimmt ist, regiert die äußeren Schicksale des Menschen. Die Natur gibt die Regeln für das animalische Dasein. Natur, Fatum und Freiheit entsprechen Körper, Seele und Geist[13].

Ephrem Syrus hatte große Mühe, Bardaiṣans Lehre vom freien Willen zu ergründen. In der ersten Rede an Hypatius sagt er, daß sich die Häretiker zwar zum freien Willen bekennen, diesen aber im Grunde einschränken, weil sie das Böse als etwas betrachten, das nicht an den freien Willen gebunden ist, sondern seinen Ursprung an anderer Stelle hat. Das Böse ist nach Bardaiṣan kein aktives Prinzip, sondern vollkommen passiv. Nur die Ausrichtung des Willens kann das Böse zum Leben erwecken, wie das reine Element Feuer die passive Finsternis entzündete. Weil unsere Welt eine Mischung aus Reinem und Unreinem darstellt, gibt es darin die Möglichkeit des Bösen. Bardaiṣan kann deshalb sagen, daß das Gute im Grunde in der Natur des Menschen liegt.

Ephrem kannte auch Bardaiṣans Anschauung vom Fatum, wie sie sich aus dem Buch der Gesetze der Länder ergibt. Im Hymnus VI contra Haereses sagt er, daß der Lauf der Gestirne nicht vom freien Willen der Gestirne abhängig ist: „Bardaiṣan ist klug, da er jenes Fatum bändigte durch ein Fatum, das größer ist, da es seine Bahn in Freiheit beschreibt"[14]. Aus diesem Hymnus geht hervor, daß Ephrems größtes Bedenken sich gegen die Einschränkung der Allmacht Gottes durch die begrenzte delegierte Macht des Fatums richtet. Meiner Ansicht nach entspricht dies genau den Vorstellungen im Buch der Gesetze der Länder. Sowohl in diesem Dialog wie in Ephrems Polemik bleibt der eine Gott Schöpfer und Gesetzgeber, der die Ordnung herstellt. In den Prose Refutations lesen wir, daß Bardaiṣan zwar sagte, die Welt sei aus einer Anzahl *ityē* entstanden, daß er aber trotzdem vom Gesetz sagt, Gott habe es gegeben[15].

---

13 Vgl. Bardaiṣan of Edessa, S. 76–95.

14 Hymnus VI, 10, ed. E. Beck, CSCO, Script. Syri 76, Louvain 1957; Übersetzung v. E. Beck, CSCO, Script. Syri 77, Louvain 1957, S. 26; vgl. Becks Kommentar zur Stelle, S. 26, Anm. 3.

15 Prose Refutations (ed. Mitchell) II, 53: 35–40; vgl. Drijvers, Bardaiṣan of Edessa, S. 134f.

Der Dialog hat eine andere Tendenz als die Polemik Ephrems, der vor allem Bardaiṣans Kosmologie als ketzerisch bekämpft. Aber die wichtigsten Ideen des Dialogs und die am Rande erwähnte Kosmologie sind Ephrem bekannt, so daß es keinen einzigen Grund gibt, den Dialog als eine sekundäre Quelle zu betrachten. Zwar darf man annehmen, daß die uns überlieferte Fassung des Dialogs über das Fatum eine ‚katholisierende' Rezension repräsentiert, aber dann hat man um so mehr Gründe, die darin enthaltenen Ideen, die denen in Ephrems Polemik entsprechen, als authentisch anzusehen.

B. Aland hat die Kosmologie für sich betrachtet und hat daraus auf eine deutliche Verwandtschaft mit kosmologischen Entwürfen in gnostischen Systemen geschlossen. Es ist jedoch falsch, einen kosmologischen Mythos isoliert zu betrachten, weil die Kosmologie eine Funktion im Rahmen einer bestimmten Anthropologie hat. Das Bild vom Menschen ist entscheidend für einen kosmogonischen Entwurf, der erzählt, wie die heutige Situation des Menschen entstanden ist und was seine Zukunft ist. Die Kosmologie verschafft uns eine feste Grundlage. In meinem „Bardaiṣan of Edessa" habe ich die genaue Entsprechung zwischen Bardaiṣans Kosmologie und seiner Anthropologie, wie sie aus dem Buch der Gesetze der Länder, den überlieferten Fassungen des kosmogonischen Mythos und den polemischen Schriften Ephrems rekonstruiert werden kann, stark betont. Geist, Seele, Körper sind Entsprechungen zu Gott, den Planetenmächten und der Materie, zu Freiheit, Fatum und unbedingtem Determinismus. In absteigender Linie von oben nach unten gibt es eine Abnahme von Aktivität und Freiheit und eine Zunahme von Passivität und Gebundenheit. Gebundenheit, Passivität bedeutet Störung der Harmonie, ist das Böse. Johannes von Dara bezeichnet exakt den Grund dieses Systems: „weil er (Bardaiṣan) das Böse von Gott fernhalten wollte"[16].

Wie Bardaiṣan sich die Schöpfung der Welt und des Menschen vorgestellt hat, ist nicht ganz klar. B. Aland hat besonders hervorgehoben, was Ephrem am Schluß der vierten Rede an Hypatius sagt, sowie Ephrems Kommentar zum apokryphen Briefwechsel zwischen Paulus und den Korinthern. Aus ihm gehe hervor, daß die Lenker, die sieben Planeten, aktiv an der Schöpfung des menschlichen Körpers beteiligt gewesen seien (u. a. wird das Verb *tqn* hier gebraucht). Namentlich darin erblickt sie deutliche Beziehungen zur Gnostik und folgert daraus, daß Zweifel an Bardaiṣans optimistischer Anschauung vom Menschen durchaus begründet sei; im Gegenteil gehöre Bardaiṣan mit seiner Lehre, daß die sieben Planeten an der Schöpfung beteiligt gewesen seien, zu den

16 „... because he wished to keep evil far from God. This idea, however, he borrowed from the ancient pagans.": Bardaiṣan of Edessa, S. 103.

Gnostikern mit ihrer „asketisch-ablehnenden Haltung gegenüber der vorfindlichen Welt". Außerdem passe er so viel besser in das allgemeine Bild der christlichen Gruppierungen am Ende des 2. Jahrhunderts in Edessa, die überwiegend gnostisch-asketisch ausgerichtet gewesen seien[17]. B. Aland hat jedoch überhaupt nicht die Funktion dieser Vorstellungen im Rahmen des ganzen Systems von Bardaiṣan berücksichtigt, sondern hat auf Grund formaler Übereinstimmungen zwischen einem Teil der Überlieferung und gnostischen Systemen die Schlußfolgerung gezogen, Bardesanes sei Gnostiker gewesen; sie hat die Gnostik zu einer Interpretationshilfe, einer Kontrollinstanz, ja zu einem „Regulativ für die Rekonstruktion des Denk- und Lehrsystems des Bardesanes" gemacht. Die Planeten sind aber in Bardaiṣans Lehre (vgl. z.B. Hymnus VI contra Haereses und das Buch der Gesetze der Länder) der Macht Gottes unterworfen, der ihnen eine begrenzte und abgeleitete Kompetenz zuerkannt hat. Es ist gewiß möglich, daß sie eine Rolle im Schöpfungsprozeß gespielt haben, und da sie über die Seele auf den menschlichen Körper Einfluß ausüben, auch als deren Schöpfer betrachtet werden. Nirgends zeigt sich aber, daß Bardaiṣan die Lenker als böse Mächte betrachtete, was sie innerhalb der Gnostik wohl sind. Das ist entscheidend für die Rolle der Planeten im Rahmen des ganzen Systems, und deshalb scheint mir die Schlußfolgerung von B. Aland nicht berechtigt zu sein. Die Planeten vollstrecken den Willen Gottes und sind keine Repräsentanten des Bösen. Die Parallelen zu dem Apocryphon Johannis sind daher bloß formaler Art[18].

Will man ein Denk- und Lehrsystem rekonstruieren, erscheint es mir als methodisch richtig, zunächst alle überlieferten Quellen miteinander zu konfrontieren, um festzustellen, ob sie ein zusammenhängendes Ganzes ergeben. Erst danach kann ein Vergleich mit anderen Systemen erfolgen. Extrapoliert man einen Teil der Überlieferung und vergleicht das Übrige auf Grund formaler Ähnlichkeiten mit z. B. gnostischen Systemen, ist der Willkür Tür und Tor geöffnet. Der hermeneutische Zirkel sollte nicht zu rasch durchbrochen werden. In diesem Zusammenhang ist noch zu bemerken, daß nur griechisch schreibende Autoren Bardaiṣan zu Valentinus in Beziehung setzen, nicht die syrischen; auch Jakob von Edessa nicht, wie B. Aland zu unrecht behauptet[19].

[17] Bardesanes von Edessa, S. 350.

[18] Vgl. Drijvers, Bardaiṣan, die Bardaiṣaniten und die Ursprünge des Gnostizismus in: The Origins of Gnosticism, ed. U. Bianchi, Leiden 1967, S. 307–314. Wichtig scheint mir, daß im manichäischen System die Befreiung der Lichtteile das Hauptanliegen ist, im bardesanitischen System hingegen die Vertreibung der Finsternis.

[19] Bardesanes von Edessa, S. 346 und Anm. 44; vgl. H. H. Schaeder, Bardesanes von Edessa in der Überlieferung der griechischen und der syrischen Kirche, in: Stu-

C. Colpe hat in einer Rezension gesagt, daß eine „vertiefte religionsgeschichtliche Interpretation" die wichtigste Aufgabe der künftigen Erforschung Bardaiṣans als Repräsentanten des syrischen Synkretismus im 2. Jahrhundert n.Chr. darstelle[20]. Ich habe früher den Standpunkt vertreten, daß Bardaiṣan kein Gnostiker war, während andere, wie Bianchi, Widengren, B. Aland, das Gegenteil behauptet haben. Ich frage mich jetzt, ob der Gegensatz gnostisch-nichtgnostisch der richtige Zugang zu einem so komplexen Ganzen wie Bardaiṣans Lehre von Mensch und Welt ist. Entleert man ein Problem nicht weitgehend seines Sinnes, wenn man es auf solche einfachen Alternativen reduziert? Etwas Vergleichbares sehen wir in der Gnostikforschung, wo ähnliche Alternativen, iranisch oder jüdisch, griechisch oder mesopotamisch diskutiert werden. Auch außerhalb des Bereiches der Religionsgeschichte ist manchmal eine solche Fragestellung aufgetreten, z. B. bei der Erforschung der sogenannten Partherkunst[21].

Die Reduktion bestimmter Elemente aus dem Systemganzen auf einen anderen kulturellen Kontext, einen griechischen, iranischen oder semitischen, ist meiner Meinung nach einer vertieften religionsgeschichtlichen Interpretation nicht förderlich. Zwar haben alle diese Kulturen mittelbar oder unmittelbar zu der Kultur von Edessa im zweiten Jahrhundert beigetragen, aber diese wurden von den Einwohnern der Stadt in jener Zeit als eine Einheit erlebt. Nur historische und wissenschaftliche Distanz gibt uns die Möglichkeit, eine Kultur, die wir als synkretistisch bezeichnen, in Elemente verschiedener Herkunft zu zerlegen. Im Grunde ist der Synkretismus ein Problem einzig für den Wissenschaftler, während die lebende Gemeinschaft sich in ihren Mythen und Ideologien immer wieder der sich wandelnden Realität anpaßt und deshalb aus dem Synkretismus überhaupt kein Problem macht. So betrachtet ist jede Art Religion synkretistisch, weil niemand in völliger Isolierung lebt und man immer wieder seine Begegnungen mit anderen oder anderen Kulturen in seiner Welt- und Lebensanschauung verarbeiten wird. Daher ist sogar vorgeschlagen worden, den Ausdruck ‚Synkretismus' überhaupt aus der religionswissenschaftlichen Fachsprache zu streichen, weil das Phänomen

---

dien zur orientalischen Religionsgeschichte, hrsg. v. C. Colpe, Darmstadt 1968, S. 130f., und Drijvers, Bardaiṣan of Edessa, S. 194f.

[20] C. Colpe, ThLZ 93 (1968), Sp. 437.

[21] Vgl. J. B. Ward-Perkins, The Roman West and the Parthian East, Proceedings of the British Academy 51 (1965), S. 175–199; vgl. D. Schlumberger, Nachkommen der griechischen Kunst außerhalb des Mittelmeerraumes, in: Der Hellenismus in Mittelasien, hrsg. v. F. Altheim u. J. Rehork, Wege der Forschung 91, Darmstadt 1969, S. 281–405.

so allgemein sei, daß er dadurch ein inhaltsleerer Begriff werde[22]. Es fragt sich also, welche spezifischen Erscheinungen dem Synkretismus im syrisch-persischen Kulturbereich eigen sind, die eine gesonderte Behandlung dieses Gegenstandes rechtfertigen. Wie können wir zeigen, daß hier von einer spontanen, manchmal sogar unbewußten Akkulturation gesprochen werden kann, ohne zu Banalitäten wie „überwiegend griechisch" oder „überwiegend parthisch" unsere Zuflucht nehmen zu müssen, zu Qualifizierungen, die der komplexen historischen Wirklichkeit nicht gerecht werden? Welche völlig eigenen Formen religiöser Weltanschauung hat dieser Bereich entwickelt, die mit allen Kulturen in Beziehung stehen, die dort ihren Einfluß ausgeübt haben, und mit den sozio-politischen Verhältnissen, die daraus entstanden? Ich bin der Ansicht, daß auch die soziale Schichtung der Gesellschaft einen Faktor darstellt, der berücksichtigt werden sollte. Die unteren Schichten der Bevölkerung haben Religionsformen gekannt, die deutliche Parallelen zu der Religion der halbnomadischen Hirtenvölker und zu der überlieferten Religion dieser Gegend aufweisen. Isaak von Antiochien hat dies in späterer Zeit in einem Augenzeugenbericht beschrieben[23]. In den höheren Schichten, denen Bardaiṣan angehörte, ist der Einfluß der griechischen Kultur ohne Zweifel stark gewesen. Edessa heißt nicht nur „die Tochter der Parther", sondern auch „das Athen des Ostens". Die Kultur des von den Parthern beherrschten Gebietes und ihrer Interessensphäre ist zum größten Teil „reines importiertes Griechentum, das nicht zuletzt hier zum Hellenismus wurde"[24]. Es scheint mir der Mühe wert zu erwägen, ob eine der spezifischen Eigenschaften der Mischkultur in diesem Gebiete nicht diejenige ist, daß Religionsformen in kultureller Hinsicht

---

[22] R. D. Baird, Category Formation and the History of Religions, Religion and Reason I, The Hague-Paris 1971, S. 142ff.; vgl. idem, Syncretism and the History of Religions, The Journal of Religious Thought 24 (1967–68), S. 42–53. Mit C. Colpe's Ausführungen über „Synkretismus als Phänomen der Kulturgeschichte und Kategorie historisch-genetischer Erklärung" bin ich im großen und ganzen einverstanden. Wichtig ist der Synkretismus-Begriff vor allem als heuristisches Prinzip zur Aufspürung von Antecedensdaten; im Bereich der alten Kulturen sind die Antecedensdaten aber oft völlig unbekannt, und das sozialpsychologische Klima kennen wir oft nur unzulänglich. Wie kann man feststellen, was beherrschend, was Besiegtes und was Gleichgewicht ist? Die Art und Weise, in der das Problem der Ursprünge der Gnostik diskutiert worden ist, bietet dafür ein gutes Beispiel: ist das Jüdische beherrschend oder das Iranische?

[23] Vgl. J. B. Segal, Edessa, the blessed City, Oxford 1970, S. 168ff.; Drijvers, The Cult of Azizos and Monimos at Edessa, in: Festschrift Widengren, Leiden 1972, S. 359ff.

[24] C. Colpe, Überlegungen zur Bezeichnung „Iranisch" für die Religion der Partherzeit, ZDMG, Suppl. I, Wiesbaden 1969, S. 1012.

mehrdeutig sind, d. h. daß sie in je verschiedenartigen kulturellen Kontexten zugleich interpretiert werden können, ohne doch ihren eigenen Charakter zu verlieren.

Eine sorgfältige Ausarbeitung dieser These ist im Rahmen dieses Vortrages nicht möglich. Ich darf mich auf einige Hinweise beschränken. Die Kosmologie Bardaiṣans enthält einige Elemente, die an die Kultur Irans, z. B. an den Zurvanismus erinnern. Seine Ansicht vom Verhältnis zwischen Gott und dem Raum entspricht der zurvanistischen Gott-Raum-Lehre. Auch die Funktion des Windes im kosmogonischen Prozeß „deutet möglicherweise auf iranischen Einfluß hin"[25]. Andererseits gibt es zahlreiche Entsprechungen zur spätantiken Philosophie, zur Stoa und zum mittleren Platonismus. Bardaiṣan wird „der Philosoph der Aramäer" genannt und aus Ephrems Prose Refutations bekommen wir einen Eindruck vom starken Einfluß der Stoa und von Philosophen wie Albinus in der Umgebung von Edessa[26]. Das kosmogonische Modell Bardaiṣans findet hier seine genauesten Entsprechungen. In Platons Timaios treten nach dem Demiurgen in einem bestimmten Augenblick die sogenannten „neuen Götter" auf, die namentlich die Schöpfer der Körper sind — Körper zu schaffen ist eine Tätigkeit, die unter der Würde eines Demiurgen liegt. Ihre Aufgabe ist es, diese Körper zu lenken (*ἄρχειν*, vgl. das syrische *mdbbr*). Der Demiurg behält sich selbst die Erschaffung der unvergänglichen göttlichen Dinge, z. B. des Nous, vor. Die neuen Götter fügen diesem Nous das Vergängliche hinzu, das die menschlichen Leidenschaften umfaßt, die *δεινὰ καὶ ἀναγκαῖα*. Den Gegensatz sterblich-unsterblich finden wir also auch in der Seele, wo er eine kosmische und moralische Bedeutung hat. Die neuen Götter sind bei Platon Astralmächte. Ich bin der Meinung, daß vor allem diese Vorstellungen des Timaios z. B. in einen jüdischen Kontext hineinpassen würden, wie bei Philo Alexandrinus in De Opificio Mundi (74) oder bei den iranisch beeinflußten Chaldäern. Das Motiv dieser Vorstellung liegt darin, daß „Gott keine Verantwortung für das Böse tragen soll" oder mit anderen Worten, daß „Gott allein die Quelle des Guten und nicht des Bösen" sein soll. Das Motiv erwähnt Philo *expressis verbis*, was an die Worte des Johannes von Dara erinnert, daß es die Aufgabe der Kosmogonie Bardaiṣans sei, das Böse von Gott fernzuhalten[27].

---

25 B. Aland-Ehlers, Bardesanes von Edessa, S. 346 u. Anm. 45.

26 Drijvers, Bardaiṣan of Edessa and the Hermetica. The Aramaic Philosopher and the Philosophy of his Time, in: Jaarbericht Ex Oriente Lux 21 (1969–70), Leiden 1970, S. 190–210.

27 Vgl. P. Boyancé, Dieu cosmique et Dualisme. Les archontes et Platon, in: Le Origini dello Gnosticismo, Leiden 1967, S. 340–356, dort alle Belege; auch U.

Es wäre interessant, einen eingehenden Vergleich zwischen Bardaiṣan und Philo vorzunehmen. Bestimmte Stellen aus dem Buch der Gesetze der Länder finden auch Entsprechungen in Philos De Providentia[28]. Bardaiṣan bleibt aber mit Philo und z. B. Numenius von Apamea im platonischen Rahmen, weil die Planeten bei ihm keine bösen Mächte werden, wie in der Gnostik und bei Mani. Das Gerüst der Kosmologie und der Anthropologie des aramäischen Philosophen stammt also aus der platonischen Tradition, wie sie in Syrien fortlebte. Bestimmte Teile dieser Tradition, z. B. die Rolle der Planetenmächte, die Elementenlehre, die negative Definition des Bösen eigneten sich für eine Mythologisierung in einem chaldäisch-iranischen oder einem semitischen Rahmen. Das Modell wird dadurch kulturell mehrdeutig: *et-et* (sowohl/als auch) tritt an die Stelle des *aut-aut* (entweder/oder). Dieser Synkretismus ist von H. H. Schaeder, dessen Name in einer Untersuchung dieses Phänomens im syrisch-persischen Kulturgebiet nicht fehlen darf, „babylonischer Hellenismus" genannt worden. Die griechischen Traditionen im ehemaligen Seleukidenreich haben einen wesentlichen Beitrag zu dem synkretistischen Prozeß geleistet, der dort bereits einige Jahrhunderte früher seinen Anfang genommen hatte, als die Perser Babylon eroberten und als die Achämeniden ihr Weltreich gründeten. Der Wechsel der Machthaber und der Kampf für die eigene Freiheit, der damit verknüpft war, hat in diesem Gebiet das Problem der Seele und der Freiheit zu zentralen Themen jeder religiösen Weltanschauung gemacht, und zwar bis in die Zeit des Islam. Bardaiṣan von Edessa ist ein würdiger Repräsentant dieses Synkretismus, weil er mit dem kulturellen Erbe des Ostens wie des Westens die zentrale Problematik der menschlichen Existenz zum Ausdruck brachte.

Bianchi, Bardesane Gnostico. Le Fonti des Dualismo di Bardesane, in: Umanità e Storia, Scritti in Onore di Adelchi Attisani, 1970 (?), pp. 1–15.

28 Vgl. P. Wendland, Philos Schrift über die Vorsehung. Ein Beitrag zur Geschichte der nacharistotelischen Philosophie, Berlin 1892, S. 27ff. Vgl. Bardaiṣan of Edessa, S. 18f.

XIII

MANI UND BARDAIṢAN
Ein Beitrag zur Vorgeschichte des Manichäismus

Seit Ephräm Syrus in seinen polemischen Schriften gegen die Irrlehrer und Irrlehren Mani in engste Beziehung zu Markion und Bardaiṣan gesetzt und namentlich Bardaiṣan Manis Lehrer genannt hat[1], ist in der Forschung wiederholt Manis Abhängigkeit von Bardaiṣan betont worden. Bekanntlich polemisiert Mani selbst in seinem *Buch der Mysterien* gegen die Daiṣaniten über das Verhältnis von Seele und Körper und über die Weltseele, wie al-Bîrûnî und Ibn an-Nadîm mitteilen[2]. In der Manichäische Chronologie bilden Markion, Bardaiṣan und Mani eine feste Reihe[3] und deshalb hat H. J. Polotsky in den in *Kephalaia* 13, 30 ff. ungenannten Erneuerern der nach Paulus verfallenen Kirche Markion und Bardaiṣan sehen wollen, worin ihm fast alle Forscher folgten[4]. Es ist auffallend, dass alle Forscher Übereinstimmungen und Unterschiede zwischen Mani und seinem Lehrer Bardaiṣan erwähnen, ohne genau anzugeben, worin diese bestehen. So schreibt F. C. Burkitt : « S. Ephraem is right when he regards the main principle of the cosmogony of Mani as derived from Bardaiṣan... But Mani and Bardaiṣan are very different in their mental outlook »[5]. O. G. von Wesendonk hat die Ähnlichkeit im Leben beider Denker stark betont, seiner Meinung nach sind beide aber selbständige Naturen mit eigenem Anliegen[6]. H. H. Schaeder hat

1. *S. Ephraim's Prose Refutations of Mani, Marcion and Bardaisan*, ed. by C. W. Mitchell, vol. I, London, 1912, p. 8, l. 5.

2. *Alberuni's India*, ed. by E. Sachau, London, 1887, p. 27, l. 12 ff. ; G. Flügel, *Mani, seine Lehren und seine Schriften*, Leipzig, 1862, S. 161 ff. H. J. W. Drijvers, *Bardaiṣan of Edessa* (« Studia Semitica Neerlandica », 6), Assen, 1966, p. 202-204 ; H. H. Schaeder, Urform und Fortbildungen des manichäischen Systems, *Vorträge der Bibliothek Warburg*, IV, Leipzig, 1927, S. 74, Anm. 3 = Id., *Studien zur orientalischen Religionsgeschichte*, hrsg. v. C. Colpe, Darmstadt, 1968, S. 24, Anm. 3.

3. H.-Ch. Puech, Dates manichéennes dans les chroniques syriaques, *Mélanges R. Dussaud*, II, Paris, 1939, p. 593-607.

4. H. J. Polotsky, *Kephalaia*, I, Stuttgart, 1940, 13, 30 ff. ; A. Böhlig, Christliche Wurzeln im Manichäismus, *Mysterion und Wahrheit*, Leiden, 1968, S. 208 ff. ; H.-Ch. Puech, *Le manichéisme, son fondateur, sa doctrine*, Paris, 1949, p. 70 und Anm. 268 ; O. Klíma, *Manis Zeit und Leben*, Prag, 1962, S. 135 ff.

5. F. C. Burkitt, *The religion of the Manichees*, Cambridge, 1925, p. 78 f. Cf. Id., *S. Ephraim's Prose Refutations*, vol. II, London, 1921, Introductory Essay by F. C. Burkitt.

6. O. G. von Wesendonk, Bardesanes und Mānī, *Acta Orientalia*, X, 1932, S. 336-363.

das Thema angerührt in *Urform und Fortbildungen des manichäischen Systems*. Dort schrieb er, dass Mani « durch Vermittlung von Marcion und Bardesanes den festen gedanklichen Unterbau für sein System gewonnen hat »[1] und dass namentlich Bardaiṣan für die Förderung des theoretischen Denkens Manis grosse Bedeutung gehabt hat. Weiter arbeitend auf diesem Gebiet, schrieb er seinen berühmten Aufsatz *Bardesanes von Edessa in der Überlieferung der griechischen und der syrischen Kirche* als Vorarbeit für eine Monographie zur Vorgeschichte des Manichäismus, die niemals zustande gekommen ist[2]. Er betrachtet Bardaiṣan als einen Vertreter der griechischen Philosophie und Wissenschaft, durch dessen Vermittlung das griechische Erbe an Mani und den Manichäismus übertragen wurde, wo es weitergelebt hat und im Dualismus und Asketismus untergegangen ist. Nach Schaeder ist das Thema Bardaiṣan und Mani nicht mehr Gegenstand einer Einzeluntersuchung gewesen ; Schaeders Thesen sind kritisiert worden und haben Beifall gefunden, H.-Ch. Puech kann darum schreiben : « Que Mani ait connu les doctrines de ses deux prédécesseurs est assuré non seulement par les ressemblances qu'offrent avec celles-ci certaines parties de son système, mais encore par les critiques que ses écrits adressent aux Bardesanites et à Marcion »[3]. Aufgabe dieses Aufsatzes ist es, die « ressemblances », « certaines parties de son système » und « critiques » näher zu bestimmen, damit das Verhältnis Manis zu Bardaiṣan etwas klarer wird. Die Lösung dieser Aufgabe wird kompliziert und erschwert, weil Bardaiṣan von Edessa in der Forschung immer eine umstrittene Figur gewesen ist bis auf heute[4]. In jüngster Zeit hat B. Aland-Ehlers sich zum Problem geäussert und ihren Beitrag beigesteuert zur Renaissance der Bardaiṣan-Studien[5]. Der Titel ihres Aufsatzes ist ein Programm, womit wir im gewissem Sinne wieder bei A. Hilgenfelds, *Bardesanes, der letzte Gnostiker* (1864), stehen, so dass die Forschung neu anfangen kann. Ihrer Meinung nach ist Bardaiṣan ein Vertreter des Gnostizismus des zweiten Jahrhunderts, verwant mit den Ophiten des Irenäus und mit Satornils Lehre, dem keine optimistische Weltansicht zugeschrieben werden kann. Vielmehr gehört er in die allgemeine Strömung der christlichen Gruppen in Edessa, die geprägt sind durch eine asketisch-ablehnende Haltung gegenüber der vorfindlichen Welt. In seiner Theologie sind viele Probleme der menschlichen Exsistenz auf unvollkommene Weise gelöst und viele Unstimmigkeiten unausgeglichen. Mani hat sein System bewusst als Verbesserung

1. SCHAEDER, *Urform*, S. 23, Anm. 1. und S. 27.

2. H. H. SCHAEDER, Bardesanes von Edessa in der Überlieferung der griechischen und der syrischen Kirche, *Z.K.G.*, 51, 1932, S. 21-74 = *Studien zur orientalischen Religionsgeschichte*, S. 108-161, *vide* dort S. 114 und Colpes Nachwort, S. 265.

3. PUECH, *Le manichéisme*, p. 69 und Anm. 268.

4. *Bardaiṣan of Edessa*, p. 1-59 : History of Research.

5. B. EHLERS, Bardesanes von Edessa — ein syrischer Gnostiker, *Z.K.G.*, 1970, S. 334-351 ; *eadem*, Kann das Thomasevangelium aus Edessa stammen ? Ein Beitrag zur Frühgeschichte des Christentums in Edessa, *Nov. Test.*, 12, 1970, S. 289-293 ; *eadem*, *Das Fortwirken der Theologie des Bardesanes im manichäischen System*, ungedruckter Vortrag, gehalten auf einem Symposium in Reinhausen bei Göttingen ; Frau Aland war so freundlich mir den Text zur Verfügung zu stellen ; dafür sei ihr herzlichst gedankt.

des ihm vorliegenden Systems des Bardaiṣan begriffen und konzipiert. Beiden versuchen, die gleichen Probleme zu lösen, beide gehören zum Gnostizismus mit seiner asketischen Lebenshaltung ; nur an den Stellen, an denen der Mythos des Bardaiṣan die ihm aufgegebenen Probleme nicht befriedigend zu lösen vermochte, hat Mani charakteristische Umwandlungen vorgenommen. Eine gerade Linie führt also von Bardaiṣan zu Mani ; der Lehrer und Schüler stehen in der selben Tradition.

Es darf deutlich geworden sein, dass die Probleme hier ganz auf der Seite der Rekonstruktion und Interpretation von Bardaiṣans Lehre liegen. Wenn er den Apologeten und Philosophen des zweiten Jahrhunderts angehört und einen christlichen Humanismus vertritt, dann sind seine Gedanken von Mani radikalisiert worden, der Erbe, an erster Stelle aber Verderber seiner Gedanken ist. Gehört der Denker aus Edessa aber zu den Gnostikern und Asketen, dann sind selbstverständlich die Divergenzen zwischen seiner Lehre und Manis Gedanken gering und beide vertreten im Grunde dasselbe Anliegen. Jedenfalls soll man bei Bardaiṣan anfangen, um die Vorgeschichte des Manichäismus teilweise aufzudecken.

Die Geschichte hat nur wenige Quellen zur Rekonstruktion der Gedankenwelt des aramäischen Philosophen überliefert, der von 154-222 nach Christi Geburt lebte und den grössten Teil seines Lebens am Hofe König Abgars VIII. verbrachte, wo er dem Kreis der vertrauten Freunde des Königs angehörte. Wenn seine Biographie und eine Menge kurzer Notizen beiseite gelassen werden, bleiben als wichtigste Quellen für seine Lehren übrig die polemischen Schriften Ephräms, der in vier Rezensionen überlieferte kosmogonische Mythos und ein Dialog über das Fatum, durchweg *Buch der Gesetze der Länder* genannt[1]. Letzteres ist geschrieben worden von einem Schüler Philippus, der in diesem Dialog die Gedanken seines Meisters über das Problem der menschlichen Freiheit und des astrologischen Determinismus darzustellen beabsichtigt. Der Wert dieser letzte Quelle ist umstritten und deshalb scheint es am vernünftigsten und methodisch am richtigsten, das *Buch der Gesetze der Länder* vorläufig ausser Betracht zu lassen und das Verhältnis dieser Quelle zu den anderen erst nachher zu bestimmen[2]. Eine zweite methodische Beschränkung ist überdies angebracht ; es ist in erster Instanz auf das Beibringen von allerlei Parallelen aus dem Bereich des Gnostizismus und verwanter geistlichen Strömungen zu verzichten. B. Aland-Ehlers ist der Meinung, dass man bei solchem Verfahren auf wichtige Interpretationshilfen verzichtet und auf die Kontrollinstanz, die im Vergleich mit verwandten theologischen Systemen gegeben ist : « Nach den uns zur Verfügung stehenden Quellen ist vielmehr ihre Nähe zu gnostischem Gedankengut und gnostische Literatur zu gross, dass hier das Regulativ für die Rekonstruktion des Denk- und Lehrsystems des Bardesanes gegeben zu

1. Cf. *Bardaiṣan of Edessa*, p. 60 ff.

2. Kritik ist geäussert worden von T. Jansma, *Natuur, lot en vrijheid. Bardesanes, de filosoof der Arameeërs en zijn images*, Wageningen, 1969, und B. Ehlers, *Bardesanes von Edessa*, S. 339 ff. ; für das Charakter des Dialogs *vide* : K. Rudolph, Der gnostische « Dialog » als literarisches Genus, *Wiss. Beiträge der M. Luther-Universität*, 1968/1, S. 105 f.

sein scheint »[1]. Selbstverständlich ist es schwierig, bei der Rekonstruktion einer Lehre mit Hilfe verstreuter Traditionsstücken auf alle Interpretationshilfen zu verzichten. Man soll sich aber davor hüten, gleich nach Systemen zu suchen, die verwandt zu sein scheinen : bei solchem Verfahren wird das Unbekannte dem Bekannten gleich und die Rekonstruktion und Interpretation wird völlig abhängig vom Bekannten, das man wählt. Wenn man Bardaiṣan in die Nähe von diskutierenden Rabbinern und Philosophen bringt, bekommt er eine andere Gestalt, als wenn mann ihm mit Gnostikern und Asketen vergleicht. Das Regulativ, gewählt auf Grund formaler Gleichheit, determiniert die ganze Interpretation ; damit sind wir bei der Methoden der religionsgeschichtlichen Schule, es wird nicht nach der Funktion von Themen und Vorstellungen gefragt, sondern nur nach äusserer Gleichheit.

Ephräms Polemik richtet sich hauptsächlich gegen Bardaiṣans Kosmologie, die auch noch in vier anderen Fassungen überliefert ist[2]. Bei einer Vergleichung von Ephräms Schriften mit der kosmologischen Überlieferung stellt sich heraus, dass beide bisweilen die gleiche Terminologie benutzen und im Grunde eine gleiche Tradition übermitteln[3]. Es ist sogar möglich, Textverderbnisse in der kosmologischen Tradition mit Hilfe der anderen Traditionen zu verbessern[4]. Inwieweit diese kosmologischen Traditionen einen selbständigen Wert haben oder nur Exzerpte aus, bzw. Zusammenfassungen und Systematisierungen von Ephräms Schriften sind, soll einer speziellen Untersuchung vorbehalten bleiben. Jedenfalls ist Bardaiṣans Kosmogonie gut bezeugt, so dass es möglich ist, diese zusammenzufassen. Im Anfang gab es vier reine Elementen, Licht, Wind, Feuer, und Wasser, ihr Herr in der Höhe und ihr Feind, die Finsternis, in der Tiefe. Die vier reinen Elementen sind in eine Ebene geordnet. Ephräm benützt das Wort *ityâ* = Seiende, um damit Gott, die reinen Elementen und die Finsternis zu bezeichnen. Ursprünglich hat das Wort eine breitere Bedeutung, wie sich auch in Ephräms Schriften gegen Bardaiṣan noch zeigt, aber in Bardaiṣans Kosmologie ist der Terminus reserviert für Sachen die « ungeworden » (ἀγένητα) sind[5]. Ephräm spricht manchmal von fünf *ityê* (Licht, Wind, Feuer, Wasser und Finsternis) mitunter von vier (nur die vier reinen *ityê*) und auch von sechs, wenn er auch Gott, den Herrn der *ityê* mitrechnet. In der kosmologischen Überlieferung wird nur von fünf *ityê* gesprochen. Ephräm kennt auch eine Ordnung der Elemente der Schwere nach : die Reihe ist dann von oben nach unten : Gott, Licht, Wind, Feuer, Wasser, Finsternis. Auch Moses bar Kepha nennt dieselbe Ordnung, wie sich

1. B. Ehlers, *Bardesanes von Edessa*, S. 350.

2. *Bardaiṣan of Edessa*, p. 96 ff. ; *cf.* A. J. M. Davids, Zur Kosmogonie Bardaiṣans. Textkritische Bemerkungen, *Z.D.M.G.*, 120, 1970, S. 32-42 ; T. Jansma, La notice de Barḥadbešabba ʿArbaïa sur l'hérésie des Daiṣanites, *Mémorial Khouri-Sarkis*, Louvain, 1969, p. 91-106 ; B. Ehlers, *Bardesanes von Edessa*, S. 337, Anm. 5 mit Verbesserungen des Textes.

3. B. Ehlers, *Bardesanes von Edessa*, p. 338. Anm. 5 mit Beispielen ; *cf. Bardaiṣan of Edessa*, p. 138 ff.

4. A. J. M. Davids, art. cit.

5. B. Ehlers, *Bardesanes von Edessa*, p. 340 ff. *Cf.* T. Jansma, Ephraems Beschreibung des ersten Tages der Schöpfung, *Or. Chr. Per.*, 37, 1972, S. 295-316.

aus seinen kritischen Fragen an Bardaiṣan ergibt, die auf die kosmologische Tradition in eigentlichen Sinne folgen[1]. Die Elemente haben eine atomaren Aufbau und haben alle eine eigene Farbe, Geruch, Geschmack, Form und Laut in übereinstimmung mit den fünf Sinnesorganen des Menschen[2]. Der Herr in der Höhe ist reiner Geist, die vier reinen *ityê* sind in einer beständigen Bewegung begriffen und die Finsternis schläft, ist inaktiv und bewegungslos und hat keine geistige Potenz. Durch eine Zufall kriecht die Wind in die Nähe des Feuers, und dies weckt die Finsternis auf, die erbrennt, einen dunklen Rauch emporsteigen lässt und sich mit den reinen *ityê* vermischt. Dadurch ist die Harmonie gestört ; ein Zufall ist die Ursache dafür, dass die Finsternis die Gelegenheit ergreift, sich geltend zu machen. Die Urordnung der *ityê* ist nicht antithetisch : Gott kontra der Finsternis, sondern zeigt eine allmähliche Abstufung. Von oben nach unten nimmt der Geist ab und die Schwere zu. Darum können die vier reinen *ityê* sowohl in einer Ebene als auch über einander geordnet sein. In beiden Ordnungsweisen behalten sie ihren Charakter als mittlere *ityê*. Sie sind rein und gehören also zum göttlichen Bereich, aber ein Zufall ist Ursache dass sie die Finsternis zu Aktivität wecken und zusammen mit der Finsternis die Materie bilden, woraus diese Welt entstanden ist. In ihrer Not schrieen die reinen *ityê* angegriffen von der Finsternis, zu Gott und Er sandte ihnen das Wort des Denkens, auch Kraft des ersten Wortes genannt, und später in der Tradition Jesu, dem Logos, gleichgestellt[3]. Das Wort des Denkens vertreibt einen Teil des Finsternis, aber eine vollständige Scheidung ist unmöglich, ein Teil der Finsternis bleibt mit den reinen Elementen vermischt. Und aus dem Gemisch schafft das Wort des Denkens die Welt.

Es ist sehr wahrscheinlich, dass der Schöpfung der Welt die Schöpfung der Planeten und Astralmächte vorhergeht, worin weniger Finsternis gemischt ist. Jedenfalls ist die Schöpfung eine Ordnung der *ityê*, wie Barḥadbešabba ʿArbaia und Moses bar Kepha sagen, « dem Mysterium des Kreuzes gemäss »[4]. Theodor bar Khonai sagt, dass das Wort des Denkens « die ganze Schöpfung machte der Dinge, die oben sind und die unten sind ». Dinge, die oben sind *(ʿlyê)*, bezeichnen in diesem Zusammenhang die Planeten und Zodiakalzeichen. Wenn man dabei in Erinnerung bringt, dass die Finsternis das schwerste Element ist, liegt es auf der Hand, anzunehmen, dass in der Zusammensetzung den Planeten weniger Finsternis beigemischt ist. Der erste Schöpfungsakt ist also eine Ordnung des Gemisches, resultierend in einer Konstellation : Gott-

1. *Cf. Patrologia Syriaca*, I, 2, Paris, 1907, 513 f. ; SCHAEDER, *Bardesanes von Edessa*, S. 139 ff. *Cf. Bardaiṣan of Edessa*, p. 96 ff. und 130 ff. ; dort alle Belege. Es ist auffallend dass sich nirgends zeigt, dass Bardaiṣan selber Gott *ityâ* genannt hat ; das tut nur Ephräm in Übereinstimmung mit seinen theologischen Auffassungen.

2. *Prose Refutations*, II, p. 214:24-215:44, 223:23-224:7.

3. *Cf.* DRIJVERS, Bardaiṣan of Edessa and the Hermetica. The aramaic Philosopher and the Philosophy of his Time, *Jaarbericht Ex Oriente Lux*, 21, Leiden, 1970, p. 206.

4. *Bardaiṣan of Edessa*, p. 102 ; *cf.* PUECH, *Le manichéisme*, p. 82 und Anm. 343, wo das « Kreuz des Lichtes » im manichäischen System besprochen wird ; hat Mani diese Vorstellung von Bardaiṣan entlehnt oder hat der Manichäismus hier auf spätere bardaiṣanitische Gedanken eingewirkt ?

Planetenmächte-Welt. Die Welt macht es der Finsternis unmöglich, weiter aufzusteigen. Wiederum ist das Resultat des ersten Schöpfungsaktes ein gestufter Kosmos : von oben nach unten gibt es immer mehr Finsternis und Schwere. In seiner vierten Rede an Hypatius bescheibt Ephräm die Schöpfung des menschlichen Körpers nach Bardaiṣan : « They suppose that its nature *(k^{e}yânâ)* is from Evil, and its workmanship from the Archons, and the cause of its arrangement is from Wisdom *(ḥekm^{e}tâ)*. And she (i.e. Wisdom) showed an image of her own beauty to the Archons, and to the Governors *(m^{e}dabb^{e}rânê)*, and she deceived them thereby so that when they saw, each of them should give from his treasure whatever he had ; and that owing to this cause their treasures should be emptied of what they had snatched away. And since Mani saw in this place that he was not able to cross the river at any other place, he was forced to come and cross where Bardaiṣan crossed » (folgt der Mythos der Verführung der Archonten) und weiter sagt Ephräm : « its (d.h. des Körpers) Architect and Regulator is God, and not the Sons of the Darkness as Mani said, nor the foolish Governors *(m^{e}dabb^{e}rânê)* as Bardaiṣan said »[1]. Wenn B. Aland-Ehlers hier von Archonten *der Finsternis* spricht, ist das nicht richtig. Hier wird sie von ihrem Vorverständnis bestimmt. Wir finden in diesem Bericht auf der Ebene des menschlichen Körpers dieselben drei Stufen wie im Kosmos : Weisheit (= Sophia), gehörend zum göttlichen Bereich ; Planetenmächte, gehörend zum mittleren Bereich, und der Körper, gehörend zum Bösen = der Materie. Jeder der Planeten steuert etwas zum Körper bei, eine Tradition, die auch später in der syrischen Überlieferung belegt und von Ephräm noch in seinem Kommentar zum apokryphen Briefwechsel zwischen Paulus und den Korinthern bezeugt ist[2]. Die Astralmächte schaffen also den menschlichen Körper, der vom Gott belebt wird[3]. Es ist am wahrscheinlichsten, dass die Astralmächte die Fähigkeit zum Schaffen besitzen, weil das Wort des Denkens in der Schöpfung zurückgeblieben ist. Ephräm führt ein Zitat des Bardaiṣan an, wo dieser sagt : « Die Kraft des ersten Wortes, die zurückgeblieben ist in der Schöpfung, diese hat alles geschaffen »[4]. Die Astralmächte geben also die Teile dieses Wortes des Denkens preis, wenn sie den Körper schaffen. Wenn Gott den Körper belebt, dann bindet diese geistige Potenz sich an die Seele, die das Leben trägt. Die Seele an sich besitzt keine geistige Potenz[5] : « Reason » as they (d.h. die Bardaisaniten) say, « is the strange Leaven that is hidden in the Soul, which is without knowledge ». Die Sünde Adams, des ersten Mensch, bewirkt deshalb nicht den Tod des Körpers, weil der Körper zur Materie gehört und *naturaliter* sterblich ist. Die Sünde Adams, der seine Freiheit, gebunden an den Geist, falsch benützt, verhindert die Rückkehr der Seele zu ihrem Ursprung. Wenn ein Mensch seinen Geist, seine Freiheit, die erst dazu geweckt werden muss, gut

1. *Prose Refutations*, I, 122:13-124:18.
2. B. Ehlers, *Bardesanes von Edessa*, S. 348 f. ; *Bardaiṣan of Edessa*, p. 189 ff.
3. *Prose Refutations*, II, p. 158:1-11.
4. *Prose Refutations*, II, p. 220:29-33.
5. *Prose Refutations*, II, p. 158:20-32 ; *cf. Bardaiṣan of Edessa*, p. 156.

benutzt, kann er zum Brautgemach zurückkehren[1]. Ephäm Syrus kennt überdies eine bardaiṣanitische Lehre, die behauptet, dass die Seele aus sieben Teilen besteht, die in vielerlei Verhältnissen gemischt sein können[2]. Das kann nichts anderes bedeuten als die verbreitete Lehre des Hinabsteigens der Seele durch die sieben Planetsphären in den Körper. Von jeder Planetsphäre nimmt die Seele etwas mit, dem Stand der Planeten entsprechend, und das bestimmt das Los des Menschen während seines irdischen Lebens. Fassen wir die Ergebnisse kurz zusammen, dann fällt das Drei-Stufen-Schema am meisten in die Augen : vor der Mischung Gott-reine Elemente-Finsternis ; nach der Mischung und dem Eingreifen des Wortes des Denkens : Gott-Planetenmächte-vermischte Materie oder Weisheit-Planetenmächte-Körper oder Geist-Seele-Körper. Es besteht hier eine deutliche Korrelation zwischen der Kosmologie und der Anthropologie. Hier spürt man die Nachwirkung der platonischen Kosmologie, wie sie im *Timaios* zu finden ist. Dort treten nach dem Demiurgen (*cf.* Bardaiṣans Wort des Denkens) die « neuen Götter » auf, die namentlich die Schöpfer der Körper sind ; Körper zu schaffen, ist eine Beschäftigung, die unter der Würde eines Demiurgen liegt. Seine Aufgabe ist es, diese Körper zu lenken (ἄρχειν, vgl. das syrische *dbbr* und *mdbbr*). Der Demiurg ist eine geistige Potenz und schaft den Nous ; die neuen Götter fügen diesem Nous das Vergängliche zu, das die menschlichen Leidenschaften umfasst. Bei Plato sind diese neuen Götter Astralmächte[3]. Im bardaiṣanitischen System verkörpert die höchste Stufe den Geist und die Freiheit, das ideale menschliche Leben ; die niederste Stufe ist dumm, unfrei und verkörpert den Tod. Al-Šahraštānī setzt die obere und untere Stufe in Beziehung zu der freien Tat und der unfreien, gezwungen Tat[4]. Ephräm kennt diese bardaiṣanitische Freiheitslehre, wie sich im sechsten *Hymnus contra Haereses* zeigt. In Strophe 9 und 10 dieses Hymnus schreibt er :

> Und wenn nun der Lauf der Sterne und Gestirne
> nicht vom freien (Willen) der Gestirne selber abhängt,
> dann lasst uns die folgende Frage stellen, die allerschwierigste :
> Wer verursacht die Bewegungen ihrer aller ?
> Wer aber in seiner Bewegung sich als unfrei zeigt,
> den mache nicht zum Herrn ; denn er ist eine Knecht ohne Füsse.
>
> Spitzfindig ist Bardaiṣan, der jenes Schicksal für gebunden erklärte
> durch ein höheres Schicksal, das in Freiheit (seine Bahn) eilt.
> Die Unfreiheit der Unteren spricht gegen ihn bei den Höheren.
> Ihr Schatten spricht gegen ihre Körper.

1. *Prose Refutations*, II, p. 164:41-165:12.
2. *Prose Refutations*, I, p. 8:4-39 : *cf. Bardaiṣan of Edessa*, p. 134 ff.
3. *Cf.* P. Boyancé, Dieu cosmique et dualisme. Les archontes et Platon, *Le Origini dello Gnosticismo*, Leiden, 1967, p. 340-356 ; U. Bianchi, Bardesane Gnostico. Le Fonti del Dualismo di Bardesane, *Umanità e Storia*, Scritti in Onore di Adelchi Attisani, 1970 (?), p. 1-15 ; *cf.* für das ganze Problem : H. J. Krämer, *Der Ursprung der Geistmethaphysik*, A'dam, 1967, *passim* u. 223 ff.
4. G. Vajda, Le témoignage d'al-Māturidī sur la doctrine des Manichéens, des Dayṣānites et des Marcionites, *Arabica*, 13, 1966, p. 30 ; für islamische Berichte über pagane Religionen *vide* : G. Monnot, Les écrits musulmans sur les religions non bibliques, *M.I.D.E.O.*, 11, 1972, p. 5-48.

Denn jene Berechnung, welche die Unteren einfing,
lähmt (auch) die Freiheit, die gelöste, der Höheren[1].

Die Gestirne hatten eine Funktion in der Schöpfung der Welt und des Menschen und ebenso in der Lenkung der Welt und des Menschenlebens. Sie sind nicht ganz frei, das ist nur Gott, und ganz unfrei, das ist die Materie. Diese Stellen aus den *Hymnen contra Haereses* und die vierte Rede an Hypatius haben inhaltlich und sprachlich enge Beziehungen zum *Buche der Gesetze der Länder.* In diesem Dialog handelt es sich um das Problem der menschlichen Freiheit und Gebundenheit. Bardaiṣan diskutiert dort mit Awida, einem Astrologen, und führt aus, dass es im Menschen drei Ebenen gibt : Geist, Seele und Körper. Der Geist verkörpert die Freiheit, der Körper die völlige Gebundenheit. Die Natur *(k^{e}yânâ)* des Körpers gehört zur Materie wo es feste Regeln gibt. Diese sind unbeeinflussbar und beschränken das menschliche Dasein. Die Gestirne bestimmen das Los des Menschen in der Welt dadurch, dass die Seele im Moment der Geburt die Planetensphäre durchquert und so aus dem göttlichen Bereich in den Körper hinabsteigt. Die Gestirne heissen darum die Führer des Menschen *(mdbbr')*. Der Geist ist an die Seele gebunden und ist die geistige Potenz, wodurch ein Mensch seine Freiheit durch gute Taten beweisen und zugleich seinen Ursprung kennenlernen kann. Der Geist verbindet den Menschen mit Gott. Das Drei-Stufen-Schema finden wir auch hier, charakterisiert durch die zentrale Stelle der Freiheit, welche korrelat ist mit dem Grad der Vermischung. Bardaiṣan sagt es so :

Die Stocheia (= Astralmächte) werden gerichtet, insofern sie (eigen-)mächtig sind. Als nämlich die Wesen *(ityê)* geordnet wurden, wurden sie nicht ihrer Natur, sondern durch die Vermischung miteinander geschwächt, (nur) ihrer eigentümlichen Gewalt beraubt und durch die Macht ihres Schöpfers gebändigt. Sofern sie nun unterworfen sind, werden sie nicht gerichtet, wohl aber insofern sie Eigenes haben[2].

Von hieraus gibt es Verbindungslinien mit Ephräms sechste *Hymne contra Haereses* und mit seinen Auseinandersetzungen über den freien Willen des Menschen. Wenn Ephräm in seiner vierten Rede an Hypatius von Archonten und Führern spricht, von der Weisheit dazu gebracht, den menschlichem Körper zu schaffen, dann hat das eine genaue Parallele im *Buch der Gesetze der Länder*, wo wir die Reihe : Weisheit (= Gott), Herrscher (*šalitânê* = Archonten), Führer *(m^{e}dabb^{e}rânê)*, Mensch finden[3].

Kosmologie und Anthropologie, Naturphilosophie und Ethik interferieren hier : vermischt = unfrei, unvermischt = frei. Das Ziel des Menschenlebens ist, die Vermischung rückgängig zu machen, das bedeutet die Finsternis vertreiben = die Freiheit dazu zu verwenden, um Gutes zu tun und dadurch die Seele die Rückkehr zu ihrem Ursprung zu ermöglichen.

1. Übersetzung von E. Beck, *Des heiligen Ephraem des Syrers Hymnen contra Haereses*, *C.S.C.O.*, 169-170, Louvain, 1957 : *vide* auch Becks Kommentar zum sechsten Hymnus, Tom. 170, S. 26, Anm. 3.
2. *Liber Legum Regionum*, ed. F. Nau, *P.S.*, I, 2, col. 548, 551 ; *cf. Bardaiṣan of Edessa*, p. 78.
3. *Liber Legum Regionum*, Col. 568.

Bisher hat sich keine fundamentale Diskrepanz zwischen Ephräms Schriften, der kosmologischen Überlieferung und dem *Buch der Gesetze der Länder* gezeigt. Wo das Grundmotiv des kosmogonischen Mythos und des Dialogs ermittelt wird, dort zeigt Bardaiṣan sein eigentliches Antlitz.

Eine Vergleichung zwischen Mani und Bardaiṣan, um Übereinstimmungen und Unterschiede herauszuarbeiten, impliziert nicht, dass es keine anderen Einflüsse auf Manis Denken gegeben hat. In Einzelfällen ist es oft schwer zu entscheiden, ob Vorstellungen Mani über Bardaiṣan oder eine andere Herkunft erreicht haben. Methodisch am richtigsten ist es, das Gerüst beider Systeme zu vergleichen und das Grundmotiv herauszuarbeiten.

In der manichäischen Kosmologie ist das Drei-Stufen-Schema bei Bardaiṣan verlassen worden ; die Finsternis ist an und für sich nicht inaktiv, wie bei Bardaiṣan, sondern hat eine eigene irrationale, chaotische Aktion. So stehen Licht und Finsternis, der Vater der Grösse und der Fürst der Finsternis einander gegenüber. Zwar ist das Licht der Finsternis überlegen, aber « cette supériorité du Bien n'implique entre les deux Substances aucune inégalité »[1]. Die mittelste Stufe der vier reinen Elemente hat Mani gleichsam verdoppelt, so dass für Lichtwelt und Finsternis fünf Substanzen oder Potenzen (nämlich vier plus eins) charakteristisch sind. In der Finsternis sind Rauch, Feuer, Wind, Wasser und Finsternis über einander gelagert, das sind drei reine Elemente zusammen mit der Finsternis. Das vierte reine Element, Licht ist durch Rauch ersetzt, womit die Finsterniswelt charakterisiert ist[2]. Dieser Rauch, *al-Humâna* in der arabischen Überlieferung[3], ist gleichsam der Geist der Finsternis, und hat selbstverständlich den Platz des Lichtes eingenommen. Alle Substanzen in der Finsterniswelt sind durch ein spezifisches Metall gekennzeichnet, einen eigenen Geschmack, eine eigene Form usw.

Das erinnert an Bardaiṣan, wo alle Elemente fünf Eigenschaften haben, korrespondierend mit dem menschlichen Sinnesorganen[4]. Der schwarze Rauch kehrt wieder in der bardaiṣanitischen Kosmogonie in Theodor bar Khonais Rezension :

> Das Feuer entzündete den « Wald » (= Hyle)
> und es ballte sich eine finstere Wolke
> die keine Geburt des Feuers war,
> und die reine « Luft » ward getrübt[5].

Die Lichtwelt ist zusammengesetzt aus fünf Wohnungen oder Gliedern des Vaters der Grösse, fünf geistigen Potenzen, als Antipode der Finster-

1. Puech, *Le manichéisme*, p. 75.

2. Puech, Le prince des ténèbres en son royaume, *Satan*, Etudes carmélitaines, 1948, p. 136-174 ; dort behandelt Puech, *Kephalaion*, XXVII und VI, wo die Finsterniswelt beschrieben ist ; *vide* auch A. Böhlig, *Mysterion und Wahrheit*, S. 245 ff. ; *cf.* Vajda, art. cit., p. 14 ff.

3. Puech, *Le manichéisme*, p. 159 ; Le prince des ténèbres, p. 158 f .; Vajda, art. cit., p. 18-21.

4. *Prose Refutations*, II, p. 223:23-224:7 ; das ist auch in den arabischen Überlieferungen über den Manichäismus bezeugt, *cf.* Vajda, art. cit., p. 12 ff. ; Puech, Le prince des ténèbres, p. 155 ff.

5. Übersetzung von H. H. Schaeder, *Bardesanes von Edessa*, S. 135.

niswelt. Wenn nun der Urmensch nach der Finsternis gesandt wird, um deren Drohungen abzuwenden, trägt er eine Rüstung aus fünf Lichtelemente *(zîwânê)* : Luft, Wind, Wasser und Feuer. Wie die Finsterniswelt den dunklen Rauch als Kennzeichen hat, so die Lichtwelt die dünne Luft. Hier finden wir also Bardaiṣans vier reine Elemente zusammen mit der Luft. Das erinnert an Bardaiṣans Kosmologie nach Theodor bar Khonai, wo von « der reine Luft » gesprochen wird[1]. Die Niederlage des Urmenschen, das Verschlungen-werden seiner Rüstung von der Finsternismächten, bedeutet eine Vermischung, wie sie in Bardaiṣans Kosmologie vorkommt. Doch gibt es wesentliche Unterschiede : Dringt bei Bardaiṣan die Finsternis in die reinen Elemente herein, durch einen Zufall geweckt, so bei Mani das Licht in die Finsternis und wird von der Finsternis überwaltigt. Die Schöpfung der Welt, die auf diese Vermischung folgt, hat folgerichtig in Bardaiṣans Denken das Vertreiben der Finsternis zum Ziel, bei Mani aber die Befreiung der Lichtteile der in die Materie gefallenen Seele. Der Ruf der vermischte Elemente in Bardaiṣans kosmologischem Mythos findet seine Parallele in dem Hilferuf des von der Finsternis verschlungen Urmenschen bei Mani. Darauf folgt das Herabkommen eines göttlichen Gesandten : bei Bardaiṣan das Wort des Denkens, bei Mani schliesslich der lebendige Geist. Diese haben aber eine verschiedene Aufgabe. Das Wort des Denkens vertrieb die Finsternis, wie alle kosmologischen Traditionen einstimmig mitteilen, und machte aus der übrigen Mischung diese Welt. Das Ziel aller folgenden Schöpfungsakte ist die definitive Vertreibung der Finsternis. Der lebendige Geist hat als Aufgabe die Befreiung des Urmenschen, der verschlungenen Lichtelemente. Das gelingt nicht völlig und deshalb sind die folgenden Schöpfungsakte auf die definitive Befreiung dieser Lichtteilchen gerichtet. Sowohl bei Bardaiṣan wie Mani ist also ein göttlicher Gesandter — sagen wir der Nous —, der Demiurgos[2]. Im Schöpfungsprozess schaffen diese Gesandten den Kosmos ; im Kosmos sind die Astralmächte, Planete und Zodiakalzeichen am wenigsten mit Finsternis vermischt. Bis hierhin besteht wieder eine weitgehende Parallelität zwischen Bardaiṣan und Mani. Die Funktion dieser Astralmächte ist aber grundverschieden. Bei Bardaiṣan haben sie eine beschränkte Freiheit — sie sind am wenigsten vermischt — und schaffen den Menschen, dazu von der Weisheit verführt. Bei Mani sind die Astralmächte Stationen auf dem Wege zu Mond, Sonne und Lichtwelt, aber die Schöpfung des Menschen ist das Werk der Archonten der Finsternis, dazu verführt vom Tertius Legatus in seiner Gestalt einer Lichtjungfrau. Es ist also völlig unrichtig, wenn Frau Aland behauptet, dass bei Bardaiṣan und Mani « Zweck der Welt ist die Ermöglichung der Befreiung der Lichtteile ». Das trifft nur für Mani zu. Unrichtig ist auch ihre Behauptung : « Lehre des Bardaiṣans ist danach die folgende : die Sophia, d.h. eine göttliche Gestalt, hat den

1. Schaeder, *Bardesanes von Edessa*, S. 137 stellt die reine Luft dem Äther gleich, was richtig ist ; wenn er aber den Äther mit dem Raum gleichsetzt, um eine Zahl von sieben *ilyê* zu erreichen, ist das falsch, *cf. Bardaiṣan of Edessa*, p. 131 ff.

2. Puech, *Le manichéisme*, n. 336 ; Schaeder, *Urform*, S. 46 ; Colp , *R.G.G.*[3], IV, Sp. 721 ; und Nachwort zu Schaeder, *Studien*, S. 255 f. ; *cf.* W. Lentz, What is the Manichaean Nous ?, *Ural-Altaische Jahrb.*, 33, 1961, p. 101-106.

Archonten der Finsternis ein Bild ihrer Schönheit gezeigt, um sie dazu zu veranlassen, das Bild nachzuformen, d.h. den Menschen zu schaffen ». Die Archonten der Finsternis spielen nur eine Rolle in Manis System ; bei Bardaiṣan sind diese Archonten Astralmächte, die in der Ordnung des Kosmos eine Stelle gleich nach Gott einnehmen. Die Wertung des Körpers ist — ganz konzequent — bei beiden unterschieden ; für Bardaiṣan ist der Körper erlösungsneutral ; dort befindet sich die Seele und der Geist, und richtige Anwendung der geistigen Gaben ermöglicht die Rückkehr der Seele zu ihrem Ursprung. Bei Mani ist der Körper Gabe der Finstermächte, und dadurch erlösungswidrig. Die Diskussion zwischen Mani und den Bardaiṣaniten über das Verhältnis von Seele und Körper bezieht sich hierauf. Sowohl bei Bardaiṣan wie bei Mani findet nach der Vermischung die Schöpfung statt durch eine geistige Potenz, die zugleich eine erlösende Funktion hat. In der bardaiṣanitischen kosmologischen Tradition wird das Wort des Denkens dem Logos oder Christus gleichgestellt. Ebenso finden wir im Manichäismus die Vorstellung von Jesus als dem Nous, Verstandeswelt-Gott. Die Gestalt Jesu ist für Mani ebenso wenig wesentlich wie für Bardaiṣan. Wesentlich ist der Geist-Begriff als schaffende und erlösende Kraft : « die manichäische Christologie muss deshalb als paganisiert bezeichnet werden »[1]. Darin sind Bardaiṣan und Mani einig : der Geist reinigt die Schöpfung[2]. Bei Bardaiṣan geschieht diese Reinigung im Körper, wenn der Mensch das Wort Gottes hält. (Joh. 8, 51 ff.)[3]. Dann hat die Finsternis, das Böse, keine Chance, sich geltend zu machen, und wird vertrieben, da sie an und für sich nichts ist, und nur Kraft hat, wenn sie geweckt wird. So geschah es vor der Schöpfung der Welt, so geschieht es auch in der Erlösung. Dann kann die Seele zurückgehen zum Brautgemach des Lichtes. In Manis System hat das Böse eine eigene Aktionsfähigkeit und deshalb ist der Reinigung im Körper unmöglich. Man soll der Finsternis entfliehen und das geschieht in der Askese.

Bei Bardaiṣan und bei Mani hat die Gnosis eine erlösende Funktion : bei dem aramäischen Philosophen ist Gnosis Verwirklichung der menschlichen Freiheit, Realisierung des Ethos, der praktischen Vernunft. Damit steht er in der Tradition der platonisierenden Philosophie, auch in deren mehr vulgären Formen[4].

Mani hat das « Szenario » der Schöpfung radikalisiert und damit Erlösung inhaltlich anders bestimmt. Das ist etwas ganz anderes als das Ausgleichen von Unstimmigkeiten oder Verbesserung eines ihm vorliegenden Systems. Es gibt eine zusammenhängende Tradition zwischen Mani und dem Philosophen aus Edessa, aber es kann nur die Rede sein von einer Kontinuität der Probleme und Motive. Daraus eine Kontinuität der Lehre zu folgern, wäre eine Rückkehr zu den Methoden der religionsgeschichtlichen Schule.

1. Colpe, *R.G.G.*³, IV, Sp. 721 ; *cf.* Bardaiṣan of Edessa and the Hermetica, p. 206.
2. *Prose Refutations*, II, p. 206:31-39.
3. *Prose Refutations*, II, p. 164:17-28.
4. *Cf.* Bardaiṣan of Edessa and the Hermetica, *passim.*

XIV

QUQ AND THE QUQITES

An unknown sect in Edessa in the second century A.D.

Since Walter Bauer in 1934, in his deservedly famous book, pointed out the 'heretical" character of the earliest Christianity in Edessa, where in the second century A.D. Marcionites and Bardesanites set the pace, [1]) our picture of religious life in this town has become considerably more complex. Thus A. F. J. Klijn distinguishes a number of loosely connected groups centred on particular persons or scriptures, including the Odes of Solomon and the Gospel of Thomas, [2]) while everything indicates that also other writings from the gnostic library of Chenoboskion either originated from the region of Syria or were known there. [3]) Jewish Christianity, whatever its exact definition may be, is also given an important place in Edessa, and direct historical connections are even thought to exist between Jerusalem and Qumran on the one hand and Edessa on the other. [4]) Bearing in mind that the

---

1) W. Bauer, *Rechtgläubigkeit und Ketzerei im ältesten Christentum*, BHTh, 10, Tübingen, 1934; second edition with a "Nachtrag" by G. Strecker 1964, SS. 6-48.

2) A. F. Klijn, *Edessa de stad van de apostel Thomas*, Baarn 1962, *passim*; *idem, The Acts of Thomas*, Supplements to Novum Testamentum V, Leiden 1962, pp. 30-33.

3) A Syrian origin of the Gospel of Thomas and the Gospel of Philip is certain. Since P. Nagel's article "Die Herkunft des Evangelium Veritatis in sprachlicher Sicht", *OLZ*, 1966, Kol. 5-14, it also becomes more likely for the Evangelium Veritatis, after H. M. Schenke, *Die Herkunft des sogenannten Evangelium Veritatis*, Göttingen 1959, had already pointed in that direction. Nagel points out a number of evident Syriacisms in the EV; but *cf.* A. Böhlig, "Zur Ursprache des Evangelium Veritatis", *Le Muséon* LXXIX, 1966, SS. 317-333.

4) Thus *int. al.* J. Daniélou, *Das Judentum und die Anfänge der Kirche*, Köln/Opladen 1964, *passim*; R. Aubert/J. Daniélou, *Geschiedenis van de Kerk I*, Hilversum/Antwerpen 1963, pp. 221 ff; J. C. L. Gibson, "From Qumran to Edessa or the Aramaic speaking Church before and after 70 A.D.", *The Annual of Leeds Oriental Society*, V, 1963-1965, Leiden 1966, pp. 24-39; *cf.* for Jewish Christians in Edessa, G. Strecker, *Das Judenchristentum in den Pseudoklementinen*, TU 70,

origins of Gnosticism are also sought in Edessa and its environment, we have a fairly complete general idea, though it is far from harmonious and clear. [5])

In none of the studies discussing the religious history of Edessa in the second century A.D. will the name of the heresiarch Quq and his eponymous followers be found, for the obvious reason that extremely little is known of him. In his edition of 1898 of the eleventh book of scholia of Theodore bar Khonai, H. Pognon annotates the passage dealing with the Quqites: "Cette secte est très peu connue". [6]) Unknown they are still at any rate in 1946, when G. Widengren speaks of "the little known sect of the Quqites", [7]) and in 1958 J. Doresse introduces the French translation of Theodore bar Khonai's passage regarding them with the words "Plus étrange était la secte des Koukéens". [8]) Obscurity combined with strangeness is attractive, and this may justify the following study, which will render the religious situation of Edessa even more complex, yet will also draw a few lines which may be hoped to increase its clarity.

The number of sources for the knowledge of Quq and his followers is restricted, yet it is greater than was thought up to the present. [9])

Berlin 1958; G. Strecker, "Zum Problem des Judenchristentums", Nachtrag I to W. Bauer, *Rechtgläubigkeit und Ketzerei im ältesten Christentum*, second edition, Tübingen 1964, SS. 245-287; H. Koester, "ΓΝΩΜΑΙ ΔΙΑΦΟΡΟΙ: The Origin and Nature of Diversification in the History of Early Christianity", *HThR*, 58, 1965, pp. 279-318; *Aspects du Judéo-Christianisme*, Paris 1965 with contributions by M. Simon, G. Quispel, J. Daniélou *et al.*, in which Qumran and Edessa are repeatedly brought into relation.

5) Thus *int. al.* Quispel, Daniélou, Doresse, Puech, Rudolph and many others; *cf.* K. Rudolph, "Stand und Aufgaben in der Erforschung des Gnostizismus", *Sonderheft d. Wiss. Zeitschr. d. Friedrich-Schiller-Universität Jena*, 1963, SS. 89-102, esp. S. 96; Edessa and the surrounding parts form the only region where all the cultures and religions, to which in turn the origins of Gnosticism are traced, have exercised influence upon each other.

6) H. Pognon, *Inscriptions mandaïtes des coupes de Khouabir*, Paris 1898, p. (209), note 1.

7) G. Widengren, *Mesopotamian Elements in Manichaeism*, UUÅ 1946, 3, p. 16.

8) J. Doresse, *Les livres secrets des gnostiques d'Égypte*, Paris 1958, p. 58; in the English translation, *The secret books of the Egyptian Gnostics*, London 1960, Doresse did not change this outlook.

9) Pognon, *l.c.*, p. (209) only names "un passage de saint Ephrem" besides the notice of Theodore bar Khonai; A. Harnack, *Der Ketzer-Katalog des Bischofs Maruta von Maipherkat*, TU IV, 1b, Leipzig 1899, S. 10 f. only knows the notice of Maruta and the four passages in the Hymns contra Haereses of Ephrem

Ephrem Syrus names Quq some four times in his Hymns contra Haereses, while he is also mentioned in Ephrem's Testament in the enumeration of all the heretics who threatened orthodoxy in Edessa, and demanded Ephrem's attention and energy. [10]) Maruta of Maipherkat (born c. 350) also devoted a passage to Quq and his followers in his heretical catalogue. [11]) A notice of much the same content, but far more detailed, is found in the Historia Ecclesiastica of Barḥadbešabba ᶜArbaïa and also in the Book of the Lamp of Darkness by Abû 'l-Barakât. [12]) Jacob of Edessa makes a short remark about him in his twelfth letter to the stylite Joḥannan of Litharb, [13]) and finally Theodore bar Khonai gives an extensive account of the heresy of the Quqites in his above-mentioned book of Scholia, an account entirely different from all the others. [14]) For a slightly better understanding

---

where Quq is named; A. Schmidtke, *Neue Fragmente und Untersuchungen zu den judenchristlichen Evangelien*, TU 37, 1, Leipzig 1911, SS. 173 ff. is acquainted with the notice of Maruta and that of Theodore bar Khonai, which he has taken from W. Bousset, *Hauptprobleme der Gnosis,* FRLANT 10, Göttingen 1907, S. 263 Anm. 2; S. 337, Anm. 2; Bousset knows the "passage de saint Ephrem" mentioned by Pognon; Puech in Hennecke/Schneemelcher, *Neutestamentliche Apokryphen I*, Tübingen 1959, S. 187 f. names all the fore-mentioned texts, and also the fragment from the 12th letter of Jacob of Edessa (incorrectly termed by him the 13th letter; H. H. Schaeder, *ZKG*, LI, 1932, S. 44, Anm. 41 even speaks of the 17th letter); Doresse, *l.c.*, p. 58 only names Theodore bar Khonai. Obviously the texts from the Historia Ecclesiastica of Barḥadbešabba ᶜArbaïa and of Abû 'l-Barakât have escaped notice. It may be that also Moses bar Kepha and Îwannîs of Dàrā have similar notices referring to Quq, but their works are largely unpublished.

10) Testament of Ephrem, *JA*, 9 série, 18, 1901, p. 298; *cf.* F. Haase, *Altchristliche Kirchengeschichte nach orientalischen Quellen*, Leipzig 1925, S. 316, and on the Testament of Ephrem in particular: A. Vööbus, *Literary critical and historical studies in Ephrem the Syrian*, Stockholm 1958, pp. 11 ff.

11) *ed.* I.E. II Rahmani, *Documenta de antiquis haeresibus*, Studia Syriaca IV, In seminario Scharfensi de monte Libano 1909, p. 111 (Syr. count), p. 78 (Latin translation); Rahmani also mentions part of the notice of Theodore bar Khonai in a Latin translation, p. XLII.

12) Barḥadbešabba ᶜArbaïa, *La première partie de l'histoire, ed.* F. Nau, *PO* XXIII, Paris 1932, pp. 194 sv.; Abû 'l-Barakât, *Le livre de la lampe des ténèbres, ed.* L. Villecont, *PO XX*, Paris 1929, p. 689-690.

13) *ed.* W. Wright, "Two Epistles of Mar Jacob, Bishop of Edessa", *Journal of Sacred Literature*, N. Series, 10, 1867, pp. 430-460; French translation by F. Nau, *ROC*, 10, 1905, pp. 278 svv.; German translation in A. Rücker, *Des heiligen Ephräms des Syrers Hymnen gegen die Irrlehren*, aus dem Syrischen übers., *BKV*², 61, München 1928, S. 13 f.

14) *ed.* H. Pognon, *l.c.*, p. 144 svv. (Syriac text), p. (209) svv. (French translation) and *ed.* S. Scher, *Liber Scholiorum*, *CSCO*, *Series Secunda*, 65-66, Paris

of Quq and the Quqites it seems desirable to examine these sources more closely, and that in a chronological order. After analysis and confrontation of the sources, a sketch of Quq's doctrine becomes possible of attainment, whereupon its place in the variegated religious scene of Edessa in the second century can be more narrowly determined, with all the lines that meet in this heresiarch or issue from him.

The sources

Ephrem Syrus (306-373), the champion of orthodoxy in Edessa, found Quqites there besides a number of other "heretical" groups, among whom Marcionites, Bardesanites and Manichaeans were most in evidence; for these three groups Ephrem's polemic supplies most valuable information, which unfortunately cannot be said of his report regarding the Quqites. Clearly this group as a whole was not very important. Ephrem says of them:

> Quq also is a mystery to the Quqites by his name,
> because he made them into pitchers, empty ones, by his doctrine. 15)
> The Quqite has added and spoiled (viz. the Scriptures). 16)
> The Quqite named it (viz. the community) after his name. 17)
> No more than the Audians
> are ashamed of the name "owl", no more are the Arians and the Quqites ashamed. 18)

Ephrem Syrus, then, has little matter to pass on regarding the Quqites. Playing upon the meaning of the word "quqa" = "pitcher", he declares that Quq made the Quqites into empty, sounding vessels, which truly do not contain the "treasure in earthen vessels" but merely mutilated Scripture, supplemented with products of their own, perhaps apocryphal or pseudepigraphical gospels. In the same way Ephrem plays upon the names of the other heresiarchs. 19) One

---

1910-1912, Vol. II, pp. (333) svv.; the text of Scher is almost identical with that of Pognon; neither edition can satisfy the requirements of scholarship; in the Institute of Semitic Studies of the State University of Groningen a new edition is in preparation.

15) *ed.* E. Beck, *Des heiligen Ephraem des Syrers Hymnen contra Haereses, CSCO*, Script. Syri 76 (*textus*), 77 (*versio*), Louvain 1957, II, 6, 5-6, p. 7 (*textus*), p. 8 (*versio*).

16) *CH* XXII, 2, p. 78 (*textus*), p. 77 (*versio*).

17) *CH* XXII, 3, p. 79 (*textus*), p. 78 (*versio*).

18) *CH* XXIV, 16, p. 95 (*textus*), p. 89 (*versio*).

19) *e.g.* with those of Mani, Bardaiṣan, Arius and Aud; *cf.* Beck, p. 89 (*versio*) Anm. 11 and 12.

strophe, Contra Haereses XXII, 2, is particularly important, for there Ephrem names Quq and the other heretics in this order: Marcion, Valentinus, Quq, Bardaiṣan and Mani. We notice that it is a chronological series, and may conclude that Quq was active in the period between Valentinus and Bardaiṣan, that is to say around 160 A.D. In his Prose Refutations Ephrem does not mention Quq at all any more, but only speaks of Marcion, Bardaiṣan and Mani, [20]) obviously those chiefly to blame for the sad lot of orthodoxy.

Maruta of Maipherkat has a passage on the Quqites in his heretical catalogue, which was afterwards added to a collection of largely spurious Acta and Canones of the Council of Nicea, transmitted to us in an Arabic version. [21]) In 1909 Rahmani edited the Syriac text of the heretical catalogue, after O. Braun had published a German translation in 1898, repeated and briefly annotated by Harnack in 1899. The Latin translation of this heretical catalogue by Abraham Echellensis, which is not entirely free of mistakes, is included in Mansi's collection of Council Acts. [22]) It is generally agreed that this heretical catalogue is indeed by Maruta, in contrast with other works ascribed to him. [23]) Maruta writes as follows about the Quqites:

Heresy of the Quqites

These resemble the Samaritans. They do not bury their dead, but when they have a dead man, they hire others to bury him. The resurrection (of the dead) they deny. They cast out lepers and sufferers from elephantiasis and other such ills. They have invented twelve evangelists with the names of the twelve apostles. They have also mutilated the whole of the New Testament, but not the Old. [24])

Barḥadbešabba ᶜArbaïa (end of the 6th century), "presbyter et interpres", "caput doctorum" of the famous theological school of Nisi-

---

20) *cf* F. Haase, *l.c.* S. 321: "Die Kukianer scheinen die älteste christliche Sekte in Edessa gewesen zu sein", words which Haase has taken literally from Harnack, *l.c.*, S. 10.

21) *cf.* for this matter H. J. W. Drijvers, *Bardaiṣan of Edessa*, Studia Semitica Neerlandica VI, Assen 1966, p. 107 f.

22) Mansi, *Conc.* II, Kol. 1058 E; Abraham calls the sect Phocalites, but this is due to a misreading of the Arabic text, *cf.* Rahmani, *Studia Syriaca IV*, p. XXX.

23) *cf.* I. Ortiz de Urbina, *Patrologia Syriaca*, Roma 1958, p. 49 and Drijvers, *o.c.*, p. 107, note 3.

24) text after Rahmani, *o.c.*, reprinted in F. Nau, Bar Hebraeus, *Sur les Hérésies, PO* XIII, Paris 1919.

bis, has a much fuller version of this notice in his Historia Ecclesiastica, running as follows: [25])

The ninth heresy is that of the Quqites. After this Quq, their heresiarch, was taken in sin with the wife of his father, he was expelled from the church and founded this heresy. He mixed the doctrine of the Scriptures with the notions of the Chaldaean system. They all believe in the Seven and the Twelve. He borrowed various things from Marcion and from Bardaiṣan and led his followers astray. Their way of behaviour is the same as that of the Samaritans. The dead they do not bury, and when they have a dead man, they hire strangers to bury him. The resurrection (of the dead) they deny. They cast out lepers and sufferers from elephantiasis and other such ills. Under the name of the twelve Apostles they have invented twelve gospels. The whole New Testament they have spoiled, the Old, on the contrary, they have not mutilated.[26])

The terminology of Barḥadbešabba and of Maruta is, at any rate in the second part of Barḥadbešabba's notice, almost literally the same, so that one naturally thinks of derivation or a common source. Barḥadbešabba is the only one to speak of the practice of astrology or a belief in astrological teachings on the part of the Quqites, and to suggest that they owe something to Marcion and Bardaiṣan.

An analogous notice in much the same words is found in the "Book of the Lamp of Darkness" of Abû 'l-Barakât (ob. 1325), whose Arabic text is almost the same as the Arabic preface to the apocryphal Acta and Canones of Nicea among which the heretical catalogue has been included. Yet this notice has a few characteristic additions. The statement is as follows:

The Sect of the Quqites

In their way of behaviour they resemble the Samaritans. They regard all things as unclean and they regard the dead as unclean and when one of them dies, they give him to someone they have hired to bury him and they remove him from their midst. If a stranger meets one of their women and desires an act of sin of her, there is nothing in their religion forbidding them to comply, but they regard it as a good work to violate some one in this manner. They do not believe in the Last Day, nor in the resurrection, nor in the Judgment. They cast out those afflicted with the itch, lepers, sufferers from elephantiasis and similar ills such as swellings of the glands and sores, those who are misshapen, such as the lame, some one who lacks a hand, is deaf or blind or has sore eyes, and they remove them from their midst. Therefore

25) *cf.* Baumstark, *Geschichte der syrischen Literatur*, Bonn 1922, S. 136; Ortiz de Urbina, *o.c.*, p. 123.

26) *PO* XXIII, p. 194 sv.

they have altered the books of the New Nestament and written a gospel for themselves under the name of the twelve apostles, without making an alteration in the books of the Old Testament (The Book of the Tower relates, that they resembled the Samaritans in their hatred of mankind, that they did not approach the dead, that they cast out the sick and misshapen, that only the pure and healthy were allowed to enter their houses of prayer and that they wrote the gospel which is put to the name of the twelve disciples. Nothing else is related of them). [27])

The Book of the Tower, commonly called *Liber Turris,* is a Nestorian Summa Theologiae and history of the Nestorian church, written in the middle of the 12th. century by Mārī ibn Sulaimān, entitled *Kitâb al-Miǧdal lil-istibṣar wal-ǧadal.* In the fourth part of the Book of the Tower is found a list of heresies, probably derived from Maruta's catalogue of heresies or an affiliated list. [27a]) On comparison, the three notices of Maruta of Maipherkat, Barḥadbešabba ᶜArbaïa and Abû 'l-Barakât respectively, show considerable resemblances beside differences and additions. They must be connected, and indeed this is already evident from the sequence of the heresies, which is exactly the same with all three authors. Considering all the peculiarities of the texts, the best solution of the problem in literary history thus posed is the following. At the time of Maruta of Maipherkat, and in all probability before his time already, there existed a collection of information about heretical groups in the Syrian-Mesopotamian region. whose author remains unknown up to the present. There is no reason to carry back all data to Ephrem, as is sometimes done. Maruta made a condensed version of this, which was afterwards added to the Acta and Canones of Nicea ascribed to him. The longer and more original version, however, continued in existence and is preserved, *int. al.*, in the notice of Barḥadbešabba. The information Maruta gives about the Bardesanites and the Manichaeans, compared with that given by Barḥadbešabba, also proves to be compressed, for Barḥadbešabba's longer version is not an elaboration of Maruta's notices; other sources confirm the soundness of Barḥadbešabba's information. [28]) If we compare the Syriac version of Maruta with the Arabic in the apo-

---

27) *PO* XX, p. 689 sv.

27a) *cf.* G. Graf, *Geschichte der christlichen arabischen Literatur,* Bd. II, *Studi e Testi 133,* Vatican 1947, pp. 200-202; and the literature there mentioned; A. Baumstark, *Geschichte der syrischen Literatur,* Bonn 1922, S.6.

28) *cf.* Drijvers, *o.c.*, pp. 106 ff.

cryphal Nicean acts, we find that the latter contains more than the former. This richer content is also found in the notice of Abû 'l-Barakât, who made use of these Nicean Acts, particularly of the preface which contains the heretical catalogue. Maruta's text, then, underwent some enlargement before assuming the shape in which it was finally embodied in the Nicean Acts, and this enlargement was presumably influenced by the existing longer version. The remarkable collation in the account of Abû 'l-Barakât also points to the existence of two versions, a long and a short one, as the text of the Book of the Tower is closest to Maruta's notice in length and content! There is no reason therefore, to doubt the reliability of these notices, since each in its own manner bears witness both to the early presence of many "heretical" groups in Syria and Mesopotamia and to the existence of an enumeration of them, which may be placed in the time of or before Maruta of Maipherkat. The spuriousness of the Acts of Nicea ascribed to him has therefore no consequences for the heretical catalogue.

The next author to claim our attention is Jacob of Edessa (about 633-708), who in his twelfth letter to the stylite Joḥannan of Litharb gives a number of particulars regarding sects of Edessa, in reply to an anxious inquiry from the pious stylite about the second Hymn contra Haereses of Ephrem Syrus and the sects mentioned there, particularly the Quqites, who are unknown to him. Jacob writes as follows:

> Now since you have also questioned your brother regarding Quq and the Quqites, I inform you of the following: five sects originated and came forth from the accursed heresy of Valentinus and each of these separately has added to and made alterations in this his heresy, more than his predecessors, viz. Valentinus, Marcion, Quq, Bardaiṣan and Mani... The sect of Quq, which is called the Quqites after him and which made many alterations, also proceeded from the adherents of Valentinus. [29]

Later Jacob himself corrects his statements and explicitly declares that the Bardesanites and the Manichaeans have nothing to do with Valentinus; for the Quqites this remark requires further examination. Jacob of Edessa, however, confirms our earlier surmise that the order in which Ephrem names the heresiarchs is chronological, by explicitly

29) Wright, *Journal of Sacred Literature* N. Series, 10, 1867, p. 26, 1.22 seqq (Syriac count); Puech mistakenly speaks of N. Series, 10, 1876 in Hennecke/Schneemelcher, S. 187, Anm. 5.

observing that the activity of these persons was largely consecutive. [30]) Our date of about 160 A.D. has thus a fairly solid foundation.

The longest account of the Quqites, and the one with the most interesting content, is found in the eleventh book of scholia of Theodore bar Khonai (end of the 8th century), who probably lived in Kaškar, a well-known residence of all kinds of "heretical" groups, both Christian and Muslim. [31]) After ten books of scholia on the O.T. and N.T., in the eleventh book Theodore gives a heresiological appendix, containing a survey of the teachings of the Greek schools of philosophy and related trends such as Orphism, [32]) of the teachings of Zoroaster [33]) and of those of a great number of in part unknown heretical groups, particularly gnostical ones. For the groups he did not know, Theodore made use of the Panarion of Epiphanius and of his Anakephalaiosis, although many differences may be observed between the notices of Epiphanius and those of Theodore: it is clear that the literary history of the matter is rather more complicated. Research into the sources of the eleventh book of scholia is surely very desirable. [34]) For his information about the groups in Syria and Mesopotamia, Theodore usually makes use of authentic sources, as a rule writings of the group itself, which he excerpts and then jeeringly comments upon. Something of the same kind is seen in his notices about the Manichaeans and Mandaeans, whom he calls Kantaeans and Dostaeans, while it is extremely probable for the Bardesanites. [35]) In the text of Theodore an authentic quotation can usually

30) Wright, *art. cit.* p. 27 (Syriac count).

31) It lay in Chinese Turkestan, a refuge for Nestorians(such as Theodore was himself, Manichaeans and many other zindiqs.

32) *cf.* A. Baumstark, "Griechische Philosophen und ihre Lehren in syrischer Ueberlieferung", *OC*, 5, 1905, SS. 1-25.

33) E. Benveniste, "Le témoignage de Théodore bar Kōnay sur le zoroastrisme", *Le Monde Oriental*, 21, 1932, pp. 170-215 and R. C. Zaehner, *Zurvan.* A Zoroastrian Dilemma, Oxford 1955, pp. 441 f.

34) Pognon, *o.c.*, p. (106) voices the supposition that Theodore made use of an extremely poor Syriac translation of the Anakephalaiosis, but many notices about sects are to be found neither in that, nor in the Panarion; here and there, *e.g.* in the notice about Simon Magus, influence of the Pseudo-Clementines may be seen.

35) *cf.* F. Cumont, *Recherches sur le Manichéisme I*, La cosmogonie manichéenne, Bruxelles 1908, *passim*; H. H. Schaeder, "Ein Lied von Mani", *OLZ*, 29, 1926, Kol. 104-107; K. Rudolph, *Die Mandäer I,* FRLANT, 74, Göttingen 1960, SS. 31 ff.; Drijvers, *o.c.*, pp. 113 ff. In the work of Theodore Puech found

be recognised by expressions such as "they say" or "they relate". These quotations, however, do not form a consecutive account; Theodore has gathered those best suited to his purpose, their demolishment. Especially the cosmological conceptions fascinated him. That is no wonder, for cosmology, in which soteriology is implied, was the great matter of controversy between Christians and Muslims on the one hand and "heretics", zindiqs, on the other. Undoubtedly this was due to the wide spread of Manichaeism, which persisted until late times. Ephrem Syrus in his Prose Refutations already combated Marcionites, Bardesanites and Manichaeans particularly upon this point, and this set of the three great heresies forms a regular and stereotype element in Muslim heresiological writings also. [36])

Theodore bar Khonai relates of the Quqites:

> They say that God was born out of the sea, that is that (sea) which lies in the empire of light and they call this the "wakeful sea" (or: angelic sea) [37]) and say that the sea of light and the earth existed before God. Now when God was born from the "wakeful sea" (or: angelic sea), he sat upon the waters, looked upon them and saw his own image in them. He stretched forth his hand and seized it. It was a spouse to him, he had intercourse with her and procreated many gods and goddesses with her. They call her Mother of Life and say that she formed seventy worlds (Aeons) and twelve rulers.
>
> Furthermore they assert that at some distance from this god, who was born from the "wakeful sea", there was something like a dead image, that is a statue without movement or life, without an idea or the faculty of thought. When god had seen that this was ugly and horrible and when this did not make a good impression on him, he conceived the plan of removing it from there and throwing it from him, but then he bethought himself: 'Since there is no life therein nor faculty of thinking nor thought to be able to wage war with me and there is not any inducement to badness found in it, it is not just that I should drive it from here. But I shall give it of my own strength and of my own movement and thought and then it will declare war upon me!'
>
> They say that he instructed the aeons to develop the flame of love and they poured forth part of their life and emitted it into this bad statue. That image now turned its soul and thought upon making war with them.
>
> And they say that the adherents of the party of Good fought forty-two battles with it. And the more the number of battles increased, the more carnal

---

fragments of an apocalypse, the Coptic text of which has now perhaps come to light in Nag Hammadi, Puech, "Fragments retrouvés de l'Apocalypse d'Allogène", *Mélanges Franz Cumont*, Bruxelles 1936, pp. 935-962.

36) *cf.* G. Vajda, "Le témoignage d'al-Māturidī sur la doctrine des Manichéens, des Dayṣānites et des Marcionites", *Arabica*, 13, 1966, pp. 1-38; pp. 113-128.

37) The Syriac word *ʿjrʾ* means "vigilans" or as substantive "angelus", *cf.* Brockelmann, *Lexicon Syriacum*, p. 523; *cf.* R. M. Tonneau, *Sancti Ephraem Syri*

forces were born, that is wild animals and cattle and creeping things of the earth...

Once, they relate, that Mother of Life descended to this statue, accompanied by seven virgins. When she had arrived there, it raised itself up and blew upon her. Its breath penetrated into her genitals, she became unclean and did not return to the dwelling of the gods, her companions. She remained for seven days in a condition of impurity and cast the seven virgins who accompanied her into the mouth of that great cavern. [38]) This swallowed them up during the seven days of the uncleanness of the Mother of Life, who threw him one of them every day. Now the gods were forced to come and save the seven virgins, whom the Mother of Life had cast into the gullet of that great cavern.

They say that the adherents of the party of Evil at set times celebrate a feast, cause these virgins to come forth and give them to their sons, and ornament themselves with the light deriving from them. That then the adherents of the party of good, their betrothed ones, descend on the day of the feast and that each of them carries off his betrothed.

They also say that the coming of our Lord to the world was for no other reason than the saving of his betrothed, who was here. They say that He carried her off and rose up from the Jordan and saw that the daughter of the Mother of Life... from Egypt. They assert regarding the other virgins that one is in Hatra, another in Mabbug and still another in Harran. Their betrothed look down on them, and when their time is come, they liberate them.

So far Theodore bar Khonai on the teachings of the Quqites, which concludes the known sources. [39])

Apart from the statements of Ephrem Syrus and Jacob of Edessa, which are only of importance for dating the group of the Quqites, the tradition falls into two distinct parts. On one side the related notices of Maruta of Maipherkat, Barḥadbešabba ᶜArbaïa and Abû 'l-Barakât and the notice in the preface of the apocryphal Nicean Acts, on the other the account of Theodore bar Khonai with all its discrepancies. A solution of the problem thus arising may be sought in various ways. One of the branches of tradition may be dismissed as unreliable, or Theodore's notice may be regarded as representing a later development within the group of the Quqites, developed from a "system" as it is rendered by Maruta *et al.* There are sound reasons, however, for not regarding Theodore's notice as a later development, but as a facet of the original system. Also for Bardesanites and

---

in Genesim et in Exodum commentarii, *CSCO* Vol. 153 (*versio*), Vol. 152 (*textus*), p. 24, L. 4-5 (*versio*), p. 32, L. 8-9 (*textus*): Vir (*i.e.* Adam) vigil (ᶜ*jr*ᵓ), quia splendore unctus, et quid sit somnus hucusque nesciens ...

38) *cf.* however Th. Nöldeke, *WZKM*, 12, S. 359.

39) text after Pognon, *o.c.*, pp. 144sv.

Manichaeans Theodore bar Khonai supplies information about their original myths, and not about later developments, which did occur, particularly among the Bardesanites. Obviously Theodore had at his disposal a great number of authentic texts of early date, 40) so that it becomes doubly important to seek for the sources of the eleventh book of scholia. Thus our obvious course is to confront the two traditions, bearing in mind that the first intends to give a summary of the doctrine and life of the Quqites without extensive discussion of their cosmology, which indeed does not appear in the other notices of Maruta either, whereas Theodore bar Khonai quotes from Quqite writings without attempting systematisation. It is not too bold a conclusion, then, that the two branches of tradition supplement one another.

There are at the same time a number of links between the two traditions which may support this hypothesis. While the first branch of the tradition (Maruta etc.) speaks of many special rules for ritual purity among the Quqites, there is a corresponding strong emphasis in the account of Theodore bar Khonai on the uncleanness of the Mother of Life, arising from the breath of evil, which makes it impossible for her to return to the world of the gods. It is this very uncleanness and its consequences which start a process of salvation, which clearly is not yet completed. The Quqites will therefore need to preserve a certain state of purity if they wish to participate in salvation. The striking combination of Jewish-Samaritan prescripts of purity, according to the tradition, with a "gnostic" concept of pure and impure is another matter, to which we shall return presently. There is another trait in the account of Theodore bar Khonai which reminds us of the Samaritans, or rather of the Samaritan Simon Magus. He came as the "great power" to save Helen. 41) Now it is highly probable that this prostitute Helen finds her prototype in the cult of Helen, the sister of the Dioscuri, who was worshipped in Samaria as goddess of the earth and the moon. 42) Even if Helen did not originally belong to the Simonian gnostic system, the fact remains

40) *cf.* n. 35.

41) *cf.* Bousset, *Hauptprobleme*, SS. 261 ff. and E. Haenchen, "Gab es eine vorchristliche Gnosis", *Gott und Mensch*. Gesammelte Aufsätze, Tübingen 1965, SS. 265 ff.

42) *cf.* L.-H. Vincent, "Le culte d'Hélène à Samarie", *RB*, 45, 1936, pp. 221-232; G. Quispel, "Simon en Helena", *NTT*, 5, 1950-51, pp. 339-345; *idem, Gnosis als Weltreligion*, Zürich 1951, SS. 45-70, esp. SS. 62 ff.

that she afterwards occupied an important and attractive place in it for the followers of Simon. 43) In Theodore's report we find the combination of the μεγάλη δύναμις, whose incarnation Simon was, and the divine maiden delivered to impurity enlarged sevenfold, when he tells us that the divine "betrothed" descend to earth at set times to save one of the maidens. One of these "betrothed" was Jesus of Nazareth, a son of god incarnate, come to carry off his female partner. Thus we find the Simonian trait of "gnostic" reinterpretation of older mythological events equally among the Quqites. Now if Abû 'l-Barakât relates that the Quqites have no objection to their wives being used by any stranger who happens along, this is directly connected with Theodore's notice about the virgins and their "betrothed ones". Any stranger may be a son of god, sent out to save his virgin, who again may be incarnated in any woman; even the divine Epinoia finally landed in a brothel in Tyre, frequented by the stranger Simon from Samaria!

Even the traditional scandal supplied by Barḥadbešabba, that Quq was turned out of the church because he put his supposed Oedipus-complex into practice, may be connected with the notice of Theodore bar Khonai, who tells us that the supreme god was born from the sea of light, from which his wife, the Mother of Life, also came forth. The Mother of Life is always mother, wife and daughter in one, 43a) which makes the proceeding of the heresiarch Quq slightly more comprehensible. Barḥadbešabba's accusation of astrology, however, is more solidly supported by Theodore's account, when he relates that the Father and Mother of Life produce many gods and goddesses; Bardaiṣan places these last in an astrological setting and even compares Father and Mother with Sun and Moon (*cf.* Henena-Selene), so that something of the kind with the Quqites is not to be dismissed in advance. Moreover, Bardaiṣan is named by Barḥadbešabba as one of those from whom Quq had borrowed; it must not be forgotten that the patres often made the same mistake as the "religionsgeschichtliche Schule", which also at once assumed borrowing whenever conceptions were found to be alike.

---

43) This is the thesis of Quispel, "Simon en Helena" and with some reservation also of Haenchen, *art. cit.*, S. 290 f.

43a) *cf.* Bousset, *Hauptprobleme*, S. 337, who has continually drawn attention to this.

In any case, there are so many points of contact between the two branches of the tradition, that we are justified in regarding them as of equal value, and supplementary to each other. On the basis of the whole tradition, a partial reconstruction of the doctrine of Quq and the Quqites has come within the reach of possibility.

The teachings of the Quqites

Since every cosmological statement is anthropologically determined, reflecting a particular outlook upon man and the world, it is methodically indicated to begin with the notice of Theodore bar Khonai. The soteriological passage at the end of it forms the required link with the information about the rules for purity of the Quqites and their sexual practices, which also demonstrate a particular outlook upon the life of man.

In the beginning there existed the light-world, also called the "wakeful sea" (or: angelic sea) and the sea of light, and its antipole the earth. The expression "wakeful sea" can be elucidated by its contrast "sleeping": waking and being awakened belongs to the world of the divine, the world of light, whence life comes, while sleeping is as a rule a metaphor for sinking down into matter. [44]) It is explicitly stated that the light-world and the earth existed before God, who was born from the life-giving sea of light. This God sat down upon the waters and saw his own image in them, a female shape, the Mother of Life, with whom he produced many gods and goddesses. Here we have, then, a certain form of the Narcissus motif. [45]) The god born from the light-world is clearly androgynous; by his "redoubling" in the mirror of the water, the female element is as it were split off, which before was contained within him. It should be remarked that in the Gospel of Mary, a writing of the Barbelo-gnostics, and in the Apocryphon of John we also find the conception of the Primordial god, the Father of Light, who sees his image in the water of the pure light; this image is his ennoia or pronoia, also called Barbelo, the Mother of Life. [46]) One gains the impression, that speculations regarding the

---

44) *cf.* G. McRae, "Sleep and awakening in gnostic Texts", a paper read at the congress on the origins of Gnosticism, held in Messina in April 1966 (to be published in the Acta); H. Jonas, *Gnosis und spätantiker Geist I*, FRLANT 51, Tübingen ^{3}1964, SS. 113-115 and register *s.v.* schlafen, erwachen, Erweckung.

45) *cf.* H. Jonas, *The gnostic religion*, ^{2}1963, pp. 161 ff.

46) *cf.* Bousset, *Hauptprobleme*, SS. 59, 87 ff., 160, 338 ff.; *Apocryphon of*

Spirit of God who moved (or brooded) over the face of the waters, as related in Gen. 1 : 2b, form the background of this image. 47) For this Spirit is at the same time Wisdom and the Mother, who form or procreate the world. Is perhaps the remark of Barḥadbešabba about Quq having intercourse with the wife of his father to be explained from this angle?

The Father and Mother of Life bring forth seventy worlds or aeons and twelve Potentates or Rulers. Twelve and seven, and consequently seventy also, are astrological numbers indicating the seven planets and the twelve signs of the Zodiac. It is noticeable that we find Bardaiṣan using exactly the same Syriac terms, while he also calls the heavenly bodies children of the Father and Mother of Life 48) whom he compares to the sun and moon. The sun then stands for the father-god, the Father of Life, and the moon for the Mother of Life, whose light is derived from the sun. The Mandaeans also have the idea that the twelve signs of the Zodiac are children of the Father and Mother of Life. 49) In any case, the Quqites concerned themselves with astrology, as Barḥadbešabba also relates, while he also links Quq with Bardaiṣan. This again affords indirect evidence of the value of the tradition of Maruta, Barḥadbešabba and Abû 'l-Barakat, also with regard to data only supplied by one of them.

Theodore bar Khonai then gives a new quotation from the Quqite cosmology, referring to the existence of a statute, entirely lifeless and without movement, intellection or thought. The image is thus described as a complete contrast to the deity himself. Of the origin of this image nothing is said. After an initial plan to remove the image, God's justice gains the upper hand, and he instructs the aeons to kindle the flame of love and give life to the statue. The image now begins a bitter contest with the aeons; the number of forty-two battles is mentioned, and from this combat there issue wild animals, cattle and

---

John (*ed.* Till), 27: 1-5; Cod. III (*ed.* Krause/Labib), 7: 9-14; Codex II (*ed.* Krause/Labib) 4: 22-28; Codex IV (*ed.* Krause/Labib) 6: 25-29.

47) Bousset/Gressmann, *Religion des Judentums*, ³1926, SS. 342-350.

48) *Book of the Laws of Countries*, *ed.* F. Nau, *Patrol. Syriaca I*, 2, col. 568; *cf.* Drijvers, *Bardaiṣan*, p. 84 ff.; Ephrem, *CH* LV, 8, 10, *cf.* Drijvers, *Bardaiṣan*, pp. 147 f.

49) *cf.* K. Rudolph, *Theogonie, Kosmogonie und Anthropogonie in den mandäischen Schriften*, FRLANT 88, Göttingen 1965, SS. 169-172. *cf.* Drijvers, *Bardaiṣan*, pp. 148 ff.

creeping things of the earth (*cf.* Gen. 1). Various questions arise in trying to interpret this quotation: what is meant by this statue? how do the "carnal forces" arise, as Theodore calls them? Who are the adherents of Good?

H.-Ch. Puech puts this statue on a level with the primordial image of man from the Apocryphon of John, which cannot move because it was formed by the seven evil archons or, in other texts, by the demiurge Jaldabaôth after the image of the supreme god, which the archons saw in the water as a reflection. [50]) Yet the situation, at any rate according to the notice of Theodore, is fundamentally different in the Quqite cosmology. The Apocryphon of John and other gnostic texts deal with the fall of Sophia, Barbelo, whose divine strength passes in part to Jaldabaôth. When the latter, with the other evil archons, has formed the image of man, this does not move and only acquires movement and life when the αὐτογενής and the four lights induce the demiurge to blow the strength of the Mother into the face of the image, after the repentant Mother herself has besought the Father partly to undo her fault by this means. In the Quqite myth there is no question yet of the fall of Sophia, which will follow later, nor of Jaldabaôth and the evil archons; on the contrary, the aeons possess divine strength because of their origin from Father and Mother both, and from considerations of divine justice they are instructed to give life to the dead statue, without being induced to do so by a divine stratagem. While there is, then, a measure of formal resemblance between the Quqite myth and the story in the Apocryphon of John, the specific gnostic touch (in the sense of Gnosticism) is lacking in the myth of the Quqites, or at least does not enter till later, when we hear of the uncleanness of the Mother of life. Moreover, the Apocryphon of John lacks the motif of battle, which for the Quqites is the direct cause of the originating of the living creatures on earth.

Yet in spite of these differences, the statue may well make us think

---

50) Puech, in Hennecke/Schneemelcher I, S. 237, where all the relevant texts are mentioned; K. Rudolph examined them in "Ein Grundtyp gnostischer Urmensch-Adam-Spekulation", *ZRGG*, 9, 1957, SS. 1-20; *cf.* also S. Giversen, *Apocryphon Johannis*. The Coptic Text of the Apocryphon Johannis in the Nag Hammadi Codex II with Transl., Introd. and Commentary. Acta Theol. Danica V, Copenhagen 1963, pp. 238-259.

of Adam the Primal Man, who is at the same time the macro-cosmos from which everything comes forth. If the first quotation from the Quqite cosmology seems to contain speculations based on Gen. 1, it is probable that the image to which the aeons give life at God's command indicates Adam, who immediately afterwards begins the revolt against God as related in Genesis. Adam is at the same time the image of the macro-cosmos, in which all living creatures on earth are contained. [51]) The great stress upon the justice of God also points in this direction, as justice is only shown to men, in this case Adam. According to the Quqite myth, man shares strength, movement and thought with God, after whose image he is, after all, created, and for that reason he can revolt against him and wage war. The adherents of the party of Good are in this context the aeons and the twelve rulers, who as children of God wage the battle with Adam. It is noticeable that the description of the way the aeons pour out their life into the image has a definite sexual tinge and reminds one of the Manichaean myth of the tempting of the archons. [52])

The result of the battle is a choice array of animals which populate the world, showing a strong aversion to animal life, which has a low origin. [53]) The general aspect betrays a particular conception of man, who can do nothing without divine strength and so becomes a rebel, which clearly points in the direction of Judaism. [54] The aversion to wild and creeping creatures also points that way. [55]) The dualism characterising this passage is therefore ethical, and not a cosmic dualism of the contrast between God and matter.

Tradition reports unanimously that the Quqites preserved the Old Testament integrally, in contrast with the New. This may agree very well with the above. Obviously the Quqites read the O.T. in a

---

51) *cf.* Bousset, *Hauptprobleme*, S. 207; Doresse, *Les livres secrets*, p. 232, 275, note 90.

52) *cf.* G. Widengren, *Mani und der Manichäismus*, Stuttgart 1961, SS. 60-62; Widengren sees the origin of this conception in Zervanism and with the Sabians of Harran; in the Syrian world, then, we find a "Vorstufe" of this myth.

53) This is also Manichaean, *cf.* Widengren, *Mani*, S. 98.

54) *cf.* Bousset/Gressmann, *Religion des Judentums*, SS. 402 ff.

55) *e.g.* Test. Naphtali 8, where it is stated that the wild animals are the instruments of the Evil one; *cf.* Bousset/Gressmann, *Religion des Judentums*, SS. 334 ff., 516; Bousset/Gressmann see an Iranian influence here. The motif of battle may also be of Iranian origin, as *e.g.* Widengren, *Mani*, SS. 52 ff.

"gnosticising" manner, especially Genesis 1, which also appears in other phenomena within Judaism or its Samaritan branch. [56])

The second part of Theodore bar Khonai's account relates the fortunes of the Mother of Life who, accompanied by seven virgins, descended to the aforesaid image, that is to the world of man. With a sexual tinge (*cf.* the aeons and the statue), it is then related how the Mother is defiled by the image, which makes her return to the world of the gods impossible. She then sacrificies the seven virgins by throwing them into a great cavern, one every day, during the seven days of her ucleanness. Part of the divine light is thus abandoned to the human world, which treats it in an unseemly manner. The seven virgins, however, have seven divine betrothed, who are thus really their brothers, who at set times come to save them, until all the particles of light have been taken back to the light-world. Jesus of Nazareth is one of them, who saved his virgin when he ascended from out of the Jordan. The other maidens are in Hatra, Mabbug and Harran. The text of all MSS of Theodore's book is corrupt here, so that an uncertainty remains; possibly one of the maidens is in Egypt. In any case, we do not know them all. [57])

As already pointed out, this quotation strongly reminds us of the Simonian gnosis, in which also the fall of Sophia, "Frau Idee", takes a central place. [58]) The Quqites, however, do not speak of one virgin, but of seven, who reside in important cult centres, where they are misused by the "ordinary" people, the adherents of the party of evil, in order to possess themselves of their light particles, according to the Quqite interpretation. One is again reminded of the adventures of Helen before she finally landed in Tyre, but also of temple prostitution, which played a part in the cult of various goddesses in Asia Minor and Mesopotamia. [59]) Just as Helen is saved by Simon, who

---

56) *cf.* Bousset/Gressmann, *Religion des Judentums*, SS. 442 ff. and the speculations in the Samaritan *Memar Marqa* (*ed.* Mac Donald).

57) *cf.* Doresse, *Les livres secrets*, p. 114 and the literature mentioned on p. 131 sv. Has the text been purposely corrupted here? The French translation of Doresse, taken from Pognon, has a confusing misprint: p. 59: "et il fit que la fille de la Mère de la vie ... (?) ... d'Égypte" should be "et il vit etc. ..."

58) *cf.* Quispel, *Gnosis als Weltreligion*, SS. 45 ff.; Jonas, *Gnosis und spätantiker Geist*, SS. 353 ff.

59) *cf.* Bousset, Hauptprobleme, S. 72, Anm. 2 and the examples named there from the cult of Syrian goddesses; *cf. Wörterbuch der Mythologie I*, Götter und Mythen im Vorderen Orient, Stuttgart 1965, S. 85 (Ištar and Inanna), 231

perhaps masks Melkart, [60]) so all the virgins have a divine saviour. In the case of Mabbug, the reference is undoubtedly to Atargatis, the Dea Syra, with her male companion Hadad. [61]) In Harran the pair may be Ningal and Sin, [62]) while in Hatra again Astarte and Baal may be conjoined. If the text also located a virgin in Egypt, that will certainly be Isis who, Epiphanius informs us, passed part of her life in the same manner as Helen in Tyre. [63]) In the traditional view of Gnosticism, Jesus of Nazareth is the saviour of Sophia. [64]) The number of seven is remarkable and is also found in other texts. In the second book Ieou the Mother of Life appears accompanied by seven light-maidens; the famous Wedding song from the apocryphal Acts of Thomas speaks of the Mother with seven bridesmaids and seven bridesmen; the gnostic Gospel of Philip speaks of the mystery of marriage and possibly gives seven as the number of marriages. [65]) The Quqites, then, have attempted to gather in a "Gesamtschau" a number of religious phenomena in the Syrian-Mesopotamian region, in towns of a decidedly pagan character, and to relate them to one another. The various cults, in which a sacred marriage perhaps played a part, become phases in a grand process of salvation, whose aim is to lead back the divine light to its origin. The salvation of the virgins clearly takes the form of marriage with their divine betrothed, and thus the conception of the Bridal Chamber comes into view, which we find in the doctrine of Barḏaiṣan, in the Acts of Thomas, the Gospel of Philip, with the Valentinians, and perhaps with other groups

---

(Aštarte); Lucianus, *Dea Syra 6, 9* relates it of Aštarte in Byblos; *cf.* G. Goossens, *Hiérapolis de Syrie*, Louvain 1943, p. 64, 129.

60) *cf.* Bousset, *Hauptprobleme,* S. 262.

61) *cf.* Goossens, *Hiérapolis de Syrie,* pp. 57 svv.; F. Cumont, *Les religions orientales dans le paganisme Romain,* [4]1929, pp. 95 svv.

62) *cf.* E. Dhorme, *Les religions de Babylonie et d'Assyrie,* Paris 1949, pp. 58-59; 85-86.

63) Epiphanius, *Ancoratus* (*ed.* Holl), 104, 11; *cf.* Bousset, *Hauptprobleme,* SS. 81 ff.

64) *cf.* H. Jonas, *Gnosis und spätantiker Geist,* SS. 359 ff. for a description of the idea in the various systems.

65) *II Ieou,* 45-47, *cf.* Bousset, *Hauptprobleme,* S. 62; *Acta Thomae* 6 (*ed.* Lipsius/Bonnet) *cf.* Preuschen, *Zwei gnostische Hymnen,* Giessen 1904, SS. 40 ff. and Bousset, *Hauptprobleme,* S. 69. *Gospel of Philip* (*ed.* Till), 112: 30-36; 113: 10-12; *cf.* E. Segelberg, "The Coptic-Gnostic Gospel according to Philip and its sacramental system", *Numen,* 7, 1960, pp. 189-200 and R. Mcl. Wilson, *The Gospel of Philip,* London 1962, pp. 118 ff.

also. [66]) This means, that the union of the virgin with her divine betrothed is representative of the union of the fallen soul with its heavenly double, which completes salvation. It has already been remarked that in the Simonian gnosis salvation has really taken place already, so that there is nothing left for man to do. [67]) The Quqites do not have this problem, since some virgins are still unredeemed. We have seen above that the sexual practices of the Quqites, as reported by Abû 'l-Barakât, are directly related to this outlook upon fall and salvation, and indeed these practices are also found with related groups. [68]) Human conduct in this field is thus imitation, renewed enactment of a mythic example, and at the same time a demonstration, a ritual anticipation of salvation. Salvation will be completed when all the virgins have been redeemed. This is the sole aim of the whole history of mankind. Presumably man's history began with the defilement of the Mother of Life, but that is not clear.

A few matters still require further elucidation: the Quqite rules of ritual purity and their gospel. As to the latter, tradition is not unanimous: Maruta of Maipherkat speaks of twelve evangelists with the names of the twelve apostles; Barḥadbešabba speaks of twelve gospels and Abû 'l-Barakât is the only one to speak of a gospel of the twelve apostles. An Ebionite gospel has been suggested in this context, or an unknown gnostic gospel, and H. Waitz has even tried to show that the remark in Maruta's notice should be connected with the astrological gnostic teachings of the Quqites, in which the number twelve plays a certain role. [69]) A gospel of the twelve apostles, for that matter, is also ascribed to the Manichaeans. [70]) It may very well be that the gospel of the twelve apostles has something to do with the place accorded to the twelve signs of the Zodiac Theodore bar Khonai

66) C. W. Mitchell, *S. Ephraim's Prose Refutations of Mani, Marcion and Bardaiṣan II*, London 1921, p. LXXVII (transl.), p. 164: 32-40 (Syr. text); *cf.* Drijvers, *Bardaiṣan*, p. 151, 152, 160; Widengren, *Mesopotamian Elements*, pp. 109 ff, where a number of texts have been collected, also from Manichaean sources; Bousset, *Hauptprobleme*, SS. 315 f. (about the Marcosians); *Gospel of Philip*, 117: 24; 123: 26 sqq.

67) Haenchen, "Gab es eine vorchristliche Gnosis", S. 290.

68) *int. al.* the Bardesanians according to Michael Syrus and Agapius of Mabbug, *cf.* Drijvers, Bardaiṣan, p. 190.

69) *cf.* Puech in Hennecke/Schneemelcher, SS. 187 f. for an exposition of this matter; H. Waitz, *ZNW*, 14, 1913, S. 46 ff.

70) *cf.* Puech in Hennecke/Schneemelcher, S. 190 f.

speaks of. Astrology teaches that these twelve signs each rule over a part of the earth. Remembering that the Quqites held to the O.T., in which the number of twelve tribes plays an important part, one might imagine that the twelve apostles, as successors to these tribes, each had part of the world assigned to them. We would then see the same pattern here as in the combining of all kinds of Syrian cults into a whole, and in the way the Quqites treat the biblical story of creation, which they also mixed with autochthonous Syrian elements. A point of particular importance is, that a gospel of the twelve apostles is ascribed both to the Christian Jews in Syria and to Quqites and Manichaeans: this points to a close relationship, particularly in Syria.[71]) Of the content of this gospel nothing is known.

The rules of ritual purity of the Quqites are connected by tradition with the Samaritans, who did indeed hold to Jewish ritual laws, but not so rigorously as is stated here.[72]) Especially dead bodies and diseases of the skin inspire the Quqites with dread, and they keep their distance from them. Abû 'l-Barakât's remark, that they would also not admit people who lacked a hand or were blind or deaf, reminds us of the customs concerning priests: a Jewish or Samaritan priest was required to be entirely whole and sound in body.[73]) A horror of corpses, joined with a denial of the resurrection, is understandable from what Theodore bar Khonai tells us regarding the "dead image", which God found to be ugly and horrible. Everything that is without life, is ugly and horrible and must be avoided. Moreover, this is an indication that the "dead image" is indeed the primordial Adam. It is not impossible that particularly affections of the skin that resemble decomposition are avoided for that reason, but no certainty can be obtained on this point.

These are the outlines, then, in so far as the sources enable us to sketch them, of a sect in Edessa in the second century A.D. that was mostly unknown until now. Of its history we know nothing whatever,

---

71) The Manichaeans or Mani himself borrowed their knowledge of books of the Bible and apocrypha from the Syrian Christians and the Christianised Jews, and they thus became acquainted with the *Gospel of Thomas* and the *Acta Thomae*.

72) *cf.* for this Bousset/Gressmann, *Religion des Judentums*, S. 199 f., 458-460; *Berakot* 47b and Moore, *Judaism I*, p. 25; see also Lev. 13.

73) *cf.* Lev. 21, 22, where it is ordained that priests may have no blemish, may not touch dead bodies, *etc.* Did the Quqites consider these Levitical rules applicable to themselves?

though it was clearly still active in Ephrem's time, if only on a small scale. After that we lose every trace. Perhaps they disappeared in the melting-pot of Manichaeans, Mandaeans and Bardesanites, which cannot always be clearly distinguished in Syria. We now still have to give a characterisation of Quq and his followers in the midst of those groups, largely gnostic ones, which were active in the second century.

The Quqites in the setting of their time

When A. von Harnack characterised the Quqites in 1899, he called them the earliest Christian sect of Edessa, who as gnostic Christian Jews confronted the Bardesanites, who represented the Christianity of the Gentiles. [74]) Harnack based this characterisation on the notice in the catalogue of Maruta. A. Schmidtke, following after Bousset, characterises them as representatives of the earliest Syrian Gnosticism of a pagan kind, consisting of a mixture of Persian, Babylonian, Old Testament, and Christian conceptions. This pronouncement Schmidtke based solely on the notice of Theodore bar Khonai, which he had found in the work of Bousset. [75]) However, if different facets of the same group are illustrated by the two branches of tradition, then these generalising pronouncements cannot be maintained in their antithetic tendency. It is very much to be doubted, whether the contrast between Christians of Jewish and of gentile extraction was indeed so vivid and was so acutely felt in the second century. A piece taken from the work of Bardaiṣan, the gentile Christian, was given a place in one of the principal literary works of Jewish Christendom, the pseudo-Clementines. [76]) It really seems impossible to work with contrasts between Christian Jews, Christian Gentiles and Gnostics in this century and in this town. The complex character of the Quqite doctrines and myths may serve as illustration.

In the first place we found certain resemblances with Bardesanite conceptions, that is to say with the Father and Mother of Life who bring forth divine children, including the planets, whose function is not considered to be negative. Probably these Quqite conceptions can even consolidate the connection between the fragments of Bardaiṣan's

---

74) Harnack, *Der Ketzer-Katalog des Bischofs Maruta von Maipherkat*, S. 10.

75) Schmidtke, *Neue Fragmente und Untersuchungen zu den judenchristlichen Evangelien*, S. 174.

76) *cf.* for this matter Drijvers, *Bardaiṣan*, pp. 60 ff.

hymns preserved by Ephrem Syrus and the rest of his teachings. The idea of the planets as children of the gods, we find indeed in the Book of the Laws of Countries, while the train of thought in this book is usually regarded as in contradiction with Bardaiṣan's views as Ephrem Syrus renders them. [77]) The two combined are found with the Quqites, whom tradition connects with Bardaiṣan.

In the second place there are lines connecting the Quqites with the Christianised Jews, since they maintain the Old Testament as it stands, which does not preclude basing speculations upon it; we find the same in the Pseudo-Clementines. [78]) The rigorous rules of purity, understandable from the cosmological and anthropological views of the Quqites, may perhaps also constitute a pointer towards Christian Jewry. Tradition connects these rules with the Samaritans, where possibly Gnosticism has one of its sources. [79]) Relationship is clearly to be discerned with the Simonian Gnosis, which may have become known in Edessa through the activities of Satornilus and Menander, who worked in Syria. [80]) The difference is, however, that Simon linked his system with one existing cult in Samaria, while the Quqites gathered many cults in the Syrian-Mesopotamian region, largely identical in form and concept, into a single creed, and included Christianity. Therefore one cannot say whether the sect was Christian or not, nor whether it was Jewish. It is Jewish with pagan and Christian elements, pagan with Jewish and Christian elements, etc. The same complexity is found with Bardaiṣan. An example is the conception of the seven saviours. On the one hand this connects the Quqites with the Jewish Christian circles of the Pseudo-Clementines with its series of prophets who succeed one another, [81]) on the other with the idea of the cyclical

---

77) *cf.* Drijvers, *Bardaiṣan*, pp. 84-86.

78) *cf.* H. J. Schoeps, *Theologie und Geschichte des Judenchristentums*, Tübingen 1949, SS. 117 ff.; *idem, Aus frühchristlicher Zeit.* Religionsgeschichtliche Untersuchungen, Tübingen 1950, SS. 1 ff.: Die Urgeschichte nach den Pseudoklementinen.

79) *cf.* H. J. Schoeps, *ThLZ*, 1956, Sp. 418 and Rudolph, *„Ein Grundtyp"*, S. 19. It is noticeable that the Jewish Christians had strict rules of purity, including a prohibition to eat meat, *cf.* Schoeps, *Theologie und Geschichte*, SS. 188 ff.; also Daniélou, *Théologie du Judéo-Christianisme I*, Tournai 1958, pp. 82 svv. points to Samaria.

80) *cf.* Leisegang, *Die Gnosis*, SS. 103-110.

81) *cf.* Bousset, *Hauptprobleme*, SS. 172 f.; Schoeps, *Theologie und Geschichte*, SS. 98-116.

appearance of the messenger of light, which appears in Manichaeism, but also in the Coptic gnostic writings of Chenoboskion. [82]) With this latter group there are more parallels: the conception of the "dead image" of the primordial Adam; the image of the "Bridal-Chamber", which we find in the Gospel of Philip and with which certain sacraments may have been connected. [83]) Denial of the resurrection is a general gnostic trait, even going beyond the limits of Gnosticism, if such limits can be defined, but in the library of Chenoboskion the Epistula ad Rheginum is explicitly devoted to this theme. It also contains clear parallels with Bardesanite teachings, thus more or less completing the circle. If we remember, too, that the idea of the "Bridal-Chamber" is also found with Bardaiṣan, as it is in the wedding hymn of the Acta Thomae, where again the Mother appears with seven virgins and seven sons (bridesmen), the unity in diversity of the many different groups is even more clearly illuminated. [84])

In spite of all resemblances with gnostic or half-gnostic systems of the second century, we must seriously enquire whether the Quqite creed belongs to the Gnosis or not. If the defilement of the Mother of Life, of which her daughters become victims, really does represent the fall of the anima, then we have to do here with a definitely gnostic system. The anti-cosmic dualism, however, is not yet fully developed: the figure of the evil demiurge is lacking; the planetary powers have not yet descended to the level of wicked archons, but are still helpers of God and constitute his army. Jewish, and possibly Iranian, is the idea that evil comes from man, since it is he who defiles the Mother (*cf.* Eve, who is defiled and violated by the archons); the world of man is divided into two groups, those who adhere to evil and those who adhere to good, that is to say the budding dualism is still ethically determined, hence the elaborate ethical system of purity of the Quqites! Neither is the creation of the world due to a fall of the deity: both the heavenly world of light and the earth existed from the beginning! Yet

---

82) *cf.* K. Rudolph, "Gnosis und Manichäismus nach den koptischen Quellen", *Wissensch. Zeitschr. d. M.-Luther Univ. Halle-Wittenberg*, Sonderheft 1965: *Koptologische Studien in der DDR*, SS. 174 ff. and the literature and texts listed there.

83) Thus Bousset, *Hauptprobleme*, SS. 315 ff. and E. Segelberg, *art. cit.*

84) The present author hopes shortly to publish a study on the connections and relationship of the Bardesanian doctrine with the gnostic writings of Chenoboskion.

it is clear that we have here one of the "Vorstufen" from which the elaborate gnostic systems of, for instance, the Apocryphon of John, Manichaeism and the Barbelo-gnostics were developed. This implies that further examination is required of the relationship between the gnostic writings from the library of Chenoboskion and the Syrian-Mesopotamian region; for at any rate part of them a Syrian origin is practically certain. [85]) In that case the sect of the Quqites helped to form the substratum and milieu, in which this Gnosticism developed. The relations between the Coptic gnostic writings and Manichaeism would then come a little more into the light of history, and also the connections between this form of Gnosticism and the Mandaeans. [86]) A further implication would be that Gnosticism is not in origin a specifically Christian phenomenon, although Christian elements may be fitted into it. The part contributed by Judaism is decidedly greater, though this does not mean that Gnosticism can be traced back to a single root in heterodox (or orthodox) Judaism. [87]) Ultimately it is an entity sui generis, to which all the religions around the Eastern basin of the Mediterranean have contributed, while its character cannot be entirely explained from one or more of those religions. [87a])

Quqite Gnosticism is often regarded as Valentinianism; it is much the same with the Bardesanian doctrine. [88]) It is obvious at first sight

---

85) *cf.* note 3 and also A. Böhlig, Der jüdische und judenchristliche Hintergrund in gnostischen Texten von Nag Hammadi, a paper read at the congress in Messina (to be published in the Acta) and *idem,* „Die Adamapokalypse aus Codex V von Nag Hammadi als Zeugnis jüdisch-iranischer Gnosis", *Oriens Christianus,* 48, 1964, SS. 44-49; *cf.* K. Rudolph, *"Gnosis und Manichäismus",* SS. 177 f.

86) Both probably drew upon the same fund of ideas and images that were current in Syria. Säve-Söderberg's research into the relations of the Mandaean and the Manichaean psalms should be continued, now that more texts are becoming available; for the *Gospel of Philip* J. E. Ménard, *L'Evangile selon Philippe,* Montreal/Paris 1964, adduced very many Manichaean conceptions in explanation.

87) Jonas has rightly pointed out more than once that Gnosticism is strongly anti-Jewish; Gnosticism is an entity sui generis, for the building of which the whole "Umwelt" supplied material, but the sum is greater than the parts of which it is composed, and displays an outlook upon man and the world of an entirely individual kind.

87a) *cf.* Th. P. van Baaren, „Towards a definition of gnosticism", a paper read at the congress on the origins of Gnosticism (to be published in the Acta).

88) Thus Eusebius, Epiphanius, Augustine and others about Bardaiṣan; *cf.* Drijvers, *Bardaiṣan,* pp. 167-185.

that the differences with Valentinianism as described by Irenaeus, are too great for this attribution to be maintained. On the one side the name of Valentinus came to stand for the archetype of heresy, which may sufficiently explain that the Quqites are assigned to his school, on the other there is yet a mesure of truth in it. These comparatively simple forms of Syrian Gnosticism formed the basis and the material upon which and from which Valentinus created his mystico-rationalistic system; it has long been clear that Valentinianism was an aristocratic shoot from a middle-class or plebeian stock. As a natural result, all kinds of gnostic groups which have preserved the material which Valentinus drew upon for his system, are given the name of Valentinianism. [89]) E. Peterson's former discussions of the relations between Mandaeans and Valentinians thus acquire a fresh interest, though in a slightly different sense than Peterson intended. [90]).

The variegated picture of second-century Edessa has become even more varied and complex, now that the Quqites also demand their place in it. Yet this increased complexity also offers the possibility of a better clarification of the whole, while the threads that meet in Edessa or go out from it may perhaps be more clearly distinguished in their historical intercrossing. The town was a meeting-place of different cultures, and thus afforded suitable nourishment to gnostic or semi-gnostic groups. [91]) The unknown sect of the Quqites may help to illustrate this, being itself both a symptom and product thereof.

---

89) *cf.* Jonas, *Gnosis und spätantiker Geist I*, SS. 358-362.

90) E. Peterson "Urchristentum und Mandäismus", *ZNW*, 27, 1928, SS. 55-98.

91) *cf.* G. Widengren, *Iranisch-semitische Kulturbegegnung in parthischer Zeit*, Köln/Opladen 1960, SS. 51 ff., Drijvers, *Bardaiṣan*, pp. 214-217 and the literature listed there, and J. Neusner, *A History of the Jews in Babylonia I*, The Parthian Period, Studia Post-Biblica IX. Leiden 1965, pp. 166-169.

XV

THE ORIGINS OF GNOSTICISM AS A RELIGIOUS AND HISTORICAL PROBLEM

The problem of the origin or origins of Gnosticism is nowadays one of the most hotly debated questions in the field of religio-historical studies, in contrast with the general inclination on the part of scholars in this field to raise no question as to the origin of religion in itself.[1] Their activities are usually confined to criticising theories developed by psychologists, sociologists or cultural anthropologists which fail to do justice to the unique, irresolvable nature of religion or to the unique forms in which it appears in history.[2] These discussions appear as it were in condensed form in the narrower field of research into the origins of Gnosticism, the problem which formed the theme of a Colloquium held in Messina in April 1966. Under the title of „Le origini dello gnosticismo" the papers and discussions of the Colloquium have now been published.[3] He, however, who expects in these more than 800 pages to find a plain answer to the question regarding the origins of Gnosticism, will be disappointed. For one thing, a great many contributions do not deal explicitly with the origins of Gnosticism, but with problems of detail, with marginal phenomena, terminological matters, or the essence of Gnosticism. It proved impossible to detach the problem of origins, especially as there is no unanimity so far as to what Gnosticism really is. Indeed, the whole colloquium suffered from considerable confusion with regard to terminology: one heard of gnosis, Gnosticism, Gnostic, pre-Gnostic and proto-Gnostic, pre-Gnosticism and proto-Gnosticism, gnosticoid etc. It is striking, therefore, that after all agreement was reached in general terms as to a definition of Gnosticism and a clearing up of the terminology,

[1] The author wishes to express his thanks to Mrs G. E. van Baaren-Pape, who has translated this article into English.

[2] See *e.g.* F. Heiler, *Erscheinungsformen und Wesen der Religion*, Stuttgart 1961, SS. 561ff.; C. J. Bleeker, *Op zoek naar het geheim van de godsdienst*, Amsterdam 1952, blz. 200 vlgg.; M. E. Spiro, Religion: Problems of Definition and Explanation, *Anthropological Approaches to the Study of Religion*, ed. M. Banton, London 1966, pp. 85–126.

[3] U. Bianchi, *Le Origini dello Gnosticismo*, Suppl. to *Numen* XII, Leiden 1967.

although objections to this were and are also raised.[1] Regarding the origins of Gnosticism opinions proved more divided than ever, as is very well seen in the various papers presented. From this point of view, they recapitulate the research that began in the previous century with Neander and strike the balance, since all standpoints defended in the course of this research were represented at the colloquium and were defended there. „Le origini dello gnosticismo," therefore, together with a number of recent publications, may well serve as point of departure for reassessing the problem of the origins of Gnosticism in correlation with the problem of its essence. For indeed, the questions regarding the origin and essence of Gnosticism prove to be correlated, and likewise the answers to these questions. Those scholars who, like G. Widengren, derive dualism in the Hellenistic world from the Iranian religions, and consider the essence of Gnosticism to be a consistent dualism, have resolved the questions of origin and essence by using a characterisation of the essence as an answer to the question of origin and vice versa[2]. When S. Pétrement holds to Harnack's old thesis that Gnosticism is the Hellenisation of Christianity, then she has answered the question as to essence by assuming Gnosticism to be a Christian heresy whose origin is to be sought in extremistic exegesis of certain pericopes of the N.T., and because of this origin Gnosticism is a Christian heresy[3]. Conceiving the essence of Gnosticism to be the fall of the divine soul into matter, U. Bianchi finds the origin of this in Empedocles and in Orphism and in their influence upon Plato, and because that is where the origin of Gnosticism lies, the „Orphic" elements constitute its essence[4]. More examples might be offered, but all the theories in this field conform to the above schema. Thus origin and essence of Gnosticism function as mutually dependent explanations and answers to the question, what the origin and the

[1] For example by Th. P. van Baaren, Towards a definition of Gnosticism, *Le Origini dello Gnosticismo*, pp. 174–180; K. Rudolph, Randerscheinungen des Judentums und das Problem der Entstehung des Gnostizismus, *Kairos* (1967), SS. 105–122; S. Pétrement, Le Colloque de Messine et le problème du gnosticisme, *Revue de Metaphysique et de Morale* 72 (1967), pp. 344–374.

[2] G. Widengren, *Le Origini*, p. 41.

[3] S. Pétrement, Le mythe des sept archontes créateurs peut-il s'expliquer à partir du christianisme, *Le Origini*, pp. 460–487; *idem*, La notion de gnosticisme, *Revue de Métaphysique et de Morale* 65 (1960), pp. 385–421, esp. p. 404; *idem*, Le Colloque de Messine et le problème du gnosticisme, *Revue de Métaphysique et de Morale* 72 (1967), pp. 344–374, esp. p. 372.

[4] U. Bianchi, Initiation, Mystères, Gnose, *Initiation*, Suppl. *Numen* XI, Leiden 1965, pp. 154–171; *idem*, Le problème des origines du gnosticisme et l'histoire des religions, *Numen* XII (1965), pp. 161–178; *idem*, *Le Origini*, p. 10.

essence of Gnosticism really are. This brings us right into the hermeneutic circle.

Others are sceptical as to the possibility of tracing the origins of Gnosticism; particularly those, who attempt to understand the phenomenon with the methods of psychology or philosophical anthropology. H.-M. Schenke states succinctly: „Gnosis ist nicht ableitbar"[1]. He does, however, give as his opinion that Gnosticism originated shortly before or at the same time as Christianity in Syria and/or Palestine, but that it arose independently of Christianity in one or more places from the interplay between one or more individuals and the community to which they belonged[2]. The origin of Gnosticism, he thinks, lies in the origin of its „Daseinshaltung" which manifested itself in certain individuals in the second century A.D.[3] Sometimes H. Jonas follows much the same direction, presenting Gnosticism as a syncretistic phenomenon in the ancient world, but with an autonomous centre, „the unity behind the multiplicity". This „unity" he sees as the „general principle", which is also the „Gnostic principle", the key for the understanding of the whole period in which Gnosticism arose and flourished[4]. A.D. Nock also greatly stresses the individualistic nature of Gnosticism, all the phenomena of which cannot be reduced to the same denominator: „what we call Gnosticism seems to me to be the aggregate of a series of individualistic responses to the religious situation..."[5] While G. Quispel has a definite opinion as to the historical origin of Gnosticism, which he places in heterodox Jewish circles, he combines this approach with that of the depth psychology of the Jungian method, and thus can say that the real origin of Gnosticism lies „in der Seele des Gnostikers"[6].

In a slightly different aspect, we again see the hermeneutic circle appear. While the first group of scholars handled the essence and origin of Gnosticism as correlated factors, the origin being found in a form of religion which historically preceded Gnosti-

[1] H.-M. Schenke, Das Problem der Beziehung zwischen Judentum und Gnosis. *Kairos* VII (1965), S. 125.
[2] H.-M. Schenke, Hauptprobleme der Gnosis. Gesichtspunkte zu einer neuen Darstellung des Gesamtphänomens, *Kairos* VII (1965), S. 118.
[3] Schenke, Hauptprobleme, SS. 118ff.
[4] H. Jonas, *The Gnostic Religion*. The Message of the alien God and the Beginnings of Christianity, sec. ed., Boston 1963, pp. 24ff.
[5] A. D. Nock, Gnosticism, *HThR* 57 (1964), pp. 256–279, esp. p. 273.
[6] G. Quispel, Das Lied von der Perle, *Eranos-Jahrbuch* XXXIV (1965), Zürich 1966, S. 11.

cism, the scholars of a more sceptical turn of mind focus their attention upon the „Gnostic" individual and his community, and these two are the correlated factors. This appears most strongly in the work of H. Jonas: Gnosticism is a syncretistic phenomenon in late antiquity, yet at the same time the „Gnostic principle" is the key to true understanding of this late classical world. It is not surprising, however, that the second group has contributed far more to a better understanding of the „Daseinshaltung" of the Gnostic, which it has submitted to philosophical and psychological examination in a series of publications[1], usually sharply criticised by scholars of the first group[2].

Yet there are certain connecting links, for clear lines of demarcation are not possible in this field. We notice that various scholars who are convinced of the possibility of deriving the phenomenon of Gnosticism from its actual historical roots, yet continually maintain that Gnosticism is something entirely new compared to all other religions in the eastern basin of the Mediterranean. Examples are A. Böhlig[3], R. M. Grant[4], and C. Colpe[5] who, looking at the historical aspect, are inclined to regard Jewish circles, or Jewish circles under Iranian influence, as the cradle of Gnosticism. One is then faced with the question what it is that is entirely new, and how this could originate. In other words, what is the „Daseinshaltung" of the Gnostic, and in what situation can it arise? In view of the above, the present article will first discuss the various definitions given of Gnosticism, then review the various attempts to find its historical or „motivgeschichtlich" derivation, and finally consider the milieu, the situation, in which Gnosticism may have originated or first manifested itself.

The essence of Gnosticism

In the first place, the Colloquium of Messina attempted to put an end to some terminological confusion, and proposed to reserve the term „*gnosis*" (gnosi, gnose, Gnosis) for the phenomenon of „knowledge of the divine mysteries reserved for an élite". In distinc-

[1] For example H. Jonas, *Gnosis und spätantiker Geist* I, Die mythologische Gnosis, 3te Aufl., Göttingen 1964; *idem, The Gnostic Religion*; G. Quispel, *Gnosis als Weltreligion*, Zürich 1951.
[2] See the review by G. Widengren of Quispel, *Gnosis als Weltreligion* in ZRGG.
[3] A. Böhlig, Der jüdische und judenchristliche Hintergrund in gnostischen Texten von Nag Hammadi, *Le Origini*, S. 139f.
[4] R. M. Grant, Les êtres intermédiaires dans le judaïsme tardif, *Le Origini*, pp. 153sv.
[5] C. Colpe, art. *Gnosis*, *RGG*[3], Bd. 2, Kol. 1649.

tion from this, „Gnosticism" (gnosticismo, gnosticisme, Gnostizismus) indicates a certain group of coherent systems of the second century A.D.[1] K. Rudolph has objected to this distinction, pointing out in the first place that „gnosis" is the term used by the Christian heresiologists to designate the phenomenon of the second century, and that every form of „gnosis" as a form of knowledge for an elite „als soteriologisches Mittel" presupposes a system, and is therefore really „Gnosticism[3]". The difficulty is, that the Colloquium wishes to use the term „gnosis" in the phenomenological sense, thus allowing an extension of the concept to embrace far distant forms of religion, far both in space and time, such as e.g. Orphism, Buddhism, the religions of the Aztecs and so on[3]. The term „Gnosticism", on the other hand, was reserved for a historical phenomenon in a particular cultural milieu. Since Gnosticism is concerned with a form of gnosis which „involves the divine identity of the *knower* (the Gnostic), the *known* (the divine substance of one's transcendent self), and the *means by which one knows* (*gnosis* as an implicit divine faculty...)"[4], that is „a type of gnosis" conditioned by the historical phenomenon of the great Gnostic systems, the definitions of the Colloquium contain a kind of short-circuit between the phenomenological and the historical approach. Rudolph attemps to eliminate this short-circuit by extending the historical phenomenon, according to the tradition of the school of Bultmann, to include e.g. trends of heterodox Judaism[5], and this is the reason why he looks upon „gnosis" as a „soteriologisches Mittel", and consequently speaks of „Gnosticism" wherever he finds this „gnosis". Generally speaking, knowledge of divine mysteries, reserved for an elite or those who consider themselves such, is a universal religious phenomenon connected with the social and political structure of the community in which the elite functions[6]. It is going too far, and leads to confusion, to label this knowledge „gnosis" or a „soteriologisches Mittel". Often this knowledge is of no value at all for the purpose of salvation, but is rather a form of

[1] *Le Origini*, p. xxvi
[2] K. Rudolph, Randerscheinungen des Judentums, SS. 106f.
[3] *Le Origini*, p. xxviii; E. Conze, Buddhism and Gnosis, *Le Origini*, pp. 651–667; G. Lanczkowski, Elemente gnostischer Religiosität in altamerikanischen Religionen, *Le Origini*, SS. 676–687.
[4] *Le Origini*, p. xxvii.
[5] Rudolph, Randerscheinungen des Judentums, SS. 112ff.
[6] G. van der Leeuw, *La religion dans son essence et ses manifestations*, Paris 1948, pp. 468svv.; F. Sierksma, *De roof van het vrouwengeheim*, 's-Gravenhage 1962, blz. 175vlgg.

(semi-)intellectual speculation or Spielerei, not intended for a deep religious purpose, but serving to maintain the elite or the sense of belonging to it. In other words, the definition of „gnosis" as given by the Colloquium is too much influenced by the historical phenomenon „Gnosticism" and Rudolph, logically pursuiung this course, finally arrives at the coincidence of „gnosis" and „Gnosticism". The conclusion must be that phenomenological categories are too general for the understanding of historical phenomena in their historical origin also, or that these categories are too much filled out with concrete historical phenomena, in this instance the Gnostic systems of the second century A.D., which are then considered as historically related to other far-off phenomena. Even if the term and concept of „gnosis" is regarded as a „soteriologisches Mittel", the category is still too general to permit the comphrehension of historical relations. Everything depends upon the way this „Mittel" is used and how it functions in the whole system, and what is regarded as pertaining to salvation. Knowledge of divine mysteries or „gnosis" cannot be set by itself any more than other motifs of the Gnostic systems: no single motif, nor even any specific knowledge, is in itself Gnostic in the sense of forming the keystone of a Gnostic system, but such elements can have a constitutive function within a certain combination of motifs, whose mutual relations and tensions give the whole system its real meaning[1].

In Messina a working hypothesis was formulated for the designation of „Gnosticism". It was concluded that the Gnosticism of the second century „involves a coherent series of characteristics that can be summarized in the idea of a divine spark in man, deriving from the divine realm, fallen into this world of fate, birth and death, and needing to be awakened by the divine counterpart of the self in order to be finally reintegrated. Compared with other conceptions of a „devolution" of the divine, this idea is based ontologically on the conception of a downward movement of the divine whose periphery (often called Sophia or Ennoia) had to submit to the fate of entering into a crisis and producing – even if only indirectly – this world, upon which it cannot turn its back, since it is necessary for it to recover the *pneuma* – a dualistic conception on a monistic background, expressed in a double movement of

[1] See H.J.W. Drijvers, *Bardaiṣan of Edessa, Studia Semitica Neerlandica* VI, Assen 1966, pp. 222ff.; *idem*, Bardaiṣan, die Bardaiṣaniten und die Ursprünge des Gnostizismus, *Le Origini*, SS. 307–313.

devolution and reintegration"[1]. This definition owes much to the views of H.Jonas, J.Daniélou and U.Bianchi[2]. The working hypothesis also sets forth that in this Gnosticism there functions a special form of gnosis, and that starting from these second-century systems the question can be raised of a pre-Gnosticism or a proto-Gnosticism. The element „pre-" is associated with the idea of certain motifs or elements found in other religions, in which there is no question yet of Gnosticism. Jewish apocalyptic or Jewish esoterism, Qumran, Christianity, Egypt, Mesopotamia etc. come to mind, from which the Gnostic systems have taken various motifs. In speaking of proto-Gnosticism some scholars, including Widengren and Bianchi, are thinking of the Indo-Iranian religions or of Orphism and the (neo-)Pythagoreans in Greece[3]. Since the term „dualism" is used in various senses, it was judged best to reserve this term for teachings containing an explicit dichotomy of principles that are fundamental to the existence of man and the world. Within this frame, different forms of dualism can be distinguished, of which the anti-cosmic dualism of Gnosticism is one. The latter sees evil as subsisting in matter, that is in the world and corporeality, whose creation is due to the fall within the divine pleroma or to some rupture in the Deity itself. This anti-cosmic dualism has an ethical aspect, either asceticism or libertinage, and a theologico-metaphysical aspect, chiefly concerning the separation made between a supreme god and the Demiurge, although not all Gnostic systems contain a Demiurge[4].

Almost inevitably, these hypotheses led to diversity of opinion and further discussion. K.Rudolph does accept the working hypothesis drawn up – „Diesen bereits von mir leicht kommentierten Darlegungen aus Messina kann man grundsätzlich zustimmen"[5], but rejects the terms „pre-Gnostic" and „proto-Gnostic" and will only speak of „gnostizierend". He considers the particular danger of these terms to be that Gnostic ideas are imposed on

[1] *Le Origini*, pp.xxvif.

[2] See *e.g.* H.Jonas, Delimitation of the gnostic Phenomenon-typological and historical, *Le Origini*, pp.90–104; J.Daniélou, Judéo-Christianisme et gnose, *Aspects du Judéo-Christianisme*, Paris 1965, pp.139–164; U.Bianchi, Le dualisme en l'histoire des religions, *RHR* 159 (1961), pp.1svv.; *idem*, *Le Origini*, pp.6ff.

[3] G.Widengren, Der iranische Hintergrund der Gnosis, *ZRGG* IV (1952), SS.97–114; *idem*, Les origines du gnosticisme et l'histoire des religions, Le Origini, pp.28–60; U.Bianchi, Initiation, Mystères, Gnose.

[4] *e.g.* the Simonian Gnosticism and other 'Samaritan' systems (Quqites) have no Demiurge.

[5] Rudolph, Randerscheinungen des Judentums, S.106.

alien phenomena, constructing a filiation which never existed. Van Baaren rejects the term „pre-Gnostic" because the first part suggests there is no Gnosticism yet, while the second part of the compound would make us believe the contrary. On the other hand he does consider „proto-Gnosticism" a „convenient term" to describe early forms of Gnosticism that precede the fully developed classical systems of the second century. „Gnosticoid", however, he deems a term demonstrating ignorance rather than knowledge. with which Rudolph will no doubt agree[1]. It should be remarked, however, that the term „proto-Gnosticism" suffers from the same disability. What are early forms of Gnosticism that precede the fully developed systems of the second century A.D.? Van Baaren, who rightly considers it impossible to give a short definition of the historical phenomenon of Gnosticism, enumerates sixteen characteristics of the Gnostic systems of the second century A.D., though not all are found in each system. Corrections or additions are possible, but not relevant here, since only the direction in which various scholars seek a solution to the existing problems is at issue. Now when he says that „Gnosticism is a historic development of the last centuries before and the first centuries after the beginning of our era", it must be remarked that the greater part of these characteristics are only found in the second-century systems, and a few of them „vereinzelt" in the centuries before. If „Gnosticism as such is an organic historic complex that cannot be satisfactorily analyzed simply by resolving it into its elements", the question arises what combination of elements is definitely necessary for the name of Gnosticism to be applicable, and which may be regarded as incidental or as elaborations. In fact, the descriptive enumeration of characteristics again gives rise to the quest for a minimum definition, showing what makes the given „organic historic complex" into „Gnosticism". Only then is it meaningful to speak of proto-Gnosticism, which historically precedes the ripe systems of the second century[2]. Moreover, it is by no means certain that Gnosticism is an „organic historic complex", for this supposes mutual filiation of the systems constituting the complex. It is true the heresiologists of the early church posit this filiation, but that is owing to their genealogical outlook upon history, viewing all phenomena according to lines of descent, be it orthodox or hetero-

[1] Van Baaren, Towards a Definition of Gnosticism, *Le Origini*, p. 177.
[2] Van Baaren, Towards a Definition, pp. 174ff.

dox. The same outlook is evident in the pseudepigraphical literature of the Gnostics, containing revelations from the earliest times, attributed to outstanding figures of those times and handed down in the line of descent. The time in which Jesus of Nazareth appeared upon earth, in whatever form it might be, also functions as the paradisial primaeval time when creation begins anew through the revelation of its true secrets. It is just because this genealogical outlook upon history is analogous with the method of the Religionsgeschichtliche Schule, that the latter has retained great influence in the field of Gnostic studies up to the present day.

As yet, the differences between the religious systems all looked upon as Gnostic are so great, that the question as to the essence of Gnosticism, *i.e.* what it is in these various systems that makes them Gnostic, becomes all the more urgent. As an example on one side one might take the Naassene preaching, and on the other the Evangelium Veritatis, both of which are accounted to be Gnostic products. This is only possible by operating with a definition of Gnosticism, so wide that very different forms are included in it; yet the more widely the net is spread, the less specific the catch! The work of Hans Jonas is a good example of this, for on the one hand he thoroughly analyses the Gnostic „Daseinshaltung" in categories such as alienation and nihilism, yet on the other hand he is thereby forced to include Plotinus and Origen among the Gnostics[1]. R. Crahay justly remarked in Messina that these categories are too formal to be set at the basis of the origin of the Gnostic concept of life[2]. Alienation is a formal anthropological structure which can be concretely presented in many different ways in religious and political systems aimed at doing away with alienation or rendering it tolerable[3]. In this context special interest attaches to those figures who are not unanimously counted among the Gnostics. U. Bianchi regards Marcion as a radical representative of Gnosticism, in contrast with von Harnack, mainly because of his anti-cosmic dualism and his eschatological tendency, although other Gnostic topoi are lacking in his teaching, such as the doctrine

[1] H. Jonas, *Gnosis und spätantiker Geist* 2, 1, Von der Mythologie zur mystischen Philosophie, Göttingen 1954, SS. 171ff.; *idem*, Gnosis, Existentialismus und Nihilismus, *Zwischen Nichts und Ewigkeit*, Göttingen 1963, SS. 5–25.

[2] R. Crahay, Eléments d'une mythopée gnostique dans la Grèce antique, *Le Origini*, pp. 323svv.

[3] *cf.* A. Gehlen, *Der Mensch.* Seine Natur und seine Stellung in der Welt, Bonn 1955; H. Popitz, *Der Entfremdete Mensch*, Basel 1953; L. W. Nauta, *De mens als vreemdeling*, Amsterdam 1960, pp. 273vlgg.

of the divine pneuma in man[1]. With this criterion, Bianchi will indeed find Gnosticism everywhere, almost like Jonas does, for the *displicentia sui* is general in the second and third century: „...contempt for the human condition and hatred of the body was a disease endemic in the entire culture of the period... an endogenous neurosis"[2]. It is not surprising, then, that merely because of a certain dualism which he considers related to that of Empedocles, Bianchi also reckons Bardaiṣan among the Gnostics, although Bardaiṣan did not develop the polarity inherent in human existence to a radical dualism, neither in cosmology nor in anthropology[3]. Similar differences appear in the matter of interpreting certain texts from the Qumran scrolls[4]. G. Quispel even goes so far as to regard the Song of the Pearl from the apocryphal Acts of Thomas and the Gospel of Thomas as non-Gnostic, accounting them a form of Christianity typical of the Syrian region and its culture[5]. These things should make us wary of calling Gnosticism an organic historical complex, as the frontiers of the complex cannot be clearly indicated, any more than the organic connections between the constitutive parts of the complex. More than ever we are dependent on monographs on the various sources for and the doctrines of that which up to the present is regarded as Gnostic, while we should on no account fill up gaps in our knowledge of one system with what we know of other systems, purely on the grounds of a common Gnosticism we attribute to them[6].

A number of further characteristics are put forward by various scholars as typical of Gnosticism. H. Schlier and others point out the strong eschatological element in Gnosticism, particularly in its conception of man. From this he would explain the missionary

[1] U. Bianchi, Marcion: Theologien biblique ou docteur gnostique?, *VigChr* 21 (1967), pp. 141–149.
[2] E. R. Dodds, *Pagan and christian in an age of anxiety*, Cambridge 1965, pp. 35ff.
[3] U. Bianchi La recherche sur les origines du gnosticisme, *Le Origini*, pp. 740svv., n. 3; *cf.* Drijvers, *Bardaiṣan*, pp. 222ff.
[4] *cf.* Bo Reicke, Traces of Gnosticism in the Dead Sea Scrolls, *NTS* 1 (1954/55), pp. 138ff.; K. G. Kuhn, Die Sektenschrift und die iranische Religion, *ZThK* 49 (1952), SS. 296–316, esp. S. 315; H. J. Schoeps, Das gnostische Judentum in den Dead Sea Scrolls, *ZRGG* 6 (1954), SS. 276–279; K. Schubert, Die Sektenkanon von 'En Fešcha und die Anfänge der „jüdischen Gnosis", *ThLZ* 78 (1953), Sp. 495–506; H. Ringgren, Qumrân and Gnosticism, *Le Origini*, pp. 379–384 and the discussion about this lecture, pp. 384–388.
[5] Quispel, Das Lied von der Perle; *idem*, *Makarius, Das Thomasevangelium und das Lied von der Perle*, Suppl. *NovTest.* XV, Leiden 1967, SS. 39–64; *idem*, Makarius und das Lied von der Perle, *Le Origini*, SS. 625–644.
[6] J. Munck wrote in 1933, *Untersuchungen über Klemens von Alexandria*, S. 2: „Anstatt neue Bücher über den Gnostizismus... brauchen wir Monographien über die einzelnen Quellen und Lehreinzelheiten zur Geschichte des Gnostizismus."

nature of the Gnostic sects and their sense of vocation, so that they were nowhere at home[1]. This point certainly deserves attention, but it is not only applicable to Gnosticism, so that it cannot serve to distinguish the essence of Gnosticism in contradistinction to other religious trends in the Hellenistic world. Just the same thing might equally be maintained of the early Christians. U. Bianchi and K. Rudolph have greatly stressed the parasitic nature of Gnosticism. Nowhere do we find a pure form of Gnosticism, always it is built on earlier, pre-existing religions or on their traditions. In this sense, one might speak of Jewish, Greek, Iranian or Christian Gnosticism, according to the religions which have supplied motifs and traditions which Gnosticism drew upon to give shape to its conception: „Der Gnostizismus hat also keine eigene Tradition, sondern nur eine geborgte. Seine Mythologie ist eine *ad hoc* geschaffene Überlieferung aus fremden Gut, das er sich seiner Grundkonzeption entsprechend amalgiert hat.[2]" H. Jonas has also continually emphasised the „Kunstmythos" of Gnosticism[3]. In the first place it should be remarked that this characteristic, again, is not exclusively Gnostic. The religious conception we meet with in the magical papyri displays exactly the same characteristic; these too „constantly operate with the debris of other people's religion"[4]. In the second place the question arises here what the relation is between the „Grundkonzeption" and the borrowed motifs. Could this Gnostic conception exist without the motifs borrowed from the religions that played a part in life in the Mediterranean area around the beginning of our era? Could the „Grundkonzeption des Gnostizismus" be expressed, for instance, by means of traditions taken from the religions of the North-American Indians or from those of the Papuans? Those who speak of a Weltgeschichte of Gnosticism will give an affirmative answer here[5]. Yet on the other hand we must, as K. Rudolph does, hold to the concept, with all needful reservation, that Gnosticism was a historical phenomenon in late classical antiquity, „eine typische Erscheinung der hellenistischen

[1] H. Schlier, Der Mensch im Gnostizismus, *Anthropologie religieuse*, ed. C. J. Bleeker, Leiden 1955, SS. 74ff.

[2] K. Rudolph, Randerscheinungen des Judentums, S. 108.

[3] H. Jonas, Delimitation of the gnostic Phenomenon, pp. 100ff.; *idem*, *Gnosis und spätantiker Geist* I, SS. 255ff.

[4] Dodds, *Pagan and christian*, p. 73; *cf.* M. P. Nilsson, Die Religion in den griechischen Zauberpapyri, *Bull. Soc. des Lettres Lund*, 1948, SS. 59ff.

[5] Le Origini, p. xxviii.

Welt"[1]. The problem then becomes whether in one or more of these religions one may not only find motifs that also function in Gnosticism, but also certain tendencies towards that which is typical of the Gnostic systems of the second century A.D. In this way K. Rudolph seeks a solution for the problem of the origin of Gnosticism, emphasising the importance of „die Zusammenarbeit von phänomenologischer und historisch-philologischer Forschung"[2]. The problem, however, is a little more complicated than it appears here, seeming no more than the ancient problem of form and content, which form the centre and the circumference of the hermeneutic circle. Collaboration of different disciplines causes the specific difficulties inherent in each, to show up more plainly. When the „phänomenologische Forschung" attempts an analysis and personal description of Gnosticism and the „historisch-philologische Forschung" goes in search of antecedents of Gnosticism, the analysis of Gnosticism shows that the motifs it borrowed, the antecedents, function entirely differently there than they did in the religions they originally belonged to. In this context, frequent mention is made of the revolutionary nature of Gnosticism which radically changes everything it borrows[3]. Jewish, Christian, Greek or other motifs, or rather motifs that are found in these religions, play an essentially different part in Gnosticism. The Creator god of Judaism becomes the evil Demiurge, and the fall of Gen. 3 becomes a decisive moment in the history of mankind's way to salvation. The number of examples may be increased at wish. One begins to wonder, then, whether it is really correct to speak of Jewish, Greek and other motifs in Gnosticism, since they have lost all connection with their origin. This difficulty is solved by referring to the heterodoxy of Jewish or Christian groups where Gnosticism originated; yet heterodoxy presupposes orthodoxy, and the latter is usually a late development[4]. This brings H. J. Schoeps to look on Gnosticism as „rein pagan", having nothing more to do with Judaism or Christianity[5]. Gnosticism, he says, is always Weltanschauung and

[1] A. Böhlig, Der Manichäismus im Lichte der neueren Gnosisforschung, *Christentum am Nil*, Recklinghausen 1964, S. 115.

[2] Rudolph, Randerscheinungen, S. 109.

[3] U. Bianchi, *Probleme der Religionsgeschichte*, Göttingen 1964, SS. 38f. Rudolph, Randerscheinungen, S. 108.

[4] *cf.* W. Bauer, *Rechtgläubigkeit und Ketzerei im ältesten Christentum*, *BHTh* 10, Tübingen 1934, *passim*.

[5] H. J. Schoeps, Judenchristentum und Gnosis, *Le Origini*, S. 529; *idem*, Zur Standortbestimmung der Gnosis, *ThLZ* 81 (1956) Kol. 420.

never a doctrine of salvation, in contrast with the aforesaid religions. Apart from the fact that Weltanschauung and doctrine of salvation cannot be separated in so unqualified a manner, since Gnosticism is pre-eminently a doctrine of salvation and consequently also a Weltanschauung, the expression „rein pagan" solves nothing; it can only be understood with reference to the doctrine of salvation of the scholar concerned, so that it is a theological statement and not a historical one. One has a perfect right to make such pronouncements, but they have no legitimate currency in the field of historical research.

In any case, it is clear from the above that motivgeschichtlich research does not lead to satisfactory results, because the motifs that are borrowed have undergone profound changes of function and content, adapting them to the specific Gnostic outlook upon man and the world, while on the other hand it is impossible to explain from the Gnostic outlook what it was that caused these particular motifs and traditions to be chosen as elements of the Gnostic myth. Nor can the problem be solved by positing that philosophically tinted Gnosticism has the earliest rights and that the later mythological Gnosticism is a symptom of degeneration[1]. Philosophy and mythology cannot be separated after this fashion; moreover the most strongly mythical elements of ancient philosophy play a great part in the Gnostic systems[2]. The view that Gnostic philosophy was gradually overrun by mythology seems to be influenced by the idea that the purest form is also the earliest, and since in certain schools of learning philosophy is accounted a purer form of human expression than mythology, the thesis is comprehensible, though its truth does not follow. Moreover, it greatly resembles the theological construction of the heresiologists that the original pure doctrine of Christianity was afterwards spoilt by pagan influences, of which Gnosticism was a product. That reflection upon the revelation led to this idea is understandable, but historically it is a fiction[3].

In such a situation it is an obvious move to search for a tertium comparationis, and in this role we commonly see appointed the general pessimism and nihilistic tenor of the late classical world,

[1] That is the view-point of F.C.Burkitt, *Church and Gnosis*, Cambridge 1932 and E. de Faye, *Gnostiques et Gnosticisme*, sec. ed., Paris 1925; *cf.* G.Widengren, *Le Origini*, p.33.
[2] *cf.* A.-J.Festugiere, *La Révélation d'Hermès Trismégiste*, 4 Vols, Paris 1949–1954; P.Boyancé, Dieu Cosmique et Dualisme, Les archontes et Platon, *Le Origini*, pp.340–356.
[3] *cf.* W.Bauer, *Rechtgläubigkeit und Ketzerei*, *passim*.

especially in the western part of Asia Minor[1]. It is true we know little of social conditions in this region at that time, and A. Adam, Van Baaren, K. Rudolph and others would wish to approach Gnosticism not only by comparative methods and from the historical-philological standpoint, but also through sociological study[2]: „Die Feststellung über Gründe und Ursachen, die zur Entstehung der gnostischen Weltauffassung geführt haben, ist nur durch eine komplexe Forschung von Sozial-, Wirtschafts-, Kultur- und Religionswissenschaft möglich[3]." This is certainly no mean task, requiring new methods and a continual confrontation of the results with those of the methods often followed in these disciplines until now.

A great difficulty that at once becomes obvious is the following. In people's actual life all those elements studied separately by various disciplines join in a more or less harmonious (or: organic?) whole, in which their function often changes. When seeking for the origin of Gnosticism this means, that for instance a distinction is made between Jewish, Christian, philosophical Greek, and possibly Iranian elements which in reality was never perceived in that way. Formerly McL. Wilson already pointed out that it was most probably through Jewish channels that other elements penetrated into Gnosticism, or that these elements worked with Judaism in giving rise to Gnosticism[4].

Even within the variegated whole formed by Gnostic and non-Gnostic Christianity sharp demarcations are impossible. Van Unnik, who has compared the doctrine about god of the apologist Aristides with that of the Apocryphon Johannis and the Sophia Jesu Christi, concludes that in the second century apologists, Apostolic Fathers and Gnostics cannot be treated as different groups[5]. H. H. Schaeder regarded Bardaiṣan as a Christian apologist, U. Bianchi looks upon him as a Gnostic, while he is in any case an exponent of his time and culture, in which many things run hand in hand that to us seem quite incompatible[6]. A given religious, cultural and social

[1] *cf.* K. Rudolph, Randerscheinungen des Judentums, SS. 109ff.; Dodds, *Pagan and Christian*, *passim*, esp. p. 57ff.
[2] Van Baaren, *Le Origini*, p. 177; A. Adam, Neuere Literatur zum Problem der Gnosis, *GGA* 1963, S. 28; Rudolph, Randerscheinungen, S. 111.
[3] Rudolph, Randerscheinungen, S. 109.
[4] R. McL. Wilson, *The gnostic Problem*, sec. ed. London 1964, p. 174.
[5] W. C. van Unnik, Die Gotteslehre bei Aristides und in gnostischen Schriften, *ThZ* 17 (1961), SS. 166–174.
[6] Drijvers, *Bardaiṣan*, pp. 213ff.

situation, then, may give rise to Gnosticism, but is by no means bound to do so. This absence of compulsion is what prevents us from tracing the historical roots of Gnosticism and giving an exact description of its causes, motifs and origins; it is also the reason why so many phenomena have a „gnostic" air about them and why it is so difficult to get a clear historical picture of the Gnostic sects and groups[1]. E. R. Dodds, who has described a number of phenomena in the time between Marcus Aurelius and Constantine – „an age of anxiety" –, continually points this out[2]. In a syncretistic culture the component parts undertake a new function in a new whole. Every attempt to derive Gnosticism from either Judaism or Christianity, or Greek philosophy and mystery religions or the Iranian religions is therefore inadequate, because it separates that which in the culture of a particular time is bound into a complex organism by innumerable links. Yet all these derivations have a certain validity, particularly when their arguments are confronted together.

The origins of Gnosticism

Iran

Although some scholars are inclined to assign the Iranian religions a part in the origin of Gnosticism, G. Widengren is the only one consistently to follow out the course set by the Religionsgeschichtliche Schule, convinced that Gnosticism is in essence and origin a phenomenon belonging to the Indo-Iranian religions, and only to be explained from these. Particularly the dualism of Gnosticism, the figure of the saviour who is at the same time Primordial Man, and who manifests himself as salvator salvatus, and the soul's ascent to heaven are regarded by him as authentic Iranian theologoumena[3]. Historically we have a hold on these in the „Song of the Pearl", in the apocryphal Acts of Thomas, in the Mandaean texts, in Qumran and in the Gnostic writings of Nag Hammadi, while Manichaeism in particular offers a pure rendering of the Iranian type of Gnosticism. In a sharp attack upon the views of H. Jonas, Widengren maintains that the pre-eminent characteristic of Syro-Egyptian Gnosticism, the evil cosmos opposed to the good God,

[1] R. P. Casey, The Study of Gnosticism, *JThS* (1935), p. 59: „A clear historical picture of these sects and their mutual relations will perhaps never be obtained."
[2] Dodds, *Pagan and christian*, pp. 18ff.
[3] Widengren, Der iranische Hintergrund der Gnosis; *idem*, Les origines du gnosticisme et l'histoire des religions.

can only be explained from Iranian dualism: „*plus* le dualisme est conséquent, *plus* le gnosticisme est originel et pur, car *plus* grande est la polarité entre Dieu et Monde". U. Bianchi has already submitted this thesis to some gentle criticism, remarking that the characteristic of Gnosticism is not an absolute dualism (polarity) between a good God and an evil world, that is to say dualism is not in itself Gnostic, but that Gnosticism is characterised by an anti-cosmic dualism, a commingling of different ontological levels, both in the world of the divine, in the cosmos and in man. This maintains the existence of the Gnostic in a delicate balance and causes the ambivalence of all phenomena, including man. Although not a necessary actor in the Gnostic drama of man and world, the Demiurge is an exponent of this ambivalence, and not a mitigation of an original Gnostic schema, as Widengren argues[1]. Bianchi does not indeed seek to detract from Widengren's views as to the Gnostic nature of the Mazdean teachings, but he does remark that especially the problems of dating Mazdean literature are particularly difficult[2]. Being no Iranian scholar I cannot judge of these matters, and will only make a few remarks from the methodical point of view. Bianchi points out the ambivalent nature of all Gnostic ideas, terming it dualism in a monistic setting, but this ambivalence is also present in the use Gnosticism makes of all existing forms of religion in the Near East. With this restriction, the expositions of Widengren have a certain validity, in the sense that to a reader or listener belonging to an Iranian milieu, the Gnostic writings will evoke certain familiar associations. In part, they make use of images and motifs which are also found in Mazdeism and Zurvanism. Considered in their function, however, the differences are great: Iranian dualism rests primarily upon an ethical basis, so that in the combat waged by the powers in the world, man can take an active part by choosing the side of Good, thus effecting his salvation. In Gnosticism, on the contrary, ethic is secondary, because there man is from the beginning irrevocably destined for good or evil. More important than the resemblances, therefore, are the differences in function, which Widengren neglects, because he strictly regards motifs and not their context. The controversy with H. Jonas is in part determined by the fact that Jonas analyses Gnosticism in the first place by means of the Manichaean and

[1] Widengren, Les origines du gnosticisme, pp. 41svv.; Bianchi, *Le Origini*, p. 25sv.
[2] Bianchi, *Le Origini*, p. 26.

Mandaean texts, which Widengren regards as forms of Gnosticism marked by Iranian influence. When Judaism or Christianity have contributed to their formation, the Iranian component still dominates over these contributions[1].

The great objection to Widengren's method is, however, that while he formally separates the comparative and the historical method of approach, he actually lets them coincide. The comparative approach shows him dualism, the figure of the salvator and of Primordial Man and the soul's ascent to heaven as characteristics of Gnosticism, and also as characteristics of Mazdeism and Zurvanism, whereupon he concludes it is a case of borrowing or influence in the historical sense; he then finds Iranian influence in the writings of Qumran *et al.*, the „Song of the Pearl" appearing as king's evidence for this historical construction based on a one-sided comparison. The song probably evoked associations in a milieu under Iranian influence, but it also did so in a Christian milieu, where the parable of the pearl was known. Yet it is going too far to deny all trace of Gnosticism to this „Song of the Pearl", regarding it strictly as an elaboration of the parable, as Quispel does after the example of A. F. J. Klijn[2]. Consequently, Quispel's method of working is in fact exactly like that of Widengren: one need merely replace Mazdeism and Zurvanism by Judaism and Christian Jewry. Everything depends, therefore, how and by whom a particular text was heard: it sounded different to a member of the Parthian feudal nobility in Edessa than it did to a Christian preacher. The polyinterpretability of myth is enhanced in Gnosticism because the Gnostic myth is also culturally polyinterpretable, it corresponds with existing themes in many religions, while it cannot be explained from these. The discussion between H. Jonas and G. Quispel about the Song of the Pearl affords a striking proof[3]. The question as to the true nature of Manichaeism gives another demonstration: the view of it varies from a Christian sect to a form of purely Iranian Gnosticism. Manichaeism can appear in both forms, and more,

[1] Widengren, *The Saviour God,* Studies presented to E.O. James, Manchester 1963, pp. 208ff.; *idem, JRAS* (1961), pp. 125ff.; *idem, Temenos* II (1966), pp. 139–177.
[2] Quispel, Makarius und das Lied von der Perle; *idem, Makarius, das Thomasevangelium; idem,* Gnosticism and the New Testament, *The Bible in modern Scholarship,* Nashville 1965; A. F. J. Klijn, The so-called Hymn of the Pearl, *VigChr.* 14: (1960), pp. 154–164.
[3] H. Jonas, Response to G. Quispel's „Gnosticism and the New Testament", *The Bible in modern Scholarship,* pp. 279–293.

mainly depending on the place where and the people by whom it is followed[1].

The main themes of Gnosticism as Widengren sees them are not exclusively Iranian; they appear in other forms in Judaism and in Orphism[2]. Widengren regards the former as having undergone strong Iranian influence, and the latter as an exponent of Indo-Iranian mysticism, as Gnosticism is also. It seems to me that the term „Iranian" then becomes so wide that it can embrace everything while explaining nothing, the danger of all one-sidedness. In conclusion one may say that Gnosticism also functioned in an Iranian milieu – the origin of Manichaeism is inexplicable otherwise – and possibly originated in a milieu of Iranian bias. The Syro-Mesopotamian region with its Parthian domination would present such a milieu. It is also the home country of the traditions about the Magians, „Les Mages Hellénisés", who crop up again in Chenoboskion[3].

Christianity

Just as Widengren cherishes the legacy left by Bousset and Reitzenstein, so does S. Pétrement that of Harnack and Burkitt. Following in their footsteps, she sees the Christian religion as the origin of Gnosticism, which does no more than elaborate certain themes of the N.T., sometimes carrying them to extremes[4]. In contrast with the religionsgeschichtliche Schule and the school of Bultmann, S. Pétrement would understand Gnosticism within the context of the development of Christian theology, and not give Christianity a place in the great current of Gnosticism. For many scholars work with a pre-Christian Gnosticism, supposed to have exercised a very strong influence on the manner in which the earliest community gave form and expression to their faith in Jezus of Nazareth[5]. R. P. Casey and H. M. Schenke are of opinion that Gnosticism originated about the same time as Christianity, that both developed in different directions from the same foundation, viz. the religious and cultural situation in the Near East around the beginning of

[1] *cf.* C. Colpe, Art. *Manichäismus*, *RGG*³, Bd. IV, Sp. 719ff.
[2] *e.g.* the theme of „Die Himmelsreise der Seele".
[3] *cf.* J. Doresse, *Les livres secrets des gnostiques d'Égypte*, Paris 1958, p. 179; M. Krause, Der Stand der Veröffentlichung der Nag Hammadi Texte, *Le Origini*, S. 67.
[4] S. Pétrement, La notion de gnosticisme, p. 391. *idem*, Le Colloque de Messine et le problème du gnosticisme, p. 372; *idem*, Le mythe des sept archontes, p. 485.
[5] Pétrement, La notion de gnosticisme, p. 404.

our era[1]. H.C.Puech sees another relation again to Christianity: Gnosticism is not the Hellenisation, but the Orientalisation of Christianity[2].

We can reduce this whole complex of relations to two questions: was there a pre-Christian Gnosticism, and were there forms of Gnosticism that are non-Christian? For non-Christian does not automatically mean pre-Christian. In spite of all the suppositions in this field, we know nothing of a pre-Christian Gnostic system. A scholar who cannot be charged with having a theological axe to grind puts it as follows: „But nothing so far published from Qumran or Nag-Hammadi lends support to the hypothesis of a pre-christian Gnostic *system*"[3]. It is certainly true that motifs present in Gnosticism can be traced back to pre-Christian times, but this does not imply the existence of Gnosticism in the true sense. The first protests we meet with against Gnostic error or its concomitants, are to be found in the N.T. This means that up to the present day it is impossible to look upon Christianity as a new shoot on the existing tree of Gnosticism. Resemblances in the images and language used are rather to be understood as stemming from the common situation in which Gnosticism and Christianity came to the fore; the N.T. speaks the language of its time, as Gnosticism does, but the same words and images do not always bear the same significance. What remains to be considered, is whether Gnosticism can be explained from Christianity, or whether they are two different entities which influenced one another and gave rise to all kinds of composite structures.

S. Pétrement sees the basis of Gnosticism in the tension between a theologia crucis and a theologia creationis, the former having come to dominate completely over the latter: Gnosticism is „un grand mouvement de révolte contre toutes les puissances, celles de la nature et celles de l'État"[4]. We understand, then, that according to her the figure of the saviour, which is fundamental to Gnosticism, is derived from Christianity as also all other Gnostic loci, such as the doctrine of the soul, the seven archons etc[5]. This,

[1] R.P.Casey, Gnosis, Gnosticism and the New Testament, *The Background of the New Testament and its Eschatology*, Studies in honour of C.H.Dodd, Cambridge 1956, pp.52–80, esp. pp.52–55; Schenke, Hauptprobleme der Gnosis, S.118.

[2] H.-C.Puech, Où en est le problème du gnosticisme, *Revue de l'Université de Bruxelles* 39 (1933/34), p.306.

[3] Dodds, *Pagan and Christian* p.18, n.2.

[4] Pétrement, La notion de gnosticisme, p.415.

[5] La notion de gnosticisme, p.399; le mythe des sept archontes, *passim*.

at any rate, does not accord with fact. The Gnosticism of Simon is plainly non-Christian and the figure of Jezus of Nazareth has no part in it. Texts were also found in Chenoboskion of a non-Christian content, and texts which had been Christianised afterwards[1]. The Gnosticism of the Quqites is non-Christian, although Jezus of Nazareth is one of the saviours who make a cyclic appearance. This group offers a good example of the way a Samaritan form of Gnosticism could be given a Christian adaptation, or how Christianity could be given a place in an existing system, in this case a very modest place[2]. This means that Gnosticism also draws parasitically upon the Christian tradition, changing its function. None the less, Christianity as a religion may have a gnosticising influence, as has been pointed out on several sides. It may very well be that great Christian activity in the second century evoked increased Gnostic activity[3].

Thus there is Christian and non-Christian Gnosticism, the term ,,Christian'' signifying no more in this context than that it makes use of Christian motifs, for ,,in the end Gnosticism is fundamentally un-Christian and un-Jewish''[4]. Yet no hard and fast lines of demarcation can be drawn: what one scholar calls Christian, another regards as non-Christian, since some do not employ these terms in a religio-historical sense when treating of Gnosticism, but in a dogmatic sense. Moreover, the plotting out of one single phenomenon ,,Gnosticism'' and another single phenomenon ,,Christianity'' is a simplification of history. Christianity of the second century is not uniform, if indeed it has been so in any century, and Gnosticism is pluriform. For this reason alone, carrying back Gnosticism to a Christianity of orthodox ,,Reinkultur'' is a construction based on a theological a priori.

Greece

When in searching for the origins of Gnosticism mention is made of the part played therein by Hellenic culture, closer specification is needed. ,,Greek'', ,,Hellenic'' and ,,Platonic'' are pretty vague

[1] Krause, Der Stand der Veröffentlichung, SS. 67ff.; R.McL. Wilson, Gnostic Origins, *VigChr* 9 (1955), p. 204; Wilson, The New Testament in the Gospel of Mary, *NTS* 3 (1957), pp. 236ff.
[2] Drijvers, Quq and the Quqites. An unknwon sect in Edessa in the second century A.D., *Numen* 14 (1967), pp. 104–129.
[3] *cf.* A. Böhlig, *Le Origini*, p. 705.
[4] Wilson, *Gnostic Problem*, p. 218.

terms, and hence they frequently appear in the works of various scholars who consider it impossible to derive Gnosticism from a single root[1]. It is a generally accepted opinion that Greek civilisation contributed in some way or another to the formation of the Gnostic myths, especially those of a more philosophical tinge. The same conclusion is also reached by R. Crahay and P. Boyancé in their contributions to the Colloquium of Messina, and both then point to Plato and Orphism as having given Gnosticism its philosophical terminology, perhaps through the intermediary of Philo Alexandrinus[2]. Now it would have been almost impossible in the first and second century of our era to formulate doctrines presented as „gnosis" without making use of the conceptual system of late-classical philosophy, which had been deeply influenced by Plato. The only thing is, that the question rises whether Gnosticism is a philosophy or a form of religion. Von Ivánka has pointed out that in this field many pseudomorphoses are to be seen, and that no clear divisions can be made[3]. When Harnack and de Faye wrote about Gnosticism, they regarded it as a philosophy of religion, a theological system adapted to the current philosophical theology of late classical antiquity, and this line is continued by H. Langerbeck, who considers Gnosticism to be in the first place an „Aufgabe der klassischen Philologie"[4]. The conclusion is then obvious that philosophical Gnosticism has the oldest rights, and the more mythological form is to be considered as a degeneration. Others, including Widengren, maintain exactly the opposite and assign the oldest rights to the mythological Gnostic systems. In any case, mythology and philosophy are not in such absolute contrast as it is suggested here, certainly not in the line of Platonic philosophy, although in each case their relation needs to be separately determined, the more so since the problem of form and content is often simplified by positing

[1] *e.g.* A. Böhlig, Religionsgeschichtliche Probleme aus einer Schrift von Nag Hamadi, *Wiss. Zeitsch. d. Univ. Halle*, Ges. Sprachwiss. Reihe 10 (1961), SS. 1325–1328; Wilson, Gnostic Origins, pp. 199ff.; K. Stürmer, Judentum, Griechentum und Gnosis, *ThLZ* 73 (1948), Sp. 581–592; W. C. Till, Die Gnosis in Aegypten, *La Parola del Passato* 4, 1949, S. 231; Schlier, Das Denken der frühchristlichen Gnosis, *NT-liche Studien f. R. Bultmann*, Beiheft *ZNW* 21 (1954), S. 67; Nock, Gnosticism, p. 277f. *et al.*

[2] R. Crahay, Éléments d'une mythopée gnostique, *passim*; P. Boyancé, Dieu cosmique et dualisme, *passim*.

[3] E. von Ivánka, Religion, Philosophie und Gnosis: Grenzfälle und Pseudomorphosen in der Spätantike. *Le Origini*, SS. 317–322.

[4] H. Langerbeck, *Aufsätze zur Gnosis*, hrsg. v. H. Dörries, *AAG*, Phil.-hist. Kl., 3te Folge, Nr. 69, Göttingen 1967, SS. 17–37: „Das Problem der Gnosis als Aufgabe der klassischen Philologie".

that the East supplied the content, the myth, and Greece the form, its philosophical wording[1]. According to the cultural climate in which Gnosticism develops, the Gnostic revelation will vary, appearing sometimes in more philosophical, sometimes in more mythological guise, but it remains a secret revelation of saving grace for those who hear it, and is not in the first place an intellectual occupation, however much intellectual play and learned ostentation may have borne a part. The core of Gnosticism is charged with a leaden gravity, loaded with the problem of existence itself, and suffering the existential crisis to the full. In Gnosticism, „gnosis" is no formal philosophy of the Platonic kind, but a means of escaping from existence, no knowledge of the world, but an attempt to anticipate the undoing of the world's creation. However strongly Gnosticism may make the impression of being philosophy, in essence it is not so, but rather an attempt to render all philosophy superfluous. Is not the origin of the misery of human existence the fall of Sophia or Ennoia? Is this not a strong anti-intellectual tendency in Gnosticism, however „learned" an appearance the system may put on? Surely it is a typical Gnostic way of giving new expression to the fundamental ambivalence of human existence? Gnosis is also the courage to be by ceasing to be as radically as possible. The dissertation of G. van Groningen, who advances the thesis that „the spirit of scientism, native to all men, a strong factor in Hellenism, evident in early pagan religions, was the basic motif in the origin of Gnosticism", therefore seems rather one-sided in its approach to the phenomenon of Gnosticism[2].

U. Bianchi has attempted to avoid these problems; he finds what he considers the essential characteristic of Gnosticism, anti-cosmic dualism, in ancient Greece already with Empedocles and Orphism. He is not the first to do so, for long ago Wobbermin and Leisegang already argued that in essence Gnosticism was a revival of ancient cosmogonic conceptions of early Greece, together with a renewal of Orphism and the Pythagorean ideas[3]. From the religions of antiquity, Bianchi isolates a phenomenological sequence, which is at the same a historical process, running through four phases: fer-

[1] This is the view-point of H.-H. Schaeder, Der Orient und das griechische Erbe, *Der Mensch in Orient und Okzident*, München 1960, SS. 107–160 (originally published in 1928).
[2] G. van Groningen, *First Century Gnosticism.* Its Origin and Motifs, Leiden 1967, *passim* and Introduction.
[3] H. Leisegang, *Die Gnosis*, Leipzig 1954, SS. 185, 269, 292, 364–365; Wobbermin, *Religionsgeschichtliche Studien*, Berlin 1896, SS. 93ff.

tility cults, mysteries, mysteriosophy, Gnosticism[1]. The first phase is centred simply on life itself and its renewal in the course of the seasons, in the second phase the concern is with the life of the individual who is initiated, the third is concerned with speculations regarding the bearer of divine life, the soul and its redemption from matter, of which Orphism is a good example, while Gnosticism concentrates entirely upon the fate and the liberation of the divine soul from the world, that originated from a fall, symbolised in the conception of the salvator salvandus. All four phases have in common that always a divine element, life, the soul, is subjected to certain vicissitudes of fate; one may therefore also speak of a historical process, in which the divine element is gradually individualised and rendered more inward. This process is accompanied by the development of dualism. Although Bianchi decidedly rejects the term „evolution" for this historical process, he has actually designed an evolutionist schema, in which the divine life becomes more and more estranged from its original milieu and the process of redemption puts on a more and more radical shape, culminating in the Gnostic resistance to the world and its powers, which have degenerated from being the „natural" milieu of life to become its antagonists. Bianchi does not indeed claim to have thus indicated the origins of Gnosticism, because he is vividly conscious of not being able to point out by what forces the historical process is dominated, but he explicitly declares that the scenario of the Gnostic drama has its origin in the cults and mysteries of the Near East and of Greece, which have been given an individualistic and anti-cosmic twist[2]. The fact that the O.T. became widely known contributed to the possibility of embodying the forces of the cosmos in the figure of Jahweh, the demiurge of this world[3]. On the other hand Bianchi holds to the concept that Orphism in particular was a Gnosticism ante litteram, because attention is there already focused on the fate of the divine soul, the demiurge of the world and the restoring of the soul to its original state[4].

There is a decided short-circuit in Bianchi's argumentation, which appears especially when he enters into discussion at the Colloquium, opposing the ideas of others. When he says that a

[1] Bianchi, Initiation, Mystères, Gnose, pp.154svv.
[2] Bianchi, Initiation, p.171.
[3] *idem.*
[4] Bianchi, Initiation, pp.167svv.

phenomenological sequence which centres upon life is identical with a historical process of which, however, we do not know the springs, he is constructing two dubious entities which function as mutually dependent explanations. Life, or the soul, is an abstraction representing what man experiences as salvation and feels as a lack, and as such it is fundamentally ambivalent. Considered in their function, the things hiding behind images such as „life" and „soul" may be very different, or in other words: the image bears different realities; the differences are determined by the milieu in which the images function. In a preponderantly agrarian community the word „life" has a different content than it has in an urban community. An attempt to invalidate these objections when setting up a phenomenological sequence of life and its vicissitudes, is to call it at the same time a historical process. Historical processes did indeed take place in the cultures of Greece and the Near East, but they did not circle round the divine life; no, this divine life may be an expression in which these processes are reflected. This reflection is again attuned to human salvation and insufficiency that are experienced in a new way owing to continual change of the historical situation. While it is thus not correct to speak of a historical process in the sense in which Bianchi uses the term here, the phenomenological sequence might also be criticised, in the first place for the reason that Bianchi can simply replace sequence by process. According to him the various phenomena form a sequence, because all are concerned with the fate in the world of the divine life. Though it might be debated whether the adjective „divine" is justified in all of Bianchi's examples, a category such as „life" is in any case too general for arranging a number of phenomena in a sequence, for it does not appear at all why the Egyptians' or the Hottentots' idea of life, for instance, has no place in this sequence. Moreover, differences in a comparison are far more important than that which at first sight seems the same. Thus if Bianchi compares terms such as „life" and „soul" as phenomena from a different context, one must first inquire which life and which soul? Just as the word „gnosis" does not mean the same thing when used by Plato or by the Gnostics and does not function in the same context, so „life" and „soul" cannot always be compared, let alone listed in the same sequence. For the characterisation and comparison of different forms of religion their concepts of salvation, after all, offer the best criterion, and the totally different concepts of salvation present in the sequence constructed by Bianchi form the best argument for considering that phenomenological and historical sequence an arbitrary choice.

We meet with the same problem in the case of scholars who look upon the mystery religions as an important source of Gnosticism, for instance H.-Ch. Puech and H. Jonas, who point out the mystic character of Gnosticism and the spiritualisation of the mystery religions, evidenced *e.g.* in the Naassene preaching[1]. All the imperfections that appear in the views of Bianchi are present here also, while formally considered terms such as „mysticism" and „spiritualisation" are quite unmeaning, as how and why are not described. Our factual knowledge of the mystery religions, moreover, is extremely slight, and what the „mysterion" is usually remains hidden. Thus, if in the Naassene preaching and among the Quqites we find motifs from the cults of the various mother goddesses, it will be necessary to determine exactly what part these figures play in the original cult, and what in the Gnostic myth. The Quqites, for instance, portray in the various mother goddesses the sublimation of sexuality, which in life is not admitted because it caused the fall[2]. To speak of spiritualisation in such a case is quite erroneous.

A variation upon the above-mentioned attempts to solve the problem of the origins of Gnosticism, is to stress the neo-Pythagorean influence, particularly upon the allegorising method the Gnostics apply to traditional writings and myths. Here we meet with the names of J. Carcopino, M. Detienne and I. Lévy[3]. It is extremely tempting to elucidate the unknown by means of another unknown factor, the neo-Pythagorean teaching, of which very little indeed is known[4]. The matter hinges mainly on the question whether the Samaritan Helena, who clearly shows lunar traits, so that she is also found as Selene, really does owe this transformation to the allegorising method of the Pythagoreans, who saw Selene in the Homeric Helen. Apart from the fact that M. Detienne has shown with considerable force of conviction that this allegori-

[1] Puech, Où en est le problème du gnosticisme, p. 296; Jonas, *The gnostic Religion,* p. 38.
[2] Drijvers, Quq and the Quqites, pp. 121ff.
[3] J. Carcopino, *De Pythagore aux Apôtres*, Paris 1956, pp. 189–221: Le symbolisme gnostique et ses origines pythagoriciennes; M. Detienne, La légende pythagoricienne d'Hélène, *RHR* 152 (1957), pp. 129–152; I. Lévy, *Recherches esséniennes et pythagoriciennes*, Paris 1965; *cf.* V. Nikiprowetzky, *REJ* 125 (1966), pp. 313–352.
[4] *cf.* G. Kafka/H. Eibl, *Der Ausklang der antiken Philosophie und das Erwachen einer neuen Zeit*, München 1928, SS. 203ff.

cal explanation after the Pythagorean manner influenced the Simonian myth of Helena, there is one typical difference: the Pythagoreans found the heroine and femme fatale of the Iliad offensive, and tried to rehabilitate her by means of allegorising. In the Simonian myth Helena is the fallen anima, Sophia, who leads the life of a prostitute in matter and is not rehabilitated by allegorising her from Helena into Selene, but is saved by the virile action of the Megale Dynamis. Thus there are very striking differences standing in the way of deriving Gnosticism or the Gnostic myth from the neo-Pythagoreans.

There is no doubt that Hellenistic philosophy influenced Gnosticism, and various Gnostic ideas can be understood by its help, while there may be „gnosticoid" traits in the philosophy[1]. Motifs from the Hellenistic mystery religions may also play a part in Gnosticism, as Orphism etc. also may. Yet Gnosticism remains an entity *sui generis*, which cannot be derived directly from forms of religion or philosophy that precede it chronologically.

Judaism

A cursory inspection of the writings by and about the Gnostics already shows that motifs taken from the O.T. and apocryphal Jewish literature abound. A. Böhlig[2], O. Betz[3], K. Rudolph[4], R. M. Grant[5], G. Quispel[6], R. McL. Wilson[7], J. Daniélou[8], H. J. Schoeps[9], A. Orbe[10] and others, each in his own way, have done

[1] Böhlig, *Le Origini*, p. 706; Dodds, *Pagan and christian*, *passim*.
[2] Böhlig, Der jüdische und judenchristliche Hintergrund in gnostischen Texten von Nag Hammadi, *Le Origini*, SS. 109–140
[3] O. Betz, Was am Anfang geschah (Das jüdische Erbe in den neugefundenen koptisch-gnostischen Schriften), *Abraham unser Vater*, Festschrift f. O. Michel, Leiden 1963, SS. 24–43.
[4] Rudolph, Randerscheinungen; *idem*, War der Verfasser der Oden Salomos ein „Qumran-Christ"? Ein Beitrag zur Diskussion um die Anfänge der Gnosis, *Revue de Qumran* 16 (1964), SS. 523–555; *idem*, Stand und Aufgaben in der Erforschung des Gnostizismus, *Wiss. Zeitsch. d. F. Schiller-Univ. Jena*, Sonderheft 1963, SS. 89–102. *idem*, Ein Grundtyp gnostischer Urmensch-Adam-Spekulation, *ZRGG* 9/(1957), SS. 1–20.
[5] R. M. Grant, Les êtres intermédiaires dans le judaïsme tardif. *Le Origini*, pp. 141–154; *idem*, *Gnosticism and early Christianity*, N. York 1959, *passim*.
[6] G. Quispel, Christliche Gnosis und jüdische Heterodoxie, *EvTH* 14 (1954), SS. 474–484; *idem*, Der gnostische Anthropos und die jüdische Tradition, *Eranos-Jahrbuch* 12 (1953), Zürich 1954, SS. 195–234.
[7] Wilson, *The gnostic Problem*, *passim*
[8] Daniélou, Judéo-christianisme et Gnose; *idem*, Le mauvais gouvernement du monde d'après le gnosticisme, *Le Origini*, pp. 448–456 („une révolte au sein du judaïsme", p. 456)
[9] Schoeps, Das gnostische Judentum in den Dead Sea Scrolls; *idem*, Judenchristentum und Gnosis, *Le Origini*, S. 535.
[10] A. Orbe, Spiritus Domini ferebatur super aquas. Exegesis gnostica de Gen., 1, 2b, *Gregorianum* 44 (1963), pp. 691–731.

valuable work in detailed research here. The same cursory inspection, however, also shows that Gnosticism had a strong anti-Judaistic bias, and G. Scholem calls it „the greatest case of metaphysical anti-Semitism!"[1] All the motifs of Jewish origin, mainly taken from the first chapters of Genesis, are given a sense in Gnosticism which is diametrically opposed to their original meaning through a kind of „Protestexegese" (K. Rudolph)[2]. It is this characteristic which prohibits the direct derivation of Gnosticism from Judaism. It is true there was an esoteric development in Judaism also, which G. Scholem calls „Jewish Gnosticism", but it was accepted by Pharisees and rabbis, and remains within the bounds of established Judaism, even if it may go off the rails in incidental cases. Scholem's terminology, however, has led to all kinds of misunderstandings and his work is sometimes read, understood and digested in quite different ways[3].

Obviously, no explanation can be found for the fact that Gnosticism is at once Jewish and non-Jewish, according to whether motifs or meanings are taken as decisive, without bringing in all kinds of historical complexes. Thus R. M. Grant traced the origin of Gnosticism to the sense of crisis in Judaism after the catastrophe of A.D. 70[4]. K. Rudolph drew attention to the uprooting of large groups of the population by the continual wars in the Near East. These people migrated to the towns, where in educated circles there developed an „Erlösungsreligosität" connected with a growing pessimism, as this is expressed in the scepticism of the Jewish wisdom tradition[5]. Especially in these circles the handling and reinterpreting of traditional writings was habitual. A. Adam's view of the origin of Gnosticism tends in the same direction[6]. In this way, the ground for Gnosticism may have been prepared in the sense of Motivgeschichte, all the more since Greek philosophy probably also became known in Gnosticism via Judaism[7]. In short, it is not possible in these centuries to divide the Jewish and the Greek, as H. Dörries has shown in a very critical review of the work

[1] cited by H. Jonas, Response to G. Quispel's, p. 288.
[2] Rudolph, Randerscheinungen, S. 117.
[3] *cf.* K. Schubert, Jüdischer Hellenismus und jüdische Gnosis, *Wort und Wahrheit* 18 (1963), SS. 455–461; Rudolph, Randerscheinungen, SS. 112ff.
[4] Grant, *Gnosticism and early Christianity*, pp. 27ff.
[5] Rudolph, Randerscheinungen, SS. 109ff.; 118ff.
[6] A. Adam, Neuere Literatur zur Gnosis, *GGA* 215 (1963), S. 31–34; *idem*, Ist die Gnosis in aramäischen Weisheitsschulen entstanden, *Le Origini*, SS. 291–300.
[7] Wilson, *The Gnostic Problem*, pp. 173ff.

of J. Daniélou[1]. The question whether these extreme developments, come about in such a fashion, should still be included in Judaism or not, is of secondary interest, and cannot be solved phenomenologically. To speak of „Randerscheinungen des Judentums", „jüdische Heterodoxie" and so on rests on the presumption, that the border of Judaism and its orthodoxy can be exactly delimited, and at present this is historically impossible. Moreover, Judaism is not a static entity during the first centuries of our era, but comprises many gradations and groups which developed or disappeared especially in these centuries. The perplexity of the problem is most evident, where we read of a „Bruch" between Judaism and Gnosticism, of an „Umwertung" of the religious traditions of Judaism from which something new was formed, *i.e.* Gnosticism, of a „transposition des idées juives" and so on. Up to the present we can do no more than state that Gnosticism arose „in close vicinity and partial reaction to Judaism", „in a zone of proximity and exposure to Judaism, where the Jewish share – besides the contribution of much transmissible material – was in essence *catalytic* and *provoking*![2]" Historically this brings us no further, though it does somewhat restrict our field of research.

Some scholars, including Th. Caldwell, G. Kretschmar and also H. Jonas, are of opinion that this „zone of proximity and exposure to Judaism" is easiest to locate in Samaria, where Simon Magus is traditionally said to have come from[3]. The Gnostic sect of the Quqites also has relations with Samaria[4], while the great part played by Seth in Gnosticism also has a Samaritan parallel: „Seths Nachkommen bilden die heilige Kette; von dem Licht, das nach dem Fall noch in Adam zurückgeblieben war, wurde durch die Heilige Kette etwas auf Mose vererbt, der das inkarnierte Licht ist"[5]. As sons of Light, the law of Moses returns the Samaritans to the status of Adam before the fall and endows them with the garment of Light. Perhaps such conceptions led to the development of the Dosithean Gnosis to which Simon Magus probably belonged,

[1] H. Dörries, *Erasmus* 15 (1963) Sp. 713–719.
[2] Jonas, Delimitation of the gnostic Phenomenon, p. 102.
[3] Th. Caldwell, Dositheos Samaritanus, *Kairos* 4 (1962), SS. 105–117; G. Kretschmar, Zur religionsgeschichtlichen Einordnung der Gnosis, *EvTh* 13 (1953), SS. 354–361; H. Jonas, Response to G. Quispel's, p. 291f.
[4] Drijvers, Quq and the Quqites, pp. 108ff.
[5] J. Bowman, *Samaritanische Probleme.* Studien zum Verhältnis von Samaritanertum, Judentum und Urchristentum, Stuttgart 1967, S. 83.

but much remains uncertain here[1]. A point of interest in any case is the replacing of the Law by Gnosis, which in a way plays the same part in Gnosticism as the Torah in Judaism.

It may be, then, that a specific form of Gnosticism developed in Samaria, but this does not mean that *the* origin of Gnosticism is to be found there. To think in terms of filiation would certainly lead us astray here, since it would imply that all the groups can be deduced from this specific Samaritan Gnosticism, of which they were an elaboration. Our knowledge of the sources does not permit of such a conclusion.

Gnosticism made use of Jewish motifs, but once this has been stated the difficulties begin, which are rather veiled than solved by the introduction of terms such as „heterodoxy", „Randerscheinungen" etc., for a crisis in the divine world is unheard of in Judaism and its borders, even in Samaria[2]. K.Rudolph offers the best illustration of the difficulties inherent in this problem, when on one hand he argues that the grounds and causes of the arising of Gnosticism as a religion *sui generis* can only be traced through the collaboration of sociology, economics, history of civilisation and history of religion, yet on the other hand still returns to the method of the religionsgeschichtliche Schule when he says „*So führte die Skepsis*, geboren aus dem Zweifel an der Macht der göttlichen Weisheit, *zur Gnosis*, und damit ausserhalb des offiziellen Judentums", a conclusion based solely on a comparative examination according to Motivgeschichte[3].

Methodical considerations

It would seem that in a hundred and fifty years the problem of the origin of Gnosticism has not advanced one step towards a solution, in spite of an immense increase of sources and a correspondingly increased stream of publications, the result of a great deal of scholarly research. The main cause of this lies in the entirely different methods by which the sources are approached, so that the same sources yield widely varying results. The epilogue of U.Bianchi to „Le origini dello gnosticismo", with the promising title of 'Perspectives de la recherche sur les origines du gnosticisme' demonstrates this very clearly, for is it not there, where the results

[1] Bowman, *Samaritanische Probleme*, SS.30ff.
[2] Bowman, *Samaritanische Probleme*, S.96.
[3] Rudolph, Randerscheinungen, SS.120f.

of research agree with his personal opinion, that he sees perspectives? Apportioning praise and criticism, he passes the colloquium in review once more. It is noticeable that one scholar can do so little with the results of another, owing to the different methods employed. There is no other branch of the religio-historical discipline where this difficulty is so evident; one need only remark the manner of quotation and the using of detached portions of some one else's researches!

Methodical clarity can only be obtained, if all the texts relating to all the Gnostic groups are worked over once more *separately* and examined according to one established system[1]. So far, nearly every scholar put different questions to the texts, depending on his own view of the phenomenon Gnosticism, and naturally this view was confirmed by the texts. Such became sufficiently evident in the above. It would seem worth while to put the same questions to all the texts usually accounted Gnostic, and that in the most simple form, to which a definite or gradated answer may be given; for instance: is an evil Demiurge referred to or not, are there speculations regarding Gen. 1 or not, do we meet with the conception of the salvator salvandus, and so on. Only by using a similar method can we approach the relationship between the various groups anew, and determine which characteristics are dominant. Such a method would certainly require the collaboration of scholars of various disciplines.

There are other matters which claim our attention in this context, and which have been unduly neglected. Motivgeschichte only considers those motifs from other religions which have been borrowed, and have usually changed their function. The principal matters taken from Judaism are cosmological and anthropological speculations based on the first chapters of Genesis. In correlation with alterations in function, it is equally important to see which motifs are not taken over, and why not. From this we many conclude just what it was that the Gnostic „protest" attacked, for protest is only possible on the basis of some extent of adaptation and compromise. We have now entered into the field of religious sociology, where all kinds of problems require to be examined anew. When Gnostic research speaks of an „elite", we first need to know what an elite was in the Near East in the second century A.D.,

[1] *cf.* Van Baaren, *Le Origini*, p.177: „It is of importance to realize clearly what question we want to put to the sources."

and how this claim was asserted. As a rule, an elite can only arrogate privileges to itself if it resigns from some other matters, or represses them. It would be worth while, for instance, to compare the claims of the Gnostics to belong to an elite, expressed in the idea of the pneumatics as the elect, with the price they had to pay for it. One often hears the regret expressed that we know absolutely nothing about the sociology of the Gnostic groups, their composition, size etc.[1] Perhaps the texts might also be examined for conceptions relating to the relationship between the individual and the community; e.g. is there any mention of „multitudes" as there is in the N.T., and similar questions. Following out these lines, a great many questions could be raised, by no means all of which it may prove possible to answer from the texts; if not, it is as well to be aware of this.

Methodically, the student of religious history cannot approach Gnosticism or a Gnostic group otherwise than as a religion, „a system of symbols which acts to establish powerful, pervasive, and long-lasting moods and motivations in men by formulating conceptions of a general order of existence and clothing these conceptions with such an aura of factuality that the moods and motivations seem uniquely realistic."[2] For a well-founded study, he needs to be preacher and unbeliever at once, and able to desist from the attitude of either. Gnosticism has been too often examined either only by unbelievers or only by preachers, and as a result we are little further advanced at present than the heresy-hunting Fathers of the Church or the Gnostics, in whom the presence of other religions elicited a crisis that had to be conjured. And is not the religio-historical discipline a phenomenon of crisis within Christianity? Particularly the search for the origins of Gnosticism affords a double demonstration of this, since it takes us back to the first turbulent centuries of our era, when the scholarly discussion of today was still a real fight for „conceptions of a general order of existence".

[1] Van Baaren, *Le Origini*, p.177; E.M.Mendelson, Some Notes on a sociological Approach to Gnosticism, *Le Origini*, pp.668–674.
[2] C.Geertz, Religion as a Cultural System, *Anthropological Approaches to the Study of Religion*, London 1966, p.4.

XVI

THE PERSISTENCE OF PAGAN CULTS AND PRACTICES IN CHRISTIAN SYRIA

SYSTEMATIC research on the persistence of pagan cults and practices in Christian Syria is beset with so many difficulties that some preliminary observations must be made on the various aspects of the theme.[1]

Although there are quite a number of pagan temples and shrines known in Syria, of which the ruins often are well preserved, the cults celebrated in these temples and other religious practices are practically unknown.[2] Except for Lucian's famous and often austere treatise on the temple and cult of the Dea Syria at Hierapolis no written sources on pagan cults and practices in Syria are available.[3] Attacks by Christian authors on their pagan opponents are mostly of a very general character mentioning pagan deities and sacrifices, but they are not informative on what really took place in a pagan temple. We know that sacrifices were made, but the whole liturgy celebrated in the temple—the prayers that accompanied the sacrificial service, the theological setting, and the ideological framework of paganism per se—is unknown.[4] Pagan myths and their cosmological and social connotations can be partly reconstructed from the known iconography of the deities as preserved in reliefs and sculptures and from the many rather stereotyped inscriptions, but no single myth or mythical tale on the *faits et gestes* of Syrian deities has been preserved.[5] Even the often long records in later Arabic literature on the so-called Sabians in Ḥarrān and their pagan cults and practices are so hard to interpret that we still await a satisfying reconstruction of their religious and philosophical system and all practices connected with it, although it seems likely that their theology may be considered a paradigm of later Syrian intellectual paganism rather than an isolated phenomenon.[6] Our sources thus are meager, often silent or contradictory, and at best make known only the surface of a whole religious world-view, but do not give any clear insight into the structural pattern on which the cult of the pagan gods and human behavior in general is based. The conflict between paganism and Christianity is a conflict between two different world-views and therefore, at least in principle, between two different ways of human personal and social behavior.[7] It is against this background that the problem of the persistence of pagan cults and practices ought to be looked at.

The Syrian area, moreover, has never been a cultural unity, and therefore it has displayed a variety of religious traditions even in late antique times after so many centuries during which the unifying tendencies of Greco-Roman culture had made themselves felt. The coastal region inherited the Phoenician cults of the various harbor cities like Sidon and Tyre.[8] The Syrian inland had famous religious centers like

Baalbek-Heliopolis, which remained pagan for a very long time, whereas the former capital of the Seleucid empire, Antioch, was strongly Christian at an early date.[9] The cities in and on the edge of the Syrian desert showed a composite religious pattern of traditional Syrian religion mostly under a strong influence from Babylon as well as the various cults of the desert population of Arab stock. Palmyra and Dura-Europos are good examples of such a mingling of cults that often belonged to different parts of the body social.[10] Although the religious pattern of Palmyra, for example, is well known, some cults and practices remain hidden from our knowledge. Offerings were made, lamps were lit to honor the gods, meals—often called sacred meals—were organized by the various thiasoi in special rooms within the temple area, altars were given to the temples as ex-voto's or officially erected, processions were held and priests ordained, but exact details of all these religious ceremonies and practices are not known.[11] The most important function of religion in a Syrian town or village in late antiquity, as in earlier times, was structuring and organizing the social network of the urban or rural society and its rhythm of life in a festal calendar. In a city like Palmyra in Syria the various tribes and clans had special relations with certain sanctuaries; the whole population was divided into four tribes—perhaps also for administrative reasons—and each tribe had a sanctuary of its own.[12] The traditional religious and social center of the city as a whole was the temple of Bêl on the ancient tell, where the cult of the theoi patroioi was celebrated.[13] There are strong indications that the relations between the different tribes among themselves and between them and the central sanctuary of Bêl were marked by processions. In this and other ways the urban area was structured along social and religious lines, and knew certain points of concentration that functioned as the highlights of all urban activities.[14]

It should be emphasized that especially during the fourth century, when Christianity became the official religion, the empire tried and at last succeeded in replacing the pagan structure of society with a Christian one: building churches instead of temples or on the very place of temples, introducing a Christian calendar with Christian feasts, and getting a grip on every aspect of life as in former times pagan culture had had. All these things had been known, but they determined a process of gradual change that involved the whole culture and society. It is therefore not surprising that pagan cults and practices as part of a whole cultural pattern persisted for a long time; it is, rather, amazing that Christianity won the victory for such a thorough change within a relatively short period.

Just as Syria was not a cultural unity in pagan times, it was not a uniform Christian country with a Christian culture in later times. Christianization proceeded through different lines at different speeds. Some cities, like Apamea and Ḥarrān, remained pagan for a long time and others, like Edessa in Northern Mesopotamia,[15] were known as totally Christian at a very early date. The countryside was won for the new faith only during the fourth and fifth centuries through the efforts of Syrian monks and ascetics.[16] There were also class differences, as the intellectual upper class remained attached to paganism for a long time because it was linked with its culture and education. Intellectual paganism had a tenacious life, especially in academic and sophisticated circles in Antioch, Apamea, and elsewhere.[17]

It is therefore impossible to speak of pagan cults and practices in Syria as a well-defined entity, just as it is impossible to refer to Christian Syria as a clear-cut religious denomination. The persistence of certain cults and practices that were labeled pagan in a society with a Christian majority is the outcome of a long process of change and religious polarization. It seems a scientific platitude to declare that pagan cults and practices have persisted in Christian Syria; this is quite natural and not amazing. The real question is what persisted and why it was called pagan in contradistinction to what was supposed to be Christian. Taking into consideration that Syria displays such a variety of cults and that the Christianization went off in various ways, it seems methodologically the best way of approaching the problem to concentrate on one special area that is relatively well known. I have chosen Northern Mesopotamia, with Edessa as center, as the cradle of early Syriac-speaking Christianity. According to tradition it was converted to the new faith at an early stage, so that the pagan emperor Julian for example, refused to honor it with a visit but went to a sanctuary in neighboring pagan Ḥarrān. In such a city the persistence of paganism can best be studied as a paradigm of what happened, why, and how.[18]

Pagan culture at Edessa should be sketched in outline to clarify the milieu in which Christianity manifested itself and at last became the dominant religion. The religious scene was dominated by the cult of Nebo and Bêl, the first the Babylonian god of wisdom and human fate, the latter the kosmokrator, lord of planets and stars, who guided the world and gave it fertility. He symbolized order in the cosmos and society, because he gave and guaranteed the laws. In his cult astrological practice kept an organic place, because astrology made known the plans and guidance of the divine creator of order, whose main feast was the New Year's festival celebrated at the beginning of April. Nebo his son stood for wisdom and the scribal art and most likely functioned as a kind of mediator between the highest god Bêl and the world.[19] Both gods were venerated at Ḥarrān, too, and it seems that the cult of Nebo had some elements in common with the doctrines associated with the name of Hermes Trismegistos.[20] It is not surprising that Nebo retained first place n the Edessene pantheon, because the city was a true academic center—called the Athens of the East—in which Greek philosophy was widely known and taught. It is most probable that the later School of the Persians at Edessa had pagan forerunners.[21] In this context I should like to stress that the language frontier between Northern Mesopotamia, where Syriac was in common use by the intellectual upper class, and Coele Syria and Antioch, where Greek was the dominant literary vehicle, did not imply a cultural barrier between a mainly hellenistic Syrian Western region and Osrhoene with its supposedly Semitic culture with only faint traces of Greco-Roman civilization.[22]

Besides Nebo and Bêl, Edessa venerated the Dea Syria Atargatis whose main sanctuary was in Hierapolis-Mabbuğ. The sacred carp in the fish ponds near the citadel are the modern remnants of her cult in which water and fish played an important role, as is understandable in the cult of a fertility goddess.[23] It can be assumed that the sanctuary of the goddess was situated north of the citadel and still existed in 384 when the nun Egeria visited the city.[24] In her cult emasculation was frequently paracticed and had a tenacious life. According to the *Book of the Laws of Countries*, a dialogue on fate from the School of Bardaiṣan, Abgar, the alleged first Christian king of Edessa, forbade this barbarous habit; nevertheless, bishop Rabbula at the beginning of the fifth century still was compelled to prohibit his clerics from emasculating themselves.[25]

Nebo and Bêl represent the Babylonian component of Edessene religion, whereas Atargatis belongs to the Aramaean layer in this region. The seminomads from the desert, who settled themselves in and around Edessa, brought their own cults of protecting spirits, the gaddê or ğinns, and of armed deities like Azizos and Monimos, who functioned as an armed escort in the desert. The veneration of the sun god Šamš and of the eagle, the symbol of the heavenly vault, also reflects Arab influence on Edessene religion.[26]

Very little is known of cultic practice, but public and private offerings and processions through the streets of the city surely were a regular spectacle accompanied with music and public acclamations. It may be assumed that the cult of all these lifegiving, foretelling, healing, and protecting deities represented the promise of a better life in the often hard and cruel circumstances of human existence in a late antique city in Northern Mesopotamia.[27]

Christianity became known in Edessa in the second century and manifested itself in the sects of Marcionites and Bardaiṣanites.[28] The latter are a local phenomenon, followers of Bardaiṣan the philosopher of the Aramaeans (154-222), who lived at the court of King Abgar the Great. Bardaiṣan tried to synthesize local paganism and astrology in philosophical disguise and the Christian faith, which resulted in a special cosmology and anthropology, in which astrological fatalism played a restricted role. Not being gnostic in the strict sense, the Bardaiṣanite doctrine flavors a kindred atmosphere.[29] Ephrem Syrus, a fervent opponent of Bardaiṣan, has preserved some fragments of authentic Bardaiṣanite hymns in his polemical poetic oeuvre, from which it becomes clear that this teacher of philosophy also intepreted traditional local cults of Atargatis and Bêl, among others, in a philosophical, sophisticated way.[30] In that aspect Bardaiṣan should be compared with the Sabians in nearby Ḥarrān who did the same. Bardaiṣan is the first example of a Christianized pagan intellectualism with strong emphasis on astrology, the fate of the human soul, symbolical interpretation of traditional myths, and an eclectic philosophy. He surely considered himself a Christian, but later generations openly accused him of adhering to pagan doctrines and practices. It seems that Bardaiṣanites, Marcionites, and Manichaeans dominated the religious scene in third-century Edessa, although what later came to be called orthodoxy was not absent.[31] Along this line of intellectual gnostic-colored, partly Christianized paganism much of pagan culture and religion persisted, especially in an academic city like Edessa. We may asume that at the end of the fourth century and the beginning of the fifth this semipagan trend was still very strong. It is even possible that in 579/80 such groups still existed in Edessa according to the record of John of Ephesos (*H.E.* III,5,15) on pagan practices at Baalbek, Antioch, and Edessa.[32] But even the Christian tradition assumed that much of this learned tradition concentrated on astrological doctrines, as becomes clear from the work of Jacob of Edessa at the beginning of the eighth century.[33]

Although the official legend of the conversion of Edessa, the *Doctrina Addai*, presents a different view for obvious reasons, the conversion did not take place as quickly as this enthusiastic propaganda would have us believe. Even the most recent version from the end of the fourth or the beginning of the fifth century contains some clues to the historical reality.[34] In a fervent sermon the apostle Addai addresses himself to the crown of Edessa and vehemently attacks the pagan deities Nebo, Bêl, Atargatis, and others. The priests of these gods are so impressed by his preaching that they destroy their altars except for the great altar in the center of the city. That may be an allusion to the fact that at the end of the fourth century the pagan temples were still standing at Edessa and still maintained their central position. In other words, the great altar symbolizes the Tyche of Edessa that is still pagan. This assumption is corroborated by an Imperial rescript of 382 of Theodosius that permitted the citizens of Edessa to assemble in the pagan pantheon, although sacrifices were not allowed (*Theodosian Code* XVI,10,3). Such a rescript of the pious Emperor can be explained only against the background of a strong and powerful pagan group to the supposedly totally Christian Edessa.[35] It is not too far-fetched to suppose that these pagans belonged to the upper class of society with its philosophically colored education. Bishop Rabbula (d. 436) destroyed the pagan shrines at Edessa or transformed them into churches. The same bishop is known as a busy builder of churches, the first since the time that Bishop Qune in the beginning of the fourth century had built the first church at Edessa.[36] Only when the churches had supplanted the former temples did Christianity get a real grip on the city population and their social behavior by offering them new places of assembly.

Even though cult ceremonies were forbidden, the population of Edessa celebrated the pagan spring festival with all pomp and enthusiasm at the end of the fifth century, according to the *Chronicle* of Joshua the Stylite: The year 809 = 497/8: "While these things were taking place, there came round again the time of that festival at which the heathen myths were recited, and the citizens took even more pains about it than usual. For seven days previously they were going up to the theater at eventide, clad in linen garments, and wearing turbans, with their loins ungirt. Lamps were lighted before them, and they were burning incense, and holding vigils the whole night."[37] The same stylite mentions the celebration of another pagan festival in the month of May (XXXIII). These festivals were accompanied by dancing and music, and obscene behavior—according to their opponents.

There are indications that the Christians tried to replace the pagan calendar of festivals by a Christian one; at Edessa (and Suruğ) the feast of the apostle Thomas might have taken the place of the pagan spring festival.[38] It is at least certain that the Christian festivals took over most of the customs of the pagan festivals such as fairs. It seems inevitable that the whole process during which Christianity at last supplanted paganism implied the taking over of a good deal of pagan practice; the practice of processions and festivals remained more or less the same, although the ideology changed. If you want to call that persistence of pagan cults and practices, there is no strong objection to that. It is, however, more a matter of continuity of culture in which no sudden changes or breaks occur, only gradual shifts.

Christianity tried, however, very hard to suppress practices that were so closely linked with pagan ideology and doctrine that they could not be allowed or taken over. Such is the case with certain forms of astrology, of sexual intercourse in honor of goddesses of love and fertility, and with magic. The words of the Apostle Addai in the *Doctrina Addai* are revealing: "Let your bodies be pure, and let your persons be holy, as is right for men who stand before the altar of God; and be ye indeed far removed from false swearing, and from wicked murder, and from false testimony, which is mixed with adultery, and for sorcerers with respect to whom there is no mercy, and from divinations, and soothsaying, and necromancers, and from fates, and horoscopes, in which the erring Chaldees boast themselves; and from stars and the signs of the Zodiac, in which the foolish are confident!"[39] It is interesting to see how stricly moral commandments are mixed with warnings against all kinds of sorcery and magic and astrology. These practices are exponents of a totally different world-view from that which Christianity cherished and held true. Astrology was not an innocent pastime as it is nowadays, but a means by which to learn the plans and decisions of Bêl and the kosmokrator, who ruled planets and stars and through them human life and fate.[40] That is the only reason why Ephrem Syrus, for example, always combines in his polemical works accusations of false doctrine with accusations of astrological and magic practice or of a shameful sexual behavior. It is also the only correct explanation for the fact that all forms of theology that developed in the Syrian area cherished the doctrine of free will against every pagan or heretical opponent.

When Ephrem in his *Hymns contra Haereses* warns against the Books of the Chaldaeans, because they make people err (V,14), or against sorcery that turns us into pagans (V,19), or against the cult of the Venus star in whose honor lewdness is committed (VIII; IX, 8), these are exactly the same objections that the church father formulates against the Bardaiṣanites and the Manichees.[41]

In the fifth century Isaac of Antioch blames the inhabitants of Beth Ḥur in Northern Mesopotamia for the same things. Even priests are not free from these practices according to the same Isaac in his homily against the soothsayers.[42] Therefore, magic and astrology mean heresy, and heresy means astrology and magical practice. A striking example is the case of Sophronios, bishop of Tella, who was condemned in 449 at the synod of Ephesos. Peterson believed that the combination of an accusation of heresy with the reproach of magical practices was a literary topos.[43] It seems, however, that at least in the Syrian area both accusations are organically connected and find their unity in the persistence of pagan religion in certain forms of religious doctrine and practice.

Accusations of and warnings against magical and related uses are always a sign of ill-defined power and competiton.[44] The same holds true for an all-pervading belief in demons such as the fourth and fifth century knew. The accusations of magic and belief in demons repeated so emphatically thus are the most convincing proof that paganism was still alive and was even believed to be a real threat for the Christian church. It is, therefore, more than a coincidence that the Christian ascetics and saints, who won the victory over their carnal body, at the same time attacked the pagan deities and demons and severely warned against magic and sorcery.[45]

Paganism persisted for centuries in the most Christian city, the blessed city of Syria. It persisted as an intellectual culture inside and outside the Christian church; it persisted in cultic practices and religious festivals that continued former traditions; it persisted in astrology and magic that were as tenacious as the despair of human freedom.

The Institute of Semitic Studies and
Archaeology of the Near East
University of Groningen
The Netherlands

1. There exists a vast literature on paganism and Christianity in Syria, but it deals mainly with various aspects of paganism per se, or of Christinaity per se, or with special problems in their interrelation, but a history of religions in Syria does not exist. W. E. Kaegi, "The Fifth-Century Twilight of Byzantine Paganism," *ClMed*, 27 (1966), 243-75, is a good introduction; cf. in general A. J. Festugière, *Antioche païenne et chrétienne: Libanius, Chrysostome et les moines de Syrie*, BEFAR, CXCIV (Paris, 1959); *The Conflict between Paganism and Christianity in the Fourth Century*, ed. A. Momigliano (Oxford, 1963). The political and cultural complexity of the Syrian area is well demonstrated by J.-P. Rey-Coquais, "Syrie romaine, de Pompée à Dioclétien," *JRS*, 68 (1978) 44-73.

2. D. Krencker and W. Zschietzschmann, *Römische Tempel in Syrien* (Berlin, 1938); G. Taylor, *The Roman Temples of Lebanon: A Pictorial Guide* (Beirut, 1967).

3. *The Syrian Goddess (De Dea Syria) Attributed to Lucian*, ed. and trans. H. W. Attridge and R. A. Oden, Society of Biblical Literature Texts and Translation, IX (Missoula, Mont., 1976); R. A. Oden, *Studies in Lucian's De Syria Dea*, Harvard Semitic Monographs, XV (Missoula, Mont., 1977); M. Hörig, *Dea Syria: Studien zur religiösen Tradition der Fruchtbarkeitsgöttin im Vorderasien*, Alter Orient und Altes Testament, CCVIII (Neukirchen, 1979); H. J. W. Drijvers, *Cults and Beliefs at Edessa*, Études préliminaires aux religions orientales dans l'empire romain, LXXXII (Leyden, 1980), 76-121.

4. F. Cumont in many books and articles offered a reconstruction of the supposedly learned theology of Syrian priests mainly based on philosophical literature; see, e.g., *Les religions orientales dans le paganisme romain*, 4th ed. (Paris, 1929), 111 ff.; *Lux Perpetua* (Paris, 1949). The solar theology as reconstructed by him does not find support in the archeological and epigraphical evidence; see H. Seyrig, "Le culte du soleil en Syrie à l'époque romaine," *Syria*, 48 (1971), 337-73.

5. To give one example, it seems clear that one of the reliefs on the crossbeams of Bêl's temple at Palmyra represents a primordial (?) fight against a chaos-monster, which also occurs in the Babylonian creation myth, but an exact interpretation cannot be given; see H. Seyrig, R. Amy, and E. Will, *Le temple de Bêl à Palmyre*, I (Paris, 1975), 87; R. du Mesnil du Buisson, "Le bas-relief du combat de Bêl contre Tiamat dans le temple de Bêl à Palmyre," *Annales archéologiques arabes de Syrie*, 26 (1976), 83-111; Drijvers, *Cults and Beliefs at Edessa*, 64 ff.

6. D. Chwolsohn, *Die Ssabier und der Ssabismus* (St. Petersburg, 1856); J. Hjärpe, *Analyse critique des traditions arabes sur les Sabéeens ḥarraniens* (Diss. Uppsala, 1972); J. B. Segal, *Edessa and Harran: An Inaugural Lecture* (London, 1963); G. Fowden, "Asceticism and the Pagan Tradition in Byzantine and Muslim Syria," *JRS* (forthcoming).

7. Cf. P. Brown, *The World of Late Antiquity* (London, 1971), 49 ff.; *idem*, *The Making of Late Antiquity* (Cambridge-London, 1978), 11 ff.

8. H. Seyrig, "Divinités de Sidon," *Syria*, 36 (1959), 48-56; *idem*, "Les grands dieux de Tyr à l'époque romaine," *Syria*, 40 (1963), 19-27; H. Gese, M. Höfner, and K. Rudolph, *Die Religionen Altsyriens, Altarabiens und der Mandäer*, Die Religionen der Menschheit, X, 2 (Stuttgart, 1970), 182 ff.

9. On paganism at Baalbek in late antiquity see Kaegi, "The Fifth-Century Twilight of Byzantine Paganism," 258f.; P. J. Alexander, *The Oracle of Baalbek: The Tiburtine Sibyl in Greek Dress*, DOS, X (Washington, 1967), 43 ff.; Damascius in Photius, *Bibliotheca, cod.* 242, PG CIII, col. 1273; John of Ephesos, *Hist. eccl.*, 3, 27, ed. E. W. Brooks, CSCO, CVI (Louvain, 1936), 114; on early Christianity in Antioch see G. Downey, *A History of Antioch in Syria from Seleucus to the Arab Conquest* (Princeton, 1961) 272 ff.; W. Liebeschuetz, "Epigraphic Evidence on the Christianisation of Syria," *Akten des XI. Internationalen Limeskongresses* (Budapest, n.d.), 492 ff.; *idem*, *Antioch: City and Imperial Administration in the Later Roman Empire* (Oxford, 1972), 224 ff.

10. On Palmyra see M. Gawlikowski, *Le temple palmyrénien: Étude d'épigraphie et de topographie historique* (Warsaw, 1973); Drijvers, *The Religion of Palmyra*, Iconography of Religions XV, 15 (Leyden, 1976); J. Teixidor, *The Pantheon of Palmyra*, Études préliminaires aux religions orientales dans l'empire romain, LXXIX (Leyden, 1979); on the cults of Dura-Europos see C. B. Welles, "The Gods of Doura-Europos," *Festschrift F. Altheim*, II (Berlin, 1969), 50-65, and many interesting suggestions by C. Hopkins, *The Discovery of Dura-Europos*, ed. B. Goldman (New Haven-London, 1979).

11. J. T. Milik, *Dédicaces faites par des dieux (Palmyre, Hatra, Tyr) et des thiases sémitiques à l'époque romaine* (Paris, 1972), contains interesting, but often too fantastic, ideas on these aspects of Palmyra's religion; it is striking that J. Teixidor, *The Pantheon of Palmyra*, does not give any attention to cult matters; see also the prudent remarks by H. Seyrig, "Les tessères palmyréniennes et le banquet rituel," *Mémorial Lagrange* (Paris, 1940), 51-58.

12. D. Schlumberger, "Les quatre tribus de Palmyre," *Syria*, 48 (1971), 121-33; Gawlikowski, *Le temple palmyrénien*, 26-52; Teixidor, *The Pantheon of Palmyra*, 36.

13. H. Seyrig, "Bêl de Palmyre," *Syria*, 48 (1971), 85-114; H. Seyrig, R. Amy, and E. Will, *Le temple de Bêl à Palmyre* (Paris, 1975).

14. One of the reliefs on the cross-beams of the peristyle of Bêl's temple represents such a procession; see H. Seyrig, "Bas-reliefs monumentaux du temple de Bêl à Palmyre," *Syria*, 15 (1934), 159-65 and pl. XIX; Seyrig, Amy and Will, *Le temple de Bêl à Palmyre*, 88 f.; it is not without interest that a fragment of an identical relief was found in the sanctuary of Allât in

the western quarter of the city; cf. Drijvers, "Das Heiligtum der arabischen Göttin Allât im westlichen Stadtteil von Palmyra," *Antike Welt*, 7 (1976), 28-38.

15. On paganism at Apamea, Sozomen, *Hist. eccl.*, 7, 15; Liebeschuetz, "Epigraphic Evidence on the Christianisation of Syria," 494 f.; G. Fowden, "Bishops and Temples in the Eastern Roman Empire A.D. 320-435," *JThS*, 29 (1978), 64 ff.; the opinion that Edessa was Christianized during the reign of King Abgar the Great (177-212) is due to a historical interpretation of the Abgar legend as told by Eusebius, *Hist. eccl.*, I, 13; II, 1, 6-8, and the so-called *Doctrina Addai* dating from the end of the 4th or even the beginning of the 5th century; see, e.g., J. J. Gunther, "The Meaning and Origin of the Name 'Judas Thomas,'" *Le Muséon*, 93 (1980), 131 ff.; the Abgar legend should, however, be understood as an anti-Manichaean work from the end of the 3rd century without any historical elements from earlier centuries; see my "Beziehungen zwischen Christentum und Manichäismus im dritten Jahrhundert in Syrien" (forthcoming).

16. Liebeschuetz, "Epigraphic Evidence on the Christianisation of Syria," 485-507; on the role of monks see Libanius, *Or.* 30, *Pro Templis*, and Sozomen, *Hist. eccl.* 6, 34; P. Canivet, *Le monachisme syrien selon Théodoret de Cyr*, Théologie historique, XLII (Paris, 1977), 205; W. H. C. Frend, "The Winning of the Countryside," *JEH*, 18 (1967), 1-14.

17. A. H. M. Jones, "The Social Background of the Struggle between Paganism and Christianity," in *The Conflict between Paganism and Christianity in the Fourth Century*, ed. A. Momigliano (Oxford, 1963), 30; Liebeschuetz, *Antioch*, 225 ff.; Festugière, *Antioche païenne et chrétienne*, 141 ff.; J.-Ch. Balty, "Julien et Apamée: Aspects de la restauration de l'hellénisme et de la politique antichrétienne de l'empereur," *Dialogues d'histoire ancienne* (1974), 267-304; Libanius, *Ep.* 1351 on the cult of Zeus (Bêl) at Apamea.

18. Sozomen, *Hist. eccl.*, VI, 1, 1; Theodoret, *Hist. eccl.*, III, 26, 2; cf. J. B. Segal, *Edessa the "Blessed City"* (Oxford, 1970), 111; G. W. Bowersock, *Julian the Apostate* (Cambridge, Mass., 1978), 92 on Julian's Letter 115 to Edessa.

19. Cf. Drijvers, *Cults and Beliefs at Edessa*, 40-75; The Cult of Nebo and Bel; *The Doctrine of Addai*, ed. G. Phillips (London, 1876), 23 (trans.) = 24, LL, 15 f. (Syriac text); Zeus-Bêl of Apamea is called *Fortunae rector mentisque magister*, *CIL*, xii, 1277 = *IG*, xiv, 2482 = *ILS*, 4333.

20. Cf. Drijvers, "Bardaisan of Edessa and the Hermetica: The Aramaic Philosopher and the Philosophy of His Time," *Jaarbericht Ex Oriente Lux*, 21 (1969-70), 190-210; *Thesaurus Syriacus s.v. nbw*, col. 2268; Drijvers, *Cults and Beliefs at Edessa*, 74 f.

21. E. R. Hayes, *L'école d'Édesse* (Paris, 1930), *passim*; there was a strong unbroken philosophical tradition at Edessa, of which the *Letter of Mara bar Serapion to His Son*, ed. W. Cureton, *Spicilegium Syriacum* (London, 1855), 43-48, is an early exponent. Bardaiṣan (154-222) represents Greek philosophy in Syriac disguise; cf. Drijvers, *Bardaiṣan of Edessa*, Studia Semitica Neerlandica, VI (Assen, 1966), *passim*, and A. Dihle, "Zur Schicksalslehre des Bardesanes," *Kerygma und Logos, Festschrift C. Andresen*, ed. A. M. Ritter (Göttingen, 1979), 123-35; Lucian the Martyr got his philosophical training at Edessa in the 3rd century with Macrinus.

22. Cf. P. Brown, "Approaches to the Religious Crisis of the Third Century A. D.," *Religion and Society in the Age of Saint Augustine* (London, 1972), 85 f.; F. Millar, "Paul of Samosata, Zenobia and Aurelian: The Church, Local Culture and Political Allegiance in Third-Century Syria," *JRS*, 61 (1971), 2-5; Syriac and Greek in the East Syrian Regions and Mesopotamia: Drijvers, "Hatra, Palmyra und Edessa: Die Städte der syrisch-mesopotamischen Wüste in politischer, kulturgeschichtlicher und religionsgeschichtlicher Beleuchtung," *Aufstieg und Niedergang der röm. Welt*, 2.8 (Berlin, 1977), 885 ff.; R. Schmitt, "Die Ostgrenze von Armenien über Mesopotamien, Syrien bis Arabien," *Die Sprachen im römischen Reich der Kaiserzeit*, *BJb*, 40 (1980), 187-214, esp. 201 f.

23. Lucian, *De Syria Dea*, 45-47; F. Cumont, *Études syriennes* (Paris, 1917), 35 ff.; G. Goossens, *Hiérapolis de Syrie: Essai de monographie historique* (Louvain, 1943), 62; Drijvers, *Cults and Beliefs at Edessa*, 79 ff.

24. *Itinerarium Aetheriae*, 19, 7 ed. H. Pétré, SC, XXI (Paris, 1948); P. Devos, "Égérie à Édesse: S. Thomas l'Apôtre, le roi Abgar," *AnalBoll*, 85 (1967), 381-400; Drijvers, *Cults and Beliefs at Edessa*, Pls. II, III.

25. According to the *Book of the Law of Countries*, *PS*, II, col. 607; cf. G. Sanders, "Gallos," *RAC*, 8, col. 1026 ff.; Rabbula of Edessa, Canon LV, ed. A. Vööbus, *Syriac and Arabic Documents Regarding Legislation Relative to Syrian Monasticism* (Stockholm, 1960), 49.

26. On the gad = Tyche see *Götter und Mythen im Vorderen Orient*, ed. H. W. Haussig, Wörterbuch der Mythologie I (Stuttgart, 1965), 438 f.; R. Dussaud, *La pénétration des Arabes en Syrie avant l'Islam*, (Paris, 1955), 110-12; D. Schlumberger, "Le prétendu dieu Gennéas," *Mélanges de l'Université Saint Joseph*, 46 (1970-71), 209-22; Teixidor, *The Pantheon of Palmyra*, 77 ff.; on armed escorts see H. Seyrig, "Les dieux armés et les Arabes en Syrie," *Syria*, 47 (1970), 77-112; on the cult of the sun god: *idem*, "Le culte du Soleil en Syrie," *Syria*, 48 (1971), 337-73; cf. Drijvers, *Cults and Beliefs at Edessa*, 146 ff.

27. J. B. Segal, "Mesopotamian Communities from Julian to the Rise of Islam," *ProcBrAc*, 41 (1955), 116 ff.; cf. *The Chronicle of Joshua the Stylite*, ed. W. Wright (Cambridge, 1882), chaps. xxxviii-xlvi on famine and plague at Edessa; see in general Brown, *The World of Late Antiqutiy*, 12 ff.

28. W. Bauer, *Rechtgläubigkeit und Ketzerei im ältesten Christentum*, Beiträge zur historischen Theologie X (Tübingen, 1934), 6-48; Drijvers, "Rechtgläubigkeit und Ketzerei im ältesten syrischen Christentum," *OCA*, 197 (1974), 291-310; *idem*, "Die Oden Salomos und die Polemik mit den Markioniten im syrischen Christentum," *OCA*, 205 (1978), 39-55.

29. See Drijvers, *Bardaiṣan of Edessa*, *passim*; *idem*, "Bardesanes," *Theologische Realenzyklopädie*, V, 206-212 (with bibliography).

30. Ephrem Syrus, *Hymns contra Haereses*, ed. E. Beck, CSCO, CLXIX-CLXX (Louvain, 1957), Hymn 55, 1-10, esp. strophe 1: "Something streamed down from the Father of Life and the Mother became pregnant with the mystery of the Fish and bore him, and he was called Son of Life"; cf. Drijvers, *Bardaiṣan of Edessa*, 144 ff.; *idem*, *Cults and Beliefs*, 79 f.; cf. E. Beck, "Symbolum-Mysterium bei Aphraat und Ephräm," *OrChr*, 42 (1958), 31, 39.

31. These "orthodox" are to be linked with Palut, who came from Antioch around the beginning of the 3rd century, and were called after him; *Doctrina Addai*, ed. Phillips, 50; Ephrem Syrus, *Hymns contra Haereses*, 22, 5-6; cf. Bauer, *Rechtgläubigkeit*, 25-27. The 42 *Odes of Solomon* and the *Apocryphal Acts of Thomas* originate in these circles which share part of their religious imagery with their opponents; cf. Drijvers, "Odes of Solomon and Psalms of Mani: Christians and Manichaeans in Third-Century Syria," *Festschrift G. Quispel* (Leyden, 1981), forthcoming.

32. Cf. Segal, "Mesopotamian Communities from Julian to the Rise of Islam," 126; cf. Downey, *Antioch*, 558 f.; 563 f.; Euagrius, *Hist. eccl.*, 5, 18; John of Ephesos, 3, 26-34.

33. Jacob of Edessa, *Hexaemeron*, ed. J. B. Chabot, CSCO, XCII and XCVII contains many examples of this learned tradition, which deserves further study.

34. *The Doctrine of Addai the Apostle*, ed. and trans. G. Phillips (London, 1876); R. Peppermüller, "Griechische

Papyrusfragmente der Doctrina Addai," *VChr*, 25 (1971), 289-301; the central motives of the Abgar Legend were borrowed from Manichaean tradition and hint at the strong position that Manichaeism held at the end of the 3rd century at Edessa; cf. Drijvers, "Beziehungen zwischen Christentum und Manichäismus im dritten Jahrhundert in Syrien," *OCA* (forthcoming).

35. *Codex Theodosianus*, ed. and trans. C. Pharr (New York, 1952), 16, 10, 17 allows *festa convivia*; cf. G. Fowden, "Bishops and Temples in the Eastern Roman Empire," 53 ff.

36. The mention of the "sanctuary of the church of the christians" in the *Chronicon Edessenum*, which was destroyed by the flood of A.D. 201, clearly is a later interpolation; cf. Bauer, *Rechtgläubigkeit und Ketzerei*, 18; *Chronicon Edessenum*, ed. I. Guidi, CSCO, I-II; Chronica Minora I (Louvain, 1903), 1-11; L. Hallier, *Untersuchungen über die Edessenische Chronik*, *TU*, IX, 1 (Leipzig, 1892); on Rabbula see G. G. Blum, *Rabbula von Edessa: Der Christ, der Bischof, der Theologe*, CSCO, Subsidia 34 (Louvain, 1969), 61-105; cf. A. Baumstark, "Vorjustinianische kirchliche Bauten in Edessa," *OrChr*, 4 (1904), 164-83.

37. The Chronicle of Joshua the Stylite, ed. W. Wright (Cambridge, 1882), xxx; cf. xxvii, xxxiii, xlvi; cf. Drijvers, *Cults and Beliefs*, 43.

38. Cf.U. Monneret de Villard, "La Fierà di Batnae e la traslazione di S. Tomaso a Edessa," *RendLinc*, 8, ser. 6 (1951), 77 ff.

39. *Doctrina Addai*, ed. Phillips, 33 f.

40. Bêl is the *Fortunae rector* (*CIL*, xiii, 1277), as is clear from the ceiling of the northern thalamos of Bêl's temple at Palmyra, which represents the god in the midst of the planets and signs of the Zodiac; cf. Drijvers, *The Religion of Palmyra*, pl. II; P. Brykczyński," Astrologie w Palmyrze," *Studia Palmyreńskie*, 6 (1975), 52 ff.

41. Ephrem Syrus, *Hymns contra Haereses*, ed. Beck, v, 14, 19; vi (against astrology and the doctrines of Bardaiṣan); vii (against astrology, the veneration of the Venus star, and Mani); viii (against astrology); ix (against astrology and lewdness in honor of Venus); xiii, 9; xviii, 9, 10, 11 (against sorcery); xli (against polytheism and Marcion, Bardaiṣan, and Mani); l, 5 (against pagan deities and Mani); it is noteworthy that the *Doctrina Addai* attacks paganism and has a strong anti-Manichaean tendency.

42. A. Klugkist, "Pagane Bräuche in den Homilien des Isaak von Antiocheia gegen die Wahrsager," *OCA*, 197 (1974), 353-69; G. Bickell, *S. Isaaci Antiocheni doctoris syrorum opera omnia*, I (Gissae, 1873), Hom. XI and XII; on the literary and historical problems connected with the various Isaacs see Baumstark, *Geschichte der syrischen Literatur*, 63-66.

43. E. Peterson, "Die geheimen Praktiken eines syrischen Bischofs," *Frühkirche, Judentum und Gnosis* (Freiburg, 1959), 333-45.

44. P. Brown, "Sorcery, Demons, and the Rise of Christianity from Late Antiquity into the Middle Ages," *Witchcraft, Confessions and Accusations*, ed. M. Douglas (London, 1970), 17-45; from this viewpoint a study of the magic bowls from the Mesopotamian area would be interesting; see C. D. Isbell, *Corpus of the Aramaic Incantation Bowls* (Missoula, Mont., 1975) for a survey of the extant material; also interesting is H. Gollancz, *The Book of Protection: Syriac Charms* (London, 1912); see the bibliography in E. M. Yamauchi, *Mandaic Incantation Texts*, American Oriental Series, ixl (New Haven, 1967).

45. For the spiritual power of the holy man see P. Brown, "The Rise and Function of the Holy Man in Late Antiquity," *JRS*, 51 (1971), 80-101; Canivet, *Le monachisme syrien selon Théodoret de Cyr*, Théologie historique, XLII (Paris, 1977), 255 ff. A striking example is Rabbula of Edessa, who in his youth tried to destroy the temples at Baalbek; Blum, *Rabbula von Edessa*, 30-32.

INDEX